C000121432

1 MONTH OF
FREE
READING

at
www.ForgottenBooks.com

By purchasing this book you are eligible for one month membership to ForgottenBooks.com, giving you unlimited access to our entire collection of over 1,000,000 titles via our web site and mobile apps.

To claim your free month visit:
www.forgottenbooks.com/free171450

ISBN 978-0-483-22005-8
PIBN 10171450

THE FORUM.

VOL. XVIII.

September, 1894—February, 1895.

NEW YORK:

THE FORUM PUBLISHING CO.

PRESS OF
THE PUBLISHERS' PRINTING COMPANY
132-138 W. FOURTEENTH ST.
NEW YORK

CONTENTS.

The Forum

SEPTEMBER, 1894.

THE LESSONS OF RECENT CIVIL DISORDERS.[1]

THE year that has elapsed since the last meeting of the Association is in some very striking particulars one of the most notable in the history of the country, and it may be well to call attention to some of the phases of its social and public life, which in a constitutional point of view appear to merit notice. They have a bearing upon the vital principles of our political institutions, and seem to indicate a necessity for reviewing the work of those whom we have been accustomed to admire and respect as the founders of liberty in the western world, and for considering and judging for ourselves whether the structure they created, and which has hitherto been the admiration of the world, is worthy of the praise it has received. The question is stated with some hesitation, because it seems presumptuous for a citizen of a country whose political institutions have been so greatly praised to seem to admit by action or suggestion that the fundamental principles of American liberty can be in need of his championship, so self-evident has their excellence appeared, and so important to the happiness and well-being of any people who have learned to consider liberty an unquestionable blessing. But the experience of the year has taught us, if we needed the lesson, that times may and will come when the fact that for a century political institutions have had beneficent operation, and the excellence of their principles has seemed unquestionable to those who have enjoyed them, may perhaps no longer be accepted as conclusive evidence of

[1] From the Presidential address before the National Bar Association.

their consistency with true liberty or with the highest good of a free people.

When such a time comes, the most fundamental principles may be in need, not merely of tacit acceptance, but of a defence that shall consist in active and aggressive warfare upon those who in disorderly or unconstitutional ways assail them. We should at all times have in mind the great truth that the customary laws and even the fundamental institutions of any country are moulded and modified by the everyday life and thought of the people, and that sometimes even the carelessly tolerated disregard of existing law, and of constitutional principles, which no one would directly propose to change, may tend in the same direction.

I wish to call attention to an obligation resting upon members of the legal profession, and which I think goes quite beyond that which under the same state of facts would rest upon citizens in general. When, as we have lately seen, so-called " industrial armies" dissolve into roving vagabonds and beggars, the absurdity of their claims and pretences makes them the subject of contempt and ridicule; but if their mischievous doctrines have taken root among any class of our people, and their demoralizing raids upon the industry of the country are likely to be repeated by themselves or by others, it is not by a thoughtless and contemptuous word that the mention of them can be wisely dismissed. Especially is this the case as regards the members of the legal profession, for a special duty rests upon them to give active and effective aid to established institutions whenever revolutionary doctrines are brought forward, or when the fundamental rights we had supposed were made secure under constitutional guarantees are invaded or appear to be put in peril. It is a low and very unworthy view any lawyer takes of his office, when he assumes that he has nothing to do with public ignorance of the duty of subordination to the institutions of organized society, or with breaches of law existing or threatened, except as he may be called upon to prosecute or defend in the courts for a compensation to be paid him.

The past year has been especially prolific in acts of violence against individuals charged with crime of a particularly horrifying character, or who had made themselves particularly obnoxious or repulsive to their neighbors, or to some specially influential or numerous class of the community. Until recently it has been assumed by some that only one section of the country was justly subject to the reproach that its public sentiment tolerated the infliction of punishment by lawless force, and that even in that section it was mostly limited to one very gross class of offences. But no one section can any longer reproach another in this particular: lynchings have recently been numerous north and south and west, and in cases where murder and sometimes only a violation of property rights was charged, as well as in gross cases of outrage upon women. Their alarming feature is that in very many cases there was no attempt at concealment, and no pretence that violence was necessary to prevent justice being cheated of its dues; they took place sometimes when legal process had already been invoked against the criminal and was leading to certain punishment; and the participants in the lawless tragedy in some cases could openly boast that those who were accounted the best citizens in the community approved the deed, and would not suffer the actors therein to be punished.

I have spoken of lynching as an offence against the life or liberty of a citizen, as commonly it is; but I desire to emphasize the fact that the extent to which the lawless restraint of personal liberty may go is less important than the public sentiment which tolerates any invasion whatsoever. Recently a man was hanged in one State as a supposed murderer; in another a State officer was publicly tarred and feathered for actions which the persons assaulting him considered inadmissible to one in his position; and in still another a delegate to a political convention was dressed in petticoats and publicly exposed to ridicule because the local community was not pleased with a vote he had cast on a question of suffrage. In the degree of wrong to the individual there was difference in the three cases, but the lawlessness, the disregard of the obligations of citizenship, and the injury to organized society were equally plain in all, and equally deserving of unqualified condemnation. It may be safely assumed that in not one of the communities in which these criminal disorders took place are life, liberty, and property—which our written constitutions undertake to protect—so secure and so jealously guarded as they were before. But the mischiefs, though greatest in localities, are by no means restricted to them, but affect in a measure the whole country.

A little while ago we were horrified by the announcement that the President of the French Republic, a man highly esteemed the world over, and a true friend of liberty, had been assassinated by an anarchist. The assassin, as an individual, had no grievance whatever to allege against his victim; he was not even pretending to redress a wrong; he was complaining of no violation, by his distinguished vic-

tim, of the liberty of himself or of any other person.   He was simply
an anarchist, and the man he murdered was the representative of law
and settled institutions,—free and just institutions, established by
and for the people themselves.   But the anarchist will have no settled institutions whatever; he will have chaos.

Now, we have anarchists in our own country; they submit to no
government if they can escape it, even if to that end they must make
use of the dagger, the bomb, or the torch; and they openly applauded
this murder.   They have gathering-places where ·by frantic appeals
to passion and prejudice they seek to make converts to their doctrines; and when anything occurs to excite other classes to a temporary disregard of law, they are ever ready and willing to swell the
ranks of discontent, and to give destructive effect, so far at least
as they may with safety do so, to their hatred of government, not
hesitating in some cases to take great personal risks.

We justly look upon these men as foes to the human race, for
their doctrines, if given full effect, would plunge us into a condition
of worse savagery than history shows to have heretofore existed.
We have no knowledge that any nation or tribe, even in the earliest
ages, has been absolutely without governmental authority which could
impose restraint upon the passions of those subject to it, and give
some protection to the community against the lawless conduct of individuals.   The anarchist, if he could have his way, would be under
no such subjection; his ideal society would be without law; and the
freedom he seeks is like the freedom which prevails among the beasts
of prey in African deserts or the jungles of India. . A people would
not simply give up their civilization by accepting his doctrines; they
would give up such restraints upon the human passions as are
found even among savages.

Every American-born citizen regards these people with horror,
and so does every man among us who has come from foreign lands
with any respect whatever for free institutions, or even for law.
When, therefore, their sentiments are openly avowed, we have very
little occasion to fear them.   But we are not infrequently reminded,
when an act of tolerated mob violence takes place, that a community
may have an abhorrence of anarchy and yet so conduct themselves
when they see the law openly and publicly set at defiance that the
respect for it which should be its chief support will become more
nominal than real, and perhaps be replaced by disregard and contempt.   If they look on with unconcern while such an act is taking

place, if they give no aid when steps are being taken for the punishment of the participants, a condition of public insensibility to this class of offences is likely to be brought about, the result of which is that whenever the community is excited, and therefore specially in need of legal restraint, the law is found to be powerless.

If every citizen who thus countenances or refuses to aid in repressing crimes of this nature would consider a little what must be the natural consequence of his action or of his failure to act, he might perhaps come to appreciate the serious nature of his fault, and to understand how little he would himself deserve the protection of the law if some mob should select him as a victim of lawless violence. He would have the conviction forced upon him that by his course he is teaching disregard of law; that the act he aids or excuses is one step in the direction of the chaos the anarchist would establish; that his example in countenancing disorder is aiding to create a public sentiment which may by and by tolerate and protect the lynching of any person whomsoever for any act bad or good which happens to arouse public animosity, or even for no other reason than that the obnoxious person has in worldly pursuits been more successful than those about him. He will perhaps reflect also that when the disorder which he countenances in a single instance becomes general, it will not be the vagabond or the beggar that lawless classes will select for victims, but the man who for any reason is important and prominent in the community.

During the summer just past, the country has witnessed a great and disastrous boycott and strike of railroad workmen. The cause was not any controversy over their own wages or their treatment by their employers; it was a " sympathetic" movement, so called, and the reason assigned was that laborers for a corporation with which some of the railroad companies had important dealings had gone upon strike.

It began with a boycott against railroad companies who made use of the cars of the corporation aimed at, and who did not discontinue their use; this being followed by a general strike, the avowed purpose of which was, by blocking the wheels of traffic, to coerce the railroad companies into taking such action as would compel the corporation complained of to submit to arbitration the charges of oppression which its employees brought against it. The strike was professedly peaceful, and the thought in the minds of the leaders appeared to be that by the men leaving the railroad service and enforcing a boycott as to such of the railroad companies as had dealings with the offending corporation, all the companies would be so completely crippled that they could no longer run their trains, and must of necessity accept the terms dictated to them.

The case was in some particulars without precedent. Its leading peculiarities were the following:

1. The railroad companies had no means of coercing the offending corporation to submit to arbitration the controversy with its workmen; they could at most only refuse to carry out certain existing contracts with it, and discriminate against it when called upon to act for it as common carriers; but either of these acts would be unlawful, and must subject them to damages and to the compulsory process of the courts. The companies struck at were therefore required to put themselves in distinct opposition not only to certain contract obligations before entered into by them, and perfectly legal when made, but to the law itself, so that, by yielding, they would naturally expect legal penalties to follow. But refusal to submit must inevitably result in great loss to the companies, for their receipts would be largely reduced, since the commerce of the country, in so far as it was in their charge, would be paralyzed in exact proportion as the strike succeeded in its aims. Meantime the offending corporation would be comparatively unharmed,—perhaps not harmed at all.

2. But, if the strike was intended to be a peaceful one, it was soon seen that the burden of the loss was to fall, not upon the railroad companies, but upon the public who had occasion to use their services. This would be, as was soon shown, a necessary result of the stoppage of railroad trains. Great numbers of passengers were side-tracked at way-stations, at some of which it was with difficulty they procured the means of subsistence; shippers of property were put to great loss by delays; and immense quantities of perishable freight were soon going to ruin on trains which the railroad managers were unable to take to their destination. California and tropical fruit by the train-load, dressed meats in similar quantities, even live cattle and horses, all belonging to private parties, were thus given to destruction by the sun and the hot winds. The suffering of innocent persons as a necessary result of what had been ordered was quite beyond estimate; the victims were found in every part of the country and among all classes of people.

3. But though it was meant that the strike should be peaceful, and the strikers, in emphatic terms, were admonished by their leaders

to make it so, its leading characteristic almost immediately came to be violence. This was unavoidable. For the time being it aimed to paralyze transportation and all commerce by rail, and the greater the consequent injury and inconvenience the greater would be the probability of success. Lawless classes, who professed to be sympathizers, but cared only for disorder, saw this very plainly, and the situation soon took on some of the features of civil war. A difficulty the leaders hoped would not be encountered, it was soon discovered was likely to prove insurmountable. Laborers out of employment were now abundant; they would covet the vacant places; and unless appeals made to them to stand with their fellow-laborers in what was assumed to be their common interest should prove successful, they must by some other means be kept from the railroad service, or the strike would fail. But the needs of the unemployed and of their families were too urgent to admit of their listening to solicitation; they came forward in considerable numbers for employment, and violence, of which they were the victims, followed. The ordinary peace authorities proved unable to protect them: the worst elements of society were soon in possession of some towns, and especially of some sections of Chicago; and not only were men anxious to perform labor upon the railroads assaulted and beaten, but the torch was applied to railroad equipment and buildings, and great destruction resulted. The leaders who were directing the strike—however anxious they may have been to avoid breaches of the peace—were powerless to calm the passions that had been aroused, and the civil commotion increased daily in magnitude.

4. One question fairly arising upon the circumstances of this strike, and which, so far as I know, has hitherto received no attention, may properly be noticed here. It concerns the rights, legal and equitable, of those who were to be affected by the strike should one be declared, and raises the question whether, under principles supposed to prevail wherever free government exists, the strike, as against them, could be fully justified without careful consideration of its probable effect upon their interests being first had, and, if practicable, an opportunity given them to urge reasons, from their own standpoint, against its being entered upon. The parties who were to be injuriously affected were: first, the railroad companies, who if they were allowed to be heard through their general managers or any authorized committee on the question, whether it would be just or reasonable to declare a strike against them for what was not

their own fault, might possibly have convinced the members of the order which was then considering the question, that the objections to it from the standpoint of their employers were altogether reasonable; second, the government of the United States, whose transportation of the mails and control over interstate commerce were to be very seriously interfered with, and perhaps the service of federal process obstructed; and third, the people of the United States, whose legal right to be transported and to have their property carried by rail was to be in part, and perhaps wholly, taken away, while the strike continued, at a cost to them which must in the end be counted by millions. The public, it would seem, might have been allowed a hearing through business organizations, such as boards of trade, or through bodies like the Farmers' Alliance; and the government had even a still stronger claim to a hearing, for it was the government of the strikers themselves, and the action which was interfered with was an action of which they, in common with all the people of the United States, enjoyed the benefit. And the government might have pointed out that if the performance of its constitutional functions was hampered now in an attempt for one assigned reason to compel the railroad companies to take some particular action, it might possibly on some future occasion, for reasons still less forcible, be rendered impossible. Success in one instance would not only strengthen those who might have in view similar action in the future, but it would indirectly aid them by diminishing the courage of resistance. But the government might also have pointed out that the declaration of such a strike would be the exercise of unchecked and arbitrary power, which, where liberty prevails, is never by law provided for, since a free people would justly pronounce it unendurable tyranny, and the strikers themselves would, as citizens, never consent to be governed by a law which would admit of it. A free government is expected to submit even the most unimportant question of legal right to the adjudication of some impartial tribunal, to make provision for the hearing of interested parties, and to take precautions that the elements of passion and prejudice shall not be suffered to control the decision.

Here were three parties, all innocent as regards the grievance in question, who if the action was to be taken after the manner deemed necessary to prevent injustice in governmental proceedings, would seem to have had a strong equitable and indeed an indefeasible right to have the effect upon themselves first considered. Now I

understand very well that the case of the ordinary strike or boycott which is entered upon for the purpose of redressing an existing
wrong or to prevent one which is threatened, is to a considerable extent different.　Such a case partakes of the nature of self-defence;
and incidental injury to third parties, if it is unavoidable, is excused
on that ground: but there was nothing in the nature of self-defence
here.　It was a third party who was supposed to have been wronged
in this instance, and, as innocent parties were to be directly struck
at and greatly injured, the very least they could justly be awarded
would be a careful consideration, by those proposing the damaging
action, of the question whether the necessary consequence, even if
they were successful in what they hoped to accomplish, might not be
that the injury to innocent parties would greatly exceed the gains,
and, if so, whether the proposal could in justice be accepted.　But
this was a question of which no notice was taken.　Innocent parties
who must necessarily suffer not only had no opportunity to protest,
but their losses were not taken into account as reasons against the
boycott and strike.　On the contrary, they were regarded as favorable features of the case, since they rendered success more probable.
But a sympathetic strike is bad in morals, and must be quite as bad
in policy where the probable injury to innocent parties will exceed
the probable benefit to the parties it aims to assist.

　　The facts here stated seem to emphasize the importance of giving
some thought to another feature of the case which perhaps is common
when the question of a considerable body of men throwing up their
employment is brought by their leaders before them, but which was
particularly prominent here.　It concerns the manner in which the
decision of the question is arrived at.

　　In theory the order to throw up the service is always supposed to
be authorized by the men called out, and to be based upon substantial reason.　In this case the reason assigned was that the obnoxious
corporation refused to submit the case made by its laborers to arbitration, which was a wrong the railroad men desired to remedy.　But
as their own employers could not compel the arbitration, and there
were legal difficulties in the way of their taking the steps the men
demanded, it would seem that the substantial reason for proceeding
in a hostile way against them must in this instance have been wanting.　An impression that such was the case must to some extent
have existed among the men who were ordered to strike, for it
seemed to be necessary to call meetings and to have them addressed

by speakers who would urge what the leaders proposed.   The method whereby at these meetings an affirmative vote is secured is worthy of attention, especially by laborers themselves, who by reason of society ties are liable at any time to be drawn into similar controversies.   They are most deeply concerned of all, since the vote to be taken may affect their interests for years,—perhaps for life.

The orders in which laborers unite are supposed to be self-governing, and the principles which apply to the action of municipal bodies, and which have become established because they conduce to justice, are applicable to them as well.   To be wisely or even safely governed, their members must proceed deliberately, and the action taken must be the result of their best judgment coolly and dispassionately applied.   In the legislative bodies of the country, from the lowest to the highest, great pains are taken by rules of order, and sometimes by statutes and constitutional restrictions, to render hasty and passionate action unlikely.   The need of these precautions is so plain that no one raises any question concerning it, and it is not infrequent that action otherwise regular is annulled by the courts because cautionary formalities have been disregarded.

If we may rely upon the reports appearing in the daily papers, the proceedings taken at the meetings called to decide upon this great movement were not deliberate and dispassionate, but the speakers who were the chief actors were expected to and did appeal, not to the reason of their audiences, but to their feelings and their prejudices. Speakers who it was thought could make such appeals most successfully were brought to the meetings for the purpose. They came to excite their hearers to action, not to reason with them.   The action taken was therefore had under the influence of excited feelings. Opposition to what was proposed was not expected, and was not patiently listened to.   There was little in the proceedings that even resembled those of a deliberative gathering.   Not only, therefore, were other interested parties not given a hearing, but even those who were deciding what should be their own action in a matter vitally affecting the interests of some, if not of all, contented themselves with listening to a passionate appeal, and responding by a hurrah. The decision thus reached was conclusive.   The general fact was that a deliberative and patient hearing was had by no one.   This was the case until it was deemed necessary to appeal to other orders also, and then the proceedings were quite different.   But when deliberate action came to be taken, different results followed.

These matters are mentioned because they bear directly upon questions of justice and right that are necessarily involved when such a movement in the industrial world is proposed. With what justice can it be entered upon when innocent parties are of necessity to be sufferers to an enormous extent therefrom, without their rights being taken into account, and their probable losses allowed due weight in reaching a decision? And how can men who live by their labor wisely or even safely throw up their employment as a means of coercion, before they have carefully considered in all its bearings what is proposed, and its effects upon their own interests, not only if it shall prove successful, but also if it fail?

5. In our notice of this great internal commotion some attention is due to a question of constitutional law which was raised by some of the governors of States. When interstate commerce was interrupted, the transmission of the mails seriously impeded, and the service of process issued by the federal courts rendered difficult or impossible, President Cleveland sent to Chicago, the point of greatest disturbance and disorder, a considerable military force to aid the civil officers and to protect the carriers of the mails and the persons and vehicles employed in interstate transportation while they continued or made efforts to continue in the performance of the customary service. This at once brought out a protest from the governor of Illinois, who insisted that the President was encroaching upon the rights of the State. The foundation for the protest is understood to have been that the duty to maintain public order and enforce the laws was a State duty which Illinois was quite able and willing to perform, and that the federal executive had no right to act in case of domestic disorder until demand was made upon him by the State legislature or executive. Governors of some other States were understood to concur in this view. When the President replied to the protest that the United States troops were sent into the States only to enforce national laws, to put an end to interruptions of the mails, to protect interstate commerce, and see that the authority of federal courts was maintained,—in other words to support the national jurisdiction and protect officers and agents in the performance of national duties,—the reply was treated as insufficient, the protest was repeated from time to time, and the consequent excitement tended to keep the disorderly elements bold and defiant, 'so that the demand was even made by some of them that the governor should employ the military power of the State to remove the federal forces.

The governor was original in the doctrine he presented for our admiration and acceptance in this case. We all remember that the right of a State to nullify an act of Congress was once claimed, and that the right of a State to withdraw from the Union at one time had a great many supporters. We all know that from the very first there have been political parties, led by able and patriotic statesmen, who have insisted upon a strict construction of grants of national authority and of the powers to be exercised under them. But in this case nullification was not suggested; secession was not thought of. The grant to Congress of the power to provide for the transportation of the mails and to regulate interstate commerce was not questioned in the least. Congress had exercised these powers, and it was not claimed that in doing so it had unwarrantably expanded them or encroached upon State rights. Congress had also provided for United States courts in Illinois, which courts were then in session, and it was not pretended that in issuing the customary process they could be lawfully interfered with or the process denied service. We see, then, that there were national duties to be performed in Illinois, national officers, agents, and courts to whom in part the performance was entrusted, and disorderly parties were interfering and rendering performance difficult, oftentimes impossible. But the position of the governor was that the maintenance of peace and the repression of disorder was a State duty, and the President was consequently guilty of usurpation when he thus without request moved troops into the State for the purpose.

We cannot admit that the position taken is even plausible. It has no warrant whatever in the federal constitution, which, on the contrary, is distinctly against it. The President is to take care that the federal laws be faithfully executed, and his doing so is not made to depend upon the will or consent of any one State. The duty is specially and in the plainest terms imposed upon him, and in the performance of it he is subordinate to no State authority. Yet, if the views of this governor were accepted as sound, the mails might be stopped at Chicago, interstate commerce broken up, and the process of United States courts refused service, unless the governor, when disorder was dominant, saw fit to suppress it or to call upon the President to do so. If the protest was yielded to, it was a concession that the governor, and not the President, was to take care that the laws of the United States were faithfully executed in his State, and, if he failed to do so, a mob might at pleasure defy them.

It seems needless to take up time in discussing this protest: the action taken by the two houses of Congress in approving in emphatic terms the action of the President was equivalent to an expression of their opinion that the protest of the governor was not only unwarranted, but was revolutionary. The sentiment of the country as expressed in its public journals and otherwise was to the same effect, and the question of constitutional law may be considered practically settled. It is fortunate that it is so; for such a protest from the executive of a great State must necessarily tend at any time to still further excite the passions of those who in a mad way are defying the lawful authorities.

6. I have had something to say of the duties of members of the bar, and I shall now add a few words as specially applicable to crises like the one here alluded to: In doing so I may perhaps without impropriety so extend what I say that it shall be applicable to all who, in important positions, and especially as members of our national legislature, are to a considerable degree dependent, for their prominence as well as for the opportunity to be useful, upon the public favor. Very often they have to deal with difficult questions in government such as those concerning political economy and finance; and we may suppose they have been selected for their positions because of their peculiar ability and fitness to do so wisely. But not infrequently we feel compelled to question, as in the daily journals we follow their public life, whether a legislator, thus presumably chosen to act independently and fearlessly upon his own mature and enlightened judgment, does not sometimes, instead of considering with deliberation the questions upon which he must act, content himself with gathering as best he may the sentiment of his constituents, and with expressing it in his public action, even when he believes it to be erroneous and possibly dangerous, and when he cannot fail to perceive that the local sentiment is the result of artful teaching, or mischievous appeals to prejudice by interested parties or by demagogues. It is easy in that way to float with a popular current, and perhaps to make sure of continued popular support. But the question must often be presented to his mind whether the current might not be altogether otherwise if in an honorable and fearless way he took steps to correct the erroneous views which, while he remains silent, are certain to control, and whether his constituents have not a right to expect of him that, instead of submitting to follow when he knows they blindly lead, he will give

his best ability to making his service as useful as possible to them and to the country, and to that end will endeavor to instruct his people when they need instruction, and so, by force of character and force of reason, to lead them.

When the man who is both a statesman and a leader shall bring the results of observation and experience to a consideration of the difficulties which beset the relation of employer and employee, and which year by year seem to grow more troublesome, he may perhaps be expected to give anxious attention to the question whether the benefits of arbitration in that class of difficulties cannot be greatly extended.   There is an impression that this is possible, and he will find laws on the statute-books of the nation and of some States having for their object to aid in the removal, by means of a tribunal of peace, of the causes of contention which now in so many cases result in disorder, and in great pecuniary loss to one party or the other, commonly to both.   He will inquire whether the benefits of such tribunals cannot by legislation be made to embrace all of what are known as labor controversies, and he will find many to urge upon him the view they hold that compulsory arbitration may be made a complete and adequate remedy when disorders prevail in the industrial world.   Some attention to this view seems not unimportant.

" Arbitration," as the word has come to us, is understood to mean the voluntary submission, by the parties to a controversy, of the matters on which they differ, to the decision of one or more impartial persons, whose award thereon shall be final.   The most notable characteristic is that the initiation of the proceeding is voluntary; such, at least, has been the understanding hitherto.   The tribunals to which the law gives compulsory power over the controversies of individuals are the courts, and even these are to deal only with questions of legal right and legal obligation; they cannot enforce mere moral duties unless the law has made such duties legal also.   But the vast majority of labor controversies involve, as between the parties to them, no question whatever of legal right.   They involve disputes over wages or hours of labor where no binding contract exists that fixes them; disputes as to continuance of the relation when one party or the other desires to terminate it, and his moral right to do so is disputed, but not his legal right; disputes as to the employment of non-union men, and the like.   If arbitration could embrace only the labor controversies in respect to legal rights, it would be of very slight value.   The award on a voluntary submission may in other cases establish a legal right which the courts can enforce, but the limits to compulsory power in this respect must be very narrow. No employer can be compelled to continue his business when, for alleged want of capital or of profits, or for any other reason, he refuses to do so; and laborers cannot be led by the sheriff to their daily task when they refuse to obey the arbitrators' award that it is their duty to continue at their work. The award may, in a sense, be binding on the one or the other; but the party obtaining it must in such case content himself with an action for damages.

If one shall say to us that it is as competent to provide laws for bringing parties unwillingly before a board of arbitrators as before a court, and to make the action of the one tribunal as much as that of the other compulsory, the answer must be that neither to the one nor to the other can powers be given to enforce against the citizen that which the law does not require him to perform. The name of a tribunal does not determine what powers may be given it; but when it is sought to obtain relief which the party summoned before the tribunal has a legal right to refuse, his consent to submit to the jurisdiction of the tribunal is indispensable. The State may even in such cases provide for investigation of the controversy by a tribunal established for the purpose, as Congress has already done, but not for a trial against the consent of the parties, and compulsory submission to the decision. This seems unquestionable.

But, passing this question, let us see what would have been the position of the late controversy if, at the time it arose, there had been a national board of arbitration and a law of Congress to compel laborers and their employers to submit their disputes to arbitration.

First, we are to bear in mind that the original controversy was between an Illinois manufacturing corporation and its laborers. The corporation gave notice that the laborers must accept lower wages than were being paid, or the losses on the business would be such that the works must be closed. The laborers called for arbitration, and the corporation replied that there was nothing to arbitrate. A strike followed. We shall dismiss this now with the single remark that, as the contract which had existed in this case was for service to be performed locally, the controversy could not come under any national law of arbitration, and the laborers, if wronged, must look to the State of Illinois for a remedy.

When the manufacturing corporation refused arbitration, a strong union composed of railway employees in various branches of service declared a boycott and went out on a sympathetic strike. It is this strike that has been so damaging to themselves and especially to the country. The immediate settlement of this, by any legitimate arbitration or by any other just means, would have been a great boon to the country and to the industrial interests involved.

But suppose a national law providing for compulsory arbitration had then existed, and the strikers had demanded the intervention of the arbitration board, what must have been the result? Obviously, after the board had looked into the case, it would have been compelled to say that under the law they could give no remedy, for it had no application whatever to the case. The strike was by railroad employees, and they and their employers were the only parties to it. But the cause of complaint which led to the strike was a controversy between other parties altogether: parties who stood indeed in hostile attitude to each other, but were not parties to this strike, and could not be brought in to take part in the arbitration demanded. The board summoned to consider this would be wholly without jurisdiction to determine or even to look into the merits of the controversy which was the excuse for the one now brought to its attention. If, therefore, the board could take any action whatever, it would be merely to report that the present strike was not based upon any complaint made against the railroad companies, that there was no controversy between the parties to it to be investigated and passed upon, and consequently the board had no jurisdiction and must dismiss the case. This would seem unavoidable.

In what is said here it must be understood that no allusion is made to the probable action of a commission such as has recently been appointed by President Cleveland to investigate and report upon the late troubles. The President has made most admirable selections for the purpose, and the country has confidence in the wisdom, the prudence, and the integrity of the men chosen; and whether their report shall or shall not fully enlighten us as to the wrongs and rights of what has already taken place, it can scarcely fail to do something toward indicating for the future more satisfactory ways of dealing with labor controversies than by instituting industrial wars. The best wishes of the country will attend the efforts they may make in that direction, and we may be certain that remedies having their approval will be truly peaceful, which a strike on a large scale very seldom is.

But if it were possible to establish compulsory arbitration in a case where the controversy was not between the parties to the strike, I should venture to ask whether parties injured by the strike, rather than those whose interests were sympathetic merely, ought not to be at liberty to appeal to the law.   Consider, for a moment, what actually occurred here.   A great many thousand persons were by the strike absolutely deprived of legal rights, and injured in the aggregate to an enormous amount thereby.   A great many passengers who had paid for being transported across the country, and who had a legal right to proceed without detention, were side-tracked without their consent, and were put to great inconvenience and pecuniary loss. A great many shippers of goods suffered loss by detention, and whole train-loads of perishable goods were in some cases ruined by delays which the strike had caused.   In every one of these and the like cases, the injury was a direct result of the strike, and in many cases the circumstances were such that there would probably be no legal remedy against the carriers.   The strike, therefore, resulted in the destruction of rights of unoffending parties who were powerless to protect their own interests or to do anything by way of restoring the normal condition of things.   Why should not the parties upon whom losses were visited under such circumstances be at liberty, under a law for compulsory arbitration, to appeal immediately to the board for an investigation of the complaints, if any, made by the strikers against the railroad companies, and to insist that the board should demand that the strike be declared off when it was found that between the parties to the strike there was no existing controversy, or none over which the board could have jurisdiction?   Why, for example, should not one of the great packers of Chicago, whose property in enormous quantities was to be ruined without his fault, and whose legal right to deliver it by rail to his customers was to be taken away, have been at liberty to demand the immediate intervention of the arbitration board, and its prompt determination that his legal rights must be respected?   Parties whose interests were put in peril might, perhaps, under such a law, with entire justice have protection given them even when the parties to the quarrel, who had struck on sentimental reasons only, did not see fit to invoke its assistance.   No class of persons—not even the laborers at Pullman—had a stronger claim to the immediate intervention of a tribunal with peacemaking powers than those who were being deprived of their rights in transportation.   A woman, for example, travelling from New York to California, with ailing children and barely means

2

enough for her journey, side-tracked and suffering for days at Battle Creek!—whose claim to the immediate intervention of a compulsory board of arbitration could be greater than hers? And she was no outside party, as the laborers at Pullman were, but was directly and immediately concerned.

In what I have here said I have endeavored to point out in few words some of the obstacles in the way of making compulsory arbitration the effectual remedy in labor controversies, which many seem to think it is in time to become. The personal liberty of both the employer and the laborer is necessarily to be respected, and every man must be left to determine for himself whether he will observe and perform such moral or sentimental obligations, or recognize such claims, as the State has never deemed it wise to convert into legal duties or legal rights. Upon these and kindred subjects a true leader may make the inherent difficulties so plain that destructive conflicts will become inexcusable and also uncommon. He can clearly show that boards of arbitration with their orders—and I may add, also, courts with their injunctions—if they heed the fundamental law of the land, can no more hold men to involuntary servitude, for even a single hour, than can overseers with the whip. But he can also point out that, by contract when the service begins, the peaceful remedies provided by law can be greatly extended; that the sudden termination or damaging change of the relation by either party can be provided against; and that any other stipulation, important for the security of rights or to guard against the consequences of misfortune, may be made part of the terms of employment. The usefulness of such contracts may be made so plain that they will from year to year become more common; and the legislation in furtherance of peaceable settlements, though it must fall far short of adequately providing for all disputes likely to arise between employers and their men, will nevertheless so forcibly express the public sentiment against existing methods that we may reasonably expect that such methods will in a little time become far less common than now, if they do not altogether cease to be resorted to. The legal difficulties in the way of a complete remedy will remain, and will be serious at almost every point; but the very knowledge of their existence will emphasize the need of precautions to prevent a resort to violent measures when arbitration is inadequate, and to give additional force to the public opinion which will look with emphatic disfavor upon any refusal of arbitration when that seems a suitable and sufficient remedy for alleged wrongs. The employer cannot be compelled to continue his business when it has become unprofitable; that is plain; but if the contract of service is for a definite time, he must expect to respond in damages if he terminates it before the time has expired, whatever may be his excuse. If the laborer leaves the service before the time of hiring is completed, he, too, may be liable in damages, and the employer must rely upon this for redress, and will be supposed to take into account the possibility that the laborer may prove irresponsible as one of the incidents necessarily affecting the pecuniary results of his business.

But perhaps the legislator or the commission who will lead us in this important work may look for the most useful results to flow from his efforts in familiarizing the classes to be affected with the thought that, if disagreements arise, peaceable measures, founded on a review of all the facts, are to settle them. The looking forward to such a settlement will of itself have a powerful influence in bringing it about; and when it comes to be fully understood that the States and the nation alike are wanting in power to force upon unwilling parties such arbitration as shall be effectual in all cases, we shall perhaps be spared the sorrowful spectacle of wholesale destruction of the rights and property of innocent third persons, which must almost of necessity result from a strike or boycott so extensive, indiscriminating, and persistent as was the case with the one above brought under consideration. Strikes are very often peaceful and harmless except to the parties immediately concerned, but peace was impossible here. And our statesman-leader, we may be sure, will never overlook the fact, or fail to give it due prominence, that there is one class of strikes that can never be settled by arbitration. That is the sympathetic strike; and the reason is obvious: the parties to the strike are not the parties to the controversy that needs to be settled; and if the sympathizers are held justified, the original quarrel still remains undetermined. A finding made by a given number of arbitrators as to the merits of the original controversy in such a case would be an idle fulmination of opinion, having behind it no force of law, and going no farther to fix a moral obligation upon any party concerned than would a like expression by any other equal number of equally intelligent members of the community.

T. M. COOLEY.

TEACHING BY TRAVEL: A SCHOOL EXCURSION FROM INDIANA TO VIRGINIA.

THE general tendency on the part of our people to oppose the introduction of all methods of instruction that do not savor of the old-fashioned mechanical routine, is, in my opinion, one of the greatest barriers to educational progress in our country to-day. This opposition is based, as a rule, upon the erroneous notion that natural methods of instruction are new and untried, and consequently experimental, and that we are not justified in converting our schools into experimental institutions. If those who are of this opinion would obtain a knowledge of the history of education, however superficial, they would soon become convinced that the "new education," so called, is by no means new; that scarcely a method càn be mentioned which has not been in vogue in one or another of the European countries for half a century or more; and that many methods still denounced in America as innovations have long been classed among the essentials by the most conservative educators of Germany.

Among these is the school excursion—the method to be discussed in the present article. Indeed, while to the uninitiated this measure may be regarded as no less than revolutionary, it is nevertheless true that excursions from two to three weeks in duration were undertaken by Salzmann with the pupils of his school at Schnepfenthal in Thuringia, when Washington was President of the United States. Since the close of the last century, the school excursion, in one form or another, has been growing in popularity in Germany, and to-day it forms a regular feature of perhaps the majority of the elementary schools of that country.

The school excursion offers the most favorable opportunity for introducing children into many branches of knowledge, as they may thereby be brought into direct contact with nature and the works of man. Indeed, the locality is exceptionally unfavorable where an abundance of material may not be found for instructing the child in geography, history, and the natural sciences. In Germany, this broad study of the environment is recognized as a distinct branch of knowledge, known as *die Heimathskunde* (home-ology), and as such is included in the curriculum of the first three years of the elementary schools.

During these years the excursions are usually of a nature calculated to familiarize the child with his home-surroundings in general. When this period is over, they become specialized into botanical, geological, geographical, historical, industrial expeditions, and so on. The ideas acquired during the general excursions of the earlier years are, in the higher grades, made to serve as a basis of comparison, and thus form material for the exercise of the imagination, while the pupil is engaged in acquiring ideas concerning things beyond his immediate reach. In some instances, however, when the study of the immediate home-surroundings has been completed, the general excursions do not cease, but are continued throughout the entire school course, becoming ever wider in their scope. Under such circumstances, beginning with the fourth school year, a study of the home, in a broader sense, is undertaken on annual outings from one to two weeks in duration.

While, in our own country, the instructive excursion is not entirely unknown, it has nevertheless as yet played only an insignificant part in American school life. In some localities a few teachers are in the habit of taking their pupils on short excursions from time to time; but thus far, I believe, nothing systematic in this direction has been attempted. In regard to the extended excursion, undertaken by *public-school* teachers with their pupils, the one here described is, as far as I can learn, the first made in the United States.

The idea of the excursion from Anderson (Indiana) was conceived last March, when, during a visit to that city, I called the attention of Superintendent Carr to the details of a seven-days excursion through the Thuringian Forest, undertaken in August, 1893, by the School of Practice connected with the University of Jena, in Saxony. This expedition impressed Mr. Carr so favorably, that he became imbued with the desire to arrange such a trip for the pupils of the Anderson schools, to be undertaken at the close of the school year. The superintendent's plans were heartily approved by the members of the Anderson board of education. By the teachers and pupils the project was received with enthusiasm; and many of the parents expressed their willingness to provide their children with the necessary funds.

As the tour was to be a pioneer attempt in our country, it was thought advisable to extend its privileges only to the pupils of the highest grammar-grade and of the high-school.   Nevertheless, the number attending the outing was seventy-eight, as follows: The superintendent, the principal of the high-school, the president and the treasurer of the board of education, fourteen teachers, nineteen grammar-school pupils, thirty-six high-school pupils, and the county superintendent.   In addition to these, there were a physician to care for the party, a stenographer to aid in keeping a record, and a few guests, including myself.   Males and females were about equal in number.

It was the principal aim of the Anderson excursion to undertake a pilgrimage to important points of historical interest, and to give to the pupils an object-lesson on as many geographical elements as possible.   With these purposes in view, no route more favorable than the one finally selected could have been found, including as it did one of the most interesting districts of our country, historically, as well as by reason of almost every imaginable geographical element. Not one of the pupils, and only one or two of the teachers, had seen the ocean or a mountain, and but few of them had ever experienced the sensation of riding on a steamboat.   One of the pupils had never been on a train.   Consequently to the teachers as well as the pupils the entire ground covered was new.   The route was as follows: from Anderson, via Indianapolis, to Cincinnati; across the Ohio to Kentucky; through Kentucky and the mountains of West Virginia to Clifton Forge, Virginia; across the Shenandoah and Piedmont valleys, via Richmond, to Old Point Comfort; thence to Newport News; across Hampton Roads to Norfolk; by train from Norfolk to Virginia Beach, returning to Norfolk by train; by boat up Chesapeake Bay and the Potomac to Washington; returning to Anderson via Cincinnati.   The distance was about 1,800 miles, the journey's duration seven days.   The cost per capita, under the special arrangement made, including fares and all expenses in hotels, boats, and trains, was only thirty dollars.   The party started from Anderson on Monday morning, June 4, at six o'clock.   A special train was furnished, connecting with the early train from Indianapolis to Cincinnati.

The country between Anderson and Indianapolis is flat, and contains no special points of interest.   Between Indianapolis and Cincinnati, however, the attention of the pupils was called to many places particularly interesting to the people of Indiana.   At North Bend the Ohio River came into view, and the hills of Kentucky—

practically the first elevations of land that the majority of the pupils had ever seen—became visible.   The train skirted the river for thirty miles, and the river shanties and steamboats proved of much interest.

The first thing of importance after leaving Cincinnati was the mag-nificent iron bridge which spans the Ohio between Cincinnati and Covington.   After reaching the Kentucky side, Point Pleasant, the birthplace of General Grant, came in sight.   By means of talks from time to time, the pupils received much information concerning the industries of the various localities through which we passed. While passing through the coal regions of West Virginia, the man-ner in which the mines were operated was explained.   The scenery all along the line was charming.   After crossing the Big Sandy and the Guyandotte rivers, the train entered the valley of the Kanawha, where the high hills began to appear.   We followed this valley to Kanawha Falls.   Here the hills became higher and higher, until we had before us a characteristic picture of mountain scenery, which naturally made a deep impression on the pupils, who before that day had seen only flat country.   Thence we passed into the New River cañon, the most picturesque part of the road.   The scenery here is very rugged.   The famous Hawk's Nest, which rises to a height of twelve hundred feet above the river, is situated near the entrance. We reached Clifton Forge shortly before midnight, and spent the night there.

On the following morning the pupils were up bright and early, anxious for their first mountain walk.   At eight o'clock, Major Jedd Hotchkiss, a well-known geologist, joined the party at the hotel.   He first delivered a short address on the geological conditions of Clifton Forge and the vicinity, which was illustrated by photo-graphs and maps.   We returned to the hotel shortly before noon, and after dinner departed for Richmond, where we had arranged to pass the second night.   The stretch of country between Clifton Forge and Richmond, a distance of one hundred and ninety-three miles, is interesting at every point.   Not only is the scenery very picturesque, but the region is one that has played a very important part in American history.

· Soon after leaving Clifton Forge, we caught a view of Elliott's Knob, the highest mountain in Virginia.   A little later the train passed through Buffalo Gap, a natural opening in the North Moun-tain, in the Alleghanies.   A ride across the Shenandoah Valley fol-lowed; and soon we entered the Piedmont Valley, which is noted for its garden-like scenery. Major Hotchkiss, who had taken an active part in the Civil War, accompanied our party for a considerable distance, pointing out various points of interest. He gave many vivid accounts of acts that took place in the Shenandoah Valley during the war, and he explained to the pupils why the valley figured so prominently in the contest. When he had left, Mr. Truitt, our regular guide, gave us much information concerning that section of the country.

In various places earthworks may still be seen. At Charlottesville we caught a glimpse of the University of Virginia, as well as of Monticello, the home of Thomas Jefferson. The train passed through Shadwell, the birthplace of Jefferson. At Afton we saw the inn where Presidents Jefferson, Madison, and Monroe, with other commissioners, met to select a site for the University of Virginia.

On our arrival at the hotel in Richmond, we found a number of citizens waiting to receive us. They kindly offered to do all they could to render our visit instructive. When our visitors had departed, a meeting was held by the teachers. During the discussion, the fact was brought out that thus far nothing had been done toward orderly arranging in the minds of the pupils the facts thus far acquired by them. It was consequently decided that before leaving the hotel in the morning, a general class-meeting should be held. Next, the programme for the following day was arranged. In order that as much as possible might be accomplished during our short stay at Richmond, it was decided that the tour of the city be made in carriages. In the morning we were driven through a number of business and residence streets, so that we might receive a general impression of the city. During this ride, a number of places of historical interest were pointed out. After this tour we drove through the park to the cemetery, where we visited the graves of many of our heroes. Among the numerous places of interest pointed out to us during the drive were St. John's Church, where Patrick Henry made his famous speech; Washington's old headquarters; the residences of Jefferson Davis, General Lee, and Chief Justice Marshall; the site of Libby Prison; statues of Washington, Lee, Stonewall Jackson, and others. As the mayor had expressed a desire to give us a reception, we called at his office after our drive. Following this, the Governor of Virginia received us in his rooms at the Capitol. The sight-seeing at Richmond was closed with an examination of many interesting historical relics. At three o'clock we boarded the train for Old Point Comfort. The ride was again an interesting one.

Soon after passing through the earthworks surrounding the city of Richmond we ran by the battlefield of Seven Pines. Next we crossed the Chickahominy River, where we obtained a glimpse of the island where Captain John Smith is supposed to have been captured. Another point of historical interest was Williamsburg, the second capital of the State. William and Mary College, the second university founded in America, is here situated. Old Point Comfort was reached at six o'clock.

In the evening a prolonged session was held by the entire party in one of the parlors of the hotel. During this session, which was devoted exclusively to recitations in geography and history, an effort was made to clinch the points thus far acquired by the pupils. The recitation in history assumed the form of a general review of the Civil War, with particular reference to the Shenandoah Valley. During the recitation in geography, the teacher endeavored to get from the pupils a connected story relating to the districts through which we had thus far travelled.

On the following morning a profitable hour was spent at Fortress Monroe. A soldier guided us around and gave us lucid explanations concerning the various points. In this instance the sight-seeing was particularly profitable, because it was accompanied by a recitation. Whenever a few points had been explained to the pupils, Superintendent Carr took charge of the classes and questioned the scholars on what they had heard. It is indeed only under such circumstances that the proper form of mental activity on the part of the pupils may be expected. When we take for granted that pupils actually observe and comprehend whatever they ought to see and understand, a grievous error is committed. The visit to the fortress was instructive geographically as well as historically. The view of Chesapeake Bay at this point, with Cape Charles and Cape Henry in the distance, is charming.

Our visit to the fortress over, we departed for Newport News. There we paid a visit to the ship-yards. The guide who conducted us through the yards explained in detail the operations and the apparatus of the dry docks. By means of the powerful pump shown to us, 150,000 gallons of water can be displaced in a minute, and the large dock pumped dry in from one to two hours. Our visit to the ship-yards was again accompanied by a recitation conducted by the superintendent.

At Newport News we boarded the boat for a twelve-mile ride

across Hampton Roads to Norfolk.   This was the first boat-ride ever taken by some of the members of the party.   It proved a very pleasant hour to them.   Time did not permit us to stop at Norfolk. We simply walked through the city to the railway station, where we entered the train for Virginia Beach.   It was at the latter place that the pupils received their first view of the ocean.   The four hours at this resort allowed us ample time to bathe in the sea, and to stroll on the beautiful beach after dinner.   The visit to the beach was one of the brightest spots of the tour.   We returned to Norfolk in time to take the boat for Washington at six in the evening.   As the night was fine,. we were able to stay on deck for a number of hours, and thus enjoy a considerable part of the sail on Chesapeake Bay;   and as we did not arrive at the capital until seven o'clock, the pupils were able, during the early hours of the morning, to appreciate a good part of the sail up the Potomac River.

While in Washington the pupils were full of enthusiasm.   They were charmed with everything they saw.   Nearly all Friday morning was consumed by a visit to the Capitol.   The party being so large, the tour of the building was made in two divisions, each in charge of a guide.   While on our rounds, we were fortunate enough to find the Senate in session.   Our morning's work was concluded by a visit to the Navy Yard, where we followed the various processes involved in the manufacture of firearms, and inspected a small man-of-war.   The afternoon was devoted to a visit to Mount Vernon. The tour of the grounds and the house at Mount Vernon was followed by a recitation, held on one of the lawns.   During this recitation the history of the Mount Vernon estate, as well as important events of the time of General Washington, were reviewed.   We returned to the city late in the afternoon.   After supper, half an hour was devoted to instruction in the hotel parlor.   The party then divided into several sections.   Some of the pupils, accompanied by a few teachers, visited the theatre;   others attended a night session of the House of Representatives;   while still others spent the evening quietly at the hotel.

On Saturday morning, before leaving the hotel, an hour was spent in a general review.   At ten o'clock we started on our tour through the city.   The places visited during the morning were the Pension Office, the Dead-Letter Office, the Patent Museum in the Department of the Interior, the Treasury Building, and the Corcoran Art Gallery.   At one o'clock the White House was reached.   As a public reception was held at the time, the tourists were afforded an opportunity to shake hands with the President.   In the afternoon, they were left free to do as they desired.   Some visited the National Museum and the Smithsonian Institution, and a large number ascended the Washington Monument.   Late in the afternoon a drive was taken through the residence portion of the city to the Zoological Gardens. On Sunday morning all were tired; nevertheless some twenty of the tourists paid a visit to Arlington.

At two o'clock in the afternoon the party boarded the Chesapeake and Ohio train for Cincinnati, on their homeward journey. The road from Gordonsville to Cincinnati had been traversed on the outward journey; but the country between Washington and Gordonsville, a distance of ninety-four miles, was new.   This part of the country was rich in points made famous by the Civil War.   The night was passed on the train.   All reached Anderson in the afternoon of Monday, June 11, just one week after starting.

Generally speaking, then, as a pioneer attempt, the Anderson excursion was a marked success.   It was, indeed, an enjoyable, interesting, suggestive, and profitable affair.   And, above all, it served to prove beyond a doubt that the school excursion is feasible in our country.   The opinion has been frequently expressed that journeys of this nature could not be successfully carried out in America, because our children, when out of the school-room, would not, like the Germans, submit to the authority of their teachers.   In regard to the pupils of the Anderson schools, this theory proved entirely unfounded; their obedience was perfect.   Indeed, too much praise cannot be bestowed upon them for their manly and womanly behavior. It was seldom found necessary to exercise any control over the young people, simply because they had learned to control themselves.   Indeed, self-control on the part of the pupils is a characteristic feature of the schools of our country.   It was the unanimous verdict of the railway employees and the hotel proprietors and clerks, that our party, in spite of its size, was one of the most orderly they had ever encountered.   During the entire excursion, the spirit manifested on all sides was excellent; every one was delighted and happy, and all looked forward with anticipation to a future trip of a similar nature.

And yet the affair was not without flaws.   While, in regard to the spirit, little was left to be desired, the same is not true of the pedagogical features.   The lack of strength on the pedagogical side, due largely to want of experience, was owing to the fact that, beyond the selection of the route, the plans were indefinite; besides, the special preparation on the part of both teachers and pupils was inadequate. In consequence of these omissions the affair was characterized by aimless sight-seeing rather than by definiteness of purpose. That travel in itself is a powerful educator, cannot be denied; yet the educational value of any given tour will depend largely upon the manner in which it is conducted. A six-months tour through the museums and art-galleries of Europe, under judicious guidance, may result in an education in history and art; while a similar tour without such guidance may lead to nothing beyond a jumble of ideas. On our excursion, lack of definiteness led to delays, and consequently to loss of time; while lack of preparation on the part of the teachers and pupils resulted in indefinite work.

In regard to the details concerning the preparation for an excursion, much can be learned from Germany, with its experience of a century in this line of work. I shall therefore add here, by way of suggestion, an outline of the method followed by the School of Practice connected with the University of Jena, whose journeys are conducted on strictly scientific principles.

At Jena we find that each expedition is preceded by a thorough preparation on the part of both teachers and pupils. In regard to the pupil, the preparation takes place by means of a series of special recitations, during which the route is carefully studied, maps are drawn, and the points to be observed are discussed in outline. Thus their minds are placed in an attitude of expectancy, and consequently in the condition most favorable to the acquisition of new ideas.

As to the teachers, the work of the journey is usually so divided that those who take an active part shall teach only during a single day. On that day, however, the one who teaches takes complete charge of all the proceedings. At a special teachers' meeting, held several weeks in advance, the particular days are selected by mutual agreement. The work of preparation on the part of the teacher now begins, and it consists in studying from maps, railway guides, books of travel, and so on, the details concerning the points of interest—historical, industrial, geographical, geological, botanical—lying within the district assigned to him. In arranging the programme for the day on which he has charge, he accounts for every hour. The programme, once made, is carried out to the letter. The sight-seeing is invariably undertaken in the form of a recitation. Lessons given on the road are particularly valuable, because they have been thoroughly prepared in advance.

It affords me much pleasure, in this connection, to be able to state that the privilege of studying pedagogy and allied subjects at Jena—the world's centre for the study of the Herbartian system—is destined soon to be extended to women.   While abroad this past summer I called the attention of Professor Rein—the professor of pedagogy—to the fact that to grant permission to American women to attend his lectures and to instruct in the University School of Practice would be doing an excellent service to our schools.   After a few consultations and before my departure from Jena he promised me, first, that without further consideration he would permit our women to instruct in the School of Practice, and, second, that as soon as the number of applicants should reach, say, ten, he would undertake to deliver privately to women lectures similar to those given before the students in the University.   Professor Eucken, of the Department of Philosophy, gave me a similar promise in regard to his lectures on philosophy and logic, and I received the further assurance that the heads of other departments would follow in the footsteps of these professors.   The admission of women to the University itself does not lie within their control.[1]

Finally, experience acquired during the Anderson excursion leads me to offer the following additional suggestions:

First, I should recommend that the classes be divided into sections, and that each section be placed in charge of a teacher taking an active part in the work.   Indeed, the teacher in charge should at all times have an eye on his pupils.

Second, I would suggest that, on a journey a week in duration, some of the time be devoted to rusticating.   A day or two spent in the woods, travelling on foot or in wagons to selected points of interest, would not only add to the enjoyment of the tour, but give an opportunity for nature studies.   By this means, also, the fatigue of a continued series of extended railway journeys would be avoided.

Now that Anderson has made the beginning, it is to be hoped that excursions from other localities will follow.   And if the preparation on the part of both teachers and pupils be thorough, there is no reason why excursions undertaken in our country should not be fully as profitable as those in Germany.   J. M. RICE.

[1] If those interested in this matter will communicate with me, in care of THE FORUM, I shall be pleased to send them further particulars.

THE PROPORTION OF COLLEGE–TRAINED PREACHERS.[1]

ON the gateway of Harvard University are inscribed the first words of the first notice of college education in British America:

> "After God had carried us safe to New-England, and wee had builded our houses, provided necessaries for our liveli-hood, rear'd convenient places for God's worship, and setled the Civill Government: One of the next things we longed for, and looked after was to advance Learning and perpetuate it to Posterity; dreading to leave an illiterate Ministery to the Churches, when our present Ministers shall lie in the Dust."

Many a tourist smiles as he reads this inscription, partly, no doubt, because of its antique form, but partly because it tells of an ideal of education which is of an antique world. What a transformation has come over that little academy, founded for the training of Puritan ministers! What an unrecognizable thing would modern education appear to the author of "New England's First Fruits"! Most of our earlier colleges, and many of our later ones, were endowed for the support of a sect and for the training of its ministers; and most of them have been led into a liberty of choice and an expansion of instruction which quite obscure the original object of the founders. What effect, one asks himself, is this new conception of education having on the profession of the ministry? Are the colleges abandoning their original function? Have we again reason to dread "an illiterate ministry when our present ministers shall lie in the dust"? What is the present relation of the colleges to the ministry? Is the talk of the time justified which assumes that the ministry has forfeited the interest of scholars, and that the colleges, in their devotion to other ends, have turned from that purpose with which they began? Those who care for organized religion may perhaps be interested in even a partial inquiry into these questions.

[1] Contributed by THE SOCIOLOGICAL GROUP, composed of the members whose names are given below. It is understood that each writer has had the benefit of suggestions from the Group, but is himself alone responsible for opinions expressed in a paper to which his name is subscribed.

CHARLES W. SHIELDS.   SETH LOW.   FRANCIS G. PEABODY.   HENRY C. POTTER.
CHARLES A. BRIGGS.   WILLIAM F. SLOCUM, JR.   THEODORE T MUNGER.   WASHINGTON GLADDEN.
EDWARD J. PHELPS.   WM. CHAUNCY LANGDON.   WILLIAM M. SLOANE.   SAMUEL W. DIKE.
CHARLES DUDLEY WARNER.

Such an inquiry does not, of course, pretend to go to the root of religious influence. It does not assume that the only useful minister is a college graduate, or that every college graduate is fit to be a minister. And yet it must be confessed that many of the religious problems of the present age call, first of all, for scholarly methods and discipline, and can be effectively dealt with only by liberally educated men. Here is the cause of much of the reaction among the educated from religion. It is not uncommonly believed that the teachers of religion are not up to their present task; that the modern minister is not, in the same sense as other professional men are, a trained and competent expert; and so the churches are abandoned by many educated men as resorts of half-educated sentimentalism and sociability. But what are the facts as to this training for the ministry? Is the popular notion of a decline of intellectual standard in the profession justified? How many Bachelors of Arts of our colleges—as a matter of fact—used to enter the profession, and how many enter it now? Where among the colleges does the source of supply seem to fail, and under what influences does its stream run full? These are the questions which have led to the collection of a few statistics which seem to indicate a reply. An adequate statistical inquiry, dealing with the whole, or even with a large part, of the American colleges, would be a very serious task, which some more competent student should soon undertake. There are simply set together here the facts of a few colleges, selected, not on any fixed principle of importance, but as being, on the whole, either best known or most accessible to inquiry. There are probably other colleges which could show equally striking figures, and which would reward a larger investigation; but to go farther would be to trespass excessively on the kindness of college officials. The following tables present the facts of twenty-eight colleges which illustrate their relation to the ministry during the last twenty-five years. No figure is given without an official guarantee behind it, so that the statement, though very incomplete, should be accurate as far as it goes.

The question presents itself in two forms, which it is convenient to keep distinct. There is, first, the question of the actual number of college graduates entering the ministry, and then the question of the proportion of these graduates to the total number of Bachelors of Arts. Are the colleges actually sending more men or fewer into the ministry as the years go by?—that is the more interesting point of view for the churches to consider. Is, on the other hand, the percentage of ministers maintained as the college classes increase in number?—that is the more interesting question from the point of view of the colleges themselves. Two sets of tables (see pp. 34,35) have therefore been compiled,—one of the actual number of Bachelors of Arts entering the ministry from each of twenty-eight colleges from 1869 to 1893; and the other of the proportion of these graduates to the whole number of Bachelors in these twenty-five years. In the case of Michigan University the facts for the last three years have not been reported; and therefore, while the statement in this case is presented as it has been kindly furnished, the results are not included in the totals, and these deal, not with twenty-eight but with twenty-seven institutions. In summing up the result of these tables of absolute and relative numbers it has seemed important to distinguish the earlier and the later movement toward the profession, so as to determine as far as possible what each college is contributing to the ministry under the most immediate influences. The tables therefore state, first, the total results for the whole period of twenty-five years, then the situation as it presents itself up to 1889, and lastly the evidence of the last five years.

Looking, in the first place, at these figures as a whole, we notice that the total result of the first table—of absolute numbers—remains practically the same throughout these years. Taking the twenty-seven colleges together, they send just about as many graduates into the university now as they have for each year during the last quarter of a century. In 1869, 123 Bachelors of Arts entered the profession, and in 1893 the number was 124. Indeed, a slight gain is indicated. During the twenty years up to 1889 the total average number was 130, and in the last five years it was 134. Taking, on the other hand, the total evidence of the second table, we have a different result. Some of the colleges considered are very large, and some very small. It is therefore not just to average their percentage. I have regarded, therefore, the whole mass of graduates of the twenty-seven colleges as one body, and have considered what proportion of that entire body has entered the ministry. Thus calculated, the percentage of the whole, as might be expected, declines, in a marked degree, from 19 per cent in 1869 to 9 per cent in 1893. It may be doubted whether this decline is peculiar to the ministry. The last twenty-five years have opened to college graduates an extraordinary number of new careers, and it is not unlikely that all the established professions would show a decline. It is to be noticed, moreover, that the decline is not peculiarly marked during the last few years. Up to 1889 the average proportion of the entire body of graduates entering the ministry was 14 per cent, and during the last five years it has been 11 per cent. This last number, therefore, represents our present general average, by which the contribution of each college may be fairly tested. Is a college sending into the ministry more than 11 per cent of its graduates? Then it is contributing to the profession more than the average of my twenty-seven colleges. Is it, on the other hand, contributing less than 11 per cent? Then it is doing less than its average part in this service. Judged by this test, the following colleges must be regarded as in this respect successful: Boston, Brown, De Pauw, Lake Forest, Oberlin, Princeton, Trinity, Tufts, Iowa, Pennsylvania, University of the South, and Wesleyan; and the following are deficient in their contributions: Amherst, Bowdoin, Columbia, Cornell, Dartmouth, Harvard, Johns Hopkins, California, Kansas, Michigan, Minnesota, Missouri, and Yale. Colby, Tulane, and Williams are fairly on the average line.

When we turn from this total result to the separate colleges, they seem to fall into five general groups. First, there are the two Southern colleges,—Tulane, and the University of the South. Unfortunately, however, neither of these contributes anything of importance to our inquiry. Tulane has a history of but ten years, and a total of but five Bachelors of Arts entering the ministry; and the University of the South in twenty-one years has sent but 19 men into the profession. This Southern group should have been much enlarged. A second group may be made of the State universities, whose charters often prohibit official relation with religion, and whose most popular courses of study are for the most part directed to what are called "practical affairs." Reports are presented from seven of these,—California, Cornell, Iowa, Kansas, Michigan, Minnesota, and Missouri; and all seven appear to be practically non-contributors to the ministry. Taken all together, they yield but 171 ministers in twenty-five years, or about one man apiece per annum; and even this contribution has declined proportionally from 6 per cent apiece for twenty-five years to 3 per cent during the last five years. A third group is made by the definitely denominational colleges, in which denominational influence is maintained as a conspicuous element of college life, and the ministry of a special communion is a special end of education. In this group may be placed Boston University

3

TABLE I.

NUMBER OF A.B.'S ENTERING THE MINISTRY, 1869 TO 1893.

COLLEGES.	Total number of A.B.'s entering the ministry.	Average per year for 25 years.	Average until 1889.	Average for last 5 years.
Amherst College	348	13.92	16.10	5.2
Boston University	64	3.76 [17 yrs.]	3.50 [12 yrs.]	4.4
Bowdoin College	58	2.32	2.10	3.2
Brown University	199	7.96	7.90	8.2
Colby University	88	3.52	3.70	2.8
Columbia College	80	3.20	3.15	3.4
Cornell University	14	.56	.6	.4
Dartmouth College	165	6.60	7.45	3.2
De Pauw University	145	5.80	5.60	6.6
Harvard University	267	10.68	8.70	18.6
Johns Hopkins University	23	1.53 [15 yrs.]	1.30 [10 yrs.]	2
Lake Forest University	41	2.73 [15 "]	2.10 [10 "]	4
Oberlin College	201	8.04	8.45	6.4
Princeton College	490	19.60	19.70	19.2
Trinity College, Hartford	172	6.88	6.35	9
Tufts College	36	1.44	1.25	2.2
Tulane University	5	.50 [10 yrs.]	.20 [5 yrs.]	.8
University of California	8	.32	.35	.2
" " Iowa	43	1.72	1.75	1.6
" " Kansas	12	.57 [21 yrs.]	.62 [16 yrs.]	.4
" " Michigan	59	2.77 [22 "]	2.85	1 [2 yrs.]
" " Minnesota	28	1.33 [21 "]	.87 [16 yrs.]	2.8
" " the State of Missouri	7	.28	.35	....
" " Pennsylvania	116	4.64	4.50	5.2
" " the South	19	.90 [21 yrs.]	.87 [16 yrs.]	.1
Wesleyan University	248	9.92	10.40	8
Williams College	169	6.76	6.80	6.6
Yale University	233	9.32	9.30	9.4
Total A.B.'s of 27 colleges entering the Ministry	3279	131.16	130.25	134.8

The total number of men who had taken the degree of A.B. at these twenty-seven colleges and who entered the ministry were as follows for the last twenty-five years:

YEAR.	Number A.B.'s entering ministry.	YEAR.	Number A.B.'s entering ministry.	YEAR.	Number A.B.'s entering ministry.	YEAR.	Number A.B.'s entering ministry.
1869	123	1875	122	1881	121	1887	116
1870	145	1876	127	1882	122	1888	120
1871	133	1877	144	1883	127	1889	127
1872	163	1878	135	1884	122	1890	131
1873	122	1879	137	1885	113	1891	153
1874	144	1880	139	1886	130	1892	139
						1893	124

TABLE II.

PERCENTAGE OF A. B.'S ENTERING THE MINISTRY.

COLLEGES.	Average per cent for 25 years.	Average per cent until 1889.	Average per cent for last 5 years.
Amherst College	21	25	7
Boston University	29 [17 years]	27 [12 years]	33
Bowdoin College	7	7	8
Brown University	18	19	17
Colby University	22	25	11
Columbia College	7	7	8
Cornell University	6	8	2
Dartmouth College	12	13	7
De Pauw University	26	24	30
Harvard University	5	5	7
Johns Hopkins University	6 [15 years]	7 [10 years]	5
Lake Forest University	73 [15 "]	80 [10 "]	60
Oberlin College	31	33	. 24
Princeton College	20	21	15
Trinity College, Hartford	38	36	47
Tufts College	13	12	19
Tulane University	10 [10 years]	10 [5 years]	10
University of California	4	5	2
" " Iowa	16	16	14
" " Kansas	4 [21 years]	5 [16 years]	1
" " Michigan	3 [22 "]	4	[2 years] 1
" " Minnesota	4 [22 "]	4 [16 years]	4
" " the State of Missouri.	4	5	....
" " Pennsylvania	22	20	30
" " the South	19 [21 years]	18 [16 years]	22
Wesleyan University	29	32	16
Williams College	16	17	10
Yale University	7	7	6
Percentage of A.B.'s of 27 colleges entering the ministry	13 +	14 +	11 −

The percentage of the A.B.'s of these twenty-seven colleges that entered the ministry for each year during these twenty-five years is as follows:

YEAR.	Percentage of A.B.'s entering ministry.	YEAR.	Percentage of A.B.'s entering ministry.	YEAR.	Percentage of A.B.'s entering ministry.	YEAR.	Percentage of A.B.'s entering ministry.
1869	19 −	1875	16 +	1881	12 −	1887	11 −
1870	20 +	1876	15 +	1882	13 +	1888	11 +
1871	18 +	1877	16 −	1883	12 −	1889	12 +
1872	22 −	1878	15 +	1884	12 −	1890	11 −
1873	16 +	1879	14 +	1885	11 +	1891	12 −
1874	18 −	1880	15 −	1886	12 +	1892	10 +
						1893	9 −

(Methodist), De Pauw (Methodist), Lake Forest (Presbyterian), Oberlin (Congregationalist), Trinity (Protestant Episcopal), Tufts (Universalist). These six colleges, taken as a group, contribute more than 30 per cent of their graduates to the ministry, and in the last five years have more than maintained this proportion. All but Oberlin show a slight increase, and Oberlin but a slight decrease. Yet the absolute contribution from the entire group is but small. Lake Forest gives in some years 100 per cent of its graduates to the ministry, but this means in absolute numbers only three men a year. The groups of six, taken together, have sent, for twenty-five years, 26 Bachelors of Arts into the profession per annum, or less than five each, and for the last five years 31, or a little more than five each.

A fourth group consists of what we may call the New England colleges, founded, for the most part, primarily in the interest of religious training, but of late years greatly broadening their range of instruction, and fruitful in many branches of liberal learning. Into this group fall Amherst, Bowdoin, Brown, Colby, Dartmouth, Wesleyan, Williams. Of these, Bowdoin, Brown, Colby, Wesleyan, and Williams just about hold their own in absolute numbers, sending in all 28 men into the ministry in each year up to 1889, and 27 men in each of the last five years. The other colleges of this group, Amherst and Dartmouth, show a marked decline in this professional service: in the case of Amherst from 16 to 5, and in that of Dartmouth from 7 to 3. The decline in the case of Amherst is a striking feature of the tables. In 1869 nearly one-half of her graduates entered the ministry; in the last five years only 7 per cent have enlisted,—a fact which some friends of the institution will welcome as an indication of greater breadth of purpose, and some will regret as a departure from the earlier tradition.

Lastly, we may group together the institutions which are generally recognized as the more important Northern universities. These are Columbia, Harvard, Johns Hopkins, Pennsylvania, Princeton, and Yale. Of these, Johns Hopkins may be left out of account, having trained in fifteen years but 23 ministers, or an average of less than two each year. Columbia College also has been a very moderate contributor, with an aggregate of 80 ministers in twenty-five years. The University of Pennsylvania, on the other hand, has had an exceptional history. The percentage of her Bachelors of Arts entering the ministry is extraordinarily high, and rises in the last five years from 20 per cent to 30 per cent. The importance of this

proportion, however, is lessened by the very limited number of
A. B. degrees conferred by this university. Thus, in 1892, 33 per
cent of her Bachelors of Arts entered the profession, but the actual
number was but five. Judged, then, by proportional figures, the
position of Pennsylvania is almost unique; but judged by actual
figures her contribution for twenty-five years is less than that of
Williams, Dartmouth, or De Pauw. There remain the three institutions which, on the whole, represent the most varied constituencies
and possess the widest national reputation. Fortunately for the
country, these three universities, Princeton, Yale, and Harvard,
maintain, in the matter we are now testing, as in most other problems of administration and aim, widely different methods and ideals.
It is therefore interesting to inquire into the apparent effect of these
differing methods on the supply of ministers. The first and most
striking fact which meets such an inquiry is the large and continuous
contribution of Princeton. For the last twenty-five years she has
trained not fewer than 19 ministers each year,—a number which
remains almost precisely the same in the earlier and the later years
of the period. Owing to the great growth of the college, however,
there has been a decline in proportional numbers, from 21 per cent
of her graduates in the first twenty years to 15 per cent in the last
five years; yet even with this decline the figures for Princeton stand,
on the whole, quite alone in the list. Yale, on the other hand, has
contributed for the whole period but nine men a year to the profession, or less than one-half the quota of Princeton; while, as in the
case of Princeton, Yale's figure remains constant throughout. Thus,
in the last five years, through the great growth of Yale College, her
proportional contribution to the ministry has dropped from 7 per
cent of her graduates to 6 per cent. Meantime the story of Harvard
in this connection shows interesting relations with both those of
Princeton and that of Yale. Taking the twenty-five years together,
Harvard is to be ranked with Yale, the annual enlistment being 10
at Harvard and 9 at Yale. During the last five years, however,
the Harvard figures rather more than double, advancing from 8 to
18; so that, while for the whole period of twenty-five years Harvard
has trained but a few more ministers than Yale, in the last five
years she has trained scarcely fewer than Princeton, and just double
as many as Yale. Moreover, while in both Yale and Princeton the
proportionate figures decline, at Harvard, in spite of her growth
from a class of 212 in 1889 to 283 in 1893, the proportion of her

graduates becoming ministers has advanced from 5 per cent to 7 per cent of each class. I am here dealing with facts alone, and deny myself much speculation about causes, but the transition in this case cannot be interpreted without reference to another movement. The change of attitude toward the ministry at Harvard University is coincident with the first years of the voluntary system in religion. The Harvard figures practically double from the year when this system began to have its full effect, and no one who is familiar with the life of Harvard University during the last five years can doubt that the increase of its graduates seeking the ministry is at least in some degree a result of regarding religion as a privilege and opportunity rather than an obligation and discipline.

If, finally, in this limited inquiry, we sum up the present situation in the different colleges, we observe that in the last five years Tulane and Minnesota have kept their proportionate contribution practically fixed; and the following show a proportionate decline: Amherst, Brown, Colby, Cornell, Dartmouth, Johns Hopkins, Lake Forest, Oberlin, Princeton, California, Iowa, Kansas, Michigan, Missouri, Wesleyan, Williams, Yale; and the following a proportionate advance: Boston, Bowdoin, De Pauw, Columbia, Harvard, Trinity, Tufts, Pennsylvania, University of the South. The largest relative decline is shown by Lake Forest; the largest relative advance by Trinity: the largest positive decline is shown by Amherst; the largest positive advance by Harvard.

Such seems to be the evidence of a few American colleges as to the movement of their relation to the ministry. There remains, however, another point of view from which the whole subject may be considered, as it were, from the opposite side. Suppose we turn from the colleges to the theological schools and consider their present condition. How do they stand in relation to the colleges? Are they recruited from the uneducated classes? Is the standard of their scholarship inferior to that of other professional schools, or is it absolutely declining? It is of course to be admitted that there are many schools for the ministry, as there are for the professions of law or medicine, which are expressly designed for non-academic students; and it is of course also true that many students pass from these schools of popular instruction to faithful and effective service. But if we turn to the more conspicuous schools of the country, we shall find that their academic standard and demands indicate a relation to the colleges which may surprise some critics of the profession.

The following table presents the condition of twelve theological schools, selected only as being most easily within reach, and reported through the extreme kindness of official representatives.

Theological Schools.	Average per cent A.B.'s 10 years.	Average per cent A.B.'s last 5 years.
Andover Theological School	77	78
Boston University School of Theology	54	53
Episcopal Theological School (Cambridge)	72	78
General Seminary of the Protestant Episcopal Church	79	74
Hartford Theological Seminary	82	78
Harvard Divinity School	74	72
Newton Theological School	57	49
Oberlin Theological School	54	45
Princeton Theological School	87	86
Rochester Theological Seminary (English Department)	62	68
Union Theological Seminary	88	82
Yale Divinity School	79	77

The average percentage of Bachelors of Arts in each school is given for the last ten years, and again for the last five years. Each student's name may be counted more than once, the figures representing not the number of separate students, but the general condition of each school in each year. The computation omits all other degrees except the Bachelors of Arts, as well as all who have entered from institutions not conferring degrees; and the net result indicates that for these ten years about 70 per cent of the students of these schools were college graduates. This means, as a matter of fact, that these schools of theology are practically administered on the post-graduate level of instruction. Their standard of antecedent education is undoubtedly higher than can be claimed for almost any school of law or medicine in this country. The best theological schools are still the best representatives of a thoroughly educated profession.

Finally, one other question presents itself, which should be of extreme interest both to the theological schools and the colleges. It is the question of the sources of supply from which the Bachelors of Arts in the theological schools are received. How is it that the ministry is reinforced by educated men? From what colleges do the seminaries draw their supply? Are the sources much the same from year to year, and in what proportion do the large and the small institutions contribute? An inquiry of this kind, extending over a series of years, would be instructive for any theological school to make, and two specimen cases have been carefully analyzed for the purposes of this paper by officers of the schools. One is the case of a large school, Union Seminary; and the other that of a small school—Hartford. In both cases the total number of Bachelors of Arts has been computed for each year. From 1883 to 1893 each student's name therefore, as before, is likely to be reckoned more than once. Each of these cases gives the same general evidence as to the movement of Bachelors of Arts toward the schools of theology. In the first place, both cases show that their main sources of supply are practically fixed. Union Seminary, for instance, since 1883, has had on its roll 1,340 Bachelors of Arts, representing no less than 122 colleges; but of these students 798, or more than one-half, have been drawn from only 16 institutions, or about one-eighth of the whole number of colleges. Hartford, in the same period, has instructed 444 Bachelors of Arts, drawn from 43 colleges; but 232 of these students, or more than one-half, have come from 4 institutions, or less than one-tenth. Moreover, Union Seminary in 1893 received 76 of its 111 Bachelors of Arts from the same colleges which in 1883 gave it 67 out of its 116 Bachelors. Thus the chief sources of supply remain on the whole constant from year to year. But on the other hand, both cases disclose a great number of subsidiary sources of supply, which are often of great importance. In 1883 Union Seminary derived its 116 Bachelors of Arts from no less than 50 colleges, and in each of the ten years since that date it has added about 7 new institutions to its list of sources, each contributing to it on the average about one student a year. The largest contributor to Union Seminary during the period considered has been Lafayette College (112 students in eleven years); and important reinforcements have come from Rutgers, from the University of the City of New York, from the University of Vermont, from Wabash College, from Park College, and from Marysville College. All these institutions should be included in any full examination of the college tendencies. Much the same story is true of Hartford. In 1883 its Bachelors of Arts came from 12 colleges, but in the last ten years it has extended its constituency at the rate of 3 colleges a year. Some of its earlier sources of supply have greatly declined. Amherst, which once sent it 20 men, now sends it but 3; Dartmouth, which in 1883 contributed 10 students, in 1893 sends but 5. Harvard College, on the other hand, has become within this period a considerable contributor to various divinity schools; to Yale (32 men in seven years), to Hartford

(25 men in ten years), and to Union (13 men in ten years); while at the same time the Divinity School of Harvard University shows a growth from 5 Bachelors of Arts of Harvard College in 1883 to 18 in 1893. Thus, an inquiry into the sources of supply of the theological schools, while it shows the importance of the large and constant contributors, discloses also the significance to the university of the constantly increasing number and humbler activity of the many obscurer colleges which make their small offerings to the higher education. These little rills refresh each year the stream which would, if it depended on its main sources alone, run a meagre course. Each year the seminaries find the range of their work enlarged by a new constituency from these less conspicuous colleges, which by these gifts to the Christian ministry go far to justify the sacrifices and the public spirit which they represent.

Looking back, then, on the data thus collected, the general impression they may give to one who cares for theological education seems to be one of reasonable satisfaction. It is, indeed, true that the proportion of Bachelors of Arts entering the ministry has somewhat declined in the last quarter of a century; but this decline, after all, is less than might be anticipated, and it is perhaps not greater than other professions have experienced. It is true, also, that some of the colleges seem to be failing as sources of supply, but, on the other hand, some are gaining in volume. Moreover, the gain appears sometimes to be most marked where the college is in the midst of modern life and interests, and the loss appears in some instances most decided in some of the most sheltered institutions. It would seem, therefore, that among the most favorable conditions for making ministers in times like ours are those where the college is most open to freedom of research, and in close relation to the needs and problems of modern society. There are many influences which still threaten the self-respect of the ministry: a pernicious system of indiscriminate aid in many seminaries, a tradition of sentimentalism in the profession, and an increasing attraction to other careers. In this state of things it is a satisfaction to believe that the best theological schools still maintain the standard of a scholarly profession, and that the call to the ministry is still heard above the noises of the time, and is still obeyed by educated young men.

FRANCIS G. PEABODY.

PRESENT INDUSTRIAL PROBLEMS IN THE LIGHT OF HISTORY.

I AM asked to deal with the causes of discontent and their true significance; with the possible lines of improvement; with the effect of the factory system; with the existence of class feeling and with the dangers to liberty—if there are any—in existing combinations of capital in trusts or corporations, or combinations of men in trades-unions and other associations.

This is rather a broad field to be covered in a Review article. In dealing with it I must appeal mainly to the reader's imagination, for I can only make a sketch; and I shall, to get the proper perspective, go back for a moment almost to the beginning of the institutions from which our own have been evolved.

Under the feudal system as it was in early days among the Teutonic races of Europe from whom we are derived, the classes protected the masses in a more or less genuine manner, demanding in return their feudal service. Our ancestors were of an independent type. They were not bound by the restrictions of any specially revealed religion, which possesses such an obstructive force in its effect upon those who are held by it. As time goes on, dogmatic theology possesses less and less hold upon the minds of their descendants. In these earlier days the merchant and the tradesman existed only in a few cities. Their prosperity was viewed with the utmost jealousy by the lords of the soil. They could not attain the possession of land outside the walls of their cities to any extent. They were not brought into direct relation with the masses of the peasants or the serfs who constituted the great body of the population. The factory system had as yet no existence. There was little or no interdependence of communities on each other.

Presently came the Crusades, promoting a wild enthusiasm among the higher classes, who were granted stay-laws in respect to their debts to the merchants; they were also permitted to mortgage their lands to the money-lenders of the cities in order to raise the outfit with which to go on the Crusade. Under the influence of this so-called religious enthusiasm, they gathered their dependents and men-at-arms about them, and went marching away to the Holy Land, where they conveniently left their bones in very large numbers,—thus perhaps rendering the best service that they could give at that time to the cause of civilization.   The hold of their class on land, which had been attained by means of force, was greatly diminished or weakened in this period, while the common men-at-arms brought back from the far East the knowledge of the cultivation of maize into southern Europe, where it is still grown under the name of Turkish corn.   They also brought back the art of weaving and dyeing, especially silks. They learned the fine art of making steel, of which the finest type was the Damascus blade.   In southern Europe the finest type was the Toledo blade, made under the instruction of the Moors, whose exclusion from Spain carried away so much of art, of literature, and of industry.

Subsequently came the great invention of gunpowder.   This was the greatest equalizer of conditions ever brought into the world.   It rendered the unarmored man the equal in force of him who had previously held dominion over all, and it enabled the development of mining in a way that had never been conceived.   Under these conditions the struggle of the masses against the classes began.   It has not yet ended,—especially in Germany, where the rule of blood and iron is still imposed by the military caste which dominates the Empire.

Glance now at the condition of the English during the Wars of the Roses.   The lords and the knights, who were the privileged class,—even the bishops—battled with each other, more than decimating their own number in single battles.   They were attended, it is true, by their squires and their retainers, but these were relatively few in number compared to those who quietly remained working in the fields or laying the foundation of modern England in the workshop, presently in the factory.   Progress ensued the faster the so-called higher classes of that type diminished in number by their own contests among themselves.   It was the non-survival of those who were not fit to rule—the suicide (sometimes, in a tournament, the duicide) of the unfit.

It is well to remember that the higher classes in England in recent years have been almost wholly recruited from among the men of affairs, not from the men-at-arms.   England owes its wealth and its present measure of welfare to the former class.

It is only when we come to the latter part of the last century that we stand at the very inception of the factory system, with which we

are now to deal.   Before we take up that question let us ask ourselves to what was the strength of England due in the conduct of the
great Napoleonic struggle.   England, with an audacity in inverse
proportion to her number, then less in the whole kingdom than ten
millions, had vainly attempted, after " the manner of a bulldog with
confused ideas," to keep dominion over our ancestors, three millions in
number, of a similar type, occupying the maritime border of a whole
continent, and as obstinate as their fathers had · been before them.
What an absurd bit of audacity that struggle now appears to us!
Yet, in spite of its absurdity, this attempt to hold the armed control
over the American Colonies might have been successful.   Had it
been so, it would have been owing to the folly of our revered patriot
fathers who controlled the finances of the Colonies for the first four
years, and who, with ideas as muddled as those of many of the present
day, nearly ruined the country with fiat money.   It was the French
and Dutch loan, negotiated in coin, that saved the patriot cause from
disaster.   There is always a material element, or an element of the
commissariat, underlying success or failure in war.   It was the rapid
concentration of the German troops by great forced marches, each
corps arriving at the right place at the right time, by which the French
were conquered in the Franco-Prussian war.   That ability to march
may be attributed to the German army sausage, without which the
German rifles would probably have failed to be effective at the right
time and at the right place.

I have put the question, What was it that gave to England, with
her small population, such a dominating power?   Was it not the very
factory system with which we are struggling?   Was it not the application of steam to power?   Was it not the invention of the blast-
furnace and the development of coal and iron?   Were not the great
mechanical forces the source of the energy which enabled England to
establish her world-wide commerce, by which she obtained the wealth
that enabled her to subsidize European states and armies, and to fight
Napoleon with money more than she did with men?   Did she not
buy the Hessians with whom she tried to conquer us?   Without that
English money-power Napoleon would never have been conquered.
Pitt was a disciple of Adam Smith.   He had planned a reform-bill
of a very broad scope.   He had planned methods for the relief of
Great Britain from the restrictions upon commerce which for centuries had deprived her of a part of her true force, so that throughout
the seventeenth century the Dutch excelled her.   All these plans for

the amelioration of the condition of the people and of commerce he was obliged to give up in order to carry on the great struggle with Napoleon. Why was it necessary? What did Napoleon himself aim at? At one time, quite early in the struggle, had he not reconstructed the map of Europe on far better lines than had ever existed before or have ever been established since? Had he not then united most of the States of Germany under the Confederation of the Rhine? Had he not excluded Austria frcm Italy? Had he not cause for many of the boasts in his grandiloquent addresses to the soldiers?

What might have been the history of Europe had Napoleon, instead of attempting to destroy the trade and commerce of England even as late as the Berlin and Milan decrees, simply recognized the fact that all nations and states are interdependent, and acted on the principle that in the great commerce among nations all men serve each others' needs? This principle was sustained even by his own great Minister of Finance, against whose counsel he adopted what was called the Continental system for destroying the commerce of Great Britain. What might have been the history of the present century if Napoleon had been as truly enlightened about the affairs of commerce as he was in the work which he did in establishing the French law on the basis of what is known as the *Code Napoléon*, or had he applied the same intelligence which he exercised in bringing men into place and power without regard to birth or previous condition, and in establishing true lines in laying out the map of Europe?

Suppose he had co-operated with Pitt in an enlightened commercial system. There would then have been no restoration of the Bourbons in France or in Italy. There would then have been no renewal of Austrian tyranny. There would then have been no disaster at Leipsic; no French Revolution of 1830. There might then have been no later Austro-Prussian war. There might then have been no Franco-Prussian war. The greater part of the burden of debt which now oppresses Europe would not have been incurred. He might then, in co-operation with Austria, in place of moving upon Moscow, have moved upon Constantinople, and shoved the unspeakable Turk out of Europe. Modern civilization, with the benefits of commerce, might have been a century in advance of what it now is. Had he established peaceful relations of mutual service after he had put men from the masses above the classes, there would now be no oppressive war-taxes as barriers between European countries, by which the very life-blood of nations is drawn away to support four million men who are now worse than wasting their lives in camps and barracks, while the women are to-day doing the scavenger-work of the streets, winding coal up from the mines because woman power is cheaper than steam power, mixing the mortar for the building trades, and living under conditions, even in the rich city of Frankfort, so abject that the water in which one man's sausage is boiled can be sold to him who has no sausage, to give a little flavor to a starvation diet.

But this was not to be.   Napoleon was conquered by the English money-power.   That power originated and rested upon coal, iron, and steel, and upon the mechanism of the factory and the workshop.   That paramount British power has culminated.   The dominion of coal, iron, and steel has come to our land.   Upon us now rests the responsibility for the use of this power.   Shall we exert it in the cause of peace, good will, and plenty, by promoting the interdependence of nations, or shall we waste it in building ships of war bearing the disgraceful name of " commerce-destroyers"?

I have in this way tried to lead up to the true aspect of the questions with which I started out.   One may now ask, What has been the greatest change in the condition of society which has been affected by these forces?   Do I go too far in my appeal to the reader's imagination if I say that it has been the elimination of friction in what Carey called the " societary circulation" of commodities? These are long words of which I am not fond.   I will put the case in a plainer way:

All that we can do is to move something.   We can make nothing. We produce or lead forth.   We could move no trains if the wheels did not stick to the rail.   We could not move the wheels of commerce at all if there were no friction due to gravitation.   There could be no movement without resistance, and yet all that we do is to apply science so as to overcome resistance.   By way of resistance comes development.   Through the action of these great moving forces all men have become interdependent.   There is no such thing as independence.   I hold in my hand the symbol of an almighty dollar.   It is tied to the standard of value of the world's commerce by redemption, and is convertible on demand.   This dollar is almighty in a sense of which few men have any conception.   I am led, through my food " fad," to which I have given so much attention, to cite the work of the almighty dollar in proof that in " the societary circulation of commodities" all that we do is to move something. We make nothing.   Distance has been sunk in a fraction of a cent a ton a mile, and the world has become one great neighborhood. I can change the dollar into dimes, nickels, and cents, and, passing around through a series of shops in Boston, I first buy four pounds of the coarser but more nutritious parts of beef. Where did it come from? From the plains of Nebraska or Texas, brought through the packing-house in Chicago to within a few rods of the door of my office. I buy a few little bones of the breast of mutton, brought from Kentucky; a pound and a half of fish from the Grand Banks; and a half a pound of bacon or pork from Illinois; a half a pound of butter or a pound of butterine from Michigan. I go to another shop and I buy four pounds of flour or meal (from which I can make a pound of bread a day) that has been brought from Minnesota or Dakota or even from Oregon or California. I buy a pound of sugar produced by the peasants of Germany in the beet-fields. I buy twenty pounds of vegetables which may have come from the maritime provinces of Canada or from the far-away Southern States, according to the season. I buy some oranges from Florida, some grapes from Ohio. I add a little tea from China or Ceylon, a little coffee from Java or South America, salt from Liverpool, pepper from Sumatra, spice from the Spice Islands, and I have expended the almighty dollar. I have placed on my table twenty-six pounds of well-balanced, varied, and nutritious food material, which I can then convert, under a flour barrel made into an oven, into the most appetizing and nutritious food with the heat developed by two cents' worth of oil from Pennsylvania or Ohio and it will give me adequate and complete nutrition for one week—three full meals a day—twenty-one meals for one almighty dollar. That dollar's worth of food, if I bought it to-morrow in Boston, would have been brought more than a thousand miles from the far-away sources that I have named.

This is the beneficent aspect of that great power of competition by which men are compelled to co-operate and to serve each other's needs whether they will or not. Yet there is discontent. There ought to be discontent. There are wrongs affecting this man who earns a dollar a day. There are wrongs for which society as a whole must be held responsible; wrongs due to putting ignorant men in places of power, who tamper with the standard of value; wrongs due to putting selfish men in places of power, who pervert the force of taxation to private ends; wrongs due to those who, by neglect of their political duties, permit cities to be misgoverned and legislators to be suborned. The discontent which does to some extent pervade great masses of people is a reflection of these wrongs, which those who are affected by them know not how to remedy. If men of intelligence fail to recognize the fact that a part of the discontent which now actuates great masses of people is well grounded, then the remedy may be a very rough one, but it will be complete.

The railway-wrecker may have laid his maleficent hand upon the railway stocks and bonds of the country. He may have perverted a trust so as to make the fortunes of those who connive at the wrong, and so as to mar the welfare of those whose trusts he betrayed. But those stocks and bonds are but loaded dice with which gamblers steal from each other in such transactions; not of course in all. Whatever happens to the stock and bonds, the railway service itself must do its work in the service of the community and under a higher law of competition than any which can be evaded,—the competition of product with product in the great markets. The railways are compelled to do the maximum service at the minimum of charge, lest there should be no work to be done that would justify the existence of the tracks.

Under the influence of this great force the charges made on all the railways of the United States have been reduced from time to time ever since the service had an existence. In the period that elapsed from 1865 to 1869 the rates were considered very low and the service was constantly improving, and becoming greater and greater. Yet, low as these rates then were, had all the railways of the United States during the last ten years been able to make a similar charge for their service, they would have earned each year for ten years a thousand million dollars ($1,000,000,000) more than they did earn. The gross difference between what the railways of the United States did earn in the last ten years, and what they would have received at the rates of 1865 to 1869, comes to over ten thousand million dollars ($10,000,-000,000), and that is a greater sum than the market value of all the stocks and bonds of all the railways even before the panic depressed them. The service which these railways rendered to each of us yesterday was to move sixty pounds of food, fuel, or fabric over one hundred miles at a charge of less than three cents. Without that service modern society could not exist.

I have referred to these matters of past history in order to lead up to the conditions of the present in our own country. The paramount control of all the imperial deposits of iron ores, of copper, and of coal, now rests with us. The development of the factory system, which has gone to such an extreme in Great Britain as to destroy the balance of occupations, to the end that more than half her supply of food must be drawn from far distant regions, has brought Great Britain into rather a dangerous condition. Her power to supply her people with food, and with the materials—mainly cotton and wool—on which so large a body of people work, depends upon her ability to sell her finished fabrics in all parts of the world; and that power of sale originated in iron, steel, and coal.

There are but two groups of machine-using nations which have as yet applied the power of metal and steam in any considerable measure. One group consists of France, the Netherlands, and Germany; their supplies of ore and coal are wholly insufficient to meet any considerable increased demand. Regarding the area of both countries, France is fertile, but Germany quite the reverse; this great body of people can barely supply themselves with their own food.

The only group which has applied the powers of coal and iron in fullest measure consists of the English-speaking people, of whom we are the larger body. The British group is in fact poorly endowed either with coal or ores of the right qualities. The supply of fine ores for making steel comes mainly from Spain and other foreign sources. Coal may not be approaching exhaustion, but is drawn from excessive depths at steadily increasing cost.

The only machine-using nation which possesses the power of producing food, fuel, and iron in excess of any possible want for generations to come, is our own. It follows that, whatever may be the delay or obstruction, this country will become within a very short time the greatest agricultural, manufacturing, shipbuilding, and commercial country in the world. As soon as these forces are allowed to take their natural and normal development, rapid progress will occur, but the forced or stimulated development of special branches of industry by legislation has brought many of the very evils upon us with which I was called upon to deal in this lecture. The collective or factory system has been forced to an unnatural development in many directions, notably in the arts to which the term "manufacturing" is apt to be limited, namely, the production of iron and steel, the textile arts, the working of metals, glass, pottery, and a few other articles which in fact constitute a small part of our manufactures.

Strikes are more apt to occur in these arts than in any others. These arts themselves and the strikes are brought into conspicuous notice by constant agitation. It may seem surprising that the col-

4

lective or factory system of work gives employment at this time to not exceeding ten in each hundred of all who are occupied for gain. More than half of our working population is devoted to agriculture, which is of necessity individual, or not collective to any extent. Here and there, there is a great field of manufacture, as of wheat in the far Northwest, but the single crop is fading out; even the production of wheat is coming into rotation in a varied system, as the great cotton plantations have yielded to varied crops and to a more intensive, or to an individual, system of cultivation. Eighteen per cent of all who are occupied for gain are engaged in professional and personal service, which is of necessity individual in its quality. Ten and a half per cent are occupied in trade and transportation, and while there are some great combinations in the railway service, that bring a small number into a union, the work itself requires individual aptitude and does not in any degree correspond to the collective or factory system. There remain to be considered the mechanic arts, manufactures, and mining. By far the larger portion in these classes are the individual mechanics, each working with personal aptitude as an artisan or as a craftsman rather than as an operative.

In the last analysis, if we put into the category of the collective or factory system all in blast-furnaces and steel-works—all the textile operatives, all who are occupied in making clothing, all the machinists and all others who can be brought together under single roofs, each doing only one part of the work, they number less than ten in a hundred. It is among these that we have to cope with most of our present difficulties. This collective work is necessary because the textile worker, for instance, performs a hundredfold more work than the individual spinner or weaver. Three persons, mainly women, in each hundred persons, supply us with all our fabrics for clothing in excessive abundance. If all this work were done on the individual principle, and the effort were made to give us an equal supply to that which we now enjoy, there would be no time left for anything else. The benefits are therefore plain. The evils consist in our long hours of work of a very monotonous kind, to some extent destructive to individualism.

Our present difficulties are not to be attributed to organization of labor, but rather to lack of organization of labor. If I am rightly informed, the total number registered in all the trades-unions is but a few hundred thousand. The organization known as the Knights of Labor in its palmiest day reached a considerable number, but it has almost faded out. There are now at least eighteen to twenty million men and two to three million women belonging to the ranks of labor, by far the greater part of whom are working on in isolation. What is most needed is that the representatives of each of the different arts shall be organized, in order that through organization each union may come to comprehend the terms of its own existence and the conditions under which its own work must be done. I even welcome the Farmers' Alliance, and the Grangers, and all that: anything better than stagnation or inertia. The farmers are learning the true lesson. The cheap-jacks who first misled them are being thrown out of the ranks. The strong men, who for a long time were themselves at first deluded as to what they could do, are learning how to lead. Step by step the organization of labor will proceed. The terms of admission to the trades-unions will become, as they were in the guilds, the possession of skill, aptitude, character, and merit. True unions will cease to attempt to reduce all their members to the dead level of mediocrity, or else all men above mediocrity will leave them and form new organizations by which the inferior ones will be beaten out of existence.

If we explore the deeper currents now actuating great bodies of men, we may see that these forces of intelligence are surely working either to the destruction of the labor organizations that are trying to work against the nature of things; or else by development they are bringing the labor organizations to a true perception of what the rights of labor really are. On the other hand, I think there is a rapidly growing perception on the part of the possessors of property as to what the duties of capital are.

Nor have I any fears of trusts. They are of two kinds. One is a mere combination of very able men, who, having obtained the control of certain enterprises, combine and hold it by doing the work for society at less cost than it was ever done before, and at less cost than it could be done except by such combination. And yet even these trusts may not be of long duration. The Standard Oil Company has worked so effectually that light is furnished us at less cost than any other important article of living, and, as I have said, a man can cook his week's supply of provisions with two cents' worth of Standard oil; yet even with that expenditure of energy I do not suppose more than five per cent—even if as much—of the real potential of the oil is converted into the work of cooking. There are other trusts and companies which are merely of a selfish order, often a fraud upon the community. Such combinations contain the seeds of their own dissolution, and may even promote—as strikes also often promote—the completion of important inventions which might have been delayed for many years except for this incentive. I know of no textile art in which the mechanism is so crude or so far behind that of others as the making of cordage. A trust which would undertake to limit the products of that art and to confine it to existing inventions could have no permanent existence. There are many other trusts too numerous to mention; but I venture to say that there is not one from which any excess of profit is or can now be derived that is not at the mercy of some one or perhaps of a hundred inventors, by whom every process that the trust controls will be invented out of existence within the next ten years.

Of all the mechanism and the processes exhibited in the first World's Fair of 1851 there is scarcely a process that has not been displaced; hardly one bit of mechanism that has not gone to the scrap-heap of old metal. Of all that was exhibited in the Centennial of 1876 very few processes remain that have not been greatly changed at lessening cost; hardly a single bit of mechanism that would not be built in a far better way at far less cost to-day. The progress of science and invention in its effect upon capital is most destructive, substituting year by year more effective examples of capital at lessening cost, by means of which the labor cost of production is diminished and the rates of wages are augmented.

Leisure, which consists in the diligent and intelligent use of time by him who earns it, has become more and more within the control of intelligent men and women as the benefits of science and invention become distributed among the great mass of the people. It is difficult to conceive the increase in productive power that has been brought about in this country since the end of the Civil War. I know of no example that will prove the progress of general intelligence more conclusively than to cite the fact that the postal receipts of this country have increased from $14,000,000 in 1865 to $80,000,000 in 1892.

The true standing army of the United States—the only one on which we can rely for effective or useful service in the future—is the great body of teachers in our common schools, academies, and colleges. Their number has increased from 229,921 in 1872 to 377,000 in 1892. The appropriations for schools between these two periods have increased from $74,234,476 to $155,000,000, and yet how far short we are in our comprehension of the duty and the responsibility which now rest upon us!

There is a vision which will become a living truth. The barriers which have separated the different groups of the English-speaking people are about to be thrown down. We shall all soon be reunited in the bonds of mutual service. We are the complement of each other; the one branch producing in abundance what the other lacks. When we are reunited in reciprocity of trade without obstruction, all the evil powers of the world must go down before us; but as yet we utterly fail to comprehend our responsibility. The false principle that commerce is aggressive, and to be dealt with as a war of industries, has even within two years been put into one of its most malignant forms. Three naval vessels of a new type have lately been tested for their speed. They cost $3,000,000 each. It costs $800,000 a year to maintain them. What are they good for? Nothing. What are they bad for? Everything. They are worthless even as cruisers, because they can carry but little coal. They are worthless even as battle-ships, because their armor is light. They are worthless for defence in our harbors. Their very name is a disgrace. They are called " commerce-destroyers." Their cost was about as great as the whole endowment of Harvard University. The annual cost of maintaining three of this vile type of piratical destroyers is more than the annual expenditure of Harvard University for all its beneficent services. Our danger does not consist now in trusts or trades-unions. It consists in such treason to the very liberty of which we boast as we have embodied in these vessels. I think this phase of ignorance, or worse, is but a passing cloud. This cloud has a golden hue of which we are beginning to comprehend the meaning. The contest in Washington is not about a few trifling dollars more or less in taxation; it is a contest with an evil influence in our body politic and a false conception of rights and duties.

All commerce is altruistic, otherwise it could have no existence. The most potent and malignant influence, which has caused more misery in the world than any false concept, except that of miscalled religion, is the error that so long has governed nearly all nations; the error that aggravated the Napoleonic contests; the error that still retains a powerful and baneful influence in our own land,—namely, that in commerce what one nation gains another loses. If we can eradicate that false idea from legislation, almost all the evils that can be cured by legislation will vanish. That is the true issue now pending. It is a part of the great struggle for freedom.

EDWARD ATKINSON.

RESULTS OF THE PARLIAMENT OF RELIGIONS.

HISTORY has scarcely any contrast to present greater or more instructive than that between " the light of burning heretics," which threw its glare over the enterprise of Columbus, and the purer splendor of a parliament of religions, which cast its radiance, four centuries afterward, over the Columbian anniversary. The human race has been wofully divided by national and other antipathies, especially by those of religion. It is remarkable, therefore, that the first universal council ever held, the first parliament of man, was a religious convention. The world appears to be determined to regard the parliament of religions as vastly significant. To Bishop Coxe, of Western New York, an earnest foe of this congress, it is still " one of the most serious events of the kind in the history of human-ity, since the wise men from the east came to the cradle of Bethle-hem." Castelar writes that, " from the beginning of the world until to-day, history has never recorded an event so momentous as this union, under one roof and one leadership and for one purpose, of the clergy of the world." A representative voice from Hindustan,—the " Indian Mirror" of Calcutta,—regards the parliament as " the crown-ing work of the nineteenth century," and " the flower of the tree of religion which mankind has so long watered and pruned." Count D'Alviella, of Brussels, regards it as a fact of great importance " that the programme of the congress was accepted by confessions so diverse and numerous, and that these were drawn to meet on a footing of equality." [1] To Professor Emilio Comba, of Rome, it seemed like reviving the spectacle of the ancient Pantheon, where the priests of many faiths met with a smile, not of cunning, but of courtesy and tolerance. And President Martin writes from the Imperial Uni-versity of Peking that " it is now evident that the greatest thing at the World's Fair was the parliament of religions, which will be re-membered when the marvels of machinery are forgotten."

Though the Congress in Chicago has had many prophecies in

[1] The equality acknowledged was "parliamentary," not "doctrinal."

literature and many preparations in history, it was, as Rev. M. J. Savage has said, " the first really ecumenical meeting the world has ever seen." Every great event is the flower of all the ages which have preceded it, but the special preparations for this meeting in Chicago were: the almost universal spread of Christian missions; the rise and study of comparative religion; the wide use of the English language, making such a conference possible; international facilities for travel; ample religious freedom in America, where church and state are separated; the attractive opportunity afforded by a world's exposition; and much hard work extending over more than three years. A broad-minded lawyer of Chicago, Mr. Charles C. Bonney, is entitled to the great and lasting honor of having origi- nated and carried to success, in spite of numerous obstacles, the entire scheme of the world's congresses of 1893. The parliament of religions was one of more than two hundred of these conventions, and, accord- ing to Mr. Bonney, " the splendid crown" of the series.

With the great peace-bell at the fair, tolling, as many hoped, the death-knell to intolerance; with the rabbis of Israel praying at that hour in all lands that the name of Jehovah might be reverenced over all the earth; with representatives of ten religions gathered be- neath one roof; and with a Catholic Cardinal repeating the universal prayer of the world's Saviour, the parliament opened on the 11th of September, 1893. It was indeed a meeting of brotherhood, where " the Brahmin forgot his caste and the Catholic was chiefly conscious of his catholicity;" and where, in the audience, " the variety of in- terests, faiths, ranks, and races, was as great as that found on the platform." As the representatives of China, Russia, Germany, Hin- dustan, Sweden and Norway, Greece, France, Africa, the United States, and the all-clasping Empire of Great Britain, from England to New Zealand, uttered their thoughts and feelings, multitudes entered anew into the spirit of the Nazarene Prophet, who seemed always to include the whole world in His purpose and affection.

Professor Toy, of Harvard, has noted the physical difficulties of bringing such a parliament together, and he shows that it might easily have been a ludicrous and melancholy failure. The promoters of the plan were surprised at their own success, though the representa- tion of the world's faiths was less complete and imposing than they had endeavored to achieve. The absence of representatives of Hindu Mohammedanism was deplored. President Miller, of Madras, who was the chairman's chief counselor, despaired for a time of securing

any Hindu representation at Chicago.   Still the religious life of India
spoke through representatives of nearly all its leading systems.
Through an address by Vivekananda, and elaborate papers by Professor D'Vivedi and S. P. Aiyangar, different types of Hinduism
were presented; Narasima, a graduate of the Christian College at
Madras, criticised Christian missions; Laksmi Narain, of Lahore,
spoke for the Arya Somaj; Gandhi, the acute Bombay lawyer, for
Jainism; Mozoomdar and Nagarkar described with great eloquence
the principles of the Brahmo Somaj; while Miss Sorabji, Rev.
Maurice Phillips, Rev. R. A. Hume, Rev. T. E. Slater, and Rev.
T. J. Scott (these last two through papers), spoke for Christianity in
India.

Buddhism addressed the parliament through more than a dozen
voices, Ceylonese, Japanese, and Siamese, including that of a Siamese
prince; the religions of China were treated in seven different papers,
the most elaborate of which was by Pung Quang Yu, Secretary of
the Chinese Legation; Zoroastrianism was described in two excellent
essays; Mohammedanism in four addresses; Shintoism in two; Judaism in twelve; and Christianity—Greek, Latin, Lutheran, Anglican,
Reformed, Liberal, New Church—in nearly a hundred.   Although
much that passed for Oriental religion was a reflection of Christian
truth and European philosophy, still the Oriental speakers were, on
the whole, fairly representative of the higher ideas of their own
faiths, if not of the popular religions.   The results accomplished surpassed the popular expectations.   Prof. Max Müller, who would
have been present had he thought the dream was to be realized, regards the parliament as "one of the most encouraging signs of the
times, the first friendly meeting and mutual recognition of all the
religions of the world."

It would have been easy to defeat the objects of this meeting by
making it chiefly a scientific gathering.   But the purpose was not to
call together the specialists in comparative religion, to produce
learned and critical essays.   Such a proceeding would have killed the
parliament.   While scholarship was everywhere apparent, technical
scholarship was not made supremely prominent, and, according to
one participant, "the peculiar charm of this meeting consisted in
this, that it did not carry with it the predominant smell of the lamp."
The parliament was not expected to furnish new facts and ideas to
life-long students of comparative religion, but it did something
quite as important by drawing popular attention to this vital theme,

and by giving the world such a demonstration of its unity and such evidences of brotherhood as had never before been witnessed.

The historian who attempts any adequate review of what the world has said of this meeting is troubled by an embarrassment of riches. The comments which have already reached the Chairman would fill more than four thousand pages like those on which this article is printed.   According to one religious journal, "when the parliament adjourned, it really began its permanent sessions.   Its utterances have continued to echo around the huge whispering-gallery of the world."   The study of these criticisms will some day be an important chapter in the progress of comparative religion.   By Professor Headland, of the University of Peking, the parliament is regarded as "one of the most stupendous events and undertakings in the religious history of the world"; valuable, among other things, in showing how strong are the great systems with which Christianity is contending, and how stupendous is the task which it has undertaken.   According to Dr. Paul Carus it will "exert a lasting influence upon the religious intelligence of mankind."   To the Archbishop of Zante it is "a strong foundation-stone for the religious temple of the future."   The secretary of the Apostolic Durbar of Calcutta, representing the Brahmo Somaj, looks upon the parliament as the realization of what that Society of the Worshippers of God has been laboring thirty years to achieve, and as an object-lesson of that dispensation which the Brahmo Somaj is now living under, and which St. Paul speaks of as "the dispensation of the fulness of time, in which he might gather together in one all things in Christ." An old Israelite in Germany, who could not read the American papers sent him by his son, an American rabbi, but who looked with wonder at the various pictures of the men and women representing such diverse faiths in the parliament, wrote back: ".The times of the Messiah have come."

According to "Le Temps," of Paris, the parliament was the most novel and amazing spectacle which America has offered.   The builder of the exposition, Daniel H. Burnham, said recently that "a thousand years hence about all that the world will remember of the fair will be the parliament"; and to President Higinbotham it is "the proudest work of our exposition."   The evident reason for this belief is that, while the fair was no novelty, the parliament was unique and unexampled, and purposed, in a great school of comparative theology, to bring the different faiths into contact and conference; to deepen the spirit of brotherhood; to emphasize the dis. tinctive truths of each religion; to show why men believe in God and the future life; to bridge the chasm of separation between Christians of different names and religious men of all names; to induce good men to work together for common ends; and to promote the cause of international peace.

From the moment of its inception the proposed congress was attacked on various grounds; and although the great majority of the religious newspapers in America have been friendly to the undertaking, and although the parliament and its literature silenced a vast deal of criticism, still the voice of condemnation and the cries of bigotry and fear have been heard in many lands. It has been stigmatized as " Bedlam," " Babel," and " a booth in Vanity Fair;" and its promoters have been likened to Balaam and Judas Iscariot! All this shows that the parliament has important work yet to do in the world.

The hyper-orthodoxy and exclusiveness which resent the classification of Christianity with other religions should not forget the historic fact that Christianity *is* one of the faiths of the world, competing for the conquest of mankind, and that, historically considered, it has not been so faultless as to defy competition and comparison. " By their fruits ye shall know them." " I shall never forget the lesson which it has been to me," writes Prof. Max Müller, " while walking through the lowest streets of Constantinople, never to see a drunken man or woman." Reasonable men perceive that comparison must be made, and missionaries in the Orient well know that defying competition is a pretty sad business. Why should there be such an apparent lack of faith in Christian truth on the part of some zealous propagandists? Why is it felt that most people cannot be suffered to learn more than one side of this question, and why should noble-hearted disciples of Christ act on the theory that Christianity is darkness rather than light, since it seems to fear such illumination as comes from a friendly comparison with other faiths? And why should those who stab the parliament with Biblical verses omit to quote the comprehensive scriptural declaration that " God is no respecter of persons, but in every nation he that feareth Him and worketh righteousness is acceptable of Him"?

Some have criticised the parliament on the ground that Christian believers must not tolerate error, by which is meant departure from the critic's own interpretations. But what are we going to do with error? Persecute it? If we are not willing to tolerate it, to listen to it, to find out the truth which may be at the heart of it, to supplement it, to enlighten it and remove it, we have no proper place in this humanitarian century. We should go back and take our stand by the side of Torquemada, or the persecuting Protestants of the sixteenth century.

The critics sometimes insist on the unique charms and claims of Christianity, implying that the Christian speakers in the parliament hid the heavenly light under a bushel. Dr. Morgan Dix thinks that the Christians who were present " were attacking the Cross of Christ," —a statement which is fairly questionable after reading the opinion of the missionary, Dr. George William Knox, that " the parliament was distinctively Christian in its conception, spirit, prayers, doxologies, benedictions; in its prevailing language, arguments, and faith." " Amid the bewildering maze of Oriental faiths represented," says one report, " Christianity shone out more luminous than ever as the universal, uplifting force of the world." Strong in its divine certainties and forces, Christianity received meekly the blows dealt at the sins of Christendom. The advances which the Christian faith lovingly made to the non-Christian representatives were no concession of weakness, but an illustration of its consciousness of truth and power. We do well to remember that " the representatives of Christianity" have been so unjust and so cruel in the past to the ancient Oriental religions that " no amount of courtesy or consideration would be excessive compensation."

No other event ever awakened so wide and sympathetic an interest in comparative religion, " the highest study to which the human mind can now devote its energies." The spectacle itself gave vividness and reality to the vague popular notions of the ethnic faiths. Scientific study of this theme has been confined to the few, and scholars are now grateful that the parliament has aroused such general interest in it on the part of educated people. Through the daily press of Chicago, which gave fifty columns each day for seventeen days to the proceedings of the congress, and through the religious press of many lands, the words spoken have already reached millions. The more permanent literary fruitage of this congress, giving its proceedings in books, with more or less fulness, has been large, more than a hundred thousand copies of these various volumes having already been taken. They have gone, not only into the great libraries, into the hands of preachers and scholars, but also into the homes of thoughtful people among the laity of the six continents.[1]

Many hundreds of lectures on the parliament have been delivered in all parts of the world. Prof. G. Bonet-Maury, who ably represented liberal French Protestantism in Chicago, has frequently spoken on the parliament in France. The eloquent voice of Father Hyacinthe has been heard extolling the high purposes of this congress. Count Goblet D'Alviella has lectured on it before the School of Social Sciences annexed to the University of Brussels, and Prof. Max Müller has made it the theme of a discourse in Oxford. In his course of six addresses in Boston, Joseph Cook stoutly championed the parliament from the standpoint of aggressive orthodoxy. The parliament has been a frequent topic of discussion in colleges and Chautauqua assemblies; and at the midwinter fair in San Francisco a congress of religions was addressed by more than twenty speakers. Among the echoes of the parliament, beside the recent Liberal Congress in Chicago, are: the proposition to hold a second parliament in Benares, in regard to which Mr. Dharmapala has already consulted the Maharajah of that ancient and sacred city; and a plan, now well under way, of holding a universal religious parliament in Jerusalem at the opening of the twentieth century.

One of the first fruits of the congress of last September is the gift of $20,000 by Mrs. Caroline E. Haskell to establish a lectureship on comparative religion in the University of Chicago, where that department is already notable. This has been followed by another noble gift by Mrs. Haskell, of $100,000 to build for the university an Oriental museum, to be devoted to lecture-rooms,

[1] It is worth while to recall that the interest in this literature comes not only from the fact that the parliament dealt with all the highest themes, and was enriched by such minds as those of Cardinal Gibbons, the Archbishop of Zante, Bishop Dudley, Bishop Keane, Mgr. Seton, Mgr. D'Harlez, Canon Fremantle, Sir William Dawson, Colonel Higginson, Principal Grant, Joseph Cook, Mrs. Chant, Julia Ward Howe, Count Bernstorff, Prince Wolkonski, Miss Willard, Modi, Mozoomdar, Minas Tcheraz, Dharmapala, Rabbis Wise, Gottheil, Kohler, Silverman, Mendes, Professors Drummond, Fisher, Bruce, Carpenter, Richey, Ely, Peabody, Albert Réville, Jean Réville, Lyon, Goodspeed, Toy, Dwight, Tiele, Townsend, Wilkinson, Terry, Drs. Schaff, Byrne, Washburn, Gladden, Momerie, Briggs, Munger, Hale, Dennis, Harris, Alger, Carroll, Post, Haweis, F. E. Clark, Mills, Abbott, Scovel, Hirsch, Paton, Pentecost, Gracey, Martin, Moxom, Jessup, Rexford, Boardman, and scores beside, but also from the fact that such varied minds were agreed in the sentiments of brotherhood which called the parliament, and which made it, as the Buddhist bishop, Right Rev. Shaku Soyen, believed, "the greatest spiritual phenomenon ever produced."

collections, and studies in the Semitic department.   A proposition now comes from a prominent English scholar that a trustworthy and interesting manual of comparative religion should be prepared for the youth in our Sunday-schools.   Still further, a religious parliament extension society has been organized, under the presidency of Dr. Paul Carus, to continue the work by promoting a sympathetic and mutual understanding of the world's great faiths.

In these days no study is of the highest value that is not comparative; and some Christians will yet discover that the strongest evidence of Christianity may be furnished by the study which many of them now fear, just as the comparative history of miracles is believed by many to be one of the best defences of Biblical supernaturalism.   If Christianity be " the only religion which faces all the facts," it has a magnificent opportunity, both in colleges and mission fields, to vindicate itself.   Its apostles need both sympathy and knowledge with regard to the faiths of the world, and the non-Christian peoples need both sympathy and knowledge in regard to Christianity.   The parliament, in some measure, answered these requirements; and where it failed,—since doubtless some of the Oriental faiths were not accurately and adequately set forth,—it has furnished a stimulus to further sympathetic inquiry.

The Orientals attending the parliament were deeply impressed by the fraternity and Christian love which invited them, furnished them hospitality, gave them a free platform, and welcomed their sharpest criticisms of Christendom.   The eloquent Buddhist, Mr. Hirai, said to me on leaving for Japan:

"I go back a Christian, by which I mean that Christianity is a religion which I shall be glad to see established in Japan.   Only let the Christian missionaries not interfere with our national usages and patriotic holidays.   I have been delighted with America and especially with its tolerance.   I expected that before I finished my address, criticising false Christianity in Japan, I should be torn from the platform.   But I was received with enthusiasm."

Mr. Gandhi, the critic of Christian missions, said: " American Christianity I like; it is something better than what we have usually seen in India."   The high priest of Shintoism, Rt. Rev. R. Shibata, and the Buddhist bishop, Zitzusen Ashitsu, write with grateful enthusiasm of their reception in America.   The international friendships knit by the Congress of 1893 are a contribution to international peace, while inter-religious good-will is a manifest help to the study of comparative theology.

While modifying some popular views of the Oriental faiths, the parliament is promoting a new and humaner interest in foreign missions, by making the ethnic systems more real, and also more definite, to millions of minds, by showing Christians that these faiths are far from dead, though they may have little life-giving power over their adherents; by setting before the Christian world the magnitude of the task it has undertaken; and by teaching it that it must make its swifter and wider conquests in the future by a better understanding and a larger sympathy, rather than by contemptuous hostility and bigoted exclusiveness. The effect of the parliament was felt immediately, in the magnificent Missionary Congress which followed it, and a new tone of kindliness and tolerance has marked many of the recent gatherings and discussions in foreign missionary societies. What Christendom needs to-day is to ponder and take to heart the truths proclaimed in the Rev. Mr. Candlin's great address before the parliament, in certain practical regards the chief address made, wherein he set forth not only the need of unity, but also the method of sympathetic approach to the foreign faiths. " The glory of Christianity," said Prof. Jowett, " is not to be as unlike other religions as possible, but to be their perfection and fulfilment." As Judaism and Christianity were reconciled in the Epistle to the Hebrews, so Buddhism and Christianity, Hinduism and Christianity, Confucianism and Christianity, Islâm and Christianity, are yet to be reconciled by some supreme minds, who shall show to India, China, Japan, Arabia, that in Christ all that is good and true in these faiths has been embodied and completed by a special revelation.

No intelligent believer in Christian missions has had his faith shaken by the stories,—some of them almost fairy stories,—which two or three delegates to the parliament related. Mr. Vivekananda and Mr. Gandhi have written and spoken against Christian missions in India, and for this we should be thankful, since their criticisms have been buried by Mr. Hume and Mr. Powers under a mountain of facts. Careful inquiry into the effects of Mr. Vivekananda's addresses before our colleges has shown that, instead of discrediting missions, he has led students to investigate with renewed interest the actual religious condition of the people whom he has eulogized. Nothing but advantage will come from hearing all sides of the missionary question. No phenomenon of the century has on the whole been more remarkable than the Christian uprising in Europe and America to give the Gospel to all lands. The splendid record of missions is starred with achievements which no amount of criticism can dim. Let Mr. Mozoomdar and others tell Christianity how its methods can be improved. Let Mr. Candlin and Mr. Hume urge a kindlier spirit in Christian propagandism; let comparative religion become a study required of all candidates for mission fields. The result can be only good. As the "Churchman" says, "it is hard to convert a man unless it is clearly understood what he is to be converted from. Light, knowledge, sympathy are necessary to all missionary work, and surely these may come from so strange a gathering as the parliament of religions." It may be that Christianity needs to be orientalized before the more cultured intellects of the East will generally accept it.

One of the best results of the parliament has been a better understanding, among enlightened minds, between Catholics and Protestants in America. When the American Catholic archbishops, with the knowledge and consent of the Vatican, decided to take part in the parliament, they did much to give the meeting its historic importance. The faithfulness with which they carried out their part of the programme, the ability, courtesy, and kindness of their speakers, made a wholesome impression on many minds; and, although the months which have followed have been filled with acrimonious attacks on the Catholic church, there has yet been a better understanding between many Catholics and Protestants in America than ever heretofore. The fanaticism and wicked folly of the methods of the American Protective Association have not destroyed the recollections of those golden days when, for the first time in history, Protestant and Catholic divines sat together in loving fellowship. The participation of the Catholic bishops made the official refusal of the English Church to participate in the congress appear almost ridiculous. But the generous and liberal sentiments spoken by Cardinal Gibbons, Archbishop Redwood, Bishop Keane, and others, were the features which particularly impressed American Protestants. Count D'Alviella reports that the Catholic journals of Europe have not reproduced these sentiments, and a strong Protestant voice in Italy inquires, If the Protestant in America is justified in his overtures of peace to the Catholic, why should such overtures be refused and condemned in Italy? Is Catholicism liberty in America and intolerance in Europe? How long will this dualism of conscience continue? Words of kindness and conciliation have been spoken by Ernst Naville in the city of Calvin, but they have met no sympathetic

response. In America, however, kindly words from Protestant pulpits are met with equal kindness by many Catholic prelates.   This
is a great surprise to Prof. Auguste Sabbatier, who, in the " Journal de Genève," says of the Catholic dignitaries at the parliament:
" Their conduct was so novel, and so in contradiction to the habitual
exclusive and uncompromising attitude of the Church of Rome, that
in France it seems incredible."   Castelar made a great sensation when
he informed a company of literary people in his own house that
leading Catholic prelates had taken part in the parliament of religions.

It required a parliament of all religions to bring together the
first modern parliament of Christendom.   An effort less ecumenical
would not have brought together the disciples of Christ.   It has often
been remarked that little sectarianism was preached at the parliament.   There Christendom proclaimed its Master.   Inevitably this
meeting which furnished the prophecy of a reunited church has had
large effect on many Christian minds.   Discussions of reunion have
been increasingly rife.   Bishop Keane says that Americans are over-
eager for speedy results, and he is almost content with saying that
" the parliament accomplished itself."   It stands as an achieved
fact, sublime, impressive, perpetual, a beacon blazing with sacred
and unwasting fire.   But facts lead to immediate results in the
world of the spirit.   Feelings are changed, and then convictions.
" The solemn charge which the parliament preaches to all true
believers is a return to the primitive unity of Christians, as a condition precedent to the conversion of the world."   With this faith in
their hearts, men are active along various lines.   The results may be
far off, but they are certain.

It was discovered that Christianity in its main divisions is in
harmony on the chief questions of doctrine and duty.   The argument of Canon Fremantle, showing that faith in the great central
truths of religion has been strengthened by the progress of modern thought, indicated also that these great truths throw into shadow
and subordination the elaborate and technical theological creeds, and
that the social movement for the common good, in which all Christians
may unite, will be recognized more and more as the main part of
religion.   The group of papers bearing on the social problem, presented by Professors Peabody, Henderson, and Ely, and Drs. Gladden
and Small, furnish the divine fire which ought to burn down the
barriers of Christian separation.   If we can centre the interest of
Christian minds, both in the greatest themes of practical ethics and

in the highest subjects of comparative theology, how divisions over pettier matters will go down! The world needs greater intellects, greater souls, greater men, and, in the divine evolution, the time appears to have come for their appearance. Attention to the supremest concerns of humanity will eliminate unholy fire from the altars at which religious zeal is ministering.

The world will not forget how the venerated Dr. Schaff declared his resolution to speak at the parliament a last word in favor of Christian unity. "He was a prophet," writes Professor Comba, from Rome, "for this word of his was his swan song." One of the chief ideas which the parliament made luminous was a reunited Christendom, the preparation for a Christianized world. Since all the religions found, as Castelar has said, "a common ground in Christianity," and since inevitably the best religion must come to the front, may we not look to see the lines of human progress centering more and more in Christ, the "unifier of humanity"? "Never before in all the earth," writes one student, "has the fact been so vividly set forth that Christianity, and it alone, is large enough to cover the whole round globe, and hold it to the heart of God." In view of the tremendous needs of modern society and the problem of the world's evangelization, Christians will certainly draw closer to each other. Of course every great movement has its reactions, and spiritual contrasts appear in close proximity. The religious world may be all borne along, like the passengers on a ship, in one direction, and yet alienations and quarrels may be intensified among the voyagers. And so in the midst of the progress now apparent we discover American Catholicism eulogizing religious liberty and brotherhood, while in American Presbyterianism appear tendencies which are "Romanizing," exclusive, and reactionary.

It was the spirit of fraternity in the heart of America which succeeded in bringing together such widely separated exponents of religion. "Enemies simply met and discovered that they were brothers who had one Father in Heaven." To speak of the deep, tender feelings awakened by the presence at the parliament of the truth-seekers of the Orient, earnest, heart-hungry, believing that they had much to teach as well as something to learn, their "faces set toward God and with some message from God;" to recall the emotions awakened during the great opening and closing hours of the parliament—would be to indulge in what many would deem a sentimental rhapsody; but it is not rhapsody to say that "the age of isolation and hatred has passed,

5

and the age of toleration and scientific comparison has come." Kindlier feelings were certainly engendered at the parliament, and many
who looked upon this meeting as a noble humanitarian measure
believe that by it prejudices were removed and certain results to
civilization made possible. Without concession, without any attempt to treat all religions as equally meritorious, without any compromise of any system of faith and worship, with no idea of finding or founding any new world-religion, with equal freedom gladly
accorded to all races and both sexes—the sessions of the parliament
continued in practically unbroken harmony. There was a vast
significance to human brotherhood in the daily recital of the universal prayer, though the unity of the parliament was that of spirit
rather than of creed. If this meeting simply effected a wider diffusion of brotherliness, it deserves, as the London "Daily Telegraph"
has said, "a place among the notable events of our age." It was
certainly a protest against exclusiveness of feeling, the ignorant
pride, the ecclesiastical aloofness, and the dogmatic haughtiness
which often prevail. It will be easier henceforth for men to feel
"that they do not sully their religious creeds and lives by permitting
them to touch any others."

The ethical unity apparent at the parliament was profoundly
impressive, and whoever henceforth makes an appeal for international righteousness may quote the universal judgment and sentiment
of this congress of religions. Doubtless many will fear that one
effect of the parliament will be still further to modify the ancient
orthodox teaching in regard to the doom of all those who have not
known and accepted the historic Christ. But this result is a benign
one. Many of the mistakes the critics of the parliament have made
would have been avoided had they gained a larger idea of the work
of Christ, as the "Original Light enlightening every man that cometh
into the world"; and there should be no hesitation to receive as a
part of the working creed of Christianity, the verses of Whittier:

> " Wherever through the ages rise
> The altars of self-sacrifice,
> Where love its arms has opened wide
> Or man for man has calmly died,
> I see the same white wings outspread
> That hovered o'er the Master's head."

Such are some of the echoes and results of this memorable meeting. The chief promoters of the parliament, grateful for what they

have been able to do, would be glad to have done something better and larger.   But most of them will be content if the words of Dr. Lyman Abbott shall be prophetic, " that the final issue of the religious parliament will be at once to broaden our conception of Christianity, and to make its acceptance both a logical and a spiritual necessity," or if the words of Prof. Grose, of the Chicago University, prove historic, that " the parliament was divinely designed to broaden the bounds of human brotherhood and charity; to bring the leaders of the world's religious thought to-day into bonds of sympathetic acquaintance and fellowship; to reveal spirit unto spirit; and to deepen the universal sense of the fatherhood of God and the brotherhood of man."

JOHN HENRY BARROWS.

THE PAY OF PHYSICIANS AND SURGEONS.

THE physician is generally sure of a good living, but he must work hard to gain it. In few professions are there so many difficulties to surmount, and so many adverse circumstances to overcome, before this end can be attained. No one denies that medicine is in every sense a noble profession, but as a mere trade it takes a low rank. One of the many reasons for this is that the medical practitioner as a rule is a poor business-man, because, from the very nature of the calling, its high duties, its grave responsibilities, its noble instincts, and its laudable aims are never to be balanced by mere cash values. As soon as a medical man descends to be a mere money-getter he sacrifices that real love for his profession which lies at the root of his scientific progress. The mere fortune-hunter is necessarily the quack. But if very few medical practitioners make fortunes, there is compensation in the great satisfaction of the work itself, in the fascination of advancement, in the ambition of useful discovery, in the triumphs of mitigating suffering, in the consciousness of adding to the length of life and in thus increasing the sum of human happiness. Fortunately for the doctor, and still more so for his patrons, he is generally satisfied to practise with these aims.

The incomes of professional men can be estimated only in an approximate way. Since the amount of money earned is considered by the public as a measure of appreciation of services rendered, there is a strong tendency to give as facts what should be, rather than what actually is. Physicians form no exception to this rule. The average annual income of a physician in full practice in a large city may be stated as $2,000, and in the smaller towns and in strictly rural districts $1,200. Two or three physicians in New York make over $100,000 each year; five or six range from $50,000 to $60,000; fifty from $25,000 to $30,000; one hundred and fifty from $10,000 to $12,000; about three hundred from $5,000 to $6,000; fifteen hundred from $2,000 to $3,000; and the remainder from $800 to $1,000.

When we endeavor to estimate the average income of the doctor, we must consider many controlling influences which bear upon his work. When he begins practice, his income is always small. The young doctor is never employed merely because he is young and anxious to earn a living. Making due allowance for the reported high appreciation of the services of the beginner, his rapid rise and phenomenal success, and his presumptuous complaint of being over-worked, we can safely estimate that he does well if at the end of his first five years of business he can meet the ordinary living-expenses of a single man. The income at that time will probably range from $800 to $1,500 per annum. Many make a great deal more money than this, but, considering those that fall short of these figures, the average is reasonable. But such incomes for beginners in medicine compare very favorably with those of the professions of theology and law.

The amount to be earned depends largely upon the locality in which a physician settles and the kind of practice he follows. What is known as general family work is the most remunerative for the ordinary practitioner. In fact, this may be taken as the standard for comparison with all other forms of professional labor. Success is easier to obtain in this line. The rewards are quickly gained, but they seldom go beyond the limit of a physical possibility of making just so many visits for a standard and moderate fee. But the physician who thus makes his own place is sure of a good and steady income, is independent of transient custom, and is secure of his position so long as he pleases his patients. While the general practitioner can establish himself during the time he is obtaining business, the specialist must get his reputation before he is a success. Hence the two kinds of practice differ very widely in their gains according as they are estimated at the beginning or at the zenith of a career. With one, the fees are comparatively small, steady, and unchangeable; with the other, the reward comes later and is more substantial. But large fortunes are never made in either.

Early success depends very largely upon whether the young practitioner settles in a rural district, a growing town, or a large city. Country practice yields more the first years, but it soonest reaches its maximum. The doctor soon gets all the business obtainable, and that is the end of it. An old practitioner in a small town in Connecticut informed me that it was impossible for him, at any time during the last twenty-five years of active practice, to collect more than $3,000 annually. Yet he lived in a large house that was his own, had a well-appointed stable, raised his own garden-truck, and

sent two of his sons to college.   He wanted but little and was consequently rich.   Many men with three times that income would
hardly have done more.   His metropolitan brother of equal age,
rank, and capabilities, with thrice the income and a proportionately
larger earning capacity, would certainly be fortunate if he owned his
brown-stone domicile and kept on the right side of his debts.   In
fact we are often surprised to learn that even a busy and fashionable
practitioner, after a long life of work, with the necessary heavy outlay for keeping his establishment in order, dies leaving his family
little or nothing for their future support.   Although these cases are
happily exceptions to the rule, they emphasize the well-worn truism
that it is what a man saves, not what he earns, that brings him comparative riches.   But the physician is too much employed in saving
lives to think as much of saving money as he should.

In respect to living expenses the medical man is very differently
situated from his professional brother of the law or of the ministry.
His office is in his residence, and this must be well appointed.   The
beginner is seriously handicapped in this regard.   Much of his
profits must go for rent and other accessory incidentals.   The young
practitioner—in New York, for instance—cannot secure good office
accommodations in a fair or respectable neighborhood for much less
than $75 of monthly rental.   If he sleeps in his office and " splits the
difference" between a bureau by day and a couch at night, he may
obtain board for an additional sum of $8 to $10 weekly, otherwise his
office is a dead loss.   In other cities, such as Philadelphia, Cincinnati, Chicago, St. Louis, San Francisco, Detroit, Boston, and Baltimore, the rents are much lower, ranging from $20 to $50 monthly,
but the fees are proportionately smaller.   In many of these localities
the offices are separate from the residences, even when the doctors
live in their own houses.   Such arrangements, of course, materially
reduce expenses of living by securing comfortable but not extravagant homes.   The young minister has his rent free, while the legal
beginner, with the nominal expense of desk-room, can prudently
secure a hall bedroom in his boarding-house.

Payment for medical services varies in different localities.   In
the large cities the fees are always comparatively higher.   But even
in New York the charges are not extravagant.   The general family
practitioner charges from $2 to $5 per visit to the patient's house.
The average of such fees for the wealthy is $5, although twice that sum
is usually demanded by practitioners whose practice is mostly limited

to that class.   Office consultations by experts range from $10 to $25, as do also consultation visits.   Visits out of town are from $10 to $20 for each hour of absence from home, plus travelling expenses, and the regular fee of $25 for the consultation itself.   Not a few, how-ever, habitually charge twice or three times these amounts and ob-tain them without trouble.   But these men are of high reputation and unquestioned experience.   Surgical operations command the highest prices, and also range according to the skill and fame of the operator, from $100 up into the thousands.   Night calls are twice the amount of day calls, whether ordinary or consultation visits.

While all this is true of the established practitioner, the younger men must be content to take one dollar in their offices, and often no more for a visit to the attic of a six-story tenement-house.   In many of the smaller towns the physician gets no more than half a dollar for an office visit, and but twice that for a call within a mile from his home.   Yet with his small expenses he manages to live comfortably, is always busy, keeps good horses, has a little home of his own, and eventually, as in the case of our good friend from Con-necticut, sends his boys to college.   With him, however, the differ-ence between a rural and a metropolitan reputation is strikingly ex-emplified, when within one day his city brother can see the same two-dollar patient and not infrequently be taken to the returning train with from $200 to $500 in his pocket.

Those physicians who confine their practice to a special branch make larger incomes than those who do a general practice.   But when we take into account the long preparation necessary, the special studies that must be made, and the time spent in attaining pro-ficiency and reputation, the difference in the end is not so great as might at first be supposed.   To make a large income as a specialist means a reputation which is substantial and widespread.   Compara-tively few gain this.   The young specialist who is working his way has a hard time to meet his current expenses until he can secure a firm foothold.   This is especially true nowadays, when the hope of ultimately large rewards coaxes so many ambitious men to enter the already crowded ranks of specialism, often without sufficient experi-ence and training, and eager to anticipate their rewards without waiting for the merit that makes them possible.   Such men, unless they have the necessarily independent income to tide them over the depressing anxieties of deferred hope, suffer a genteel martyrdom which is the more aggravating in that it has the forced semblance of prosperity. In the waiting and wishing for practice they hover around the free dispensaries and freer clinics, eagerly give their services to the so-called poor, and thus directly and indirectly re-act the fable of the worm that strives to flourish by consuming its own vitals.

These strugglers often submit to real privations, living a bohemian life, lodging in poor quarters, dining at cheap restaurants, subletting their offices, earning money by odd literary jobs, playing in orchestras, dabbling in art, acting as medical attendants to rich travellers, and doing such other things as may not divorce them entirely from their professional calling. With pity be it said that very many never get beyond these emergencies, and become lost in the great army of the unsuccessful and unfortunate.

The pay of the profession in different countries averages about the same when the relative cost of living is taken into account. In England the guinea fee is the standard for the office consultant, twice that amount for outside work, and a proportionate reduction for visits to the poorer classes. But in the great cities, London, Paris, Berlin, and Vienna for instance, the larger amounts go to the titled physicians and surgeons who from time immemorial have controlled the best business.

The fees in Paris for surgical operations run from $200 to $5,000. Except that the latter sum is not infrequently paid, there is no difference as compared with American or English rates. Still, there are only three or four surgeons in Paris who can command such prices, and only two who are reputed to make $100,000 a year. We have probably an equal number who could aggregate that yearly amount in New York. In Paris, $5,000 may be considered as the maximum fee for operations, such being the ruling in a recent case in which a suit was brought for $10,000 for such a surgical service. The Parisian fee for a surgeon called in consultation is $20, whether in his office or at the house of the patient. The consulting physician receives somewhat smaller pay, the amount ranging from $12 to $20 per visit, while at his office it is from $4 to $10. The highest annual income of a French physician is $40,000, although the late M. Charcot is reported to have made much more. The general practitioner in Paris averages $2 per visit, but in aristocratic circles he demands $4. Allowance must also be made for smaller living expenses in Paris than in London or New York.

In comparing our fees with those of the German physician and surgeon it is well to understand that, although a German mark is reckoned as equivalent to twenty-five cents, its purchasing value in Germany equals our dollar here. Thus the German family doctor, while he nominally gets but 2 marks for an office visit, can really count on $2 of actual worth to him. The specialists of Berlin and other large German cities charge from 5 to 10 marks for outside calls. The first-class medical authorities, who are necessarily professors in the universities, charge 20 marks in their offices and 30 for house visits. Taking into account the facts that competition is less active in Germany than in America; that the ratio of physicians to the population is about 1 to 1,400; that the living-rates are much lower; that even the highest medical dignitaries live, breathe, and have their offices in the upper and cheaper apartment flats, we can easily allow that the average German can have enough over ordinary profits for his beer and tobacco. All other things being equal, we can count the average earnings of the German family doctor to be about 5,000 marks, and the consultant's and professor's income 10,000 marks.

Some of the physicians of highest repute obtain enormous amounts for attendance on the nobility and the wealthier classes. Royalty often rewards them with a title besides, which gives a peculiar social stamp to their work, makes them men of acknowledged reputation, and floats them at once on the top wave of the fashionable swim.

A reputation in London means a reputation for all Great Britain and a good part of Europe besides. The Queen of England would never think of consulting any but her Court physicians, unless under a forced emergency. Some of the fees paid by royalty have been eminently befitting the giver and taker. The late physician to the Prince of Wales received for four weeks' attendance at Sandringham, during the illness of his distinguished patient from typhoid fever, not only the usual title of baronet, but a fee of £10,000. Sir Morell Mackenzie is reported to have received more than twice this amount for his treatment of the late Emperor Frederick of Germany. Dimsdale, a prominent practitioner of London in 1762, was called thence to St. Petersburg to inoculate the Empress Catherine II., for which he received not only the equivalent of $50,000, but an extra $10,000 for travelling expenses, the title of baron, and a life pension of $2,500 yearly. His Royal Highness the Nawab of Rampur, India, recently paid an English army surgeon £50,000 for a three-months occasional attendance in an ordinary attack of rheumatism. This is said to be the largest fee ever paid for medical services in that so-called heathen country. Verily even the benighted races can afford us profitable object-lessons for imitation! The late Sir Andrew Clark, Gladstone's physician, often charged $1,000 for running down from London to Liverpool, and the late Sir William Gull commanded equally high rates for similar services. Although this fee appears to be a princely one, with men whose earning capacity was as large as was theirs, the inconveniences attendant on a sudden journey are very great, and the loss sustained by the interruption of the routine of many days of subsequent business scarcely covered the abstract profit. A Russian surgeon charged a wealthy notable of Odessa $6,000 for opening an abscess of the hip, the time occupied being about ten minutes. And better still, while on the same visit, he took a chance shot at another patient in the shape of a similarly simple operation, for which he received nearly $1,500 more, certainly enough extra to pay the fee of the railway porter on his homeward journey.

But in all this it is not so much the doing as the knowing how to do. When the French peasant said that there were not ten francs' worth of paint on Rosa Bonheur's "Horse Fair," he was incapable of valuing high art. "Five dollars for amputating the leg," said the surgeon, "and nine hundred and ninety-five for knowing how,' —and the victim was thankful accordingly.

In giving testimony to the value of professional time, in a recent suit in London, a leading surgeon maintained that $150 was a fair charge for a day's absence; that $2,000 should be paid for a trip from London to Paris, and $150 or $200 per day extra while there. Contrast these fees with those paid the late physicians who watched so faithfully over our lamented Garfield. For three months' services of the entire staff, but $25,000 was paid, and then only after an amount of abuse, by buncombe Congressmen, for alleged unskilled treatment—and almost murder—on the part of the surgeons, which was a disgrace to the nation. Much has been said of the expensive physicians in attendance upon General Grant, but the whole amount paid did not exceed $18,000. Of this Dr. Douglas received $12,000, two-thirds of the entire sum, as he was the only one who gave up his business and tendered his undivided attention for five months to the service of the patient. As General Grant was virtually a poor man at the time, only the most reasonable and ordinary fees were charged by the other members of the staff, which it is proper to say were promptly and thankfully paid by the family.

American millionaires are as a rule quite liberal with their physicians, but the attendant who has only one patient must necessarily have something for the sacrifice of his other business. The sums range from $60,000 to $100,000 yearly, with the usual luxurious surroundings. One physician received $87,000 for attending the daughter of a millionaire for two months; another, $60,000 for a yachting cruise of less than six months; and another $2,000 for intubation—an operation performed in a few seconds. A distinguished ear specialist was paid $5,000 for a flying trip from New York to St. Paul, and still another physician received $25,000 for a similar professional visit involving a trip from Philadelphia to San Francisco. When we add to these the gifts from grateful patients, ranging from an inkstand to a house, the widest possibilities are offered for the discharge of the most elastic obligations that exist between giver and taker. There are, however, many exceptions to these rules, which are notable as proving that wealth and generosity are not always synonymous terms. A distinguished physician, not long ago, sued for $2,500 for ten days' service in a Southern town in a case of typhoid fever, but the jury allowed barely $1,500.

When we compare the high fees in medicine with those received for legal services, it is difficult to make a reasonable comparison. It must be conceded that the ordinary doctor makes a surer and better income than the ordinary lawyer, but when the high fees are reached the shoe is surely on the other foot. In law, however, the less you do the more you get. There is, in fact, an inverse ratio of fees to services which is startlingly apparent. Talk of $50,000, $60,000, and $100,000 in single fees in a lifetime!—such amounts are often multiplied many times over in the practice of leading lawyers. No usual pay for a skilful and dangerous operation brings $25,000 or $30,000 to the lucky surgeon; yet such sums are not uncommonly paid for legal services in the defence of wealthy criminals. The slayer of Jim Fisk paid to his lawyer $200,000,— a good year's work for a professional man. The late Hall McAllister received a fee of $20,000 on a compromised case and did not even appear in court. No more time was occupied than in amputating a leg for which probably $1,000 would be charged by a surgeon of equal eminence and skill. The late John B. Felton received from James Lick $50,000 for setting aside his first deed of trust, the work of a few hours. A young and inexperienced attorney asked $5,000 for a breach-of-promise case that did not last a week. In the settlement of estates, in the drawing of articles of incorporation for large and wealthy syndicates, the lawyer's fees often reach $100,-000. A notable illustration was afforded in the recent reorganization of the Sugar Trust, which gave its attorney a little fortune for a week's work. The legal fee in the Lux estate exceeded $250,000, and yet we can hardly conclude that services to the estate of a rich man are worth so much more than those for saving his life. In fact we are forced to assume that such services are paid for out of all proportion to their real value.

But these large rewards carry with them their own penalty. The leading element of mere money-making has infused into legal practice a purely commercial aspect which saps its real professional character. Companies are now forming to monopolize these extravagantly large gains and divide them among hundreds of members or stockholders in their concerns. Thus we have title-guarantee and trust companies, lawyers' title and insurance companies, through which legal advice is doled out by the yard and sold by measure. Thus, every evil has its remedy. The pendulum swings too far, and then the spring snaps. Happily there is no such tendency in medicine. One reason for this is that the service of the doctor is of a more personal character than that of any other professional man. There can be thus no machine work liable to be monopolized by a capitalized syndicate. The quacks can make pills by the wholesale, it is true, but they never can fit them to the individual case. There are no automatic machines for amputating limbs, auscultating chests, or diagnosticating diseases. The doctor has a monopoly of his name and his methods, his skill and his judgment, which no power can gainsay, and thus his personal fee is guaranteed against infringement by outside influence. This is his comfort and his right.

Comparing his pay with that of the minister, he has the advantage of being in business for himself, and is, in a great measure, independent of individual patrons. He can be progressive up to the limit of the highest possibilities and increase his income proportionately. The minister, as a rule, goes through a lifetime of hard work subject to the whims of fault-finding members of his flock, liable to dismissal if he puts the hay too high for the little horses, gets what content and support he can from a small fixed salary here, and must offset it merely with the hope of a better life hereafter.

So, all told, the doctor is not so badly off if he can get what is really due him. But every one knows that he loses a great deal in bad debts. He is generally the last to be paid, but, strange to say, is the first to be called when there is real trouble in the family.

> "Three faces wears the doctor: When first sought,
> An Angel's,—and a God's, the cure half wrought:
> But when, that cure complete, he seeks his fee,
> The Devil looks less terrible than he."

The peculiar and personal services of the physician have much to do in explaining this lax system of payment. A main difficulty lies, in most cases, in the separation of the purely philanthropic element from the strictly practical one. He is called more as a friendly helper in time of dire emergency than as a mere tradesman. He cannot demand a retainer before he assuages the pain of an infant's colic. He has no time, in case of hæmorrhage, to mention his fee; consequently his work is mostly done on credit, especially as he is the last man who is expected, after saving a life, and amid the profusion of heartfelt thanks, to discuss the purely material element in the equation. But it does not take him long to discover that he cannot live on sentiment alone. He soon learns that he must do business on business principles. His patients must be taught to pay promptly. Nowhere but in England and in France is this system perfectly enforced, and yet no complaints are made. No patient would think of consulting an English or Parisian physician without leaving his fee upon the table. Happily for both parties in the contract this practice is becoming fashionable with the leading consultants in all the large cities of this country. Where pecuniary credit must, from the circumstances of the case, be imperative, there is no reason why the doctor should not in the end get all that is due him. Although the value of his services can never virtually be fixed by his patrons, he should nevertheless fix them for himself. This gives them a strictly business aspect. If the charges are always just and reasonable, no deductions are necessary. In cases of disaster, misfortune, accident, or sickness, the consequent loss of money affects only one side in every other business, and why should there be any exception in the case of medical services when rendered to a man sick and out of work? Even the actual death of the patient is a gain to the undertaker, who is always paid on the spot, and whose profits almost equal those of the plumber, the policeman, or the political boss. It may be pertinent in this connection to mention in passing that sometimes the doctor forestalls the fees of the grim and unwelcome man of crape. A curiously unique instance of this occurred to the writer, in which two children of a family were happily saved from death by a timely operation. The father, although a poor man, viewed the situation so philosophically that the probable expenses of the funeral were calculated and presented to the doctor as his fee, with the extra satisfaction to the parent of having the two children thrown into the bargain. This certainly was a clear gain all around.

Aside from the want of business tact on the part of the medical attendant, there are many other considerations which bear upon the amount of fees collected. The law of demand and supply affects medical services as well as other salable commodities. When the profession is so overcrowded in this country that there is only one physician to five hundred inhabitants, when the incomes are averaged, the individual recipients can scarcely expect to be millionaires.

Then comes the hospital and dispensary abuse. This takes thousands of dollars from the physician which rightfully belong to him. He is always ready to help the really poor, to give his services gratuitously to hospital, dispensary, and clinic, but naturally objects to imposition by those who can, but will not, pay for treatment. This abuse of medical charity is so notorious that it is considered to be the principal if not the only reason why competent young medical men cannot get a fair start and make an ordinary living in our large cities. In New York, for instance, the clinics and dispensaries wrongfully absorb almost all the available business of the young practitioner. It is not an uncommon thing to see women dressed in sealskin sacques and decked with diamonds boldly claiming the free treatment intended only for the deserving poor. Many of these come in cabs, and importunately demand prompt attention, while the poor doctor who gives them free advice comes and goes on a five-cent car-fare. But this grave abuse is winked at by the leading institutions, and complaints avail nothing. The fact is, there are in the larger cities more hospitals and dispensaries than are necessary. In New York this is unquestionably true. One-half the number would respond to all the charity work that is really needed. The medical profession does more than its share of philanthropic work in these institutions. There is not a surgeon in attendance on any of the larger hospitals who does not perform operations which would aggregate in money value from $50,000 to $100,000 yearly. The only material return is an increased experience and dexterity which he can use in such outside work as the hospitals permit him to do.

Another serious obstacle to legitimate income is the quack-medicine trade. Quackery is medical practice commercialized, and therefore prostituted. It thrives because the victims are in the majority and are easily reached by lying advertisements. "What is the proportion of sensible people in this crowd?" asked a patent-medicine man of a physician. "About one in ten," was the answer. "I take the nine and leave the one to you," said the quack. This represents the majority which help to make the quack rich. The nostrums cost almost nothing; but the capital is used in advertising; in publishing portraits of the idiots and feeble-minded who imagine themselves cured; in placarding fences; in defacing scenery; in circulating manufactured certificates; in ridiculing scientific medicine; in alarming the credulous; in claiming false discoveries; and in vaunting impossible results. But these are the men who make the money. Medicine to them is the nickel-in-the-slot machine. The diagnosis is ready-made to suit every need, and even otherwise sensible people are being educated into quackery, and into the belief that every man can be his own doctor and not have a fool for a patient.

To sum up these conclusions, we must admit that medicine pays in its own good way. The mere fee is its smallest recompense. The ancients believed that the man who healed his fellows was next to the gods.

GEORGE F. SHRADY.

MACAULAY'S PLACE IN LITERATURE.[1]

MACAULAY, who counted his years of life by those of this century, may fairly claim to have had the greatest body of readers and to be the most admired prose-writer of the Victorian age. It is now nearly seventy years since his first brilliant essay on "Milton" took the world by storm. It is exactly half a century since that fascinating series of "Essays" was closed, and little short of that time since his famous "History" appeared. The editions of it in England and in America are counted by thousands; it has six translations into German, and translations into ten other European languages. It made him rich, famous, and a peer. Has it given him a foremost place in English literature?

Here is a case where the judgment of the public and the judgment of experts is in striking contrast. The readers both of the Old and of the New World continue to give the most practical evidence that they love his books. Macaulay is a rare example of a writer all of whose works are almost equally popular and believed by many to be equally good. "Essays," "Lays," "History," "Lives"—all are read by millions: as critic, poet, historian, biographer, Macaulay has achieved world-wide renown. And yet some of our best critics deny him either fine taste, or subtlety, or delicate discrimination, catholic sympathies, or serene judgment. They say he is always more declaimer than thinker—more advocate than judge. The poets deny that the "Lays" are poetry at all. The modern school of scientific historians declare that the "History" is a splendid failure, and it proves how rotten was the theory on which it is constructed. The purists in style shake their heads over his everlasting antitheses, the mannerism of violent phrases and the perpetual abuse of paradox. His most indulgent friends admit the force of these defects, which they usually speak of as his "limitations" or his "methods." Here, indeed, is an opportunity for one of those long-drawn antitheses of which Macaulay was so great a master. How he would himself have revelled in the paradox—"that books which were household words

[1] Copyright also in England.

with every cow-boy in Nevada and every Baboo in Bengal were condemned by men of culture as the work of a Philistine and a mannerist"; "how ballads which were the delight of every school-boy were
ridiculed by critics as rhetorical jingles that would hardly win a prize
in a public school"; "how the most famous of all modern reviewers
scarcely gave us one example of delicate appreciation or subtle analysis"; how it comes about "that the most elaborate of modern histories does not contain an idea above the commonplaces of a cram-
mer's text-book"—and so forth, in the true Black-and-White style
which is so clear and so familiar. But let us beware of applying to
Macaulay himself that tone of exaggeration and laborious antithesis
which he so often applied to others. Boswell, he says, was immortal,
"*because* he was a dunce, a parasite, and a coxcomb." It would be a
feeble parody to retort that Macaulay became a great literary power
"*because* he had no philosophy, little subtlety, and a coarse taste."
For my part, I am slow to believe that the judgment of the whole
English-speaking race, a judgment maintained over more than half a
century, can be altogether wrong; and the writer who has given such
delight, has influenced so many writers, and has taught so much to
so many persons, can hardly have been a shallow mannerist or an
ungovernable partisan. No one denies that Macaulay had a prodigious knowledge of books; that in literary fecundity and in varied
improvisation he has never been surpassed; that his good sense is
unfailing, his spirit manly, just, and generous; and lastly that his
command over language had unequalled qualities of precision, energy,
and brilliance. These are all very great and sterling qualities. And it
is right to acknowledge them with no unstinted honour—even whilst
we are fully conscious of the profound shortcomings and limitations
that accompanied but did not destroy them.

In a previous paper we discussed the permanent contribution to
English literature of Thomas Carlyle; and it is curious to note how
complete a contrast these two famous writers present. Carlyle was
a simple, self-taught, recluse man of letters: Macaulay was legislator, cabinet minister, orator, politician, peer—a pet of society, a
famous talker, and member of numerous academies. Carlyle was
poor, despondent, morbid, and cynical: Macaulay was rich, optimist,
overflowing with health, high spirits, and good nature. The one
hardly ever knew what the world called success: the other hardly
ever knew failure. Carlyle had in him the elements that make the
poet, the prophet, the apostle, the social philosopher. In Macaulay

6

these were singularly wanting; he was the man of affairs, the busy politician, the rhetorician, the eulogist of society as it is, the believer in material progress, in the ultimate triumph of all that is practical and commonplace, and in the final discomfiture of all that is visionary and utopian.   The Teufelsdröckhian dialect is obscure even to its select students: the Macaulay sentence is plain as that of Swift himself. Carlyle's gospel is full of passion, novelty, suggestion, theory, and social problems.   Macaulay turned his back on social problems and disdained any kind of gospel.   He had no mission to tell the world how bad it is: on the contrary, he was never wearied with his proofs that it ought to be well satisfied with its lot and its vast superiority in all things to its ancestors.

The great public, wherever English books penetrate, from the White Sea to Australia, from the Pacific to the Indian Ocean, loves the brilliant, manly, downright optimist; the critics and the philosophers care more for the moody and prophetic pessimist.   But this does not decide the matter; and it does not follow that either public or critic has the whole truth.   If books were written only in the dialect and with the apocalyptic spirit of " Sartor," it is certain that millions would cease to read books, and could gain little from books if they did.   And if the only books were such " purple patches" of history as Macaulay left us, with their hard and fast divisions of men into sheep and goats, and minute biographies of fops, pedants, and grandees, narrated in the same resonant, rhetorical, unsympathetic, and falsely emphatic style—this generation would have a very patch-work idea of past ages and a narrow sense of the resources of our English language.   There is room for both literary schools, and we need teachers of many kinds.   We must not ask of any kind more than they can give.   Macaulay has led millions who read no one else, or who never read before, to know something of the past, and to enjoy reading.   He will have done them serious harm, if he has persuaded them that this is the best that can be done in historical literature, or that this is the way in which the English language can be most fitly used.   Let us be thankful for his energy, learning, brilliance.   He is no priest, philosopher, or master.   Let us delight in him as a fireside companion.   In one thing all agree—critics and public, friends and opponents.   Macaulay's was a life of purity, honour, courage, generosity, affection, and manly perseverance, almost without a stain or a defect.   His life, it was true, was singularly fortunate, and he had but few trials and no formidable obstacles.

He was bred up in the comfortable egotism of the opulent middle classes; the religion of comfort, *laisser-faire*, and social order was infused into his bones. But, so far as his traditions and temper would suffer, his life was as honourable, as unsullied, and as generous, as ever was that of any man who lived in the fierce light that beats upon the famous. We know his nature and his career as well as we know any man's; and we find it on every side wholesome, just, and right. He has been fortunate in his biographers, and amply criticised by the best judges. His nephew, Sir George Trevelyan, has written his life at length in a fine book. Dean Milman and Mark Pattison have given us vignettes; Cotter Morison has adorned the "Men of Letters" series with a delightful and sympathetic sketch; and John Morley and Leslie Stephen have weighed his work in the balance with judicial acumen and temperate firmness. There is but one voice in all this company. It was a fine, generous, honourable, and sterling nature. His books deserve their vast popularity and may long continue to maintain it. But Macaulay must not be judged amongst philosophers—nor even amongst the real masters of the English language. And, unless duly corrected, he may lead historical students astray and his imitators into an obtrusive mannerism.

Let us take a famous passage from one of his most famous essays, written in the zenith of his powers after his return from India, at the age of forty—an essay on a grand subject which never ceased to fascinate his imagination, composed with all his amazing resources of memory and his dazzling mastery of colour. It is the third paragraph of his well-known review of Von Ranke's "History of the Popes." The passage is familiar to all readers, and some of its phrases are household words; it is rather long as well as trite. But it contains in a single page such a profusion of historical suggestion; it is so vigorous, so characteristic of Macaulay in all his undoubted resources as in all his mannerism and limitations; it is so essentially true, and yet so thoroughly obvious; it is so grand in form, and yet so meagre in philosophic logic, that it may be worth while to analyze it in detail; and for that purpose it must be set forth, even though it convey to most readers little more than a sonorous truism.

"There is not, and there never was on this earth, a work of human policy so well deserving of examination as the Roman Catholic Church. The history of that Church joins together the two great ages of human civilization. No other institution is left standing which carries the mind back to the times when the smoke of sacrifice rose from the Pantheon, and when camelopards and tigers bounded in the Flavian amphitheatre. The proudest royal houses are but of yesterday, when compared with the line of the Supreme Pontiffs.   That line we trace back in unbroken series, from the Pope who crowned Napoleon in the nineteenth century to the Pope who crowned Pepin in the eighth; and far beyond Pepin the august dynasty extends, till it is lost in the twilight of fable.   The republic of Venice came next in antiquity.   But the republic of Venice was modern when compared with the Papacy; and the republic of Venice is gone, and the Papacy remains.   The Papacy remains, not in decay, not a mere antique, but full of life and youthful vigour.   The Catholic Church is still sending forth to the furthest ends of the world, missionaries as zealous as those who landed in Kent with Augustin, and still confronting hostile kings with the same spirit with which she confronted Attila.   The number of her children is greater than in any former age.   Her acquisitions in the New World have more than compensated her for what she has lost in the Old.   Her spiritual ascendancy extends over the vast countries which lie between the plains of the Missouri and Cape Horn, countries which, a century hence, may not improbably contain a population as large as that which now inhabits Europe.   The members of her communion are certainly not fewer than a hundred and fifty millions; and it will be difficult to show that all the other Christian sects united amount to a hundred and twenty millions.   Nor do we see any sign which indicates that the term of her long dominion is approaching.   She saw the commencement of all the governments and of all the ecclesiastical establishments that now exist in the world; and we feel no assurance that she is not destined to see the end of them all.   She was great and respected before the Saxon had set foot on Britain, before the Frank had crossed the Rhine, when Grecian eloquence still flourished in Antioch, when idols were still worshipped in the temple of Mecca.   And she may still exist in undiminished vigour when some traveller from New Zealand shall, in the midst of a vast solitude, take his stand on a broken arch of London Bridge to sketch the ruins of St. Paul's."

Here we have Macaulay in all his strength and all his limitations. The passage contains in the main a solid truth—a truth which was very little accepted in England in the year 1840—a truth of vast import and very needful to assert.   And this truth is clothed in such pomp of illustration and is hammered into the mind with such accumulated blows; it is so clear, so hard, so coruscating with images, that it is impossible to escape its effect.   The paragraph is one never to be forgotten, and not easy to be refuted or qualified.   No intelligent tiro in history can read that page without being set a-thinking, without feeling that he has a formidable problem to solve.   Tens of thousands of young minds must have had that deeply coloured picture of Rome visibly before them in many a Protestant home in England and in America.   Now, all this is a very great merit.   To have posed a great historical problem, at a time when it was very faintly grasped, and to have sent it ringing across the English-speaking world in such a form that he who runs may read—nay he who rides, he who sails, he who watches sheep or stock *must* read—this is a real and signal service conferred on literature and on thought.   Compare this solid sense with Carlyle's ribaldry about "the three-hatted Papa," "pig's wash," "servants of the Devil," "this accursed nightmare," and the rest of his execrations—and we see the difference between the sane judgment of the man of the world and the prejudices of intolerant fanaticism.

But, unfortunately, Macaulay, having stated in majestic antitheses his problem of "the unchangeable Church," makes no attempt to provide us with a solution. This splendid eulogium is not meant to convert us to Catholicism—very far from it. Macaulay was no Catholic, and had only a sort of literary admiration for the Papacy. As Mr. Cotter Morison has shown, he leaves the problem just where he found it, and such theories as he offers are not quite trustworthy. He does not suggest that the Catholic Church is permanent because it possesses truth: but, rather, because men's ideas of truth are a matter of idiosyncrasy or digestion. The whole essay is not a very safe guide to the history of Protestantism or of Catholicism, though it is full of brilliant points and sensible assertions. And in the end our essayist, the rebel from his Puritan traditions, and the close ally of sceptical Gallios, after forty pages of learned *pros* and *cons*, declares that he will not say more for fear of "exciting angry feelings." He rather sneers at Protestant fervour: he declaims grand sentences about Catholic fervour. He will not declare for either of them; and it does not seem to matter much in the long run for which men declare, provided they can be kept well in hand by saving common sense. In the mean time the topic is a mine of paradox to the picturesque historian. This is not philosophy, it is not history, but it is full of a certain rich literary seed.

The passage, though a truism to all thoughtful men, was a striking novelty to English Protestants fifty years ago. But it will hardly bear a close scrutiny of these sweeping, sharp-edged, "cock-sure" dogmas of which it is composed. The exact propositions it contains may be singly accurate; but as to the most enduring "work of human policy," it is fair to remember that the Civil Law of Rome has a continuous history of at least twenty-four centuries; that the Roman Empire from Augustus to the last Constantine endured for fifteen centuries; and from Augustus to the last Hapsburg it endured for eighteen centuries. There is a certain ambiguity between the way in which Macaulay alternates between the Papacy and the Christian Church, which are not at all the same thing. The Papacy, as a European or cosmical institution, can hardly be said to have more

than twelve centuries of continuous history on the stage of the
world. The religion and institutions of Confucius and of Buddha
have twice that epoch; and the religion and institutions of Moses
have thirty centuries; and the Califate in some form or other is nearly
coeval with the Papacy. The judicious eulogist has guarded himself
against denying in words any of these facts; but a cool survey of
universal history will somewhat blunt the edge of Macaulay's trenchant phrases. After all, we must admit that the passage as a
whole, apart from the superlatives, is substantially true, and contains
a most valuable and very striking thought. With what a wealth of
illustration is it enforced, with what telling contrasts, with what
gorgeous associations! How vivid the images, how stately the personages, who are called up to heighten the lights of this tableau of
the Vatican! Ancient and modern civilization are joined by it; it
recalls the Pantheon and the Colosseum; it gave sanction to the
Empire of Charlemagne and to that of Napoleon, it inspired Augustin, and confronted Attila; Venice is a mere modern foundation;
the Church is older than Hengist and Horsa, Clovis, or Mahomet;
yet it stretches over the Atlantic continent from Missouri to Cape
Horn, and still goes on conquering and to conquer. And the climax
of this kaleidoscopic " symphony in purple and gold"—the New Zea-
lander sketching the ruins of St. Paul's from a broken arch of London Bridge—has become a proverb, and is repeated daily by men
who never heard of Macaulay, much less of Von Ranke, and is an
inimitable bit of picturesque colouring. It is very telling, nobly
hyperbolic, no man can misunderstand it, or forget it. The most
practised hand will not find it easy to " go one better than" Macaulay
in a swingeing trope. It is a fascinating literary artifice, and it has
fascinated many to their ruin. In feebler hands, it degenerates into
what in London journalistic slang is known as " telegraphese." A
pocket encyclopedia and a copious store of adjectives have enabled
many a youth to roar out brilliant articles " as gently as a sucking
dove." But all men of power have their imitators, and are open to
parody and spurious coining. Now, Macaulay, however brilliant
and kaleidoscopic, is always using his own vast reading, his own warm
imagination, his unfailing fecundity, and his sterling good sense.

Turn to the style of the passage—it is perfectly pellucid in meaning, rings on the ear like the crack of a rifle, is sonorous, rich, and
swift. One can fancy the whole passage spoken by an orator: indeed it is difficult to resist the illusion that it was " declaimed" before

it was written. We catch the oratorical tags and devices, the re-peated phrase, the incessant antithesis, the alternate rise and fall of eloquent speech. It is declamation—fine declamation—but we miss the musical undertones, the subtle involutions, the unexpected bursts, and mysterious cadences of really great written prose. The term "the Republic of Venice" is repeated three times in three lines: the term "the Papacy" is repeated three times in two lines. Any other writer would substitute a simple "it" for most of these; and it is difficult to see how the paragraph would lose. The orator aids his hearers by constant repetition of the same term: the writer avoids this lest he prove monotonous. The short sentences of four or five words interposed to break the torrent—the repetition of the same words—the see-saw of black and white, old and young, base and pure—all these are the stock in trade of the rhetorician, not of the master of written prose. Now, Macaulay was a rhetorician, a con-summate rhetorician, who wrote powerful invectives or panegyrics in massive rhetoric which differed from speeches mainly in their very close fibre, in their chiselled phrasing, and above all in their dazzling profusion of literary illustration. If it was oratory, it was the oratory of a speaker of enormous reading, inexhaustible memory, and con-summate skill with words.

There is nothing at all exceptional about this passage that has been chosen for analysis. It is a fair and typical piece of Macaulay's best style. Indeed his method is so uniform and so regular that any page of his writing exhibits the same force and the same defects as any other. Take one of the most famous of his scenes, the trial of Warren Hastings, toward the end of that elaborate essay, written in 1841. Every one knows the gorgeous and sonorous description of Westminster Hall, beginning—"The place was worthy of such a trial." In the next sentence the word "hall" recurs five times, and the word "which" three times, and is not related to the same noun. Ten sentences in succession open with the word "there." It is a perfect galaxy of varied colour, pomp, and illustration: but the effect is somewhat artificial, and the whole scene smells of the court up-holsterer. The "just sentence of Bacon" pairs off with "the just absolution of Somers"; the "greatest painter" sits beside the "great-est scholar of the age"; ladies have "lips more persuasive than those of Fox"; there too is "the beautiful mother of a beautiful race." And in the midst of these long-drawn superlatives and glittering con-trasts come in short martial phrases, as brief and sharp as a drill-ser-

jeant's word of command. " Neither military nor civil pomp was
wanting"—" The avenues were lined with grenadiers"—" The streets
were kept clear by cavalry." No man can forget these short, hard,
decisive sentences.

The artificial structure of his paragraphs grew upon Macaulay
with age. His " History of England" opens with a paragraph of
four sentences. Each of these begins with " I purpose," " I shall";
and the last sentence of the four has ten clauses each beginning with
" how." The next paragraph has four successive sentences beginning
" It will be seen"—and the last sentence has again three clauses each
beginning with " how." The fourth paragraph contains the word,
" I," four times in as many lines. This method of composition has
its own merits. The repetition of words and phrases helps the perception and prevents the possibility of misunderstanding. Where
effects are simply enumerated, the monotony of form is logically correct. Every successive sentence heralded by a repeated " how," or
" there," or " I," adjusts itself into its proper line without an effort
of thought on the reader's part. It is not graceful; it is pompous,
and distinctly rhetorical. But it is eminently clear, emphatic, orderly, and easy to follow or to remember. Hence it is unpleasing to
the finely attuned ear, and is counted somewhat vulgar by the trained
lover of style, whilst it is immensely popular with those who read
but little, and is able to give them as much pleasure as it gives
instruction.

The famous passage about Westminster Hall, written in 1841,
may be compared with the equally known passage on the Chapel in
the Tower which occurs in the fifth chapter of the " History," written
in 1848. It begins as all lovers of English remember—" In truth
there is no sadder spot on the earth than that little cemetery." The
passage continues with " there" or " thither" repeated eight times; it
bristles with contrasts, graces and horrors, antithesis, climax, and
sonorous heraldries. " Such was the dust with which the dust of Monmouth mingled." It is a fine paragraph, which has impressed and delighted millions. But it is, after all, rather facile moralizing; its rhetorical artifice has been imitated with success in many a prize essay
and not a few tall-talking journals. How much more pathos is there
in a stanza from Gray's " Elegy," or a sentence from Carlyle's " Bas-
tille," or Burke's " French Revolution"!

The habit of false emphasis and the love of superlatives is a far
worse defect, and no one has attempted to clear Macaulay of the

charge. It runs through every page he wrote, from his essay on Milton to the Death of James II., who valued Lord Perth as "author of the last improvements on the thumb-screw." Indeed no more glaring example of Macaulay's *megalomania* or taste for exaggeration can be found than the famous piece in the "Milton" on the Restoration of Charles II.

"Then came those days, never to be recalled without a blush, the days of servitude without loyalty and sensuality without love, of dwarfish talents and gigantic vices, the paradise of cold hearts and narrow minds, the golden age of the coward, the bigot, and the slave. The king cringed to his rival that he might trample on his people, sank into a viceroy of France, and pocketed, with complacent infamy, her degrading insults, and her more degrading gold. The caresses of harlots and the jests of buffoons regulated the policy of the State. The government had just ability enough to deceive and just religion enough to persecute. The principles of liberty were the scoff of every grinning courtier, and the Anathema Maranatha of every fawning dean. In every high place, worship was paid to Charles and James, Belial and Moloch ; and England propitiated these obscene and cruel idols with the blood of her best and bravest children. Crime succeeded to crime, and disgrace to disgrace, till the race, accursed of God and man, was a second time driven forth, to wander on the face of the earth, and to be a by-word and a shaking of the head to the nations."

This is vigorous invective, of the style of Cicero against Catiline, or Junius attacking a duke ; it is brilliant rhetoric and scathing satire. At bottom it has substantial truth, if the attention is fixed on Whitehall and the scandalous chronicle of its frequenters. It differs also from much in Macaulay's invectives in being the genuine hot-headed passion of an ardent reformer only twenty-five years old. It is substantially true as a picture of the Court at the Restoration; but in form how extravagant, even of that! Charles II. is Belial: James is Moloch; and Charles is *propitiated* by the blood of Englishmen!—Charles, easy, courteous, good-natured, profligate Charles. And all this of the age of the "Paradise Lost" and the "Morning Hymn," of Jeremy Taylor, Izaak Walton, Locke, Newton, and Wren! Watch Macaulay banging on his antithetic drum—"servitude without loyalty and sensuality without love"—"dwarfish talents and gigantic vices"—"ability enough to deceive"—"religion enough to persecute." Every phrase is a superlative; every word has its contrast; every sentence has its climax. And withal let us admit that it is tremendously powerful, that no one who ever read it can forget it, and few even who have read it fail to be tinged with its fury and contempt. And, though a tissue of superlatives, it bears a solid truth, and has turned to just thoughts many a young spirit that was fascinated by Charles's good-nature and impressed with the halo of the divine claims of kings.

But the savage sarcasms which are tolerable in a passionate young reformer smarting under the follies of George IV., are a serious defect when used indiscriminately of men and women in every age and under every condition. In his " Machiavelli," Macaulay hints that the best histories are perhaps " those in which a little of fictitious narrative is judiciously employed." " Much," he says, " is gained in effect." It is to be feared that this youthful indiscretion was never wholly purged out of him. Boswell, we know, was " a dunce, a parasite, and a coxcomb"—*and therefore* immortal. He was one of " the smallest men that ever lived," of " the meanest and feeblest intellect," " servile," " shallow," " a bigot and a sot," and so forth—and yet " a great writer, *because* he was a great fool." We all know what is meant; and there is a substratum of truth in this; but it is tearing a paradox to tatters. How different has Carlyle dealt with poor dear Bozzy! Croker's " Boswell's Johnson" " is as bad as bad can be," full of " monstrous blunders"—(he had put 1761 for 1766) " gross mistakes"—" for which a school-boy would be flogged." Southey is " utterly destitute of the power of discerning truth from falsehood." He prints a joke which " is enough to make us ashamed of our species." Robert Montgomery pours out " a roaring cataract of nonsense." One of his tropes is " the worst similitude in the world." And yet Macaulay can rebuke Johnson for " big words wasted on little things"!

Neither Cicero, Milton, Swift, nor Junius ever dealt in more furious words than Macaulay, who had not the excuse of controversy or passion. Frederick William of Prussia was " the most execrable of fiends, a cross between Moloch and Puck "; " his palace was hell"; compared with the Prince, afterwards Frederick the Great, " Oliver Twist in the workhouse, and Smike at Dotheboys Hall were petted children." It would be difficult for Mark Twain to beat that. " The follies and vices of King John *were the salvation* of England." Cranmer was peculiarly fitted to organise the Church of England by being " unscrupulous, indifferent, a coward and a time-server." James I. was given to " stammering, slobbering, shedding unmanly tears," " alternating between the buffoon and the pedagogue." James II. " amused himself with hearing Covenanters shriek"; he was " a libertine, singularly slow and narrow in understanding, obstinate, harsh, and unforgiving." The country gentleman of that age talked like " the most ignorant clown"; his wife and daughter were in taste " below a stillroom maid of the present day." The chaplain was a mere servant, and was expected to marry a servant girl whose character had been blown upon.

But it ought to be remembered that all of these descriptions are substantially true. Macaulay's pictures of the Stuarts, of Cromwell, of the Restoration and its courtiers, of Milton, of William III., are all faithful and just; Boswell *was* often absurd, Southey *was* shallow, Montgomery *was* an impostor; Frederick William *did* treat his son brutally; the country squire and the parson two centuries ago *were* much rougher people than they are to-day. And if Macaulay had simply told us this in measured language of this kind, he would have failed in beating his lesson into the mind. Not only was " a little of fictitious narrative judiciously employed," but not a little of picturesque exaggeration and redundant superlatives. Carlyle is an even worse offender in this line. Did he not call Macaulay himself " squat, low-browed, commonplace"—" a poor creature, with his dictionary literature and his saloon arrogance"—" no vision in him"—" will neither see nor do any great thing"?[1] Ruskin, Freeman, Froude, and others have been tempted to deal in gross superlatives. But with all these it has been under the stimulus of violent indignation. With Macaulay the superlatives pour out as his native vernacular without heat or wrath, as a mere rhetorician's trick, as the favourite tones of a great colourist. And though the trick, like all literary tricks, grows upon the artist, and becomes singularly offensive to the man of taste, it must always be remembered that, with Macaulay, the praise or blame is usually just and true; he is very rarely unfair and wrong, as Carlyle so often is; and if Macaulay resorts too often to the superlative degree, he is usually entitled to use the comparative degree of the same adjective.

The style, with all its defects, has had a solid success and has done great things. By clothing his historical judgments and his critical reflections in these cutting and sonorous periods, he has forced them on the attention of a vast body of readers wherever English is read at all, and on millions who have neither time nor attainments for any regular studies of their own. How many men has Macaulay succeeded in reaching, to whom all other history and criticism is a closed book, or a book in an unknown tongue! If he were a sciolist or a wrong-headed fanatic, this would be a serious evil. But, as he

[1] Froude's "Carlyle," I. 192.

is substantially right in his judgments, brimful of saving common sense and generous feeling, and profoundly well-read in his own periods and his favourite literature, Macaulay has conferred most memorable services on the readers of English throughout the world. He stands between philosophic historians and the public very much as journals and periodicals stand between the masses and great libraries. Macaulay is a glorified journalist and reviewer, who brings the matured results of scholars to the man in the street in a form that he can remember and enjoy, when he could not make use of a learned book. He performs the office of the ballad-maker or story-teller in an age before books were known or were common. And it is largely due to his influence that the best journals and periodicals of our day are written in a style so clear, so direct, so resonant. We need not imitate his mannerism; we may all learn to be outspoken, lucid, and brisk.

It is the very perfection of his qualities in rousing the interest of the great public which has drawn down on Macaulay the grave rebukes of so many fine judges of the higher historical literature. Cotter Morison, Mark Pattison, Leslie Stephen, and John Morley all agree that his style has none of the subtler charms of the noblest prose, that his conception of history is radically unsound, that, in fact, it broke down by its own unwieldy proportions. Mr. Morison has very justly remarked that if the " History of England" had ever been completed on the same scale for the period intended, it would have run to fifty volumes, and would have occupied one hundred and fifty years. As it is, the eight duodecimo volumes give us the events of sixteen years, from 1685 to 1701; so that the history of England from Alfred would require five hundred similar volumes. Now, Gibbon's eight octavo volumes give us the history of the world for thirteen centuries; that is to say, Gibbon has recounted the history of a century in nearly the same space that Macaulay records the history of a year. There cannot be a doubt that Gibbon's " Decline and Fall" is immeasurably superior to Macaulay's fragment, in thought, in imagination, in form, in all the qualities of permanent history; it stands on a far higher plane; it will long outlast and overshadow it. Compared with this, Macaulay's delightful and brilliant pictures are mere glorified journalism.

Macaulay, who was no braggart, has put it on record that his conception of history was more just than that of Hume, Robertson, Voltaire, and Gibbon. It is perfectly true that his conception was

different from theirs, his execution was different, and he does not address the same class of readers.   But his conception of history was
not just; it was a mistake.   His leading idea was to make history a
true romance.   He has accomplished this; and he has given us *a historical novel drawn from authentic documents.*   This is, no doubt, a
very useful thing to do, a most interesting book to read; it is very
pleasant literature, and has a certain teaching of its own to a certain
order of readers.   But it is not *history.*   It sacrifices the breadth of
view, the organic life, the philosophy, the grand continuity of human
society.   It must be a sectional picture of a very limited period in a
selected area; it can give us only the external; it inevitably tends to
trivial detail and to amusing personalities; it necessarily blinds us to
the slow sequence of the ages.   Besides this, it explains none of
the deeper causes of movement; for, to make a picture, the artist
must give us the visible and the obvious.   History, in its highest
sense, is the record of the evolution of humanity, in whole or in part.
To compose a historical novel from documents is to put this object
aside.   History, said Macaulay in his " Hallam, " " is a compound of
poetry and philosophy. "   But in practice, he substituted word-paint-
ing for poetry, and anecdote for philosophy.   His own delightful
and popular " History of England " is a compound of historical romance
and biographical memoir.

Macaulay's strong point was in narrative, and in narrative he has
been surpassed by hardly any historian and even by few novelists.
Scott and Victor Hugo have hardly a scene more stirring than Macaulay's death of Charles II., Monmouth's rebellion, the flight of
James II., the trial of Titus Oates, the inner life of William III.
This is a very great quality which has deservedly made him popular.
And if Macaulay had less philosophy than almost any historian of
the smallest pretension, he has a skill in narration that places him in
a fair line with the greatest.   Unfortunately, this superb genius for
narration has rarely been devoted to the grander events and the noblest chiefs in history.   Even his hero William III. hardly lives in his
canvas with such a glowing light as Charles II., Monmouth, and
Jeffreys.   The expulsion of James II. was a very poor affair if compared with the story of Charles I. and the Parliament.   If Macaulay
had painted for us the Council Chamber of Cromwell as he has
painted the Whitehall of Charles II.; if he had described the battle
of Naseby as well as he has pictured the fight of Sedgemoor; if he
had narrated the campaigns of Marlborough as brilliantly as he has

told that which ended at the Boyne—how much should we have had!

But it could not be. His own conception of history made this impossible. It is well said that he planned his history "on the scale of an ordnance map." He did what a German professor does when he tries to fathom English society by studying the "Times" newspaper day by day. The enormous mass of detail, the infinitesimal minuteness of view, beat him. As he told Johnson, he runs into " big words about little things." Charles' mistress, her pug-dog, the page-boy who tended the dog, nay, the boy's putative father, occupy the foreground : and the poet, the statesman, and the hero retire into the middle distance or the background. What would we have given to have had Macaulay's "History of England" continued down to his own time, the wars of Marlborough, the reign of Anne, the poets, wits, romancers, inventors, reformers, and heroes of the eighteenth century, the careers of Walpole, Chatham, Pitt, Burke, Fox, Nelson, Wellington, Brougham, Bentham, and Canning—the formation of the British Empire—the great revolutionary struggle in Europe. The one thought which dims our enjoyment of this fascinating collection of memoirs, and these veracious historical romances, is the sense of what we might have had, if their author had been a great historian as well as a magnificent literary artist.

FREDERIC HARRISON.

HOME–LIFE IN INDIA: CHILD–MARRIAGES AND WIDOWS.

DIFFERENT nations have adopted different customs suited to their climate and physical and mental developments. Many things that are good in America are considered barbarous in India. But unhappily for India, though she is the cradle-land of civilization, she has not made the progress which the Western nations have made with the starting capital borrowed from her. The reason is, that India has for a thousand years been the most unfortunate country on the surface of the earth. Owing to the report of her fabulous riches, almost every Western nation in turn has invaded her. Then, again, her religion has kept her progress in check. It is fair to say that if the Western nations had adopted severely religious methods—had really observed Christianity in its original spirit—they would never have made their marvellous progress. During the period when religion had its strongest hold on them, men were burned in Europe for making scientific researches. But as soon as the Europeans liberated themselves from this absorbing devotion to religion, they made progress. The Americans especially are the most progressive nation, and have in some respects left the Europeans behind because they have not been hampered with religion. They have, indeed, found an outlet for their religious fervor in sending missionaries to India, Japan, China, and Africa. I have observed everywhere in the United States that practical men do not permit religion to interfere with their progress. Religious superstition has been the curse of India. Customs, manners, trades, and every-day life are all regulated and dominated by religion. Any habit or custom that once gets religious sanction is very hard to change.

My readers may naturally ask why I dwell upon the subject of religion instead of going on with my proper subject. I wish at the beginning to record my conviction that on the one hand it is not devotion to Christianity that has made the Western nations what they are, and that on the other hand it is devotion to religion that has kept the Hindus back.

To give a fair idea of Hindu women and marriage-customs I must go far back to the ancient times and see how and why customs changed. There was a time when the Hindu lady was educated, and when there were no child-marriages. Some of the "Upanishads," speculations on philosophy, were written by ladies. There are books written by ladies also on mathematics and other abstruse subjects. Of course they did not write sensational novels, but they were taught music and dancing: *dancing*, not jumping, hopping, and skipping round a hall in the arms of strangers. There were no child-marriages at that time, and the young lady had liberty to select a husband herself.

There were four kinds of marriage: first, the marriage in which the father gave his daughter to the bridegroom according to religious rites; next, marriage in which the young lady made her own selection; third, marrying by elopement; and last, marrying the bride by force. These two latter were not acknowledged as lawful. In the old books we read that the lady in the princely ranks used to select her husband, and when a daughter came of age, the king appointed a day for the selection of a husband for her, and sent invitations to all the kings and princes. The kings and princes came with their retinues, each wishing to win the fair lady. They met in a very large pavilion, and showed their skill in archery and also their physical power. Then the father or the brother of the lady escorted her to the pavilion and showed her each prince in turn, describing his power and wealth as well as his personal qualifications; and he asked her to select the one that she liked best. The bride then chose whom she liked, and put on his neck a garland of sweet-scented flowers which she carried in her hands. Then the religious part of the marriage was conducted by the Brahmin priests, who were a necessity in all social as well as religious ceremonies. The marriage festival continued for several days, all the princes and kings assembled joining in the rejoicing.

The young princess used to make a vow that she would marry the prince who excelled in aiming an arrow at the mark. A large pot filled with oil was placed in the pavilion, and a fish was hung over it, turning round. The prince who hit the right eye of the fish with the arrow without looking directly at the fish, but at the reflection of it in the oil, was to be the husband of the princess. Owing to this custom, the princes used to practise archery, and they became masters in dexterity. In some cases regular "courting" took place, and there was an exchange of love-letters.

It seems that the system did not prove a good one in the warm climate, where women develop very early, and it was changed, and the giving of the daughter by the father is the prevailing method at present. Especially among the Brahmins did this change from the ancient custom take place. The warrior caste, though they do not follow the ancient custom of allowing their daughters to select their husbands, do not marry them so early as the Brahmins. Some classes follow the Brahmins' custom to the present day, and marry their daughters early.

The Brahmin has to get his daughter married before she attains puberty. This custom has crept into religion. The Hindu religion strictly forbids single life for woman or man: especially must the woman be married. Hence there are no old maids in India. Sometimes one may meet an old "cranky" bachelor, who has remained unmarried because he was too poor to marry, or because his character was not good; but even these are seldom found except in the lower classes. If a man is not married at the latest by his twenty-fifth year, his reputation suffers. It is a belief that those who have a son go to heaven, when the son, after the death of his parents, performs the spiritual rites. However this may be, whether they go to heaven or not, this severe rule tends to a strict cultivation of home-life.

Owing to this rule, if a Brahmin's daughter attains puberty before marriage, the father is disgraced; he loses his caste, and no one will marry the girl. Thus, when a poor man has more than one daughter, it is a misfortune for him. The Hindu father himself has to find out a suitable husband for his daughter, so he goes to a gentleman who has a son. He first makes inquiries about the family, the property, the health and education of the boy. Then he asks the father of the boy to marry his son to his daughter. The father of the boy asks for dowry, and the amount of this is fixed according to the means of the man who asks for it and not of the man who gives it; that is to say, if the father of the boy is very rich, he asks thousands of dollars. Hence the Hindu father of a girl has to spend much for the marriage of his daughter, for he always wishes to see her married into a rich family.

In recent times it has come about that a college education has raised the value of the boy in the marriage-market. If the boy has passed the university examination and has obtained the degree of B. A. or of M. A., the father raises the sum of dowry. He says: "You see, my son has just passed the examination, and many people

7

are seeking his hand for their daughters." Hence the boy commands a high price.

In America the young woman selects a husband who can supply
all her wants; and let me say that these wants seem to me to be so
many that many men do not dare marry. Many women also do not
seem to wish to marry because they want men who can spend money
for their fancy. Young men look to the hand of a rich man's
daughter, and the young woman looks to the hand of the rich man's
son,—in other words, they marry the purse of the " old man."

Well, when the Hindu contract is made, the priest (who is an
astrologer) is to be consulted as to the tallying of the stars of the boy
and the girl. If he says Yes, then the contract is settled, and they
proceed to make preparations. Sometimes, if the stars do not agree,
the astrologer fixes them all right when he is paid a little money; and
this money is generally paid by the bride's father. When all things
are settled, the mother of the boy or the nearest relative goes to see
the girl and gives her ornaments, and a dinner is given by the girl's
father as a promise of marriage. Then the astrologer fixes a day for
the marriage. The day is fixed at least a month before the marriage.
Then the father of the girl raises a big canopy especially for the marriage ceremony. This costs a great deal of money, for it must be as
beautifully adorned as possible, to please the public,—and the public
is very critical in such matters. This custom of erecting a big canopy
prevails most, even among the poor, on the Malabar coast.

Then the party of the bridegroom comes to the place where the
bride lives, and stops in a big house or a temple. The bride's father
has to arrange for all this. Sometimes the whole expenses, even the
railway fares, are borne by the bride's father; and then the bridegroom's party is often a very large one. The bride's father has
to look to the comforts of the whole party. They are to be treated
as guests. On the evening of the appointed day, the bridegroom
rides on an elephant, or a horse, or in a palanquin, and a long procession is formed. Torches and flower-gardens made of wax and
paper are carried by men on their shoulders. Nautch girls dance before the bridegroom. Band music is played, and fireworks are set
off. It is a beautiful sight to see this procession. Many carriages
filled with children with picturesque dresses lead it. When the procession is at a little distance from the house of the bride, a halt is
made, and the bridegroom and all his company sit on cushions and
mattresses, waiting for the father of the bride. He also comes with a

procession, with torches and fireworks, to greet the bridegroom. This greeting is called a "greeting beyond the limits." This ceremony cannot be performed in big cities, but it is observed in small towns. Properly performed, it takes place at the time of the arrival of the bridegroom in the town, but usually, for the sake of convenience, it is performed on the day of the marriage.

The bride's father greets the bridegroom, presents him with a new dress, a cocoanut, and many other things, and returns to his house. Then again the procession moves on. By the side of the bridegroom walks his sister with a silver lamp, and all the ladies lead the procession, the gentlemen following. In some parts of India the ladies sing marriage songs. When the bridegroom comes near the door, the father of the bride again comes to receive him. He presents him a cocoanut and promises to give him his daughter in marriage. This promise is the betrothal. Then he takes the hand of the bridegroom, and escorts him to the seat which is raised in the middle of the canopy, and seats him on it. This raised seat is made beautiful, having small ornamental pillars and a charming arch and a small dome overhead. The whole canopy is illuminated. On the right of the groom sit all the ladies, on the left hand all the gentlemen are seated on cushions. The nautch girls, in two parties, dance before the ladies and gentlemen. The bands play, and when the appointed time arrives (the time of the marriage must be observed to a second, and therefore there is always a great deal of bustle among the ladies to adorn and make the bride ready); the bride is escorted and brought before the bridegroom by her mother and sister. She stands in the presence of the bridegroom, who also stands, and a yellow piece of cloth is held between them. Meanwhile rice (colored red) is distributed in small quantities to all the guests assembled to be ready to throw it on the pair in token of their blessing. When the time arrives, the family priests on both sides repeat three times: "*Su muhurta Sâwadhán.*" They address the bridegroom: "This is the good time; be careful henceforward": and all the guests reiterate this and throw the rice at the pair.

Then the yellow cloth is removed, and the bride and bridegroom stand face to face. Then the father of the bride stands near and repeats the Sanskrit sentences which mean: "The bridegroom is not deformed, has not lost caste or has not been polluted, and is healthy. To him I give my daughter in the presence of God, fire, and the priests." The bride's father says: "My daughter is healthy;

she has a brother.[1] She is not of the same family as the bridegroom. This my daughter I give to you. Protect her as her father did."

Then the bridegroom promises: "In religion, in money, conjugal rights, and in salvation I will never leave her." This promise is made three times, and he knows that he now has a wife, and that he must love and take care of her. And he does this sacredly when, later, he lives with her. After this the sacred fire is kindled, and the bridegroom's and the bride's scarfs are tied together with a knot. The bridegroom takes the hand of the bride and walks seven times around the fire. This is called "the seven steps." All the while the priests chant the Vedic *muntras*. There are many minor ceremonies after this, and they continue for four days. On the fourth day the bridegroom takes the bride to his house with the same pomp as when he came for her. The young pair ride together, the wife sitting by his left side. The bride stays there one night with her mother-in-law, and returns to her parents. After some months she is sent back to her husband's house for a few months. While living there she occupies her mother-in-law's or sister-in-law's room. She does not even speak to her husband. The utmost modesty is to be observed by a Hindu woman. She must not talk loudly or giggle and laugh in the streets. The young pair thus religiously married love each other from childhood, and that love becomes stronger when developed and is everlasting.

When the girl becomes of age, another ceremony—the consummation of the marriage—is performed, and then the wife and husband live together.

An impression seems to prevail in Western countries that there is no love between the Hindu wife and husband. The truth is, the Hindu families are the happiest in the world. The Hindu woman, having been tied to the lot of the man early, thinks only of him. His happiness is her happiness. She loves her husband devotedly. In the Western nations I observe that the man works from morning to late in the night to earn money. He has no rest. Who enjoys the benefits of his money? His wife. While he is struggling to get the almighty dollar, his wife is enjoying the luxuries and the leisure it buys. If she cannot get the newest fashion of ornaments or clothing, she is often unhappy, and consequently, if the husband cannot

[1] To have a brother for a girl and a sister for a boy is considered good luck; and this is to show that there is no family defect; in some families no male child is born.

buy them, he, too, is made unhappy. Moreover, the women in America seem to have greater liberty than the men. The young girl is brought up by her mother to think that she is equal to man and in some respects superior to him. She reads love novels, spends much time at her toilet: she wears in her bonnet flowers, feathers, dead birds, seaweeds, moss, horns, thorns, big needles; and in her dress, pins, hooks, ties, iron and brass bars, clips, stitches, and what not; and on her bosom I have seen her wear a living lizard fastened with a thin chain. Her waist is laced tight by a corset, which makes her pant for breath. Thus equipped, she sallies forth to make conquests of young men's hearts. She seems to me (pardon me, I write without offence) to lack the mild and delicately sweet look that even the commonest Hindu woman has. Her look is bold and defying to the man. This is all owing to the innate feeling that she is equal to the man. In her pride she has forgotten woman's part. There are, of course, many exceptions. But most women in America seem to be—what shall I call it?—"manified." She falls in love (at least she supposes so) with a young man who takes her to the theatre, and whom she finds possessing means enough to buy her dresses of the newest style, and she marries him. I speak of the average woman that I have observed during the year that I have been in the United States. When they love and court, they have a "good time." Why good? Because it is the best time they spend in their lives, for love sometimes ceases after marriage.

If I may speak a moment of one of your institutions, the Western people have no idea, nor can they even imagine, with what abhorrence and shock the Hindus look on divorce. It is the most disgraceful thing for a Hindu to go to court and make any charge against his wife. No woman or man in India, except of the lowest class, would go to the divorce court. It brings disgrace even to the distant relatives; hence there are no divorce cases.

In India the woman is brought up from her childhood in the mildest way possible, and is taught the home duties,—to love her husband and to obey him. Sometimes—I will say in one case out of a million—there is a disagreement, and the wife goes to live with her parents; but such cases are very, very few: I might almost say there is no such case. Of course the widow has not the privilege of remarrying except in the lowest classes. But the man can marry again. I confess that the custom of forbidding the marriage of widows is a heartless custom, yet it has saved us from the scandal of divorce cases. In India the man has the better of it; in America the woman has the better. But in India, a quarrel between husband and wife is made up on the evening of the day it occurs. O Western Civilization and Liberty, you drive away the modesty of women wherever you go! You have entered India, and your influence is already felt even there!

The greatest care and anxiety of the Hindu mother is to bring up her daughter to home-life, and to make her a good housewife. When a girl is seven years of age, the mother teaches her to cook and to clean the pots. Hindus have two kinds of washing: one is the daily washing of every-day apparel; for the clothes are changed every morning after bathing. Every Hindu must bathe before he takes his meals. Religion requires that no food be cooked before the person who cooks it has bathed. Hence every woman must bathe before she cooks. A woman first gives a bath to her children; then she takes a bath herself, and thereafter goes to cook. The clothes are changed and washed every day. The little girl washes the smaller clothes on a stone and hangs them for drying. She assists her mother in many small things: she sweeps the kitchen; she fetches the utensils; she cuts and slices vegetables; she pounds and grinds the spices; she takes out the small pebbles from the rice and cleans it in water; and, in short, she does all the petty work, assisting her mother. If she has an infant sister or brother, she feeds it, and lulls it to sleep in the cradle. She gathers flowers and weaves them into wreaths with which the Hindu women adorn their hair. The mother teaches her to sew, and to embroider, and to make her toilet, which is simple. She has no paints on her cheeks and no hooks and thorns in her hair. She adorns her hair with ornamental flowers made of gold. These are fixed on the knot of hair. A small, round mark of red paint is made on her forehead. The absence of this mark from the forehead of a woman indicates that she is a widow, for widows have not the privilege of wearing it. By the time she is fifteen, she learns all things pertaining to general housekeeping and cookery. The mother teaches her to prepare cakes, puddings, and sweetmeats. Hindus, especially Brahmins, cannot eat bazaar-made sweetmeats in which water is mixed. She also teaches her to make preserved pickles and other things for use in the rainy season, which begins at the end of May and lasts to about the middle of October. In short, the mother makes her daughter a good housekeeper before she goes to live with her husband. Often she chides her daughter and says: " You will bring discredit on me when you go to your husband's. Your mother-in-law will judge me by your behavior." She is very particular in not allowing her to talk loudly, or to laugh, even at home, at the pitch of her voice, as I have heard American women do even in the streets. Of course "high-caste" American ladies do not laugh in the streets. Yet, as a general rule, it is not considered indecent here as it is in India. I have used the word "caste" because the ladies in America, I observe, have caste prejudices, perhaps quite as strong as in India.

No love songs are taught to a girl. The Hindus do not even sing them in the presence of their women. The girl, after twelve, is not allowed to talk to boys, except to the nearest relatives or family friends, and to these only in the presence of the elders. A young woman cannot go out alone. She is accompanied by an elderly lady, even to the temples and marriage ceremonies. A Hindu lady is not allowed to go to the theatre with other gentlemen than those of her own family; and no Hindu woman—even the poorest, or those of the lowest caste, *not even the dancing girls*—would go on the stage as actresses. Female parts are taken by boys. The Hindus, even the poorest, would not allow their daughters to work in shops or stores and leave them to the mercy of employers. If the parents of a girl are dead, the relatives take care of her until she is married.

The Hindu woman brought up under these strict rules naturally makes a good housewife. When, in turn, she has children, she brings them up in the same way. In the afternoon she talks with her neighbors, mends or sews the clothes, or embroiders, or rests, while her children play. The ladies have their gatherings in India, where they meet and enjoy themselves. Men do not mix in them. At home the Hindu woman has to look to the household duties, and the whole management of the house rests with her. She makes the list of all things required, and the husband or a servant goes and buys them. She does not go shopping.

Of course some of the rules are very strict, but they bring a good result in home-life. Where is a happier home than the Hindu's? The wife loves her husband; the husband loves his wife and children. The Hindu woman's sole desire is to bring happiness into the family, and therefore she is self-denying. Foreigners having no access to Hindu society can have no idea of the bliss of the family life. The members of the family cling to each other. The Hindu feels a family separation with a keenness that Western civilization can hardly appreciate.

In India, as long as the parents are alive, the sons, though married and with children of their own, do not separate, but live in the same house and under the command of their parents. Sometimes the mother-in-law is oppressive, but the daughters-in-law, brought up as they are to that life, quietly submit to her. The earnings of all the sons are given to the father, who manages the household. After the father's death, the property is equally divided without reference to the largeness or smallness of the earnings of individuals. Sometimes the brothers also live together with their families. There are thousands of families living together for five or six generations. This patriarchal system is gradually dying away, owing to the progress of Western material civilization.

The hotels and restaurants, to a certain extent, seem, to an observer from a distance, to have spoiled the home-life here in the cities of the United States. Many rich people live in hotels. Ladies, leading their children by the hand, followed by the husband, go to the restaurant and sit at the table like invited guests.

The Hindu woman is as fond of ornaments as the American is of dress. First, the father and the father-in-law give her ornaments at the marriage. Then the husband buys her more, as many as he can. Generally this is the investment of his earnings. These are the savings, and when in need the wife gives him these willingly. The husband, according to law, has no claim on these ornaments. This is the woman's personal property, and the law cannot attach it for the husband's debts. Therefore the husband, as a provision for her after his death, gives her ornaments. This system saves them from being robbed by the bank. Much gold is used in making bangles. Pearls and diamonds are used according to the means of the families. A very poor woman generally has many dollars' worth of gold ornaments, which in time of need are very useful.

But there is one heartless social-religious custom: the widows are not allowed to re-marry. This is a very, very cruel rule, and it has got hardened and fixed by religious sanction. A woman, after her husband's death, is a most pitiable thing. She cannot take part in marriage ceremonies or any others. She must shave her head, and she must not use ornaments. She must live an ascetic life. This is the precept; but all widows do not shave their heads, especially young widows. It is a belief that the soul of the husband cannot enter heaven unless his wife shaves her head! She is the most miscrable of creatures. But the impression which prevails in America that they are treated badly, is erroneous. The mother and father of the widow look to her with a sigh, and pity her. Sometimes a bad-tempered mother-in-law may treat her badly; but as a general rule she is treated with the utmost sympathy. The ill-treatment of a wife or a widow may occur in the lower classes in any country, but these cases cannot be taken as a criterion.

The Brahmins of the present day feel this very keenly, and the reformers are trying to uproot this cruel custom. Some years ago a law was passed by the government acknowledging the heirship of children born of a widow from her second husband, to his property. Some Brahmins have come forward and boldly introduced widow-marriage. But it is not acknowledged by the orthodox party, which is still very strong and excommunicates the reformers. Yet every year two or three marriages of widows take place among the Brahmins. At first there was a great sensation at such a marriage, but now the fierce outcry against it is dying away. Gradually the Hindus are leaving behind some of their old customs. To unloose the orthodox ideas will take some time, but a day will come when all widows will re-marry. We are fast adopting Western manners—except religion, for the young Brahmin of the present day holds fast to his religion, but he is a very broad-minded man. We are making progress. Thirty or forty years ago, if a Brahmin touched or shook hands with a Christian, he was obliged to take an oath and to change and wash his clothes. Now the Brahmins mix socially with the Christians to a degree. The old orthodox priests and ladies still keep their prejudices, but the liberal party is growing. To touch a beef-eater is polluting. But even this prejudice is dying, except among the ladies and in some remote villages and towns and among the very orthodox.

There are schools for boys and girls in every town and village, established by the government, in which primary education—reading, writing, simple arithmetic, and geography—is taught the boys; and the girls, in addition to the above subjects, are taught cooking, sewing, and embroidery. The girls' schools are separate from the boys'. Generally the teachers in the girls' schools are women; but, where women cannot be had, men take the place. I am sure that a time will come when all our Hindu women will be educated as they were once. They will have liberty, too. Secret love-letters will fly from woman to man; there will be divorces and all the necessary and consequent evils of Western high civilization. But these things will not come with great rapidity.

In conclusion, I must request my American readers to pardon my remarks on their social customs. I have felt obliged to speak plainly because erroneous reports seem to have been brought by missionaries, who cannot know the best social life in India. We should not judge one another harshly. I have seen the beautiful home-life of the cultivated Americans. I have been very kindly and very hospitably treated. I have lived as a guest in one family for more than a month, and when I left them I shed tears. I know that there is a genuine and sweet home-life in America, but the tendency is to live in hotels and restaurants. The presence of so many old maids and bachelors, each disliking the other,—these things force me to think none too well of Western methods of bringing up girls. We have no hotels or restaurants in India. Years ago, when I was quite a lad, a relative of mine returned home from Bombay. Among other things, he told us that there were houses where they sold food for money. The village people could not believe it. Cooked food sold! It was a surprise to us. We never took money for feeding people, and never made a business of it. Any traveller was a guest wherever he went. In Sanskrit the word " guest" means "`atithi`," or " one who knows no date." Hence no appointment of date. He can come any time. " *Tithi* " means date, and " *a* " is equal to " *wu* " or " no. " But owing to railway and steamship communication and the progress of Western civilization, this custom of hospitality, which is a part of Hindu religion, is also gradually dying away, except in towns. In some big cities there are now " feeding-places"—I cannot call them hotels. We have no equivalent word for such, as we had not the custom of selling food to a stranger. My purpose in telling this is to show that the hotels and restaurants, though very convenient for a traveller, have, together with the manner of bringing up children, especially girls, with too much of independence, injured the home-life of America.

But again, I beg pardon. I am very grateful for the hospitality and kindness that I have received in America during my visit to this grandest nation on the earth. The American ladies surpass their sisters in India in education. It was a very agreeable surprise to me to hear ladies here discussing social, philosophical, and political subjects in a thorough way. In this respect our ladies are far behind them, and I wish that they, too, were educated, as they will again be in time.

Purushotam Rao Telang.

UNIVERSITY TRAINING AND CITIZENSHIP.

It is hard, amidst a multitude of counsellors, to make up our own ideal of what a university should be. We have been so often bidden, by young and old alike, to make our university instruction like that of Germany, that we have more than half consented to try the experiment. And yet we are by no means sure of our purpose in that direction. Once and again we have been made to think a good deal about the advantage that a young fellow gets from reading widely and systematically with a tutor, as the men do at the English universities. We like the close contact between teacher and pupil, and the rather liberal and unscholastic way of handling many books, which such a method of instruction seems to secure. The French system, too, we can appreciate and wish for when we are in the humour. We like the French spirit and sense of form, and we hold our judgments open to suggestions as to the best way of imparting vitality of that sort to our own instruction. All the while, however, it is our temper to put varied and vexatious restrictions on these, as on other, international exchanges. There is a very heavy duty on imported ideals. It costs us more than they are worth to subject them to our customs and get them fairly on the market. There is no great demand for them. The young men who really want them go abroad, if they can, to get them.

And yet we have no university ideal of our own. We are not even sure that we wish to create one. We ask ourselves, Do we want universities of a distinctively American type? It is the first impulse of most scholarly minds to reply with a plain and decided negative. Learning is cosmopolitan, and it would seem at first thought like stripping learning of its freedom and wide prerogative to demand that the universities where it makes its home should be national. Let the common schools smack of the soil, if they must, but not the universities! Must not the higher forms of scholarship follow everywhere the same method, in the same spirit? May not its doctrines constitute always a sort of international law of thought? Is it not a kind of freemasonry which has everywhere like degrees and a common ceremonial? Certainly truth is without geographical boundary, and no one could justly wish to observe a national bias in the determination of it.

It must be remembered, however, that scholarship is something more than an instrument of abstract investigation merely. It is also an instrument and means of life. Nations, as well as individuals, must seek wisdom: the truth that will make them free. There is a learning of purpose as well as a learning of science; for there is a truth of spirit as well as a truth of fact. And scholarship, though it must everywhere seek the truth, may select the truths it shall search for and emphasize. It is this selection that should be national. It is a question of emphasis and point of view; not a question of completing the circle and sum of knowledge. A wise man will choose what to learn; and so also will a wise nation. Not all learning, besides, is without a country. All physical science is international, so are also all formal parts of learning; and all philosophy, too, no doubt, and the laws of reasoning. But there is, besides these, a learning of purpose, to be found in literature and in the study of institutions; and this it is which should be made the means of nationalizing universities, being given the central and coördinating place in their courses of instruction.

In order to be national, a university should have, at the centre of all its training, courses of instruction in that literature which contains the ideals of its race and all the nice proofs and subtle inspirations of the character, spirit, and thought of the nation which it serves; and, besides that, instruction in the history and leading conceptions of those institutions which have served the nation's energies in the preservation of order and the maintenance of just standards of civil virtue and public purpose. These should constitute the common training of all its students, as the only means of schooling their spirits for their common life as citizens. For the rest, they might be free to choose what they would learn. Being thus prepared for their common life together by schooling in the same ideals of life and public action, they might the more safely be left to prepare for their individual and private functions separately and with undisturbed freedom.

It is the object of learning, not only to satisfy the curiosity and perfect the spirits of individual men, but also to advance civilization; and, if it be true that each nation plays its special part in furthering the common advancement, every people should use its universities to perfect it in its proper rôle. A university should be an organ of memory for the State for the transmission of its best traditions. Every man sent out from a university should be a man of his nation, as well as a man of his time.

This idea of a balance between general and special training has been temporarily lost sight of by the necessity to make room for the modern scientific studies. We have adopted the principle that a student may freely choose his studies, and so make the most of his natural tastes and aptitudes; and the length we go in applying the principle is determined, it would seem, rather by historical accident than by reasoned policy. If we are conservative, we insist that at least every Bachelor of Arts shall submit to a drill in both Greek and Latin. If we are 'liberal,' we permit the substitution of a modern language for one of these. If we are radical, we give the pupil *carte blanche*, and let him choose for himself what training he will have. But, whether we be conservative, 'liberal,' or radical, we are willing to confer other degrees besides Bachelor of Arts, and, under another label, to send men forth from the university who have taken nothing from it but a drill in laboratories and instruction in the use of tools. We have lost all idea of a common standard of training for all the men alike who seek to be accredited to the world by an academic degree.

Not only so, but in our controversies about the matter we have allowed ourselves to be driven into an awkward and even untenable position. We debate the relative values of a classical training and a scientific, as if it turned wholly upon the question of the development of the individual mind as a good working instrument. Can the man who has received a purely scientific training, from which all the nice discriminations of taste and of delicate judgment that come from the critical study of languages have been left out, use his mind as well as the man who has had these; as well as the man who has been schooled to submit his faculties to the subtle and refining influences of style and syntax, the elevating influences of delicate feeling, and the vivid passion of poet and orator? The question cannot be answered. The one may use his mind quite as well as the other: it depends upon what he uses it for. He uses it differently: that is all. The values represented by the difference cannot be satisfactorily assessed.

The difference is even very difficult to express. But no doubt it can be illustrated. The man who has been trained only in science or in technical and narrow lines—however well equipped or variously within those lines—is confined to them, not because he lacks knowledge, but because he lacks sympathy and adaptability. The scientific spirit and method, in academic instruction, hold their votaries very rigourously to a single point of view, and the more this spirit and method are submitted to and served, the more restrictive does their mastery become. It is presently impossible for those who are their willing and habituated subjects to understand whereof other men speak when they urge considerations which cannot be subjected to exact tests or modern standards. The men who have been inducted into literature and language, on the other hand, while they have obtained little marketable knowledge, have obtained both drill and an opened view of life. They have, so to say, breathed and analyzed the common air of thought that the better minds have lived in from the first. They have, in greater or less degree, become citizens of the intellectual world, and have examined with some critical care and a little discrimination the documents by which that citizenship is evidenced and secured. They cannot, however, make themselves so immediately useful in the practical tasks of the world of business as the men of the laboratories, the shops, or the purely professional schools; and they are thought, by those who have special training or capacity, to know nothing. They can use their minds, but there is nothing in them to use. They possess, at most, only a point of view. They are like good soils that have been prepared for planting, but as yet contain no edible harvest. The best light of the world has shone upon them; they have been watered by the tears of old songs, quickened by the passion of deeds done long ago; but no merchantable thing has yet been sown in them, and the man of science brings his quick crop first to market.

Certainly we have come to the parting of the ways, and there is nothing for us but to choose a direction. The graduates of our universities no longer go forth with a common training which will enable them to hold together in a community of thought. Some of them are trained in science, some in letters; some well and broadly trained, many ill and narrowly, with a hard technicality and mean contraction of view. Scarcely one of them has been fully inducted into the learning which deals with the common experiences, the common thoughts and struggles, the old triumphs and defeats of the men of his race in the past: their dreams and awakenings; their ambitions, humours, confidences, liberties, and follies: the intimate stuff of their minds and lives in past generations, when others were in like manner graduated from college and brought face to face with life and the unthinking mass of men.

The study of institutions and of English literature furnishes the only practicable common ground for the various disciplines of the modern university curriculum; but fortunately it has much more to commend it than its practicability.   It would furnish also an ideal principle of unity.   Such studies are practicable because they are not open to any serious utilitarian objection.   They do not involve the long and tedious acquisition of any dead language: their tools are of easy use by any one.   They bear directly upon such practical matter as a man's usefulness as a citizen and his influence and acceptability as a member of society.   He can understand other men so much the better, command their sympathy the more readily, aid them and obtain their aid the more efficiently, for comprehending affairs and appreciating the common movements of sentiment and purpose.   Such a community of plan is ideal because the great spiritual impulses and values which young men get when properly trained in the classics can be gotten in part from the splendid and various literature of our own tongue, rich as it is with treasures both new and old; because men trained to the exact standards and accustomed to the precise measurements of science, its cold dispassionateness and cautious reserve of judgment, can get from that literature an imagination for affairs and the standards by which things invisible and of the spirit are to be assessed; and because the men trained in the classics can get by it their pilotage into the modern world of men and ideas.   It makes the classicist more practical and the scientist less narrow and pedantic; it is capable of giving to things technical an horizon and an elevation of spirit, and to things merely scholarly or æsthetic a thrill and ardour and discipline of life.

Every university, therefore, which would educate men as well as drill them, should make the reading of English literature in many sorts and much variety, under energetic and quick-witted tutors, compulsory from entrance to graduation; and the study of institutions under suggestive lecturers compulsory throughout at least the latter half of every course for a degree.   It can be done, and sooner or later it must be done, if only to prevent disintegration and the utter separation and segregation of educated men in respect of their ideals of thought and conduct.

But this is the view only from inside the university.   The greater arguments, from without, are supplied by the life of the modern world and the exigencies of national existence. The world in which we live is troubled by many voices, seeking to proclaim righteousness and judgment to come; but they disturb without instructing us. They cry out upon this point or upon that, but they have no whole doctrine which we can accept and live. They exaggerate, distort, distract. But they are dangerous voices, for all they are so obviously partial and unwise, because we have no clearly conceived standards of common thought to which to hold them. Those who hear are as ignorant and as fanatical as those who speak. A college man who has studied only the classics can no more criticise them than the man who has studied only science or the man who has studied nothing at all. Even the man who has read political economy and history has nowadays, very likely, read no literature. He can only cry out from his corner that these would-be teachers now everywhere on the platform are guilty of errors in logic and misconceptions of historical fact in all their revolutionary talk; and no one cares to listen to his pedantic and scholastic corrections: for these, they say, are matters of life and death, in which we need, not dialectic, but deliverance.

There is no corrective for it all like a wide acquaintance with the best books that men have written, joined with a knowledge of the institutions men have made trial of in the past; and for each nation there is its own record of mental experience and political experiment. Such a record always sobers those who read it. It also steadies the nerves. If all educated men knew it, it would be as if they had had a revelation. They could stand together and govern, with open eyes and the gift of tongues which other men could understand. Here is like wild talk and headlong passion for reform in the past,—here in the books,—with all the motives that underlay the perilous utterance now laid bare: these are not new terrors and excitements. Neither need the wisdom be new, nor the humanity, by which they shall be moderated and turned to righteous ends. There is old experience in these matters, or rather in these states of mind. It is no new thing to have economic problems and dream dreams of romantic and adventurous social reconstruction.

And so it is out of books that we can get our means and our self-possession for a sane and systematic criticism of life: out of our own English books that we can get and appropriate and forever recreate the temper of our own race in dealing with these so hazardous affairs. We shall lose our sense of identity and all advantage of being hardheaded Saxons if we become ignorant of our literature, which is so full of action and of thoughts fit for action.   We must look to the universities to see to it that we be not denationalized, but rather made more steadfast in our best judgments of progress.   To hear the agitators talk, you would suppose that righteousness was young and wisdom but of yesterday.   How are the universities correcting the view, and aiding to make this nonsense ridiculous?   How many of their graduates know anything clearly to the contrary?   How many of them know when to laugh?

Of all things that a university should do for a man, the most important is to put him in possession of the materials for a systematic criticism of life.   Our present methods of training may easily enough make *tabula rasa* of a man's mind in respect of such matters.   The reasoning of the scientific method, for all but a few constructive minds, is analytical reasoning.   It picks things to pieces and examines them in their ultimate elements.   It is jealous, if not quite intolerant, of all traditional views; will receive nothing, but test everything; and its influence is very marked and pervasive.   It produces, for one thing, an overweening confidence in the pure reasoning faculty. Now, it happens that the pure reasoning faculty, whose only standard is logic and whose only data are put in terms of determinable force, is the worst possible instrument for reforming society.   The only thing that makes modern socialism more dangerous than like doctrine has ever been is, that its methods are scientific and that the age also is scientific.   Two-thirds of our college graduates are not taught anything that would predispose them against accepting its logic or its purpose to put all things into a laboratory of experiment and arbitrarily recombine the elements of society.

The 'humane' spirit of our time is a very different thing from the *human* spirit.   The humanity which we nowadays affect is scientific and pathological.   It treats men as specimens, and seeks to subject them to experiment.   It cuts cross-sections through the human spirit and calls its description of what is thereby disclosed moral essays and sociological novels.   It is self-conscious and without modesty or humour.   The human spirit is a very different thing. It has a memory and a sense of humour.   It cannot read Ibsen after having read Shakespeare, any more than it can prefer sugar and butter and flour and sweets separately, in their individual intensity, to their toothsome and satisfying combination in pudding.   Its literature is that which has the one flavour for every generation, and

8

the same broad and valid sagacity. It regards the scientific method of investigation as one, but only one, method of finding out the truth; and as a method for finding only one kind of truth. It sees the telling points of the socialistic argument, but it knows some old standards of justice that have outlived many programmes of reform and seem still sound enough to outlast these also. "It's a mad world, my masters!" but it takes a nice balance of judgment and a long view of human nature to determine where the madness lies.

The worst possible enemy to society is the man who, with a strong faculty for reasoning and for action, is cut loose in his standards of judgment from the past; and universities which train men to use their minds without carefully establishing the connection of their thought with that of the past, are instruments of social destruction. Of course no man's thought is entirely severed from the past, or ever can be. But it is worth while to remember that science is no older than the present century, and is apt to despise old thought. At least its young votaries are: not because they are 'scientists,' but because they are only scientists. They are as much pedants, in their narrowness, as the men trained exclusively in the classics, whose thought is all in the past.

The training that will bring these two extremes together can be obtained by a thorough familiarity with the masterpieces of English thought and with the efforts of human genius in the field of institutions. A body of men thus made acquainted with their species is needed, to give us, at the centre of our political and social life, a class with definite and elevated ideals and a real capacity for understanding the conditions of progress: a power making for stability and righteousness against the petty and ineffectual turbulence of revolution.

We mistake the service of literature when we regard it as merely æsthetic. A literature of such variety as our own is nothing less than the annals of the best thought of our race upon every topic of life and destiny. Even our poets have had an eye for affairs; their visions have been of men and deeds. And, as for reading in the literature of institutions, no self-governing people can long hold together in order and peace without it. It is noteworthy that what remains the greatest text-book of English law, invaluable in spite of all the modern changes which have been hurried forward in the century since it was written, was written for laymen. Blackstone intended his lectures for the gentlemen of England: to enable the men of Oxford to take a place of intelligent authority in society when they should come into their own.   With the spirit of our sane litera-ture in us, and the strong flavour of our institutional principles present in all that we do or attempt, we shall be broad men enough, be our special training, in tools or books, what it may.   Without this, we can but go astray alike in our private judgments and our public functions.

It would not be necessary to erect a new university to try the experiment of such a synthesis of university courses; though that would be worth doing, were the means made sufficient for a really great object-lesson in the right motives of education.   Anybody can establish the modern sort of university, anywhere.   It has no neces-sary nationality or character.   But only in a free country, with great traditions of enlightened sentiment and continuous purpose, can a university have the national mark and distinction of a deliberate espousal of the spirit of a noble literature and historic institutions. Such a university would be a National Academy,—the only sort worth having.   The thing can be done, however, without troubling a millionaire to appropriate to himself the glory of a unique function of greatness in the development of education.   It can be done by only a comparatively slight readjustment of subjects and instructors in the greater of the universities we already have.   It can even be done upon no mean scale by every college whose resources are at all adequate to the ordinary demands of education.

It may be made the basis for the synthesis now so sadly lacking in university plans.   Better than any other discipline, it can be made the meeting point for all degrees: where candidates in every sort may get their liberalizing outlook upon the world of thought and affairs.   More worthily than any other can it be made the means of nationalizing the men whom the universities send forth to represent the power and worth of education.   In no better way can an Ameri-can university obtain a distinguishing function in the world.

As a practical means of university reorganization, such a plan would sacrifice nothing of our present academic freedom.   The study of the literature and institutions of our stock could be made the common feature of all the schools of a modern university without cutting off any essential part of the separate groups of studies we have been at such pains to develop.   It would not prevent, or even embarrass, specialization.   It is susceptible of being joined alike to classical studies and to technical training; and it would not be incongruously joined to either.   It would serve ideally, besides, as the centre of those compromise and middle courses of study, half way between the classical and the scientific, which the peculiar conditions of the day have constrained the colleges to offer.   It would make all courses in a good sense 'liberal' without requiring any wholesale reconsideration of the provisions we have already made to train men for the special tasks of practical life.

The serious practical question is, How are all the men of a university to be made to read English literature widely and intelligently, as this plan presupposes?   For it is reading, not set lectures, that will prepare a soil for culture: the inside of books, and not talk about them; though there must be the latter also, to serve as a chart and guide to the reading.   The difficulty is not in reality very great. A considerable number of young tutors, serving their novitiate for full university appointments, might easily enough effect an organization of the men that would secure the reading.   Taking them in groups of manageable numbers, suggesting the reading of each group, and by frequent interviews and quizzes seeing that it was actually done, explaining and stimulating as best they might by the way, they could not only get the required tasks performed, but relieve them of the hateful appearance of being tasks, and cheer and enrich the whole life of the university.

WOODROW WILSON.

So general is the idea among laborers that they will be persecuted by their employers unless they are sheltered under the folds of a "union," that an instance of employees organizing for the advancement of the interests of their employers is unique enough to deserve the consideration of the thoughtful as well as the attention of the curious. In the European countries where conditions have become fixed by custom and changes are restricted by the oversupply of labor, strikes fail because of the lack of moral support accorded the strikers or the eagerness with which several unemployed men would grasp at every vacated place; and a boycott is practically made inefficient by the large number of persons engaged in a small way in all the trades and industries. This feeling of helplessness on the part of the laborers one would think might naturally prompt silent if not open defiance, and the desire to promote the welfare of the employer would be foreign to the mind of the employee. Still this wish seems to have prevailed at Antwerp—one of the oldest of the busy places of Europe—in the establishment there of those guilds or societies known as the "nations."

By the enactment of laws favorable to the free importation of foreign wares, Antwerp early in the fifteenth century became an important port, as can be learned from the reports of the embassies sent by various courts to attend the regal festivities which frequently took place there. But the delays in discharging vessels and the frequent losses to merchandise from unskilful handling threatened to outweigh beneficent legislation and advantageous position. The dock-hands and porters became careless, in the belief that plenty of work would always await them; but an awakening came when some of the united traders erected buildings of their own, where they could not only store their goods but house their workmen and horses as well. Two of these structures are still standing—the "Maison Hanséatique" and the "Maison de Hesse." The result of the awaking of the laborers to a proper apprehension of the danger of the loss of work, and the consciousness that sooner or later it would fall into the hands of strangers, was the establishment in 1442 of a company of 'longshore-men who assumed the name " Les Grecs," a name which, with merely those changes incident to change of language, the society has borne from that year to the present time.   This was the first of the fifty " nations" now in active existence at Antwerp.

A " nation" is a corporation of workmen forming a limited soci-ety in which every member is also a stockholder.   The society is not only limited in membership, but it is restricted also in functions. First of all, the " nations" work only at the docks, loading or un-loading vessels or hauling merchandise to or from ships; secondly, each " nation" will handle only certain articles of commerce, and again, only those articles which come from or are destined for a certain port.   For example, the " Katven nation" will unload wool that comes from Buenos Ayres, but a vessel charged with wool from Australia can secure the services only of the " Zuid nation."   One " nation" puts on board ordinary Belgian sugar; but if the sugar is specially refined and intended for candy, its loading is the work of another " nation."   The underlying principle of this elaborate differ-entiation of labor is that a society with restricted lines of work can become especially proficient in those lines, can acquire the best im-plements and appliances for their performance, and thus give to their employers the best possible service.   In no instance has this monop-oly given an excuse for extortionate charges or forcible increase of prices.

Every one of these societies upon its organization must give bond to abide by the regulations prepared by the port officers, and a special rule fixes for a term of years—usually ten—the tariff of charges, and any attempt to violate this rule would result in an im-mediate abrogation of the society's privileges.   On the other hand, every vessel entering port is obliged to employ the appropriate soci-ety; but this compulsion is evidently in the best interests of shippers, as can be seen from what follows as well as from the fact that the maritime trade of Antwerp is increasing at the rate of one hundred thousand tons per year.   Every " nation" is a stock company, but no one can hold stock who is not an active working member.   As a member he obeys implicitly the orders of his superiors and profits by his own labors as well as by the labors of his associates.

The officers are a dean and as many assistant deans as may be necessary,—there being one dean in the smaller societies of twenty or thirty members, and two or three in those of fifty or sixty,—and a secretary and such additional officers as are found essential in each society. They are elected annually and are eligible for re-election, but serve without extra compensation. Every organization has its own by-laws; but since they are not published, and dismissal would be the penalty of their promulgation, very little is known about them. The "nations," however, appear to be very wisely governed regarding the duties and obligations of the members to one another; for it is known that fines are imposed for certain offences. For instance, if a member fails to report each morning, unless sick, he pays eighty cents; if the absence occurs twice within a month the fine is two dollars; while the next repetition would result in dismissal. Again, if one member summons another, against his will, as a witness, he must pay an honorarium of four dollars for every day, and the same amount is demanded in case one member causes the arrest of a colleague.

The nearest approach to an authentic financial statement is obtained from the decennial report which each "nation" must submit to the local authorities showing its nominal assets and liabilities. From the accounts rendered in 1890 it is seen that the richest "nation" had a capital of $180,000, divided into shares of $5,000 each; and the next richest had a capital of $168,000, divided into shares of $4,000. Of the actual assets the world at large knows nothing, except that they consist of a number of magnificent draught-horses (perhaps the best in the world), wagons, stables, and such appliances as are needed in their work. The Belgian law requiring every firm and corporation to file a balance-sheet annually does not apply to the "nations," because they have no standing in the local courts. In their articles of incorporation they bind themselves to submit all differences between themselves and their employers to arbitration. Yielding their right to sue, they become exempt from being sued.

The outward workings of a "nation" resemble somewhat a patriarchal form of government. On every work-day morning all the members who are able assemble at headquarters half an hour before time to begin work, and receive assignments for the day. This allotment of tasks is made by the dean and is not subject to open criticism or refusal, but he is doubtless guided by a knowledge of every man's special fitness or some consideration of his recent labors. Those for whom there is no work have the day free without suffering any diminution in their share of the society's profits, but they are not allowed to hire themselves to others, the idea being that they keep themselves fresh for the probable duties of the morrow. In the evening, those who were occupied report at the office, and a record is made by the secretary of the place and of the character of the work, rather as a check upon the work than upon the workmen. When the task is finished the dean collects the entire amount due the society and places it in bank as a part of the general fund. At the end of the month the net receipts are equally divided among the members, regardless of the number of idle or employed days of each. Usually there is a maximum limit to the sum paid to each member for his share of the month's profits; that is to say, if the receipts would justify a larger dividend he would receive only $80, the overplus remaining in the general fund to help over those months when the earnings are less. Likewise those who are unable to work because of sickness or injury received in the discharge of duty fare equally with the others. This benefit, however, is restricted to a definite number of months, usually four.

The " nations" sustain individually—or collectively in some cases —orphan asylums for the maintenance of the children of those who die from illness contracted or injury received while engaged at work. As the number of accidents is large and the lives of men engaged in such heavy work is short, these institutions are always well filled. The city, rightly appreciating the contributions that the "nations" make to the mercantile prosperity of Antwerp, assist in the support of these asylums or in educating their occupants.

When a member dies his share is sold at auction for the benefit of his heirs. Shares in the more prosperous nations command a premium, according to the condition of the society. In this sale no preference is shown a son of the deceased should he be a bidder. Since no member can own more than one share, there is always an evenly distributed power with no possibility for control on the part of any one except through the weight of personal influence. And as each member is also a shareholder, when he looks after his own interests by assiduous and well-directed labor, he is contributing to the welfare of all. With the increase of work they do not add to their membership and thereby risk a loss or at least a depreciation in the value of their stock in case of any untoward movement in trade, but they employ laborers, thus becoming themselves employers, or rather contractors. Those " nations" that also load vessels have their own expert stevedores, as well as their own blacksmiths and wagon-makers; but in no case are these members.

When a vessel passes Flushing, a telegraphic message is sent to the port-officer at Antwerp, giving the approximate size of the ship and the character of her cargo. A place at the dock is at once assigned to the ship, and the appropriate "nation" is notified, so that by the time she takes her place at the dock the men are ready to take her in hand. As soon as the first member of the "nation" places his hand upon the cargo, the whole "nation" becomes responsible for it, as well as for any damage that the ship may sustain through careless discharging. Thus it is that the largest vessel as well as the tiniest craft can confidently ascend the Scheldt knowing that no delays await her because of strikes or useless bargaining for reduced rates. It is this confidence together with other exceptional facilities that is making Antwerp the first maritime city on the continent of Europe and enables her to handle fourteen thousand tons of merchandise every day.

J. H. GORE.

HOW TO BRING WORK AND WORKERS TOGETHER.

THE other day a man, a German house-painter, committed suicide in West Forty-ninth Street, New York. I suppose that it is not very often that the readers of THE FORUM are asked to concern themselves about an ordinary, every-day suicide; for I may as well say at once that this one had nothing to redeem it from the reproach of being hopelessly common. Suicides belong in the category of crime, which the newspapers are blamed for exploiting *ad nauseam*. I am not at all sure that that view is correct, or justified even by the sensational stories that are published. Suicides sometimes preach sermons to which society, to its injury, turns a deaf ear. Any wrong unredressed works injury to society, and back of a good many suicides there is somewhere wrong—injustice. That the wrong was unintentional, the result perhaps of twisted, unnatural conditions for which no one was directly or wholly responsible, makes it only the more important that we should see the truth and know what causes produce such effects.

This suicide that I speak of was a case in point. The little family now broken up lived happily enough until the man lost his job last fall and failed to find another. From that time on troubles crowded upon them. Worry laid him upon a sick-bed from which he did not rise until the winter was far spent. What little they had saved against a rainy day was then long since gone. The wife had to go out washing to earn bread for them all. Happily she was strong and cheerful. But her husband, not so light-hearted, suffered at the sight and at his inability to help. As the days of his convalescence passed and he went about again, he sought work with the desperation of a man whose life was at stake. And it was. Worn out in body and mind by the hopelessness of his search, he broke down under the last disappointment and killed himself. He said to his wife before he died that he could no longer bear to see her work as she did, when he was unable to help her.

That was his story, and there was no reason for doubting it,—certainly not because of its strangeness. There were more cases of that kind last winter and in other winters that have gone before. There are thousands looking as anxiously and as vainly for work as he, even to-day. But the feature in his case to which I invite attention is that the work had been looking persistently and vainly for him all the time. The job wanted him quite as badly as he wanted the job. They simply had not found each other. *There was no place where they would naturally both go in search of what each wanted.* And so the job to-day is not done, and the man is dead, a suicide.

How do I know this? Because I had the job to give. I had been searching for a painter of just his kind many weeks and had not found him. I had a reason for searching which makes me write down the story of it here. I have a little house out on Long Island that needed painting. It needs that periodically. Two years ago, or three, when it was in that state last, it happened that all the painters in my neighborhood were busy. I went three or four weeks vainly trying to get one, and then one day my business as a police reporter led me to a tenement on the west side of New York where a house-painter had that day killed himself because he could not find work. There was no other cause. He was neither a drunkard nor an idler. He simply was unable to find work by which to support his family. That very day I had tried hard to hire the services of just such a man as he, but I could not. I made up my mind then that, when next I needed a painter, I should look for a man in his plight. If there was one, I had no doubt that I should find him.

More than a month ago, my house being in need of painting again, I set about the quest. I inquired here and I inquired there, of this charity committee and of that, but did not find what I wanted. I had almost concluded that all the city painters were at work, and, being unable to wait longer, I sent for one of the village workmen. I left him that morning at work, to find upon my arrival at the office the story of this second painter's suicide.

It was a coincidence, of course; but such coincidences are not meaningless. The meaning of this one was plain. Had there been such a place as I spoke of, where the man and the job would naturally go in search of each other with mutual confidence, these two lives would not have been wasted. For suicide, apart from its moral aspect, is waste; and this was wicked waste, seeing how badly the lives so recklessly thrown away were needed scarce half a dozen miles away. There was a failure here of the social machinery which surely required adjustment.

The way of adjustment was as clearly indicated as the need of it. I pointed out in THE FORUM at the time of the first painter's suicide that one great need of the poor in New York was a thoroughly repre-sentative, really adequate labor bureau, where what there was of work in bad seasons could be made to go as far as it would. It does not do so now. We have employment bureaus, but I would have an employment bureau to which everybody would come as a matter of course, feeling perfectly sure that whether he wanted work or work-men, if they were to be had he would get them there. We have as a legacy from the last hard winter, the Charity Pawnshop and the Wayfarers' Lodge, excellent in their way; but they are both at the wasteful end of the problem how to deal with poverty; and so are most other ways charity has devised. The ounce of prevention, always so precious, would be the Employment Bureau. Why have we not one?

I do not mean a municipal enterprise. I would rather have none. Neither do I mean a money-making or newspaper-advertising scheme, nor yet a charity with the charity sticking out all over it, but a friendly, capable, aggressive concern that should really endeavor to cover the field, to inform itself about the labor market in town and out of town, and make such tragic blunders as these I have men-tioned impossible.

Relief committees are well enough for an emergency, but they make no pretence to the kind of grasp of the situation that I speak of. They speedily feel the want of it. As to the employment bureaus that exist—I mean those that are in the field to benefit mankind, not to make money—I have no desire to discredit them; but I maintain that they are miserably inadequate. They content themselves mostly with registering applicants. As well might a general hope to overwhelm the enemy with his morning roll-call—very imposing, no doubt, and satisfying, but hardly substantial enough for a fight. The labor unions' offices are perhaps an excep-tion, but they cover only so much of the field as has been reached by organization, and that is neither the bigger nor the needier end of it.

In what way could such a bureau be launched with the best promise of success? Why not, by the way, call it a " labor exchange" rather than " bureau"? All trades and branches of business have their exchanges where the exact state of the market for their special wares here and abroad can be ascertained at any time. The only market that is without official quotation or attention of that sort is the most important of all, the labor market, though upon its state depends the well-being of the whole community. It is left to balance itself somehow, and it does after a fashion. What that fashion is I have had occasion to observe since I have lived out on Long Island. There has been no spring these eight years past, and I presume not before them in the memory of man, that has not found us suffering for help to dig our gardens and to mow our lawns. We have had work for twenty men whom we could not get, and yet in the city, only eight miles away, a hundred times twenty able-bodied men were at that time walking the streets begging for work, with no one to direct them to us. I am not thinking of tramps—there are always enough of them—but of men who wanted work and wanted it badly.

But about the way of establishing the exchange that shall bring the two together. Two ways are open: by private means, or by public provision. If the latter, it must needs be a State concern; as municipal action is neither desirable nor in the least probable. It is not desirable, because politics would be too apt to get mixed up with it, and because it would not be likely to reach far enough, in which case it would be merely the old failure on a larger scale. Against the danger of politics, the State's authority is not sure protection; but on the other hand it furnishes the only guarantee that the bureau would be planned on a really useful scale. The State has now in its labor statistics and the machinery by which they are collected the very material for such a bureau, without which it would be a mere registry office of no value.

In any event a private concern would need some sort of connection with these State offices as a means of informing itself of the situation. It is to be noted also that a State bureau would have the support and co-operation of organized labor, which might be wanting in any other case. The labor organizations championed a State employment bureau in the last New York legislature. These considerations weigh against any supposed socialistic tendencies in action by the State. For that matter, why should there be more socialism in a State employment bureau than in a State bureau of labor statistics? And may not one with perfect consistency deny the claim that the State is bound to furnish work for its unemployed, and yet applaud its efforts to help its starving citizens to help themselves? That is all the employment office would do for them, and on economic grounds it might well be considered good politics.

The "Ohio experiment," as it was called, is instructive on that point. In April, 1890, the State of Ohio, under pressure of the labor organizations, established by law free employment offices in the five cities of Cincinnati, Cleveland, Columbus, Dayton, and Toledo. They were made a part of the Bureau of Labor Statistics. The superintendents were to report weekly to the commissioner in charge, and they were to exchange lists of " help wanted" and " situations sought" with each other. There was some delay through a provision in the law which settled the expenses of the offices on the cities in which they were; but, despite this, the first six months made the following showing: Applicants for work numbered 20,136, a little over one-third of them women. Employers had registered a demand for 18,154 persons—somewhat more than half women. Nearly fifty per cent found what they wanted. The total number who secured situations through the offices was 8,982, of which number 5,575 were males, and 3,407 females. The entire cost of conducting all the offices was less than $5,000.

"If," says the commissioner in his report, "the 8,982 persons who secured work through the free public employment office had obtained it through the private employment agencies, it is fair to assume that the cost of such services would have averaged $3 per capita for males, and $1 for females, or a total of $20,132; and by deducting from the latter sum the cost of maintaining the free public employment offices, there is a balance of $15,132, which has been saved to the willing yet poor and needy working men and women by the State law."

From the above figures it would appear that domestic servants and those looking for such help made immediate use of the offices. And so, in fact, the superintendent of the Cleveland bureau reports in the following year (1891): " Persons employing females for domestic service have nothing but the highest praise for the office." Not so the private intelligence offices, whose fraudulent practices the officials had denounced from the outset. The fight with these was in full swing, but it did not last long. Already in 1892 they had been cleared out entirely from three of the five cities. Only in Cleveland and in Cincinnati a few yet survived.

In the second year of the experiment the free employment offices found work for four out of every nine applicants, and for every four vacancies there were five to fill them. After two and a half years, on January 1, 1893, the commissioner reports the plan as having passed the experimental stage. On business as well as on humane grounds he pronounces it a success. A total of 81,464 had applied for work, and 63,564 for " help." In 38,352 cases these demands had been made to fit each other. The National Convention of

Officials of Bureaus of Labor Statistics, held in Denver in May, 1892, recommended the plan for consideration to their respective State governments.

Two things are especially noticeable in this statement. One is the strikingly large percentage of employers demanding help, with so many seeking work. In 1890 the "help wanted" was 90.2 per cent of the "situations wanted." In 1891, which was a bad year with a great dearth of work, it was yet 67.52 per cent of the "situations wanted," while 45.2 per cent of the latter secured the coveted work. In 1892 the registered demand for help footed up 82.36 per cent of the requests for work. Nothing further need be said in justification of the experiment. It is the story of my painters over again. The other thing that arrested my attention was this, that in less than two years the bureau had run into a rut, out of which it had to be pulled by the removal of all the five superintendents on account of "lack of interest and enthusiasm." That was evidently the political end of it; but as their chief, the commissioner, had himself been changed in the interval, I shall not say upon whom politics fell heaviest. It'is worth noticing, however, that it was there.

The Ohio experiment is likely to be urged upon other legislatures this coming winter, among them that of New York. The labor men proposed it last year at Albany, but it was then ignored. Whatever be the result at the next session, it is worthy of the most serious discussion. Something of the sort should be started in New York city at all events. It may be that it will be left to private benevolence to take the first step. In that case two conditions are to be insisted upon in advance: that the movement shall inspire confidence from the start, and that the benefits it would confer shall be entirely free. All the rest may be left to work itself out as the plan develops. But at the start it should gather to its support all the best elements in the community. In fact it should partake of the character of a citizens' movement for a great emergency. The emergency is quite certain to be great enough both to warrant and to demand it, and to a greater or less extent it will always exist in New York city.

Some years ago the Society for Improving the Condition of the Poor, if I am not mistaken, saw the need of such a bureau and discussed a plan to start one. ' Why it was shelved I do not know. The Society is one which might well take the initiative in an undenominational movement of that sort by inviting kindred organizations to join. The East Side Relief Committee is another. The point is that it should possess the fullest confidence of the public. I am certain that there is no way in which the condition of the worthy poor could be improved more readily and effectively. Tramps would not obstruct it. They would give the employment bureau a wide berth. I can see no objection to it, and no hindrance save the red tape that would inevitably spin itself out of such an organization and would have to be kept down to the useful point. But I can see great good to come from it. It would enormously simplify the work of the Relief Committee, which we shall need again, and in fact render much of it unnecessary. The soup-house would be finally and happily eliminated from our winter landscape, and the pauperization avoided that is the sad legacy of the best-meant efforts in behalf of the needy.

Who knows what effect the better understanding of the labor market which such an Employment Exchange would help to bring about might have in preventing the ignorant strikes that add so much to the undeserved suffering of the great body of workers who have nothing? With half of those seeking relief really wanting work, as is always the case, and with work going begging around the corner, as happens often enough to demonstrate that the whole business is a huge misfit, it seems to me that an employment bureau of the kind I have described is not only a logical necessity, but concrete Christianity and common sense rolled into one.

JACOB A. RIIS.

The Forum

OCTOBER, 1894.

SOME REASONS WHY THE AMERICAN REPUBLIC MAY ENDURE.

THE governments which have been called republics have not, as a rule, exhibited the kind or degree of durability which we desire for our own free government. The American Republic has now lasted more than a hundred years; and little Switzerland maintains a precarious existence by favor of powerful neighbors jealous of each other; but the so-called republics of Greece, Rome, and Italy, and two French republics, have perished. Mexico and the republics of Central and South America are insecure and ineffective governments. On the whole, in spite of our instinctive faith in free institutions, we cannot shut our eyes to the fact that the auguries which can be drawn from history are not favorable to the real permanence of any republic.

When we set out to seek reasons for believing that our republic will live longer than other governments which have borne that name, and will altogether escape decline and fall, we cannot but be dismayed to see what great powers and resources the older republics possessed, and what splendid achievements they made, without winning stability and perpetuity from all these powers, resources, and achievements. The Republic of Athens, for example, had an art and a literature which have proved themselves immortal. In sculpture and archi tecture Athens is still supreme; its literature still inspires and guides philosophers, poets, and men of letters in nations unborn when Greece was in her prime. Now art and literature are among the supreme achievements of the human race; yet the example of Athens demonstrates that they cannot of themselves safeguard a republic.

9

We must not attempt to console ourselves for this painful fact by the thought that an effeminate and peaceful people might excel in art and literature, and that the absence of forceful national qualities might account for the instability of such a people's government. The story of the Roman Republic invalidates this theory. For generations the Roman Republic was the strongest government on earth; and even now, as we examine the elements of its strength, it seems to us that they might have given durability to that powerful commonwealth. In the first place, it had an admirable body of public law which determined justice between man and man and between man and state; and that body of law was so wise and ample that to-day it is the basis of the public law of the greater part of the populations of Europe. This great system of jurisprudence survived, indeed, the nation and the government which gave it birth; but did not give undecaying life to the nation which created it. Moreover, the Roman Republic possessed the most superb army which has ever existed—an army whose conquests were more extensive and more lasting than the conquests made by the arms of any other state, ancient or modern. The Roman army has never been equalled either as a fighting force or as a colonizing force; yet that army did not assure mounting vitality to the Roman commonwealth: on the contrary, it was one of the means of its downfall.

There are some short-sighted people who expect systems of public transportation and intercommunication to secure nations from disintegration; but again the history of Rome teaches the contrary. Rome had a transportation system which, considering the means at the disposal of the engineer at that time, has never been equalled. The Roman roads covered the greater part of Europe and northern Africa, and considerable portions of Asia; and they were so well constructed that parts of them remain to this day. Some of the Roman bridges have stood for twenty centuries unharmed by flood and weather. But this transportation system, vast and perfect as it was, did not prevent the decline and fall of the Roman power.

One might suppose that a nation strong and rich enough to carry out immense public works, such as aqueducts, baths, temples, palaces, and theatres, would necessarily possess also the means of giving durability to their form of government; but the experience of Rome proves that we can rely in our own case on none of these things. The Roman aqueducts, for example, which brought water to all their principal cities, are unequalled to the present day for size, massive-ness, and boldness of conception,—partly, to be sure, because the Roman engineers were forced to erect huge structures of masonry, since they had not learned to make large metallic pipes. Rome teaches conclusively that magnitude and splendor of public works have no tendency to guarantee the permanence of a state.

The Italian republics have still another lesson for us. Venice, which possessed an architecture of wonderful beauty, and an art in painting which still remains pre-eminent, developed these fine arts by means of a widespread commerce, which gave its citizens wealth, dignity, and power. It was, moreover, a martial republic. Its very merchants wore swords. Its paintings and palaces are still the admiration of the world; but its commerce has disappeared, and the Venetian Republic has long been obliterated. Successful commerce, and fine arts following in its train, provide no security for national perpetuity.

Most of the national resources and achievements which have now been mentioned have a certain material or physical quality. Perhaps we can discern in history some immaterial force, some national senti-ment or passion, which can. be relied on to give permanence to national institutions.   There has been one power in the world on which men have greatly relied for the security of governmental and social institutions,—namely, the power of religious enthusiasm; but what does history teach with regard to the efficacy of this sentiment to give security to states? It is easy to find instances of concentrated religious enthusiasm in unified national forms. The Hebrew religion was of this sort. It bound together by a simple faith and a common ritual all the members of a race which possessed extraordinary vitality and persistence; but did it give permanence to Judea? Even as a province or a principality, Judea has disappeared. The race persists, but without a country or a capital. The Arabic civilization was carried from Asia through Africa into Spain by the Moslem religious enthusiasm; and it was a civilization which had fine arts, chronicles, and for the higher classes a delicate and luxurious mode of life. Its soldiers have never been surpassed for fervent devotion. But this concentrated religious zeal, effective as it was for conquest, did not preserve the Arabic civilization, which has disappeared from the face of the earth. Christian experience points to the same conclusion. Spain, for example, drove out the Moors and the Jews, exterminated the Protestants, and made itself Roman Catholic unitedly and fer-vently; but that single Roman Catholic belief and ritual did not preserve for Spain its once pre-eminent position in Europe. On the contrary, Spain, become single in religious opinion and practice, languished, retrograded, and lost place among the leaders of civilization. In the present century it is a striking fact that the three nations which have given the greatest proofs of constitutional vigor,—namely, Germany, England, and the United States—are those which in religions opinions and practices are very heterogeneous, so that no concentrated religious fervor can possibly melt and unite all their people. We cannot believe, then, that religious enthusiasm, however unified and concentrated, can guarantee the permanent existence of a state.

Great public powers, splendid arts, noble literature, wide-spread commerce, and exalted religious sentiment have, then, all failed to secure the continuance of states. Perhaps a humbler achievement of recent times may prove more effectual,—namely, the achievement of general, diffused physical well-being. There seem to be a good many social philosophers in these days who believe that the general diffusion of physical comforts, and the accessibility of easy modes of life for large numbers of people, will have some tendency to give permanence to the institutions under which these material goods are secured; that the power which man has won over nature through the study of chemistry, physics, and natural history means stability for the institutions under which these conquests have been achieved. May not these theorizers be right? Will not growing wealth, ease, and comfort guarantee the state, provided that these advantages be within reach of the many? The answer to this question must depend on the spiritual use made of added physical comfort. A nation is after all but the agglomeration of an immense number of individuals, and the moral condition of a nation can be nothing but the result of the morality prevailing among the individuals who compose it. Comfort, ease, and wealth must have on a nation almost the same effects that they have on an individual. Now, softness and ease of life do not always make for manliness and virtue. It is not generally supposed that riches increase the probability of enduring vitality for a family or a social class. The common opinion is that wealth and luxury make it, not easier, but harder to bring up children to serviceable citizenship. All persons who have been concerned with education during the past forty years—which is the period of most rapid increase in diffused physical comfort for all classes, and in wealth and luxury for considerable numbers—recognize that great efforts are necessary in order to bring up successfully the children of the luxurious classes; because they lack the natural training to service which children get in families where every member has habitually to contribute to the common maintenance. It is harder, not easier, for the rich man than for the poor man to bring up his children well. Families of moderate means have a great advantage over the rich in this respect. In this matter of material well-being there is surely some question concerning the profitable degree of comfort and ease. By common consent there is a degree of it which debilitates rather than invigorates. The general fact seems to be that the effect of material prosperity on the development of an individual or the duration of a family depends on the use made of added wealth and comfort. When added material resources produce in the individual, or in the family, additional mental and moral resources, all the additions work together for good; otherwise added wealth is a hindrance and not a help. When a mechanic, a clerk, a farmer, or a laborer doubles his income and his expenditures, it does not necessarily follow that the mode of life of himself and his family will be purer, more refined, and more intellectual. It may be elevated, or it may not be. In the same way it would be the intellectual and moral effects of a higher degree of physical ease and comfort enjoyed by a whole people which would determine whether the material gain were a good thing or an evil. If diffused prosperity made a people lazy, selfish, and sensual, as it easily might, it would not contribute to the permanence of their nationality or their government. It is not the climates which are always soft, warm, and caressing which produce the most vigorous races of men. While we see plainly that extreme poverty is an evil and a danger alike for the individual, the family, and the state, we can place no reliance on diffused physical well-being as a source of public security, until we can be assured of its effects on the motives, affections, and passions of the people. There is no sure hope in either increase or redistribution of wealth.

If, then, we would find reasons for believing that the American Republic will live, when other republics have not lived, we must seek for intellectual and moral causes of permanence which are comparatively new in the world, or at least which have much fuller play in recent than in elder times.

The first moral cause of permanence of which the American Republic has the advantage is the principle of toleration in religion—a principle which, though not recently enunciated (nobody has ever stated it better than William the Silent), has been very recently put in practice, not by any means in all parts of the civilized world, but in a few favored regions, and notably in the United States. On one of the tablets of the Water-gate at Chicago was written this sentence: "Toleration in religion the best fruit of the last four centuries." This statement is no exaggeration, but the literal truth. Toleration in religion is absolutely the best fruit of all the struggles, labors, and sorrows of the civilized nations during the last four centuries. The real acceptance of this principle cannot be carried back more than fifty years. Even now it is not accepted everywhere,—far from it; but it is accepted in the ,United States more widely and completely than in any other country, and here lies one of the chief hopes for the permanence of our institutions. We are delivered from one of the'worst terrors and horrors of the past. What suffering our race has endured from religious wars, persecutions, and extermina‐ tions! From these woes, and from all apprehension of them, the people of the American Republic are delivered. We owe to this principle, however, much more than deliverance from evils; for it is a positive promoter of good-will and mutual respect among men and of friendly intercourse unembarrassed by religious distinctions. That this beneficent principle has freer play here than it has ever had elsewhere gives one firm ground for believing that our Republic may attain a permanence never before attained.

Another mental and moral force which makes for the permanence of our institutions is universal education. This is a new force in the world, not in action in any land before this century. It has not existed more than twenty years in such a civilized country as France; it dates only from 1871 in England. It is not yet true that education is universal even in our own country; but the principle of universal education finds general acceptance, and the practical results approxi‐ mate more and more, as time goes on, to the requirements of the theoretical principle. In all civilized countries continuous effort is made to bring the practice up to the level of the theory. Within three generations immense progress has been made; and it now seems as if a perfectly feasible development of this principle in practice must work a profound change in human society within a compara‐ tively small number of additional generations. Must we not hope everything from this new factor in civilized life,—from the steady cultivation in all classes of correct observation, just reasoning, and the taste for good reading? Must we not hope to be delivered from a thousand evils of ignorance and unreason which now oppress us?

It is reasonable to expect that even the evils of inherited vicious tendencies and habits will be mitigated by universal education. It is always through the children that the best work is to be done for the uplifting of any community. When we consider how few years in the history of mankind this practice of general education has prevailed, and to how few generations it has ever been applied, we cannot but find in this new practice great hope for the development of the intelligence and morality needed to secure the permanence of free institutions. It is a commonplace that republican institutions are built on education; but we hardly realize how new that commonplace is. Plato taught that the industrial and producing classes needed no education whatever. None of the republics which have died had anything more than a small educated class. The masses of their people grew up and lived in crassest ignorance. The great change in regard to the education of the people which the present century has witnessed is not confined to mere primary instruction. That primary instruction is of course the most widely diffused, and imparts to the masses the art of reading, which is the principal vehicle for the subsequent cultivation of the intelligence. Beyond this primary instruction about five per cent of all the children in the United States receive the more elaborate training of secondary schools and normal schools. Of this five per cent a fair proportion attend colleges and universities. This attainment of secondary, or higher, instruction by one child in twenty in the United States is quite as novel a social fact as the attainment of primary instruction by the other nineteen. Universal suffrage prolongs in the United States the effect of universal education; for it stimulates all citizens throughout their lives to reflect on problems outside the narrow circle of their private interests and occupations, to read about public questions, to discuss public characters, and to hold themselves ready in some degree to give a rational account of their political faith. The duties of republican citizen-ship, rightly discharged, constitute in themselves a prolonged education, which effectively supplements the work of schools and colleges.

A third reason for believing that our institutions will endure is to be found in the fact that a better family life prevails among our people than was known to any of the republics which have perished, or, indeed, to any earlier century. The family, not the individual, is the tap-root of the state, and whatever tends to secure the family tends to secure the state. Now family life—under which term may properly be included all the complex relations between husband and wife, and parents and children—is gentler in this century, and particularly in the United States, than it has ever been.   Family discipline has become, even within thirty years, much gentler than it ever was before.   The relations of husband and wife have also become juster.   In the savage state the superior physical strength of the man, his greater freedom from occasional or periodical bodily limitations, and his greater enterprise and boldness, made the relation of husband and wife very like that of master and slave.   Civilization has steadily contended against that savage inheritance; and has aimed through public law at the emancipation of the weaker sex and the establishment of equality in the relation of the sexes.   A single illustration— the laws affecting the transmission of property—must suffice.   American legislation on this subject is the justest the world has seen. Under the feudal system it was almost necessary to the life of that social organization that, when the father died, the real estate—which was generally the whole estate—should go to the eldest son over the head of the mother; for the son inherited his father's responsibilities in war, in productive industries, and in society.   The son, not the wife, was the husband's heir.   In France to-day, if a man dies leaving a wife and children, a large share of his property must go to his children.   He is not free under any circumstances to give it all to his wife.   A prescribed portion must by law go to the children over the head of their mother.   The children are his children, and the wife is not recognized as an equal owner.   It is the man who is the head of that group of human beings, and a large share of his property must go to his children.   Again we see in public law an assertion of the lower place of the woman.   But how is it in our own country?   In the first place we have happily adopted a valuable English measure, the right of dower; but this measure, though good so far as it goes, gives not equality, but a certain protection.   Happily, American law goes farther, and the wife may inherit from the husband the whole of his property.   She must receive a part of it; but he, under certain restrictions intended to prevent frauds on creditors, may give her the whole.   On the other hand, the wife, if she has property, may give the whole of it to the husband.   Here is established in the law of inheritance a relation of equality between husband and wife,—a relation which is the happiest, justest, and most beneficent for the man, the woman, their children, and the state.   It is an indirect advantage of our laws and customs concerning the inheritance of property that they promote the redistribution of wealth accumulated in single hands. The custom of treating all children alike in testamentary dispositions obviously tends in this direction; and the practice of leaving property to women promotes the redistribution of wealth, because women are, as a rule, less competent than men either to keep money or to make it productive. There is a real safeguard in these customs against the undue increase of wealth and luxury. That gentleness and justice in family life should have been greatly promoted under the American Republic, not among a small minority of the people, but among the masses, may well give us a lively hope for the permanence of the institutions under which these benefits have been attained. Whatever regulates wisely the relations of the sexes, and increases domestic happiness, increases also social and governmental stability.

Pursuing the idea that the promotion of diffused happiness promotes governmental stability, we observe next that certain means of public happiness have recently been liberally provided in many American communities at public expense with great intelligence and by deliberate design. During the last twenty-five years strenuous efforts have been made in many municipalities to promote public happiness by giving opportunities to the multitude for the enjoyment of fresh air and natural beauty. One of the most striking social phenomena in the United States of recent years has been the sudden creation of public parks and playgrounds, constructed and maintained at public expense. At bottom the meaning of this sudden development is that the people seek to procure for themselves, and are procuring, increased means of health and happiness. They have still much to learn in regard to utilizing the means provided, for our native population does not take naturally to fresh air, family holidays, and out-of-door meals. They have been too long unwonted to these wholesome delights. This public park and garden movement has only just begun; but the improvement made within twenty years gives the strongest possible hope for the rapid spread of this wise public policy. European municipalities have often been enabled to provide themselves with parks and gardens by appropriating royal domains, estates of nobles, or disused forts and fortifications. The democratic American communities have enjoyed no such facilities, but have been obliged to buy the reservations—often at great cost— and create or restore the needed beauties of park or garden. That the democracy should manifest both the will and the capacity to accomplish such beneficent and far-seeing undertakings is a good

omen of durability for that form of government. The provision of
free libraries and museums of natural history and fine arts at public
expense, or by the combination of private endowments with public
appropriations, is another evidence of the disposition of the democracy to provide the means of public cultivation and enjoyment.
Much of this good work has been done within the past forty years,
and very little such work was ever done before by a popular government. The American cities have also grappled intelligently with the
serious problems of water-supply, sewerage, and preventive medicine,
although the suddenness and volume of the movement of the population into large towns and cities have greatly increased the normal
difficulty of these problems.

Another new and effective bulwark of the state is to be found in the
extreme publicity with which all American activities are carried on.
Many people are in the habit of complaining bitterly of the intrusion
of the newspaper reporter into every nook and corner of the state, and
even into the privacy of home; but in this extreme publicity is really
to be found a new means of social, industrial, and governmental
reform and progress. As Emerson said, " Light is the best policeman. " There are many exaggerations, perversions, and inaccuracies
in this publicity; but on the whole it is a beneficent and a new agency
for the promotion of the public welfare. Such publicity has become
possible partly through man's new power over nature, as seen in the
innumerable applications of heat and electricity, and partly through
the universal capacity to read. For almost all social, industrial, and
political evils publicity gives the best hope of reasonable remedy.
Publicity exposes not only wickedness, but also folly and bad judgment. It makes crime and political corruption more difficult and far
less attractive. The forger, burglar, and corruptionist need secrecy
for two reasons: first, that they may succeed in their crimes; and
secondly, that they may enjoy the fruits of their wickedness. The
most callous sinner finds it hard to enjoy the product of his sin if he
knows that everybody knows how he came by it. No good cause
ever suffered from publicity; no bad cause but instinctively avoids
it. So new is this force in the world that many people do not yet
trust it, or perceive its immense utility. In cases of real industrial
grievances or oppressions, publicity would be by far the quickest and
surest means of cure,—vastly more effective for all just ends than
secret combinations of either capitalists or laborers. The newspapers,
which are the ordinary instruments of this publicity, are as yet very

imperfect instruments, much of their work being done so hastily and so cheaply as to preclude accuracy; but as means of publicity they visibly improve from decade to decade, and, taken together with the magazines and the controversial pamphlet, they shed more light on the social, industrial, and political life of the people of the United States than was ever shed before on the doings and ways of any people. This force is distinctly new within this century, and it affords a new and strong guarantee for the American Republic.

Within the past fifty years there has been developed for the conduct of business, education, and charity an agency which may fairly be called new,—namely, the corporation. Although a few charitable, trading, and manufacturing corporations were of earlier origin,—some of which became famous,—the great development of corporate powers and functions has all taken place within fifty years, since the application of the principle of limited liability. Thousands upon thousands of corporations are now organized in the United States, and are actively carrying on a great variety of industrial and social operations. Millions of Americans get their livings and pass their lives in the service of these corporations. As a rule, the employees of corporations receive wages or salaries, and have no further interest in the business. We are so familiar with this state of things that we do not realize its absolute novelty. It has practically been created within the lifetime of persons who are not yet old. In the service of corporations there is seldom any element of personal devotion, such as existed in other times between subject and sovereign, or between retainer and feudal chief; but there is a large element of fidelity and loyalty, which is becoming of greater and greater importance in the formation of the national character. A considerable portion of all the business, charity, and education carried on in the United States is well conducted by the faithful and loyal servants of corporations, as every one will plainly see, so soon as he takes account of his own contacts in daily life with the work of corporations, and compares them with his contacts with the work of individuals or of partnerships. This corporation service affords a new discipline for masses of people; and it is a discipline of the highest value toward inducing stability and durability in governmental institutions. The service of a town or city, of a state, or of the national government is really a kind of corporation service, carried on at present, to be sure, under unfavorable conditions, the public service being subject to evils and temptations from which private corporation service is for the most part exempt, and yielding to those who pay its cost less for their money than they get from any other kind of corporation. In all probability these unfavorable conditions will prove to be temporary. From the frequent occurrence of strikes on railroads and in mines we get an impression that there is little fidelity in the service of corpora- tions; but it must be remembered that the organization of American railroads and mining companies is, with some notable exceptions, very inferior to the organization of other corporations, and that the laborers in the lower grades of these two employments are distinctly of an inferior sort.   Most of these railroad and mining corporations have never adopted any of the means which European experience has shown to be efficacious for attaching their employees permanently to their service.   For the most part they claim the right to act on the brutal principle of instant dismissal without notice or cause assigned. If we direct our attention to the banks, trust companies, insurance companies, manufacturing corporations, colleges, universities, en- dowed schools, hospitals, and asylums of the country, we shall realize that the quality of corporation service is really good, and that the great majority of corporation servants exhibit in high degree the admirable virtues of fidelity and loyalty.   The successful career of the new companies which insure fidelity is an interesting corroboration of this observation.   Even the railroads and the mines exhibit from time to time fine examples of fidelity on the part of large bodies of their employees, in spite of extremely adverse conditions, such as the presence of serious bodily danger, and the seductions of unions which claim to represent the permanent interests of workingmen.   There can be no better preparation for faithful and loyal service to the government than faithful and loyal service to a corporation which con- ducts a business of magnitude and recognized utility.   In these days of comprehensive trusts and far-reaching monopolies we see clearly that such agencies directly prepare the way for govern- mental assumption of their powers and functions.   The wider and more comprehensive the monopoly, the stronger becomes the argument for the assumption of that business by the government.   Indeed, the government is the only agency which should be trusted with a com- plete monopoly.   At any rate, the presumption is in favor of govern- ment conduct of any business which has complete possession of the market.   The corporation, then, is not simply a means of aggregating small capitals and utilizing them in large blocks; it is also an agency for training masses of people to the high virtues of fidelity and

, loyalty—virtues which cannot but secure the state.   At the present stage of progress, with all corporations so new in the world, society suffers through them various evils, such as oppressive monopoly, destructive competition, political corruption, and occasionally in- efficiency and obstructiveness; but on the whole this new agency is of incalculable value to modern society, and will prove in time to come a real buttress of free institutions.

The recent attempts to carry out general strikes in industries which produce or distribute necessaries of life have demonstrated that society will not endure a suspension of labor in such industries for more than a few days.   The reason is that men are much more dependent on each other than they used to be.   The extreme division of labor, which has more and more characterized the normal industrial methods in civilized states since the beginning of the present century, has brought about a mutual dependence of man on man and com- munity on community, which is a strong guarantee of the permanence of free institutions.   Adam Smith dealt with this great subject of the division of labor in 1776; but the present century has seen the principle wrought out in detail, and carried through every branch of industry,—indeed, the last fifty years have witnessed extensive new applications of the principle.   In the savage state each family is toler- ably independent of every other, as regards food, clothing, and shelter. Fifty years ago a New England farmer raised on his own farm most of the materials which supplied him and his family with food, cloth- ing, fire, and shelter; but now, when three-fifths of the population of New England live in large towns or cities, when the New England farm no longer produces either wheat or wool, and when every urban household imports the whole of its food and clothing, and all its materials for light and heat, the dependence of every little group of New-Englanders on numerous other persons, near and remote, has become wellnigh absolute.   All civilized mankind lives under similar conditions of interdependence.   The sense of dependence is of course mutual, and with it goes some recognition of common aims and hopes among the different sorts and conditions of men.   This sense of common interests is something very different from the sentiment of human equality.   It is a feeling of unity, not of equality.   It has a firm foundation in facts; whereas the notion that men are equal is plainly false, unless it be strictly limited to the political significance of equality, namely, to equality before the law and in regard to the right of suffrage.   It is a feeling which leads naturally to a sense of human brotherhood.   In a family the feeling of mutual dependence and mutual support is one of the roots of family affection.   In the same way in the larger human brotherhood the mutual dependence which division of labor has brought about strengthens the feeling of unity. The doctrine of human brotherhood has been taught for thousands of years.   It is all contained in two words—" Our Father"; but, though accepted by seers and philosophers, it has been little realized in practice by the multitude.   There are many signs of the wide and steady spread of the realized acceptance in practice of this doctrine.   The theory, long current in the world, gets more and more applied in institutions, in business, and in society.   The fact of intimate mutual dependence extends to different states and nations.   A federation of states like the American Union affords a favorable field for the practical realization by masses of people of the truth of the affirmation St. Paul frequently repeated, "We are members one of another."   It gives excellent opportunities for observing that the misfortune of one state is invariably the misfortune of all; that no state can suffer in its crops, or its industries, or its moral standards, without involving the others in loss and damage.   Under a federated government like our own, the conditions under which such deductions as these may be made are simpler than they can possibly be when the experiences of different nations, living under different forms of government and under different legislation, must be compared.   In spite, therefore, of local and sectional jealousies and oppositions, the American people have come to accept as literal truth St. Paul's statement, "And whether one member suffer, all the members suffer with it."   The doctrine is old; but the realization of the doctrine is new.   This realization of an ancient truth marks again the progress of society toward practical acceptance of the conception that there is a genuine unity of aims and hopes among all men, an acceptance which of itself will prove a stout bulwark of free institutions.

We now come to certain abstract considerations which, though to some minds they will doubtless seem intangible and unsubstantial, probably supply the firmest grounds for hopeful anticipations concerning the future of free institutions.   In recent times serious changes have taken place in regard to the highest hopes, aspirations, and ideals of mankind.   These ideal conceptions have been slowly wrought out in the minds of students, philosophers, and poets, and have been cherished by the few; but suddenly, within the past two generations, they have found acceptance with multitudes of men.   This sudden acceptance is the combined result of the rapid progress of scientific knowledge during the last fifty years, and of the general ability of the people to read. These changes of expectation, aspiration, and faith are of course only moral forces; but they are forces which greatly affect the sum of human happiness. As has already been repeatedly intimated, the stability of governments depends largely on the just answer to the question—Do they provide the necessary conditions of happy human life? The first change of expectation which claims attention is the changed sentiment of the people toward what is new and therefore untried. The American people as a rule approach a new object, a new theory, or a new practice, with a degree of hope and confidence which no other people exhibits. The unknown is to the savage terrible; the dark has been dreadful, and evil has always been imagined of it; many highly civilized people have an aversion to things novel; but for us Americans so many new things have proved to be good things, that we no longer look on what is novel with suspicion and distrust. Our continent is new, and has proved to be. rich; our machinery is new, and has proved to be useful; our laws are many of them new, but they have proved helpful. The people have traversed many wilds and wastes, but have passed them with safety, and found good in the unexplored and unknown. The untried is therefore for us no longer terrible, or, at least, to be suspected. Hope and expectation of good spring in our hearts, as never before in the hearts of former generations or in earlier ages.

Furthermore, the changes which have taken place in the realized doctrines of Christianity concerning the origin and nature of man are very reassuring for those who believe in the possibility of developing a nation of freemen capable of orderly self-government. The old conceptions of the fall of man and of the total depravity of the race were good foundations for the regime of a beneficent despot, but not for the regime of self-governing freemen. The modern doctrine of the steady ascent of man through all his history is necessarily welcome to republicans, because it justifies their political beliefs. Again, enlarged knowledge of the nature of the universe, and a more accurate view of man's humble place in it, have also contributed to the prevalence of a humane philosophy which is a security for good governments. It was, on the whole, an unwholesome conception that the universe was made for man, and that he was the rightful master of it all. Out of that prodigious piece of ignorant assumption came many practical wrongs toward animals and inferior races of men. To a more cheerful outlook the gradual triumph of science over many terrors and superstitions has contributed, as has also the growing power of men to resist or moderate the effects of catastrophes like storms, droughts, famines, and pestilences.   The earth and the universe are brighter and less terrible than they were.   There is even a greater brightening in man's spiritual landscape.   No cherished ideal of our race has undergone a more beneficent change during the present century than the ideal of God; and this change makes strongly for the happiness of mankind.   The Christian Gospel has just begun to be realized. We have just begun to understand that God is love.   He has been an awful ideal of justice and wrath,—an angry deity whose chief functions were punishment and vengeance.   The world He made was full of evil; the men He made were all depraved, and most of them hopelessly so.   This ideal of divinity, however influential, did not increase human cheerfulness and joy.   Although it lingers still in creeds, consecrated formulæ, and ancient hymns, it has practically ceased to be believed by considerable numbers of men, both churched and unchurched.   The ideal which replaces it· is one of supreme power and love, filling the universe, working through all human institutions, and through all men.   This deal promotes happiness and joy.   It is not new; but it is newly realized by multitudes.   Now, these beneficent changes in the spiritual conceptions of large numbers of men have taken place since our country took on its present governmental structure; and they have lent ·and will lend to that structure a firm support, because they contribute generously to the happiness and· true spirituality of the people.

Finally, the object of religion and the aim of its ministers have become wonderfully different, since the American Republic was established, from what they were in ancient or mediæval times, or even down to the opening of this century.   The religions of the ancient world had very little to do with morality.   They were propitiatory and protective.   The Christian religion and its ministers for the last fifteen hundred years were chiefly concerned with the conciliation of an offended God, the provision of securities for individual happiness in a future life; these securities being attainable by persons whose mode of life in this world had been of questionable or even vicious quality, and the offering of joys in another world as consolation or compensation for sufferings or evils in this.   Since the beginning of this century a revolution has occurred, which has been felt in almost every branch of the Christian church and in almost every Christian nation, but has had a broad sweep in the United States. The primary objects of religion and its ministers in our day and country are more and more to soften and elevate the characters and lives of men in this world, and to ameliorate the common lot. The improvement of character and conduct in the individual, in society, and in the state during this present life is now becoming the principal aim of many churches and their ministers. The progressive churches are all of this mind; and even the most conservative—like the Roman Catholic and the Presbyterian—plainly exhibit this tendency. By the multitude of the unchurched also it is generally understood that there is no angry God to propitiate, and that the only way to take securities for the morrow, whether in life or in death, is to do well the duties of to-day. Religion, by devoting itself to the elevation of human character, becomes a prop and stay of free institutions, because these rest ultimately on the character of the citizen.

These, then, are some of the new principles and forces which make for the permanence of the Republic: toleration in religion; general education; better domestic relations; attention to the means of public health and pleasure; publicity; corporation service; increased mutual dependence of man on man, and therewith a growing sense of brotherhood and unity; the greater hopefulness and cheerfulness of men's outlook on man, the earth, the universe, and God; and finally the changing objects and methods of religion and its institutions. It is the working of these principles and forces, often unrecognized, which has carried the Republic safely through many moral difficulties and dangers during the past thirty years. These things, and not its size and wealth, make us love our country. These things, we believe, will give the American Republic long life. These bulwarks of the commonwealth will prove all the stronger and more lasting, because women as well as men can work on them, and help to transmit them, ever broader and firmer, from generation to generation.

CHARLES W. ELIOT.

10

HAS ORATORY DECLINED?

THERE has been of late frequent allusion to, and some discussion of, the decay or decline of oratory in recent years, and of what has been the cause. It is much easier to determine the fact than to answer the far more important question, why it has declined. There can be no doubt that the *volume* of public speaking has in this country, and I am quite sure elsewhere, vastly increased, outrunning all other expansion—whether of territory, of population, or wealth, or any other element of growth. Take as a test a single long session of Congress, that national meter of public speaking, and compare it with one fifty years before it. The Congressional oratory of the session of 1839–'40 covered 1,405 pages of the " Congressional Globe;" that of the session of 1889–'90 covered 11,568 similar pages of the " Congressional Record." And this may be taken as a fair rate of increase during the same period at any point where public speaking may be treated as a calling. But, while all oratory is public speaking, all public speaking is very far from being oratory. The plain inquiry raised is whether there is as much oratory in the public speaking of the present day as in the past, and whether it is declining in quality or is held up to the standard of the earlier days of the Republic. What is the standard that shall determine that quality? Herein lies the main difficulty.

Whether public speaking which combines oratory and eloquence is in a state of decline or decay is a question of much importance and cannot enlist too much attention. It cannot be doubted that it has undergone great change, whether compared with the little that has come down to us from ancient orators, or with what comes within the memory of those still living. In the overflow of public speaking of the present day no one looks for, or would think of finding, anything which would remind him of Fisher Ames or Daniel Webster. But would he not, nevertheless, find very much which is entitled to live with the imperishable productions of the past, because, like them, they are marvellous instrumentalities in producing great and abiding results? One would hesitate before he would say that, judged by such a test, oratory or eloquence is moribund. We are thus led directly to the conclusion that the value of public speech, and, consequently, of whatever of oratory or eloquence there is in it, depends upon its purpose and its adaptation to the accomplishment of that purpose. This is what Webster means when he speaks of a theme which is "something greater and higher than all eloquence," which causes "the graces taught in the schools, the costly ornaments and studied contrivances of speech to shock and disgust men, when their own lives and the fate of their wives, their children, and their country hang on the decision of the hour." The "subject and the occasion" are as essential as the man to the production of any great and enduring utterance of speech. Mr. Boutwell, himself one of the best illustrations of modern oratory, asserts the same truth when he says that "the great orators have appeared and the great orations have been delivered in revolutionary periods." These occasions cannot be created to order, but themselves wait on the order of the universe.

A review of the last half-century of our history, while it will disclose a great change in method and manner of public speaking as well as in the conditions under which it has been maintained, will not, it is confidently believed, sustain the charge that the man has not shown himself equal to the occasion or the theme. He could not be called upon to rise above them, and he can have no agency in creating either. He who longs for another Chatham or Burke or Webster or Phillips or Beecher must be patient till there again arises such an occasion as Conciliation with the Colonies, or Nullification, or the Anti-Slavery Struggle, or the Cause of the Union at home and abroad. We have had, only a generation now past, the greatest of all crises in our history, and there have come down to the present, with its record, some great orations which will live as long as any others in the English language. But there are not many such. The reason there were not more is not difficult to find. The country was not carried through that great crisis by much speaking. The debate closed when the first gun was fired at Sumter, and valor, not oratory, thereafter swayed the fortunes of the Republic. But still there were times during the war when gloom and despondency so shut out the light and weighed upon the spirits that thoughts of compromise found entertainment in the minds of faint-hearted and timid public servants. Then the subject and the occasion appealed to the loftiest powers of the orator, and the response was worthy of the theme. The oration of Henry Winter Davis on the Value of the Union, pronounced in the House of Representatives at one of these critical moments, in the grandeur and force and the lofty patriotism which inspired his utterances, will suffer in comparison with none of the great orations, ancient or modern, which have become classic standards. Thaddeus Stevens and Charles Sumner, E. D. Baker and William Pitt Fessenden, Roscoe Conkling and Oliver P. Morton, have each left in the permanent records of that momentous period convincing testimony that the subject and the occasion then, as in the days of the undisputed supremacy of oratorical power, found worthy and effective utterance. The glory of the battle-field, which these efforts made possible, has been chronicled in merited terms, but the cause has yet to make fitting acknowledgment of its obligation to these great leaders of the public heart and conscience.

The period before the war—that which may properly be termed the preparatory period—illustrates in a striking manner the truth that the standard of oratorical attainment is dependent quite as much upon the subject and the occasion, over which the speaker has no control, as upon the man himself. The great questions at issue, which culminated in the war, were worthy of the highest powers of the most devoted patriot, for they threatened the very life of the Republic. That the orators of those days fall in no particular behind the highest standards cannot be disputed. Sumner and Beecher and Wendell Phillips on the one side, and Yancey and Benjamin and Breckinridge on the other, stirred multitudes, aroused passions, and fired the public heart in terms not less eloquent than the loftiest productions of Fox or Pitt, of Patrick Henry or John Adams.

But when the overshadowing question of slavery and its threatened domination had been put to rest, the subject and the occasion, which had been the inspiration of their eloquence, also passed away, and with them the ability of these orators to hold an old-time audience or pronounce an old-time oration. After the war was over, Wendell Phillips, the most consummate of all platform orators, who had been wont to speak on great living issues to uncounted multitudes, looking down one evening from the stage upon a very thin and scattered audience, exclaimed to a friend by his side, "It is no use. I shall be obliged to purchase a stereopticon." The man was there in complete armor, but there was no great theme or impending peril to kindle the fires in which burning words are forged. Eloquence in a calm is *vox et præterea nihil*. It is for this reason that platform eloquence, once of a very high order, has so nearly disappeared. When the public mind was at a white heat, the material was at the command of the public speaker, and he could mold and weld and shape formidable weapons before which opposition was sure to give way. But he cannot order the material or create the occasion, and therefore the platform orator has little opportunity in days of peace and quiet. There have been attempts in recent years to revive the power of the platform in the service of ephemeral issues which disturb for a little while the otherwise unruffled surface of things, but the effort has been attended with no lasting results, nor has it brought forth any genuine product worthy the name of oratory.

Comparative pulpit oratory, if such a phrase be allowable, furnishes striking proof that the subject and the occasion, more than all else, inspire the speaker and determine the character and place among oratorical efforts of what he utters. The great theme of the pulpit orator, and its vital importance to every listener, remain ever the same, though change shall overtake all else in the lives of men. It waits for no felicitous occasion or unusual emergency, but is always present and imminent, claiming precedence of all else that can appeal to the conscience or judgment. The genius of the speaker is at all times challenged to its utmost in the presentation of the truths it embodies, and is the measure of his rank among those to whom it is committed to promulgate their real significance. Whatever failure, therefore, in maintaining the high rank pulpit oratory has held in the past, can with truth be fastened upon that of the present day, must be laid in large measure at the door of the speaker himself, and little of it can be traced to any other source.

Now what is the fact? Has pulpit oratory declined? Is it weaker in its presentation of the great truths it has in charge?—are its arguments less powerful?—is the language in which they are sent home to the judgment and conscience more feeble, the diction less clear, the imagery less impressive, or the metaphor less striking than in the sermons and addresses of the great divines who have gone before? One would hardly answer these interrogatories in the affirmative. The expounders of religious thought have never spoken in purer or loftier strains of eloquence and power than at the present day.

Congressional oratory, with which I am most familiar, has undergone essential change during the last forty or fifty years. Whether that change has been deterioration and decline, or simply the adoption of new and widely different methods forced upon it by new conditions, will admit of much difference of opinion. The fact can hardly be questioned that the ablest orators who were wont, fifty years ago, to hold Congressional halls in breathless silence, for their hour, would be talked out of doors if it were possible to put them in competition with any one of a score of the leading speakers in either House to-day. The mind will no more work under strange conditions than will the muscles in a strange harness. We have but to glance at some of these changes in the conditions forced upon Congressional speakers of the present day to realize how little at home and ill-at-ease an orator of the old school would be, and consequently how poorly he would be likely to acquit himself, if called upon to address the modern House of Representatives in its new hall and under its recent methods.

Those who saw the transfer of the members from the old hall of the House of Representatives to the new one were able to notice at once a marked change in the style and methods of speaking which that transfer compelled them to adopt. The Thirty-fifth Congress met in December, 1857, in the old hall, a beautiful, compact, semi-circular assembly-room, with the Speaker's desk in the centre of the arc, and the members in seats forming concentric half-circles with aisles radiating from the Speaker's chair, each seat being a settee reaching from aisle to aisle, with one continuous desk in front divided into compartments, but extending the entire length of the seats. There were 234 members then, there are 356 now. These filled the seats thus compactly arranged, and were equally under the Speaker's eye, and almost within touch of each member when he spoke. It was in this hall that the great orators of the first fifty years of the Republic, the Clays, Calhouns, Websters, and Choates, and later John Quincy Adams and S. S. Prentiss, spoke. This hall, with all its memories and inspirations, was exchanged for one of several times its area, rectangular in form, with the Speaker's desk midway of one of the sides,—the room being the inside of an iron box dependent on a skylight for its light and on a force-pump for air, with galleries running up the four sides on an inclined plane like flanges, and having a seating capacity for 1,500 people. The seats of the members were scattered over this large area, each with its own separate desk, and so isolated that there was a free passage round each desk, with an open space midway between the rows of seats the entire length of the hall. A committee had reported that the acoustic qualities of the hall were perfect, and that a whisper at the Speaker's desk could be distinctly heard in the remotest corner of the gallery. They were silent as to what volume of voice would be necessary to arrest the attention of men on the floor; for no experiment of that kind had been attempted, and the effect of the new habits which were to follow the new conveniences of members had occurred to no one. With the beginning of the new year the members took possession of their seats and of all the conveniences and opportunities that went with them. Is it strange that the first thought of each, as he surveyed his little realm, was business, and that his first order was for a supply of what was necessary for carrying it on, however wide the range or varied the character of its possible demands upon the time or thought of a politician?

If Mr. Gladstone's idea be accepted that the faculty of the orator is "the power of receiving from an audience in vapor what he pours back upon them in a flood," what chance is there for him before such an audience amid such surroundings? It was soon demonstrated. The first speech delivered in the new hall was by one who was well equipped for his part, and had won elsewhere the reputation of a brilliant public speaker. But he made little impression and his speech is forgotten. He caught no inspiration from the place or from the faces of his audience scattered, isolated, listless, warmthless. Others tried it with little better success. The members being furnished with facilities so tempting for the discharge of official duty and other labors, the hall soon assumed the appearance of a Congressional workshop. It became next to impossible for a member on his feet to arrest attention by any oratorical effort however meritorious. Gradually, speaking at length from briefs gave way to written essays read from the desks of members as sermons are from the pulpit.

This transfer from the discomfort of the old hall to the luxury of the new proved too radical a change, and some new arrangement became necessary. Several members who went abroad during the summer vacation came back with the conviction that conformity to the plan of the House of Commons, the substitution of benches for the chairs and desks of members, was the remedy; and a penance little short of hair-cloth and spikes was the penalty. Now a member could not even read a speech with any comfort. This was carrying reform to the other extreme, and it thwarted the very purpose for which it was instituted. The members would not fix their attention on the public business by compulsion, and spent more of their time in complaining of their inconveniences than they bestowed upon what they were assembled to transact. When the hot summer months came round, the new close plush-cushioned seats became well-nigh intolerable, and they disappeared at the end of the Congress. The House returned to the original plan of desks and chairs, but re-arranged so that 356 members were seated in the space originally occupied by 234. This arrangement still continues.

There are other changes affecting the chances for oratorical achievement since the days of the old hall, yet to be noticed. The hour rule was in those days an iron rule, and the hammer was as sure as fate to come down on a speaker even in the middle of a sentence. This rule is now so frequently and so easily evaded that it is practically a dead letter. Speeches are now prepared without reference to it, and are spread over as much space in circumlocution, tabulation of figures, and quotations, as time and assistants can command. No man can be eloquent even for an hour, much less for four or five, with "leave to print" at the end. If a speaker knows beforehand that all he can say must be said within his hour, and that nothing can be added beyond that limit, he will study brevity which is the soul of wit, clearness of statement which is the power of argument, simplicity of language which is the key of speech that is effective, and then will stop. It is said that the writing of telegraphic messages, now so common, has brought about a marked improvement in brevity, conciseness, and clearness of style among business men. The reverse is a habit much more easily fallen into, especially when one imagines that his ability is to be measured by his much speaking.

The habit of greeting speakers with applause, which, in this country and especially in Congress, is of recent origin, is having a marked effect upon the character of the oratory of legislative bodies. It was not tolerated for a moment fifty years ago in the House of Representatives, and is not now in the Senate. But it has come to be the daily food of the orators of the House, and every speaker seems to measure his own success by the volume of it which he is able to elicit. Party friends also are always ready to make sure that he does not, in this regard, fall short of any opponent who has preceded him. The consequence is that the temptation to prepare speeches for this effect is too strong to be resisted, and the orator studies all the arts and methods and tricks of diction most calculated to call forth sudden and unrestrained manifestations of approval. The direct effect has been to bring the speaking of legislators to the level of stump oratory on the prairies, where applause serves to fill the sails of the speaker and toss him about as the wind does a dory at sea.

One will look in vain for true and genuine eloquence in any length of oration delivered under such influences, punctuated though it be with parenthetic outbursts of uncontrolled applause all carefully recorded. The effect upon the character of public speaking has been a great increase in quantity, but a failure to elevate or even sustain the standard of the past in any of the qualities which constitute real oratorical power and true eloquence.

A change in the method of conducting business in legislative bodies, which has become general, must also be taken into account. Legislation by committees, instead of by the whole body, is the prevailing method of the present day. Almost the entire consideration and shaping of the most important measures which now come before legislative bodies is done in the committee room before they are reported for action. Little more than ratification of committee work remains after a measure leaves the committee room. There are exceptions, but this is the rule. Consequently the opportunity for debate is greatly abridged, and for extended oration almost entirely cut off. Nobody ever hears of the oratory or eloquence of a committee room. Add to this modern method that other invention of recent years, which takes up legislation thus prepared in the committee room, and puts it in charge of another committee of three to determine beforehand when it shall be considered by the bodies who are to pass upon it, for how long a time, and in what shape, and by what number of supporters and opponents, to be selected as prize combatants are selected by the opposing sides in a ring, and the hour by the clock when such consideration shall cease,—does any one conceive it possible that anything deserving the name of oratory or eloquence can be the outcome of such a contest? Shackled oratory will surely limp and halt and fail, and drafted or pre-announced oratory will fare no better. A speaker who gives notice beforehand that he is about to be indignant, or that in so many minutes he will proceed to weep, would be as likely to carry his audience with him into agonizing sympathy, as would the legislator called in strait-jacket under such a rule to fill his allotted time and then to yield to another impatient for his turn, while neither the requirement of the argument, nor the inspiration of the theme, but the hammer of the clock above his head is to determine the end of what he is to say.

Oratory should not be confounded with debate in this connection. While the former sometimes breaks out in genuine power, and true eloquence appears in the latter, yet the occasion is rare, and there is a vast amount of debate in which there is no oratory. They are distinct faculties. Debate is contention, oratory is persuasion. The one attacks the reasoning powers, the other plays with the emotions; the one would knock down an opponent while the other would charm him. They are not often found working hand in hand. Debate has not suffered as oratory has under the influences which change has wrought on the public life of the country during the last fifty years. On the contrary, the field of controversy has been very much enlarged during that period. Everybody stands ready to dispute everything, and to require a reason for each new step or position in the progressive life we are living. This gives debate its opportunity, and stimulates it to the highest activity. Besides, debate, to be effective, must be concise, direct, and pointed. It cannot be verbose, or wander or soar, if it would hold the ear of this hurrying generation. Life is short, and there is only time to reach for the pith of the matter in hand. The rest is counted as chaff. It stirs the blood, also, bad as well as good, more than any other form of discussion, and a taste of blood always arouses the carnal heart. The very conditions we have been considering as unfavorable to the cultivation and practice of the art of oratory have had the opposite effect upon that of debate. It has become more general in practice, and has attained a higher degree of power and effectiveness, taking the place, in a sort of hand-to-hand contest, of elaborate and lengthy oratorical efforts in support or condemnation of issues arresting public attention. The intensity which, during the war period, wherein every impulse, and every undertaking, every passion and every purpose, were stirred, found voice through this channel rather than through the calmer and more elaborate and studied medium of the prepared oration. It has been equally so during the period which has followed, in which material development and progress have largely absorbed thought and purpose to the exclusion of all things not contributing to this end. In each of these periods the shortest cut to conclusions took precedence of all other methods of determining action. When great interests are staked on promptitude, the public ear will tolerate nothing but yea, yea, and nay, nay. Tropes and metaphors, rhetoric and eloquence are wasted at such times, and the roughest form of expression, if it hits or hurts in accordance with the public pulse, will win its way over all other methods of public address, however polished and elegant.

During the period we have been considering so unpropitious for high attainment in oratorical art, there has come into use another method of public address which has little claim to oratorical merit, and is quite in contrast with the method of debate now so universal. It has nevertheless gained such foothold side by side with it, that it cannot be passed over without consideration. The practice of addressing the public by the reading of speeches written out in full beforehand did not originate in a desire to display through this means oratorical power, but rather from a consciousness of a lack of it. I speak of this practice outside the pulpit. Men making no claim to oratorical gifts have nevertheless found themselves in positions which, as they judged, made it incumbent upon them to address the public. And a wise use of the faculties they did possess would seem most naturally to dictate this method. The subject-matter itself is also sometimes of such nature as to require this method of treatment before the public even by an accomplished orator. Outside the limited uses here indicated there has still sprung up a habit of reading to the public written speeches in place of the spoken oration to the extent that it has become the rule and the extempore speech the rare exception. The largest quantity and the poorest quality is thus most easily disposed of, and the market and the taste alike suffer. The supply is inexhaustible, and the ability of the critic to cull from it whatever of value there is in it is baffled in the surfeit. There can be no genuine oratory in such productions, and an eloquent utterance is as rare as a kernel of wheat in the chaff that is scattered by the wind.

Still farther deterioration has this noble and godlike art suffered in legislative bodies of late by that counterfeiting process called "leave to print"—a refuge for the dumb and the simple, whose product, measured by any standard of oratory worthy the name, is of little more value than "green goods." There are exceptions to all rules and there have been orations of great merit, brought before the world by this method, which will survive the accidents of birth and take rank with the best, but they are very rare. Some modest and unostentatious treatment of a great theme or some great thought will rescue such an effort from a mass never read, but merely passed to the credit of the authors by the page or the pound. The public is being over-fed with this cheap food, and it palls the appetite. The effect has been worse than so much waste. It has not only displaced all opportunity for genuine oratory to exert its legitimate influence upon the public mind, pushing it discouraged and disgusted from the field, but it has caused a much lower estimate to be put upon the value of that great and rare faculty as a force in the direction of human affairs.   The public does not readily distinguish between these lifeless and worthless words which are inundating the land, and those great and grand periods with which orators in the past have swayed multitudes and touched the public conscience.   Tired of this kind of talk it would gladly turn its back on all talk.   It has come to hunger and thirst for facts that are patent, and new truths which scientific research is daily revealing without the aid of this faculty. The counterfeit has discredited the genuine coin, and both the good and the bad are for the time alike under the ban.

The conditions and influences unfavorable to the maintenance of that high standard of oratory heretofore attained in this country which have been thus far considered may be deemed by some to be incidental and only temporary, likely to cease as change follows change in the order of method and development to which all life among us is subjected.   There are, however, other influences, destined to have marked and lasting effect upon the future of public speaking in this country, concerning which there is no ground for belief that they will ever weaken, but on the contrary there is every indication of increasing force and effectiveness.   The stenographer, the telegraph, and the daily press, great and all-pervading revolutionary forces in modern life, have not spared this, the noblest of all instrumentalities for influencing the judgment and touching the conscience of mankind.   They bring the nation, and sometimes the whole English-speaking world, into the presence of the orator, to be moved by his words or to cast those words out if unworthy.   He therefore takes less and less heed of the few in his actual presence, and is led, in what he has to proclaim, to consider more and more its effect upon those beyond the narrow circle of actual vision who will at their leisure critically weigh each word on the printed page almost as soon as he shall have done.   This has a direct effect upon prepared oratorical effort.   Random, unpremeditated public speech is not caught up and sent abroad.   That alone which promulgates some striking thought in attractive color, some argument in new armor, or some new problem of life, is taken up by these new forces and carried to the understanding of multitudes miles away.   This leads every one who would speak to the generations, and not to the groundlings merely, to make more careful preparation.

Contrast these opportunities and aids of high oratorical art of the present day with the conditions with which it was surrounded fifty years ago. When Webster pronounced that greatest of his orations, the reply to Hayne, there was no power printing-press in existence, nor railroad in this country, nor was the telegraph thought of, and what we call stenography was not known till nearly ten years afterward. While there is no doubt that Mr. Webster spoke after long and profound study of his subject, yet he was compelled to speak at last without opportunity for immediate preparation, and from a brief hardly more than a modern sheet of note-paper. And when he was done, all that remained on paper of that grandest of English orations was this brief and the imperfect and detached notes taken by Mr. Seaton by a method of his own which would now be discarded as useless. With this brief and these notes, and by the help of his wife, who had listened to the speech and could recall its most striking passages, and also by aid of Mr. Webster's own recollections, Mr. Seaton undertook the work of writing out this unsurpassed effort. Friends who were listeners were called in, and paragraph after paragraph submitted to the test of their memory, and altered or rewritten as doubts were thrown on the accuracy of the original draft. They were called in also to aid in the choice of phrases and sentences the most impressive, regardless of the original notes. It was not until a month after its delivery that this work of reproduction was completed and the speech first published as it now appears, even in a Washington newspaper. The public was kept in waiting for this long period before it could read and weigh this great argument, the fame of which, as described by those who had listened to it, had spread far and wide. It was nearly six weeks before anything beyond what was in letters of friends, and fugitive extracts produced from memory, reached Boston. If Mr. Webster could re-enter the Senate Chamber to-day and speak as he did then, before he could resume his seat untold multitudes from Portland in Maine to Portland in Oregon would be reading what he had said. The speech of that day was delivered to the Senate and to those within the sound of the orator's voice. It was its extraordinary character alone that rescued it for the country and the coming generations. Mr. Winthrop says that Mr. Webster spared no labor in the writing out of his speech after delivery, to make it as perfect and impressive as possible to readers in all coming time as it had been to hearers at the moment, in order to satisfy a public expectation not justified by the shorthand report of Mr. Seaton. This report is still preserved in the Boston

Library, so that every reader of the speech in its present form can appreciate the value of the final finish. This great example makes clear the necessity which forces the most gifted orator to conform to the changes of condition which surround him. This final finishing of sentences and phrases, this re-statement of argument after delivery, is not possible now. If done at all they must be done before the orator speaks, for every sentence is transferred with photographic accuracy to paper, and published to the world by the stenographer as soon as it falls from the lips of the speaker, passing instantly beyond recall.

Another illustration, taken from the practice of speakers in that same Senate Chamber more than twenty years later, will make more clear the methods forced upon the most gifted orators by conditions with which they are surrounded. It will also show how they have been compelled, as these conditions have become more effective, to greater care and painstaking beforehand to guard against the effect of possible slips, hesitations, and tripping in speech and argument which, once made, could never be recalled. In the summer of 1852 I visited Washington, reaching there on the day on which Mr. Seward read from manuscript one of those orations full of profound political philosophy, and eloquent in the enforcement of great political truths, for which he was so justly celebrated. In the evening I called with many others to pay my respects and offer my congratulations. Among these callers was Mr. Sumner, whose first political speech had then been waited for by impatient friends for some time. As he offered to Mr. Seward very warm and hearty congratulations and commendations of the speech just delivered, Mr. Seward remarked to him, " By the way, Sumner, where is that speech you were going to make? I thought you would have delivered it before now." Mr. Sumner replied, " I have it all written out, but I have n't committed it to memory perfectly yet." Here were two great and justly cele- brated orators, but of distinctly different types, and each found himself compelled to train his peculiar powers for the most effective work in subordination to surrounding conditions. Mr. Seward had none of the graces and could practise none of the arts in delivery which win and captivate and chain the hearer, and never turned aside to attempt either. Mr. Sumner was in his delivery richly endowed with the highest qualities of the oratorical art. The one was listened to be- cause no one could afford to lose a word he uttered, while the con- summate oratory of the other, as well as the matter of his oration itself, won the hearer to his side. Thus, by writing out in full be-

forehand with great care and elaboration what they had to say, they
were both able to secure every word and phrase and sentence for all
who may hereafter read them in the precise form and shape they chose,
on the fullest deliberation, to have them presented; while Mr. Sumner,
by committing his production to memory, was able to add to the force
of the argument itself all the grace and art and fire of oratory of
which he was so consummate a master.   This last was Mr. Everett's
method during his entire public life, and his last great oration on
Washington was in manuscript at home while he was reciting it in
all parts of the country from memory with all the grace and eloquence
and polish of diction that had been fashioned and put upon paper with
care in his own study.   But the exacting duties of his public service
compelled Mr. Sumner early to give up this laborious practice of committing his speeches to memory, and, except in debate, led him to
deliver from manuscript whatever he had prepared to speak at any
length.   While, for the reasons given, public speakers have come
more and more to the method of committing to paper beforehand
whatever they design to present to the public on important occasions,
the practice of reciting from memory is passing out of use and is
seldom resorted to by any noted speaker of the present day.   All
conditions and influences have for many years tended directly to the
substitution of the manuscript for the extempore delivery of speeches.

From this inquiry the conclusion is evident.   The lack of interest in the old ways of the orator, and their gradual disuse by public
speakers, which have been cited as evidence of the decay of the art
itself, are really but changes in method forced upon them by the new
conditions and influences which have superseded and driven the old
out of use.   The orator has not command of the conditions of success; he is more their servant than their master, and must wait upon
them, not they upon him.   " The man, the subject, and the occasion"
is the order in which Webster places the three great elements essential for the attainment of the highest triumphs of oratory.   This
order should be reversed, if there can be any order where each is
indispensable.   Given the subject and the occasion—the exigency
and the opportunity—and the man has never yet failed the nation in
all its history, while, for lack of these, great oratorical power has
waited and slumbered.   These are the trumpet-calls to which the
brain-power and the soul of the orator will respond, and they will
wait on no other summons.   There is no occasion to lose faith in his
future because we do not find him in his old haunts or hear him

making vain efforts on old instruments long since out of tune. He is not a plaything for the entertainment of an hour, but a force capable of great achievements. Like the poet, he is born, not made; and the rare faculties with which he is endowed, given to the few, are withheld from the many, but they are still given in as large measure as ever. They wait for great exigencies and fitting opportunities. When these shall arise they will come forth with unimpaired power. That power will not be put forth in old-time methods and it may not be for old-time uses. But these faculties, like all others with which man is endowed, are destined for a higher state of development and perfection, and, whenever the need shall be upon them, will assert an advanced rank and a wider influence than ever yet attained.

HENRY L. DAWES.

IS THE BRITISH EMPIRE STABLE?

THE British Empire is a political creation unparalleled in the world's history, not only by its extent and population, in both which respects it is slightly surpassed by China, but because, with an area of more than 10,000,000 square miles and with 352,000,000 inhabitants, it is scattered over the whole globe. Starting westward from Queenstown, we land at Halifax on English soil; the Canadian Pacific Railway carries us across the whole American continent to Port Moody; we cross the Pacific to Hong-Kong, and thence reach North Borneo, Singapore, and Calcutta. Passing by rail through India, we meet, in continuing our road from Bombay, the British settlements in the Persian Gulf, Aden, Perim, Suakim, and Berbera in the Red Sea; Egypt and Cyprus are practically in English hands; the rocks of Malta form the central station of the naval British power in the Mediterranean, of which Gibraltar guards the entrance. And such a voyage leaves untouched numerous important parts of the Empire, East Africa, Mauritius, Zanzibar, the dominion of the Cape, the settlements on the western coast of Africa, the British Antilles, the Bahamas, Guiana, Honduras, the Falkland Islands, and Australia.

This extensive Empire embraces all zones from the icy wildernesses of Hudson Bay to the tropical jungles of India and the mahogany forests of Honduras; there is scarcely a product which a British province does not bring forth in excellent quality; and not less various are the degrees of civilization of its inhabitants, from the Kaffirs of the Cape to the highly cultivated citizens of Toronto or Sydney. We find, with Christians of all confessions, 200,000,000 Hindus, about 70,000,000 Mohammedans, and 8,000,000 Buddhists; and the Bible is printed in 130 languages and dialects represented in the Empire. India and the Crown colonies are under an absolute government; Canada and the Australian States enjoy democratic constitutions; Quebec is a French-speaking province; in the Cape colony the Dutch nationality prevails,—yet, notwithstanding such promiscuously tessellated elements, the government, with rare exceptions, maintains order, and no sign of dissolution is visible.

It is evident that such an Empire must be pre-eminently colonial:
11

of its total area the mother-country occupies scarcely one-eightieth, and counts about one-ninth of the whole population; and London, with its 4,500,000 inhabitants, is the capital of the vast aggregate of countries which acknowledge British sovereignty. What is still more remarkable is that this Empire should be a comparatively young one. It took the Romans nearly a thousand years to build up a state which, at the time of its highest development, was small compared to the present English commonwealth, while the beginnings of Great Britain are scarcely two hundred years old. In the age of the discovery of the New World, England took no part in the conquests made by Spain, Portugal, and Holland; the buccaneering raids upon Spanish settlements under Elizabeth can be considered only as an apprenticeship for British seamanship. It was the religious persecution under the Stuarts which first led to the establishment of the colonies of Virginia, New England, and Maryland, to which, under Charles II., were added the Carolinas and Pennsylvania. But it was Cromwell who, by the conquest of Jamaica from the Spaniards, became the real founder of that policy which led to such success.

The principle of the colonial policy of those times—a principle long followed by England—was to extort as much profit as possible from transatlantic possessions for the mother-country. But this system at last became impossible by reason of two great facts. The first was the rapid growth of the United States. As, in their vast dominion, immigrants found the freest economical motion and full possession of all political rights, the same could not be refused to the British colonies with a population of European descent; and Canada, the Australian settlements, and the Cape received autonomy and free constitutions. This was rendered the more necessary by the second fact,—the changed condition of the immigration into these colonies. When the Pilgrim Fathers settled in North America, England was not overcrowded; they went to live on creeds which were not tolerated at home. But when the mother-country became too small for its fast-increasing population, emigration began, and thousands crossed the ocean in order to find new chances in life and to live under free institutions. The happy results of this colonial development reacted on the mother-country: the privileged commercial companies were suppressed; the civil disabilities of Catholics and Dissenters were abolished; the navigation act, the corn laws, and protective duties were repealed; and English industry and commerce as well as colonial growth underwent an unparalleled expansion.

When, in 1836, the first white settlers came to Victoria, they found but camps of the aborigines; now the colony has more than 1,000,000 inhabitants, and Melbourne is the fourth city of the British Empire. New Zealand, where 60 years ago the Maoris held their war-dances and devoured their prisoners, now has 700,000 inhabitants. All the Australian colonies have a population of 4,000,000, with a budget of £30,000,000 and a total commerce of £144,000,000. Canada, also, which, unlike Australia, had no gold to attract immigrants, shows a rapid growth. Its commerce in 1891–92 amounted to $250,000,000, and is fast increasing, owing to the completion of the Canadian Pacific Railway, which is now the shortest route from England to eastern Asia. Moreover the progress of these countries is backed by well-nigh inexhaustible resources. The Cape Colony is constantly expanding; it has now a population of 2,000,000, and its mines of gold promise to become the richest of the world. These great provinces will speedily become powerful nations which in future times may outweigh in importance many of the present European states. At the same time there seems no prospect of their separation from the mother-country, with which they are connected by language, blood, religion, a common civilization, and strong material bonds.

England is day by day more dependent upon colonial purchasers. Australia buys British manufactures at the rate of £8 per head; the Canadians at the rate of £2 per head; while Frenchmen buy 9s. 3d. a head, and the Germans 8s. 4d. The colonies, on their side, furnish large quantities of food and raw materials to England. It must not be forgotten that in these colonies, as well as in all others, property to an enormous extent is in English hands. All colonial public debts have been borrowed in London; railways and public works have been constructed mainly by English money; vast British capital has been sunk in mortgages on colonial land and its cultivation; and 88 per cent of Australian shipping belongs to English owners.

But it must not be presumed that in the face of this peaceful expansion England has abandoned her policy of enlarging her foreign possessions by force and diplomacy. Leaving out of consideration the extension of the South African colony, which is greatly due to conquest, and notwithstanding many backslidings, her expansion is still going on, as the following acquisitions testify: the Strait-Settlements, in 1819; the Falkland Islands, 1837; Aden, 1839; Hong-Kong, 1843; Labuan, 1846; Perim, 1855; Lagos, 1861; the Dutch possessions on the Gold Coast, 1872; the Fiji Islands, 1879; Delagoa Bay,

1881; North Borneo, 1883; a large part of New Guinea, 1884; the Nigerland, 1886; Zanzibar and British East Africa, 1890; Uganda, 1894; not forgetting Cyprus and Egypt. The same policy has prevailed in the Indian Empire, which surpasses in importance all British colonies and forms the very centre of gravity of England's power.

Ethnographically speaking, India holds a population of 291,000,-000, inhabiting the peninsula up to the northern and western mountain ranges; politically it means the British dominion over this vast mass of men, in which it forms the sole connecting link. The English are the ruling caste, but a caste consisting of an infinitely small minority of scarcely 200,000. If, nevertheless, they are implicitly obeyed by this population of different races and creeds, so that a sole Resident administers districts of 2,000,000 inhabitants without ever encountering resistance, the reason is to be found in the masterly organization of the government. By its nature it is autocratic, but the autocracy is an intelligent absolutism resting upon a bureaucracy carefully trained for its task. It secures order and liberty to all creeds, but suppresses energetically all aggressive manifestations of one against another, and at the same time has done away with some of the most offensive excrescences of religious fanaticism. By skilful irrigation and a railway network of 17,283 miles, and by promoting industry and trade, the wealth of the country has been greatly developed. While formerly whole regions were decimated by famine, India has now become one of the foremost wheat-exporting states; its total commerce is £195,500,000. The government has established an efficient system of education: every village has its school managed according to race and creed, and every district a higher school; there are 82 colleges with 9,000 students, directed by three universities. Lastly, the government possesses an excellent army having a British nucleus of 73,000 combined with 125,000 natives, to which, in time of war, contingents of the semi-independent princes are added.

Leaving aside the minor colonies, even this bird's-eye view shows what a mighty edifice is this constantly expanding British Empire. Yet, as it is not a compact mass like the United States or Russia, but, by its dissemination over all parts of the world, forms a highly complicated and artificial structure, it is eminently vulnerable and exposed to special dangers. If peace should prevail for an indefinite period, there would be probably little chance of seeing its integrity impaired; but as we cannot hope to have entered upon this millennium, war remains the great test of the strength of states. The principal Continental governments are prolific in peaceful assurances, and, not-withstanding their colossal armaments, they are probably sincere. Unfortunately these assurances do not add much to the confidence of the nations, because many causes for conflict exist, and it remains very doubtful whether this prolonged tension and the oppressive economical strain of this military preparedness will not result in an outbreak which under existing circumstances would assume such tre-mendous proportions that England could scarcely remain neutral. As a single example we may take the chance of a war in the Mediter-ranean, where France and probably Russia would be opposed to Italy and Austria, while England has declared that she cannot suffer an alteration of the *status quo*. The question, therefore, cannot be avoided, how in such a case she will be able to weather the storm.

In this respect we must first consider that circumstances have totally changed since the times in which she obtained her position as a great world-power. Then armies were comparatively small, and the English, strengthened by paid foreign auxiliaries, could play a promi-nent part; but now, in the face of the enormous Continental armies raised by universal service, the English army, which adheres to the principle of free enlistment, dwindles into next to nothing. This was seen in the Crimean war, when with all her exertions England could put into the field little more than 50,000 men, who fought with gallantry but could have achieved nothing without their allies. Since this experience the government has abstained from active interference in the great struggles which have changed the map of Europe; nay, it tamely submitted when Russia, during the Franco-German war, arbitrarily denounced the neutralization of the Black Sea, which had been one of the most important clauses of the treaty of Paris. After the treaty of San Stefano, Lord Salisbury, indeed, declared that England would not tolerate its execution; but while two army-corps sent to Constantinople would have sufficed to annihilate the decimated Russian army, the government contented itself with dispatching the fleet and a few Indian regiments to the Bosporus, and then quietly went to the Congress of Berlin. After the Congress, Lord Beacons-field declared that if England had spoken decisively there would have been no war; but she did not speak decisively, and the net result of the peace with honor was that England pocketed Cyprus. The Egyptian expedition of 1882 may appear as an exception to this policy; but when Mr. Gladstone, forced by public opinion, undertook it, he had not to fear resistance from other powers.

Apart from this short campaign, which offers no proof of what an English army could do against trained European troops, England's policy has been to avoid conflicts, and it was but natural that her rivals should profit by this tendency. Both France and the United States have treated her with little ceremony in recent disputes, but it was Russia, above all, who profited by the certainty that England would not go to war, by her conquest of Central Asia. The successive strides she made in this direction gave great uneasiness to English statesmen; but they did not offer any active opposition, and allowed themselves to be lured by the promises of Prince Gortschakoff—which were broken as soon as they were given—and by negotiations which proved abortive. A Russian general appearing at Kabul, in order to conclude an alliance with the Ameer of Afghanistan for the invasion of India, while a Russian army was advancing from Samarcand for the same purpose, forced Lord Salisbury to meet Russia's demands half way by a secret convention with Count Schouvaloff; but meanwhile the Russians steadily advanced through deserts hitherto believed inaccessible, until they stood at the Afghan frontier, and soon afterward, under the eyes of the British commissary, ejected the Afghans from Penjdeh. After protracted negotiations the Afghan frontier was at last settled, and Russia not only remained in possession of Penjdeh, but advanced three miles nearer to Herat.

In recent times England has done much to redeem the faults of the past. As long as India was surrounded by deserts, there was little danger in her limits being undefined; but with the approach of Russia, her interest in the intervening countries has enormously increased. After discovering that the Himalayas, hitherto believed unsurmountable, had passes by which the Russians might advance from the north, Gilgit, a place in the Pamirs of great strategical importance, was occupied. When strategical roads are completed, the Indian army will be able to outflank a Russian advance from Herat; and as the western frontier has been greatly strengthened, and a railway built to Quetta, from which Candahar can be easily reached, a Russian attack, carried on so far from its strategical base, would seem to have little chance for success.

But if India be considered safe against Russia alone, there is danger of its being placed between two fires. The French desire to balance in Indo-China the position they formerly lost on the Ganges peninsula; they have conquered Cochin-China, Annam, Cambodia, and Tonquin, and in 1893 they compelled Siam to cede the whole territory on the left bank of the Mekong. Economically these conquests are worthless to France, because she has no colonists, and the commerce is in English and German hands. But from the political and military points of view her new position is of considerable importance, particularly because she acts in concert with Russia.

Admitting that France would have great difficulty in bringing a respectable army into the field in Asia,—that on the contrary a strong English squadron could render French Indo-China as isolated as Tahiti,—the very fact of her aggressive policy, like that of Russia, is disquieting to the Indian population, which is already swayed at one moment by gusts of Eastern fanaticism, and at another, in its higher classes, by Western ideas of the most advanced type. In time of peace the government may easily keep downt urbulent feelings, as Islam and Hinduism—the one stronger in faith, the other in numbers—create a sort of equilibrium. But if, in a great war, a mutiny should coincide with foreign aggression, the government would have to rely mainly upon the army against both.

Turning to the other colonies, we have to distinguish between the naval and military stations,—such as Gibraltar, Malta, Aden, Hong-Kong, Esquimault, Halifax, Bermuda, or coaling-stations, as the Seychelles, Singapore, etc.,—which are supported as garrisons for imperial purposes, and those which are empires themselves,—Canada, Australia, and the Cape. Their defence on land is based upon the principle that, as they risk being involved in England's wars with other powers, the obligation exists to protect them within certain limits; so the government sends out a certain force which garrisons the important strategical positions, and forms at the same time a nucleus around which the colonists can rally, and which assists them in their military organization. Of the three, the Cape has probably the least to fear: access is difficult for foreign squadrons; it has no powerful hostile neighbors; and, independently of its garrison, it possesses a force of sturdy volunteers trained in wars with the natives. As to Australia, an invasion seems equally impossible, but its numerous ports have to rely mainly on the protection of the British fleet.

It is different with the Dominion of Canada, which alone of the three has a neighbor, the strength of which compared to its own is about ten to one. The loyalty of its population cannot be doubted, and when, in 1862, a conflict with the United States was threatened in the "Trent" affair, all classes showed their determination to maintain their allegiance, although the terrors of war would in the first instance have fallen upon themselves.   But it must not be forgotten that the United States could not then have spared an army to invade Canada.   If, however, a war between England and the great Republic should now take place, Canada would undoubtedly be doomed.   Such a war is extremely unlikely: that of 1812 was mainly due to the impolitic conduct of the British government; and although the two nations have sometimes seemed to be on the verge of war, their disputes have always been peacefully adjusted.   In a war with other foreign powers England would take good care not to violate American interests, and the United States would adhere to its policy of non-interference in foreign conflicts.

As regards naval and military stations, they have first to rely upon the strength of their fortifications, which varies greatly; but principally upon the support of the fleet, without which most of their garrisons could be starved.   All minor colonies are in a similar position, and this leads to the key of the situation: namely, *that the British Empire as it stands is safe only so long as it has supremacy at sea;* that defeat at sea would be an unmeasured catastrophe and national ruin.

What is supremacy at sea?   An unvanquished fleet against which the attack of the enemy has no chance.   But here again circumstances are totally changed.   When England, in the Napoleonic war, had destroyed the French and Spanish and captured the Danish fleets, she was the omnipotent mistress of the sea and had the monopoly of commerce, which furnished the sinews sustaining the war.   Her naval supremacy remained uncontested up to comparatively recent times. Even in 1846 Lord Palmerston could threaten in Paris that England would sweep the French fleet from the seas; but since the Second Empire the latter has made constant progress, and it cannot be doubted that at present it is a very formidable power.   Besides, Russia, Germany, Italy, Austria, and the United States have respectable fleets.   The Admiralty report of 1890 states that in 1807 England had 207 battle-ships, and all other powers 180, whereas now she has but 45 real battle-ships, while France has 34 and Russia 15. Of first-class cruisers she has 18, the two other powers 9 and 11; of armored coast-defence vessels she has 17, of which 8 are permanently abroad, France has 14, and Russia 16.   The House of Commons indeed has, by the Naval Defence Act of 1888, increased the fleet by. 70 ships, which will be finished now, and has unanimously voted (April 11, 1894) £30,000,000 for an extraordinary addition to the navy in order to make it strong enough to face the coalition of any two powers. Mr. Goschen declared that then England alone would be equal to any emergency; but whether that would be the case remains to be seen, for if the British fleet is the strongest, it has also to fulfil an exceptional task of exceptional magnitude. Captain Mahan [1] insists on the necessity of concentration of effort; and he is certainly right, as the command of the sea can be secured only by victory in great pitched battles. But such a concentration is particularly difficult for England, having her fleet scattered in ten stations for protecting her colonies and commercial interests; and if these are to be defended against hostile expeditions they can only partially be drawn upon to strengthen the central force. The distances of some of these squadrons would render it difficult to bring them on the spot in the right time, whereas France has the greatest part of her navy concentrated at Toulon and Brest.

Blockades are now of little importance except against powers which have no navy to defend themselves. The use of steam renders a blockade much stricter than in the time of sailing-ships; but blockading squadrons must be constantly supplied with coal, while the blockaded ships can easily replenish their bunkers, can choose the moment for attack, have considerable advantages for the use of torpedoes, and may retire to give their companies rest, while the crews of the blockading squadron are worn out by fatigue. After Trafalgar the British were able to shut up the French warships in their ports for years, but an effectual blockade is to-day so difficult that, according to Admiral Sir Geoffrey Hornby, all the ironclads of England would not be able to blockade Toulon.

Capturing the enemy's merchantmen and national cargoes can certainly do much harm, but its advantage has been exaggerated. In our days, as soon as war is declared, the telegraph informs all ships liable to seizure, and they enter the nearest national or neutral port; the result being that the whole commerce of the belligerents goes into neutral hands, because their flag covers the cargo. This would be particularly the case with England, as her navy is not able to protect her commercial marine, amounting in 1891, with that of the colonies, to 26,085 ships of 12,427,596 registered tons and £970,000,000 of sea-borne trade. To protect this vast host of vessels scattered over the waters of the globe, there are 111 cruisers adapted to such service. In the next great war she has to sustain, England will

[1] "The Influence of Sea-Power upon the French Revolution and Empire," 1892.

realize that by her insular position she is in a condition differing from all other countries.   The latter, when their maritime communications are cut, can draw their supplies by rail, but England alone must import goods only by sea, and importation is an absolute necessity.   While in 1803 the import of corn was three per cent, it now reaches two-thirds of what she requires to feed her population.   In the same way English industry would come to a standstill if the import of raw materials was arrested.   According to Lord George Hamilton's calculation, England has to draw the food of her population for 189 days from foreign parts, and an interruption of the import of raw materials would throw 5,000,000 workmen out of employment.   The "Quarterly Review," April, 1894, admits that the stopping of imports would suffice "to starve us into making an ignominious peace with the enemy at his own terms."

The probable enemies of England know perfectly that this is England's most vulnerable point, and they would do all in their power to intercept the supply of provisions, while their own commerce would be much less exposed to English attacks, because they could lay up their ships in port.   Admiral Elliot has declared that the great expense incurred by France and Russia in building swift cruisers is mainly directed against British commerce.   Admitting that the enemies of England would not be able to reduce her population to starvation, they could still inflict upon it great harm, and this question does not belong to the future, but is imminent.

We leave out of consideration a real invasion of England. Although Lord Wolseley, in 1888, thought it quite possible that the French within a short time might collect a considerable force in their northern ports and transport it in one night, French naval authorities are of contrary opinion,[1] for in order to undertake such a perilous adventure the assailant must at all events have the absolute command of the Channel; and the same applies to Admiral Aube's barbarous plan of small cruisers, ubiquitous by speed and numbers, evading the hostile force and destroying undefended cities.

The decisive point remains the strength of the English battle-fleet; and what this is even the naval experts are not able to say. War alone can decide that question.   The strength of a fleet for attack and defence depends not only upon that of the ships and their

---

[1] Admiral de la Réveillère, in an article in the "Marine Française" of 1893, said: "Aucune personne de bon sens ne songera à nous voir assez maîtres de la Manche pour opérer un debarquement et pour ravitailler une armée debarquée."

number, but quite as much upon its armament and manning. In this respect the English battle-ships have recently shown unpleasant shortcomings. The 110-ton Armstrong and the 68-ton Woolwich guns have proved inferior to French and German guns; and the recruiting system does not furnish a sufficient number of trained crews. England on a peace-footing has but 44,000 men, a force which cannot be suddenly increased. While France, employing in peace 25,000, has a reserve of 113,000 trained and disciplined men, England has a nominal reserve of 23,000, of which only a small part would be available when wanted. Even if the whole reserve force could be collected, the greater part are very imperfectly trained and would be quite new to the life and exercises of a man-of-war. Other merchant seamen, if there were any to be had, would be still more ignorant, so that beyond the 44,000 England has only the coast-guard on which dependence can be placed. Even the quality of the enlisted men decreases. Accidents have become frequent: the "Howe" in 1892 ran ashore in clear weather; the catastrophe of the "Victoria" and the "Camperdown" is still fresh in the memory; in the naval review of 1889 there were three collisions; and in the manœuvres of 1891 only three ships of the defensive squadron came out without accident. Ironclads being very complicated instruments, the handling of which demands thoroughly experienced men, this deficiency must render the mobilization of the fleet slow. In the manœuvres at Toulon in 1891 the French Mediterranean squadron was ready to take the sea twenty-four hours after the order had arrived, and had a reserve division of twenty-four ships.

As to fortifications, only the Thames is efficiently defended; those of the other ports are antiquated in construction and armament. If the enemy could take Woolwich, the whole material of the fleet would be in its hands. Shortly before the Russo-Turkish conflict Lord Beaconsfield said that if England once went to war her resources would be practically inexhaustible; but the question is, whether she would have time to develop those resources.

To-day the fate of war is decided by a few great battles. France, after the peace of 1871, has shown of what resources she is possessed; yet after a six-months campaign Thiers was obliged to declare to the Assembly of Bordeaux, "La France reconnaît qu'elle n'a plus d'armée." It is the same in maritime war. Two great defeats would be fatal to the naval power of England, which is in fact her only power. It remains to be seen whether the above-mentioned deficiencies will be removed in time by the recent Imperial and Naval Defence Acts.

The British Empire has been built up under the leadership of an intelligent aristocracy, a form of government which, as the example of Venice and Holland shows, is eminently fit for such a task. That aristocracy still exists, but it has long since ceased to govern. Gradually England has passed down to a crowned democracy. But it cannot be said that the experiment, first to give power to the masses and then to "educate our masters," has particularly well succeeded. It is one thing to give manhood suffrage to a new country, where the largest part of the population is agricultural, mostly owners of their farms, well educated, and therefore conservative; and another thing to grant it in England, where more than fifty per cent of the population live in cities, and the landed property is in the hands of comparatively few large owners and is cultivated by poor laborers. Under such circumstances the masses not only rule the elections, but practically disfranchise the higher, more intelligent, and wealthy classes. The English democracy has disappointed its friends; it has not brought forward a single notable man; it has not cared much for Imperial interests, which by its leaders are ridiculed as "jingoism," but mainly for the class-interests of the workingmen. Moreover it is swayed by sudden changes: one parliamentary election can overthrow a whole policy; and this is the reason why foreign powers are little inclined to conclude alliances with England. In former wars, England, in order to make up for the insufficiency of her army, gave subsidies to her allies; but what British Minister would now have the courage to demand such grants from Parliament?

Will the English democracy, in the face of the dangers of the present situation, have the intelligence to see that in a war not only England's greatness, but the very existence of her Empire, would be at stake? Will, in that emergency, the old fighting spirit of John Bull revive in the masses, and make them ready to bear the necessary sacrifices? Or will they follow the cry for peace at any price, and adhere to Cobden's opinion that it would be a perilous adventure to hold India, and that the colonies are only good for providing places for the younger sons of the aristocracy? That is the question which will ultimately be decisive for the future of the British Empire.

F. HEINRICH GEFFCKEN.

FUNDAMENTAL BELIEFS IN MY SOCIAL PHILOSOPHY.

A SCIENTIFIC person dislikes creeds. Science is not religious revelation but a progressive unfolding of truth. When I am asked, "What is your social creed?" I naturally reply, "I have no creed." When the editor of THE FORUM asks me for an article on my creed, I am obliged to answer that I have none. What have I to do with a creed in economics or, more strictly speaking, general sociology? For it is in reality a sociological creed that is wanted.

Yet more mature thought reveals to the man of science that he may after all go too far in his opposition to a statement of his opinions. As the result of his studies, and, in a case like the present, also of his experiences in life, he may have reached certain conclusions of value to others. There may be no impropriety in a statement of these conclusions provided it is understood that he reserves the right to change his opinions if longer investigation and riper experience reveal mistakes. It is in this spirit that I consent to state briefly my views concerning some of the most fundamental problems presented by modern society in the United States.

No economic topic of a practical nature occupies a more prominent position in the public mind at the present moment, than strikes. What do I think about strikes? When we review industrial history it is scarcely possible to avoid the conclusion that strikes have been a necessary evil. They are a species of warfare and must be viewed somewhat in the same light in which we look at war in general. War has been a terrible scourge to the human race and has brought in its train more misfortunes, both to victors and vanquished, than people generally understand. At the same time it has frequently happened that war has been preferable to other evils, and no historian could be found who would deny that it has produced, along with vast wretchedness and misery, some good results. Not all strikes have been failures, and it has happened before this that the firm resistance of employees to wrong and oppression has been productive of results valuable alike to themselves and their employers. An orderly, well-conducted strike implies labor organizations, and labor organizations in their earlier period find their chief activity in industrial warfare and in the preparations for such warfare. The older trades-union was largely an organization of men bound together to accomplish their purposes by means of actual strikes or threats of strikes. I say " largely" because other purposes and very important ones have always been connected with labor organizations of any importance.

But conditions have changed. Formerly the trades and occupations of wage-earners were so distinct and separate that those employed in any one craft need have little reference in their struggles to wage-earners outside of their own ranks. Machinery has changed all that and broken down the barriers between the various occupations of wage-earning men and women. When the shoemakers in the great shops in Massachusetts have struck, they have been replaced with comparatively little difficulty by farmers' sons and daughters never before in a manufacturing establishment, and in a few months, if not indeed in a few weeks, the employers have been able to carry on their work as well as before. It seems clear, then, that the very foundation on which old-fashioned striking trades-unions rested has given way. The field of their operations seems to be a more restricted one than has been supposed by those who have considered merely older conditions. Labor organizations are a necessity, but they should change their methods to correspond to our present economic life, making more of other features than heretofore and less of strikes.

When we come to certain primary institutions like railways, telegraphs, gas-works, and the like, upon the continuous operation of which the general welfare is dependent in marked degree, the public interest becomes paramount, and public authority, if it discharge its functions, will not tolerate strikes. Anarchy means no government, and it is genuine anarchy for a great community to stand quietly by while undertakings of fundamental importance are paralyzed by the strife of different parties engaged in their operation. There is every reason why society should not tolerate such suffering as this involves. What we have recently witnessed in railway strikes is barbarism and not civilization. We should not, in this matter, allow a discussion of abstract rights to interfere with determined action which will prevent the recurrence of events like those referred to, which are nothing less than a national disgrace and humiliation. Some way or another, these peculiarly public industries must be kept in continuous operation, and this must be effected while ample protection is afforded to all interests involved. If wrong and injustice are done to employees, effective means must be discovered to remedy them without a disturbance of domestic peace.

But this statement of the problem—that is to say, continuous operation of the industries in question and justice to all interests involved, capital and labor alike—calls to mind practical difficulties which industrial civilization in general, but especially in our own country, has met, and which we have to overcome. Let us always remember that we are Americans and dealing with American conditions. A solution of the problem which in the case under consideration might perhaps be found in England or Germany, may be no solution at all in the United States. Without sharing in any anti-English sentiment, it seems to me that our writers on economic topics, especially our writers of text-books, have forgotten the elementary fact just stated, and have been too exclusively under the influence of English thought; and that they have not supplemented what they have learned from English masters, by a large and varied American experience. The conduct of some of our writers resembles that of an inventor who, having constructed a large and expensive machine, should become enraged because it would not perform the purpose which called it into being. The inventor says: "It ought to work. It conforms to the principles of the books. It is a shame and an outrage that it does not work as it should." But we reply: "My dear fellow, all your talk and all your rage do not alter the main fact. You have overlooked either some principle or some peculiarity in your material. We do not want your machine." Writers and speakers are filled with indignant amazement because the ordinary rules which govern the relations between employed and employers, and between both and the general public, do not hold in the case of these industries with which we are dealing. Is not the reason because we have overlooked fundamental principles and fundamental facts? Let us see.

The peculiarly public industries with which we are dealing are the so-called natural monopolies. Two or three are national in the scope of their operation, some are chiefly local in their activity, while a few are too extensive to be called local, but are not nevertheless strictly national in character. Roughly, they correspond to our three chief political units, the nation, the commonwealth, and the town or city. These undertakings are: streets and highways of all sorts, the means of communication and transportation, and lighting-plants. Every one thinks, of course, of railways, telegraphs, telephones, harbors, canals, street cars, elevated urban railways, gasworks, electric-lighting plants. These are monopolies because they can be managed as a unit, and competition is so partial that it does not afford adequate protection to the public. All rivalry and emulation are by no means excluded. Monopoly does not mean that, but it does mean an absence of adequate protection to important public interests. Moreover, reference is had to these industries in their maturity, not in their early stages of development. Railways, in our country, give difficulty to those who do not grasp the principles of monopoly, because our railway systems are not yet fully developed, although every fair-minded person will admit that even now they are not regulated by normal competition, which excludes destructive industrial war as well as combination. Naturally we cannot enter upon the very difficult theory of monopoly, and attempt to elaborate it. Much work remains to be done before we have a complete theory of monopoly, and the treatment of this subject would require a large work if it approached exhaustiveness. Nevertheless some things have been made clear.

Experience in the United States has demonstrated that there are two—and only two—ways of dealing with monopolies. We have, in the main, a choice only between private ownership and operation with control by government, and government ownership and operation. One or the other our courts and our legislatures have decided we must have; and their decision has been wise, as it has been forced on them by hard facts. Waterworks in our cities very generally illustrate government ownership and operation, whereas our railways afford illustration of control by government united with private ownership and operation. Government control simply takes the place of the regulation by competition which obtains in agriculture, manufactures, and commerce. This control is, by the necessities of the case, pushed further and further every day. It has not yet included labor; but as the principles of monopoly must in time make themselves fully felt in the relation of the industries in question to labor, and as public interests are paramount, as already indicated, it can be only a question of time when what we have seen in the efforts of the courts to keep our railways in operation will be further developed. Whatever we otherwise think of the injunctions recently issued by the courts, we must acknowledge that they are a step in the right direction.   The force operating to bring under the control of government the relations between employed and employers in the case of monopolistic undertakings is like a law of nature which will override all opposition.

The question we have to answer is this: Which is better, government ownership and operation with the control naturally and spontaneously resulting therefrom, or private ownership and operation with government control forced on the owners and managers?   The question is complex, and the answer is a difficult one in regard to which men may well differ; but it should receive the careful and conscientious attention of all who have any qualifications calculated to help them to throw light on the problems involved, and above all things it should be considered dispassionately.   Whichever alternative we choose, we have complicated problems without end to solve; and this simply calls again to mind the fact that modern civilization is at best an arduous process.

It has seemed to me that the difficulties inherent in minute and detailed public control of private property, especially under American conditions, have been too generally underestimated.   First of all, we must remember that private property naturally carries with it the right of exclusive control over the objects of property.   A large part of the benefits of private property results from this exclusive control. The farmer exerts himself with diligence and reaps reward or bears loss according to the wisdom with which he exercises his control over his own operations.   The anomalous condition of public control over private property is that we ask men to take the responsibilities of private property without its prerogatives; and protests from managers of railways and other similar enterprises are not surprising.   Now what are the managers of such property going to say, if, having taken away from them the right to control their relations to the general public, we take from them the right to control the labor they employ?   Will not the present friction, already disastrous, between government and powerful private interests, be increased many fold? Were any suggestions thrown out during the recent strike investigation in Chicago which would lead us to think otherwise?   Already, at least one railway president insists that the government should purchase railway property if it assumes the right to control it.   What may we expect will be the attitude of railway managers if we continue our policy of perpetual interference with private railway property?

12

But we have difficulties in the way of control which are seldom alluded to. Of necessity, the special expert knowledge must for the most part be on the side of those over whom it is desired to exercise this control. Is this a promising experiment? Can ignorance control knowledge?—inexperience, experience? A German professor, with experience in public life in his own country, tells me how successfully in some instances this control has been exercised in Germany; but I reply: "America is not Germany. Can you, with American conditions, expect similar results? If you do, it seems to me you do not know our country. We have to deal with American farmers and American workingmen. Whatever you may think of them, they are facts, very real, very important."

But we have further to notice the immense power which these natural monopolies inevitably wield. When towns and cities contend with them, we have the spectacle of weakness attempting to exercise control over strength. What must we expect? Let us freely admit that in their moral qualities railway owners and managers are quite equal to the rest of the community, while wiser and stronger than most of their fellow citizens: can we, then, expect beneficial results? If the federal government is stronger than the natural monopolies it seeks to control, can they not treat with it almost as a co-ordinate power?—and is this beneficial?

Now let us take the question of corruption in public life, and let us freely admit the share of this corruption connected with the control in question, for which public authorities must bear the blame; let us take the view most favorable to the private parties controlled, and must we not admit that, with our American conditions, this corruption is to a great extent an inevitable result of the conflict of interest produced by the American policy? Not only must we protest against solving this question by considerations which hold in England and Germany, but we must likewise protest against a solution based merely upon the facts of life in New England and the Middle States.

The difficulties in the way of public ownership and management are vast. Such ownership and management imply changes and readjustments in our political conditions. Additional safeguards against undue centralization may possibly be necessary, for local self-government needs to be further developed rather than restricted. No danger must be suffered to threaten the American commonwealth. The civil service must be developed far beyond what we have as yet seriously considered, for it would be folly indeed to think of the enlargement of the functions of government mentioned, with our present civil service.   Every one, however, will admit that, were it necessary, we could maintain a military service of one million men. Is it true that, should we set about it, we could not devise measures to maintain a civil service of one million men?

The acquisition, by the public, of the private property involved, without wrong to any one, suggests numerous difficulties.   All these difficulties and obstacles in the way of the socialization of natural monopolies deserve most careful consideration; but, after all, which alternative suggests the greater difficulties?   Which course promises most for the future?

Should it be decided that government ownership, immense as are its difficulties, is on the whole preferable, it will then be necessary to pass on to details: but it does not seem likely that such a decision will be reached except for some local monopolies, and perhaps the telegraph and telephone, in any near future.   It may be one genera-tion—it may be two generations—hence, before the public will be fully persuaded; and in such matters prediction is extremely unsafe.   The change may never come, while it is possible that it may come sooner than I have anticipated.   It is well for us, however, to have clear ideas in regard to the goal which it would be desirable to reach, could we attain it, in order that we may approximate as nearly to it as possible.

It should, however, be distinctly understood that a belief in the policy of socialization of national monopolies does not involve indorse-ment of every scheme for carrying into effect this policy.   If a party arises which demands the socialization of natural monopolies, we may well ask ourselves what kind of leadership has this party.   Has it in its leadership such mental capacity and such moral qualifications that it would be expedient to turn over the government to it, especially when so doing involves grave changes, requiring the best brains and ripest experience of the nation to effect them with safety?   Further-more, we may ask, what else does this party couple with the demand for the socialization of monopoly?   Has this party ideas which seem to us wildly impracticable in regard to money and public finance? If so, we may conclude that adherence to older parties is preferable to support of a party deficient in leadership, and which couples unsound planks with one which, differently brought forward, might command our support.

Furthermore, it should be clearly understood that the policy of socialization of natural monopolies does not carry with it any idea of spoliation. Whatever we think about that policy, we should all, it seems to me, insist on full payment for all property taken from private owners.

A still more fundamental question is that suggested by the word "socialism," which is something so radically different from my general thought, that the competitive field of industry—that is, in the main, agriculture, manufactures, and commerce—is suitable for private effort, and the field of monopoly for public activity, that only shallow thinkers can confound the two. Socialism, however, is not so much a single question as a series of questions, vast and intricate. Socialism is indeed a philosophy of society supported by many very able men. I have held and still hold that the study of socialism is most useful, and that on several accounts. First of all it gives us a standpoint from which to survey existing institutions, and enables us to understand them and weigh in the balance their merits and demerits. It is general principle that indirect methods, both in science and industry, are speedier and more effective than direct methods. A critical study of socialism not only interests a student in the study of present society, but gives an aid in this study which it is difficult to find elsewhere. This is a position which was taken long ago by John Stuart Mill, and subsequent experience has only confirmed what he stated when he expressed the opinion "that the intellectual and moral grounds of socialism deserve the most attentive study, as affording in many cases the guiding principles of the improvements necessary to give the present economic system of society its best chance."

Socialism has also been a force which has stimulated the consciences of many and transformed beneficially the lives of not a few. Again, socialism has furnished a needed corrective to certain anarchistic tendencies in our life.

On the other hand, the agitation of socialism as it has been too frequently conducted has tended to an undue exaltation of manual toil, a depreciation of the brain work which alone can render mere physical exertion fruitful, and to class separation and hatred, and has at times turned away the attention of the masses from true remedies for evils which afflict them. The difficulties in the way of socialism seem to me to be insuperable. First of all there is the difficulty in the way of the organization of agriculture, which has never yet been squarely faced by socialists. Then, socialism once organized, there remains difficulty in securing that distribution of annual income which would give general satisfaction and at the same time promote progress. There is reason to apprehend that under socialism those pursuits upon which the progress of civilization depends would not be amply supported, and that the result of socialism would thus be a non-progressive society. If this is true, then the masses would ultimately suffer, even if we admit that their condition at first would be improved.

Finally, it is my opinion that the concentration of dissatisfaction under socialism would be revolutionary in character. As I have stated in my recent work on "Socialism and Social Reform," "the outcome of socialism then, it is to be apprehended, would be such an amount of dissatisfaction that one of two things would happen: either socialism would result in a series of revolutions, reducing countries like England and the United States to the condition of the South American republics, and rendering progress impossible; or the dissatisfaction would cause a complete overthrow of socialism and a return to the discredited social order."

I have stated my views in regard to anarchy so often and so emphatically that it is difficult for me to do more than to repeat what I have said elsewhere. Anarchy comprises the sum and substance of all evils of a social nature. Every step in the direction of anarchy is a calamity. The propaganda of anarchy is a terrible evil, leading to disturbance and insurrection. The evils which flow from anarchy or even the propaganda of anarchy are not incidental, but proceed from the very nature of the doctrine. Progress depends upon obedience to law and constituted authorities, and anarchy in its very nature is rebellion. Anarchy is lawlessness elaborated into a social philosophy, and anything more diametrically opposed to my own social philosophy is to me scarcely conceivable.

But this consideration of anarchy raises the question, Upon precisely what foundation does the opposition to anarchy rest? Anarchy is the negation of the state. What is the source and sanction of the authority of the state? Is the state a mere aggregate of individuals accomplishing their purpose simply by brute force? Does might make right? If it does, then is not the question between anarchy and its opponents simply a question of superior force? But if might does not make right, what does make right? Has the state an ethical nature? If the state is itself non-ethical, can the power which it exercises have an ethical element? But if it is devoid of an ethical element, can it rest upon anything less than mere brute force?   The doctrine of the Christian church has been from time immemorial that the state is a divine institution and that its authority comes from God.   If this is true, then we have a ground of opposition to anarchy which appeals alike to intellect and heart.   Is this a true doctrine or is it not?   Is it a doctrine which science can recognize?   If science does not recognize it, what does science put in its place?   I do not attempt to answer these questions, although I think a sufficiently clear answer can be found in my various writings; but I commend them to the careful consideration of the readers of the present article.

Finally, if my views have, as the editor of THE FORUM thinks, a public interest, probably it may be well for me to say a few words about the future progress of society.   No sane man can claim that in our social arrangements we have as yet reached perfection.   Every one acknowledges that there is room for improvement in literature, art, religion; but, strangely enough, some seem inclined to resist the conclusion which follows from the nature of man and the conditions which surround him, that there is room for improvement and possibility of improvement in our industrial relations.   We have made advance in the past, and we shall certainly make progress in the future.   It is inconceivable that industrial society two hundred years from now will be like the industrial society of to-day.   It is eminently desirable that right-minded and intelligent persons should work for improvement and endeavor to render change—which must come in some way or another—as little injurious and as beneficial as possible.

First of all, the necessity is suggested of careful, conscientious study.   The importance of study is generally felt, and the educational institutions of the land are moving in the right direction in the development which they are giving to all branches of social and political science.   We need trained men in the pulpit and the press, and especially in legislative halls.   Careful, impartial, thoroughly scientific study of the actual facts of life is to-day one of the most striking needs of the civilized world.

Such study and observation as have been already made show clearly that there is no panacea for individual and social ills.   There is no royal road to a happy condition of society, but the road is long, arduous, and often painful.   There is no possibility of escape from toil and suffering.   Mitigation and gradual improvement are the utmost which we can hope for, and it is a duty of all those who have the ear of the masses to tell them this plain truth even if it be not altogether palatable. To arouse false hopes and to cultivate illusions result only in increased suffering. At the same time there is enough which can be accomplished, to stimulate all to put forward their best efforts, and to give encouragement in the midst of the weary struggle for better social conditions.

The eighteenth-century doctrine of essential equality among men is, in my opinion, pernicious. It seems to me that it has been a most fruitful cause of misfortune and misdirected social effort. It nourishes false hopes and turns attention away from facts of the utmost moment. There is no more marked social fact, no one more momentous in its consequences, than the essential inequality of men. Men are unequal in power, capacity, requirements; and the more one thinks about it the more marvellous do all these inequalities appear. Any social action based upon an assumption of equality is mischievous. It is especially the feebler members of the community who suffer under the doctrine of essential equality, because, as has been well said by a jurist, " Nothing is more unequal than the equal treatment of unequals." The doctrine of equality also weakens the feeling of responsibility on the part of those who are superior to their fellows either in their persons or their fortunes, whereas a frank recognition of inequalities and of the favored position of a few must tend to awaken in them a feeling of responsibility.

As far as my general social philosophy is concerned, I may then say that I am a conservative rather than a radical, and in the strict sense of the term an aristocrat rather than a democrat; but when I use the word " aristocrat," I have in mind of course not a legal aristocracy, but a natural aristocracy; not an aristocracy born for the enjoyment of special privilege, but an aristocracy which lives for the fulfilment of special service.

RICHARD T. ELY.

ELY'S "SOCIALISM AND SOCIAL REFORM."

THERE is a set of current conceptions as to the relation between political economy, socialism, and legislative reform which have been fostered by writers like Carlyle or Ruskin, Kingsley or Maurice, which are reflected in many of the most popular novels and sermons of the day, and to which Professor Ely, in his recently-published book, "Socialism and Social Reform," has lent the weight of his authority. These conceptions may be formulated as follows:

1. Political Economy makes the individual an end, in and for himself; in other words it is a gospel of Mammon and a glorification of selfishness.

2. Socialism substitutes collective aims for individual ones. It is the result of a moral reaction against the traditional political economy,—a reaction which is taking hold of the masses, and which they are inclined to carry to an extreme.

3. The only way to prevent matters from being carried to such an extreme is for the wealthy and intelligent classes to adopt a great many socialistic measures on their own account, before the control of our social machinery is taken out of their hands.

The first of these conceptions is an entire mistake. Political Economy does not regard the individual as an end in himself. It does not glorify the pursuit of wealth except so far as this pursuit serves the interests of society as a whole. The great work of Adam Smith was an inquiry into the causes of the wealth of nations; and subsequent economists have followed in his footsteps. They have shown that the collective prosperity of a nation is far better fostered by the individual freedom and enlightened self-interest of its members than by any complicated system of police government. They have shown that, in the industry of modern civilized nations, the man who serves himself intelligently is generally serving others, even when he has no intention or consciousness of so doing. But in all this the individual freedom is treated as a means to social welfare rather than as an end in itself.

This development of individualism in economics is part of the general trend of modern thought and modern life. A few centuries ago, the principle of individual freedom was not recognized in law or in morals, any more than in trade. It was then thought that liberty in trade meant avarice, that liberty in politics meant violence, and that liberty in morals meant blasphemous wickedness. But as time went on, the modern world began to see that this old view was a mistake. Human nature was better than had been thought. Man was not in a state of war with his Creator and all his fellow-men which it required the combined power of the church and the police to repress. When a community had achieved political freedom, its members on the whole used that freedom to help one another instead of to hurt one another. When it had achieved moral freedom, it substituted an enlightened and progressive morality for an antiquated and formal one. When it had achieved industrial freedom, it substituted high efficiency of labor for low efficiency, and large schemes of mutual service for small ones. Constitutional liberty in politics, rational altruism in morals, and modern business methods in production and distribution of wealth, have been the outcome of the great individualistic movement of the nineteenth century.

Professor Ely quotes with apparent approval the Bishop of Durham's statement that " individualism regards humanity as made up of disconnected or warring atoms. " This is not only untrue : it is exactly the reverse of the truth. This idea of disconnected and warring atoms represents the traditional theological standpoint instead of the modern individualistic one. The individualist holds that, as society develops, the interests of its members become more and more harmonious; in other words, that rational egoism and rational altruism tend to coincide. In fact his chief danger lies in exaggerating the completeness of this coincidence in the existing imperfect stage of human development, and in believing that freedom will do everything for society, economically and morally.

These mistakes and exaggerations of individualism have given a legitimate field for socialistic criticism, both in morals and in economics. Some of the ablest economists on both sides of the Atlantic have done admirable work in pointing out where the evils arising from individual freedom may exceed its advantages, and when society must use its collective authority to produce the best economic and moral results. Such has been the work of John Stuart Mill, of Stanley Jevons, of Sir Thomas Farrer, of President Andrews, and of the leaders of the German " Historical School. " Men of this type recognize that the point of issue between them and their opponents is not a question of ends, but of means. Both sides have the same object at heart; namely, the general good of society. One side believes that this good is best achieved by individual freedom in a particular line of action; the other side believes that the dangers and evils with which such freedom is attended outweigh its advantages. The good and evil are often so closely balanced that economists on either side find the utmost advantage in studying the criticisms of their opponents as a means of avoiding or correcting their own errors.

But the name "socialist" is rarely applied to a critic of this stamp. It belongs by current usage to a far larger body of people who dislike, misunderstand, and try to ignore, the results of economic experience. They are, as a rule, men who see clearly the existence of certain evils in modern industrial society which some economists have overlooked, and others have deplored as inevitable. They rush to the conclusion that economic science regards these evils with indifference, and that its conclusions and purposes are therefore immoral; while they claim for themselves, more or less consciously, a superior moral purpose because they are trying to right visible wrongs by direct state action. This is, in its general nature, the so-called moral reaction against the teachings of economics.

This reaction is in fact not so much a moral as an emotional one. It is not due to the fact that the socialist hates moral evils which the economist of the old school regards with apathy. It is rather the result of a difference in mental constitution which leads the economist to calculate the large and remote consequences of any measure and ignore the immediate details, while the socialist feels the details so strongly that he refuses to work out the indirect consequences of his action. It is an old saying that men may be divided into two classes, one of which is so occupied looking at the woods that it does not see the trees, while the other is so occupied with the trees that it does not see the woods. The attitude of some of the economists toward questions of social reform is not inaptly typified by the former class; that of their socialistic critics by the latter.

Of course it will not do to undervalue the emotional element in dealing with economic matters, as men of the more purely intellectual type are sometimes prone to do. Reasoning about human conduct is full of chances of error; and if the outcome of such reasoning is to leave a considerable number of human beings in hopeless misery, society is justified in demanding that every premise and every infer-

ence in the chain of reasoning be tested, and every rational experiment be made to see whether such a consequence is really inevitable.
Instances have not been wanting when the conclusions of the economists have proved wrong, and the emotions of the critics have been
warranted by the event. The factory legislation of England furnishes an historic example. The economists, as a rule, condemned
this legislation as wrong in principle and likely to do harm; but the
results showed that these economists had overlooked certain factors of
importance with regard to public health and public morals which vitiated their conclusions and justified public opinion in disregarding them.

But while the men of emotion may sometimes be right and the
men of reason wrong, the chances in matters of legislation are most
decidedly the other way. It is safe to say that the harm which has
been done by laws based on unemotional reasoning is but a drop in
the bucket compared with that which has been done by laws based on
unreasoning emotion. The tendency to overvalue feeling as compared with reason is a far greater danger than the tendency to undervalue it. For legislation is essentially a matter of remote consequences. The man who tries to reason out these consequences will
occasionally make mistakes; the man who refuses to reason them out
will habitually do so. The good which state interference does is
often something visible and tangible. The evil which it does is
much more indirect, and can only be appreciated by careful study.
The man who has his mind so fixed on some immediate object as to
shut his eyes to the results of such study, is almost certain to advocate too much state action. He may succeed in passing a few good
laws, but he will be responsible for a vastly larger number of bad ones.

The danger from this source is increased by the fact that so many
good people make very little distinction between what is emotional
and what is moral. They think that calculated conduct is selfish
conduct, and that unselfishness can exist only in the emotional as
opposed to the intellectual sphere. Many a man gives charity to a
pauper upon impulse and thinks he is doing a good deed, when he is
really shutting his eyes to the consequences of an evil one. "Virtue," says a French writer, "is more dangerous than vice because its
excesses are not subject to the restraints of conscience." There is a
great deal of legislation, and a great deal of socialism, to which this
remark will apply. Its promoters believe themselves to be actuated
by moral ideas, when the chief ground for this belief is the absence
of intellectual ones.

Perhaps the most plausible argument urged in favor of the superior morality of the socialistic system is that it would teach people to think more than they now do of sympathy as an industrial force, and less of self-interest. It is urged that a belief in the principles of the commercial world tends to make people selfish, while a belief in socialism tends to make them sympathetic. This view is hardly justified by the facts of history. In Europe, all through the Middle Ages, charity was regarded as a right and business as a wrong; but those ages were marked by strife rather than by sympathy. The attempt to restrict business transactions and to suppress self-interest as a commercial factor stood in the way of mutual service. The assertion of the duty of charity did not produce a better system of mutual service, as the advocates of socialism would have us believe. It put intolerable burdens upon some classes—especially the agricultural laborers—in order to support other classes in comparative idleness. Though the ideals of socialism may be attractive, its methods have been demoralizing; and this is the really important thing to consider in judging the moral character of socialism as an economic system.

Let us compare the moral effect of the commercial and the socialistic theories of value. The commercial theory is that the value or proper price of an article is based on the needs of the market; that is, upon the utility of additional supplies of that article to the consumers. The socialists object that the results of this theory are unjust, and that some people get a large price for what has cost them very little effort; while others expend a great deal of effort and can command only a small price in return. They would have us adopt a theory of value which should make the price depend on the sacrifice of the producer rather than on the needs of the consumer. At first sight the socialistic theory seems the more just; and the emotional man is pretty certain to pronounce it morally superior to the commercial theory. But the intellectual man, who traces the consequences of the two views, finds that the commercial theory leads men to produce what others want in as large quantities as possible, and with the minimum expenditure of labor; while the socialistic theory leads men to spend as many hours as possible over their work and dole out the smallest possible quantities of what other people want. Whatever may be thought of the assumptions of the two systems, the industrial results of the commercial theory are efficiency, progress, and service to others; while those of the socialistic theory are inefficiency, antiquated methods of work, and restriction of service to others.

Judged in the light of economic history, the "high ideals" which, to quote the words of Professor Ely, "socialism has placed before the masses of the people, and which they have absorbed," are based partly on erroneous assumptions and partly on demoralizing ones.

But there is still another point to be considered. Even if we regard the socialistic views as erroneous and demoralizing, the fact remains that they are held to a greater or less extent by a large number of people—perhaps a majority of the voters in the United States. What is a wise man to do under these circumstances? Shall he make concessions to this sentiment lest a worse thing befall him? Professor Ely most explicitly urges that this should be done. From this view the writer is compelled to dissent emphatically, alike on grounds of morality and of policy. He believes that the courageous answer to this question is the prudent one, and that that answer is, *No*.

Let us not be misunderstood. If, on careful inquiry, it appears to a thinking man that the public good will in any particular case be better served by the adoption of socialistic means rather than of individualistic ones, he ought to favor their adoption, whether this policy commands five votes or five million. But if he does not believe that the public good will be served by such a policy, and lends his countenance to its adoption because he is afraid to oppose the emotional demand which stands behind it, his conduct is a mistake from whatsoever point of view we regard it.

In the first place, it is likely to strengthen rather than weaken the demand for more radical changes. You cannot compromise with an emotion as you can with a differing opinion,—witness the difficulties of arbitration in labor disputes. An emotion is stimulated rather than satisfied by concessions. Such concessions are taken as evidence, not of a spirit of accommodation, but of weakness,—and, on the whole, rightly so. If the conservatives yield to a popular clamor which overawes but does not convince them, the people are justified in assuming that their previous toleration of evils was due to indifference and not to an honest conviction that it was impossible to stop them by state action. In sacrificing their own better judgment, the conservatives give up their strongest weapon of defence, and gain absolutely nothing.

Nor do we find, except in rare instances, that the failure of an experiment in over-legislation lessens the demand for similar action in the future. The failure will be attributed not to the fact that there was too much state action, but too little. Disasters and losses connected with state railroad control are made so many arguments in favor of state railroad ownership. The difficulties and failures of co-operation under the existing system of industry lead to a demand for a "co-operative commonwealth." No socialistic experiment is proved a failure, in the eyes of its promoters, until all other simultaneous experiments have been stopped. It is just here that individualism has its greatest advantage for the progress of the community. It tries to leave people free to make their own mistakes; trusting that the successful experiment will be followed and the unsuccessful one abandoned, and that the community will thereby profit from the errors hardly less than from the successes of its active members. Though this ideal of the individualist is nowhere fully carried out, it is unquestionably true that economic individualism has enabled nations to learn and profit by the success or failure of industrial experiments far more rapidly than any socialistic system with the collective action which it necessitated. The world's great inventions and improvements, material and moral, have been made by individual initiative, and adopted reluctantly by organized governments of any form whatever.

It is because of this success in serving the community that individualistic economics holds the position which it does at the present day. It is not because the leaders of industry or the exponents of the traditional political economy are popular, for they are not. It is because their work proves constructive and preservative of human happiness, while that of their opponents is unsuccessful or destructive. It is doubtful whether President Cleveland, three months ago, was any more popular than President Debs; but President Cleveland represented intellect while President Debs represented emotion, and we have seen what came of the contest. A nation must let intellect rule over emotion, whether it likes intellect or not. The alternative is political and industrial suicide. The proof of intellect and the condition of holding power is success in foreseeing the future. "There is one quality in a general which every soldier understands, and that is success."

Whenever a republic undertakes to carry on a war, there is always a popular demand for more vigorous action than the judgment of the best trained officers can approve. An emotional public

sentiment mistakes the caution of a general for apathy, and stigma-
tizes his scientific foresight as the result of cowardice or treachery.
Too often, under the influences of such a sentiment, a Fabius is displaced by a Varro, a McClellan by a Pope, or a Johnston by a Hood.
A Gates is allowed to snatch away the well-earned laurels of a
Schuyler, and even to menace the authority of a Washington. But
sooner or later science finds its vindication in a Cannæ or a Camden,
a Manassas or an Atlanta. It is not by yielding to popular demands,
as did Burnside at Fredericksburg or Lee at Gettysburg, that generals
preserve their authority and their cause. It was a great deed when
Thomas held his position at Chickamauga for hour after hour against
the assaults of ever-increasing numbers, amid imminent peril of destruction; but it was a far greater deed for himself and for the
Union, when, fifteen months later, he held his position at Nashville
for week after week, under increasing popular clamor for premature
action, and in the hourly peril of ignominious removal. The statesman who, under the pressure of popular clamor, modifies his calmer
scientific judgment to suit an emotional demand, barters the possibility of a Nashville for the probability of a Fredericksburg.

This illustration will serve to show why economists as a body
look with distrust on those who appeal from the conclusions of history and deduction to those of popular sentiment, and will explain a
great deal of this alleged intolerance and exclusiveness. It is not
true that economists make the individual good an end in itself.
Nothing but ignorance of their writings can excuse this belief. Nor
is it true that they reject socialistic means for the promotion of the
public welfare. Those who adopt an extreme position in this matter
are to-day in a minority. But they strongly disapprove the attempt
to " popularize" economics by giving too much weight to the conclusions of uninstructed public sentiment. It is not toward the theories
of the socialists that their hostility is exercised, nor even toward
their practical proposals, but toward their methods of investigation
and the manner of their appeal to the public.

ARTHUR T. HADLEY.

STUDIES OF THE GREAT VICTORIAN WRITERS:
III.—DISRAELI'S PLACE IN LITERATURE.[1]

IN the blaze of the political reputation of the Earl of Beaconsfield we are too apt to overlook the literary claims of Benjamin Disraeli. But many of those who have small sympathy with his career as a statesman find a keen relish in certain of his writings; and it is hardly a paradox to augur that in a few generations more the chief of the new Tory Democracy may have become a mere name, whilst certain of his social satires may still be read. Bolingbroke, Swift, Sheridan, and Macaulay live in English literature, but are little remembered as politicians; and Burke, the philosopher, grows larger in power over our thoughts, as Burke, the party orator, becomes less and less by time. We do not talk of Viscount St. Albans, the learned Chancellor: we speak only of Bacon, the brilliant writer, the potent thinker. And so perhaps in the next century, little will be heard of Lord Beaconsfield, the Jingo Prime Minister: but some of Benjamin Disraeli's pictures of English society and the British Parliament may still amuse and instruct our descendants.

It is true that the permanent parts of his twenty works may prove to be small. Pictures, vignettes, sketches, epigrams will survive rather than elaborate works of art; these gems of wit and fancy will have to be picked out of a mass of rubbish; and they will be enjoyed for their vivacious originality and Voltairean pungency, not as masterpieces or complete creations. That Disraeli wrote much stuff, is true enough. But so did Fielding, so did Swift, and Defoe, and Goldsmith. Writers are to be judged by their best; and it does not matter so very much if that best is little in bulk. Disraeli's social and political satires have a peculiar and rare flavour of their own, charged with an insight and a vein of wit such as no other man perhaps in this century has touched—so that, even though they be in sketches and sometimes in mere *jeux d'esprit*, they bring him into the company of Swift, Voltaire, and Montesquieu. He is certainly inferior to all these both in wit and passion, and also in definite purpose. But he

[1] Copyright also in England.

has touches of their lightning-flash irradiating contemporary society. And it seems a pity that the famous " Men of Letters" series which admits (and rightly admits) Hawthorne and De Quincey, could find no room for the author of " Ixion in Heaven," " The Infernal Marriage," " Coningsby," " Sybil," and " Lothair."

Disraeli's literary reputation has suffered much in England by the unfortunate circumstance of his having been the leader of a political party.   As the chief of a powerful party which he transformed with amazing audacity, as the victorious destroyer of the old Whig oligarchy and the founder of the new Tory democracy, as a man of Jewish birth and alien race, as a man to whom satire was the normal weapon and bombastic affectation a deliberate expedient for dazzling the weak—Disraeli, even in his writings, has been exposed in England to a bitter system of disparagement which blinds partizans to their real literary merit.   His political opponents, and they are many and savage, can see little to admire in his strange romances: his political worshippers and followers, who took him seriously as a great states- man, are not fond of imagining their hero as an airy satirist.   His romances as well as his satires are wholly unlike anything English; and though he had brilliant literary powers, he never acquired any serious literary education.   Much as he had read, he had no learning, and no systematic knowledge of any kind.   He was never, strictly speaking, even an accurate master of literary English.   He would slip, as it were, unconsciously, into foreign idioms and obsolete words.   In America, where his name arouses no political prejudice, he is better judged.   To the Englishman, at least to the pedant, he is still a somewhat elaborate jest.

Let us put aside every bias of political sympathy and anything that we know or suspect of the nature of the man, and we may find in the writer, Benjamin Disraeli, certain very rare qualities which justify his immense popularity in America, and indeed in England. In his preface to " Lothair" (October, 1870), he proudly said that it had been " more extensively read both by the people of the United Kingdom and the United States than any work that has appeared for the last half century."   This singular popularity must have a ground. Disraeli, in truth, belongs to that very small group of real political satirists of whom Swift is the type.   He is not the equal of the terri- ble Dean; but it may be doubted if any Englishman since Swift has had the same power of presenting vivid pictures and decisive criti- cisms of the political and social organism of his times.   It is this

13

Aristophanic gift which Swift had.   Voltaire, Montesquieu, Rabelais, Diderot, Heine, Beaumarchais had it.   Carlyle had it for other ages and in a historic spirit.   There have been far greater satirists, men like Fielding and Thackeray who have drawn far more powerful pictures of particular characters, foibles, or social maladies.   But since Swift we have had no Englishman who could give us a vivid and amusing picture of our social and political life, as laid bare to the eye of a consummate political genius.

It must be admitted that, with all the rare qualities of Disraeli's literary work, he hardly ever took it quite seriously, or except as an interlude and with some ulterior aim.   In his early pieces he simply sought to startle the town and to show what a wonderfully clever young fellow had descended upon it.   In his later books, such as "Coningsby," "Sybil," and "Tancred," he wished to propound a new party programme.   "Lothair" was a picture of British society, partly indulgent and sympathetic, partly caustic or contemptuous, but presented all through with a vein of *persiflage*, mockery, and extravaganza.   All this was amusing and original; but every one of these things is fatal to sustained and serious art.   If an active politician seeks to galvanise a new party by a series of novels, the romances cannot be works of literary art.   If a young man wants only to advertize his own smartness, he will not produce a beautiful thing.   And if a statesman out of office wishes to amuse himself by alternate banter and laudation of the very society which he has led and which looks to him as its inspiration, the result will be infinitely entertaining, but not a great work of art.   Disraeli therefore with literary gifts of a very high order never used them in the way in which a true artist works, and only resorted to them as a means of gaining some practical and even material end.

But, if Disraeli's ambition led him to political and social triumphs, for which he sacrificed artistic success and literary honours, we ought not to be blind to the rare qualities which are squandered in his books.   He did not produce immortal romances—he knew nothing of an ingenious plot, or a striking situation, or a creative character—but he did give us inimitable political satires and some delicious social pantomimes; and he presented these with an original wit in which the French excel, which is very rare indeed in England.   Ask not of Disraeli more than he professes to give you, judge him by his own standard, and he will still furnish you with delightful reading, with suggestive and original thoughts.   He is usually inclined to make

game of his reader, his subject, and even of himself; but he lets you
see that he never forgets this, and never attempts to conceal it.   He
is seldom dull, never sardonic or cruel, and always clean, healthy,
and decent.   His heroines are ideal fairy queens, his heroes are all
visionary and chivalrous nincompoops; and even, though we know
that much of it is whimsical banter and nonsensical fancy, there is an
air of refined extravaganza in these books which may continue to give
them a lasting charm.

The short juvenile drolleries of his restless youth are the least
defective as works of art; and, being brief and simple *jeux d'esprit* of
a rare order, they are entirely successful and infinitely amusing.
" Ixion in Heaven," " The Infernal Marriage," and " Popanilla," are
astonishing products of a lad of twenty-three, who knew nothing of
English society, and had had neither regular education nor social
opportunities.   They have been compared with the social satirettes of
Lucian, Swift, and Voltaire.   It is true they have not the fine touch and
exquisite polish of the witty Greek of Samosata, nor the subtle irony
of Voltaire and Montesquieu, nor the profound grasp of the Dean.
But they are full of wit, observation, sparkle, and fun.   The style
is careless and even incorrect, but it is full of point and life.   The
effects are rather stagey, and the smartness somewhat strained—that
is, if these boyish trifles are compared with " Candide" and the " Let-
tres Persanes."   As pictures of English society, court, and manners
in 1827 painted in fantastic apologues, they are most ingenious and
may be read again and again.   " The Infernal Marriage," in the vein
of the " Dialogues of the Dead," is the most successful.   " Ixion"
is rather broader, simpler, and much more slight, but is full of
boisterous fun.   " Popanilla," a more elaborate satire in direct imitation of " Gulliver's Travels," is neither so vivacious nor so easy as
the smaller pieces, but it is full of wit and insight.   Nothing could
give a raw Hebrew lad the sustained imagination and passion of
Jonathan Swift; but there are few other masters of social satire with
whom the young genius of twenty-three can be compared.   These
three satires, which together do not fill 200 pages, are read and re-
read by busy and learned men after nearly seventy years have passed.
And that is in itself a striking proof of their originality and force.

It is not fair to one who wrote under the conditions of Benjamin
Disraeli to take any account of his inferior work: we must judge
him at his best.   He avowedly wrote many pot-boilers merely for
money; he began to write simply to make the world talk about him,

and he hardly cared what the world might say; and he not seldom wrote rank bombast in open contempt for his reader, apparently as if he had made a bet to ascertain how much stuff the British public would swallow. "Vivian Grey" is a lump of impudence; "The Young Duke" is a lump of affectation; "Alroy" is ambitious balderdash. They all have passages and epigrams of curious brilliancy and trenchant observation; they have wit, fancy, and life scattered up and down their pages. But they are no longer read, nor do they deserve to be read. "Contarini Fleming," "Henrietta Temple," "Venetia," are full of sentiment, and occasionally touch a poetic vein. They had ardent admirers once, even amongst competent judges. They may still be read, and they have scenes, descriptions, and detached thoughts of real charm, and almost of true beauty. They are not, in any sense, works of art; they are ill-constructed, full of the mawkish gush of the Byronic fever, and never were really sincere and genuine products of heart and brain. They were show exercises in the Byronic mode. And, though we may still take them up for an hour for the occasional flashes of genius and wit they retain, no one believes that they can add much permanent glory to the name of Benjamin Disraeli.

Apart from the three early burlesques, of which we have spoken —trifles indeed and crude enough, but trifles that sparkle with penetration and wit—the books on which Disraeli's reputation alone can be founded are "Coningsby," "Sybil," and "Lothair." These all contain many striking epigrams, ingenious theories, original suggestions, vivacious caricatures, and even creative reflections, mixed, it must be admitted, with not a little transparent nonsense. But they are all so charged with bright invention, keen criticism, quaint paradox, they are so entirely unlike anything else in our recent literature, and they touch, in a Voltairean way, so deeply to the roots of our social and political fabric, that they may long continue to be read. In the various prefaces, and especially in the general preface to "Lothair" (of October, 1870), Disraeli has fully explained the origin and aim of these and his other works. It is written, as usual, with his tongue in his cheek, in that vein of semi-bombastic paradox which was designed to mystify the simple and to amuse the acuter reader. But there is an inner seriousness in it all; and, as it has a certain correspondence with his public career and achievements, it must be taken as substantially true. "Coningsby" (1844) and "Sybil" (1845) were written in the vigour of manhood and early days of his political ambition, with an avowed purpose of founding a new party in Parliament. It must be admitted that they did to some extent effect their purpose—not immediately or directly, and only as part of their author's schemes. But the Primrose League and the New Toryism of our day bear witness to the vitality of the movement which, fifty years ago, Disraeli propounded to a puzzled world. "Lothair" (1870) came twenty-five years later—when he had outlived his illusions; and in more artistic and more mellow tones he painted the weaknesses of a society that he had failed to inspire, but which it gratified his pride to command.

" 'Coningsby,' 'Sybil,' and 'Tancred,'" says he in his grandiose way, "form a real Trilogy.' "The derivation and character of political parties,"—he goes on to explain—was the subject of "Coningsby." "The condition of the people which had been the consequence of them"—was the subject of "Sybil." "The duties of the Church as a main remedial agency" and "the race who had been the founders of Christianity" (although, if we are to believe the Gospels, the murderers and persecutors of Christ and His Apostles)—were the subjects of "Tancred" (1847). "Tancred," though it has some highly amusing scenes, may be dismissed at once. Disraeli fought for the Chosen Race, their endowments and achievements, with wonderful courage and ingenuity. It was perhaps the cause which he had most deeply at heart, from its intimate relation to his own superb ambition and pride. But it has made no real way, nor has it made any converts. Thackeray's "Codlingsby" has almost extinguished 'Sidonia.' And the strange phantasmagoria of the Anglican Church, revivified by the traditions of Judaism, and ascending to the throne of St. Peter is perhaps the most stupendous joke which even Disraeli had ever dared to perpetrate. In the preface to "Lothair" we read:—

"The tradition of the Anglican Church was powerful. Resting on the Church of Jerusalem, modified by the divine school of Galilee, it would have found that rock of truth which Providence, by the instrumentality of the Semitic race, had promised to St. Peter."

Whatever this jargon may mean, the public has allowed it to fall flat. It seems to suggest that the Archbishop of Canterbury, by resuming the tradition of Caiaphas, as "modified" by the Sermon on the Mount, might oust the Pope of Rome as was foretold by the Divine young Jewish reformer when he called the fishermen of Galilee. It is difficult to believe that Disraeli himself was serious in all this. In the last scene, as Tancred is proposing to the lovely Jewess,

their privacy is disturbed by a crowd of retainers around the papa
and mamma of the young heir. The last lines of "Tancred" are
these:—" The Duke and Duchess of Bellamont had arrived at Jerusalem." This is hardly the way in which to preach a New Gospel to a
sceptical and pampered generation.

But, if the regeneration of the Church of England by a re-Juda-
izing process and return to the Targum of the Pharisees has proved
abortive, it must be admitted that, from the political point of view,
the conception announced in the "trilogy," and rhapsodically illustrated in "Tancred,"—the conception of the Anglican Church reviving
its political ascendancy and developing "the most efficient means of the
renovation of the national spirit"—has not proved quite abortive. It
shows astonishing prescience to have seen exactly fifty years ago that
the Church of England might yet become a considerable political
power, and could be converted, by a revival of Mediæval traditions,
into a potent instrument of the new Tory Democracy. Whatever we
may think about the strengthening of the Established Church from
the point of view of intellectual solidity or influence with the nation,
it can hardly be doubted that in the fifty years that have passed since
the date of the "trilogy," the Church as a body has rallied to one
party in the State, and has proved a potent ally of militant Imperial-
ism and Tory Democracy. Lord Beaconsfield lived to witness that
great transformation in the Church of the High and Dry Pluralists
and the Simeonite parsons, which he had himself so powerfully organised in Parliament, in society, and on the platform. His successor
to-day can count on no ally so sure and loyal as the Church. But
it was a wonderful inspiration for a young man fifty years ago to
perceive that this could be done—and to see the way in which it
might be done.

"Coningsby" and "Sybil" at any rate were active forces in the
formation of a definite political programme. And this was a programme which in Parliament and in the country their author himself
had created, organised, and led to victory. It cannot be denied that
they largely contributed to this result. And thus these books have
this very remarkable and almost unique character. It would be very
difficult to mention anything like a romance in any age or country
which had ever effected a direct political result or created a new
party. "Don Quixote" is said to have annihilated chivalry; "Tartuffe" dealt a blow at the pretensions of the Church; and the "Marriage of Figaro" at those of the old *noblesse*. It is possible that

"Bleak House" gave some impulse to law reform, and "Vanity Fair" has relieved us of a good deal of snobbery. But no novel before or since ever created a political party and provided them with a new programme. "Coningsby" and "Sybil" really did this; and it may be doubted if it could have been done in any other way. "Imagination, in the government of nations" (we are told in the preface to "Lothair") "is a quality not less important than reason." Its author trusts much "to a popular sentiment which rested on a heroic tradition and which was sustained by the high spirit of a free aristocracy."

Now this is a kind of party programme which it was almost impossible to propound on the platform or in Parliament. These imaginative and somewhat utopian schemes of "changing back the oligarchy into a generous aristocracy round a real throne," of "infusing life and vigour into the Church as the trainer of the nation," of recalling the popular sympathies "to the principles of loyalty and religious reverence"—these were exactly the kind of new ideas which it would be difficult to expound in the House of Commons or in a towns-meeting. In the preface to "Coningsby" the author tells us that, after reflection, the form of fiction seemed to be the best method of influencing opinion. These books then present us with the unique example of an ambitious statesman resorting to romance as his means of reorganising a political party.

There is another side to this feature which is also unique and curiously full of interest. These romances are the only instances in which any statesman of the first rank, who for years was the ruling spirit of a great empire, has thrown his political conceptions and schemes into an imaginative form. And these books, from "Vivian Grey" (1825) to "Endymion" (1880), extend over fifty-five years, before his political career seemed able to begin, in the midst of it, and after it was ended. In the grandiloquent style of the autobiographical prefaces, we may say that they recall to us the "Meditations" of Marcus Aurelius, the "Political Testament" of Richelieu, and the "Conversations" of Napoleon at St. Helena.

In judging these remarkable works, we ought to remember that they are not primarily romances at all, that they do not compete with genuine romances, and they ought to be read for the qualities they have, not for those in which they fail. They are in part autobiographical sketches, meditations on society, historical disquisitions, and political manifestoes. They are the productions of a statesman aiming at a practical effect, not of a man of letters creating a work of imaginative art. The creative form is quite subsidiary and subordinate. It would be unreasonable to expect in them elaborate drawing of character, complex plot, or subtle types of contemporary life. Their aim is to paint the actual political world, to trace its origin, and to idealise its possible development. And this is done, not by an outside man of letters, but by the very man who had conquered a front place in this political world, and who had more or less realised his ideal development. They are almost the only pictures of the inner parliamentary life we have; and they are painted by an artist who was first and foremost a great parliamentary power of consummate experience and insight. If the artistic skill were altogether absent, we should not read them at all, as nobody reads Lord Russell's dramas or the poems of Frederick the Great. But the art, though unequal and faulty, is full of vigour, originality, and suggestion. Taken as a whole, they are quite unique.

"Coningsby; or, the New Generation" was the earliest and in some ways the best of the trilogy. It is still highly diverting as a novel, and, as we see to-day, was charged with potent ideas and searching criticism. It was far more real and effective as a romance than anything Disraeli had previously written. There are scenes and characters in the story which will live in English literature. Thackeray could hardly have done better than 'Rigby,' 'Tadpole' and 'Taper,' 'Lord Monmouth.' These are characters which are household words with us like 'Lord Steyne' and 'Rawdon Crawley.' The social pictures are as realistic as those of Trollope, and now and then as bright as those of Thackeray. The love-making is tender, pretty, and not nearly so mawkish as that of 'Henrietta Temple' and 'Venetia.' There is plenty of wit, epigram, squib, and bon mots. There is almost none of that rhodomontade which pervades the other romances, except perhaps as to 'Sidonia' and the supremacy of the Hebrew race—a topic on which Benjamin himself was hardly sane. "Coningsby," as a novel, is sacrificed to its being a party manifesto and a political programme first and foremost. But as a novel it is good. It is the only book of Disraeli's in which we hardly ever suspect that he is merely trying to fool us. It is not so gay and fantastic as "Lothair." But, being far more real and serious, it is perhaps the best of Disraeli's novels.

As a political manifesto, "Coningsby" has been an astonishing success. The grand idea of Disraeli's life was to struggle against what he called the "Venetian Constitution," imposed and maintained by the "Whig Oligarchy." As Radical, as Tory, as novelist, as statesman, his ruling idea was "to dish the Whigs," in Lord Derby's historic phrase. And he did "dish the Whigs." The old Whigs have disappeared from English politics. They have either amal-gamated with the Tories, become Unionist Conservatives, henchmen of Lord Salisbury, or else have become Gladstonians and Radicals. The so-called Whigs of 1894, if any politicians so call themselves, are far more Tory than the Whigs of 1844, and the Tories of 1894 are far more democratic than the Whigs of 1844. This complete trans-formation is very largely due to Disraeli himself. And the first sketch of the new policy was flung upon an astonished public in "Coningsby," just fifty years ago. No doubt, the arduous task of educating the Conservative Party into the new faith of Tory Democ-racy was not effected by "Coningsby" alone. But it may be doubted if Mr. Disraeli would have accomplished it by his speeches without his writings. As a sketch of the inner life of the Parliamentary system of fifty years ago, "Coningsby" is perfect and has never been approached. Both Thackeray and Trollope have painted Parliament and public life so far as it could be seen from a London club. But Disraeli has painted it as it was known to a man who threw his whole life into it, and who was himself a consummate Parliamentary leader.

"Sybil; or, the Two Nations," the second of the trilogy (1845), was devoted, he tells us, "to the condition of the people," that dismal result of the "Venetian Constitution" and of the "Whig Oligarchy" which he had denounced in "Coningsby." "Sybil" was perhaps the most genuinely serious of all Disraeli's romances; and in many ways it was the most powerful. Disraeli himself was a man of sympathetic and imaginative nature who really felt for the suffering and oppressed. He was tender-hearted as a man, however sardonic as a politician. He had seen and felt the condition of the people in 1844. It was a time of cruel suffering which also stirred the spirits of Carlyle, Mill, Cobden, and Bright. It led to the new Radicalism of which Mr. Gladstone and Mr. John Morley are eminent types. But the genius of Disraeli saw that it might also become the foundation of a new Toryism; and "Sybil" was the first public manifesto of the new departure. The political history of the last fifty years is evidence of his insight that, to recover their political ascendancy, a Conservative Party must take in hand "the condition of the people," under the leadership of "a generous aristocracy," and in alliance with a renovated Church.   These are the ideas of " Sybil," though in the novel they are adumbrated in a dim and fantastic way.   As a romance, " Sybil" is certainly inferior to " Coningsby."   As a political mani-festo, it has had an almost greater success, and the movement that it launched is far from exhausted even yet.   One of Disraeli's comrades in the new programme of 1844–5 was a member of the last Tory cabinet and may well be a member of the next.   And when we con-sider all the phases of Tory Democracy, Socialistic Toryism, and the current type of Christian Socialism, we may come to regard the ideas propounded in " Sybil" as not quite so visionary as they appeared to the Whigs, Radicals, Free Traders, and Benthamites of fifty years ago.

In " Lothair," which did not appear until twenty-five years after " Sybil," we find an altered and more mellow tone, as of a man who was playing with his own puppets, and had no longer any startling theories to propound or political objects to win.   For this reason it is in some ways the most complete and artistic of Disraeli's romances. The plot is not suspended by historical disquisitions on the origin of the Whig oligarchy, by pictures of the House of Commons that must weary those who know nothing about it, and by enthusiastic appeals to the younger aristocracy to rouse itself and take in hand the con-dition of the people.   In 1870, Mr. Disraeli had little hope of realis-ing his earlier visions, and he did not write " Lothair" to preach a political creed.   The tale is that he avowed three motives, the first to occupy his mind on his fall from power, the second to make a large sum which he much needed, and the third to paint the manners of the highest order of rank and wealth, of which he alone amongst novelists had intimate knowledge.   That is exactly what we see in " Lothair." It is airy, fantastic, pure, graceful, and extravagant.   The whole thing goes to bright music, like a comic opera of Gilbert and Sullivan. There is life and movement; but it is a scenic and burlesque life. There is wit, criticism, and caricature; but it does not cut deep, and it is neither hot nor fierce.   There is some pleasant tomfoolery; but at a comic opera we enjoy this graceful nonsense.   We see in every page the trace of a powerful mind; but it is a mind laughing at its own creatures, at itself, at us.   " Lothair" would be a work of art, if it were explicitly presented as a burlesque, such as was " The Infer-nal Marriage," or if we did not know that it was written to pass the time by one who had ruled this great empire for years, and who within a few years more was destined to rule it again.   It was a fanciful and almost sympathetic satire on the selfish fatuity of the noble, wealthy, and governing orders of British society.   But then the author of this burlesque was himself about to ask these orders to admit him to their select ranks, and to enthrone him as their acknowledged chief.

As the rancour of party feeling that has gathered round the personality of Beaconsfield subsides, and as time brings new proofs of the sagacity of the judgments with which Benjamin Disraeli analysed the political traditions of British society, we may look for a fresh growth of the popularity of the trilogy and "Lothair."   England will one day be as just, as America now is, to one of her wittiest writers. He will one day be formally admitted into the ranks of the Men of Letters.   He has hitherto been kept outside, in a sense, partly by his being a prominent statesman and party chief, partly by his ineurable tone of mind with its Semitic and non-English ways, partly by his strange incapacity to acquire the *nuances* of pure literary English. No English writer of such literary genius slips so often into vulgarisms, solecisms, archaisms, and mere slip-shod gossip.   But these are after all quite minor defects.   His books, even his worst books, abound in epigrams, pictures, characters, and scenes of rare wit.   His painting of Parliamentary life in England has neither equal nor rival. And his reflections of English society and politics reveal the insight of vast experience and profound genius.

FREDERIC HARRISON.

THE CONTENTED MASSES.

THOSE who think that it would be easy for our industrial discontent to ripen into social revolution have not taken account of
the largest element in our national polity, the people outside of the
great cities. The provinces are the silent partners of the great cities.
But, though silent, they hold most of the proxies; and in every great
crisis in the republic it is they that have had the last word. The
provinces are not yet prepared to upset the present industrial scheme
on the chance that a few desperate agitators with a smattering of
knowledge, backed by an intrepid vanity, may instantly provide a
better. And this holds true in the West as in the other parts of the
country. There is a very common belief that the West is in a state
of sullen revolt against the present, and willing to turn its hand to
any vagary in finance or sociology. But this is true, not of the
West, but only of limited portions of the West. In sections of the
Northwest, where men without a penny have bought farms, mortgaging them, expecting out of the money thus raised to pay for farms,
stock, and machinery (very likely loading themselves down with both
chattel and farm mortgages), and year after year have reaped hardly
enough from their scorched acres to pay the interest on their debts,—
there discontent, like weeds, is a sure crop. The farmer has risked
everything on the climate, and the climate has played him false.

But a very different state of things is the rule in sections with
kindlier skies. Such a section is the State of Iowa. A survey of
the State, and especially of one section thereof (chosen because it is
the section that the writer knows best) may give Eastern readers a
fairer idea of a Western community than they sometimes have.
The State of Iowa has a population a little under 2,000,000 souls.
Of these, 1,587,827 were born in this country, which scores one
point for the State. It scores another in the character of its foreign-
born population, who come from Germany, Sweden, and Great
Britain, rather than from the mongrel races of Southern Europe.

Iowa has no bonded debt, and has a floating debt of only a few hundred thousand dollars. It is one of the great rural States, producing

the largest amount of corn and swine, standing second in the production of flax, and ranking among the foremost six in the raising of
wheat. Nature has given the State a beautiful rolling country, a
soil of wonderful fertility, a climate admirably adapted to agriculture
and health, albeit very warm in summer and very cold in winter, a
bountiful provision of mines and forests, and a noble privilege of
rivers. But its greatest good fortune has been the sturdy honesty
and energy of its settlers, from 1846 until now.

Scott County is one of the river counties in the eastern part of
Iowa. It claims to be the most prosperous of Iowa counties, but
very likely Polk or Dubuque, or half a dozen other counties, would
not indorse the claim; and it is not for an Iowan to take sides in an
unseemly manner.

But there is no question that it is one of the wealthiest and most
thriving of the counties. It has all the gifts of nature and of conduct
belonging to the interior, with " the reason firm, the temperate will"
of its own. It has never been swept from its moorings by any
" craze"; it has never had a " boom;" it believes in honest money, in
a moderate use of the good things of life (including wine, spirits,
and malt liquors), in the full payment of debts, and in the protection of individual rights and property. It has a population of
43,164, and has within its borders one city—Davenport—with a
population of 30,000, and several villages. The total recorded real-
estate mortgage debt in force January 1, 1890, was $1,450,355,
making the average for each person $72. The average amount of
debt for each person in the State is $104; and the counties of the State
range in their per capita debt from $36 in Dallas and $49 in Henry
to Osceola's $208 and Woodbury's $258.

A simple arithmetical calculation will show that the Scott County
citizen has more than three times as much property per capita as he
has debt, and this without taking into account the large diminution
in mortgages made by the great crop of 1891. It is not likely that
as much as 20 per cent of the farms are encumbered. The rate of
interest has fallen to 6 and 7 per cent from the 30 to 50 per cent that
used to claw the life out of the old settler.

The Scott County poor-house sheltered on the first day of 1890
45 wretched fugitives from the battle of life. On the first day of
1891 there were 37 men and 5 women; on the first day of 1894 the
number was only increased by one woman; so that whether or no the
hard times pressed heavily on the poor, they did not crowd them

into the poor-house. It is quite safe to compute the number of different people receiving aid from the county during the year as well under 1,000.

It is a charitable county, with a spirit of neighborliness and a Western good humor even in its public benevolence. There is an old women's home established by the beneficence of a woman, the late Mrs. Clarissa C. Cook; and a home for worn-out old farmers of the county, which was given and endowed by Nicholas Fejervary, one of the prominent citizens of the county. Both establishments are carefully and generously conducted, and are provided lavishly with comforts and in many cases with luxuries. The old women and the old men visit their friends at will; and a generous supply of car-tickets on the street railways of the city is distributed. Once, in the old women's home, the question of permitting the inmates to take patent medicines came up; and the medicines were unanimously allowed. "It may shorten their lives," said the chief speaker in their behalf, philosophically; "but they will have enough more comfort taking the stuff while they do live to make up for it!" For the same kindly reason snuff was held not to be contraband; and a veteran old smoker is allowed to smoke her pipe in the safe seclusion of the cellar. An industrial home in the city of Davenport is carried on by a long-established relief society to which all religions and all nationalities contribute both money and the workers' time.

The county and the town, indeed, have rather a perilous reputation for "being good to the poor," which has attracted more attention than the almoners of their bounty desire. Not only the poor within their gates have town and county helped, but almost every cry of distress, be it fire, or water, or wind, or pestilence, or hunger that has appealed to the compassion of the world during the generation since the war, has met with a response from hearts and purses.

To the writer it is a further proof of well-being that the county should be so scantily provided with Populists. Prosperous communities may be Republican or they may be Democratic; but they never are of the party of calamity. It is the unsuccessful men and the communities slipping down hill, that grasp at rainbows.

Much of the solid conservatism of Scott County is due to the large German element. The better class of Germans bring from their own paternal government a passionate love of personal liberty. It is needed in these days of "the new slavery"; when the sanctity of individual rights is flung away like old rags, and promoters of a new hand-made millennium would punish greed, cruelty, and brains with the same Artegal's flail.

Contented we are, as most men. Even the farmer is contented —for a farmer. For even as horse-trading allures the most honest of men into double-dealing, so does dependence on the Lord in the matter of rain and sunshine mysteriously incline a man to gloom. Making this allowance for his profession, the Scott County farmer is cheerful. He has reason. There are few better farms to be found. The land rolls in gentle hills, richly wooded, and threaded by streams where the sleek cattle stand knee-deep, under the willows. As they lift their heads to watch the traveller, he may notice how many Jerseys are among them. Now, the hay-fields shine with a flaxen stubble like a child's head; the corn is tasselling above the drooping green leaves; the oat-fields and the barley-fields are bare; but the great barns are full. Amid the grain-fields are great sweeps of green spikes—the famous Scott County onions, and fields of potatoes; and the hillsides are trellised with vines. There are many orchards; and small fruit does well, as do most vegetables. The onions, melons, and strawberries of the county have a noble repute. The onions are known the world over, we please ourselves with thinking. The strawberries' reputation is circumscribed by their own fragility; but our strawberries, especially those from one long-established farm, are of exceptional size and flavor. Farm land in the county sells for an average price of $45 to $65 an acre—without buildings. With buildings their price is added. Farm-houses are of wood, well weather-boarded and shingled and painted. Immense barns, with their dark-red sides and sloping roofs, give a touch of homely plenty to the landscape. Here and there a windmill noiselessly swings its great blades. There is likely to be a hedge of Lombardy poplars shading the front yard and the well-sweep, and old-fashioned marigolds and sweet-williams thriving close to the rows of onions and tomatoes in the large kitchen-garden. Poor and small is the house that has not its piazza and its window-screens.

What the county needs most is good roads. The dirt highways are in fair order for eight months out of the twelve; during the remaining four they are the cause of discomfort, loss, anger, and profanity. They make the farms lonesome, they prevent the hiring of help for the farmer's wife, they interfere sorely with the marketing of crops, they wear out wagons and horses and men's souls. Yet in spite of his roads the Scott County farmer lives in great comfort.

His daughter has a piano, and his wife a silk gown. The pioneer farmer is disappearing. A few remain among us, rugged old Spartans, unlettered, but full to the brim of a homely and sarcastic shrewdness wrung out of life itself instead of books, weather-beaten and toil-beaten into an outward grimness, but with the kindest hearts in the world. Such a man, but of the heroic mould, was Governor Kirkwood; and a humbler example of the type is " Uncle Zimri Streeter," or " Old Blackhawk," who probably jested more bad bills out of existence than any Iowa legislator. It was he who defeated an exemption law once with a single sentence. " Mr. Speaker," he drawled, in his slow, melancholy voice, " I hope our benevolent friends will not tinker up the law so as to prevent a feller from payin' his debts if he wants to!"

The farmer of to-day is an educated man. He has travelled; he reads the magazines and the papers; and his wife, who is likely to be better educated than he, is beginning timorously to decorate her house. The State University, hampered though it has always been by inevitable poverty, has yet, thanks to the wisdom of its regents, and to a president of remarkable gifts as an executive officer, acquired a brilliant staff of instructors, and has kept in touch with the latest methods of education. There are also more than twenty colleges scattered through Iowa,—a feeble folk many of them but; some of them (especially Iowa College, at Grinnell) conducted by men of ability and strong character; and all of them opening a door into a wider life for the country lads who flock to them. Most of the students have one advantage over students with fuller purses in the famous colleges: they come, they are not sent, and they come with a very eager and persistent desire to learn.

Not long ago, going from one Iowa town to another in the day-coach, where all classes meet, I grew interested in the conversation of two farmers behind me,—so much interested, in fact, that I presently changed my seat to the one behind them in order to secure a view of the speakers. One was an elderly man in black broadcloth rather dusty about the coat-collar. He mopped a strong, brown, kindly face, with a very large white handkerchief. The other's tidy blue coat, russet belt, and pink shirt gave him so sophisticated an air that I assigned him to a city until I heard him refer to " my farm." They began the talk by some valuable statistics (I regret that I should forget them) about horses. The elder man, who had a rich baritone voice with a wide register of inflections, held that there was no profit in raising what he called "scrub stock." He used the current *argot* of the soil, but in an educated sort of way, as if for its picturesque force rather than for lack of more correct and formal phrase. The young man's voice was lighter, but mellow and pleasant, with a distinct Western accent; his grammar was good, and he talked fluently; once he quoted Browning, and the elder said that was sense, and asked who was the poet. To the young man's answer he returned a slow nod. "Yes, I've heard tell of him. Nothing difficult to understand 'bout *that*, is there? I haven't much use for poetry, but my daughter belonged to a club, kind of literary club. She went to the university."

"So did I," said the young man; "I took the course in general science."

"Found it helped you out on the farm, too, didn't you?"

"Oh, my, yes! There is no use talking; a farmer, to make money, now-a-days, needs to be an educated man,—a bit of a scientist and a good deal of a business man."

"That's so," agreed the elder man, emphatically; "a man, to be a farmer, can't know too much. But for a man that does know something and has got horse-sense to the bargain, there's plenty of money left in farming, still."

Then they drifted into politics, and I was minded to admire equally the younger man's knowledge of history, which he had in very good trim, and the homespun sense of the old man, who had learned from his own experience.

They were both married, and they both, in thoroughly American fashion, extolled their wives. One confided that his wife always was nervous when he was away, "travelling," although in general a woman that took everything easy, nursed the whole family through scarlet fever, and he (the husband) never saw her look down-hearted once; and the other sympathized with a recital of *his* wife's never wanting him to drive fast horses. They had never met in the flesh before, but during the hour I sat behind them they cemented a solid acquaintance. Yet for all their artless *bonhomie*, I do not envy the rogue who shall presume on it.

The young man was a Republican, and the old man a Democrat; but by uniting in abuse of the Populists they skimmed safely over the ice. Both were "honest-money men," as they called themselves; both believed in a moderate relaxation of the tariff; and both admired him whom with real if not outward respect they named "Old Man

14

Cleveland." Why the one should be a Democrat and the other a Republican I cannot say, except as the fat monk who vainly starved himself said to the lean monk who ate to sad satiety with as little advantage to his state, "It was the will of God!"

These good fellows came from the interior. So much the better for the interior, thought I; but we have their like on many a Scott County farm. In the interior the farmer has a far harder life than with us; because the farmer of the far Western counties has not yet emerged from the pioneer stage. The farmer of Scott County is what the farmer on myriads of homesteads, farther West, will be in another generation. At the old settlers' reunions they tell of farmers making their own plough-beams and handles, and of men of substance scouring the country to raise twenty-five cents needed to take a letter out of the post-office. Garland has described these dramas of toil and struggle, to the life; and he, better than any one, has painted the eternal and varying beauty encompassing the toilers. But it should be remembered that he is painting the lives of the first husbandmen of the soil,—the pioneers, the men who have literally to dig their farms out of the earth. Their "ferocious" toil gives place to a gentler pastoral as the country becomes developed.

Three-fourths of the population of Scott County are not rural, but urban, belonging to the 30,000 Davenport residents, not counting the odd thousand in Le Claire and the hundreds in the smaller villages that dot the whole country at small intervals.

Davenport is situated picturesquely on the Mississippi, where the river widens and flows about the island of Rock Island. Opposite the town, on the Illinois side of the river, are the pretty cities of Moline and Rock Island. The three towns are a centre of more than 60,000 people, and, as Davenport is the largest, her accessible population is reflected in the large business done by her banks as well as in her handsome shops and her daily journals.

Once the country all about the city was the resort of innumerable flocks of grouse and ducks. Boys would go out before breakfast and come back with a brace of prairie-chicken at their belts. But now—

"They drum no more, those splendid springtime pickets;
    The sweep of share and sickle has thrust them from the hills:
They have scattered from the meadow, like partridge in the thickets—
    They have perished from the sportsman who kills and kills and kills!"

The meadows where they used to beat their *reveillé* are turned into gardens, and their only shelter now would be among the potato or melon vines.´ Davenport is become a manufacturing town,—not enough of one yet, however, to stain the skies. The Davenporters are accustomed to say that in no town of its size are there handsomer shops, solider banks, or more contented and prosperous working-people. The manufactories are not on so large a scale as the great works in Moline, but are more diversified. They include lumber, agricultural implements, flour-mills, glucose, metal wheels, sashes and blinds, barrels, foundries, pumps, and some smaller industries. The town streets are carved through the bluffs, and their sticky soil is paved with brick or macadamized. Trees are everywhere,—on the boulevards which skirt the humblest streets; shading beautiful lawns or tiny yards and flower-beds; growing in the little parks that make the children's playgrounds,—maples, elms, birches, and oaks: it would seem as if every householder in town, and his father before him, must have planted them! It is the wholesome aim of the Western architect to build detached houses; and in the Western towns every house of any pretensions has its own wide lawn and its own trees. The poorest cottages in Davenport, if they are owned by the dwellers, are sure to have green grass around them and a garden in the rear. And the wee lawns will be kept as daintily as the larger ones. Window gardens prosper, and the Virginia-creeper stipples the church walls with green in summer and the vividest scarlet in autumn. Many towns have costlier mansions; but no Western town of my knowledge has such a universal trim smartness. In summer, when the lawns are shaven and the windows brave with gardenias and geraniums and every graceful, creeping, green vine, and the fresh paint helps the old houses to a new youth, the town is like a pretty woman in a clean print gown, with a flower in her belt.

There are not many great fortunes in the town, and no fortune swollen in a day; the gentry of the place are unassuming people who read more than the people of great cities, who travel a great deal (not always to Europe), who give many small companies among themselves, and only give one or two balls in a lifetime—on great occasions, such as the coming out of a daughter or the marriage of a son. The younger men and women study their apparel and would pass muster in any of the cities; but the older and richer a man grows the more he is likely to evolve his own ideas of comfort in his clothes. The town has many clubs of all kinds. The women have literary clubs. The men have the usual club, with rather a plainer home and a better cook and wine-cellar than such clubs have in the

smaller cities. There is a shooting-club to which most of the prominent citizens belong, whether they shoot or not; and an outing-club,
which has beautiful grounds and a pretty club-house, and is trying
to teach the Davenporters to bowl on the green. Thanks to the
60,000 people within range of the bill-poster's brush, there are
amusements of a good class during the winter; and not only the
richer people, but most of the wide circle known as "well-to-do," go
to Chicago if any peculiar dramatic or musical attraction appear. It
is a town (like all Iowa towns) where the personal qualities have
more to say about the individual's position than either money or
family. Yet, more than in many Western towns, family is regarded,
and certain decayed gentle-people live in a posthumous grandeur and
respect. Being so small a town, all circles touch. Employers know
their men, and the men have a more familiar acquaintance with their
employers than is possible in the immense establishments of the cities.

Mr. Howells' traveller from Altruria, before he shakes the dust
of our country from his feet and goes away to weep over us, should
come for a brief space to a Western town. There he might find
manufacturers who voluntarily advance wages, and workingmen who
voluntarily work over-time. In fact, the place for a workingman
who wishes to live in peace and rise in the social scale is not in the
cities, but in the small towns. The Iowa workman's condition is
being investigated with much care and judgment by the present
labor-commissioner, Mr. O'Bleness. He has sent out reports of a
hundred and fifty circular letters sent to workingmen asking them in
regard to their earnings, their membership in labor unions, their
savings, and their ownership of their homes. I have the last two
reports before me. They deal with a hundred men. The first fifty
reported an average annual wage-income of $624. The wages ran from
$26.87, received weekly by locomotive engineers, to the $3 of a clerk.
Twenty-three of the fifty owned their homes, only six having any
encumbrance on them. The average mortgage was $360. The
average monthly rental was $9.45, and the average number of rooms
occupied by each family was five. Eighteen reported savings, averaging $221.72 during the year. This first fifty lived in the larger
towns; the second fifty had neither as high wages nor as high rent
to pay. They averaged $517.72 wages yearly, and paid an average
rent of $5.97. The average number of rooms occupied was the
same. In the latter fifty the rooms ranged from ten to two.
Twenty-one owned their homes. Ten had mortgages on them. Two

of the homes had ten rooms each. Sixteen reported savings averaging $194.43. Two men had saved $400 each,—a fireman and a butter-maker. A stationary engineer on $6 a week, with a wife and family, somehow pinched $100 out of his tiny income. Twenty-seven of the first, and fourteen of the second fifty, belonged to labor organizations. Those who did not belong, and condemned them (which some did, roundly), generally did so on account of their strike feature. A farm laborer expressed the common feeling concisely: he did not join "because," said he, "I think they cause men to lose good jobs quite often."

Studying these reports, one is struck by two features in the evident high average of the condition of the writers, both in intelligence and comfort, and the exceeding cheapness of the living in Iowa towns and villages, which have made this possible in spite of wages which in some cases would scare a Pullman striker. After all, Micawber is a safer guide for the workingman than Marx; and the waiting philosopher's dictum that it is the sum saved, and not the sum received, that counts, is surer than the iron law of wages.

Davenport is known in labor circles as "the scab town." I spoke of the nickname once to some mechanics at work on a house. It was during the great strike, at the critical moment when Mr. Sovereign had advised the Knights of Labor to lay aside their tools and meditate.

"You have not struck, I see," said I. "Struck!" repeated a painter who was oiling woodwork with a skilful hand. "I guess it would be like hunting a needle in a haystack to find a man who has struck in this town. We ain't that kind of fools!" I ventured the remark that I had heard there were not many union men in town; it was called the "scab town." The men laughed. "I guess that's right," said a carpenter; "but all the same there's not a town in the country where more workingmen own their homes, or where there's more workingmen's money in the savings-bank or invested in shares in factories." "Now you're talking," chimed in the painter; "nor there ain't a town where there's a kindlier feeling between employers and their men,—no, sir!"

There is one distinct advantage that the provincial workingman enjoys; he counts for more as an individual. Besides the physical helps of better air and cheaper living, he has the indefinite but steady working help of respect from the other classes. The workingman in the city is flattered by the politicians and the newspapers; but he is not respected. In the country, John Smithers, the best foreman

in the shop, is consulted by the head of the firm, has his wages paid
when he is ill, knows every one on his street, and is asked to run for
alderman, not as a labor candidate, but as the best man of his party.
In the provinces, the workingman is a man and a citizen before he is
a workingman; in the cities he is fast growing to be a workingman,
not only first, but last.

I recall an alderman, a worthy man who had won a little competency with his own hard hands. When he was nominated, he rose
in his working-clothes and cast a friendly glance over the room.
"Well, boys," he said, "you know me. I ha'n't the eddication to
make a grand speech, and ye've heard that little cretur over there"
(contemptuous wave at an opponent) "say I cudn't write me own
name widout helpin'. Maybe I can, and maybe I cannot; but wan
thing I *can* do; if you elict me, I can git Rock Island Street put into
shape so there won't no more tames stick there!" He was elected.

A typical workingman of our Western town often goes by my
window. He is a carpenter who has become in a modest way a mas-
ter-builder. He does not look to be thirty years old, but he' has
already bought him a house, with a yard and a garden and a little
barn where he keeps his horse. Before I knew him I was sure that
he had plenty of work, he always walked with such a light, swinging
step and showed his white teeth so cheerfully at the children that he
met. After a while I grew to know him, and to fall into desultory
talks with him about the weather, the new house on the corner, and
finally the great strike. From his talk I soon perceived that he not
only read the papers and the magazines, but more serious works;
and, as is common with the workingman when he does read, his
reading was not the usual skimming, but serious study. He had
forged out for himself an opinion, sometimes not in the least that
which his writer would have presented to him for the mere glance of
an eye, but in every case a careful, thoughtful judgment, distinguished generally for that quality we in the West term "horse-sense."
"No," said he, "I never joined a union; I never was willing to
chase a man out of a job just because he didn't belong to a union;
and I never was willing to farm out my liberty to any set of talkers,
either. I believe that doing a good job will get a man better wages
and keep them for him better than any union on earth. And sometimes I think the employers would treat the men better if they
weren't for ever and ever being riled up by walking-delegates and
committees. First, these fellers stir up the men to think they are

being awfully abused, and then they mad the employers, who are losing money (which doesn't put a man in good temper anyhow), until they get their backs up, and then there's a strike. I think it would be better if employers would explain things more to the men,—just talk to them as man to man. American workmen ain't unreasonable, and when they have confidence in a man they'll take a pretty stiff reduction and bear it, particularly if he promises them to put wages back as soon as business will justify him. I tell you it *pays* an employer to treat his men fair and square. There isn't a class of people in the world that will go through more and be truer to a man they believe in than the workingman; and there are some employers right in this town have found that out!"

Some day, if he lives, this young mechanic will have a number of employees of his own; he will be a contractor; he will accumulate property; he may represent us in the legislature. Well, we shall be safe in his hands.

The workingman's best opportunity in the provinces is this fluidity of conditions. Not only does it make an Arabian Nights' elevation possible to the poorest; it has a farther-reaching, more subtly-pervasive power: it mingles all classes together, and creates that indescribable atmosphere of human friendliness which is the deepest spiritual charm of the West. An intimate acquaintance with less-favored lives is the surest cement of society; perhaps that is why its structure stands firmest in the quiet Western provinces. For this open-handed willingness to touch other lots and "help those who cannot help again," this feeling that nothing human is foreign to any man or woman, and the divine hopefulness that accompanies it, are as Western as our prairies and our sky.

And that is why we of the West, in spite of all her crude and violent faults (so patiently and perspicuously explained to us by our true friends of the East), love her and believe in her. The little segment of the West that I have tried to describe is not in Altruria; it is in Iowa, and it is quite content with its geography. It is founded on the rights of the individual rather than those of the community; it has no sympathy with socialistic dreams; it is just a Western town of honest, hard-working, kindly, decently selfish men and women who are not working for the golden age of brotherhood, but to provide for their families; yet nowhere do I know of any place where there is less friction between the classes, or where all classes help each other more along our rough and checkered road.   OCTAVE THANET.

THE SIGNIFICANCE OF THE JAPAN–CHINA WAR.

JAPAN has entered upon the present war with China with the negative purpose of protecting her own interests in particular, and of preserving the general and permanent peace in the East. But the war really has a wider significance,—it is a struggle between progress and stagnation. Japan's success means the extension of modern civilization into Corea, and the opening of her wealth to the world. China's success, on the other hand, means the continuance of Corean incapacity; and this, sooner or later, is likely to yield to Russian despotism.

Those who are not familiar with recent diplomacy in the East, and depend on the daily dispatches, may be at a loss to know the real cause and the significance of the present crisis. As most of the dispatches come through Chinese and English hands, they are sometimes grossly distorted. Both in English and American papers I find arguments to show that Japan is wantonly disturbing the peace in the interest of national ambition. I freely admit that Japan has an ambition to become the leading power in the East, and to be classed among the great nations of the world. Indeed, because of the impulse of this ambition, she has made progressive strides during the last thirty years. But it is a gross mistake to infer that Japan has wantonly precipitated the present trouble. Ever since Japan came into close contact with foreign countries, her established policy has been to elevate her position only through peaceful means, such as the introduction of railway, telegraphic, and postal systems; the establishment of national compulsory education and competitive examinations for the civil service; the revision of the entire fiscal and monetary system; the radical improvement of the police and jail systems; the enactment of new and enlightened criminal and civil laws; the adoption of new methods of judicial procedure; the reconstruction of local government; the promulgation of a written constitution, and the substitution of a parliamentary government for the absolute monarchical government. As to the foreign relations, all political parties in Japan have had it in their creed to " endeavor to strengthen the commercial relations with foreign countries, and to avoid diplomatic complications as much as possible."

It is only since the ever-increasing pressure of the territorial aggrandizement of the European powers was keenly felt that Japan began to strengthen her military equipment: it is only since the collision between Russia and England began to affect the vital in-terests of Japan that she adopted a definite foreign policy.　To understand this policy, we must glance at the recent history of in-ternational relations in the East.

During the last forty years the seat of the Eastern question has been constantly moving from the West to the East: from Eastern

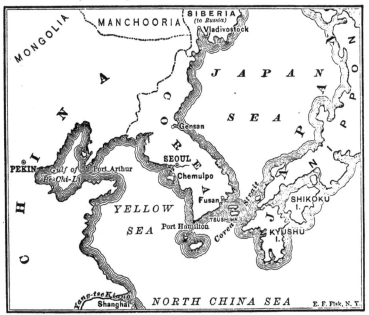

Europe to Central Asia, thence to Eastern Asia and the North Pacific. Russia in 1858 succeeded in obtaining from China the cession of eastern Siberia, with Vladivostock as her port on the Pacific.　This gave Russia an outpost for undermining British interests in the South China Sea.　Thus the North Pacific became the seat of the struggle between England and Russia; and Russia has ever since been strength-ening the defences at Vladivostock with all possible speed.　The build-ing of the famous Trans-Siberian railway is part of the grand scheme of defence.　Russian activity does not, however, stop here; on the con-trary, she is acting toward Corea in an ever-increasingly aggressive spirit, her immediate desire being to get·a better seaport than Vladi-vostock, which is ice-bound for weeks every winter, and she is further trying to get out to the Yellow Sea through Manchooria and Mongolia.

Now let us look at the English side. Previous to this period England had been extending her interests in South China at the expense of China. But now Russian encroachments upon British interests, from both Central Asia and the North Pacific, have caused England to perceive the necessity of forming an alliance with China. Sir Charles Dilke, the author of " Problems of Greater Britain," says:

"There can be no doubt that an alliance between England and China in Central Asia is a natural result of the present state of things. Russia and China have 4,000 miles of common frontier, and England and China desire to maintain the *status quo*, and are able to strike powerful blows for its maintenance. China will have for some years to come a considerable superiority over Russia at certain points upon the frontier, and could take offensive action against Russia more easily than either Great Britain or Afghanistan. . . . The alliance of China, which is very important in a general scheme of imperial defence, has, however, little bearing upon this special problem. . . . On the other hand, in the policy of attacking Russia on the Pacific, which for some years to come, until her means of communication are complete, will be the most effective way of meeting an attack by her on us, the Chinese alliance would be of moment and would paralyze the Russian advance."

Thus we easily see the importance for English interests of the Anglo-Chinese alliance; it lies not only in the fact that by this arrangement England secured a strong ally for the protection of her South-China trade against the Russian attack, and for the prevention of the Russian inroads through Manchooria and Mongolia, but also and chiefly in the fact that by reason of this alliance England can, in the event of war with Russia, deal a heavy blow upon Russia at Vladivo-stock. Notwithstanding Russia's strenuous efforts to strengthen her position on the Pacific, the defence of Vladivostock is yet far from being complete. Several years must elapse before the great Siberian railway is completed. It is therefore evident that Russia could not single-handed withstand the attack of the combined Anglo-Chinese fleets. But as long as Russia regards Vladivostock as an essential portion of her empire, and one from which the future descent upon the Pacific is to be made, she must fight to the bitter end to keep that port. Therefore the policy of attacking Russia at Vladivostock would be as effective in paralyzing the Russian advance in Central Asia as the attack made by England in the Crimea. Such have been until lately the relations between England, Russia, and China.

In view of this situation great was the surprise when it appeared this year that a Russo-Chinese *entente* had been entered into.   This much is known about the *entente*, that China has tacitly acquiesced in Russia's accepting a port on the northern coast of Corea, as a coal-ing-station, on condition that the Russian troops should be removed from a portion of the Pamirs over which China claims territorial sovereignty.   It is not improbable that this secret understanding may go further and lead to an entire change of the balance of power in Central Asia and the Pacific.   Its immediate result, however, is the precipitation of the collision of the British and Russian interests in the Pacific.   It compels England to push further her policy of attack-ing Russia from the Pacific before the Siberian railway is completed. The feasibility of this policy depends, in the absence of the Chinese alliance, upon the success of England in securing a seaport in Corea within reach of Vladivostock as a base of operations.   It was with this in view that England, in 1885, occupied Port Hamilton, on the southern coast of Corea, during the threatened breach with Russia on the Murghab question.   England abandoned it only because the clearest possible understanding was reached that China would continue to be friendly to England and withstand with her the Russian en-croachments.   Should the necessity again occur, England would have no hesitation in seizing any seaport on which she could lay her hands,— a necessity now arising in view of the recent Russo-Chinese *entente*. Thus we see that Central Asia and the North Pacific are closely con-nected strategically, and in case of a collision between Russia and England the Japan Sea would become a battle-field for the fleets of these rival powers and their allies.   Such a conflict would inflict an immense amount of damage on the combatants and an injury upon the whole world.   But the countries which would suffer most are Japan and Corea, both of which lie between the combatants.

It therefore became an imperative necessity for Japan to adopt a definite policy to meet the impending crisis.   Some among her leaders argued that Japan could most advantageously join the Anglo-Chinese alliance; while others proposed that Japan should form a triple alliance with Russia and France.   But either course is not with-out serious drawbacks.   Therefore, after deliberate consideration, Japan reached the conclusion that in the present state of affairs she ought to remain aloof from any alliance, but do her utmost to pre-vent an outbreak between Russia and England on the Pacific.   To make this policy effective, Japan found it absolutely necessary in the first place to have an army and navy powerful enough to make her voice a casting-vote between the contending parties; and, in the second place, to secure Corea's independence against the encroachments of any power.   If you examine the map of the East, you will easily see that Japan and Corea hold the key of the North China Sea and the Japan Sea respectively, in Tsushima and Fusan.   If they are fortified strongly, the Japan Sea becomes impregnable from any southern attack.   Port Hamilton, even if occupied again by the British, would be rendered useless as an offensive station for the attack at Vladivostock.   In like manner the Russian fleets would not be able to get out to the China Sea.   From the strategical point of view, Tsushima and Fusan can be compared with Constantinople in the Mediterranean, and Corea itself to Turkey or the Balkan Peninsula. The importance of their situation would be greatly increased by the completion of the Siberian railway.

Under these circumstances Japan has spared no effort to fortify the island of Tsushima.   It is now placed in direct communication with the nearest Japanese naval station, and also with the nearest military land station.   At the same time Japan has been doing her best to increase her naval and military forces.   Her navy is already strong enough to inflict a heavy blow on any power in the Pacific, perhaps· of such severity as to make her voice the casting-vote in the Pacific question.   In this manner she would be able to keep the gate of the Japan Sea shut to both English and Russians as long as Corea maintains her independence and Fusan remains unoccupied by either of them.

But how about Corean independence?   Is Corea strong enough to resist an unlawful seizure of Fusan or any other important port by any foreign power?   No.   About the helplessness and incapacity of the government enough is known.   If left alone Corea will before long fall into the hands of some aggressive foreign power,—a fate which Japan can positively not allow.

If once Corea, or even the port of Fusan, should fall into the hands of Russia or England, Japan's situation in the Pacific would at once become precarious.   Not only would the Japan Sea be turned into a battle-field of the rival powers, in the event of an outbreak between England and Russia, but also the defence of Tsushima Island against the aggressive hand of either Russia or England would become eminently difficult; for the distance between Tsushima and Fusan is less than fifty miles, and the power which seized one of them would naturally try to occupy the other, which forms with it the gate of the

Japan Sea. Japan, therefore, found it imperatively necessary to lend her support to Corea to secure the latter's independence.

Besides these considerations of international interest, however, Japan has an old historical relation with Corea which imposes upon her certain moral obligations to lend her support to Corea. It is not necessary here to refer to events of far-off ages, such as the importa-tion of the Corean civilization into Japan. It is sufficient for the present purpose to recall what Japan has done for Corea in compara-tively recent years. It was Japan that first opened the Hermit King-dom to the beneficent influences of modern civilization: it was Japan that introduced Corea to the world as an independent State. Such being the case, it is the duty of Japan to help the little kingdom to secure its independence and to grow in prosperity and power.

Under these circumstances it is not at all surprising that Japan adopted a positive policy for the maintenance of Corean indepen-dence. To carry out this policy two measures must be taken: in the first place, internal affairs in Corea must be thoroughly reformed so that she can develop her resources for self-protection; and in the second place her independence must be guaranteed by the powers in-terested. But the latter measure is supplementary to the former, and must go together with it. Of the states concerned in Corea, Japan and China have the largest interests,—interests, too, that are almost identical. It is therefore to the advantage of China as well as of Japan that the two countries should co-operate in guaranteeing Corea's independence without drawing in any third power. If an interna-tional device like a congress of nations, including other powers than China and Japan, is to be called at all to guarantee Corea's indepen-dence, it must be resorted to only as the last means.

In pursuance of the policy defined above, Japan has never wavered during the last twenty-five years. Why, then, is not a joint control of Corean affairs feasible? Is not China ready to act harmoniously with Japan? Or, if co-operation is impossible, cannot China alone be trusted to supervise Corean affairs in the joint interest of China and Japan? The answer is that China cannot be trusted, as bitter expe-rience has shown to the Japanese in the past ten years.

What is that experience? Since 1876, commerce between Corea and Japan has steadily increased until Japan became the principal commercial country represented in Corea, and the number of Japanese residents became larger than that of the citizens of all other countries put together. Naturally the Japanese influences gradually increased, and several schemes of reform and improvement have been introduced and wrought out. Meanwhile, this state of things aroused China's jealousy and suspicion to the utmost. She spared no efforts to obstruct and defeat all the schemes of reform and improvement introduced through Japanese influences. In spite of the fact that Corea's independence had been recognized by foreign powers, and China herself has on two occasions explicitly disavowed any responsibility for matters concerning the Corean government, first to the French and secondly to the Americans, China has always tried to revive her worn-out sovereignty over Corea.

Thus the conflict between two rival influences went on until it culminated in the cruel and terrible *coups d'état* of 1882 and 1884. On each occasion the Japanese Legation in Seoul, the capital of Corea, was burned, and the Japanese representative was obliged to flee for his life. If Japan wished to protect her interests at the point of the bayonet she had grounds for doing so. But the desire to keep on good terms with China induced her to settle the matter amicably. The trouble, therefore, was eventually settled in the Tien-Tsin convention of 1885 between Li Hung Chang and Count Ito, who was then the Japanese ambassador and is now prime minister. The convention was a distinct disavowal on the part of China of any suzerain rights over Corea, and a mutual acknowledgment by both countries that neither should interfere by force of arms in the affairs of Corea without notifying the other. In other words, this convention established a concurrent negative guarantee of Corean independence.

In fact, however, this convention had no moral weight in restricting the dealings of China with the Corean government. China managed to station her soldiers in Seoul, as before, disguised as merchants. She exercised her alleged suzerainty over Corea without showing any sense of responsibility. Japan tried in vain to keep on good terms with China and to get China's concurrence in reforming Corea. Almost all schemes inaugurated through Japanese influence had to be abandoned. The first post-office on the modern plan, which was established at Seoul in 1884, was destroyed, it is said, by people incited by Chinese agents. The new mint, which was erected in 1889 for the purpose of reforming the Corean currency, was shut up soon afterward, owing to the active opposition of China. Time and again legitimate commerce has been deliberately interrupted, entailing a large loss, particularly upon Japanese merchants. What is worse, China secretly exercised practical suzerainty over the Corean kingdom.

With the development of foreign trade and foreign intercourse, the Corean spirit of independence might have grown, but Chinese domineering completely checked such growth.   China interferes unscrupulously in Corean domestic affairs, but she is irresponsible.   The Coreans, therefore, feel only the weight of China's hand without receiving its support.   The only administrative privileges they enjoy with some measure of freedom are those of extortion and peculation. In this way a kingdom with a fertile soil, a temperate climate, abundant mineral resources, and above all a most advantageous geographical position, remains in an utterly impoverished condition, and, with an area of 79,000 square miles and a population of 11,000,000, is made incapable of continuing its own existence.

In all this, China is directly playing into Russian hands; for this helplessness is exactly what Russia wants.   Russia has long since viewed Corea as an apple ripening to its fall, and China as a gardener not strong enough to guard it or to pick it up; and Russia saw the opportunity and approached Corea with hidden hands.   Ever since the opening of Corea, her foreign trade has been carried on in three open ports,—Fusan, Chemulpo, and Gensan; but in 1886, two years after the *coup d'état* above referred to, Russia succeeded in persuading the Corean government to open a market for overland trade.   Thus was opened the first door for the customary " sapping" policy of Russia, which had so well succeeded previously in Eastern Europe and Central Asia.   And mark that the Corean representative in this negotiation was a German by birth, and was made the adviser of the Corean government for foreign affairs by the influence of Li Hung Chang!

How, then, under these circumstances, can Japan recognize, contrary to her long-standing policy, the Chinese claim of suzerainty over Corea and entrust the guardianship of Corea in China's hands alone? The immediate cause of the present crisis in the East is an attempt on the part of China to assume just such a function as her prerogative. To this we now turn.

Since 1884, as we saw, China's influence in Corea has rapidly increased, while the influence of Japan has correspondingly diminished.   China has long been looking for an opportunity to thwart completely the policy of Japan, and once for all to place Corea in a definite relationship of dependency toward herself.   Finally, this opportunity presented itself. [1]   The Corean people, who have been for a long time groaning under the extortion and maladministration of the officials, were in the spring of this year driven to desperation.   A number of men who called themselves the Tong Hak party rose in arms. The insurrection increased in size and strength so rapidly that the government troops were repeatedly defeated. Greatly alarmed by this, the pro-Chinese party, which then had the control of the government, applied for Chinese assistance. It is believed that it was through the instigation of the Chinese Resident, Yuan, that the Corean government took this course. The request was immediately responded to, and a body of Chinese troops embarked for Corea. But China did not give any notice of her intention to dispatch troops to Corea until the first batch had actually landed there.

This is a plain breach of the spirit, if not of the letter, of the Tien-Tsin treaty, for the treaty, in order to be effective, must be understood to require a previous—not a subsequent—notice of the dispatch of troops into Corea. Japan considered it useless to complain seriously against such a matter. The treaty itself had long since become a dead letter. It had no moral weight in restricting the crafty dealings of the Chinese government. As soon as the Japanese government received the notice from China, it sent an immediate answer that it would also send troops for the protection of Japanese subjects and interests, deeming it necessary and having the privilege of doing so. It is not improbable that the Chinese viceroy, who remembered that the Japanese government did not send any troops to Corea on a similar occasion in 1884, supposed that it would be less able on this occasion to send any considerable body of soldiers, on account of the constant struggles of internal Japanese politics. Perturbed by the unexpected result, however, the viceroy resorted to his customary diplomacy. A series of declarations that a large Chinese force had left China for Corea was made on the one hand; on the other a request was made for the withdrawal of the Japanese troops.

At this point the Japan government declined China's request, and at the same time made a proposal for united action with the object of effecting thorough reforms in Corea, saying:

"On account of its geographical situation, the ever-increasing disorders in the Corean kingdom materially affect the vital interests of both China and Japan, and threaten to create a dangerous crisis; therefore Japan proposes, in concert with China, to persuade Corea to introduce thorough reforms in her internal government, so that all danger of future disorders may be avoided; and, in thus acting, Japan's object is purely to promote the independence of Corea and maintain peace in the East."

This expedient furnished the only chance of an amicable and satisfactory settlement of the Corean question. But China positively rejected this proposal, and at the same time demanded the withdrawal of the Japanese troops simultaneously with those of China, on the ground that the insurrection had been quieted.

The presence of the Chinese and Japanese forces in Corea might have quieted the insurrection for a while. But unless radical steps were taken to remove the existing causes, similar disturbances would perpetually recur with all their international contingencies. The simultaneous withdrawal of the troops meant by no means the re-moval of the existing causes, but merely the prolongation of their existence. China's secret domineering would, as ever, crush inde-pendent aspirations. China's corrupt influence would check forever the growth of progressive tendencies. The extortion and maladminis-tration of local officers would prevail as before. The intrigues of fac-tions would threaten, as ever, to involve resort to alien interference.

The history of the ten years since the Tien-Tsin convention conclusively proves the futility of a concurrent negative guarantee of Corean independence. The only effective method of securing Corean independence is the immediate adoption of the policy of posi-tive guarantee. But China having positively declined to take any concerted action for that purpose, Japan at once decided on its sole responsibility to undertake the task of placing Corean affairs once for all upon a basis consistent with the programme of independent de-velopment. Japan immediately approached the Corean government and recommended the adoption of internal reforms, such as the complete reorganization of the civil service and the financial and police systems, the remodelling or rather the establishment of an army and navy, the introduction of means of communication, and the like. The Corean government showed an inclination to accept the proposal. If China had then stopped all further attempts to block Japan's course in Corea, the dispute would have been checked and the present crisis might have been avoided. But of course such acquiescence meant to China an imposition upon herself of a certain measure of self-efface-ment in Corea. China would not suffer this. She then solicited the mediation of foreign ministers. But in the presence of the fact that China had positively refused concerted action, and of the fact that the Chinese Resident and Commander in Corea still continued to declare Corea a dependency of China, Japan naturally shrank from accepting any premature though kindly meant mediation of third powers. At the same time Japan is not utterly insensible to the urgent desire of all the Western powers for peace. She would have agreed to a com-

15

promise, if there were any fair means by which her original policy toward Corea could be carried out in substance. Negotiation followed negotiation until the suspense was broken by China's resumption of a menacing attitude.

In accordance with the methods of Chinese diplomacy, China had been collecting a considerable army, in order to enforce by intimidation her demand for the withdrawal of Japanese troops. She now made a second and peremptory demand that Japan should withdraw her army and fleet from Corea by July 20. Failing in this, it was announced that China would send her force at once by land and sea. To this ultimatum Japan replied that, since all the leading Western powers were urgent for peace, she would accede to the demand of China in substance, if the latter would promise to enter into a treaty negotiation with Japan for the satisfactory settlement of the Corean affair; but that, pending an amicable settlement, she would consider an advance of China's fleet as an act of war.

At the same time the Corean government, at the instigation of China, changed its front on the question of reform and refused to accept the proposal of the Japanese government; although the king himself was inclined to accept it. Then followed the skirmish at Seoul, the firing by the Corean soldiers upon the Japanese garrison, and the war was begun. This was on the 23d of July. What has since happened is known to all.

Such are the causes and the situation of the present crisis in the East. Such is the policy of Japan. It has been alleged that the Japanese government has, to some extent, made use of the opportunity to distract the attention of her own discontented political parties. But nothing can be more erroneous than to imagine that this is the cause of the present war. The Japanese government is honestly executing the will of the nation. If circumstances require, Japan may, for a considerable length of time, station her troops in Corea as a garrison. But it is none the less erroneous to imagine that Japan secretly harbors any intention of annexing Corea. Not only her sense of honor, but the strongest considerations of interest, forbid such action. The question at issue is solely whether the national life of Corea shall be allowed to continue in independence and progress.

Indeed, Japan's primary object is not to fight China, but to secure Corean independence. Therefore, if China in the future, either as the result of her own reflections or at the instance of Western powers, gives up further endeavor to circumvent Japan's policy in

Corea, and offers to take concurrent action with Japan in giving a positive guarantee of Corean independence, Japan will be only too glad at any time to give up a burdensome warfare.

It has been supposed by some that the Japanese government has made use of the present trouble in order to divert the attention of the discontented party chiefs from domestic problems.   But nothing can be more erroneous.   There is another erroneous notion: that the " veneer of civilization" which Japan has put on " cannot withstand the friction of war"; that " if Japan is successful in the present war, the consequences will be important, not only in checking her republican development, but in seriously complicating her foreign relations"; that while Japan has been busy in her arduous task of assimilation and development of modern ideas, " there has been always on the part of the Western nations a half-amused feeling that it was all a pretty farce." These apprehensions arise from the Western distrust of the solidity and sincerity of the rapid progress made by Japan during the last thirty years,—a distrust resting on the erroneous assumption that Japan has attempted to make a sudden bound from a state of semi-civilization to one of complete civilization.   Let me try in a few words to disprove this erroneous assumption.

Though for hundreds of years Japan remained practically in seclusion, and her civilization naturally developed slowly and in her own way, yet she was all this time steadily improving in the conditions of her national life, her intellectual and social refinement,—above all in the development of the artistic talent of the people and in preparing herself for the immediate adoption of any new idea or system with which she might come in contact.   There was not wanting even a political training.   Though the people were subject to the feudal sway for centuries, yet their political instinct was allowed to develop itself under a peculiar system of local government.   It was this social culture and this political training which enabled the Japanese to perceive clearly the opportunity to accomplish the great task of national reconstruction in 1868.   As to the solidity and sincerity of the changes wrought, history again bears testimony.   There is no possibility of a " reversion to barbarism," however high the war fever may run.   Although this war, if successful, may prolong for a short while the official life of the present clan government, it is utterly unwarrantable to say that " it will check the republican development" of the country.

MICHITARO HISA.

TEACHING GREEK AS A LIVING LANGUAGE.

THERE can be no doubt that the study of the classic languages, and of Greek more especially, is indispensable to the formation of a truly cultured mind. If, therefore, it be admitted that the tuition of Greek ought to continue to form part of the curriculum of a liberal education, then the consideration of the mode of teaching and the manner of pronouncing that language is a matter of primary importance. The reason both of the efforts to suppress the study of Greek, and of the blessed contentment with the so-called "ancient pronunciation," is to be sought in the prevailing fallacy that it is a "dead language." This notion is so deeply rooted in the minds even of students of Greek, that it will appear at first a paradox to maintain the contrary. It will nevertheless be my purpose to examine in the following pages the several questions thus raised; and I hope to be able to produce such evidence as will supply light sufficient for their satisfactory solution.

And first, with regard to the benefit and utility of the study of Greek, the whole question turns, of course, upon the condition in life for which a youth is being prepared. If only instruction is being aimed at,—namely, the acquisition of a certain amount of information calculated to equip simply a bread-winner,—it would be useless to waste his time upon the study of the classic tongues. By the same process of reasoning, Euclid, algebra, and, for the matter of that, gymnastics also, should be eliminated from the course of studies of those who are not likely to find such branches of training immediately productive of dollars in the careers which they intend to follow. But I maintain unhesitatingly that no truly liberal education is possible without the study of Greek. It is impossible to imagine a polished gentleman devoid of knowledge of it.

This is not a new "fad." It is an incontrovertible fact, co-existent and co-extensive with Western civilization. The Romans sought by every means to encourage the prevalence of Latin over their Grecian and Eastern conquests. But the Greek language, by virtue of its inherent superiority, not only maintained its own, but made a triumphal entry into Rome itself, and cast its magic spell upon the city to such an extent that no Roman was deemed to have received a befitting education unless he knew Greek. And Cato, after combating this invasion during the better part of his life, found himself compelled to learn Greek during his old age. The benefits of this tendency were soon made manifest; for it was only through Greek that Latin literature was enabled to rise into eminence. During the Renaissance the study of Greek literature was the main factor in the intellectual awakening of the Western world; and it is the result of the accumulated experience of many centuries, which has maintained Greek to this day as the corner-stone of all academic training.

At the same time, there were never wanting those who expressed a self-satisfied contempt for a knowledge which they did not possess. This attitude of mind is well expressed in the tirade attributed, in the "Vicar of Wakefield," to the Principal of the University of Louvain, who is made to say:—

"You see me, young man; I never learned Greek, and I don't find I ever missed it. I have had a doctor's cap and gown without Greek; I have 10,000 florins a year without Greek; I eat heartily without Greek; and in short, as I don't know Greek, I don't believe there is any good in it."

But the answer is manifest. Academic training is an end in itself, not a mere preparation for a trade or profession. As Professor S. H. Butcher [1] has pithily said:—

"Its aim is not to turn out doctors, clergy, lawyers, merchants; but men—and now women also—with thoroughly trained minds, minds fortified and enlarged by different discipline, and fitted, not for this or that profession, but for the conduct of life."

The study of Greek is not only a study of language, or of poetry, or of philosophy, or of art; but a study of the spirit which, in ancient Greece, animated all those various expressions of intellectual life, and produced the highest form of intellectual development ever witnessed. And to quote Professor Butcher [2] again:—

"One great charm of Greek literature is, that in reading it we seem to be present at the first awakening of the universal human reason; we seem to watch and overhear it as it became conscious of itself. It does not yet speak quite like a book. It is thinking aloud. It debates with itself, as with an antagonist."

In fact, there is in Greek literature an inspiring, ennobling, stirring, life-giving genius which no other human language can supply. This

[1] "Some Aspects of Greek Genius," p. 201: London, 1891.   [2] *Ibid.*, p. 192.

was felt by the great thinkers and writers of all ages, not least by James Russell Lowell, a typical American himself, and an ardent advocate of the study of Greek.   He writes:—

"One of the arguments against the compulsory study of Greek—namely, that it is wiser to give our time to modern languages and modern history than to dead languages and ancient history—involves, I think, a verbal fallacy. Only those languages can properly be called dead in which nothing living has been written. If the classic languages are dead, they yet speak to us, and with a clearer voice than that of any living tongue. If their language is dead, yet the literature it enshrines is crammed with life as perhaps no other writing, except Shakespeare's, ever was or will be. It is as contemporary with to-day as with the ears it first enraptured, for it appeals not to the man of then or now, but to the entire round of human nature itself. . . . We know not whither other studies will lead us, especially if dissociated from this; we do know to what summits, far above our lower region of turmoil, this has led, and what the many-sided outlook thence."

It would be easy to multiply opinions of this kind, the authority of which is incontrovertible.   But enough has been said to establish the utility and the benefit to be derived from the study of Greek.

Yet, there are many men of culture and of eminence, mostly professors and students of mathematics and natural science, who, while admitting all this, advocate eliminating Greek from the curriculum of academic studies, and applying to modern languages the time now devoted to it; or, at least, making Greek an optional subject, except in the case of philological and theological students.   This opposition can hardly be said to be directed against the Greek language itself; it is argued rather that its study entails eight or nine years of onerous and fruitless labor,—a labor of Sisyphus,—at the end of which time the results obtained are, in most cases, poor, not to say imperceptible. We are bound to admit that these arguments are mainly valid.   But they fail to touch the real cause of mischief: they aim at ending what needs only mending.

The manner in which Greek is taught in America and in England is the laborious, pedantic, and antiquated method of three centuries ago; it ends by torturing out of the pupil all love for a language in which he sees nothing more cheering than the dry theory of the rules of grammar.   As has been well said,—

"We have tried to mummify Greek, which is still alive, tying it up with the bandages of a dead language, so that in our hands it has ceased to breathe, and can only express itself in such painful sounds as were never heard and cannot by any means be understood in its native country."

This system is now virtually condemned, since it is admitted on all

hands that some remedy must be applied.   The solution of the difficulty should therefore be sought in a radical reform of the existing
method of teaching Greek, whereby its acquisition may become more
rapid, its study more attractive, and its results more manifest and
more abundant.   To ensure these advantages Greek should be studied
as any other living tongue.

In the case of every other language, except Greek, it is admitted
that the only rational and scientific method of becoming acquainted
with its ancient literature is to master first its living form, and then
to go backward,. so to say, learning the tongue in its entirety.   No
one tries to learn English or German by beginning with Chaucer or
the " *Nibelungenlied.*"   Yet the difference between those mediæval
forms of the two languages and their present style is, if anything,
greater than the deviation of the Greek of to-day from the style of
the classics.   And, as we shall presently see, Greek literature has
been transmitted in unbroken succession to the living descendants
of the Greek race, and is studied by them at the present day as an
integral part of a continuous whole.

A writer, familiar with what is vaguely styled " modern Greek,"
as well as with the mode of tuition followed in Greece, explains
that—

"—the grammars used in the gymnasia of Greece are similar to those used
in the gymnasia of Germany and the public schools of England.   Many of them
are simply translated from the German.   Therefore, to study Greek as a living
language would require no change of grammar; the slight differences in the
future and infinitive of the verbs could easily be explained *vivâ voce*, as they
present no difficulty.   The principal difference is in the style of the written
language, which is simpler than the classical, to which it thus forms an easy
introduction."

It is in an elementary book of this simpler style that pupils of
the communal schools in Greece begin to read and write.   In the
Hellenic schools (a three-years course) they are first initiated into
the classics, beginning with the stories of the *Scholasticoi* and the
fables of Æsop, and gradually advancing to the " Anabasis" of Xenophon, Plutarch's " Lives," Homer's " Iliad," and parts of Herodotus.
In the gymnasia (a course of four years) they take up Demosthenes,
Thucydides, the tragic poets, and Pindar.   During these seven years
the curriculum naturally includes the other usual branches of a liberal
education, preparatory to a university course.   But a fairly assiduous
student, by following this course of Greek, leaves the gymnasium
_amply equipped in the knowledge of the Greek tongue, which he

should then be able to master easily in all its various forms, and to write it in a scholarly style.

If this system were adopted wherever Greek is taught, its study would be rendered not only easier, but more attractive and more interesting to the pupil; it would, free his mind from the sense of awe, difficulty, and uselessness which is inseparable from the notion of a dead language. The reproach that valuable time has been wasted would disappear; for he would have acquired, with the advantages of a classic training, a living language spoken all through the Levant, possessing a contemporaneous and daily increasing literature and an ably conducted newspaper press.

Not only this, but it will be found that the best, indeed the only sure way to the full comprehension of the niceties and many of the idiomatic sayings in the classics, is through the knowledge of the Greek of to-day. This has been set forth with irresistible force by Coray in his immortal introductions to the Greek classics which he edited, and it has been admitted by many foreign Hellenists, learned enough to appreciate the importance of the study of Greek as an entirety. Many instances might readily be cited of the ludicrous misconceptions, by foreign commentators, of words and expressions in the classics, which any Greek peasant would understand as form- ing a part of his own vernacular. It is the knowledge of Greek as now spoken which alone can render the study of classic Greek easy, pleasant, and profitable.

The chief obstacle to be apprehended to the introduction of this method is the prejudice of the teachers themselves,. who are bound to a misleading tradition, both by habit and by interest. It would be too much to expect of them a voluntary disavowal of their past, and an acknowledgment of their present insufficiency; for the reform of the barbarous pronunciation of Greek now in use in English schools and universities is, of course, an inevitable corollary to the adoption of the system suggested. The pupils themselves would experience no more difficulty in pronouncing Greek as the Greeks do now, than they experience in learning to speak French or German. It is less easy to expect of teachers wedded to a false tradition a ready denun- ciation of its errors.

The difficulty, however, might be overcome if they were con- vinced, as they might easily be, that a few weeks' application would enable them to become familiar with the Greek pronunciation of to- day, and with the slight differences between the contracted classic and

the more analytic recent Greek forms.   This would add to their lin·
guistic stock one more living tongue, and would enable them to teach,
as such, the most beautiful and most perfect form of human speech.

The gradual transition from the old to the new method of tuition,
which we advocate, would be facilitated, and its success ensured, by
attaching to each school or university a well-educated native Greek,
whose duties would be confined to teaching professors and pupils the
actual pronunciation of Greek, and to exercising them in reading and
conversation; while the grammatical and critical elucidation of the lan·
guage would still be left in the hands of the professors, who would
soon be qualified to impart it in its genuine pronunciation.   Professor
John Stuart Blackie, of Edinburgh, has for many years past followed
this system, and I commend the following weighty remarks of his:—

"I undertake to prove that by learning Greek in the natural and true way,
as a living language, by a direct appeal to the ear and response by the tongue,
thinking and speaking in Greek from the first lesson, a greater familiarity with
that noble language will be acquired in five months than is done now by the
assiduous labors of as many years.   Nature is always right: schoolmasters and
scholars are sometimes wrong."

To go further—schoolmasters and scholars were never more wrong
than in their misleading conception of what constitutes " ancient"
Greek, so called.   In the minds of university men, and perhaps more
in the minds of outsiders, " ancient" Greek is limited to Homer
(about 1000 B.C.), Hesiod (born 950 B.C.), Pindar (b. 517 B.C.),
Herodotus (b. 480 B.C.) and all the poets and prose-writers of the
golden age of Attic literature, from Sophocles (b. 498 B.C.) down to
Callimachus (b. 227 B.C.).   About the end of the third century B.C.,
Greek literature began to decline.   Nevertheless Dionysius of Hali·
carnassus (b. 50 B.C.), Strabo (b. 60 B.C.), Plutarch (b. 50 A.D.),
Lucian, who flourished in the second century of our era, Athenæus
(b. 188 A.D.) and Diogenes Laertius (b. 179 A.D.), whose writings
date from the third century, are all included in " ancient" Greek.
The Greek New Testament—written, of course, during the first decades
of the Christian era, though in an admittedly debased style as com·
pared with the classic Greek—is none the less studied along with
other " ancient" Greek texts, and in the minds of many passes mus·
ter as such.

And yet, in all that constitutes style and idiom in language, there
is as great a difference between the Greek of Hesiod and the Greek of
Plutarch as there is between the Greek of Xenophon and the style of

a Greek newspaper of to-day.   And again, there is as much similarity between a text-book of geography, as now taught in the gymnasia of the Greek kingdom, and the Greek of Strabo, as there is between the Dialogues of Lucian (b. 135 A.D.) and the Comedies of Aristophanes (b. 430 B.C.).   More than this, it may safely be presumed that if a student were strictly confined, in his study of Greek, to the Odes of Pindar, he would experience as great a difficulty in understanding the text of Herodotus, if set to it without any preliminary preparation, as he would in following the sense of St. John's Gospel or a "modern" Greek philosophical treatise, such as Dr. Therianos's life of Coray.   He would probably find the Greek of the New Testament the less comprehensible of the two.

Now, what is the explanation of the existing strange confusion of facts?   It is to be sought in the old academic tradition which was based on the delusion that Greek had died, as a literary language at least, and which limited the study of Greek to what are admittedly its classic authors; it furthermore adopted as a test standard those authors who wrote in Attic Greek, not only during the great Athenian age, but as late as the second and third centuries after Christ.

It would be both scientifically correct and practically accurate to style the Greek of such authors "classic" or "Attic"; but to define it as "ancient," and to include in that definition what may well be called the prehistoric Greek of Homer (1000 B.C.), and the Greek of the Atticizing authors of the third century of the Christian era,— to the exclusion of the Hellenistic Greek of the first century, the Greek of the Byzantine period, and the Greek of our own time, all of which is loosely and indiscriminately considered "modern,"—is to transgress against all scientific truth and to ignore the incontrovertible facts of history.

No one doubts nowadays that the classic texts which have come down to us no more represent the popular idiom of those times than the classics of France, Germany, or England can be considered as written in the respective colloquial styles of those countries.   Classic authors never reproduce the popular spoken and written language of their times.   And we know that with the Greek classics more especially, both prose-writing and poetry were considered as demanding the care and finish of a fine art.

The fact that the entire demos of Athens not only followed with perfect ease the dramas and songs of their poets and the harangues of their orators, but were quick to seize every nicety and detect any flaws in them,—this undeniable fact is an isolated instance of the existence of an intellectual aristocracy unrivalled in ancient Greece itself, and unmatched in any other epoch or country. On the contrary we have every evidence that in ancient Greece there existed, not only a vernacular, a variety of local idioms and provincialisms, but also entire dialects, special to certain parts of the Greek world, which have not all been preserved in classic literature. Dr. Coumanoudes, the learned professor at the Athens University, has collected from inscriptions and other sources, and published in the form of a dictionary, ten thousand Greek words not met with in any Greek text known to us, and not included in any Greek lexicon. Words, again, and forms of speech used in Homer and some of the earlier poets, disappear in the classics, but are in constant use in the mouth of the people in Crete and other parts of Greece at the present day.

We know also that, from the Alexandrine epoch forward, the Attic dialect, which by reason of its literary excellence and superiority had come into common use, began, in consequence of this very reason, to lose much of its elegance and subtlety, and was gradually disfigured by the introduction of provincialisms; and that from this mixture there arose, already in the third century B.C., the " common dialect," which varied in point of purity and presents different degrees of development, according to the date and the ability of the authors who used it.

Coming to a later epoch, we find that some of the best verses in the Anthology, in point of purity of style and elegance of form, are admittedly the compositions of Byzantine scholars, whose proficiency even in classic Greek is conceded by that merciless detractor of the Greeks of the Eastern Empire. Gibbon says:—

"In their lowest servitude and depression the subjects of the Byzantine throne were still possessed of a golden key that could unlock the treasures of antiquity —of a musical and prolific language, that gives a soul to the objects of sense, and a body to the abstractions of philosophy."

This golden key has never fallen from the hands of the Greeks; and the Greek language has suffered no break of continuity. In the whole course, even of its late history, not a generation passed by without leaving some written record of its life and work, some monument of its literary activity; so that we have a complete and unbroken chain of evidence of the unity of Greek literature, even during the darkest days of its decay.

The Greek language has never ceased to live. Latin indeed—in spite of its exclusive adoption for liturgical purposes by the Roman Church to this day, and in spite of its special use up to a compara- tively recent time for certain courtly and legal functions—Latin has died out as a spoken and written language. Its different dialects, having been debased, were merged into local idioms, and have devel- oped into the Romance languages of modern Europe, which now deviate from the mother tongue so materially as each to require a different grammar, a special dictionary, and a separate study for its acquisition; and no one of these offshoots of Latin approaches the parent stock so closely as the Greek of to-day does that of Plato or Xenophon. Latin, having thus died, has undergone no change. Greek has changed from age to age because it has continued to live. But its changes have been, so to say, exterior, not organic; super- ficial, not fundamental. It is not the dead shrub, that survives only in its offshoots; but the mighty oak, which, after the glow of sum- mer, has shed its leaves in the autumn, has hibernated in winter, to blossom forth again with the returning spring. Of the Greek lan- guage it may indeed be said, "*plus ça change, plus c'est la même chose.*"

After reaching the highest pitch of excellence—a perfection so supreme and ideal as to remain forever the one unrivalled model of human speech—the Greek language declined, decayed, and became degraded almost beyond recovery; but it has again been resuscitated; it has been regenerated and cleansed from the effects of a long barbar- ous oppression; and it now reverts more and more every day to its original purity and beauty; thus faithfully recording, in its own vicissitudes, the glories and the misfortunes of the Greeks themselves. As it rose to its greatest perfection and beauty with the victories of Marathon and Salamis and the splendors of the Periclean age, so it declined under the Romans; it decayed with the Byzantine Empire, it was lowered almost beyond recognition under the tyranny of the Turks; only to take again a new life to itself, and thus herald the regeneration and signal the freedom of new Greece. For it is a remarkable feature in the survival of Greek language and literature that it preceded and prepared the political regeneration of the people; it did not follow as a result, but it was a cause. No other language presents, in the successive degrees of its literature, so faithful a reflex of the contemporary condition of the nation; and no other nation has, for an uninterrupted space of three thousand years, maintained its language so continuous and so little changed; evincing thereby once more an inherent tenacity and vigor of life which has scarcely been witnessed in any other race.

If but for this, the study of the Greek language in its entirety offers a special interest and promises great profit. It presents many variations, yet it constitutes an indisputable whole. The Greek of Homer, the Doric Greek (Pindar), the Greek of Ionia (Herodotus), the most perfect and most elegant form of Greek in its Attic classicism, the Alexandrine, the Hellenistic, the Byzantine, the Romaic, the Neo-Hellenic Greek of to-day,—all are interwoven forms and inseparable parts of one and the same language, no one epoch, no one phase of which can be adequately mastered or sufficiently appreciated without the concurrent study of all the other portions of the language. Between no two of them is the difference greater than between the English of Chaucer, the German of Gudrun and the "*Nibelungenlied*," or the French of the "*Chanson de Roland*" and the "*Chanson de la Rose*," and the present style of those languages. Yet the space of time which separates mediæval from modern European literature amounts to about as many centuries as the Greek tongue counts thousands of years of uninterrupted literary life.

These facts have not escaped the notice of scholars who, being versed in every epoch of Greek literature, are qualified to speak with authority as to its continuity. Let us listen first to the eminent historian, the late E. A. Freeman. He wrote in the "Fortnightly Review" of February, 1879, as follows:—

"There is something more in the Greek tongue, something more abiding, something which more nearly touches the general history of mankind, than is to be found in that view of it which looks on it as dead, ancient, classical, cut off from modern interests of every kind. I claim for the Greek its place on the exactly opposite ground, because it is not dead, but living : because it is ancient, it is mediæval and modern no less."

Similar is the testimony of Professor Jebb, of Cambridge, a distinguished scholar in modern no less than in ancient Greek:—

"Old and new Greece are bound together by language. Latin, passing into Romance languages, was more or less disintegrated. Greek was for centuries rude and ungrammatical, but it was always itself and itself alone .. . . In the organic matters of structure and syntax, Greek has never made a compromise with any other language. . . . During the last eighty years the Greek language has been returning more and more to the old classical type. . . . The chief difference now remaining between old and modern Greek is one which exists between old and modern generally,—the old is synthetic, the modern is analytic. Thus it has been the unique destiny of the Greek language to have had, from prehistoric times down to our own, an unbroken life. Not one link is wanting in this chain which binds the new Greece to the old."

J. Gennadius.

A SOUTHERN WOMAN'S STUDY OF BOSTON.

WHEN a Southern visitor goes to Boston, after the first novelty of sight-seeing is over, the chill of the Northern manner and temperament often causes a qualm of homesickness. The stranger feels lonely; her presence is unnoticed unless she gets in somebody's way; and in the early stages of acquaintance she finds it a waste of ammunition to be as cordial as she would be in the South under similar circumstances. When this discovery is made and acted upon, she gets along better, and finds herself respected in proportion to the earnestness with which she appears to be attending to her own business. If any serious trouble overtakes her, she will often be agreeably surprised by a real kindness from some one who had hitherto not only seemed densely reserved but blind to her existence.

She soon conceives a genuine admiration for the spirit of the multitude of brave women around her, living alone, without family ties in the present and scarcely a hope of them for the future, managing with moderate talents and immoderate perseverance to make a respectable support from their trades and arts, and to extract also a fair amount of pleasure from their lives, the press of competition rarely crowding out a resolute struggler. Boston men are helpful to their women. There are not enough men to marry them all, but cheerful and liberal instruction is given in all the ways and means of wage-earning. Woman's equal right, as a human being and fellow-citizen, to possess all she can honestly acquire and to learn all she can possibly absorb, is recognized everywhere in the radius of Boston civilization. If some sweet little feminine privileges, granted as freely as air in the South, are ignored, a looker-on cannot long resist the conclusion that the finger of destiny is pointing that way. The more "rights" women get, the fewer will be their privileges. They must take their choice between them.

In Boston a woman is valued socially in proportion to what she knows and can do well, or, to put it correctly, what she has the reputation of knowing and doing well. In the society of the South, a knowledge of school-books, an appreciation of the fine arts, and a proper acquaintance with English literature, are always politely *assumed* to be a part of a lady's equipment, as her hats and gloves are, whether she is well stocked with them or not; and the degree to which her womanhood adorns and benefits her surroundings marks her value in the mind of the public. A woman who remains un-married may command the highest respect, but it must be admitted that unless she have some special mission of charity in her family circle or outside of it, she has a dull middle life and old age com-pared with the middle life and old age of her Boston contemporaries.

If it could be a pleasant thing anywhere for a woman to grow old, it would be so in Boston. In that city spinsters and widows, if they are ambitious and even tolerably healthy, never consider it too late to find a vocation. They ·would take up botany, china-painting, sloyd, or political economy at sixty with a refreshing independence of their age. I have seen a pupil of seventy at one of the prominent schools of oratory, her fellow-students, mostly in the teens, treating her with a beautiful comradeship, instead of staring at her with sup-pressed smiles as if she were a kind of "freak." They recognized only her plucky defiance of Father Time's limitations by a larger measure of applause when she recited her pieces than they usually accorded to the younger members of the class.

Relations between the sexes are more romantic and picturesque in the Southern States than they are in New England; the old, and, as must be conceded, the natural ideal of marriage for everybody making youth and beauty the chief attractions.

Boston girls stop dancing in the early twenties, a survival of Puritan decorum probably forbidding that kittenish sport to belated damsels of thirty-five and upwards. In Washington and Baltimore very mature women dance, but they are not so likely to be chosen in wedlock when past the first bloom as New England women are,—if these last marry at all. Southern bachelors and widowers associate the idea of love and marriage only with young women, although fully expecting to be accounted eligible themselves until they wither on the stalk. A Boston man forgives and may even forget a woman's advancing years if she is bright and interesting and can make him feel always that he knows more than she does.

A Boston girl wintering in Georgia was kept in a continual flutter of astonishment at the facility with which the "knights" made love to her; a woman from any quarter of the globe likes to be convinced that she is fascinating, and this one was for a while inclined to believe in the homage she received. But she presently discovered that the

Georgians were merely indulging in a chivalrous habit, paying tribute to her youth and beauty.   Yet it is observable that a real lover makes a deep impression on one of these same Boston maidens,—who can get along so comfortably without the admiration of the opposite sex, when need be,—and she can reciprocate his feelings.   She is no more independent of him than a girl from any other zone would be, and she makes a devoted if not a demonstrative wife.   It is noticeable also that as a rule she rejects the overtures of an unwelcome suitor with due consideration for his feelings.   Not only the scarcity of men in society, but the time-honored custom of announcing engagements, cause her to regard the whole matter of courtship with greater seriousness than girls in the South regard it, where, until a comparatively recent period, there were plenty of men, and the public was allowed only to speculate upon the state of a young lady's affections and the direction of her preference even until her trousseau was fairly under way at her dressmaker's.

The attention which the Boston maiden has given to learning in her girlhood is likely to continue with modifications after marriage. It has become a habit, and is often an inherited taste, several generations of Bostonians having cherished an ambition to take the lead in that line.   The standard is no higher now than that of the best-educated persons in other cities; but a high standard in proportion to the population existed there earlier, until it has given a sort of chrism to the mental atmosphere.   It is a mistake to conclude that a taste for knowledge interferes with the home.   The Bostonians admire success of all things, they want solid comfort, they appreciate money and material advantages to a high degree, and have a keen perception of the road which leads to all these things.   Among a diversity of types, if there is such a figure as the typical Boston woman, she would hardly be found neglecting the interests of her home—*ergo* her own interests—for seances, lecture-platforms, and laboratories: she would not consider such a course practical.   What is peculiar to her organism might be said to be her capacity for attending to the mental and the material at the same time; this is due in part to her being less emotional and impulsive than many of her sex.   It is the stress of emotion that wears out human tissue with the greatest rapidity.

As a rule, in Boston, as everywhere, the more a woman really knows—not the more she pretends to know or wants to be thought to know—the more capable she is as a wife and mother.   Certainly a woman will not love and respect her husband less for understanding the bearings and claims of his profession; their house will not be less cleanly and comfortable for her comprehension of the laws that govern drainage and ventilation; she will press her infant to her heart with no less devotion for having examined bacteria with a microscope and investigated the sterilization of liquids; her growing boy will even be less likely to die a violent death from some rash experiment of his own for her having attended emergency lectures; and her young daughter may get even more pleasure out of her girlhood for her mother's having absorbed the optimistic philosophy of Emerson.

It is a very pleasant thing in Boston to see all ages, after the first dancing heyday of youth is over, meeting on the neutral impersonal ground of an interest in subjects and pursuits. Ideas having no age, the old keep fresh longer, and the inexperienced lose some of their crudeness. There is a free interchange of opinion about everything. Nothing in the heavens above, the earth beneath, or the waters under the earth, escapes inquiry; nothing is taken for granted simply because it has heretofore been accepted. Southern guests of active intelligence feel a novel sense of emancipation in this opening of doors that were at home kept shut and securely bolted during seasons of friendly reunion; the fear always existing that if they were left ajar something likely to hurt traditional beliefs and prejudices might escape.

On the other hand, the survival of the Puritan temperament in Boston makes many persons afraid of being too pleasant for the maintenance of sincerity and for the good of their neighbors. This restriction often causes a lack of spontaneity, a stiffness and heaviness in drawing-rooms, where the intelligence and kindly feeling are more than sufficient to produce an opposite effect. The element of graciousness, considered an essential part of the Southern home training, is too often at a minimum. New Englanders accept this graciousness of manner on the part of Southerners with an indulgent air,—a little doubtful of it at times, but on the whole rather pleased and amused by it, as they are by the soft vowels and dialect.

The grandest attribute of the Boston public is its profound regard for the sacredness of selfhood,—for individuality as a formative power; and, as a consequence, character concentrates to a focus. As might be expected where scientific curiosity is a factor so potent, it often plants its standard on unscientific territory, and interest in theories proven or beyond proof becomes a craze. Exotics are especially welcome. The Grand Lama of Tibet, turning off yard upon yard

16

of mysticism on a brass prayer-wheel,—if only he would be careful to observe the decencies of New England life through the week,—would draw a large and attentive audience at Music Hall on Sunday, and make an earnest band of converts to the wonder-story of his reincarnations. He would leave his most cordial blessing behind him, and take away a good subscription for the mysterious lamaseries in his native land.

There are retrogressive as well as progressive ideas in the New England "Athens": the cults of India and of Egypt flourish in a mysterious twilight within a few blocks of the Institute of Technology and Boston University. It is the paradise of Irregulars in every line. It is in the old South End that the haunts of occultism are most fully represented; the Esoteric Society has its name over one doorway; and Solar Biology is a sort of annex to this cult, mingling Astrology with Buddhism. Once, strolling into a meeting of the Esoteric Society, I saw "Solar Biology" inscribed above an intricate chart on which a diagram of the human body was connected by lines and geometrical figures with the signs of the zodiac. A thin, mild-eyed man rose on the platform and opened the meeting with these words: "I invite all here present to unite for three minutes in a silent invocation and wish for the benefit of *some one else.*" There was a sublimity in those three silent minutes in which selfishness had no part. When before had the stranger seen a hundred persons all forgetting the mighty Ego at the same time and lifting up their souls in wishes for others? Few mortals could sustain the unique grandeur of such a prelude, and it is not surprising that the address which followed it proved vague and untenable.

Many helpful elevating things are to be found in these mystical philosophies; most thinking persons are ready now to acknowledge psychic force as a reality: but the step from the sublime to the ridiculous is easily taken, and the credulity of some who are shrewd and clear-sighted in the every-day business of life does sometimes provoke a smile. A Boston dressmaker may be given to mixing divers systems of thought in a mysterious hash and dilating upon the sevenfold nature of man while fitting a customer. "You like a short cut on the shoulders?" said one, taking a pin out of her mouth and brandishing her scissors aloft. "You're not feeling so well this winter? So many people are upset in their health now! Talk about 'grippe,' it is a great perihelion among the planets that causes it all! The disease was due to planetary influence. You just sit down when you get home, and let the divine work right through you" (as if referring to some active yeast-powder); "*I* woke up with a bad sick-headache the other day, and I didn't know what I *should* do, for I had to move that day; but I got through it all with the aid of this truth and lemon-juice."

The fashionable Bostonians of the Back Bay and suburbs are conservative, and do not tend to the radical phases of occultism. They are rarely to be seen in the beautiful Temple the Spiritualists have erected, but quite a number have become interested in the higher aspects of Theosophy as presented to them by distinguished Oriental gentlemen who have tarried long enough in the city. Mind-reading, telepathy, and psychic research attract others; and some aristocratic chronic invalids, after vainly trying all the pharmacopoeia of the doctors, have been restored to health by the mental cure for disease. Among advanced physicians, hypnotism as a remedial agent is a burning question; it may become fashionable in a few more years, and Boston "Regulars" will be the first to offer patients the choice between a pill and a mesmeric sleep, a "suggestion" of relief expected to work as well as the pill at from two to five dollars a suggestion.

The South keeps a firm grip on calomel and quinine, persuaded that nothing else will fit its climate, and is still too orthodox in religious belief to make the occult in any shape a factor in practical affairs, fearing that the devil may be lurking at the bottom of it. The ghost is still kept in his winding-sheet, and is enjoyed only with a mysterious thrill over the twilight fire. An access of scientific curiosity would be a stimulus to the growth of the South in many directions, although, so far as the ghost is concerned, it might be a waste of time, the only positive result of the skilled inquiry into his constitution going on in so many places being a decline of the fear of him.

There is only one exception to the statement that prophets of all races, climes, and proclivities are welcome to bring their teachings to Boston so long as their conduct is according to Boston standards. This is the Pope of Rome. No matter how angelically he might behave while promulgating his doctrines, he would inspire a red-hot antagonism too deeply burned in to have been caused only by the recent feud about public schools. This is another inheritance from those old Pilgrims who crossed the sea for freedom to worship and freedom to persecute. Throughout New England, persons who are liberally disposed in every other direction enjoy a fling at priests and nuns as bugaboos. The educated Southerner cannot exactly participate in this aversion, having found her acquaintances among the

Roman Catholic families of Baltimore, Washington, Mobile, New Orleans, and a certain belt of Kentucky, as agreeable, refined, and law-abiding as citizens of other creeds, without horns or hoofs on their persons, or trap-doors and secret passages in their institutions.

An impression has gone abroad that Boston critics are terribly severe to encounter; in reality printed criticism is mainly generous. When real ability and earnest effort are behind failure, the governing spirit of the press there is always ready to credit the failure as a preliminary, a step in evolution. "Evolution," by the way, is still the latest word in Boston. Nobody need try to succeed there in anything without excellence, but excellence alone will not ensure success: it must be "fadded" by the leading set. A fad once properly inaugurated is promoted for the nonce to the pedestal of a cult, and then no sort of eccentricity of manner or of setting constitutes a barrier. If the lucky originator of a full-fledged fad should be a woman, she might don a short black-serge dress and white stockings to give her evening entertainments, talk straight through her nose from under a big poke bonnet (although the Bostonians do not themselves affect white hose and a nasal twang) ; and her audience would lose the sense of the comical and applaud the idea she represented, the mere medium for it becoming secondary. *The idea*, in and by itself, is a more vital and controlling force than in any city of modern times; there is something glorious in its prerogative.

When it comes to real originality, with all their appreciation of a good thing that is new, the new good thing is more likely now to come to Boston for recognition than it is to spring into being there, and there are more brilliant and versatile conversationalists in some of the large Southern cities. The following of fads is menacing originality to such a degree that a halt is being called in some directions. It is seen at last that the reading of Browning and the praying to understand him may take up too much of the limited span that can advantageously be given to poetry; that the painstaking acquisition of Delsarte gestures throughout the system may not leave room enough for the unexpected in feeling and manner, and (though it is still a heresy to say so) the votaries of the Impressionist School of Art may some day be willing to banish to their attics some of the vivid sketches of the blue and pink rocks, the lilac houses, and canary-colored grass, that it is now the fad to see in the landscape. It is not the desire or the real nature of Boston women to be superficial; they are thoughtful and earnest in temperament and get a great deal out of life in one way and another—so much that they might get more by attempting less,—this is what they are finding out.

No end of curious incongruities strike the Southerner in Boston, arising from the prevalence of a certain amount of book-learning and an educated middle class. Among persons who have had the best school training, but not the best early social advantages, often heart and manners do not seem cultivated up to the brain, a mellowing process throughout being needed. The neighbor at a boarding-house table who discusses Comte's altruistic philosophy at dinner may grunt a reluctant "good-morning" the next day; it may require several months of proximity for his civilities to reach the point of passing the vinegar-cruet. The man who explains the glacial theory so lucidly to his son as they look toward the skating-pond on the Common may be practically frozen to the end seat of the car at the same moment, and allow ladies who are encumbered with hand-bags and umbrellas to struggle across his knees. These painful surprises rarely occur in "Dixie"; if the area of education is less widely distributed there among the masses it is more likely to be found an even thing in the individual.

As a sort of anti-climax to this, one sometimes notices in Southern society a needless hesitation about displaying knowledge and individual tastes, lest somebody in the circle should be bored or made to feel deficient. Often this consideration for the general social ideal has a narrowing influence upon persons conscious of possessing talent or marked bias and longing for an outlet; many—women especially— attempt to fit themselves into grooves that are too small for them rather than be thought "peculiar." The Boston fashion of taking all the candles from under bushels, of letting no talents be buried in napkins, is more conducive to growth and happiness. As a matter of course, where there is an apotheosis of culture, shams of the real thing also will often be found. Many persons pay for winter sittings at Trinity Church, and season tickets to the Symphony concerts, because they wish to be credited with good taste.

The beautiful custom of treating governesses as equals prevails in Southern families; they are honored guests in country neighborhoods, sharing the social distinction of the daughters of the house; and from such a standpoint it certainly looks like an inconsistency in suburban Bostonians of high degree that they tacitly assign a subordinate position in their homes to the chosen exponents and exemplars of highly prized culture. This is very English.

Anglomania has grown to be second nature in some cases. The

best way to make a favorable impression at the start on persons of a certain set is to mistake them for Englishmen. The imitation is not bad,—the rough suit, the unbecoming hat, the arms akimbo as if hung by loose springs to the shoulders, and last but not least the *basso profundo* enunciation, the long *à* being *de rigueur*. Some Anglo-maniacs out-English the English by pronouncing " and" as *ànd*. One female Anglomaniac asked an American naval officer if he did not think the British flag the most glorious one to sail under!

The Bostonians are hospitable to strangers if they consider them worth knowing, and are careful to return any attention that has ever been paid to themselves or their kindred in another city. The very easiest way to ensure a volley of hospitality and to gain the heart of the place is to let it be understood that the stranger appearing there has been the victim of oppression, of some deep, deadly wrong else-where. Then a universal throb of indignation will strike tenderness and passion in a flash from the New England nature as nothing else will. The object of sympathy may be red, white, or black. Boston sometimes gets " taken in" through her active sympathies for the sup-posed victims of other less enlightened communities.

Boston women usually have a lurking conviction that the stranger among them has more time to spare for visiting than they have, and the stranger soon concedes this to be a fact. Never was a set of women more desperately worked, more solemnly, awfully driven, between the conscientiously fulfilled duties of the home and the Ethical Reform societies, "Nineteenth-Century-Thought" classes, Associated Charities, concerts and clubs. Their clubs would in them-selves furnish a liberal education to any woman privileged to attend and capable of assimilating them all with her mental digestion. The " Elderblow Tea," given in Brookline every fortnight during the winter, is one of the most charming club reunions, membership being restricted to " settled" ladies, many of them even elderly, and all pos-sessed of great refinement and cultivation. No matter how busy Boston women may be, they always find time to call on strangers who are distinguished for something, even if these chance to be sojourning in the tabooed South End, which is usually spoken of as if it were located at the end of creation, although the new-comer soon discovers that it is but a few minutes' walk from the halcyon " Back Bay" district.

Admiration for talent, for successful intellectual and artistic enterprise, is a distinctive feature. Residents who have attained celebrity in a literary way become a limited aristocracy carefully graded and not expected to return calls; aspirants in the various embryonic stages crowding in on their reception days to pay willing tribute.

A Southern lady long residing in Cambridge contributes an amusing anecdote illustrative of the intensity the pursuit of cults sometimes acquires, finally crowding to the wall the merely superficial social obligations. An intellectual representative of an historic Massachusetts family had been owing her a visit for a long time, and, the two meeting one day by chance, the derelict Miss Blue-Blood feared an immediate reproach. " Oh dear!" she exclaimed; " I've been intending to call on you for ever so long, but it is one of those nasty jobs that I can't seem to accomplish!" A moment more, and she was joining in the laugh at her own expense, apologizing for her apology. She had not meant to be discourteous; she knew only that she was gasping for time to do everything, and, when cornered, frankly came out with the unvarnished truth.

A Southerner of passably even temper will get along quite well now in political discussions, most of the old issues being safely dead, unless he has the hard luck of being housed with a posse of Wendell Phillips radicals during a Presidential campaign, when they will hold him personally responsible for evils in the South which may have had their origin in evils at the North a hundred years before he was born. Radicals of this stripe are becoming rare.

Boston loves to probe, to reconstruct; and when her conscience is convicted of wrong at home she turns the lance as mercilessly against herself. There is an oversoul, as it were, of Boston, which the higher order of citizens looks up to, and holds before the eyes of the people, and there is something noble in the continual effort made to keep the city up to this ideal. A community devoid of a good opinion of itself could never amount to much in the world's opinion. Boston is conceited, but so are New York and Chicago. How was it with Rome and Athens? And, since their day, how has it been with England, Virginia, South Carolina?

Delightful dinners are given by Bostonians who have escaped from their ancestral cuisine, but the ordinary cooking of the people is distasteful to a Southern palate: there are too many pies; too many codfish are caught; too many beans are baked; too much brown bread is made on Saturday nights. It is quite probable, however, that the insipid " boiled dinners" are more wholesome than the fried dishes that prevail in the South.

It is a perpetual surprise to see Boston women getting along comfortably with so few servants. There are some with fair incomes who do not keep a nurse for a first baby after it is six weeks old. Of course, if the nursery fills up, extra help becomes necessary. One discharged her nurse when her baby was two months old, resuming her favorite botanical studies, and this without neglecting the human specimen. If he was not always accommodating enough to sleep, cook held him while mamma botanized. There are young professors who marry on a regular salary of $850. With some small outside assistance from "coaching" and other work, they go to housekeeping in one of the suburban towns; and if the wife is gifted with "faculty" they get richer instead of poorer as the years go by, she doing the housework and managing to know something about her husband's special branch besides. Many a well-dressed Northern woman with a pretty home and a small family will say in the course of conversation: "I do the cooking myself. Oh, yes! I wouldn't be bothered with training a girl; they waste more than they are worth." This is wherein a bracing climate, with an inherited habit of waiting on themselves, accounts for much with the New Englanders.

Southern women will do quite as much for love—what have they not done since the war? They have even driven mule-carts to the woods and felled the trees for fuel to burn; but it is certain that as soon as they find themselves able financially to employ somebody accustomed to manual labor and glad to be paid for doing it, they will take advantage of the opportunity. A Southern lady will do without a servant—necessity obliging her—just as she would do without a leg or an arm, and try to make the best of a hard lot, but she cannot be said to regard a servant in her house as an evil. On the contrary she is more likely to feel grateful to that functionary for giving her a chance to accomplish something outside the drudgery of life.

The best domestic service in Boston is that of Scandinavians. On the part of some persons there is a decided repulsion felt toward the Negro in household relations. His constitution, as the Southern people know, who had him to train for two hundred years,—shiftless, irresponsible, faithful, and affectionate,—is still a mystery. New England understands him only when he gets to studying law, medicine, or engineering, and is called "Mr.,"—in other words, when he assumes the conditions of the white man.

A great deal has been said about the relative generosity of the New England and the Southern natures. If a neighbor's house were burned and he left destitute, the conscientious effort to help him, even at some personal sacrifice, would be much the same in the two regions. Boston has felt every stricken city in the land to be a near neighbor and contributed nobly to its relief.   But the Southerner is more generous, less questioning, when it comes to purely impulsive giving. If asked for a quarter he feels prompted to hand it over at once, thinking the sum too trifling to be worth talking about; if his pocket-book is empty he is very sorry.   A quarter looks larger to the average New Englander even when he has more quarters.   He has a conscientious feeling that " the case ought to be investigated."   This logical giving is more commendable as a system, but sometimes the other temperament is capable of a sudden generous overflow that comes like a tidal wave mighty enough to sweep away in one divine moment all the boundary lines of hate and prejudice.

Bostonians do not claim that their beloved city is cosmopolitan like Paris, like New York and Washington.   They prize it more for not being cosmopolitan, and, with all its progressive ideas, it retains some of the characteristics of the early New England village.

If outsiders as they now are, go to Boston as it now is, to live and not to visit, and wish to be even moderately contented, they must acquire a serious aim if they fail to bring one with them.   They must " grapple" it to their " souls with hoops of steel," they must live and be prepared to die still grappling.   They may miss some of the sweet amenities of their ancestral homes, the glow of impulsive friendship and spontaneous demonstration, the balm of a softer climate; but nowhere on the planet will a satisfied head come nearer to being a substitute for a satisfied heart, nor could there be a better place for a disappointed life to attain the conviction that life, if only as a means of development, is worth living.

FRANCES ALBERT DOUGHTY.

CAN RAILROAD RATES BE CHEAPENED?

No single result of recent discussions of the various topics collectively termed the "railway problem" is more apparent than the disappearance of the purely superficial notion of a continuous combat between a small body of railway proprietors, on the one hand, and, on the other, the general public, whose interests were considered to require the very lowest rates. A clearer insight into the relations between railroads and their patrons has demonstrated a surprising identity of interest which requires harmonious sentiment and action in order to promote the prosperity of all.

According to the latest information furnished by the Interstate Commerce Commission, the number of employees in the railway service on June 30, 1893, was 873,602, from which it may safely be estimated that not less than 3,500,000 persons are directly supported from the proceeds of railway transportation. When the number of producers and others required to supply railway operatives and their families with the necessaries of life is considered, it becomes apparent that a very large body of our citizens is dependent for prosperity almost wholly upon that of the railways.

A brief examination of the present financial condition of the railway system is sufficient to show that the charges for railway transportation now in force do not produce excessive revenue, and that any changes toward lower charges, which are unaccompanied by measures of radical economy in operation, will render the business unprofitable and consequently be detrimental to the public interest.

During the decade from the beginning of 1884 to the end of 1893, 74,348 miles of railway, operated by 311 independent corporations, and capitalized at $3,853,371,000, passed from the control of stockholders into that of receivers appointed by the courts, on account of the failure of the rates obtained for transportation to provide sufficient revenue to meet the expenses of operation, taxes, and interest. Of this total, 29,476 miles (40 per cent of the mileage), capitalized at $1,758,836,000 (46 per cent of capital), was placed in charge of receivers during the year ending December 31, 1893. The entire railway mileage operated by receivers on that date was 40,279, and the par value of its stocks and bonds $2,217,656,000, constituting 23 per cent and 21 per cent respectively of the total railway mileage and capital in the United States.

During 1893, twenty-five railways, operating 1,613 miles of road, and represented by $79,924,000 of capital stocks and bonds, were sold under foreclosure, while the number thus sold during eighteen years from 1876 to 1893 inclusive was 551, their aggregate length 57,283 miles, and their capitalization $3,209,126,000. The crop of foreclosures that must inevitably follow the enormous number of receiverships created during 1893 is not yet ready for harvest. When its data become available they will afford an appalling presentation of the financial condition of a large portion of our railway system.

According to the latest data furnished by the Statistician of the Interstate Commerce Commission, during the year ending June 30, 1893, railway stocks having a par value of $2,859,334,572, or 61.24 per cent of the total stock capital, received no dividends; and no interest was paid on mortgage bonds amounting to $492,276,999, or 10.93 per cent of the total, nor upon $204,864,269 of income bonds, being 82.56 per cent of the total.

The average rates of dividend and interest during 1893 are not yet known, but during 1892 they were as follows: Dividends on preferred stock, 2.73 per cent; on common stock, 2 per cent; average on all stock, 2.11 per cent; interest on funded debt, 4.75 per cent; interest on unfunded debt, 1.47 per cent; average rate of return to capital of all classes, 3.38 per cent.

The ratio of return to invested capital in the form of dividends on capital stock has declined with great rapidity during the last twenty years. In 1871, with 44,614 miles of railway, the dividends paid averaged $1,265 per mile of line; in 1882, with 107,158 miles, dividends were only $952 per mile; while in 1893, with 176,461 miles, dividends had declined to an average of $572 per mile. Comparing the years 1883 and 1892, it is found that the mileage of the latter year was 55 per cent greater than that of the former, the gross earnings 45 per cent greater, and the net earnings 20 per cent greater; but the aggregate sum paid in dividends had actually declined more than 20 per cent. The decline in the average amount of dividends per mile of line equalled 48 per cent of the average of 1883.

The rates charged for railway transportation have shown a con-

stant downward tendency so extensive as to afford considerable evidence in support of the contention that they are regulated by forces
beyond the control of managers or owners.   During the six years
covered by the reports of the Bureau of Statistics of the Interstate
Commerce Commission, the average rate per ton per mile charged for
the transportation of freight declined from 1.001 cents to .878 cent,
and that per passenger per mile from 2.349 cents to 2.108 cents.
Inconsiderable as these reductions appear, when stated in this form,
they amount to a saving to the public upon the traffic carried during the year ending June 30, 1893, of $115,113,377 on freight, and
$34,292,134 on passenger traffic; or a total of $149,405,511 in one
year,—an amount exceeding by 48 per cent the aggregate of all dividends paid during that year.

   An investigation of the charges exacted for the transportation of
freight by rail during the period from 1852 to 1892 inclusive was
recently made by Mr. C. C. McCain, the Auditor of the Interstate
Commerce Commission, and an acknowledged authority upon the
subject of railway rates.   The results of his work were published as
a Senate Document in connection with the Finance Committee's Report on Prices and Wages, and show a decline which has been constant
and considerable and has included all sections of the country and all
articles of commerce commonly offered for shipment by rail.

   Notwithstanding these extensive reductions and the unfortunate
financial condition of so many railways, there is a continuous popular
demand for still cheaper transportation.   It is on account of this demand that many States have resorted to legislation prescribing maximum rates, and other even less defensible measures which are believed
by many to be unfavorable alike to the railways and the public.
This, too, is to be assigned as the chief reason for the existence of
numerous State railway commissions clothed with authority, more or
less effective, to require reductions in rates within the boundaries of
individual States, and of the Interstate Commerce Commission with
similar power in regard to rates upon traffic between States.

   The public desire for cheaper transportation is both reasonable
and natural.   The carrier of goods is a middleman between producer
and consumer, and consequently obnoxious to both.   While it is to
nobody's interest that the business of transportation should become
unprofitable, its charges are a principal part of the friction incident
to the processes of exchange and distribution; and the best interests
of all, therefore, require their reduction to the lowest practicable

minimum. Consequently the public will be well served if, from a critical observation of current railway methods, there shall be discovered important particulars in which they can be so reformed as to allow radical economies in operation, as by that means alone can the reductions in rates which have so far characterized the development of the railway system be continued without reducing all companies to the condition of bankruptcy already confronting a large number.

The expenses incident to the struggle for traffic between competing lines could undoubtedly be reduced, if not entirely eliminated, by better methods of conducting transportation. Prominent among these is the outlay incident to the system of paying commissions to influence the routing of traffic in favor of particular lines. Authentic statistics concerning the amounts thus expended are exceedingly difficult to obtain, as the efficiency of such practices in securing business obviously depends largely upon the degree of secrecy attained, as, if the rate of commission allowed becomes known, it will generally be met by competing lines, and agents will no longer have any reason to favor a particular route. From an investigation made by the Interstate Commerce Commission several years ago, it appeared that during the year ending June 30, 1889, 108 companies paid commissions amounting in the aggregate to $1,729,492, of which $1,097,130 was paid by nine roads. As high as $20.70 is alleged to have been paid for the sale of a single second-class ticket from Chicago to San Francisco. Annual, largely-attended conventions of ticket-scalpers from all parts of the country afford evidence that these expenses are sufficient to support a considerable army of parasites.

Another extravagance resulting from the struggle for traffic is that required to maintain the multitude of outside agencies and travelling agents, whose sole occupation is to secure the routing of passengers and freight by their respective lines. So important are the expenditures resulting from these causes, even during seasons of comparative harmony between rival lines, that the number of such agencies is frequently restricted by contract. In one of our principal Atlantic seaboard cities at which nine railways compete for westbound passenger traffic, a contract is known to have been in force limiting to seven the number of agencies each should be allowed to maintain. Obviously a system of joint agencies would have accorded the public equal if not superior service at an enormous saving in expense. During those too-frequent periods of fierce and unbridled competition popularly denominated "rate-wars," each participating road has its freight and passenger agents in every important city in the country, at a total expense for rents, clerk-hire, advertising, etc., which can scarcely be estimated. During a single year, when rates were fairly maintained, four roads operating westward from Chicago paid $1,283,585 for maintaining outside agencies and advertising, and one road from New York expended $871,291 for similar purposes.

Much economic waste arises from the competition of long and circuitous routes for traffic which would naturally go by more direct and shorter lines. As an example of this class of competition, that for freight traffic between New York and New Orleans may be cited. This traffic is actively sought by various lines operating in whole or in part by water, and in consequence the rates obtainable are extremely low; yet in spite of this fact 94 all-rail routes are known to seek actively to secure it. Of these the shortest and most direct is by way of Philadelphia, Baltimore, Washington, Lynchburg, Bristol, and Chattanooga, the entire distance being 1,340 miles. In contrast to this, the longest route, involving a total haul of 2,051 miles, is by way of Buffalo, New Haven, Ind., St. Louis, and Texarkana. Estimating the cost of carrying a minimum carload of 24,000 pounds at the basis per ton per mile furnished by the Statistician of the Interstate Commerce Commission for the year ending June 30, 1892, the cost for the shorter route is $77.18; for the longer, $118.14,—or an excess over the minimum of necessary expenditure for each carload carried by the longer route of $40.96, or 53 per cent. This illustration is typical of the entire transportation system, and many equally startling instances could be shown. Between Omaha and St. Paul, with a short-line distance of 373 miles, traffic is carried by a competing line whose distance is 734 miles. Between Chicago and New York there are 21 routes ranging from 912 to 1,376 miles; from Chicago to Montreal, 10 routes ranging from 837 to 1,400 miles; from Omaha to San Francisco, five routes varying from 1,865 to 2,724 miles; and from Chicago to Jacksonville, Fla., 63 routes ranging from 1,097 to 1,644 miles in length. These are not merely possible routes, but are all actually competing for traffic between the points named. A case recently decided by the Interstate Commerce Commission illustrates this practice in one of its many phases. A shipper located at Ritzville, Wash., offered a carload of wheat for shipment to Portland, Ore., which the railroad declined to accept, except upon the understanding that it should be carried on its own line over the Cascade Mountains, through a long tunnel to Tacoma, and thence to destination, a total distance of 480 miles, over an expensive and circuitous route having many costly grades, although in connection with another railway there was a shorter route of only 311 miles, mostly along the Columbia River, with few and light grades. The Commission, in an opinion rendered by Chairman Morrison, sustained the contention of the complainants that it is the right of every shipper to demand that his goods be carried over the least expensive route. While it may be true that the shortest is not necessarily the cheapest route, yet it cannot be doubted that a considerable saving would result from forwarding all traffic over whatever routes should be found by careful experiment to be the cheapest.

Railway revenues are constantly wasted in order to maintain competitive train service, both passenger and freight, which is wholly unnecessary for the accommodation of the public or the demands of traffic. Between Chicago and Omaha, 22 passenger trains, or 11 each way, are run on every day except Sunday, and 16 run seven times a week. As there are only about 200 passengers per diem in each direction, it is evident that half as many trains would afford ample accommodation with sufficient margin for local traffic. Upon the basis of the estimated cost per mile for running passenger trains, furnished by the Interstate Commerce Commission, the cost of running a passenger train from Omaha to Chicago is about $400, and the saving resulting from reducing the number of trains one-half would amount to $1,539,200 per year. Similar duplication of service exists between Chicago and Kansas City, Chicago and St. Paul, St. Louis and Kansas City, and in many other localities. Similar data are not available regarding freight service, but it is certain that while an ordinary locomotive will readily haul from twenty-five to thirty loaded cars upon level road, the actual average trainload of about 182 tons is far too low. The statement that the most economical use of railway facilities would require that every locomotive should haul a full train of completely loaded cars, and that great savings can be effected by measures tending to secure that result, does not need further amplification.

Large sums are also expended annually in maintaining separate and duplicate organizations with the requisite official machinery for each. Though reform in this direction may seem less practicable, there is no doubt that, could it be effected, large savings would result.

It will be observed that all the wasteful expenditures enumerated are in some way connected with competition between carriers for traffic, and it will not be surprising, therefore, that its elimination in a greater or less degree is suggested as the means through which the radical economies which are a necessary preliminary to further reductions in rates are to be effected.

The measures which have been suggested to attain this end are railway associations, pooling, consolidation. These will be found to be satisfactory in exact proportion to the degree in which they are successful in suppressing competition. Railway associations not founded upon the principle of division of traffic or earnings have proved ineffectual because they do not sufficiently protect the traffic or revenues of the weaker lines. Pooling, when permitted, was charged with responsibility for the construction of unnecessary lines which could serve no useful end, but were built upon the purely speculative anticipation of being able, by piratical methods, to obtain a share of the pooled traffic. Consolidation, if carried far enough, would render unnecessary the payment of commissions to secure traffic and the maintenance of expensive agencies; would cause all traffic to be forwarded by the cheapest routes; would do away with unnecessary train service and empty trains; would wipe out duplicate organizations,—in short, would abolish all competition. It might also render imperative a decision upon the question whether the government shall own the railways.

H. T. NEWCOMB.

The Forum

NOVEMBER, 1894.

POLITICAL CAREER AND CHARACTER OF DAVID B. HILL.

THERE is no other man, so conspicuous in public life as Senator Hill, about whose personal qualities so little is known. He was an avowed candidate for the Presidency in 1892, and had a solid delegation to the National Democratic Convention in his favor from the most powerful State in the Union. He has for the past two years been the most conspicuous individual figure in the United States Senate. He is now again the Democratic candidate for the governorship of New York, with the expectation that, if elected, he will be a prominent candidate for his party's nomination for the Presidency in 1896. He has been before the public constantly for nearly ten years as a politician of untiring activity and high ambition. What is a proper measure of this man? To answer this question is to explain what it is that Mr. Hill represents in American politics; and this can best be done by tracing his political career from its beginning to the present moment, judging his character and purposes by the outward manifestations of them which he himself has made.

Mr· Hill began his political career in 1863. He was seventeen when he entered a law office and began the study of his profession. He was twenty when he became an active ward politician in the city of Elmira. He devoted much more time to politics than to his profession, showing more ambition to become a ward leader than to advance himself as a member of the bar. From the first he showed an aversion to polite society, to books, and to studious ways in life, seeking friends and companions among those elements of city population which delight in ward politics. These he organized into compact bands of personal followers, and used them to advance his political ambition. He was soon chosen a justice of the peace, was sent as a delegate to a State convention, and in due time was chosen a member of the State legislature, and finally mayor of the city of Elmira. Simultaneously with his advancement a change for the worse came over the politics of his ward. It had a large floating vote and a considerable negro vote when he became active in its affairs. Both these elements speedily became purchasable, and the methods of his ward soon became those of all parts of the city. In Elmira he played his part with skill and address. He was on familiar terms with the " boys." The volunteer firemen were his friends, and he cultivated the popular game of base-ball, thereby acquiring the only passion, aside from politics, that he is known to possess. He had already become a commanding local figure, fast making himself known to the Democrats of the State by constant attendance at State conventions.

As a political leader Mr. Hill early put in operation the principle that if you cannot succeed with your own party you may seek success by means of a coalition, open or secret, with the opposing party. From the beginning, too, he preferred as agents and allies the disreputable rather than the respectable elements of the community. One of his most intimate friends and chief lieutenants was a man who had been dismissed from the Union army, and who subsequently, as a pension-agent, was convicted of gross frauds and sentenced to the penitentiary. When he became a member of the Assembly in 1871, Mr. Hill allied himself with the followers of Tweed, voting with them on all the Tweed measures designed to rob New York city, opposing the repeal of the Erie Classification Act under which Fisk and Gould had gained possession of the Erie railway. He got control of an Elmira newspaper, and the pension-agent mentioned above took $10,000 worth of its stock for some person not named, who subsequently turned out to be Tweed. It is fair to say that he did not owe this quick success in politics—he was one of the youngest members when he first entered the Legislature—to mere manipulation of the politics of Elmira, nor to mere popularity with the firegoing, ball-playing youth of western New York. Intellectually he was worthy of the place. He had risen at the bar, and was a jury advocate of no mean ability. He was far better equipped as a legislator than many fellow-members older both in years and experience. He clearly possessed every requisite for public life except character.

He was re-elected in 1872 to what was known as the Reform

Legislature. It was here that he met Mr. Tilden. Tweed could no longer be of service to the aspiring young politician. He recognized the man of the hour and clung to him. It was in Chemung County as yet that he was strong, and not beyond it. He had indeed won the favor of Mr. Tilden, but while the latter was Governor he did not avail himself of Mr. Hill's services. While Mr. Tilden controlled the party in New York, Mr. Hill was an opponent of Tammany Hall. He was a member of the State Committee when it was under the leadership of Manning and Whitney. He was a foe of John Kelly. He doubtless held the view that Tammany Hall did not and could not represent the Democratic party of the city of New York, and that Democrats who were not members of that organization had the right to participate in the primary elections of their party. During seventeen years, beginning in 1871, the doctrine prevailed in the Democratic party that the organization was the instrumentality for carrying out the will of the voters. The leaders of the party succeeded in preventing the Tammany machine from obtaining recognition as the party organization in the city. While this idea prevailed, Mr. Hill accepted it, although during most of that time his opinion on that subject was not sought. He was depended on for carrying caucuses and conventions, and the admiration which Mr. Tilden undoubtedly entertained for him was due to the fact that he was a consummate master of machine politics. In his own city of Elmira he had constructed a machine which excited the wonder of his local associates, and in 1882 enabled him to be elected mayor in opposition to the Republican candidate, who, a year before, had been elected.

This success made him the Democratic candidate for the lieutenant-governorship in the same year. But from that moment his course in politics took a different and a sinister direction. A high ambition mastered him, but a rivalry that seems to have compelled him to discard all appearance of political virtue also took possession of him. A new object of popular regard had entered the political arena, and Mr. Hill felt that his own advance was checked if not finally and definitely obstructed. It was natural that he should have sought Mr. Cleveland's nomination and election to the Presidency in 1884; for the promotion of Mr. Cleveland, whose extraordinary victory in 1882 he had shared, made him the Governor of New York.

Since March, 1885, his career has been in full view of the public. He has turned his back upon the leaders with whom he was once associated. He allied himself with Tammany Hall and joined in the

partisan ribaldry with which Mr. Cleveland's civil-service-reform professions and practices were greeted by disappointed office-seekers. He
had a part of the machine with him, and the people against him. It
had been said that his administration of the office of mayor of Elmira
was " businesslike," and, during the campaign of 1882, Mr. Cleveland and he were spoken of by stump orators and party newspapers as
the " two reform mayors. " Nevertheless, the inference was general that
Mr. Hill was a small politician and quite too inconsiderable a person to
be governor of the State. There had then been no Democratic candidate for that office of such slight repute. Whatever rewards might have
been considered meet for the useful politician who looked after details,
organized machines, and carried caucuses, the governorship was not
one of them. Mr. Cleveland's election to the Presidency advanced
Mr. Hill to an office for which, otherwise, he might still be struggling.

No sooner was he governor than he began a partisan struggle
with the Republican legislature. He recommended himself to many
of his fellow-Democrats by.the intensity of his partisanship. It was,
however, not a partisanship founded upon belief in political principi-
ples. Mr. Hill's opinion on the tariff question, or on any other issue
of moment, was unknown when he became governor, and is unknown
yet. In the autumn of 1885 it was known that he represented nothing which had brought to Mr. Cleveland the votes of the Independents, but that he did stand for all that was base and selfish in New
York politics. But he had won the friendship and applause of
Democrats of the baser sort from one end of the country to the other.
Mr. Cleveland had been in power only a few months, but the land
was filled with the wailing of the disappointed, and the *disjecta mem-
bra* of the shipwrecked office-beggars. Mr. Hill gathered them into an
army of personal followers. He was the desperate leader of desperate
fortunes. When he opened his campaign in Brooklyn he uttered the
sentence, " I am a Democrat,"—which has since become famous. He
meant: " I am different from the person you have foolishly placed in
the White House. " He was elected governor by 11,000 plurality,
and this was pointed to as an indication that he was more popular in
the State than Mr. Cleveland, who the year before had carried it by
a plurality of a little more than 1,000. But his opponent was Ira
Davenport, a man of excellent character, who had offended Mr.
Thomas C. Platt in the memorable struggle between himself and Mr.
Conkling with President Garfield in 1881. Davenport was the victim
of Platt, and Hill was the beneficiary.

An episode growing out of this campaign will suffice to indicate Mr. Hill's personal character. Hasty men have called him honest because they assume that he is poor. Whether his poverty is fact or fiction is not known to the writer of this article. But it may be well to consider the degree of honesty shown in the transactions which were revealed in the inquiry into the Aqueduct contracts, and to consider how far Mr. Hill's pecuniary negotiations with the firm of O'Brien & Clark and the Democratic State Committee can be reconciled with the standard of probity which should be found in the governor of the State. Governor Hill secured $15,000 on two notes in 1885, which, it is asserted, was paid over to the Democratic State Committee, of which John O'Brien was chairman. The first note—for $10,000—was indorsed by William L. Muller, Hill's partner and political agent, and by John O'Brien and Heman Clark, contractors doing business under the firm name of O'Brien & Clark. It was cashed by O'Brien. The second note—for $5,000—was indorsed by Muller and Alton B. Parker. It was cashed by John Keenan, who held and divided the spoils in the Broadway railroad case, and who for years was a fugitive from justice in Canada. O'Brien paid both notes. Hill never paid a dollar on them. In return for this he secured a contract for work on the New York aqueduct for O'Brien & Clark, from the Commission which he had appointed, the notorious Rollin M. Squire being its head. This contract was given to the firm at Governor Hill's request, in spite of the fact that its bid was $54,000 higher than the lowest bid. O'Brien & Clark sold out the contract for a profit of $30,000. The taxpayers, however, were forced to pay $54,000 to take up Governor Hill's notes, amounting to $15,000. All this appears in the evidence taken in the investigation of the Aqueduct Commission, both Mayor Grace and Comptroller Loew testifying to the solicitation of the contract for O'Brien & Clark.

Circumstances had grown to be adverse to the development of Mr. Hill's good character. Mr. Cleveland was the representative of the best elements of his party, and Mr. Hill was therefore forced to depend upon other sources of strength for the advancement for which he had already begun to intrigue. He soon made an alliance with Tammany, and entered upon the task of constructing a machine which has since become the most perfect instrument of its kind known to the political history of the country. The scandals of the Aqueduct Commission can be traced directly to his first efforts in the building of this machine.

During his term as governor he continued his war with the Republicans who controlled the legislature. He insisted that they should pass a law providing for a new census and a new apportionment, but neither side would consent to anything that would not give its party an advantage, and so, between the two, the Constitution, which required a census in 1885, was disobeyed. Mr. Hill has always manifested his contempt for civil-service reform, and, whenever he was able to evade the law while he was governor, he availed himself of his opportunity. His hostility to the reform was manifested most characteristically in his opening speech of the present campaign at Syracuse, when he attempted to account for the corruption of the New York police force by pointing to the fact that appointments to it are governed by civil-service regulations, ignoring the evidence recently brought to light of the defiance of those regulations, and of the law itself, by his friends and supporters in Tammany Hall. As governor, he also opposed all attempts to secure ballot-reform, inventing difficulties, and discovering a constitutional objection which was worthy of the cunning brain of a criminal practitioner.

In 1888 he was again nominated for the governorship. His machine was not so perfect as to prevent the sending of a Cleveland delegation to St. Louis, but he sympathized with Tammany's opposition to the President, and it is generally believed that he traded with the Republicans for his own profit, and to the defeat of the head of his party's ticket. Notwithstanding his assurance of his devotion to his party, it was almost universally believed that he was quite capable of making a bargain of this kind. At all events, he received 15,000 more votes than were cast for Mr. Cleveland, while Mr. Warner Miller received 17,000 fewer votes than were cast for Mr. Harrison. The figures of the election of 1885 show that at that time he was a much weaker candidate in New York State than Mr. Cleveland; for while he had a plurality of 11,000, his total vote was nearly 34,000 less than that which was cast for Mr. Cleveland for the governorship in 1882, and over 62,000 less than that which was cast for Cleveland for the Presidency in 1884. The New York "Tribune" said that he "succeeded only because he was able to sell a Presidency for a governorship." Mr. James M. Varnum, Chairman of the Republican Convention, speaking of the appearance of Mr. Cleveland and Mr. Hill on the same platform, said: "If Mr. Hill . . . had not thought more of himself than he did of his party, Grover Cleveland would now be President of the United States, and you all know it."

It was in the campaign of 1888 that Governor Hill obtained full control of the Democratic machine on the plea that the campaign in the State was primarily for the governorship, and therefore the State Committee should be in the hands of his friends. In 1891 the machine was perfect. It controlled the great cities, and they, in turn, controlled the State. Croker in New York, McLaughlin in Brooklyn, Murphy in Troy, and Sheehan in Buffalo, commanded the divisions, and Governor Hill was general-in-chief of the army of hungry marauders. It did not matter what the Democratic voters wished to declare at their primaries. The Governor, with a mastery of detail, and an industry in his single purpose which few good men wish to possess, had placed his emissaries in command of the town and county committees throughout the State. Subsequently laws were passed which deprived the voters of the conduct of their own primaries, and transferred the power—up to that time always in the hands of the people—to the local party organization. This was accomplished, however, after the election of Governor Flower.

After the election of 1891, when it was discovered that the State Senate was evenly divided between the two parties, with a few districts in doubt, a scheme was set on foot by the Democratic party managers to manipulate the local canvassing-boards in those districts, and thus secure certificates of election from them for the Democratic candidates. From the first, Governor Hill gave hearty support to this scheme. When the clerks of two county canvassing-boards declined to sign the certificates for the Democratic candidates, on the ground of fraud, Governor Hill summoned them before him and removed them from office. The Supreme Court of the State sustained the view of the refusing clerks by declaring the canvasses fraudulent and illegal, and ordering new ones. One of these fraudulent returns, signed by a secretary *pro tem.*, was sent to Albany and filed in the State office. The Supreme Court, its General Term, and the Court of Appeals, all declared this return to be the "result of an illegal and erroneous canvass," and directed that if a legal return should be sent to the State Board of Canvassers that body should canvass it. Such a legal return was sent by mail, was delivered in the office of the Governor, Comptroller, and Secretary of State, and was taken from the mails in those offices by Isaac H. Maynard and a county clerk who acted with the approval of Governor Hill. When the State Board of Canvassers met, this legal return was missing. Judge Maynard was present and sat in silence when the question as to its whereabouts was raised. The Board, in defiance of the decrees of the courts, then proceeded to canvass the illegal return, and in that way stole a majority of one in the Senate. The members of the Board have been adjudged guilty of contempt for this act, both by the Supreme Court and by its General Term. It was shown by affidavits offered in the contempt proceedings that the decision to canvass this illegal return was reached at a meeting between Governor Hill, Judge Maynard, and one other person. The Bar Association of New York city, through a committee of nine of its most eminent members, seven of whom were Democratic, investigated Judge Maynard's conduct in taking the legal return from the mails, unanimously declared it to be " entirely without any warrant or justification in law," and pronounced his offence to be " one of the gravest known to the law," coming under the Penal Code as grand larceny in the second degree, punishable by imprisonment for not more than five years, or by a fine of not more than $500 or both. Judge Cullen of the Supreme Court, in reviewing the same act, grouped Governor Hill and Judge Maynard as equally guilty in the crime. When Judge Maynard was nominated for election to the Court of Appeals bench, upon which he was sitting by appointment from Governor Flower through Mr. Hill's influence, Hill took the stump in his behalf, declared the theft of the returns to be " an act of simple justice," denounced the Bar Association as a " brainless set of namby-pambys," and asserted that Maynard's nomination was demanded by " justice, honor, propriety, and the usages of our party."

Having gained control of the State, and having nothing to fear from the opposition of the Democratic voters at home, Senator Hill became an avowed candidate for the Presidential nomination of 1892. He had retained the admiration of Democrats who are enemies of Mr. Cleveland, and he undertook to present himself to the South as a statesman worthy of their support for the highest office in the country. His tour through the South was a failure. But he owned New York. Governor Flower was his obedient tool. At Mr. Hill's dictation he had appointed Isaac H. Maynard to fill a vacancy on the Court of Appeals bench. He had retained Hill's men in office. He was Hill's man himself. He signed the bills that fastened the rule of the corrupt machine upon the party and the State. When he had prepared everything to his satisfaction, Mr. Hill ordered his machine to elect a delegation to the National Convention that should be unanimously in favor of his nomination. He wanted New York secure for the impression that his apparent mastership would make in other States.

It was largely for this reason that the Convention was called to meet on the 22d of February. The plan worked to the point expected, but Hill had gone one step too far in his autocratic rule, and, from the day that the call for the "Snap Convention" was issued, his power in politics began to wane. The Democratic party revolted against the Hill machine. The "Anti-Snap" or May Convention was called, and the enrolment of protesting Democrats against the February Convention and its packed delegation was so great that the National Convention declined to credit the predictions of Hill's messengers and delegates to Chicago that Mr. Cleveland could not carry the State if he were nominated.

Mr. Hill was defeated in the Convention, but he returned to New York with power enough to compel the friends of Mr. Cleveland to give over the management of the campaign in New York to his machine, over which presided those geniuses of political depravity— Edward Murphy, Jr., and William F. Sheehan. Whether or not the State machine was loyal, its efforts were directed to securing a majority in the Assembly that would favor the preposterous senatorial ambition of Edward Murphy, Jr. This, at least, was the result of the contest, and Mr. Murphy became Senator Hill's colleague against the protests of Mr. Cleveland, of every Democrat who had a political conscience, and of every citizen of New York who was proud of his State and wished to see it worthily represented in the Federal Senate.

During his seven years as governor, Mr. Hill vetoed three carefully drawn ballot-reform measures in as many successive years, and finally gave his approval to a measure which was drawn to meet his objections, and which is the present law of the State, universally recognized as one of the most defective of the thirty-seven similar laws now in operation. He vetoed also three measures designed to restrict and regulate the liquor traffic by increasing the license fee, and making other reasonable and conservative changes, taking occasion, in doing so, to assail with abusive language the advocates of them. After pursuing this course for three years he advocated an excise bill which the liquor-dealers' association had drawn to meet their own desires, and it became a law with his signature. There is no record of any measure of reform, especially in city government, becoming a law with his approval. Neither is there any record of a measure designed to increase the powers and add to the enrolments of the most corrupt municipal machines, like those of Tammany Hall in New York, the McLaughlin ring in Brooklyn, and the Sheehan

266 POLITICAL CAREER AND CHARACTER OF DAVID B. HILL.

faction in Buffalo, failing to become a law because of his opposition. So persistently did he oppose all measures in the interest of good government, that during the closing year of his career as governor the advocates of all such measures became weary of bringing them before the legislature.

Mr. Hill cut scarcely any figure in the Senate in 1892. He had not been long in his seat before he deserted it and went to Albany to manage the midwinter convention which he had called to elect delegates to the National Democratic Convention in support of his candidacy for the Presidency. During the struggle in Congress for the repeal of the Sherman Silver Act he made speeches which were in favor of free silver coinage, but voted finally in favor of repeal. When the Wilson tariff bill reached the Senate he was one of the first Senators to take the field against it. His first formal speech against it was directed almost entirely at the income-tax feature of it. He opened his speech with an attack upon the foreign policy of the Cleveland administration, especially in Hawaii, saying it was a blunder, and a natural consequence of selecting a Republican for Secretary of State. He avoided saying that he should vote against the Wilson bill, simply declaring that he stood ready to support any reasonable measure of tariff-reform framed within the lines and based upon the principles of his formerly expressed views. He said in concluding: " The failure of the tariff-revision means the defeat, the demoralization, if not the division and the annihilation of our party." From that time forward he did all that he could to delay and defeat the bill. He voted in favor of making it a more liberal measure of tariff-reform only when he knew that his vote would be powerless. Thus he voted with three Populist Senators in favor of free iron ore, making the total vote in the affirmative four. He advocated putting lead on the free list, after the Democratic canvass had decided against it, and got two votes besides his own in support of that proposition. He dodged nearly all the votes on the details of the sugar schedule, only recording his vote when he could get individual prominence by so doing. He refrained from voting unless the Senate put wool on the free list. He advocated the putting of coal on the free list, knowing that the Democrats were committed against it, and got four Populist and two Republican votes besides his own in the affirmative. On the proposition to strike sugar from the free list, he refrained from voting. He opposed a proposition to put barbed wire on the free list. When the income-tax provision was reached in the Senate he again denounced it, and when the tariff bill came up for final passage he voted against it. In his speech he censured the Democratic majority in the Senate for its course in disregarding his advice, saying that leaving the income tax in the bill was in his opinion a blunder which "imperils the possibility of permanent Democratic success in any northern State for many years to come;" and that, "as between a Populistic income tax on the one hand, and a Republican tariff law on the other, I choose the latter as the least of two evils." Though he had not voted for free wool, and had antagonized free barbed wire, he rebuked the Democratic majority for not putting more free raw materials in the bill. Finally he declared that the bill was "satisfactory neither to the Democratic party nor to the country," and thus characterized it:

"This is not a Democratic bill, I am sure; it is not a distinctly Republican bill; it is not a Populist bill entire, but it is a mixture of all—it is a rag-bag production—it is a crazy-quilt combination—it is a splendid nothing."

When the final vote was taken, Mr. Hill was the only Democrat recorded in the negative with the Republicans.

Before closing the record of Mr. Hill's career in the Senate, it remains to add that he opposed the confirmation of two appointees of President Cleveland for the Supreme Court bench, both of whom were eminent lawyers, of unimpeachable ability and fitness, who had served on the committee of the Bar Association of New York city which had condemned Judge Maynard. Mr. Hill regarded their appointment, after this proceeding against a nominee of their own party, as a personal affront to himself, and persuaded the Senate to reject both nominations.

In the Senate all his alliances have been with other parties than his own. He joined the Populist and Silver Senators in his opposition to the Sherman repeal bill, and he worked with both Populists and Republicans in his efforts to defeat the tariff bill. It will be remembered that in explaining his vote against that bill he said he preferred the McKinley bill to it as "the least of two evils," and spoke of the bill itself as a "splendid nothing." This was on July 3. Barely three months later, on September 25, he was saying of the same two tariff bills, in a speech as presiding officer of the Democratic convention which nominated him for governor,—

"The enactment of the McKinley tariff law was the culminating atrocity of Republican recklessness in legislation, a measure so extreme, so selfish, so unreasonable that I hazard nothing in asserting that conservative and fair-minded Republicans everywhere regretted the party exigencies which seemed to demand its passage. It was the very personification of protectionism run mad. Throwing off all disguises, it was the inauguration of a huge scheme of governmental partnership with private business interests. Without retracting a single word which I uttered in the Senate in criticism of the measure [the Senate tariff bill], of its strictly tariff issues it may truthfully be urged that it is a vast improvement over the McKinley law. It is true that it does not embody the full measure of tariff reform, but nevertheless is safe, moderate, reasonable."

Not a word was to be found in this speech about the income tax.

This is the record of Mr. Hill's life, and it reveals so clearly the elements of his personality that comment is scarcely necessary. Throughout the whole of it the same tendencies appear. From the beginning of his political career in the third ward of Elmira, down to the present moment, he has shunned not merely intellectual but respectable society, and sought for intimates and followers among the lower classes, the tricksters in politics. While governor, and aspiring to a Presidential nomination, he selected as the editor of his personal newspaper organ a man who had served a term in the penitentiary. He has seldom been seen at a social gathering or dinner in the house of an eminent or respectable member of society. Not a single conspicuous act in the interest of good government or pure politics can be found in his career. He has been the first American politician to build up a political following and to base his hopes of political preferment entirely upon the worst elements of the population. He not only has not sought respectable support in constructing his power, but has openly defied it. When he was nominated for the governorship a few weeks ago, so completely had he cut himself off from the respectable elements of even his own party, that the Vice-President of the United States was the only man of either National or State eminence who ventured publicly to congratulate him.

Mr. Hill is a man of great intelligence, whose character depends upon circumstances. A clever newspaper writer once compared him with Jay Gould, saying:

"Gould's purpose is the accumulation of wealth. Hill's is the obtaining of political power. And for twenty-five years there has been no thought or action of his life which has not been centred in his purpose."

There are no pursuits like money-getting and politics for affording opportunities for dishonesty; and when a young man whose character depends upon circumstances chooses either one of these careers, it is not difficult to foretell the end.

So much for this spectacular and artificial political career. As for Senator Hill himself, he has reached the zenith of his career.

He has no moral resources. A product of machine politics, his career may at any time be closed by the same artificial forces that have made it; nothing is less secure than a machine-built success.

But there is one question of greater importance in connection with this political career—the question of the survival of the Democratic party as a political instrument of utility. Now whether it be desirable that the Democratic party should survive as an active and respectable force, is a matter of permissible difference of opinion. But there can be no difference of independent opinion regarding the certainty of its defeat for many a year in contests for control of the national government, if it mistake Senator Hill's artificial success for statesmanship; and in proportion as Democratic orators and newspapers throughout the country encourage him, or even tolerate him, do they give evidence of their party's old-time infirmity. And the Democratic party has not such a reputation for wisdom that it can afford to make an unnecessary display of ignorance; nor has it so firm a grasp on great principles that it can afford to slip one inch from its already insecure hold on them.

Least of all can the party afford to follow the one man in its ranks who has in the most spectacular way repudiated its pledges to tariff-reform whereupon it won its only victories within the lifetime of a generation. The tariff-reform tide was the last tide in national politics. The next will be a tide of municipal reform. As Senator Hill is the only Democratic Senator who voted against the party's single great principle, so he is the most conspicuous and successful product of corruption in municipal politics. If the cities of the State of New York had not been governed corruptly, as they have been, no such career as Mr. Hill's would have been possible. A small municipal boss himself, it has been by the help of the municipal bosses whom he has served that he has prospered.

Every thoughtful man knows that the three subjects of political vitality now before us are the tariff, the currency, and municipal government. It is very unfortunate for the Democratic party that its most conspicuous personality is a man without convictions on any of these subjects, and who has done violence to right thinking and right conduct regarding all three of them. Mr. Hill's career is important, therefore, as a measure of the stupidity and the criminal tendencies of the Democratic party. It revives the old question whether the party can ever be trusted.

" INDEPENDENT. "

SHOULD SENATORS BE ELECTED BY THE PEOPLE?

In order that those who do the writer the honor of reading this contribution to the study of a very important question may thoroughly understand in what way and to what end the Senate of the United States came to be composed as it is, I beg the reader's indulgence to begin with some generalities of theory and historic events, which, however well known, can hardly, especially in these days, be too often repeated.

The establishment of all good government has been designed. to secure liberty and justice. To do this, restraints and counterpoises have been proved, both by philosophy and by all human experience, to be absolutely indispensable. If too much power is vested in the Executive, there is a constant tendency toward usurpation and tyranny. If too much power is left with the people, or their immediate delegates, unchecked, there is continual gravitation toward frequent and ill-considered changes in the laws, as temporary maladies that no law can cure, or crude speculative theories, may disturb the content or excite the day-dreams of the people,—such as fiat money, loaning government money on real-estate security, and the great multitude of nostrums that socialism and anarchism propose as specifics for evils that are inherent among men as social animals, and that no act of legislation can possibly cure. Self-knowledge and self-control are, and always have been, as necessary to the welfare of communities and states as to individuals. All this is as obvious and trite as it is fundamental; but, as one of the old State Constitutions of more than one hundred years ago puts it, " a frequent recurrence to fundamental principles" must be the duty and safeguard of every society that wishes to be free and happy.

It has been upon such considerations that written constitutions have been framed and adopted in establishing governments of the people, declaring inalienable rights, separating governmental powers and duties into three divisions,—legislative, executive, and judiciary, —and dividing the legislative power between two separate bodies *differently constituted and composed by different processes of popular action,* and setting bounds and barriers against the preponderance of any one of such divisions, and imposing restraints upon any sudden change in the constitutions themselves.   It was upon such principles and under such conditions that the great, and then unique, Constitution of the United States came into existence in 1787.

The Convention that framed it was constituted by the separate and independent action of all the thirteen original States (excepting Rhode Island, which sent no delegates), upon the solemn appeal of the Continental Congress, made after seven years of bitter experience in war and three in peace, during both of which periods the need of the fundamental elements and adjustments of a government adequate to the preservation of the liberties of the people, the administration of personal justice, and the stability of the whole republic, were made fully and often painfully manifest.   The men who composed the Convention were possessed of all that knowledge which the histories and careers of all other civilized countries and peoples could furnish; they represented all the principal occupations of civilized society and all the phases of political philosophy—monarchical in one direction, and so-called pure democracy in the other.   It was presided over by " His Excellency, George Washington, Esquire," as he is styled in the Convention Journal.   The Convention labored assiduously from the 25th of May until the 15th of September, 1787, when the completed Constitution was agreed upon and signed by representatives of all the States, excepting Rhode Island, which, as has been said, took no part in the Convention.   Almost every example and method of government was examined and discussed.   The *apparent* conflicts of interest, and the *real* jealousies existing between large states and small ones, were to be accommodated or overcome,—undue centralization, on the one hand, as well as the fatal weakness of a mere league of states on the other, were to be guarded against.   To accomplish all these supreme ends, it was easy for those learned, experienced, and patriotic men to agree that the new government should be composed of three independent departments,—legislative, executive, and judicial; and that the legislative branch should be composed of two independent parts, each having a negative on the other.   But the composition of the two houses was a subject of extreme difficulty.

The States, without regard to geographical dimensions, population or wealth, freedom or slavery, were, under the Confederacy, absolute equals, and the national powers scarcely extended to, or operated personally upon, any of the citizens of the States.   At last, after considering and reconsidering nearly every variety of propositions, it was agreed that the House of Representatives should be chosen directly by the people and in proportion to the number of inhabitants in each State, excepting two-fifths of the slaves.   And after similar tribulations of proposal and discussion, it was settled that the President should be chosen on the principle of having regard, chiefly, to the population of the various States.   So far, then, it was a government based upon capitation, and, in one part of it, required to be constituted by the direct vote of the people,—the weight and force of *numbers alone*.   It was obvious that if the other branch of the legislature were constituted in the same way, either as to the number from each State or the direct method of election, there would be a perpetual tendency toward the effacement of State rights and State sovereignty in respect of local affairs, and the establishment of a national democracy by government, practically, *en masse*, where the weight of the mass in one part of the country might, and probably would, dominate over other parts, and might in the end destroy the peaceful liberties of all, as has been the ever-repeating experience of ill-balanced and unchecked forms of government,—democracy succeeding conservatism and liberal order; the commune succeeding democracy; anarchism overturning the commune; and a single despot or brace of despots springing from the cabals and corruptions of communism and anarchy to be the masters of all.

To establish a secure barrier against such tendencies and dangers, the constitution of a second legislative branch composed of persons having a different constituency, and representing the independent equality of the States, was a supreme necessity.

In the Convention every aspect of the question was considered, and nearly or quite every possible method of accomplishing the purpose was suggested.   In the first draft of a Constitution submitted by Edmund Randolph, of Virginia, it was proposed that the Senate be elected by the House of Representatives " out of a proper number of persons nominated by the individual legislatures." [1]   Mr. Dickinson, of Delaware, and Roger Sherman, proposed that the senators " ought to be chosen by the individual legislatures." [2]   Mr. Wilson, and Mr. Morris, of Pennsylvania, proposed that the senators " be elected by the people *in districts* to be formed for that purpose." [3]   Mr. Sherman and Mr. Ellsworth moved that in the Senate " each State shall have

[1] Convention Journal, p. 67, May 29.
[2] P. 105, June 7.   [3] P. 106, June 7.

one vote."[1] Mr. Wilson and Mr. Hamilton moved that voting in the Senate "ought to be according to the rule established for the first branch" (the House of Representatives).[1] Mr. Hamilton proposed that Senators be elected " by electors chosen for that purpose by the people,—in order to this, the States to be divided into election districts."[2]

These various propositions were considered in Committee of the Whole, which on the 19th of June reported to the whole House a scheme which provided that the members of the Senate " ought to be chosen by the individual legislatures."[3] *This proposition was agreed to, unanimously, in the Committee of the Whole;*[4] and in the whole House it was agreed to in connection with another proposition, by nine States to two, when it first came up on June 25.[5] This difference is accounted for by the struggle then pending as to whether the States should vote in the Senate as in the existing Confederacy, *i.e.*, each State having one vote. When the question again came up on August 9,[6] there does not appear to have been any difference of opinion as to the wisdom of choosing senators by the State legislatures. The only difference was as to the amount of representation each State should have; and on September 17, " on the question to agree to the Constitution in order to be signed, all the States answered Aye."

It will be seen that the proposal to elect senators by the people was brought forward and considered deliberately, and as deliberately and almost, if not quite, unanimously dismissed. The debates[7] show how calmly and fully the whole subject was considered, and how nearly unanimous the great statesmen and patriots who composed the Convention were in deciding against the proposition, which " these new charmers who keep serpents" have now revived.

The essential and underlying idea of the structure of our national government is that in its relations to the people in respect of the subjects committed to it by the Constitution, and no others, it is a government operating upon *persons*, and that in respect of all its other relations with the people of the several States it affects them in their *collective character as States.*

The ultimate sovereign power of a free state must and should always reside in the people. But a wise people who wish to remain free and sovereign never undertake the task of exercising their sovereignty otherwise than by selecting representatives responsible to them, to do all acts of governmental sovereignty, save in passing *ad*

[1] Ibid. p. 112, June 11. [2] P. 130, June 18. [3] P. 135. [4] P. 106.
[5] P. 147. [6] Pp. 237, 238. [7] Madison Papers.

18

referendum upon their Constitutions.   It is true that in some of the Swiss republics and in a few of the States of our Union some laws have been passed to take effect upon the approval of the people, but these are rare exceptions.   The legislature of a State, then, is the depositary of the whole mass of the sovereign power which the people, as such, have set forth and defined in its Constitution.   It expresses the *will* of the State; the Executive executes that will; and the judiciary, in cases of dispute, decides what that will is.   In constituting and exercising such a sovereignty, the people of a State never elect either branch of their legislature by the popular vote of all the citizens on a general ticket: that step remains to come in when the dream of the socialist shall be realized.   The reason is obvious. Such a method would be purely the voice of an aggregation of mere numbers regardless of intelligence, property, and business interests, as well as of that innate sense of the value of the geographical distribution and separation of the various parts of a State into small communities substantially homogeneous.   This notion begins with the nature of man himself as a separate individual; it is the foundation of the family, the town, the county, and of the State also, in our great republic.   Upon it rests the division of States into congressional districts, which took place in 1842, after fifty-three years of experience had demonstrated the evils of the system of electing members of the House of Representatives from each State by a vote *en masse*,—a system to which no one is yet wild enough to propose a return.   The government of a State is instituted for the benefit of the whole people, and not for that of party, nor for that of a majority of its people alone; and the act of a State in choosing its senators is one of the most important parts of its governmental duty.   Both reason and experience prove that an election by a majority of all the people of a State is radically a different thing from the choice of the same officers by the people (through their representatives) of the separate political divisions of it.   In respect of members of the House of Representatives and of the State legislatures, the vast majority of citizens will agree that such a system of mass voting would be unendurable, and dangerous to, and at last destructive of, good government, and even liberty itself, as rational men understand the term.

If these conclusions be true as regards the election of members of the House of Representatives and the members of the State legislatures, is it not equally clear that the founders of the republic adopted the best possible—and indeed imaginable—method of choosing the members of the national Senate? They believed that the liberty and happiness of the people of the several States—States which they foresaw would finally embrace a continent in their benign sway—could only be preserved by such divisions and subdivisions of the sources and methods and exercise of political power as they adopted and provided for. A century of experience has demonstrated the wisdom of their marvellous plan.

But a new school of politicians has now appeared who profess to believe that the Fathers were mistaken in their theory of the surest foundation of our national republic, and that the system they adopted has not, in regard to senators, worked well,—that the senators have not been the choice of, and have not represented, the great body of the people of the States that elected them, and therefore that elections of senators should be had by the suffrage of all the voters in the State *acting together*. One test of the truth of the first statement is the fact that of the less than 900 persons who have served as senators since the government was organized in 1789, more than 200 have been members of the House of Representatives—substantially one-fourth.

State	Number of Senators since 1789	Have served in House of Representatives	Serving in House subsequent to Senatorial term	State	Number of Senators since 1789	Have served in House of Representatives	Serving in House subsequent to Senatorial term
Alabama	18	7	..	Montana	2	..	..
Arkansas	14	3	..	Nebraska	7	2	..
California	19	6	..	Nevada	5	..	..
Colorado	7	2	..	New Hampshire	38	15	1
Connecticut	34	18	1	New Jersey	34	9	2
Delaware	29	11	..	New York	38	15	..
Florida	11	1	..	North Carolina	27	10	1
Georgia	37	16	..	North Dakota	3	1	..
Idaho	3	1	..	Ohio	27	9	..
Illinois	23	9	..	Oregon	13	5	1
Indiana	22	13	..	Pennsylvania	33	14	1
Iowa	10	5	..	Rhode Island	32	7	1
Kansas	10	2	..	South Carolina	32	11	1
Kentucky	35	17	3	South Dakota	3	1	..
Louisiana	28	7	2	Tennessee	30	9	..
Maine	20	11	..	Texas	13	4	..
Maryland	34	15	2	Vermont	23	9	1
Massachusetts	33	24	4	Virginia	38	20	..
Michigan	18	7	..	Washington	2	1	..
Minnesota	11	5	1	West Virginia	10	2	..
Mississippi	27	8	1	Wisconsin	10	3	..
Missouri	18	3	1	Wyoming	2	1	..

Only two States—Montana and Nevada—have not been thus represented, while more than one-half of the senators from Massachusetts,
Connecticut, Indiana, and Maine have been members of the House
of Representatives; and, in addition to these, a very large fraction
of the senators have been governors and judges elected by the
people in their States.   These facts show that it has been almost
universally true that those chosen as senators have possessed the
confidence, not only of the legislative representatives of political
divisions of the States, but of the whole body of the people as well.
The second part of the assertion of the persons who have seen a
new light, as they think, is that sometimes "senators do not represent their States."   This is true; but, happily for all the States and
their people, *a senator, once chosen, becomes a senator of the United
States*, and is not the mere agent of the State that chose him.   And,
as to the State itself that chose him, it has happened, and will happen again, that a gust of passion or a misguided opinion has taken
temporary possession of a majority of the people of a particular State,
which the senator, in his bounden duty to all the States, has disregarded.   This was one of the very incidents that the patriots of
1787 foresaw and provided against by legislative elections and a
long time of service.

Again, the new school of constitution-makers say that they think
the Senate has become a body of rich men who gained their places by
corrupting legislatures in a pecuniary way.   But to any one acquainted
with the personality of the Senate as it has existed for a generation
and is now, such a statement is known to be absolutely destitute of
foundation.   The proportion of rich men in the Senate is not greater
than that which exists in every State and community in the whole
country where the honors and responsibilities of public office are
shared alike by the rich, the comfortable, and the poor.   As a perfect millennium has not yet been reached, it is doubtless true that some
(but very few) men have secured election as senators by pecuniary
persuasions, or, to put it roughly, have "bought their places" with
money,—a crime of the worst character both in the buyer and in the
seller.   But alas, this is not a peculiarity belonging to the office of
senator alone.   It has happened equally or more often in elections
to the House of Representatives, as well as in State and municipal
elections.   A legislative election of senators, therefore, is not the
cause of this great evil.   In the nature of things, it must be worse
in popular elections, for the members of a legislature must, in the

choice of the senator, vote openly, so that the constituents know whether or not their representatives have followed the general judgment of the particular communities they represent,—a matter of vital importance in all representative government. But in popular elections, where each citizen is acting in his personal character only, it is equally important that he have the right to vote secretly, notwithstanding that he may be bribed in spite of every precaution that the law may adopt to prevent it. And when we go back of the regular act of a government election and reach the " primaries" and the district, the county and State conventions, all barriers and safeguards are left behind, and the corruptions of riches and still more of trading machines and office brokerage, have their easiest and most abundant field of achievement in selecting candidates.   To cite examples to the intelligent reader would be a waste of time.   The real people of this republic of States and citizens—those who believe in liberty and order as inseparable, who believe in the value of individual endeavor and frugality, and, as a consequence, in the right to save earnings and to have homes and houses and lands and schools and churches— should consider:—

First, that the Constitutional provision for the choosing of two senators from each State by its legislature was wisely designed by the States that founded the government, as one of the corner-stones of the structure necessary to secure the rights and safety of the States.

Second, that a legislative instead of a popular election was adopted as necessary to the expression of the deliberate will of the State in its character as such, represented in all its parts in the way in which its own constitution distributed power.

Third, that the people of the several political divisions of the State should have the right to express their choice separately through their legal representatives, as they do in making laws, and not be overwhelmed by a mere weight of numbers that might occupy only a corner of the State and possess interests and cherish ambitions quite unlike those of all the other sections of the commonwealth.

Fourth, that the Senate as it has existed for a century has demonstrated the wisdom of the mode of its constitution.

Fifth, that its members have been as free from any just accusation of corruption, either in their election or in their course as senators, as any equal number of men connected with public affairs on the face of the earth, or connected with all the employments of private life.

Sixth, that as the election of senators by the State legislatures must be by open public voting, the danger of bribery, or the misrepresentation of constituents for other causes, is reduced to a minimum, and stands in strong contrast with the election of senators by the direct vote of the whole mass of voters in the several States, and especially in States where political parties are nearly equal in numbers.

Seventh, that, whatever evils now and then happen under the present system, they do not arise from any fault in the system itself, but from the fault of the body of citizens themselves,—non-attendance at caucuses and primaries; non-attendance at registration and at the polls; slavish fidelity to party organizations and party names; a contributing to and winking at the corrupt use of money at nominating conventions and elections; and the encouragement or tolerance of individual self-seeking in respect of getting possession of offices, all of which are truly public trusts.

Eighth, that in ninety-five instances out of a hundred, if there be an evil or inadequate senator or other officer in the public service, it is because the power that elected or appointed him—his State or community—has been either grievously negligent or else is fairly represented. We must believe that the people's government is a failure and a delusion, to think otherwise.

Ninth, and finally, there is neither reasonable nor plausible ground, then, for taking the grave step of disturbing the exact and solid balance of the powers and functions of our national Constitution, which has in these respects given us a century of security, of State representation, and of State rights, as well as a wonderful national progress as a people.

GEO. F. EDMUNDS.

OLIVER WENDELL HOLMES.

THERE are some reasons for believing that Old Chronos is not indifferent to certain coincidences and sequences in the order and connection of our human lives. It has been an almost universal custom to set apart in a company by themselves the poets Bryant, Emerson, Longfellow, Whittier, Holmes, and Lowell,—I name them in the order of their birth; and, while some one now and then has endeavored to swell the number of this company by additions at the farther or the nearer end, few have been persuaded of the judiciousness of the proceeding. And it is certainly an interesting fact that the date of the death of Dr. Holmes, October 7, brings us within a month of the centennial of Bryant's birth, November 3. These poets in their going have not stood upon the order of their coming, or Lowell would yet have another decade of our fond regard. The survival of Holmes beyond all the others is not, however, without a certain aspect of propriety. If not the youngest in years, he was the youngest of them all in heart. In that charming bit of reminiscence called " Cinders from the Ashes," he tells of the little ghost at Andover, whose ticket he bought for Boston: " But the little ghost whispered, 'When you leave this place you leave me behind you.'" But he never left that cheerful little ghost of his boyhood behind him. Wherever he went, that urchin travelled in his heart.

Schiller's assurance that the immortals never appear alone gets ample confirmation from the year of Holmes's birth, 1809, which was more prodigal of greatness than any other that I can recall. The immortals of that year were Lincoln, Darwin, Tennyson, Gladstone; and Holmes is not unworthy to be named with these. Lincoln, we may be sure, would have valued him as highly as any contemporary. A man who could " shake the midriff of despair with laughter" was just the man for him. Like Bryant, Emerson, and Lowell,—like Longfellow and Whittier in a less degree,—he was much more than poet. Like Bryant and Lowell, he was much more than both poet and general man of letters, while unlike Whittier he was nothing of a reformer, except as he held fast to a reformed theology. Had he done only what he did as a good physician and medical professor, his record would have been highly honorable, and his reason for not dividing his practice, when he was urged to do so, would have witnessed to the goodness of his heart. It was that he had only one patient left, an indivisible unit. If he had been cut off in 1857, when he was forty-eight years old, his rank among our poets would have been very different from what it is now, and among our prose-writers he would have had no signal place. He would have been generally regarded as a distinguished medical professor and practitioner who occasionally "dropped into poetry," and had a few times gone down many fathoms deep and brought up a priceless pearl. Such an one was "The Last Leaf," in whose blended humor and sentiment many thousands besides Abraham Lincoln have found something piercing to the heart. Landor's "Rose Aylmer" does not awaken any tenderer chord than the stanza Lincoln loved so much:

> "The mossy marbles rest
>   On the lips that he has pressed
>   In their bloom,
> And the names he loved to hear
> Have been carved for many a year
>   On the tomb."

But no other poem of Holmes's first period (before 1857) approximates the delicacy of this, which has to perfection Beecher's "two babies in one cradle," laughter and tears, one waking the other, a conjunction which is the secret of the true society-verse. The aptness of the form for such an order of ideas has been attested by many happy imitations by the masters in this kind. Mr. Stedman has reminded us that Holmes came by inheritance and survival into possession of the manner of the Queen Anne and Georgian poets, and that he lived to see his fashion come in again. So did the old lady with her bonnet; but she flattered herself that she had brought back the fashion. So did not Holmes; but he was no less grateful to the whirligig of time. His loyalty to Pope's rhymed pentameter was the first article of his poetical creed. He theorized that it was the measure of our natural respiration. His use of it, habitual to all his longer poems on great public occasions, went far to justify his admiration, which, in truth, was not for the measure as such, but for its possibilities. "In his hand the thing became a trumpet." Holmes knew well enough that poetry intended to be read aloud or recited, as even his longer poems generally were, must be simple, eloquent, rhetorical, ornate. Acting upon this knowledge he became the pet of college commencements and the literary societies in the 'forties and 'fifties. The immediate impression must have been delightful, so incessant was the sparkle of the wit, so sonorous the appeal to the instinctive associations of the patriot and the collegian. But there was no " lead-poisoning" in things of this sort for coming generations; no pledge of a posthumous reputation. They would not have given Holmes a permanent rank with our other major poets if he had not gone on to better things. Nor would those poems which are still, no doubt, " the delight of generous boys," where, if he did not write " as funny as he could," he wrote in such a jocund way, with such animal spirits and such pure absurdity, that he was to the majority the poet of " The September Gale" and things of that breezy quality, " The Height of the Ridiculous," his private spur of the Parnassian Mount, than which he could no further climb. There were some, no doubt, who recognized a vein of purer fancy cropping through the classic satire and the persistent jollity. It was unmistakably there, and it was what Holmes always valued in himself above all things. To be a poet was the mark of his high calling, and he prized affectionately and gratefully the moments that brought to him some happy consciousness that he was something more than humorist or satirist or laughing philosopher. His " Chambered Nautilus" was more to him than many One-Hoss Shays.   " When I wrote that," he said, " I did better than I could."

One has only to compare Holmes's poetical production for the 'forties and earlier 'fifties with that of the 'thirties, to see that he was losing ground. He was producing less, and its character was getting more and more occasional. The exigencies of his practice and professorship were severe, and then, too, he was a lyceum-lecturer, in which relation it was not the hardness but the softness of his lot—the feather-beds—that tried him most. But that and much other chastening which for the present seemed not to be joyous worked out for him many pleasant fruits of popularity when he began to exercise himself as the Autocrat and Professor of the Breakfast Table. He was as sternly anti-orthodox as such a genial soul could be: but for one orthodox doctrine, that of regeneration, he should have had a warm appreciation; for in 1857, when the " Atlantic Monthly" was established, and he began to write for it, he had his own re-birth. A little while ago we should have compared it to Mark Twain's Map of

Paris, and said, "There was never anything like it;" but the author of "Peter Ibbetson" and "Trilby" furnishes a striking parallel. It was not only that the prose lucubrations, some of whose "seeds and weak beginnings" were entreasured in an old portfolio, were a fresh, delightful revelation; the correlated growth and exuberance of his poetic faculty was not less remarkable. We have had twice the amount of poetry from him in the last thirty years, as in the thirty years preceding, and its variety and average quality have been as superior as the amount. In the "Autocrat" we had his most perfect poetry for poets, that of "The Chambered Nautilus," and that masterpiece of logical construction, at once the deacon's and his own, "The One-Hoss Shay," and in "Contentment" a most frank confession of his honest liking for life's fair and pleasant things, and with these many others nearly or quite as good. He compared "The Professor" and "The Poet" to the wine of grapes that are squeezed in the press after the first juice that runs of itself has been drawn off. Like Thackeray he "wrote in numbers, for the numbers came," and such necessity is not always the mother of literary invention, or her offspring are a feeble folk. The mechanism of the Breakfast Table creaks a little in the "Autocrat" Series, and it becomes more stridulent under the Professor's elbows and the Poet's. But with every abatement they were a source of boundless pleasure, and they had in them a lot of saving grace. The story of Iris lay across the Professor's table like a gleam of tenderest light. The egotism was evident, but it was so easily resolved into a sympathetic appreciation of the reader's happiness that we could hardly wish it less. The toryism was unmistakably present, but so naked and unashamed that to blush for it would be absurd. And what shafts there were at folly and pretence; what pleasant talk of books and learning; what genial social wisdom; what airing of pet theories; what charming interfusion of the medical professor's blood into the poet's veins, as in that noble poem "The Living Temple"; what aphorisms and reflections that will be current till the patent on them has run out and they pass into the universal wisdom of mankind; and last, but not least, how much of serio-comic criticism of the creed and temper of that theology and religion which New England had inherited from Calvin, and which her own Edwards had made more intolerable.

Dr. Holmes's activities were so various, and the diamond clearness of his mind presents so many facets to the light, that it is difficult to speak of him with any adequacy within such limits as a writer for

THE FORUM would not lightly overpass. But there are some things that are so evident that they must occur to every one who views the Autocrat with an observing eye. First the ungracious negative, that he was not found among the abolitionist or anti-slavery prophets with Bryant, and Emerson, and Longfellow, and Whittier, and Lowell. He was of that Boston tea-party which shut its doors on Charles Sumner and Wendell Phillips. He was a Union-saver of the most aggravated type. Like Webster, he loved the Union so much that he would bind it firmer with the chains of negro slavery. He had a panegyric for Webster, for whom Whittier had had his " Ichabod" like lightning out of heaven. In 1843 he wrote:

> "Chiefs of New England! by your sires' renown,
> Dash the red torches of the rebel down,
> Flood his black hearth-stone till its flames expire,
> Though your old sachem fanned his council fire."

Who was the rebel, who the old sachem of this spirited demand? The rebel was the abolitionist, and the old sachem was John Quincy Adams. But his eyes were couched when Sumner was struck down, and when the war so initiated became general, no one saw more clearly that liberty and union were one and inseparable. His Boston oration of 1863, " The Inevitable Trial," brought forth fruits meet for repentance in no stinted fashion. In the terrible winter of 1860-61, when so many hearts were failing us for fear, his songs rang out like trumpets for the preservation of the Union and the beating of rebellion down. Lowell was not more patriotic, though with a more infallible predilection for showing his patriotism by his loathing of whatever meant his country's shame.

The good woman of a familiar story, who was called up at a spiritual sitting, and, while admitting that the heavenly society was very good, added, " But it isn't Boston!" was a woman after the Autocrat's own heart. " Homesick in Heaven" is the subject of one of his later poems, the best of which is the homesickness, not the proffered consolation. It is quite impossible to conceive of him as not homesick in heaven for his beloved Boston, whatever Franklin and Irving, Lamb and Thackeray and Steele may do to cheer his heart. Boston does not seem Boston without him. The State House or the Common would not be more sadly missed. His muse loved what Lamb called " the sweet security of streets," and yet she had her outings and came back from them with her apron full of flowers. He loved trees of famous girth, and those " wooden preachers" were exceptionally interesting among the many he had known, but in general the nature that he loved best was the more civilized sort, such as he found *intra muros*, when the springtide came swelling into Beacon Street and cast its foam of blossoms at his doors. It was for her symbolic value that nature was most dear to him; and yet it may be doubted whether Longfellow had so much first-hand unliterary love of natural things. The gods made him scientific as well as poetical, but to draw the mystic line dividing his science from his poetry would be a difficult matter. The two were interfluent streams.

The amount of Whittier's occasional poetry was absolutely large, but relatively small compared with that of Holmes, who has more than one hundred occasional pieces, not counting those inspired by great events—about one-third of all he ever wrote. It was not strange that he was so much desired—his taste, his tact, his ingenuity were so infallible. He could adapt himself with equal facility to the most various demands: occasions of greeting and farewell to scholars, poets, ambassadors, generals; country fairs and city celebrations; dirges for heroes; the anniversaries of—

—"mighty poets in their misery dead,"

or still alive and yet in misery because their turn was coming soon—I do not mean to die, but to respond. But the occasions which elicited his happiest productions were those pertaining to his Alma Mater and the class of '29. No other of our poets has had such a feeling for his university. Harvard did well to give him every honorable degree but that of S. T. D., and there were excellent reasons why that should not have been withheld. She never had a son who loved her more. And as for the class of '29, was ever class so fortunate?

> "You see me as always, my hand on the lock,
>   The cap on the nipple, the hammer full-cock;
>   It is rusty, some tell me; I heed not the scoff;
>   It is battered and bruised, but it always goes off."

It went off at more than forty successive meetings of the class. There were but nine survivors when the last Quinquennial Catalogue was published, and now there are but four. It is pathetic to imagine how soon he might have sung his annual song *solus cum solo*. When one recalls the enthusiasm and expressiveness and the contagious glee with which the poet read his own verses or recited them in public, and then turns to such a class-meeting poem as "The Boys," he wonders that when they heard it the old men's heart-strings did not snap under the tension of the great emotion with which it must have filled them to the brim. But these college and class-meeting poems have something in them that will long survive Samuel May, the veteran abolitionist, or that other Samuel,—

—"a young fellow of excellent pith—
Fate tried to conceal him by naming him Smith—"

who wrote "My country, 'tis of thee," or any other who may prove the last to go. For they are as full of happy comradeship as an egg is full of meat. We have all been saying lately that the comradeship in Mr. Du Maurier's "Trilby" is altogether sweet and good, whatever else is true of the book; and the spirit of Dr. Holmes's college poems answers to the spirit of comradeship in "Trilby" as face answereth to face in water.

The literary work of Dr. Holmes would amply justify itself if it had done nothing more than add immeasurably to the happiness of our contemporary life. Life is not so full of pleasantness, and the pessimists in these last days are not so few nor so well disposed toward such pleasantness as we have, that we can afford to be ungrateful for any increment; and for such an increment as that of Holmes's health and joy and cheer how can we be sufficiently grateful? No one in America has done so much as he to cheer us with sweet, guileless laughter. But both consciously and unconsciously he was set for the defence and propagation of a gospel that was indeed "tidings of great joy to all people." The fact that his father intended him for the ministry has affected many people as extremely funny in view of what he came to do and be as time went on. But the ministry as a class do not object to wit and humor, and there have been clergymen quite as humorous and witty as Dr. Holmes without damage to their cloth. What is more to the point, however, is that his predilection for preaching was immense, not less than Thackeray's, and that he did a great deal of it from the pulpit of the "Atlantic Monthly," and from other elevations. And he was the preacher of a very liberal theology. Like Bryant, and Emerson, and Longfellow, and Lowell, he was connected with what President Eliot calls "the unsectarian sect called Unitarians." But they all sat much more lightly to it than he, and no one of them ever felt so sternly bound to oppose the traditional orthodoxy and to set forth his liberal opinions, let who would hear him or forbear. He was not lacking in courage for the expression of his opinions, and its effect upon his publisher's statements was to him a matter of supreme indifference. Much of his liberal preaching

was incidental.   He was so full of it that it came quickly to the surface on the slightest provocation.   His table-talk and poems furnished
him with vehicles of expression equally serviceable to the end he had
in view.   Occasionally, as in the paper on Jonathan Edwards and
that called " The Pulpit and the Pew," he spoke with much more
elaboration.   These papers give forth no uncertain sound.   We are
admitted in the latter to as complete a confidence as we could possibly
desire.   He says:

"The real, vital division of the religious part of our Protestant communities
is into Christian optimists and Christian pessimists.   The Christian optimist in
his fullest development is characterized by a cheerful countenance, a voice in
the major key, an undisguised enjoyment of earthly comforts, and a short confession of faith.   His theory of the universe is progress; his idea of God that he
is a Father with all the true paternal attributes, of man that he is destined to
come into harmony with the keynote of divine order, of this earth that it is a
training-school for a better sphere of existence."

He goes on to describe the Christian pessimist, and then says:

"The line dividing these two great classes zigzags its way through the religious community, sometimes following denominational layers and cleavages,
sometimes going, like a geological fracture, through many different strata.   The
natural antagonists of the religious pessimists are the men of science, especially
the evolutionists, and the poets."

There can be no question where he conceived his proper place to be.
He was emphatically a Christian optimist.   His was the major key,
the cheerful countenance, the short confession of faith, the undisguised enjoyment of earthly comforts.   And as he conceived that
Robert Burns " did more to humanize the hard theology of Scotland
than all the rationalistic sermons that were ever preached," so without any slightest disrespect to Dr. Holmes we may conceive that he
did more by the incidental Christian optimism of his poetry and
literary prose to humanize the hard theology of New England than
by such deliberate rationalistic preaching as that of his " Jonathan
Edwards" and " The Pulpit and the Pew."   How much he did it is
impossible to say.   But as Poet, Autocrat, Professor, he found his
way to many a breakfast-table, many a sitting-room and library,
where the formal literature of a liberal theology would have been
hopelessly shut out.   And in many instances it must have eaten away
the substance of the wintry creeds as the south wind eats away the
drifts of snow that linger till the April days.

And still we have not touched the deepest spring of Holmes's
influence upon his time.   If this influence had reached its maximum

as a solvent of the Puritan theology, it would have been a modest factor in the evolution of New England thought and life as compared with the poetry of Whittier. Whittier did much more than Holmes to soften the Puritan theology, but Holmes did vastly more. than Whittier to soften the Puritan temper of the community. And here was his most characteristic work. He was neither stoic nor ascetic; neither indifferent to life's sweet and pleasant things, nor, while hankering for their possession, did he repress his noble rage and freeze the genial currents of his soul. His was " an undisguised enjoyment of earthly comforts"; a happy confidence in the excellence and glory of our present life; a persuasion, as one has said, that " if God made us, then he also meant us," and he held to these things so earnestly, so pleasantly, so cheerily, that he could not help communicating them to everything he wrote. They pervade his books and poems like a most subtile essence, and his readers took them in with every breath. Many entered into his labors, and some, no doubt, did more than he to save what was best in the Puritan conscience 'while softening what was worst in the Puritan temper and what was most terrible in the Puritan theology. But it does not appear that any one else did so much as Dr. Holmes to change the social temper of New England, to make it less harsh and joyless, and to make easy for his fellow-countrymen the transition from the old things to the new. And it may be that here was the secret, in good part, of that great and steadily increasing affection which went out to him in the later lustrums of his life. It was recognized, or felt with dim half-consciousness, that here was one who had made life better worth the living, who removed the interdict on simple happiness and pure delight, who had taken an intolerable burden from the heart and bade it swell with gladness in the good world and the good God. Whatever the secret, it is certain that no man among us was more widely loved, or will be more sincerely mourned. As he enters on another life beyond the grave, we seem to enter on another here. An epoch seems to end with the completed century of our six major poets. But whatever the new time may have in store, it must be something better than it could ever be without the heritage of their immortal songs.

JOHN WHITE CHADWICK.

IMPOTENCE OF CHURCHES IN A MANUFACTURING TOWN.

MR. JUSTICE MASON, commenting upon the exhibit of religious life in a New England town, made in an article in THE FORUM for March, remarks with judicial precision that it is an approved method in the study of economic and social principles to observe their application first under conditions of extreme simplicity, and to reason therefrom of their effect under more complex conditions where their operation is less open to observation.

The article under comment traced the history of religious segregation in a New England village, and sketched the present secularized condition of the churches and the decadence of religious life in a community torn by religious dissension and rivalry. The principle of sectarianism was here seen in operation under simple conditions. A dozen miles from the village is a manufacturing town with a population approximating one hundred thousand. When the student undertakes to observe the operation here of the principle of division in religious life, he finds it immediately widening out into results of the most startling character, which, however, have not heretofore been attributed to the agency which he, coming with a previous knowledge of its work in a more primitive community, clearly discovers to be their cause. He sees the idea of division, introduced and recommended by a divided Church, accepted by the population of a city, and given manifold application, until all conception and possibility of united action are gone, and municipal interests are given over to the clash, no longer merely of many religious bodies, but of many social classes, arrayed against each other on every conceivable issue and pretext of issue. He discovers with what readiness men who have been taught to think of themselves not as Christians, but as Catholics or Protestants, and not even as Protestants, but as Congregationalists, or, with another title of division, Orthodox Congregationalists, as Episcopalians or may be Methodist Episcopalians, or, with even a third mark of distinction, African Methodist Episcopalians,—he discovers the readiness with which such men go on and

think of themselves not as men, but as "bosses" and operatives; if
"bosses," again either as owners or agents; if operatives, no longer
as operatives only, but as weavers or spinners.   He sees those who
should constitute the moral force of the city divided and subdivided
and divided again until they are incapable as toy soldiers against organized crime and united greed.   He sees—a monument to division—
the city an aggregation of houses on ill-made and worse-kept streets,
with no great buildings reflecting its united character as a city, its industries subject to periodical paralysis, its social life unendurable, its
political events general debauches, spotted physically with festering
sores, a city suffering every species of misgovernment at the hands
of officials who mock the warring factions from whose indignation
they are secure.   He sees, in short, religious division no longer
merely resulting in religious disaster, but effecting public calamity.

The city of Fall River, Massachusetts, may be regarded as a typical manufacturing town.   It has a population of ninety thousand.
One-half of this is Roman Catholic, the other half being made up of
Protestants and those who profess no religious faith.   The churches
and mission chapels and Sunday-schools maintained by the Protestants are distributed among fifteen denominations as follows:

Protestant Episcopal...5	Primitive Methodist...3	Friends 1
Baptist................7	Christian..............3	African Methodist Epis-
Orthodox Congrega-	Unitarian Congrega-	copal................1
tional..............6	tional..............1	Christian Science......1
Methodist Episcopal...7	United Presbyterian...1	Latter-Day Saints.....1
Presbyterian..........4	New Church..........1	Advent................7

The Protestant clergy number twenty-eight.   The table attempts
to show the probable order of the denominations with respect to size,
the bodies numerically larger preceding those numerically smaller.
The position of the Episcopal Church is accounted for by the presence
in the city of large numbers of English operatives.   It is impossible
to give anything like an accurate tabulation of totals of members belonging to the several denominations.   The Young Men's Christian
Association considers that there are, all told, twenty-five thousand
Evangelicals (by which it means Trinitarian Protestants), attached
and unattached, in the city.   It has been estimated at the Ministers'
Meeting that five thousand people are in attendance upon Protestant
services Sunday by Sunday.   At present the popular place of worship is the Baptist Temple.   This structure, which rejoices in a new
organ and an attractive preacher, stands on the principal business
19

street, its front being occupied by four shops—an arrangement which is becoming lamentably frequent in American cities. It is an arrangement made necessary by the heavy and needless expense of maintaining many separate church establishments. A block away on the same street is a Methodist church; at least, the sign of one is displayed on the street, and, by crossing, one may see the roof of a church back of the row of shops which occupy the best portion of the lot. The Methodist church also has four shops, but it is to be credited with maintaining a wider entrance than do the Baptists, into the spiritual reserve.

Either of these locations affords a splendid opportunity to lift, out of the midst of the sordid life of the street, a great, solemn witness to the invisible, the spiritual. Could but these two congregations forget their fancied differences, and set up a common household, they would be strong enough to do for this city what Trinity Church and Grace Church do for New York, and what St. Paul's Church does for Boston,—make, where most it is needed, a dignified and worthy protest against the engrossment of men forever in getting and spending; afford an inviting retreat out of the turmoil of barter and selfishness, to which men might repair for a little thought of more enduring things. As it is, passing throngs merely see the signs of a feeble folk, who acknowledge their defeat and hide themselves, who ingloriously hang on behind prosperous and triumphant materialism.

The testimony of those who have tried to enlist the Protestant denominations in united undertakings is that one who looks for any spirit of unity in Fall River is fated to look in vain. This week, a non-denominational mission in Flint Village, the poorest quarter of the town, is abandoned for lack of funds. A coffee-house, in the conduct of which several denominations have lately associated themselves, is a happy fact; its success, however, is doubtful.

There is an Associated Charities organization, the work of which, though under good management, is pitiably inconsequential. It has been embarrassed with conflicts with city physicians and other health officials, who were Roman Catholics, and were not disposed to receive orders from a somewhat assuming Protestant affair. The city has a Young Men's Christian Association which strives heroically, against sectarian narrowness, to make a place for itself, and a rather inconspicuous society known as the Young Men's Union. Last summer a nurse attached to the Massachusetts Emergency and Hygiene Association worked here under the direction of the Board of Associated Charities. There has lately been established a Methodist deaconesses' home. This practically sums up the work done by Protestants in Fall River.

A comparison of this showing with that which Roman Catholics are able to make is much to the embarrassment of the Protestants. Inferior to them in wealth and education, Roman Catholics, because united, are far in advance in every Christian activity. Their churches are the most conspicuous objects in the city. At least two of them every Sunday contain each as many worshippers as are present in all the Protestant churches combined. They have at present fifteen churches, and they are building on magnificent sites two more which will be larger than any now standing. In these churches thirty-two masses are said on every week-day, and between thirty-five and forty every Sunday. The most prominent hill-top is crowned with a group of Roman Catholic charitable institutions. They support an English and a French orphan asylum, a college, and several convents. They have about ten thousand children in parochial schools. They maintain a Catholic Union, which affords young men a club house and gives them lectures and concerts in the season; they support some ten boys' clubs, all well housed. They frequently astonish the Protestants of the city with evidences of their prosperity and charity. I record one rather striking instance. The High School some years ago received from a family of the city a gift to which was attached the condition that the family should have a veto power over appointments to its teaching staff. This has always been understood as intended to exclude Roman Catholics. Last year an effort was made by Protestant gentlemen to establish a scholarship in this school. The effort failed, but as soon as it had been abandoned the scholarship was founded by the subscriptions of Roman Catholics.

The most serious limitation upon the Roman Catholic Church is that its communicants are drawn mainly from one of the two classes which compose the world, so far as Fall River is concerned. It has no influence among the employers of labor; it is the church of the laborers. Conscious of this fact, and taking no pride in it, it is careful not to antagonize the corporations, even to the extent of denouncing their selfishness and injustice. It has no opportunity to impress the rich, and, its policy—the best one, I doubt not—being not to commit itself to a partisan position, it is prevented from doing its duty to the poor. The importance of this we shall see later. Let us now observe the great Roman-Protestant schism at work in municipal politics.

In the autumn of 1892, Fall River, voting under the local-option statute of the Commonwealth, adopted the policy of no license for liquor-selling. Great was the joy in the high places of morality when, the prohibition going into effect, every liquor-shop was closed. The officials had no apparent difficulty in enforcing the law. If there was illicit selling, the public did not discover it. It is doubtful if a glass of liquor was sold in the city for two weeks. Then, as if by magic, the doors opened. Every semblance of restraint was taken off, and intoxicants were sold as openly as groceries and dry-goods. The mayor was charged with receiving bribes for protection given to violators of the law. He had made a large addition to the police force, himself nominating the new members. This force became a band of mercenaries paid out of the public treasury to further his private ends. In the aldermanic chamber the president of the board told the mayor that " all kinds of liquor were being sold in victuallers' shops, tenement dives, boozing-dens, and hell-holes, seven days in the week, and by his authority," and received no denial. This is an old story, with no original incidents in its early course. The interest comes later.

The following autumn the mayor was a candidate for re-election. A month before the election, a committee, representing the Protestant ministers of the city, had a hearing in the city hall: laying before his Honor evidence of violation of the law, they asked him to pledge himself to an attempt to enforce it. They gave him the location of five hundred and forty places which had paid the United States liquor tax, and in plain words impeached him of perjury and bribe-taking. The answer of this man to the serious charge of official connivance at violation of law was an attack on the law. He did not believe in it. Therefore he would not enforce it. In the face of the fact that the city had voted to sacrifice revenue to the amount of a hundred thousand dollars annually, for the sake of freedom from the saloon evil, he had the impudence to declare that the people did not want the law enforced, and that the vote was merely an expression of disgust with the limitation statute. The law of Massachusetts allows but one saloon to every thousand souls. " Take off the accursed limitation," cried the mayor to the assembled clergy. He appealed to them to aid him to secure its repeal, and he shamelessly admitted every charge they had made. "I don't say that liquor is not sold. I say that it is sold. I make no apology for my conduct. The people will record their verdict later."

No better case than this could have been desired. The pages of this article may contain little that is complimentary to Fall River, but they make no reflection so severe as that its people are ready to repudiate and nullify law. There is but one sentiment among decent people with regard to law and its enforcement, and the majority of the citizens of Fall River are decent people. A vigorous campaign was at once begun in behalf of the opposing candidate, and its issue was confidently expected to vindicate law.

It is not to be doubted that it would have done so, had not another question been permitted to displace the one which should have been settled at the polls. The American Protective Association made its appearance. Mayor Coughlin happens to be a communicant of the church from which this association "protects" America, and it took up the fight against him, not because he was a perjured and lawless official, but because he was a Roman Catholic. The Protestant ministers from their pulpits, properly enough, denounced the mayor, but unfortunately some of them were led to denounce his religion. The pastor of the First Methodist Episcopal Church, for example, in the course of a sermon proclaimed that "the Roman Church is the greatest menace to the government," that "political Romanism means destruction to American institutions," and so on. The Pope's toe, the Jesuits, the plotting priests, and kindred subjects of familiar sound, were discussed in places of worship. A daily paper supporting the mayor retorted with the customary alliteration, "Blatant bigots!" and the issue had ceased to be moral, having become religious.

The result, of course, was the solidifying of the Roman Catholic vote for Coughlin. The most worthy and able Democrat in Fall River, though Coughlin's political enemy, was led, solely by the raising of the religious question, to support him, and scores followed. The Roman Catholic clergy, several of whom, at least, I have assurance would have given their influence against the mayor, were prevented from doing so; "L'Independance," a French Republican paper, bolted the ticket of its party because it represented the American Protective Association; and Mayor Coughlin was re-elected.

Consider the significance of this bit of history. If ever angels of darkness fear that vice is about to be struck down, crime visited with punishment, they need but remind those about to strike that they are of different Christian names. Since this election, which was a crisis in the affairs of the city, the filth of its politics has grown unspeakable; to-day it is an offence to the nostrils of Massachusetts. Since this their triumph, encouraged by the growing heat.of the religions issue, lawlessness, bribery, and vice do not have even the decency to hide themselves. Let us get clearly in mind the lesson of the election from which all this dates: *When the ecclesiastical issue is raised, moral issues must go unsettled. When the divided households of Christ's Church lift their hands against each other, crime goes untouched and undismayed.*

At the city-hall hearing the mayor proposed to the ministers a question which, though it was of no significance for his purpose, is, on quite other grounds, worth getting an answer to. Why, the mayor asked, this sudden interest in the enforcement of this particular law? Why not have equal interest in that of other important statutes, such as those for the protection of operatives? I desire to examine into the ground of the mayor's question.

A great line divides the population of Fall River into two classes. This is a vastly more apparent division than is usually to be found, because there is here but one industry,—that of cloth-making. Every man, woman, and girl in the city either is, or is not, an operative. If he or she is an operative, he or she not only works, but goes to church, buys, finds companionship, dresses, and lives as an operative. The designation is fastened upon each one, and is laid off neither day nor night. There are twenty-five thousand who bear this name. Over against these are the owners, agents, and " supers." The attitude of these two classes is of one of mutual suspicion, hatred, and war. The unquestioned assumption is that their interests are necessarily opposed; their dealings with each other proceed upon that assumption. Each is eager for chances to take an advantage of the other. It is not difficult to guess which is more successful at this. It cannot be otherwise than that operatives are stupefied by their work: to pass one's days, beginning in childhood, amid the din of looms and mules, making a few ever-recurring movements of arms and bodies, reduces men to something akin to the machines they operate. The " supers" know this, and commonly believe that they can reason with their men on but one subject, and when they are in but one condition,—upon the subject of food, and when their stomachs are empty. They therefore view with equanimity the exercise of the only defensive measure operatives know of,— the strike,—and usually turn it to their own profit. The city is now going through the miseries of a protracted strike; for two months the spindles have not turned. The point in dispute is one easily susceptible of settlement, but manufacturers unable to agree, and operatives organized separately as weavers and as spinners, complicate the situation.

Looked upon as natural enemies by the corporations, employees are the victims of many frauds. One inspector and one female assistant are detailed by the State for this district, and it includes the city of New Bedford. This is entirely inadequate for the task of enforcing the statutory regulations as to ventilation and other sanitary provisions, fire-escapes, the employment of minors, the Particulars Act, and other measures of protection.

The mayor's question referred to all this, and had its reason in a hundred cruel wrongs that need somebody's attention. Why do not the churches interest themselves in this?

The answer seems a harsh one to give, but it is the facts that give it: because, under the sectarian system, the expense of operating the many churches is great, and no appreciable share of it can be borne by the poor. The churches therefore are mainly churches of the well-to-do, and the majority of the pastors are occupied with their proper parishioners, the well-to-do. The exceptions to this statement do not prevent its being the explanation of a lamentable fact. Let it be remarked that it is unfair to blame the clergy. They are the servants of the congregations which hire them. They have each registers, not of the souls within their cures, but of the members who compose their congregations. I am aware that liberal-minded and hard-working ministers may feel their duty to be also to others; it is a happiness to know that the Episcopal Church—in theory, at least—knows no " members"; but the practical outworking of the system is this: a minister must serve the society by which he is employed. The pastor of the Central Congregational Society, which is known as " the Manufacturers' Church," learned this when he returned home after having uttered in another city the views of a Christian socialist. So did an assistant employed by this society to look after a mission congregation, when once it drew out his sympathies and set him to writing for the city press warm articles in behalf of labor, until his employers persuaded him to think better of it.

It would be wrong to seek to give the impression that the operatives have no attention from the churches. Those of them who are
Roman Catholics are looked up if they do not present themselves at
mass. Those who are Protestants have a few churches,—for the most
part small and weak affairs,—over which are faithful ministers, and a
few missions, at which to obtain religious privileges. Most of the
manufacturers are to be described conventionally as Christians, and
some of them send their wives to the missions, on the self-sacrificing
principle of Artemus Ward, who freely devoted all his wife's relatives to the service of his country. And this is best. Few workmen would permit their children to receive religious instruction from
the men whom they look upon as being engaged in grinding and
squeezing them during the week. And when Christian work among
the operatives is being spoken of, it should be said that three names
—that of a big-hearted schoolfellow of Cardinal Gibbons and Archbishop Corrigan, himself working away in the humbler station of a
parish priest; that of a Scotch Presbyterian, who talks the same fearless words among the poor, in the pulpit, and in the State House;
and that of a young man who sacrificed much to give his accomplishments to the homely duties of rector of the English operatives'
church—are spoken with affection in many a tenement in Fall River.

But when the best is done, a body of sixty clergy working the
same ground in sixteen unsympathetic squads, manifestly cannot
begin to touch a hundred thousand people. I want them relieved
from blame, but I want the system of which they and thousands of
human souls are the victims, visited with the wrath which it deserves.

I have talked with groups of the better-looking operatives on the
street. They say, not with bitterness, calmly, as if from settled conviction, "Go to church! There is no church for us. Churches can't
be run without money, and we have none. Why don't we go to the
churches on the hill? Because, when we have gone, our wives got
such looks as cut them for weeks after. We don't see much good
in churches. Hardly think Jesus Christ would know they were his."
Some of the language is more vivid than it is necessary to make it
here, but on every side it was plain that the churches had lost their
influence by reason of their devotion to their respective constituencies rather than to men. Those who dream Christ's dream of one
catholic Church shudder at the thought of constituencies. The streets
are full of religious debatings, and of arraignment of churches and
ministers. Religion is up for trial, and the prospects for the judg-

ment are not reassuring to those who cherish it.   The charge is justifiable that a daily result of its administration by a divided Church is
the creation of unbelief in its claims and in those of its Founder.
Jesus saw what would follow division when he prayed for his apostles,
their successors, and those who should believe, that they might be
one.   His petition was, "as thou, Father, art in me, and I in thee,
that they also may be one in us: that the world may believe that thou
hast sent me."   Otherwise, was the unspoken reflection, the world
will not believe.   The issue of events proves his prophetic insight.

A further and more specific inquiry into the ability of a divided
Church to do its work will show how inevitable is the world's unbelief.   It must be admitted that the first duty of Christianity is to
the bodies of men.   Jesus seems to have preached few sermons, but
to have healed many men.   Relieving bodily misery was his daily
occupation.   He came that men might have life more abundantly, in
a real and physical sense.   He bade his Church care for the temples
of men's souls, and preachers say that it is his Holy Spirit who gives
us strength and skill to battle with disease.   It is inconceivable how
a Church which has no concern for the bodily welfare of men can
have any holy anxiety as to their spiritual condition.   But this needs
no argument.   With such care as sixteen religious bodies can give
them, how do the operatives of Fall River live?
We will begin our inquiry, entirely without selection, at the
Richard Borden mill tenements.   They stand on Rodman Street, between two alleys.   There are sixteen blocks arranged around a court;
the blocks have six tenements each.   You can enter the court with dry
boots if you tiptoe on an isthmus, and jump; for the village is built
on low ground, and pools of standing water abound.   If you ask at
the first tenement on the right, you will be told that there are four
bedrooms and a kitchen, and that four sleep in each room.   Operatives live in bedrooms and kitchens.   They pay here seven dollars a
month; this means to the corporation a rental of $8,000 annually—
five per cent interest on $160,000.   Four to a room is perhaps an
unusual number for this particular village.   They are not often willing to tell how many share a tenement; it will average here, perhaps,
ten, though the patrolman thinks more.   The population of the court
is about one thousand.   The buildings have been painted a cheap
color which might have been selected for its dinginess; the court,
however, is always gay with hundreds of fluttering garments of many

colors; clothes-lines cross it in every direction. Looking in at entries, the plastering of the walls is seen to be discolored and broken, and the stairs bare and dilapidated. The court is littered with refuse; one threads one's way among unsavory heaps. Along under the eaves of every block is a ridge composed of potato-parings, egg-shells, and garbage; the universal rule is to pour the kitchen-emptyings out of the window. This description must pause, however, for it dare not tell how the centre of the court—which is the playground of children and the thoroughfare for all—is occupied. A photograph would shock the world. In certain details of filth, hideous indecency, and indescribable shame, this place is probably not matched outside of Fall River anywhere in what we call civilization. And in the centre of all stands a pump. The air is pestilential, and the place revolting to every sense. The heart sickens at the sight of the crowds who sit on stoops and hang out at windows, and gaze at their common misery. God in heaven! how is it permitted for girls to look upon this? The saloon is a retreat of which we should do wrong to deprive these men. For their women, there is no refuge but the streets. For them, immorality is almost inevitable from childhood. And among them all, hatred of the rich, and rage against life, are inevitable. In such a place what can men do but sit on the steps and curse their employers; what can women do but nurse their cripple babies and wish them dead?

Leaving this place, you pass a block where a dozen families draw water from a single faucet, the condition of which may be judged from the statement of the patrolman that to fill a pail from it requires several minutes. You see many blocks worse than those of the Borden mills. "Little Canada," the property of the American Linen Mills Company, is unspeakable. It would be an abuse to house a dog in such a place. The Slade mill tenements stand in a swamp; they do not compare favorably with old-time slave-quarters of the poorer class. Speak to one of the many heads that crowd the windows:

"All idle here?"

"All, sir."

"What do you pay?"

"A dollar ten a week. Three bedrooms and a kitchen. There's no money coming in now, so there's none to go out. But they've got it down against us. Lower the rent when we are out of work? No, sir. They're so busy cutting wages they've no time to cut rents."

The first floor of the Globe mill tenement blocks is deserted.

The tenants were overpowered by rats. At one of the upper windows is a box filled with soil in which stands a leafless geranium.

I have entered these abodes, in some cases with a physician on his rounds. In one room were three cots, two supported on soap-boxes, the third being made up on the floor. From one of these sprang a sick boy to kiss the hand and kneel for the blessing of the priest. The doctor calculated that fifteen men would occupy the room that night. The rent-man was at the door.

In another place there was typhoid fever in one room scarcely big enough to turn round in, while in the next the family was gathered; a washing was being done in one corner, supper was cooking in another, children were peeling potatoes on the floor, and an infant was crying on a shelf under the window. The brother of the sick man here died last week. It is almost impossible ever to save them.

Into such a room as this you may see a boarder come, bringing a piece of meat. He will cut it on the bare table over which kerosene has been spilled, lay it on the stove-top, and presently take it in his hands and eat it. There seems to be no cupboard or larder, and the loaf of bread is generally pushed back on the table in a heap with the lamp and the soap-bar. Sometimes it is kept in the pot; I never saw it on the floor; the potatoes are kept there.

So live thousands of men, women, and children in Fall River. Who is to blame? Many are to blame. Among others, the divided Church is to blame. It may be said that the city government is to blame. But who is to blame for the government? Indisputably, in Fall River, the divided Church.

But the case against the Church is worse than this. The man who might stop a crime, and does not, is guilty of the crime. Where there is ability, there is responsibility. The Church might stop the crime of permitting men to live as these do; it does not. Fall River is not a great city, where it is impossible to get into houses and to find men. It is easily possible here to know every alley, tenement, room, and man in the city. A united Church could throw into the tenements a powerful body of ministerial patrol, and give adequate inspection. Its sixty clergy, united, organized, and backed by the entire Christianity of the city, could clear out these places in two weeks. Moreover, to say nothing of what it could force the corporations to do in the way of better tenements, it could itself afford financial help which would prevent the worst miseries of the city. The money which, under its present conduct, it wastes, in five years would house every operative in decent, comfortable quarters. The Church here administers annually at least a quarter of a million of dollars. I impeach it of misuse of sacred funds. Not one-half of what is expended is necessary for the maintenance of worship with better music, greater accommodations, and a larger corps of ministers than at present. The other half should go to the suffering and the poor. It belongs to the category of crime to appropriate it for the gratification of personal fancies for this or that doctrine, custom, or form.

Even stronger is the indictment against the Church for indirect blame. Fall River is the product of the idea of division. What it needs is to hear the gospel of the race's unity. Corporations and operatives must be taught that their interests are one; that industry can prosper only when its prosperity is an object to both; that it can survive only upon condition of reciprocal sympathy and help. Specifically, employers ought to learn that to take better care of their men, to house them better, would be to make them actually more valuable workmen. All should be impressed with the lesson that the industrial world will be, as now it is, perplexed and bewildered, that wages will be unsettled, and dividends uncertain, till the great social and economic truth of the unity of the human family is learned.

Now, exactly that is the message of the Church; the proclamation of that is just its business on earth. God is the Father of men; therefore men are brothers—how glibly we say it! It is indeed the gospel; it is indeed the salvation of the world; the world political, social, commercial. How can the Church preach that humanity is one, when it is itself rent with schism? How can it persuade men to unity, unless it is united? The Church was founded to stand as the type and prophecy of what the race should be. These are serious words. It is questionable if an institution is worth maintaining when it fails to do that for which it was instituted. No one doubts that, in Fall River, Christianity is comforting hearts and lightening burdens, that happy homes are being blessed by its precious light; but no one who looks the facts in the face can doubt that Christianity as it is at present administered is incompetent for the work which its Master put it into the world to do. It is doubtful if an institution rendered incapable of duty by its divisions can much longer command the love or the service of men who would love and serve it. The duty of loyalty, even to the Church, depends upon the Church's loyalty to its duty.

WILLIAM BAYARD HALE.

GEORGE INNESS: THE MAN AND HIS WORK.

"INTENSE" was the word chosen by the Swedenborgian minister who delivered the address over the body of the late George Inness, to characterize the subject of his discourse, and he could not have found a better. It gives the key to the painter's life and work.

In the United States, at the end of the first quarter of the century, there was no art, there were no artists. This meant not only that there were no models and no teachers, but that to the American public art was not conceivable as a career, a profession, or even a livelihood. Painting, to most people, meant portrait-painting, and it is doubtful whether there was in one of the chief cities an established and fashionable portrait-painter, while the travelling portrait-painter was socially and pecuniarily much in the position long afterward occupied by the strolling photographer before he was submerged by the rising tide of amateurism. There was, however, one consolation to be got even from the depressing circumstances of the environment. It was quite certain that no active-minded boy who grew up in that environment would become a painter except from a real vocation and through "the strong propensity of nature." The later multiplication of facilities for studying art, it need scarcely be pointed out, much weakens this guarantee.

George Inness was born May 1, 1825, on a farm two miles and a half back of Newburgh, on the Hudson,—the fifth of thirteen children. That he was of Scotch descent was attested to all who knew him in later life—not so much by his name, unmistakable as that was, as by the Scottish qualities he had inherited, prominent among them the hereditary taste for theological disputation. He did not come, however, of a line of farmers. His grandfather had been engaged in the West India trade. His father had prospered in business in New York as a grocer, and had retired to the Newburgh farm for the benefit of his health. But he again removed his family to New York city while George was still an infant, and in 1829, his health again requiring attention, he removed to Newark, and it was in Newark that the painter's boyhood was passed. George was sent to the Academy, but when he was thirteen his teacher reported that he would not " take education"; and thereupon his father opened a grocery in Newark, and put the lad in it as a shop boy, but this experiment also was a failure.   There is no further record that the elder Mr. Inness tried to make his son conform to what he himself regarded as the ways of usefulness and respectability.   On the contrary, he tried to further him in his ambition.   Newark possessed at least one drawing-master, a Mr. Barker, who dabbled also in color, and the boy was given into his charge, and the bright hope of a mercantile career was finally abandoned.   At this time George could not have been more than sixteen, for he remained a pupil of Mr. Barker until the latter himself announced that the boy had learned all that Barker had to teach, and the family returned again to New York in 1843, when the art-student was eighteen.   His elder brother James was established in Pottsville, Pa., as a schoolmaster, and George went to spend with him the summer of 1844, painting furiously at what his eyes found to paint while the daylight lasted, and conversing with equal ardor after nightfall, as became his life-long wont.   The studies were as crude and as niggling as might be expected, but it is significant that even then he should have confided to his brother that his grievous trouble was to represent " the action of the clouds,"—a problem which probably did not vex any of his contemporaries; and equally significant that he should have thrown down his brushes in despair, exclaiming: " Oh, if I could only get that down without paint. "

It was about this time that George took refuge in the asylum of almost all American youths of that time of an incorrigibly artistic bent—an engraver's shop.   Engraving was at least a trade that gave promise of a livelihood, had at least a recognized name to go by, and so was on a much more respectable footing than mere " mooning about. "   Inness learned the trade, like Durand before him, like Kensett, like Casilear, like others his coevals, and actually executed some engravings.   It was not aversion—at least not wholly aversion —that led him to abandon it, but an alarming break-down in his health, which had never been robust and now succumbed to frequent attacks of epilepsy.   Meanwhile his father had married again and moved back to New York, and the young artist lived at home, and satiated in the domestic circle his appetite for theological controversy. His mother had been a zealous Methodist, his step-mother was an equally zealous Baptist, and her brother was an ardent and proselytizing Universalist. There was in this conjunction ample fuel for the disputation in which he liked to relax his mind after the day's work was done. The day's work in those years was painting in the studio of Régis Gignoux, perhaps the best-instructed landscape-painter in this country at that time, a graduate of the schools of Paris, whose pictures may still be seen in many of the older-fashioned American collections.

It is not easy to perceive that Inness owed anything to him but those rudiments of painting that were then common property in France and mysteries in America. The earliest Inness that I have seen is of the year 1847. It would not be noticeable, naturally, except for his subsequent success, but when one is led by that to take notice of it, he cannot fail to see that the unskilful attempt is the attempt to represent action—the action of clouds, the action of waves—in an otherwise conventional composition. This was as far as possible from the aim of most of the American painters at that time. The influence of Thomas Cole was still paramount. The "Course of Empire" and the "Voyage of Life" were recent, and, though Cole himself was an Englishman, were among the boasts of the country. Inness must have been familiar with them very early, since the series of the "Voyage of Life" was finished when he was twelve years old, but they do not seem to have impressed him as they impressed his contemporaries and gave direction to the "Hudson River school." The most obvious of the tendencies which Cole impressed upon American landscape-painting was to the production of panoramas, and more generally to what has been scornfully called "view-hunting." The art of Mr. Church, the only one of the living whom I allow myself to name, is obviously panoramic, and Mr. Church, who was indeed for two years a pupil of Cole, is the most faithful as well as the most distinguished continuator of the Cole tradition. But indeed one has only to visit any American collection assembled before 1869 to see the prevalence of the panoramic land-scape and the universality of "view-hunting." Neither can one help seeing the influence of the engraver's way of looking at things in the way of the engravers turned painters and producers of tinted engrav-ings. The "school," indeed, exerted an effective pressure to produce panoramas upon men who were by no means panoramically inclined. Mr. Kensett, for example, who, though an engraver, was not a rep-resentative of the Hudson River school, since he studied painting in England and exhibited at the Royal Academy before he exhibited

at the National Academy, found it necessary in New York to do
" important works," in which we look in vain for the real Kensett,
whom we still find with gladness in the idyllic " bits," touched
with the—

> —" melancholy grace
> Brought from a pensive though a happy place."

But the idyls had as little as the panoramas to teach the painter
who at nineteen had been baffled by the " action" in nature. It was
in his definition of a picture always, both in theory and practice,
that it should comprehend only what could be seen all at once; and
this definition of itself almost excludes the panorama. I know
scarcely another " view," in the sense of the tourist or the older
American painter, among all his works, than the " Delaware Valley"
(1863) in Mr. Clarke's collection; and this picture is saved from
being a panorama not only by the moderate dimensions of the
canvas, but by the unification of the picture through ". tone," so
that it becomes " possible"—to use the artist's own phrase—" to
unity of vision," and thus falls within his own definition of a picture. And as his subjects were restricted in space to what could
be seen all at once, so they were restricted in time. The fact he
thought best worth representing, that for fifty years, with increasing and at last with astonishing success, he struggled to convey in
pigment, was, that the aspect of nature which he strove to fix was
evanescent and momentary, and that it was its very transiency and
elusiveness that to him gave its most appealing charm. It was a
different thing that he was trying to do, and a more difficult than
was aimed at by the painters for whose " important works" it seemed
that nature might have been giving day-long sittings for a fortnight.
The bursting dawn as it broke, the fading twilight as it waned, the
clouds that chased each other in the air or their shadows over the
hillsides or the meadows, the " change of glare and gloom," the
movement of nature, was Inness's subject from first to last, though
it was not till long after the first that his skill sufficed to make his
intention clear, and not till toward the last that he could really fulfil
his intentions, and then never so as to satisfy himself. As was inevitable with his intense and impetuous temper, he passed by turns
from elation to despair. He said once: " My love for art is killing
me, but it is what keeps me alive: it is my blessing and my curse."
Just before he sailed on the voyage from which he was not destined

to return, he was at his nadir, and he expressed the depth of his despondency by the declaration—perfectly sincere, but perfectly incredible—that he would never take a brush in hand again. So wide to the artist is the difference between his vision and his realization of it.

While still under his father's roof, or at least while still dependent upon his father, he had married, but he lost his wife while she was still his bride. In 1850 he married the lady who is now his widow. The marriage was very probably a reckless performance, from the point of view of worldly prudence, in which the painter was always the least capable of men. But he had by that time attracted some believers in his art, among them Mr. Ogden Haggerty, then a very well known and prosperous auctioneer in New York, whose admiration for the painter and belief in him led him to constitute himself his patron, and to assume the responsibility of disposing of his product, a responsibility that the painter at any period readily devolved upon whoever chose to assume it. There never was an artist more absorbed in his art and less careful of its pecuniary results. It was through the good offices of Mr. Haggerty that he was enabled to make, in 1851, his first visit to Europe, and was introduced for the first time to the world of art. The next two years were spent in Italy, and in 1854 he went abroad again, this time to Paris. It was upon this visit, doubtless, that he really came to know the works of the French landscape-painters of Fontainebleau, and the study was of great help to him and of great influence upon him. The vogue of the leaders of the school was just firmly established. Rousseau had won the cross of the Legion of Honor—which in France denotes such an establishment—in 1852; Diaz in 1851; Corot a few years earlier. Here the open-eyed American saw how what he was trying to do under every disadvantage of solitude and remoteness had been done by men who had every advantage of tradition and co-operation. He saw examples of "tone," of the harmonious relation of colors, he saw what "values" were, the force of objects represented in their relation to each other. He found that a truer, deeper, and more impressive representation of nature than he had known before was possible. He learned the lesson that the Fontainebleau painters had to teach, not by way of imitation, which was absolutely impossible to him at any time, but by analysis. He was learning to write his own hand. To make his own what he found in French art was not a short task for the American painter.

20

There is an Inness even of 1855, which shows little of the solidity
and vitality of the Fontainebleau painting or of his own later work,
and which betrays the result of the artist's "wander-years" only in a
more completely harmonious tonality than he could have then have
acquired or seen at home.

Upon his return from Europe, or not long after, the painter took
up his residence in a suburb of Brooklyn, and opened a studio in
New York; and the duties of his manager and man-of-business were
assumed for a time by his brother Joseph. Among those who believed in his pictures and bought them in those years were Simeon
Draper, Henry Ward Beecher, George Ward Nicholls, George M.
Vanderlip, Fletcher Harper, Jr., J. Abner Harper, and his friend
and fellow-artist, Samuel Colman. But in spite of these and other
believers those were evil days for the painter. It was in those days
that a sudden call for money would produce an irruption of Inness
into some hospitable studio or parlor, with a picture under his arm
to be pledged for a fraction of its value, or to be bought on the
buyer's own terms. After five years of zealous experimentation in
his art, disturbed by the "cares of bread," he determined upon a
flight to Boston, where, as has happened to other artistic Nazarenes
of New York whom their townsmen found too peculiar, he was in
more honor than in his own country. Williams & Everett, of Boston, who also had a branch in New York, were the chief buyers of
Inness among the dealers, and among the principal buyers of Innesses
for the love of them were Messrs. Harrison E. Maynard, Edward
Maynard, and Thomas Wigglesworth of Boston. So in 1859 the
family was established in Medfield, eighteen miles from Boston,
and in Medfield the head of it lived and painted till 1864. It was
there that the news came of the outbreak of the war, which excited
more enthusiasm in no Northern State than in Massachusetts, nor in
any inhabitant of Massachusetts than in the landscape-painter of
Medfield. Mr. Inness may be said to have lived in a chronic condition of excitement, but he was, perhaps, never more excited than
when the news of the firing upon Sumter reached the village, for he
was not only a fervent American but an Abolitionist from his youth
up. He declared that Medfield must raise a company, and that to
raise a company it was necessary to indemnify by bounties the families of the volunteers. He went straightway into Boston, collected
from his agents every dollar they would advance upon his pictures
in their possession, offered the proceeds to the bounty fund, insisted

that a platform should be erected from which he might address his fellow-citizens, and addressed them accordingly, calling upon the "men of valor and men of muscle" to volunteer. He himself volunteered, but was balked by the medical examination. He insisted that the spectacles he was never seen without were not really necessary to him, but when the examiner, who had been handling ploughboys all day, gave the artist a vigorous blow upon the chest to test his lungs, the volunteer fainted dead away, and the company he had done so much to raise marched away to the war without him.

In 1864, at the suggestion of Marcus Spring, a friend and patron, the painter again returned to New York, living in Eaglewood, N. J., until 1867, when he removed to Brooklyn. In 1870 he sailed once more for Europe, for the longest of his sojourns, which lasted until 1876, when he returned to Boston and the next year to New York, in which, or in the environs of which, he thenceforward resided. His pecuniary troubles were not over. The old-fashioned American collector, in so far as he was not extinct, looked askance at the novel and questionable style of Inness, while the buyer of French landscapes demanded French names to them. Meanwhile the painter, with untiring industry and ever-increasing facility, was producing landscapes which wandering artistic Frenchmen gladly recognized as worthy to be ranked with the noblest contemporary work of Europe.

It was the suave and harmonious "Golden Sunset," painted in 1865 and shown at the Paris exhibition of 1867,—now in Mr. Clarke's collection,—that first drew European attention to the American painter. It was the spectral and yet real "Winter Morning at Montclair," painted in 1882, in the same collection, that attracted the admiration of M. Benjamin Constant,—an admiration so strengthened by his inspection of other works of the artist that he induced Messrs. Boussod, Valadon & Company to arrange to have a collection of the artist's work consigned to Paris for sale. Mr. Inness was freed from pecuniary care only during the last decade of his life, and the enfranchisement began with the purchase by the late Roswell Smith of the large "Niagara" for $5,000. It was this that determined his removal to Montclair, and after that time the painter was free to pursue his art in his own way. He had grown up to a far freer and more complete expression of his impressions of nature than he had attained before, and his public had grown up to an appreciation of his art. He was especially fortunate in these latter years in devolving the mercantile responsibilities of his art upon Mr. Thomas B.

Clarke, who was induced to undertake them by his own hearty ad-miration of and belief in the painter whose pictures he had been buy-ing for many years for love of them, and whose labors in Inness's behalf were also largely of love.   The result of them was that for the last few years the artist attained the enviable state of being able to dispose of whatever canvases he offered at studio prices, while the purchaser had the comfortable assurance that the auction price would not be less than the studio price.   One purchaser who paid $400 for an Inness sold it at auction within a few months for $1,600.   "The Grove of Oaks," for which the painter received $200, was sold again for $1,500; and a picture was bought for $200, for which the buyer afterward refused an offer of $2,500 from Mr. Seney.   In the later years the studio price of an Inness, 30 inches by 45, his most frequent canvas, was $2,000, and the price at auction was some hundreds higher.   The painter had, through the long years of ob-structed expression and of uninterrupted striving, attained a surpris-ing fluency and facility of brushwork, and his mind always teemed with subjects.   So one does not greatly marvel to be told that his income in these latter years was larger than that of any living land-scape-painter.   At all events, he was put finally out of reach of the " cares of bread. "

Among the chief buyers of the later Innesses were Mr. George I. Seney, Mr. R. H. Halsted, Mr. William H. Fuller, Mr. H. Dalley, Jr., Mr. Benjamin Altman, and Dr. Ferdinand of New York, Mr. James W. Ellsworth and Mr. Potter Palmer of Chicago.   But there is scarcely a town in the United States where there are collectors of pictures where there is not now an example of Inness to be seen and studied.   Mr. Clarke's collection, which is easily the most complete and most representative, numbers twenty-five, and includes the "Winter Morning," the "Gray Lowery Day," the "Nine o'Clock," and covers the period from 1863 (the "Delaware Valley") to 1894 ("After a Summer Shower," the last completely finished Inness). Mr. Halsted has eighteen, from the serene and almost "classical" "Valley of the Olive Trees" (1867), to the magnificently free and vital "Tenafly Oaks" (1893).   Mr. Ellsworth has twelve, Mr. Palmer has nine, Mr. Altman has eight, Mr. Dalley has eight, the estate of Roswell Smith has six, Mr. Wigglesworth has six.   The Metropol-itan Museum has four, of which but one is in the fullest sense rep-resentative.   There is one in the Corcoran Gallery at Washington, one in the gallery of the Long Island Historical Society ("The Old

Roadway," given by Mr. Seney), and one in the Boston Museum. Perhaps 250 canvases of all dates, sizes, and kinds remain to the painter's estate.

Considering his incessant industry, and, in his maturity, his great facility, even this goodly number seems small. It would have been larger but for a habit that arose from one of his most characteristic traits. That trait was an intense preoccupation with what concerned him at the moment, amounting to a conviction that it was the only thing in the world worth doing or thinking about. The resultant habit was the habit of trying to express this upon whatever material happened to be at hand. If there was nothing else available than one of his own most valuable pictures, so much the worse for the picture. He must even wreak his present inspiration upon that. It is said to be literally true that one of the remaining canvases contains twenty-five separate and superimposed pictures. There is another that was begun as a "Morning Hunting Scene," and that in its final phase was a "Summer Afternoon." In most cases the later pictures were developments from the earlier. A new notion of the treatment of some particular "passage" led to a reconstruction of the whole. So long as a picture remained in the studio it was not finished to the painter's mind nor safe from his hand. At any time he might take a fresh dash at it and render it unrecognizable. So well was this habit understood among the habitual buyers of Innesses, that they would lie in wait for the "state" in which a canvas satisfied them, and artfully convey it out of the reach of the painter's study of perfection. Sometimes, however, the new picture bore no relation whatever to the old. His son-in-law and studio-companion relates that one morning in the winter of 1882, Mr. Inness, departing on a visit to Montclair, and foreseeing that he could not help painting, seized a canvas upon which a striking and promising composition was already "laid in." To the remonstrances of his friend that it would be a pity to efface this, and that it would take but a few minutes to procure a fresh canvas, he turned an inattentive ear and sallied forth with the canvas upon which now appears the "Winter Morning at Montclair."

This intense absorption in the matter in hand, and this exclusion of all other things from consideration, were of the utmost value to the painter as a painter, and so to us, his public; but even in his art they prevented him from being a teacher except by example, or even a counsellor. "I can get no good of Inness," a younger painter

once exclaimed, who had asked his advice; "he does not help me
to paint my picture; he insists upon my painting his." The concentration that is admirable and enviable in an artist is the negation of
the notion of a man of the world. In his case it amounted to an in-
capability to conceive that there could be any other point of view
than his own of the moment. The tact, the light transition, the
give-and-take of conversation, were impossible to the strenuous
Inness, who was as much "possessed" when he talked as when he
painted. Conversation, in the proper sense, was almost out of the
question with him. He either sat silent or he harangued. When he
talked about art, he was always suggestive and interesting; but art
was not his favorite topic, and a remark, or a few remarks, prefatory
to his real topic, were all that could be had from him. One writer
did, indeed, extract from him a clear and tolerably systematic confession of his artistic faith, and published it in "Harper's Magazine"
for February, 1878. But one suspects that the interpreter must have
been very patient as well as very faithful and sympathetic, and have
gone through many sittings to cull the detached remarks about painting to which he has given consecutiveness and unity. The paper is
extremely well worth reading, both for the express explanation of
the painter's own artistic standard, and for the implicit reference to
that standard in his criticisms upon other painters. Here is the express explanation:

What the painter tries to do is simply to reproduce in other minds the impression which a scene has made upon him. A work of art does not appeal to
the intellect. It does not appeal to the moral sense. Its aim is not to instruct,
not to edify, but to awaken an emotion. This emotion may be one of love, of
pity, of hate, of pleasure, or of pain; but it must be a single emotion, if the
work have unity, as every such work should have, and the true beauty of the
work consists in the beauty of the sentiment or emotion which it inspires. Details in the picture must be elaborated only fully enough to reproduce the impression that the artist wishes to reproduce. When more than this is done, the
impression is weakened or lost, and we see simply an array of external things,
which may be very cleverly painted and may look very real, but which do not
make an artistic painting. The effort and the difficulty of the artist is to combine the two, to make the thought clear and to preserve the unity of impression.
. . . Some persons suppose that landscape has no power of communicating
human sentiment. But this is a great mistake. The civilized landscape peculiarly can; and therefore I love it more and think it more worthy of reproduction than that which is savage and untamed. It is more significant.

The specific and laudatory criticisms of his favorite French painters that follow are in line with this definition. Delacroix was the
master whom Inness most of all admired, and it is possibly signifi-

cant that the picture of Delacroix that he selected for praise in the paper just quoted from, and that he never tired of praising, should have been an allegory—" The Triumph of Apollo," from a ceiling in the Louvre.   One who knew him only by his talk might have expected him to deal largely in allegory in his own work, so symbolical and mystical did his talk represent everything in Nature.   But in fact, while his pictures were suffused with his personal sentiment, there is in them very little of express allegory, save in a few titles, such as " The New Jerusalem," a battlement of sun-gilded clouds upon the horizon, or the sombre " Valley of the Shadow of Death," which was reproduced, with Walt Whitman's verses upon it, in " Harper's Magazine," two or three years ago.

It seemed that his talk was the safety-valve of the freaks and fantasies of the man, and enabled him to preserve the sanity and balance of his art.   It was astonishing talk at all times when he gave himself full swing.   Brought up in an atmosphere of polemics, the dogmatic and supernatural sides of religion had taken a great hold upon him.   In his early manhood he had joined the Baptist Church. In riper years he became a very friendly investigator of " Spiritualism" expressly so called.   His resort to Swedenborg was perhaps due to his association with William Page, the painter, mildest and most winning of the lay expositors of the " Arcana Cœlestia. "   Whatever led him to the Swedish mystic, Mr. Inness came to revel in him, and, when he was in good spirits, to administer bad quarters of an hour to those who did not revel.   At such seasons he was, in sooth, as Garrick's brother said of Johnson, " a tremendous companion. "

He easily united with his adherence to Swedenborg an unquestioning credence of the grosser " manifestations" of the mediums.   Naturally the assumption that supernatural visitations were as credible as the police-court news was " unto the Greeks foolishness. "   I happened to be the third when Inness encountered one Greek, who had himself rather a turn and talent for monologue.   But he was straightway overborne by the painter, who was excited by a recent " manifestation" that he had witnessed or read of, and was presently in full Swedenborgian swing.   My friend opposed to the torrent a countenance of calm but obvious incredulity, without the least effect, and at last walked to the book-shelf, and took down a volume in which he immersed himself.   But he was not to be let off so.   The rapt declaimer turned upon him at a crisis of the discourse with an explosive " Don't you think so, Mr. ——?"   " Mr. Inness," returned

the Greek, with extreme tranquillity and deliberation, " I think nothing about it except that the whole subject wearies me inexpressibly."

There is another story that is too characteristic not to be told.
The painter had been spending one of his latest summers in New
Brunswick, and had met there a well-known Canadian, who, as he
halted in Montreal on his way home, bade him to a dinner-party
given in honor of some distinguished Australians—a very distinguished publicist among them—who were about to cross the continent.   As is known, the " single tax" excites much interest and discussion in Australia, and Inness had become an ardent Georgeite.
The talk at dinner turned upon the tax, and the Australian view was
expounded at length by the distinguished publicist.   Inness sat
quite silent, his burning black eyes, under his black and shaggy
" fell of hair," fixed upon the speaker, who talked the more complacently in the consciousness of so appreciative a listener.   Hardly
had the door been closed after the ladies, however, when from the
silent corner the appreciative listener's forefinger shot out at the
chief speaker, as it had been a highwayman's pistol, with " Did you
mean what you said?"—and then followed an oration in the course of
which it is averred that the orator stood upon every one of the vacated
chairs.   The party in the drawing-room were startled at last by the
sudden irruption of the sitters, those large antipodean men huddled
like their native sheep, and bearing in their faces evidences of alarm,
while behind them, rounding them up like an active collie, came the
small nervous American, still declaiming.

But it was not in hard painting and hard talking alone that the
artist expounded his wonderful energy.   He wrote voluminously,
especially in his later years, theological and spiritualistic rhapsodies
and mysteries in prose and in verse not much less formless, and he
has left masses of manuscript.   But he had not undergone in this
the discipline to which he had subjected himself in his own art.
His meaning, we must believe, was clear to himself, but he had not
learned how to make it clear to others.   In spite of an occasional
striking thought, the prose is incoherent and unreadable, and the
verse is not more important, in comparison with the author's real
work, than the unpublished " Fallacies of Hope" from which Turner
extracted mottoes for his pictures compared with the pictures themselves.   But as an additional proof of its author's exuberant and inexhaustible vitality the results of his literary labor form a remarkable
document, and increase the wonder that a bodily machine originally

so frail should have lasted, at such a tremendous pressure, for all but seventy years.

This same vitality, it seems to me, is the dominant note in his art. This may be divided, as with most individual painters who live to old age, into three periods. The first—the apprenticeship—was, in Inness's case, unusually long and toilsome, from the unfavorableness of his surroundings. It took him ten years or more to find his hand-writing, which the American art-student of to-day, with his immeasurably better facilities, can acquire in less than half that time, unless it happen to him to acquire his teacher's. In his middle career he subordinated all things to unity of impression, and became a master of "tone." As he grew riper in mind and more skilful of hand, he attempted to gain more variety and truth of color, more "objective force," as he puts it, without losing unity, and this was the attempt that, with varying success, engrossed the last decade and more of his life. So confident was he that tone and resplendence could be united that he proposed in his last years to paint landscape with the three primary colors alone. But evidently this was but "theory playing its usual trick upon the artist," and a wise instinct held him back from the actual attempt. That his work should be unequal was quite inevitable. But the vitality that was the note of the successes was hardly less marked in the failures, and the successes were very great indeed. In a country in which any other than the literary form of artistic expression was popularly understood or even recognized, they would have made the painter's work one of the national possessions. The high seriousness with which he took his art is attested by two striking facts. In all the mass of his work it is impossible to point to a "pot-boiler," on the one hand, or to a conscious *tour de force* on the other. It is within bounds, I think, to say that he thoroughly believed in every one of his pictures while he was painting it, and equally within bounds to say that he painted nothing to exhibit his technique, even when his technique was at its best and ripest. The idea possessed him; the execution needed to be merely adequate. That an artistic life so full, so devoted, and so successful can be lived in America ought to go far toward reconciling American artists to their discouragements.

MONTGOMERY SCHUYLER.

THE EASTERN WAR, AND AFTER: A MILITARY STUDY.

"Don't never prophesy onless you know."

THE Mongols cover a larger part of the area of the globe than any other race; they make up nearly half its population. It is well for Europe that the predominant trait of the Turanian is inertia; if the Chinese had the colonizing instinct which many centuries ago drove the Aryans outward from their Asian plateau, there would to-day be nothing left of our civilization, even had they afforded our ancestors the leisure to create one. The "backbone of the earth," as the range on the west of their habitat has well been called, could scarcely have arrested their migration. But they are, as a rule, a stolid set of men, fatalists by religion, satisfied with their little present, or, if not satisfied, making no effort to improve it. There is perhaps nothing which shows the inertness of the Mongol more than the fact that the sampan population of Canton, with its two millions of people, numbers over two hundred thousand souls. A sampan is a "slipper" boat plying for hire, owned by and housing a family whose members pass their entire lives therein, no more thinking of leaving their floating home than a serf tied to the soil dreams of quitting his lord's land. If you hire a sampan, you get aboard with the whole family, and while you cross the harbor may be actual witness to a birth, a marriage, or a death. How long would a European Aryan thus live?

One of the surprises encountered by the traveller when he is first cast among Mongolians is their physical development. Americans are wont to judge their bodily structure by the specimens in the laundry-shops of Sam Lee or Wi Ping; and the loose clothing of the China-man conceals his brawny arms and legs when he has them. Seeing Thibetans in the Himalayas—stocky chunks of men with an abnormal muscular development—had not brushed away my idea that the Chinaman was rather a slim, unmuscular Oriental, something like the willowy Hindu; but when I landed in Singapore and first saw numbers of coolies stripped to their work, I was thunderstruck at their massive proportions. The Chinese are commonly said to be a diseased race, a people permeated with blood-poisons: but one does not see it in the average specimen, and one does see at every street corner men with limbs and torsos like a Sandow, men who would be marked down for football-players in any American college.   Not but what disease is always an accompaniment of so crowded a population; not that its manifestations fail to impress you: but the Chinaman, far from being a taper-fingered mortal, is a tough, sturdy, fine fellow, with thews and sinews like an athlete, and plenty of ambition and courage—within his racial lines.   Nor have I found any exception to the rule.   The Mongol, from the borders of India, where, going east, you first strike his homely coarseness, to the confines of Japan, where you say good-by to his lovely cherry-blossoms and his smiling bows, is everywhere, in physique, the same strong, enduring man.   The Chinaman is filthy in mind, body, and estate; the Japanese is equally clean; but in mere physical quality they are very much alike.   That the Mongol's nervous structure is less fine than the Aryan's is evidenced by the fact that the average Chinaman will endure unblenched the pain of a surgical operation which would seriously compromise the reactionary power of most white men; and this, if anything, adds to his value as a mere human animal.

. But there be Mongols and Mongols; and perhaps no two European Aryan nations are quite so dissimilar in their traits and tendencies as are the inhabitants of the mainland of eastern Asia and those of the adjacent islands of Japan.   The lapse of generations since the continental dwellers put over to the islands is one reason for the difference.   It does not take many generations to work a climatic change in races—look at the spare, quick, nervous Yankee, who in eight generations has been transformed from the beefy, easy-going Briton,— and all isle-dwellers are apt to develop a peculiar type.   Religion is another reason; and while Shinto is not Christianity, it has produced a people with more qualities approaching those which are undoctrinally taught by the New Testament than can be found within what we are wont to entitle Christian lands.   If honest helpfulness, unending amiability, loyalty to the powers that be, filial piety in its highest expression, law-abiding steadiness, and a keen sense of honor be not fair equivalents of Christian virtues, where shall we find them?

The history of the Japanese testifies to abundant courage; their internal wars have been long and bloody.   It is hard to reconcile this quality, which is the usual comrade of the grosser virtues, with their hyper-artistic sense.   That the Japanese, as a people, lead the world in their feeling for the beautiful, seems now to be an accepted fact; and it must be confessed that there springs from this temperament that lack of practical directness which always characterizes the true æsthete. The business instinct is quite apart from the artistic; and the Japanese, when he promises you a thing for to-morrow, fully meaning at the moment to deliver it as agreed, may actually put you in possession of your property at some time between now and Christmas, or he may not. Now the Chinaman will do as he agrees; not that he has half the good intention or kindly feeling toward an outer barbarian which the other possesses; but he has found that honesty is practically the best policy, and he always pays his note when due. So well recognized is this difference that the cashier of every large commercial house in the treaty ports of Japan wears a pigtail. Business is business with the Chinaman—always; with the Japanese it is not so—if the chrysanthemums be in bloom.

One cannot expect all the cardinal virtues in one man; nor do you get them in the Japanese. He is far behind his distant cousin of China in all which makes for orderliness; but the latter can in no sense be compared to him in those qualities which make life worth living. The "Jap" has the "mañana" of the Spaniard, or the "pacienza" of the Brazilian, always on his lips; time is as nothing to him, and he will arrest the chariot of state to pen (or rather paint) a poem on a piece of rice-paper and hang it on a flowering plum-tree.

This long initial digression is not wasted if it conveys to those who do not know them the idea of the divergent characters, aims, and habits of the two nations who are now fighting in the Corea: the idea of the fatalistic but utilitarian Chinaman; the idea of the æsthetic, unmethodical Japanese. And the wonder of it all is that the latter, despite his tendency to carelessness, has adopted and is fast assimilating our practical Western civilization, while the former, with all his sharp-cut tendencies, still adheres to his Eastern ignorance; the one has got arms of precision and an able navy, while the latter, barring a small modern equipment, is still in the era of junks and stink-pots.

Now it is rather odd that the Chinese have not further adopted European inventions. To be sure, they have (or had) a few iron-clads; but they are by no means as well equipped as the Japanese, with a tenth of their population. They have (or had) a few brigades of troops drilled according to the modern method; but only a fraction of the aggregate of their little enemy. Whether it be their bureaucratic structure of government which makes changes hard to introduce, or those peculiar racial characteristics the sum of which is utter passiveness, it is hard to say.   One might guess that a nation where a man condemned to be beheaded can buy a substitute for a few pieces of silver, and thus satisfy an easy criminal code and his own convenience, had scarcely arrived at the perceptivity of electric search-lights and melinite shells.   But this does not satisfy the inquiry; and one is at a loss to explain to himself the true inwardness of what one might call Chinese astigmatism in viewing the value of our modern devices.   The larger the body, the more slowly, proportionately, will it move.   The greyhound is more active than the bullock.   Is it the volume of China, the impossibility of penetrating the whole mass with any one idea except conservatism, which keeps her so backward?   It is only on the coast that there are any European ideas to-day; and what all China possesses of our modern machines and methods would scarcely equip a nation of ten million souls.

With Japan it is just the reverse; and while islanders are more get-at-able than continentals, it is little short of a miracle what she has accomplished since Perry rapped at her front door only so far back as 1854.   It is hard to state the utter dissemblance between the Japanese and ourselves.   Some one has truly observed that when you speak French or German you are only speaking English by using a new set of words.   " How many people are there in the hotel?" would be almost word for word the same in any of our Aryan tongues.   But when you have to say, " Honorable guests under roof how many as to?" it argues a new form of thought, not language. And from what is to us an abnormal form of thought as well as life, the Japanese had to start in order to adopt our modern civilization. They have swallowed our inventions with wholesale gluttony; but their digestion is good, and they have assimilated them.   Every centre in Europe and America is full of Japanese students of our arts and manufactures.   Among the best customers of our trading-marts are the merchants of their treaty ports.   All who were familiar with what Japan has been doing knew how it would be; but she has fairly startled the world by the speed and splendor of her mobilization and the sharp and effective directness of the offensive movement to, in, and about Corea.   How is it that a nation confessedly unbusiness-like, which adjourns from work at regular short intervals to play under the flowering trees, which twists a wistaria into a valid excuse for a popular holiday, has been able to make strides in civilization involving such exceptional stewardship, such unswerving directness, and such unremitting labor? The answer to this lies in the fact that Japan possesses its share of able men, and, above all, a dutiful people.

At the head of old Japan were the daimios, or nobles; beneath them the samurai, or gentry; and to the wants and wealth of these the heimin, or peasants,—nine-tenths of the population,—contributed all their toil and gain save only a bare subsistence. Though Japan now possesses that portfolio of civilization, a written constitution, the demarcation between the two upper classes, which have much inter-mingled, still remains.

The Japanese have no decalogue; their commandments are but two: Obey the Mikado; Love and obey your parents,—having done which they may follow their own sweet wills within the pale of the law, for nothing is wrong which does not inflict hardship on others. Simple as is this rule of life, it has, in Japan at least, shown its ability to produce a people happy and happy-making; a fair proof that too many laws tend to confusion. The second commandment, inculcating filial piety, is carried out in its broadest sense; the first is observed blindly; but in old Japan the orders of the Mikado trickled down to the commoner through several mouths, and they were wont to reach him as construed by his immediate lord. While to the European who only sees the railroad-opened cities, old Japan is a thing of the past, it suffices to go a day's 'ricksha journey from the tourist track to discover that modern Japan is confined mostly to the governing class of the capital and to their immediate surround-ings. Where the Japanese has cut his hair à la brosse, and wears a derby and a " boiled rag," he is, or is trying to be, Europeanized; when you get to regions where the paint-brush queue points at you from the top of his poll, and he wears a kimono and walks home from his bath in puris naturalibus, there is old Japan still resident. And the time-honored motto of old Japan is unquestioning obedience.

Japan is a bigger country than we imagine. In area and in population it equals Great Britain and Ireland; and its strength lies in the absolute subservience of the people to one man's will, or to that of one small set of men,—the Mikado and his ministers. How-ever much we may hear of the efforts of Japan to make a representa-tive government, or however pertinently she may show, as in this war, that she has adopted European methods, the people will for

many generations remain the patient, law-abiding, duteous folk of
yore.   And so long as this exists, and the peasant retains his hardy
courage and exceptional power of endurance, Japan will be able to
deal a. blow out of all proportion to her weight.

The Japanese is brought up to work, to bear burdens, to be
patient under exhausting toil, to live on little, and to keep his temper.   This latter has been so long inculcated, that babies never cry.
If a child tumbles and hurts itself, every one laughs, and it is surprised into laughing too.   The six-year-old boy carries his six-
month-old sister;   the ten-year-old girl works with her two-year-old
brother strapped to her back, to keep him out of mischief.   Add
to this the fact that the peasant is healthy and sound, and what can
better produce an infantry able to march to the end of the world?
He is plain, your Japanese, but the stuff is there.

The tone of the Japanese people is artistic, but the man of action
in Japan possesses strength, intellectual and moral.   A land where
strong men too much abound may be torn by faction; this has not
happened in new Japan, though in olden days the history was made
up of the quarrels of rival shoguns.   Since 1854 her course has been
moulded by few men, but able ones.

Japan proudly dates her autonomy back beyond the Christian era.
Tenshi-Sama, God of Heaven, whom we call Mikado, is the fountain
of all authority, but centuries ago he was compelled to delegate this
to a " ring" of his powerful subjects, known as shoguns.   The last
family of shoguns, the Tokugawas, reigned two hundred and fifty
years, and up to 1868 the Mikado was a sort of Pope, infallible, but
confined to a species of Vatican.   In 1868 the Satsuma and Choshu
clans rose against the Tokugawas and wrested their power from
them; since when the " Sat-Chos" have been absolute rulers; and
it is they who have built up the new Japan.   Count Ito, who represents the progressive idea, but who does not wish the power to pass
from the Sat-Cho ring;   Count Itagaki, the head of the radicals;
Count Okuma, leader of the Liberal party, which would make the
government responsible to Parliament; and many others,—are truly
able men; and they will lay aside their political disputes to work
success out of their present complications.

A twofold ambition inspires Japan: to make herself a first-rate
Power in the eyes of Europe, as by her native wealth, her territorial
extent, and her population she may properly aspire to become if she
adopts our ways; and as a sequence, by placing herself in the sister-

hood of nations, to demand the revision of her treaties, especially that part which claims ex-territoriality, or the right of Europeans to be tried by Europeans for acts committed on Japanese soil. Her war in Corea is inspired perhaps as much by a Jingo desire to make a mark, and thereby prove her claim to equality in the European economy, as by any feeling of having been imposed upon by China. She intends to be ranked no longer as an effete Mongol, and is fast proving her case. It may be seriously questioned whether Japan has taken a wise step in entering upon this Corean war; but, being in it, what are her chances of eventual success?

About China I know little. Who does know much? There is no new China; the proverbial hills are no older nor more inert. Though she has an immense territory, a dense, immeasurable population, and a species of negative force, the events of the past generation show that, despite the adoption of a few European methods, she has so slowly assimilated what she has taken, that she has been forced to yield to the successive demands of several of the Powers, though backed up by a naval and military display no less than grotesque when viewed from the light of armaments destined for the European theatre of war. The true cause of this supineness I cannot pretend to give; China is like a mammoth pachyderm; the blow from an elephant-hook which would kill a horse, merely makes the monster flap his ears; and it seems as if the body of China was not homogeneously sentient.—as if the nervous system of the mass was so subdivided that a lesion to one part did not reach the nervous centre of the whole structure. Nothing that China has done of late years demonstrates her capacity to act as one body. Her crew does not pull together, however bulky each oarsman. Granted the strength, the prowess of the Chinaman. That he can face death with stolid indifference is true. But that is not the desideratum of modern war, and, once demoralized, the Chinaman decamps. In no age has immobility won against activity. The Persian hosts could not resist the handful of Macedonian sarissas, or the passionate charges of Alexander's few Companions. Tilly's dense Spanish battalions were broken by the three-deep Swedes of Gustavus. Heavily manned works have been easiest taken by thin and active lines of skirmishers pushed on in quick succession. Assuming China to rise in her might and to deliver a blow at Japan with a directness in any sense comparable to her weight, the result could not be doubtful. But she has never done this; can she do it now? I see nothing to make me believe that she can or will. The European equipment is no greater than Japan's, and it has been, in the initial engagements on land and water, smashed by the intelligent violence of the Japanese. To be sure, Corea is an easy battle-ground for Japan; but her landings have been admirably made, and while her division of forces at Ping Yang was not quite defensible, it succeeded,—and that is better. And at the Yalu fight, despite Admiral Ting's bravery, and the fact that he had two battle-ships and almost as great tonnage and average speed of vessel, he was bested by Admiral Ito by initiative and skilful energy.

The Corean war, so far, is rather interesting than great. In the absence of grave contests elsewhere, it looms up into undue prominence. Much talk was devoted to Big Bethel, when some of the battles around Petersburg—a score of times more deadly—were barely noticed. By no means to underrate Count Yamagata and his gallant divisions, the Ping Yang battle was no huge affair, except in its results. How it can be compared to Sadowa, as I have seen done, it is hard to say; for though battles are not properly measurable by numbers or losses, these have a certain bearing on the subject which may not be overlooked. Many a brigade has fought to a standstill with a loss out of all proportion; but you would not liken its struggle to the Moskwa or Gettysburg. The Yalu battle was greater as being typical of a new naval method. I see that the experts are drawing conclusions from the latter, to the effect that to attack is the policy of the future. But this is no discovery; to attack has been the policy of all great soldiers from Cyrus down. No vast result has ever been accomplished by defensive strategy or tactics. The trend of events sometimes dictates a defensive policy. Circumstances may bring results to a man who waits, but it is not he who has won them. The Yalu fight has shown no more the desirability of attack than a hundred battles on land and sea for the past five-and-twenty centuries. It is of more interest to know how the attack was made, whether "all along the line," or on some one spot in the Chinese front; what was the percentage of hits; and what the actual effect of the fire was on each and all the ships. Perhaps its lesson is that many small and swift are better than few heavy and slower vessels,—shall we say cruiser instead of battle-ship?

There are two dangers to Japan. One lies in her overreaching herself in her over-eagerness for success. This is the graver. To learn when you have won enough is the hardest lesson of all. The

other danger lies in foreign intervention.   Who shall have Corea is a
question which interests all the Powers,—England and Russia most.
Like the Balkan peninsula, England feels that Russia must not have
it; but Russia wants it none the less.   May Japan play the part of
Turkey and hold it so that neither the lion nor the bear shall prowl
therein?   These be questions of international policy which it be-
hooves me not to answer—even if I could.

   Another question is as to how far the Corean war may stimulate
China to arm *à l'Européenne*, and how much danger such an act
might threaten to Oriental, and, as a next step, to European peace?
There lurks no danger in Japan.   She has but forty million souls,
and even if aggressive could do no harm.   But China, the vast, the
incalculable?   This matter has already been partially answered by
the above.   Races are either migratory or they are not.   Some races
have been spasmodically migratory, as when led by some viking,
thirsting for war and plunder; others have been consistently migratory, tempted by the colonizing instinct.   China has never been
either.   The influx of Chinese on our Pacific slope has brought us
scarcely a bubble of the froth on the surface of the population of that
vast nation.   And had the immigration of these dirty folk not been
checked, while their advent might have produced a prejudicial effect
on California, it would scarce have deluged America.   Their migration hitherto has been individual, not national.   Unless the Celestial
changes the character he has possessed for generations untold, I should
have no fear of his becoming inflated with the idea of conquest.   His
rôle is defence: "What we want is to be let alone!"   China has
able men, but they are not at the helm of state to-day.   Their work
does not dovetail, even when of the best.   Li Hung Chang has not
succeeded, because his hands were tied; nor is he the first able man
to fail; and in any case the ability of the Chinese does not run on the
lines of modern practice.   Nor is China rich in the sense that she can
spend millions on such armaments.   Her recent expense-account, despite treasures said to be hoarded in Pekin and Moukden, had to be
footed by robbery of the people; while Japan raised her loan three-
fold.   There seems to be neither centralization, energy, nor antagonism in China sufficient to lead her to create a dangerously great army
or navy.   Moreover, these things mean years of preparation and outlay.

   At the outbreak of hostilities Japan had on foot and ready for
duty in the outland five divisions, what we should call army corps,

or a total of one hundred thousand men; and at their head a general staff composed of officers mostly trained in Germany. The reserve and landwehr could not be included in the tale of forces to be sent on a rapid foreign expedition, but were more than equal to home defence. This hundred thousand men, thoroughly organized and equipped in modern style, and with an *esprit de corps* bred of thorough discipline, was well ahead of any army China could throw into Corea. At sea, Japan likewise felt stronger than the enemy, and, though this was more doubtful, has since proven herself to be so in personnel, manœuvring, and marksmanship. Moltke's motto, "March in separate columns; unite for battle," was evidently the Japanese scheme for operations in Corea; their divisions worked on several lines; and against the Chinese the plan culminated in success. Yet, in front of an active enemy, unless you know just where he is and are convinced that he cannot fall on you in detail, this motto may not be construed too broadly. From Ping Yang, for quite a period, an able captain might have seriously disturbed the Japanese concentric manœuvres. The latter relied on their speed; they were right; and it is a truism that an operation crowned by success shall not be criticised. Ping Yang was a Sedan on a rather small scale in all but results.

This ancient city is an important strategic point. At this very place, some three hundred years ago, China won from Japan the control of Corea. From here leads a road northward, substantially following the coast, which it strikes at Sin-Chin, and thence continues on to the Yalu river, a hundred and twenty miles from Ping Yang. From the further bank of the Yalu, a better road runs a hundred and seventy-five miles further to Moukden, capital of Manchuria, parent of the present Chinese dynasty, and the Mecca of the Chinese pilgrim. But these roads are poor at any season; in many places two carts cannot pass each other; the many rivers are bridgeless; and through the rice-growing districts they are at times so deep as to be impassable. Other Corean roads there are practically none. The rainy season in northern Corea is over in September, leaving a number of weeks for campaigning before the winter snows set in. The Japanese are stubborn marchers, and the distance to Moukden, apart from military or other obstacles or delays, might be made in little over three weeks. The invaders must, however, consider not only the advance, but the feeding of an army in Moukden; and this is a practicable thing by water, if the Japanese take Niu-Chwang and keep control of the sea.

Manchuria, though its home of origin, is not without rebellious feelings toward the Chinese Imperial family, which, in its turn, has done little to conciliate the province. It was only so late as 1891 that the Manchurian rebels, who were projecting no less than a march on Pekin, were luckily stopped at Kin-chu-fu by the Chinese army. This antagonism is all in favor of the Japanese, and if they can take Moukden they will have struck a sufficient blow at China to warrant their claim to Corea.

Not only are soldiers gratified with the Japanese strategy, but the thoroughly civilized manner in which these Europeanized Asiatics have gone to work stands out in marked contrast to the mediæval methods of the Chinese, whose wrath at being beaten seems to have threatened the security of all foreigners within her borders. The effect of the moderation of Japan has been to commend her cause to the entire world.

It is quite within the possibilities that there may be intervention between China and Japan, on the part of the Powers, jealous lest any change in the strength or aim of either contestant may disturb the balance of power in the Orient, or, what is more to the point, the current of trade. Proposals to this effect are already afoot. Should intervention take such form that Japan must accept it, it would so far alter the conditions that the merely military situation would count for no more than a make-weight in the final forced settlement. Should the contestants be left alone, the probabilities run strongly in favor of the islanders. They will scarcely face the rugged and difficult territory between Ping Yang and Moukden with its severe winter climate. But Moukden is readily turned by a descent on Niu-Chwang, and the configuration of the theatre of war affords excellent means of coöperation by the Japanese army and navy; they will probably command all the waters west of Corea, as well as their communications with home ports; they can now readily move their troops by sea; Corea seems to be fairly won; they have the initiative; they have more modern troops, arms and vessels than the continentals. And though it is true that there is matter in nature which continues to compress before a blow or a missile, so that this can penetrate its substance only so far; while China may have a density of population and a stolidity of racial traits which would make it impossible for any army to march through the length and breadth of her land without coming to grief; yet, in view of the nearness to the coast of Tientsin and Pekin, in view of the historical certainty that well-led,

.well-armed troops may safely defy mere numbers; in view of the fact
·that the Chinese fleet will not be able for at least some months to hold
head to the Japanese vessels convoying transports; in view of the personal equation, the strongest force in war, and which in this instance
is markedly with the islanders; in view of the momentum acquired
by the attacking party and of the good cheer as against loss of morale
following the initial battles; in view of the almost certainty that
China will not put out any efforts commensurate with her bulk,—it is
equally within the possibilities that Japan may dictate peace at the
capital of Manchuria or of China.   I am inclined to think, however,
that the Japanese would be wiser to aim for Moukden than for Pekin.
Their claim would be urged with equal force at either place, and
with far less danger at Moukden.   In fact all they have started out
to get they may rightfully claim when their occupation of Corea is
made secure.   For this brilliant consummation there is yet one thing
wanting—a leader.   At least three-quarters of the value of an army
or a navy resides in the mental and moral equipment of one man.
This suggestion of the possibilities must be Celtically answered by
a query:

Has Japan a Von Moltke?   We shall see.   *Finis coronat opus.*

THEODORE AYRAULT DODGE.

PARIS, *September 27, 1894.*

STUDIES OF THE GREAT VICTORIAN WRITERS:
IV.—THACKERAY'S PLACE IN LITERATURE.[1]

THE literary career of William Makepeace Thackeray has not a few special features of its own that it is interesting to note at once. Of all the more eminent writers of the Victorian age, his life was the shortest: he died in 1863 at the age of fifty-two, the age of Shakespeare. His literary career of twenty-six years was shorter than that of Carlyle, of Macaulay, Disraeli, Dickens, Trollope, George Eliot, Froude, or Ruskin. It opened with the reign of the Queen, almost in the very year of " Pickwick," whose author stood beside his grave and lived and wrote for some years more. But these twenty-six years of Thackeray's era of production were full of wonderful activity, and have left us as many volumes of rich and varied genius. And the most striking feature of all is this—that in these twenty-six full volumes in so many modes, prose, verse, romance, parody, burlesque, essay, biography, criticism, there is not one which can be put aside as worthless and an utter failure; not one that falls from his consummate mastery of style; not one that it is irksome to read, to re-read, and to linger over in the reading.

This mastery over style—a style at once simple, pure, nervous, flexible, pathetic, and graceful—places Thackeray amongst the very greatest masters of English prose, and undoubtedly as the most certain and faultless of all the prose writers of the Victorian age. Without saying that he has ever reached quite to the level of some lyrical and apocalyptic descants that we may find in Carlyle and in Ruskin, Thackeray has never fallen into the faults of violence and turgidity which their warmest admirers are bound to confess in many a passage from these our two prose-poets. Carlyle is often grotesque; Macaulay can be pompous; Disraeli, Bulwer, Dickens, are often slovenly and sometimes bombastic; George Eliot is sometimes pedantic, and Ruskin has been stirred into hysterics. But Thackeray's English, from the first page of his first volume to the last page of his twenty-sixth volume, is natural, scholarly, pure, incisive, and yet gracefully and easily modulated—the language of an English gentleman of culture, wit, knowledge of the world, and consummate ease and self-possession. It is the direct and trenchant language of Swift: but more graceful, more flexible, more courteous.

And what is a truly striking fact about Thackeray's mastery of style is this—that it was perfectly formed from the beginning; that it hardly ever varied, or developed, or waxed in the whole course of his literary career; that his first venture as a very young man is as finished and as ripe as his very latest piece, when he died almost in the act of writing the words—" *and his heart throbbed with an exquisite bliss.*" This prodigious precocity in style, such uniform perfection of exact composition, are perhaps without parallel in English literature. At the age of twenty-six Thackeray wrote " The History of Samuel Titmarsh and the Great Hoggarty Diamond." It was produced under very melancholy conditions, in the most unfavourable form of publication, and it was mangled by editorial necessities. And yet it can still be read and re-read as one of Thackeray's masterpieces, trifling and curtailed as it is (for it may be printed in one hundred pages); it is as full of wit, humour, scathing insight, and fine pathos in the midst of burlesque, as is " Vanity Fair" itself. It is already Thackeray in all his strength, with his 'Snobs,' his 'Nobs,' his fierce satire, and his exquisite style.

Modern romance has no purer, more pathetic, yet simpler page than the tale of the death of poor Samuel Titmarsh's first child. Though it is, as it deserves to be, a household word, the passage must be quoted here as a specimen of faultless and beautiful style.

"It was not, however, destined that she and her child should inhabit that little garret. We were to leave our lodgings on Monday morning ; but on Saturday evening the child was seized with convulsions, and all Sunday the mother watched and prayed for it: but it pleased God to take the innocent infant from us, and on Sunday, at midnight, it lay a corpse in its mother's bosom. Amen. We have other children, happy and well, now round about us, and from the father's heart the memory of this little thing has almost faded ; but I do believe that every day of her life the mother thinks of her first-born that was with her for so short a while : many and many a time she has taken her daughters to the grave, in Saint Bride's, where he lies buried ; and she wears still at her neck a little, little lock of gold hair, which she took from the head of the infant as he lay smiling in his coffin. It has happened to me to forget the child's birth-day, but to her never ; and often in the midst of common talk, comes something that shows she is thinking of the child still,—some simple allusion that is to me inexpressibly affecting."

Could words simpler, purer, more touching be found to paint a terrible, albeit very common sorrow! Not a needless epithet, not a

false note, not a touch over-wrought! And this is the writing of
an unknown, untried youth!

This exquisitely simple, easy, idiomatic, and nervous style marks
all Thackeray's work for his twenty-six years of activity, and is
equally perfect for whatever purpose it is used, and in whatever key
he may choose to compose.   It naturally culminates in " Vanity Fair, "
written just in the middle of his literary career.   Here not a word
is wasted: the profoundest impressions are made by a quiet sentence
of a dozen plain words that neither Swift nor Defoe could have surpassed.   I know nothing in English literature more powerful than
those last two lines of the thirty-second chapter of " Vanity Fair."
For four chapters the story has pictured the scene in Brussels on the
eve of Waterloo.   The women and non-combatants are trembling
with excitement, anxiety, fear, whilst the cannon roar all day in the
distance—Amelia half distracted with love, jealousy, and foreboding.
And the wild alternations of hope, terror, grief, and agony are suddenly closed in the last paragraph of chapter 32.

"No more firing was heard at Brussels—the pursuit rolled miles away.
Darkness came down on the field and city : and Amelia was praying for George,
who was lying on his face, dead, with a bullet through his heart."

Take all the great critical scenes in the book, and note how simple,
and yet how full of pathos and of power, is the language in which
they are described.   There is the last parting of George and Amelia
as the bugle rings to arms.

"George came in and looked at her again, entering still more softly. By
the pale night-lamp he could see her sweet, pale face—the purple eyelids were
fringed and closed, and one round arm, smooth and white, lay outside of the
coverlet. Good God! how pure she was; how gentle, how tender, and how
friendless! and he, how selfish, brutal, and black with crime! Heart-stained
and shame-stricken, he stood at the bed's foot, and looked at the sleeping girl.
How dared he—who was he, to pray for one so spotless! God bless her! God
bless her! He came to the bed-side, and looked at the hand, the little soft hand,
lying asleep; and he bent over the pillow noiselessly towards the gentle pale
face."

The whole tragedy of their lives is given in miniature in this
touching scene; and yet how natural and commonplace are all the
effects of which it is composed, how few and simple the words which
describe such love and such remorse.   It is hard to judge in ' Vanity
Fair" which are the more perfect in style, the pathetic and tragic
scenes or those which are charged with humour and epigram.

And the scene after George's marriage, when old Osborne burns
his will and erases his son's name from the family Bible—and the

scene when Osborne receives his son's last letter—" Osborne trembled long before the letter from his dead son"—" His father could not see the kiss George had placed on the superscription of his letter.   Mr. Osborne dropped it with the bitterest, deadliest pang of balked affection and revenge.   His son was still beloved and unforgiven."   And the scene of " the widow and mother," when young Georgy is born, and the wonderful scene when Sir Pitt proposes marriage to the little green-eyed governess and she is scared into confessing her great secret, and the most famous scene of all, when Rawdon Crawley is released from the sponging-house and finds Lord Steyne with Rebecca alone. It is but a single page.   The words spoken are short, brief, plain— not five sentences pass—" I am innocent," said she—" Make way, let me pass," cried My Lord—" You lie, you coward and villain!" said Rawdon.   There is in all fiction nò single scene more vivid, more true, more burnt into the memory, more tragic.   And with what noble simplicity, with what incisive reticence, with what subtle anatomy of the human heart, is it recorded.

" Vanity Fair" was written, it is true, under the strain of serial publication, haste, and anxiety, but it is perhaps, even in style, the most truly complete.   The wonderful variety, elasticity, and freshness of the dialogue, the wit of the comic scenes, the terrible power of the tragic scenes, the perfection of the *mise-en-scène*—the rattle, the fun, the glitter of the Fair are sustained from end to end, from the first words of the ineffable Miss Pinkerton to the *Vanitas Vanitatum* when the showman shuts up his puppets in their box.   There is not in all " Vanity Fair" a single dull page that we skip, not a bit of padding, no rigmarole of explanation whilst the action stands still.   Of what other fiction can this be said?   Richardson and even Fielding have their *longueurs*.   Miss Austen is too prone to linger over the tea-table beyond all human patience.   And even Scott's descriptions of his loved hills grow sometimes unreadable, especially when they are told in a flaccid and slovenly style.   But " Vanity Fair" is kept up with inexhaustible life and invention, with a style which, for purity and polish, was beyond the reach of Fielding, Richardson, or Scott.

" Esmond" was composed with even greater care than " Vanity Fair," and in the matter of style is usually taken to be Thackeray's greatest masterpiece.   Its language is a miracle of art.   But it is avowedly a *tour de force*—an effort to reproduce an entire book in the form and speech of a century and a half preceding.   As a *tour de force* it is wonderful; but in so long a book the effort becomes at last too visible, and undoubtedly it somewhat cramps the freedom of the author's genius.   Thackeray was not a born historical romancist, as were Scott and Dumas; nor was he a born historian at all.   And when he undertook to produce an elaborate romance in the form and with the colouring of a past age, like George Eliot, he becomes rather too learned, too conscientious, too rigidly full of his authorities; and if as an historian he enters into rivalry with Macaulay, he somewhat loses his cunning as a novelist.   Thackeray's force lay in the comedy of manners.   In the comedy of manners we have nothing but " Tom Jones" to compare with " Vanity Fair."   And though Thackeray is not equal to the " prose Homer of human nature," he wrote an English even finer and more racy.

In " Esmond" we are constantly pausing to admire the wonderful ingenuity and exquisite grace of the style, studying the language quite apart from the story; and we feel, as we do when we read Milton's Latin poems or Swinburne's French sonnets, that it is a surprising imitation of the original.   But at the same time " Esmond" contains some of the noblest passages that Thackeray ever wrote, scenes and chapters which in form have no superior in English literature.   That sixth chapter of the second book, in the cathedral, when Henry Esmond returns to his mistress on the 29th of December, on his birthday.   " Here she was, weeping and happy.   She took his hand in both hers; he felt her tears.   It was a rapture of reconciliation"—" so for a few moments Esmond's beloved mistress came to him and blessed him."   To my mind, there is nothing in English fiction which has been set forth in language of such exquisite purity and pathos.

" Esmond" too, which may be said to be one prolonged parody of the great Queen-Anne essayists, contains that most perfect of all parodies in the English language—" The paper out of the 'Spectator'" —in chapter third of the third book.   It is of course not a 'parody' in the proper sense, for it has no element of satire or burlesque, and imitates not the foibles but the merits of the original, with an absolute illusion.   The 341st number of the " Spectator," dated Tuesday, April 1, 1712, is so absolutely like Dick Steele at his best, that Addison himself would have been deceived by it.   Steele hardly ever wrote anything so bright and amusing.   It is not a 'parody': it is a forgery; but a forgery which required for its execution the most consummate mastery over all the subtleties and mysteries of style.

In parody of every kind, from the most admiring imitation down to the most boisterous burlesque, Thackeray stands at the head of all other imitators. " The Rejected Addresses" of James and Horace Smith (1812) is usually regarded as the masterpiece in this art; and Scott good-humouredly said that he would have taken the death of Higginbottom for his own verses. But Thackeray's " Novels by Eminent Hands" are superior even to the " Rejected Addresses." " Codlingsby," the parody of Disraeli's " Coningsby," may be taken as the most effective parody in our language: intensely droll in itself, it reproduces the absurdities, the affectations, the oriental imagination of Disraeli with inimitable wit. Those ten pages of irrepressible fooling are enough to destroy Disraeli's reputation as a serious romancer. No doubt they have unfairly reacted so as to dim our sense of Disraeli's real genius as a writer. When we know " Codlingsby" by heart, as every one with a sense of humour must do, it is impossible for us to keep our countenance when we take up the palaver about Sidonia and the Chosen Race. The " Novels by Eminent Hands" are all good: they are much more than parodies; they are real criticism, sound, wise, genial, and instructive. Nor are they in the least unfair. If the balderdash and cheap erudition of Bulwer and Disraeli are covered with inextinguishable mirth, no one is offended by the pleasant imitations of Lever, James, and Fenimore Cooper.

All the burlesques are good, and will bear continual re-reading; but the masterpiece of all is " Rebecca and Rowena," the continuation in burlesque of " Ivanhoe." It is one of the mysteries of literature that we can enjoy both, that the warmest admirers of Scott's glorious genius, and even those who delight in " Ivanhoe," can find the keenest relish in " Rebecca and Rowena," which is simply the great romance of chivalry turned inside out. But Thackeray's immortal burlesque has something of the quality of Cervantes' " Don Quixote" —that we love the knight whilst we laugh, and feel the deep pathos of human nature and the beauty of goodness and love even in the midst of the wildest fun. And this fine quality runs through all the comic pieces, ballads, burlesques, pantomimes, and sketches. What genial fun in the " Rose and the Ring," in " Little Billee," in " Mrs. Perkins' Ball," in the ,"Sketch Book," in " Yellowplush." It is only the very greatest masters who can produce extravaganzas, puerile tomfooleries, drolleries to delight children, and catchpenny songs, of such a kind that mature and cultivated students can laugh over them for the fiftieth time and read them till they are household words. This is the supreme merit of " Don Quixote," of " Scapin," of " Gulliver," of " Robinson Crusoe." And this quality of immortal truth and wit we find in " Rebecca and Rowena," in the " Rose and the Ring," in " Little Billee," in " Codlingsby," and " Yellowplush." The burlesques have that Aristophanic touch of beauty, pathos, and wisdom mingled with the wildest pantomime.

A striking example of Thackeray's unrivalled powers of imitation may be seen in the letters which are freely scattered about his works. No one before or since ever wrote such wonderfully happy illustrations of the epistolary style of boy or girl, old maid or illiterate man. There never were such letters as those of George Osborne in " Vanity Fair" —that letter from school describing the fight between Cuff and Figs is a masterpiece—the letters of Becky, of Rawdon, of Amelia—all are perfect reproductions of the writer, as are scores of letters scattered up and down the twenty-six volumes. Nor must we omit, as part of the style, the author's own illustrations. They are really part of the book; they assist us to understand the characters; they are a very important portion of the writer's method. None of our great writers ever had this double instrument: and Thackeray has used it with consummate effect. The sketches in " Vanity Fair" and in " Punch," especially the minor thumb-nail drolleries, are delightful—true caricatures—real portraits of character. It is true they are ill-drawn, often impossible, crude, and almost childish in their incorrectness and artlessness. But they have in them the soul of a great caricaturist. They have the Hogarthian touch of a great comic artist.

One is tempted to enlarge at length on the merits of Thackeray's style, because it is in his mastery over all the resources of the English language that he surpasses contemporary prose writers. And it is a mastery which is equally shown in every form of composition. There is a famous bit of Byron's about Sheridan to the effect that he had written the best comedy, made the finest speech, and invented the drollest farce in the English language. And it is hardly extravagant to say of Thackeray that, of all the Englishmen of this century, he has written the best comedy of manners, the best extravaganza, the best burlesque, the best parody, and the best comic song. And to this some of his admirers would add—the best lectures, and the best critical essays. It is of course true that he has never reached or attempted to reach the gorgeous rhapsodies of De Quincey or the dithyrambic melodies of Ruskin. But these heaven-born Pegasi can-

THACKERAY'S PLACE IN LITERATURE.

not be harnessed to the working vehicles of our streets. The marvel of Thackeray's command over language is this—that it is unfailing in prose or in verse, in pathos or in terror, in tragedy or in burlesque, in narrative, in repartee, or in drollery: and that it never waxes or flags in force and precision throughout twenty-six full volumes.

Of Thackeray's style—a style that has every quality in perfection: simplicity, clearness, ease, force, elasticity, and grace—it is difficult to speak but in terms of unstinted admiration. When we deal with the substance and effective value of his great books we see that, although Thackeray holds his own with the best writers of this century, he cannot be said to hold the same manifest crown of supremacy. One of his strongest claims is the vast quantity and variety of his best work, and the singularly small proportion of inferior work. Fielding himself wrote pitiful trash when he became, as he said, a mere "hackney writer"; Richardson's "Grandison" overcomes most readers; Scott at last broke down; Carlyle, Disraeli, Dickens, and Ruskin have written many things which "we do not turn over by day and turn over by night," to put it as gently as one can. But Thackeray is never below himself in form, and very rarely indeed is he below himself in substance. "Pendennis" is certainly much inferior to "Vanity Fair," and "Philip" is much inferior to "Pendennis." "The Virginians" is far behind "Esmond." But of the more important books not one can be called in any sense a failure unless it be "Lovel the Widower" and "The Adventures of Philip."

Thackeray's masterpiece beyond question is "Vanity Fair"— which as a comedy of the manners of contemporary life is quite the greatest achievement in English literature since "Tom Jones." It has not the consummate plot of "Tom Jones"; it has not the breadth, the Shakespearean jollity, the genial humanity of the great "prose Homer"; it has no such beautiful character as Sophia Western. But "Vanity Fair" may be put beside "Tom Jones" for variety of character, intense reality, ingenuity of incident, and profusion of wit, humour, and invention. It is even better written than "Tom Jones"; has more pathos and more tragedy; and is happily free from the nauseous blots into which Harry Fielding was betrayed by the taste of his age. It is hard to say what scene in "Vanity Fair," what part, what character, rests longest in the memory. Is it the home of the Sedleys and the Osbornes, is it Queen's Crawley, or the incidents at Brussels, or at Gaunt House:—is it George Osborne, or Jos, or Miss Crawley, the Major or the Colonel,—is it Lord Steyne or Rebecca?   All are excellent, all seem perfect in truth, in consistency, in contrast.

The great triumph of "Vanity Fair"—the great triumph of modern fiction—is Becky Sharp: a character which will ever stand in the very foremost rank of English literature, if not with Falstaff and Shylock, then with Squire Western, Uncle Toby, Mr. Primrose, Jonathan Oldbuck, and Sam Weller.   There is no character in the whole range of literature which has been worked out with more elaborate completeness.   She is drawn from girlhood to old age, under every conceivable condition, and is brought face to face with all kinds of persons and trials.   In all circumstances Becky is true to herself; her ingenuity, her wit, her selfishness, her audacity, her cunning, her clear, cool, alert brain, even her common sense, her spirit of justice, when she herself is not concerned, and her good-nature, when it could cost her nothing—all this is unfailing, inimitable, never to be forgotten.   Some good people cry out that she is so wicked.   Of course she is wicked: so were Iago and Blifil.   The only question is, if she be real?   Most certainly she is, as real as anything in the whole range of fiction, as real as Tartuffe, or Gil Blas, Wilhelm Meister, or Rob Roy.   No one doubts that Becky Sharps exist: unhappily they are not even very uncommon.   And Thackeray has drawn one typical example of such bad women with an anatomical precision that makes us shudder.

And if Becky Sharp be the masterpiece of Thackeray's art amongst the characters, the scene of her husband's encounter with her paramour is the masterpiece of all the scenes in "Vanity Fair," and has no superior, hardly any equal, in modern fiction.   Becky, Rawdon Crawley, and Lord Steyne—all are inimitably true, all are powerful, all are fearful in their agony and rage.   The uprising of the poor rake almost into dignity and heroism, and his wife's outburst of admiration at his vengeance, are strokes of really Shakespearean insight. It was with justice that Thackeray himself felt pride in that touch. "*She stood there trembling before him.   She admired her husband, strong, brave, victorious.*"   It is these touches of clear sight in Becky, her respect for Dobbin, her kindliness to Amelia apart from her own schemes, which make us feel an interest in Becky, loathsome as she is.   She is always a woman, and not an inhuman monster, however bad a woman, cruel, heartless, and false.

There remains always the perpetual problem if "Vanity Fair" be a cynic's view of life, the sardonic grin of a misanthrope gloating

over the trickery and meanness of mankind.   It is well to remember
how many are the scenes of tenderness and pathos in " Vanity Fair,"
how powerfully told, how deeply they haunt the memory and sink
into the heart.   The school life of Dobbin, the ruin of old Sedley and
the despair of Amelia, the last parting of Amelia and George, Osborne revoking his will, Sedley broken down, Rawdon in the sponging-house, the birth and boyhood of Georgy Osborne, the end of old
Sedley, the end of old Osborne, are as pathetic and humane as anything in our literature.   Mature men, who study fiction with a
critical spirit and a cool head, admit that the only passages in English romance that they can never read again without faltering, without
a dim eye and a quavering voice, are these scenes of pain and sorrow
in " Vanity Fair."   The death of old Sedley, nursed by his daughter,
is a typical piece—perfect in simplicity, in truth, in pathos.

"One night when she stole into his room, she found him awake, when the
broken old man made his confession. 'O, Emmy, I've been thinking we were
very unkind and unjust to you,' he said, and put out his cold and feeble hand to
her. She knelt down and prayed by his bed-side, as he did too, having still hold
of her hand. When our turn comes, friend, may we have such company in our
prayers."

And this is the arch-cynic and misanthrope, grinning at all that is
lovable and tender!

It is too often forgotten that " Vanity Fair" is not intended to be
simply the world: it is society, it is fashion, the market where mam-
mon-worship, folly, and dissipation display their wares.   Thackeray
wrote many other books, and has given us many worthy characters.
Dobbin, Warrington, Colonel Newcome, Ethel Newcome, Henry
Esmond, are generous, brave, just, and true.   Neither " Esmond," nor
" The Newcomes, nor " The Virginians" is in any sense the work of a
misanthrope.   And where Thackeray speaks in his own person, in
the lectures on the " English Humourists," he is brimful of all that is
genial, frank, lenient, and good-hearted.   What we know of the
man, who loved his friends and was loved by them, and who in all
his critical and personal sketches showed himself a kindly, courteous,
and considerate gentleman, inclines us to repel this charge of cyni-
cism, that he is a satirist—a great satirist, but a cruel mocker at
human virtue and goodness.

This is, however, not the whole of the truth.   The consent of
mankind, and especially the consent of women, is too manifest.
There *is* something ungenial, there *is* a bitter taste left when we have
enjoyed these books, especially as we lay down " Vanity Fair."   It

is a long comedy of roguery, meanness, selfishness, intrigue, and affectation. Rakes, ruffians, bullies, parasites, fortune-hunters, adventurers, women who sell themselves, and men who cheat and cringe, pass before us in one incessant procession, crushing the weak, and making fools of the good. Such, says our author, is the way of Vanity Fair—which we are warned to loathe and to shun. Be it so: —but it cannot be denied that the rakes, ruffians, and adventurers fill too large a canvas, are too conspicuous, too triumphant, too interesting. They are more interesting than the weak and the good whom they crush under foot: they are drawn with a more glowing brush, they are far more splendidly endowed. They have better heads, stronger wills, richer natures than the good and kind ones who are their butts. Dobbin, as the author himself tells us, "is a spooney." Amelia, as he says also, "is a little fool." Peggy O'Dowd, dear old goody, is the laughing-stock of the regiment, though she is also its grandmother. "Vanity Fair" has here and there some virtuous and generous characters. But we are made to laugh at every one of them to their very faces. And the evil and the selfish characters bully them, mock them, thrust them aside at every page—and they do so because they are more the stuff of which men and women of any mark are made.

There are evil characters in Shakespeare, in Fielding, in Goldsmith, in Scott: we find ruffians, rakes, traitors, and parasites. But they are not paramount, not universal, not unqualified. Iago is utterly overshadowed by Othello, Blifil by Alworthy, Tom Jones by Sophia Western, Squire Thornhill by Dr. Primrose, the reprobate Staunton by the good angel Jeanie Deans. Shakespeare, Fielding, Goethe, Scott draw noble and generous natures quite as well as they paint the evil natures: indeed they paint them better; they enjoy the painting of them more; they make us enjoy them more. Take this test: if we run over the characters of Shakespeare or of Scott we have to reflect before we find the villains. If we run over the characters in Thackeray, it is an effort of memory to recall the generous and the fine natures. Thackeray has given us some lovable and affectionate men and women: but they all have qualities which lower them and tend to make them either tiresome or ridiculous. Henry Esmond is a high-minded and almost heroic gentleman, but he is glum, a regular kill-joy, and, as his author admitted, something of a prig. Colonel Newcome is a noble true-hearted soldier: but he is made too good for this world and somewhat too innocent, too transparently a child of nature. Warrington, with all his sense and honesty, is rough, Pendennis is a bit of a puppy, Clive Newcome is not much of a hero, and as for Dobbin he is almost intended to be a butt.

A more serious defect is a dearth in Thackeray of women to love and to honour. Shakespeare has given us a gallery of noble women; Fielding has drawn the adorable Sophia Western; Scott has his Jeanie Deans. But though Thackeray has given us over and over again living pictures of women of power, intellect, wit, charm, they are all marred by atrocious selfishness, cruelty, ambition, like Becky Sharp, Beatrix Esmond, and Lady Kew; or else they have some weakness, silliness, or narrowness which prevents us from at once loving and respecting them. Amelia is rather a poor thing and decidedly silly; we do not really admire Laura Pendennis; the Little Sister is somewhat colourless; Ethel Newcome runs great risk of being a spoilt beauty; and about Lady Castlewood, with all her love and devotion, there hangs a certain sinister and unnatural taint, which the world cannot forgive, and perhaps ought not to forgive. The sum of all this is, that in all these twenty-six volumes and hundreds of men and women portrayed, there is not one man or one woman having at once a noble character, perfect generosity, powerful mind, and lovable nature; or one man or one woman of tender heart and perfect honour, but has some trait that tends to make him or her either laughable or tedious. It is not so with the supreme masters of the human heart. And the world does not condone this, and it is right in not condoning it.

But to say this, is not to condemn Thackeray as a cynic. With these many scenes of exquisite tenderness and pathos, with men and women of such loving hearts and devoted spirits, with the profusion of gay, kindly, childlike love of innocent fun, that we find all through Thackeray's work, he does not belong to the order of the Jonathan Swifts, the Balzacs, the Zolas, the gruesome anatomists of human vice and meanness. On the other hand he does not belong to the order of the Shakespeares, Goethes, and Scotts, to whom human virtue and dignity always remain in the end the supreme forces of human life. Thackeray, with a fine and sympathetic soul, had a creative imagination that was far stronger on the darker and fouler sides of life than it was on the brighter and pure side of life. He saw the bright and pure side: he loved it, he felt with it, he made us love it. But his artistic genius worked with more free and consummate zest when he painted the dark and the foul. His creative

22

imagination fell short of the true equipoise, of that just vision of *chiaroscuro*, which we find in the greatest masters of the human heart. This limitation of his genius has been visited upon Thackeray with a heavy hand. And such as it is, he must bear it.

The place of Thackeray in English literature will always be determined by his "Vanity Fair": which will be read, we may confidently predict, as long as "Tom Jones," "Clarissa," "Tristram Shandy," "The Antiquary," and "Pickwick." But all the best of his pieces, even the smaller *jeux d'esprits*, may be read with delight again and again by young and old. And of the best are—"Esmond," "The Newcomes," "Barry Lyndon," the "Book of Snobs," the "Hoggarty Diamond," some of the "Burlesques" and "Christmas Books" and the "English Humourists." Of these, "Esmond" has every quality of a great book, except its artificial form, its excessive elaboration of historical colouring, and its unsavoury plot. Beatrix Esmond is almost as wonderful a creation as Becky Sharp; though, if formed on a grander mould, she has less fascination than that incorrigible minx. "The Newcomes," if in some ways the most genial of the longer pieces, is plainly without the power of "Vanity Fair." And if "Barry Lyndon" has this power, it is an awful picture of cruelty and meanness. The "Book of Snobs" and the "Hoggarty Diamond" were each a kind of prelude to "Vanity Fair," and both contain some of its essential marks of pathos and of power. It is indeed strange to us now to remember that both of these books, written with such finished mastery of hand and full of such passages of wit and insight, could have been published for years before the world had recognized that it had a new and consummate writer before it. The "Book of Snobs" indeed may truly be said to have seriously improved the public opinion of the age, and to have given a death-blow to many odious forms of sycophancy and affectation which passed unrebuked in England fifty years ago. And the "Burlesque Romances" and the "English Humourists" have certainly assisted in forming the public taste and in promoting a sound criticism of our standard fiction.

Charlotte Brontë dedicated her "Jane Eyre," in 1847, to William Makepeace Thackeray, as "the first social regenerator of the day." Such language, though interesting as coming from a girl of singular genius and sincerity, however ignorant of real life, was excessive. But we may truly assert that he has enriched our literature with some classical masterpieces in the comedy of cotemporary manners.

FREDERIC HARRISON.

THE TEMPERANCE PROBLEM: PAST AND FUTURE.

NEVER before has there been such widespread interest in public control of the liquor traffic as is felt to-day. Thoughtful minds have long recognized immoderate drinking to be closely connected, either as cause or effect, with various social miseries; but energetic reformers are now utilizing the results of experience as well as research in a practical way. Movements for throttling the well-nigh intolerable social curse are operating with a vigor hitherto unknown. Sharp conflicts have recently taken place in the ancient stronghold of Puritanism and in South Carolina, and now from the broad West we hear the din of marshalling forces. Over sea, Norway, Sweden, Finland, and Switzerland are pausing on vantage ground, while England is forming ranks for a struggle from which a rational regime must eventually emerge. We may especially take courage from the latter movement, for it has assumed organic shape in the formation of a "Public House Reform Association," and is being fathered by such eminent men as the Bishop of Chester, the Duke of Westminster, Lords Aberdare and Thring, Judge Thomas Hughes, and Messrs. Joseph Chamberlain, J. G. Talbot, and George Wyndham. As in Massachusetts, the Norwegian system of control has been accepted for the plan of campaign. Indeed the distinguishing feature of this and nearly all other latter-day movements is the substitution of evolutionary reform for total and instantaneous repression.

The United States has been a fertile field for experiment. Diverse systems of control have been tried. Individual States, and still oftener separate communities, have changed their policy several times within a comparatively short period. Has this experience any definite lesson to teach?

In seven American commonwealths prohibition is the prevailing form of control. This term indicates withdrawing the right to manufacture and sell spirituous and malt beverages from domiciled residents within the borders. In the sense in which it is incorporated in American practice, it does not further attempt to regulate the conduct of individuals. A man may buy liquor in another State and have it shipped to him, provided it is destined for his own private use. Still more, he may purchase it surreptitiously from a fellow-resident without rendering himself liable to punishment. It is the manufacturer and the seller, not the consumer of drink, who are placed under the ban. Prohibition is now the law of seven States,—Maine, New Hampshire, Vermont, Iowa, Kansas, North Dakota, and South Dakota. Four of these—Maine, Kansas, and the two Dakotas—have prohibition amendments to their constitutions. Prohibition has been tried and abandoned in Delaware, Rhode Island, Massachusetts, Connecticut, Indiana, Nebraska, New York, Illinois, and Ohio.

All the States in which prohibitory legislation obtains to-day are relatively sparsely populated. The largest urban community in any of them is the city of Des Moines, Iowa, which contains 50,093 people according to the last census. But it is in large cities where the liquor traffic is hardest to control. Therefore I think it is perfectly fair to make answer to the friends of prohibition that the soundness of their views has not been sufficiently apparent from practical experiments. New York, Ohio, Illinois, Massachusetts, and Rhode Island are the only States containing large city populations which have been under a prohibitory regime, and they have abandoned it.

The chief difficulty with all restrictive measures directed against social vices is to secure their enforcement, or, indeed, their moderate observance in urban centres. People should take account of this, remembering that virtue can never be inculcated by legal enactment. Its springs are in the human heart, and before they will flow they must be struck with the rod of a quickened intelligence. Marching too far in advance of public sentiment always renders success problematical—in this country for the added reason that existing conditions of municipal government are ignored. With civic spirit at so low an ebb, and supineness the attitude of the police, we cannot rely upon enforcement of or rigid conformity to law. Neither ought we to blame public authorities too severely. There are usually motes in our own eyes as well as beams in the eyes of representatives of the body politic. Depositing the ballot is too often accompanied on our part by a thrill of satisfaction that duty has been done, whereas it should be understood as having only just commenced. We should reflect that a majority vote for prohibition establishes a new legal misdemeanor, and that unless there is hearty and effective co-operation to secure enforcement, damage is more likely to be done than good accomplished. Disrespect for law is the most dangerous of all things under a democratic form of government, and those who assist in making laws which, for one reason or another, cannot be enforced, assume weighty responsibilities.

The control of the liquor traffic is a moral and social question and has no place in the arena of politics. It is greatly to be feared that making prohibition a political issue has compelled the liquor interests to seek political means of defence. But, whatever the cause, the result has been an alliance with the dominant party, or the lower elements of both political parties, which has degraded American politics to the lowest depths.

Another favorite American method of dealing with the liquor traffic has been through local option. This, by many, is called prohibition in its more rational form. The advantages claimed are that the small area to which it applies renders its introduction easier. There is not only a strong local feeling behind it, but concentration of attention upon a limited territory brings greater likelihood of rigorous enforcement. Again, the movement advances slowly, and ground once gained rarely has to be surrendered. Local option represents evolutionary advance, whereas prohibition is cataclysmic. Opponents of local option enumerate among its drawbacks:

1. That drinking is made a local question, whereas it ought to be considered from a national point of view.

2. The ethical basis of the problem is lowered to mere expediency.

3. It has only been successful in practice in country districts, and then at the expense of adjoining neighborhoods.

Local option has been tried in several States. Better results seem to have been achieved in Massachusetts than elsewhere. In several of the Southern States, also, a feeling of satisfaction with its operation has been expressed, though generally the areas to which it has been confined are almost exclusively country districts. The experiences of Michigan and Missouri give a reverse side to the picture. In the former an important contention of critics seems to have been justified. The ratio of licenses to population in places not under local option increased, during the last census period, eight per cent.

High-license is the method most in favor for large cities, where restrictive measures have been practised at all. Advocates claim that it is the only effective form of control as demonstrated by experience. It may be applied to places where prohibition and local option would both fail, and it reduces the number of saloons within measurable limits, both as to number and geographical situation.

It is true that where a really high license fee has been charged, dram-shops have notably decreased.   In Omaha, in 1881, the license fee was raised from $100 to $1,000.   At that time the ratio of licenses to population was 1 to 267.   In 1891 it was 1 to 600.   The experience of St. Paul is almost equally significant.   During the six years from 1886 to 1892, when a similar change took place, the ratio of licenses to population declined, becoming 1 to 367 instead of 1 to 152. In Philadelphia results have been even more remarkable.   Previous to the enactment of the Brooks law in 1888 there was one license to every 160 inhabitants.   In 1891 the proportion was 1 to 600. This favorable statistical showing, be it noted, applies to three States where the license fee is fixed at $1,000.   Other high-license cities require only $500, and it is undeniably true that no such conspicuously useful results have there been attained.   There seems to be somewhere a normal limit of efficiency, and whenever the sum charged is below the line the useful effects of control are lessened.

Perhaps the most effective form of high-license prevails in Pennsylvania and Massachusetts.   To my mind there are two reasons for this.   In the first-named State, while the number of permits is not limited by law, complete discretion is vested in the licensing commission, which is composed of judges in courts of secondary instance. Massachusetts has recourse to limitation, Boston being allowed one license to every 500 of population, and every other city one license to every 1,000 persons.   Legal limitation of number, and especially a high-class commission of judges, are features which should accompany every high-license regime.

Opponents of this plan dispute the fact that it has been much of a success anywhere.   Again, they assert that it forges more closely the alliance between liquor and politics.   Licensing-boards have usually a distinct political element in their composition, so that in the distribution of privileges the political bummers may be properly looked after.   Furthermore, it is alleged that consolidation of liquor interests more readily occurs, and " tied houses" become substitutes for individual tap-rooms.   Finally, those who take the high ground that license fees represent blood-money, so to speak, contend that enhanced revenues are a salve to the conscience of the weak-kneed brother, and lessen his practical interest in the suppression of liquor-drinking.

The latest form of experiment is that inaugurated by South Carolina under the law of December 24, 1892.   Though recently declared unconstitutional by the Supreme Court of the State, reference to it may not be out of place.   Private liquor-selling is abolished, and a State dispensary system substituted.   At least one of these dispensaries is opened in every county not under local option, and in the cities of Charleston and Columbia more are provided for.   A State board of control, composed of the governor, comptroller-general, and attorney-general, is the highest business authority.   A State commissioner, who is believed to be an abstainer, is appointed by this body, as well as county boards of control, which are composed of three members serving for two years, and who are likewise teetotalers. Dispensaries are opened by the county boards of control upon motion of a majority of freehold voters.   The State commissioner purchases the liquors (under a saving political clause which gives preference to manufacturers and brewers doing business in the State), and the State chemist analyzes the beverages to see if they are pure.   They are then done up in packages varying from five gallons to half a pint in size, shipped to the county dispensaries, and sold at prices not exceeding 50 per cent profit.   Considerable formality is required in the purchase of drink.   The dispenser must demand a written or printed request, properly dated, stating the age and residence of the signer for whose use the liquor is requested, as well as the quantity and kind required.   The certificate is then attested and put on file.

At first glance one would think that a law which lengthened the time between drinks would not be very popular with a South Carolina governor.   The present incumbent, however, in his last annual message, urges the following claims in support of his dispensary system:

1. The element of personal profit is destroyed, thereby removing the incentive to increased sales.

2. A pure article is guaranteed, and it is subject to chemical analysis.

3. The consumer obtains honest measure of standard strength.

4. Treating is stopped, as the bottles are not opened on the premises.

5. It is sold only in the daytime.

6. The concomitants of ice, sugar, lemons, etc., being removed, there is not the same inclination to drink.   The closing of the saloon, especially at night, and the prohibition of sale by the drink, destroy the inducements and seductions which have caused so many to be led astray and enter on the downward course.

7. It is sold only for cash, and there is no longer "chalking up" for daily drinks against pay-day.   The workingman buys his bottle of whiskey Saturday night, and carries the rest of his wages home.

8. The local whiskey rings, which have been a curse to every municipality in the State, and have always controlled municipal elections, have been torn up root and branch, and the influence of the bar-keeper as a political manipulator is absolutely destroyed.   The police, removed from the control of its debauching influence, will enforce the law against evil-doing with more vigor and a higher tone; and greater purity in all governmental affairs must result.

Were the history of this unique measure not so well known, the contentions of Governor Tillman might be more generally accepted. It is a fact that the plan had its origin in an effort to raise revenue, not in the virtuous desire to reduce the consumption of drink. Prohibitionists were cajoled into its support by promises that the coming enactment would be a stepping-stone to their ideal. It is much to be feared that the local whiskey rings, which the governor denounces, may give place to a State politico-liquor machine. The claim that the consumer will obtain an honest measure of drink, standard in strength and quality, may have local grounds for favor, but one can hardly accept it as possessing great moral weight. Taking from the tippler his ice, lemons, and sugar may be a hardship, but it is not a positively reformatory measure. Selling only in the daytime and for cash, the abolition of treating, the weeding out of gambling-dens and other immoral concomitants of the saloon, are undoubted advantages.

There has been an absurd confounding, in the minds of many people, of this South Carolina experiment with the Scandinavian system of controlling the liquor traffic. Points of similarity do exist, but modes of operation and effects are quite different. The cardinal principle of the South Carolina plan is State monopoly of all sale of drink; that of the Norwegian plan is local control through commercial companies organized often by the best and most patriotic citizens, who renounce all profits and take merely the ordinary rate of interest on the small amount of capital invested. Wherein both of the plans agree, and where both, in my judgment, strike at the root of the whole matter, is in eliminating private profit from liquor-selling. But here the parallel ceases. These local companies in Norway engage in the traffic in order that they may control it and restrict it until such time as municipalities may do away with licensing altogether. So well has their aim succeeded that the great majority of inhabitants of the Scandinavian peninsula are to-day under a no-license regime. In South Carolina the profits go to the State, and the very conception of the measure reposes on the idea of relief to taxpayers. Indeed, Governor Tillman apologetically remarks that the revenues are not yet as high as they will be. A State monopoly makes liquor-selling a part of the machinery of the government, and therefore gives to it a more or less permanent existence. The essence of the other plan is liberty to abolish the traffic whenever a community is ready, but, in the mean time, to regulate it so that the least possible damage may be done. Another most significant difference between the two systems is that State dispensaries involve regulation by political appointees.   In Norway every vestige and semblance of political influence is eliminated.   Indeed, to my mind, the absolute separation which has been practically effected between liquor and politics is a most conspicuous merit.   Again, Scandinavian control brings about progressive reform by educating public opinion.   The South Carolina plan, being nearly prohibitive in character, is a measure too far in advance of public opinion to be accepted and enforced to-day.

The minor points of similarity represent borrowings from Scandinavian practice.   They include reduction in the number of places of sale, early closing, selling only for cash, and furnishing pure liquor.   Presumably, also, gambling and immorality are divorced from dispensaries, as they are in every instance from the companies' liquor-shops abroad.   The South Carolina plan offers avenues of political interference and possibilities of corrupt exploitation.   Revenue and partisan convenience may easily become dominant motives. In these vital features it must be distinguished from the system abroad, from which it is often popularly and erroneously supposed to have borrowed likeness.

Notwithstanding the variety of American experiments in controlling the drink traffic, results in a general way show that practically nothing has been accomplished.   In 1850 the consumption of all kinds of liquor averaged 4.08 gallons per inhabitant; in 1892 it was 17.04 gallons,—considerably more than a fourfold increase. During this period the consumption of spirits diminished, it is true, from 2.25 to 1.50 gallons per capita, but beer-drinking advanced from 1.58 to 15.10 gallons per head of population.   Wine-drinking increased only slightly, namely, from 0.27 to 0.44 gallons per capita.   Taking the year 1874, chosen because at that time the first Swedish company—the Gothenburg—secured the licenses for retail sale of spirits (only sales over the bar were given in 1865), and making a comparison with the present, the consumption of spirits and wines with us has remained stationary, but beer-drinking has very much more than doubled.   It is true that during the last half-century the United States has received large accessions of population from countries where beer is the national beverage, and doubtless some will say that, since spirit-drinking has not advanced, it is unfair to assume deterioration in habits.

There is another significant fact to which attention must be called.

Returns of the prison population in the United States show an increase of 358 persons per million inhabitants during the last census period.   The advance has been greatest in the North Atlantic Division, which contains our largest city populations.   Exactly what proportion of criminality springs from drink is a question which, so far, has not been accurately determined.   The best studies, however, go to show that tippling is a prolific source of wrong-doing,—indeed, probably the most potent factor in petty crime.

Here, then, is a summary of our situation.   Prohibition, local option, State monopoly, high-license, and low-license, have been tried,— most of them during long periods and in various sections of the country.

1. The consumption of liquor has increased, and the prison population is advancing.

2. The ratio of licenses to inhabitants, in large cities, often now attains disgraceful proportions.

3. The alliance between liquor and politics is being drawn closer and closer.

There exist three leading alternatives in future action.

1. Hopelessly to give up the struggle, at least for the present, and allow the evil to become unendurable, trusting to a great wave of moral enthusiasm to sweep it entirely away.   Municipalities exercise this method to free themselves from political corruption, but it is generally noticed that spasms of virtue come at longer intervals, while relapses follow more speedily and are more severe.   Generally speaking, the last condition of the patient is worse than the first.   Such doctrines are so dangerous in the field of politics that none but the nonchalant American, who has been nourished on the belief that nothing can permanently undermine his country's greatness, would dare to profess them.   They cannot for one moment be admitted in dealing with grave moral issues, because, ere long, recuperative virtue would be debauched and silenced.   No! things cannot go on as they are; they must not be allowed to grow worse.

2. Numbers of people, while candidly admitting that present conditions are not satisfactory, are so wedded to preconceived notions, or attached to a narrow system, that they will not hear of moving outside of regulation methods.   They may be partisans of a faith-cure, such as prohibition, especially when applied to large cities.   More, perhaps, believe in very mild homœopathic treatment, and so recommend high-license, forgetting that a consolidation of liquor interests and the exercise of political favoritism are necessary incidents there-

to.   Instead of removing private gain, the impulse to it is stimulated by rendering success uncertain unless business is pushed and resorts are made more seductive.   Early-closing is an impossibility under high-license, because, if you charge a man well for the privilege of selling drink, you cannot, under any pretence of equity, deny him the opportunity to exercise the trade during the more profitable hours. No-license—or local option, as it is usually called—cannot be successfully enforced in the case of large municipalities unless there is some adjacent community upon which to unload the burden.   I doubt very much if Cambridge could have shown such good results, did not a bridge span the stretch of water between it and Boston.

3.   The third alternative—and I believe the only admissible one— is to study impartially the liquor problem from all points of view, and adopt those methods which have been proven most efficient in practice as measures of progressive, if not ideal, reform.   Nothing can be more rational than this; nor, indeed, can success be reasonably expected from any other policy.

The formation of a national Committee of Fifty on the study of the liquor problem was briefly noticed in the March number of THE FORUM.   Distinguished men in clerical, professional, academic, and business stations, representing all shades of opinion, have banded together for the purpose of thorough and rational study.   When results are reached and published, the American people will have data for judgment which have never existed before.   To my mind, one reason why so little solid advance has hitherto been made is that the liquor problem has been largely dealt with from the standpoint of sentiment.   Sentiment is undoubtedly a tremendous force, but, like other motive powers, unless it is usefully directed, no progress can be made.   A locomotive with furnace blazing and lever drawn may remain at a complete stand-still.   It must have a track upon which to run if ground is to be traversed and a goal reached.   Now, this Committee of Fifty, if it does nothing else, will certainly lay the track.

As regards practical measures we need not wait for its possible suggestion.   Light is already available; and, as in days of old, it comes from the east.   The Norwegian system of public control, modified slightly to meet American conditions, is the best and safest plan to adopt so long as licensing has to be practised, and I think it would be a pretty sanguine person who would not admit that that will be for a good while yet.   It represents the only effective means of minimizing the evils of the traffic in large cities, and it includes admirable provisions for encouraging no-license in country districts and smaller towns.

Each local governing community regulates its own practice. If no licenses are permitted, a formal vote to that effect settles the question; but, where licensing is to go on, a monopoly of saloon and retail trade up to a certain limit—in Norway 10½ gallons, and in Sweden 66 gallons at one sale—is conceded to a commercial company whose shareholders are usually individuals or institutions of high standing, and whose management is conducted in the strictest possible manner for the public interest. All profits beyond the current interest on capital are distributed among institutions for furthering public weal, or to lessen the social and moral burdens to which inordinate alcoholic indulgence gives rise. Public interest being substituted for individual gain, all rules of management, such as limitation in the number of places of sale to the lowest possible limit, with consequent removal of temptation to drink, refusal to sell in such quantities that intoxication may ensue, early week-day and absolute Sunday closing, disposal of goods for cash only, destruction of political alliances, of gambling, and of every immoral accessory,—these are some of the salutary consequences of this rational regime. Testimonies of efficiency are numerous and overwhelmingly conclusive:

1. No single community in Scandinavia has ever tried the plan and afterward abandoned it.

2. Liquor-selling has been abolished, except in the case of a comparatively small number of privileged licenses, which are held for life and cannot be expropriated, throughout the country districts and smaller communities of Norway and Sweden.

3. Membership in total-abstinence societies has risen from a meagre coterie to over 300,000 in the two countries.

4. Even the radical temperance party has not sought to abolish the regime, and its leader, in writing to me not long ago, officially expressed his earnest preference to this over all other systems where the sale of liquor was permitted at all. The real effort of the party is being directed toward securing a law which shall make it unlawful to sell any beverage whose alcoholic content is more than 25 per cent.

5. Chiefs of police have been led to see " that the difference between conditions under the old and new order of things is as the difference between night and day." Provincial governors, foreign

ministers and consuls have likewise expressed their approbation with but one dissenting voice.[1]

6. The testimony of undeniable fact, which is more eloquent and conclusive than the best-founded opinion, shows that the consumption of spirits in Sweden has been reduced from 14.2 to 6.8 quarts per inhabitant from the time the first company received its complete monopoly of retail and bar sale of spirits, and in Norway from 6.8 to 3.3 quarts. The reformatory influences of the regime have brought Sweden down from the second to the seventh, and Norway to the lowest place, as regards per capita consumption of spirits, among the thirteen most civilized countries of the world, while we in the United States still occupy the rank of tenth. Need anything more be said to convince the doubter that this system points the way to Rational Temperance Reform?

[1] This criticism came from Mr. T. Michell, British Consul-General at Christiania. His report is one of the grossest misrepresentations of facts that ever emanated from an official pen, yet notwithstanding very clear evidences of faulty analysis it has been widely utilized by persons not understanding or not in sympathy with the Norwegian system. Particularly has a writer in "The Voice" been unwittingly misled into drawing inferences from quotations which one familiar with the facts recognizes as illogical, distorted, or untrue. But the public should be informed of a few incidents to which Mr. Michell's ridiculous but unfortunate work has given rise. Popular indignation in Norway was immediately aroused, and Mr. H. E. Berner, of Christiania, a temperate man, and universally recognized as the highest authority on the Norwegian system, was commissioned to prepare an official refutation. In a letter received not long ago, Mr. Berner remarked :

"In regard to the very incorrect report about the Norwegian *Samlag* (company system) by Mr. Michell, I may state that I was requested by our Home Department to formulate a reply to it, and this reply has been sent to the English Foreign Office, through our legation in London. The Foreign Office has also asked permission to publish my reply. I do not think the Norwegian authorities will do anything further in the matter."

Mr. Thomas M. Wilson, of Bergen, also wrote shortly before his death :

"Mr. Michell's consular report has been well refuted by the Norwegian press, and the government has forwarded an official refutation of it to Lord Rosebery. Besides that, the leading British residents in Norway have prepared a memorial pointing out the absolute advantages of the system practised in Norway, and requesting the withdrawal of the report from circulation. The memorial will be presented very soon, and has been numerously signed. The report is just as untruthful, biased, and incorrect as it well can be."

When a document is officially repudiated, directly by one government and indirectly by another, besides being protested against by the writer's resident compatriots, is it not time that all who prize fairness and uprightness in controversy should cease quoting it? I feel sure that most writers who have used these data have done so without the knowledge of the above facts. Still they are only partially excusable, for the report bears unmistakable intrinsic evidences of absurd and illogical induction.

The only reliable gauge of efficiency to apply to any system for controlling the liquor traffic is per capita consumption of drink. Even this does not offer a mathematical standard of accuracy, for it is a well-known fact that changing economic conditions will cause wide fluctuations.   Indeed the British chancellor of the exchequer is accustomed to use this " spirit barometer" in his budgetary estimates of national prosperity.   Nevertheless, individual consumption of drink is a sound, if only an approximate test.

Statistics of drunkenness are valueless as an index, because law, strictness in enforcing regulations, artificial incentives to take up offenders, such as giving a part of the fines to the police, and the progressive popular intolerance of inebriety which usually follows a reforming regime, all play an important part.   Again, published statements of convictions are rarely differentiated to show how many times the same person was arrested.   This is exceedingly important as indicating whether the actual number of persons drinking to excess is on the increase, or whether professional tipplers are simply indulging more freely.   Furthermore, the area to which the system applies must be studied as a whole, and not individual districts alone. It is evident that if there be no-license in the country, and license in the towns, the former's more jovial inhabitants will utilize occasional visits to the cities to drink to excess.   Statistically such offences belong to the place where they are committed.

Statistics of pauperism abound with even more treacherous pitfalls to the unwary.   Everywhere public sense of responsibility toward the unfortunate has deepened during the last three decades. The logical result is that this class is not only being better cared for, but more are helped.   To find the pauper constituency increasing does not necessarily argue deterioration of habit, growing failure of self-respect, or the application of sentimental methods in relief. The concentration of population in urban centres represents in no small degree a flocking together of the unfit.   Here public institutions to care for those who fail in life's struggle exist in large numbers, accounting in a measure for the anomaly of increasing urban and declining rural poverty.

. Methods of enumerating the poor vary in different countries and at different periods.   As an illustration, in Sweden, during recent years, those receiving gratuitous hospital or dispensary treatment figure in the pauper record.   Take another case showing divergence in systems of registration.   In Gothenburg, if the head of a family is helped by having his rent paid from the poor rates, the whole family are inscribed as paupers. Supposing there are eight children, and that both parents are alive, there would be ten recipients of relief. If rents were paid in this manner monthly during eight months, the record would show eighty paupers; if weekly during the same period, three hundred and fifty. Figures which indicate that one person in every nine inhabitants of a thriving commercial city is a pauper ought to create suspicion in any discerning mind. Yet the totals are accepted and quoted by the writer in "The Voice" and by the secretary of the English County Brewers' Society as evidence that unparalleled poverty is somehow or other closely connected with the Gothenburg system of liquor traffic. Nothing can be more easily distorted than statistical data. Sir Charles Dilke in one sense was right when he said, "There are three degrees of untruth,—a fib, a lie, and statistics." Crime bears a positive relation to drink, but the terms of this relation cannot be expressed in mathematical language. There is always a tendency among the lapsed, who appreciate the practical value of sympathy, to lay their misfortunes to tippling.

We come back, then, to the statistics of per capita consumption of liquor, so as to apply the only real test of efficacy to the Scandinavian method of control. In 1874 the average amount of spirits drunk per individual in Sweden was 3.55 gallons, in Norway 1.7 gallons (1876), in the United States 1.51 gallons. In 1892 the corresponding quantities are 1.7 gallons for Sweden, 0.82 gallons for Norway, and 1.50 gallons for the United States.

But what about beer? Has consumption of this beverage increased? It has; but that is a phenomenon everywhere discernible, and in the United States to a far greater degree than in Scandinavia. During practically the same period of time as the dates above mentioned, the consumption of beer advanced, in Sweden from 4 gallons to 7.05 gallons per capita, in the United States from 6.99 to 15.10 gallons, while in Norway it remained almost stationary at less than half the amount of the present annual per capita consumption in this country.

Such is the testimony of facts,—facts that are as pertinent as they are incontrovertible. Their teaching should be laid deeply to heart. All opponents of the liquor evil should cast aside their prejudices and struggle valiantly in behalf of a system which is at the present moment practicable, and which alone provides an avenue for the realization of high ideals.

E. R. L. GOULD.

WILLIAM L. WILSON AS A TARIFF-REFORM LEADER.

ALTHOUGH the tariff act which has taken the place of the McKinley act does not keep the promise of the Democratic party, and is marred by "concessions" to protected interests, which are really surrenders, it is a distinct gain to the country, and it is the first tariff law that has been enacted in nearly forty years which recognizes the rights of consumers and the needs of commerce, and is not entirely devoted to the enrichment of favored manufacturers.

Mr. William L. Wilson is appropriately the chairman of the Ways and Means Committee when this is accomplished. He is the one member of the House of Representatives who should be in this place when this first step is taken away from McKinleyism. There is but one other man in Congress of whom one instinctively thinks in the hour of this small triumph,—and Mr. Mills is in the Senate. Mr. Carlisle, the first leader of the determined tariff-reformers, since Mr. Kerr, to be elected Speaker, is the head of the Treasury. Mr. Morrison, the first chairman of the Ways and Means Committee to formulate in a bill the tariff-reform contest which began in 1875 with the election of Mr. Kerr to the speakership, is out of the struggles and contests of politics.

Mr. Morrison's bill was defeated by protectionist Democrats in the House of Representatives; but when Mr. Mills became chairman of the Ways and Means Committee the protectionist Democrats had so dwindled in numbers that they could not prevent the majority from carrying out its purposes. The effort to reform the tariff has been defeated by the protection sentiment in the Democratic party, but that sentiment has been growing weaker since the day that it was able to help the Republicans to defeat the Morrison bill. Even now, when it is strong enough in the Senate to force through the sugar schedule, it is not strong enough to refuse free wool, free lumber, and other relief from taxation.

With this great change of sentiment Mr. Wilson has had a good deal to do. He is more than part of the movement for tariff reform; he has been among the leaders from his first appearance in the House, until now he is the foremost,—the survivor of the group which with-stood Mr. Randall and his fellows until their forces went to pieces, dissipated by the adverse sentiment of their party. It would be impossible to describe the manner of man Mr. Wilson is without recalling the struggle which has gone on within the Democratic party, and especially among its members in the House of Representatives, for the last ten years. The history of that contest is the history of Mr. Wilson's political career. His attitude in it and toward every phase of it, notwithstanding apparently unfavorable conditions in his district, has been marked by an elevation of mind and nobility of character that place him among the American statesmen of whom the country has reason to be proud.

It was in 1883 that Mr. Wilson entered Congress. He was forty years old. He had been a soldier, a teacher, and a lawyer, but it is easy to read between the lines of his brief biography the strong tendency of his mind toward active politics. His training fitted him to be a college professor, but his inclination led him into the contests that centred about his political opinions. He was graduated at Columbian University at Washington, and had begun the study of law when the war broke out. He at once abandoned his books for the army. When the war was over, he became a professor at Columbian University; but a more active career was destined for him, and when the lawyers' test oath in West Virginia was repealed, he returned to Charlestown, W. Va., and began to practise. He was soon in politics. In 1880 he was a delegate to the Democratic National Convention, and was an elector-at-large on the Hancock ticket. Two years later his scholarship was in demand in West Virginia, and he was elected President of the State University; but his importance in politics, and probably his own strong inclination for the study of political questions, once more prevailed, and he was elected a member of Congress a few months after he had accepted the presidency of the University. Even now, after his service in Congress is in its twelfth year, the conflict between the pleasures of letters and philosophy, and the activities of the political struggle, is renewed. This time, judg-ing from his speech before the nominating convention at Martinsburg, Mr. Wilson would probably have chosen to accept the invitation to resume the presidency of the University, so suddenly and quickly laid down in 1882, if it were not that his duty demanded that he should not abandon the cause whose first triumph, disappointing but important, has been won under his leadership.

23

Those who recall Mr. Wilson when he first entered the House of Representatives will remember that he soon made a deep impression on the leaders, with whom he very quickly stood on an even footing. The reputation of the Virginian "scholar in politics" had reached Washington before him. The story of his earnest and courageous campaign for tariff-reform among the coal-miners of West Virginia was known, and much was expected from the young man who had come out of his president's chair to become a militant politician in a contest whose inherent difficulties were known, if the long years in which it was to endure could not be counted, and if the treacheries and betrayals of its pretended friends could not be foreseen. The appearance of the frail, small body may have been disappointing; but the disappointment did not last long, for at once there was an occasion for the display of a kind of courage which most politicians sadly lack, —the courage which leads a man to do what he thinks is right without regard to the consequences to himself. In his recent speech at Martinsburg, before the shouting enthusiasts who nominated him for the seventh time, Mr. Wilson said this:

"No man could worthily approach such a work [tariff-reform] without putting away from him any petty personal ambition and any selfish concern for his own political future. No man could hope for any measure of real success who was not willing to dedicate to such a task every power of body and mind, with an humble invocation for strength and wisdom from the unfailing Source of strength and wisdom.

"I cannot claim to have risen to the full height of this duty, but I have never faltered in the belief that you, my friends and constituents, expected and desired me to enter upon my work in this spirit, and in this spirit to persevere to its close. I knew that you were tariff-reformers without reservation; I knew that the Democrats of West Virginia were not protectionists for West Virginia, and reformers and free-traders for other States. But even if I had known otherwise I should not have gone aside one step from what was to me the clear pathway of duty to all the people."

If at its beginning he had deliberately chosen this sentiment for the rule of his career, his course in the House of Representatives would have abundantly justified it, for he has never considered his political future for a moment in determining his conduct on any question of importance, and he has really dedicated " every power of body and mind" to the task of relieving the country from the wasting burden of protective taxes. In the last session, when he was the leader of the tariff-reform forces, his spirit of devotion was of the character that has made its possessors remembered in history. Husbanding his strength, undermined and almost consumed by illness, he never spared it when the hour came for putting it forth, and he kept his faith through a period of conflict, disappointment, constant threat of defeat, and ever-present anxiety.

In December, 1883, the issue of tariff-reform was first clearly defined and hotly contested within the Democratic party. It had been somewhat vaguely regarded as Democratic policy before then, but other questions had kept it in the background, and the protectionists, under the leadership of Mr. Randall, had diligently assisted the Republicans to preserve sectional differences, in order that economic differences might be submerged. Mr. Kerr had tariff-reform in his mind when he was chosen Speaker in 1875, and Mr. Morrison, his chairman of the Ways and Means Committee, had determined that it should be made the leading policy of the party. But Mr. Kerr died, and when Mr. Randall became Speaker he did not reappoint Mr. Morrison as chairman of the Ways and Means Committee, but put Mr. Fernando Wood in that place and gave him a committee incapable of any action on the tariff. When the Democrats next controlled the House of Representatives, the issue was explicitly defined. The contest between tariff-reform and protectionism may be said to have begun. It had been thoroughly understood that some Democrats were protectionists, but no revenue-reformer believed that they held their allegiance to the manufacturers above their loyalty to their party, whose revenue-reform platform they had accepted, and even above their duty to the country. That protectionism was not to give up its power to make tax-laws for the profit of its beneficiaries without a struggle was certain, but that it had succeeded in corrupting both parties, and that its agents in the party which professed to be for tariff-reform were better protectionists than Democrats, and numerous enough to defeat their party's political principles, was very far from the thoughts of those who preferred Mr. Carlisle to Mr. Randall as Speaker of the Forty-eighth Congress. They thought that with the Democratic majority, a revenue-reform Speaker and Committee of Ways and Means, a tariff bill would surely pass the House, and that the resulting dispute between the Representatives and the Senators would determine the issue for the Presidential campaign of 1884. Events have shown how greatly they were mistaken.

Mr. Wilson's attitude in the struggle for the speakership was soon defined, and at the same time there began to appear evidences that the protected interests intended to exert all their power to divide the Democrats on the issue and to make their business interests the interests of the country.   A protected manufacturer was at the head of the Democratic National Committee, and the majority of his associates sympathized with him and sustained him.   Congressmen in close districts were threatened with a loss of the votes of Democratic workingmen, or with a denial of their portions of the Democratic campaign fund, if they considered the country instead of the manufacturers, and were promised Republican votes and abundance of campaign funds if they followed Mr. Randall.

Mr. Wilson came from a close district.   His first election was won by a plurality of ten.   He represented a population largely composed of coal-miners.   His State was apparently controlled by a company of able and shrewd politicians and speculators, Republicans and Democrats.   Among them were Senator Henry G. Davis, a Democrat; Stephen B. Elkins, a Republican; Arthur P. Gorman, a Democrat; and with these Mr. Blaine was closely associated. Mr. Wilson was at once threatened with defeat at home if he voted for Mr. Carlisle for Speaker, but he had gone into public life for the purpose of aiding in what seemed to him to be the pressing and needed task of tariff-reform, and public life had no charm for him if he were to spend it in denial of his principles and in servile obedience to corporations that had gained their wealth and power at the expense of the vast army of consumers, and by taking from the people the right to tax themselves for themselves.   The pressure that was brought upon Democratic Congressmen by the protected interests in behalf of Mr. Randall was surprising, but more surprising than this to the average politician was the firmness with which Mr. Wilson and some others like him declined to permit his political future to sway his convictions.   He voted for Mr. Carlisle, and left the future to be cared for when the time came, trusting in the people who had elected him to Congress.

From this time on, Mr. Wilson has been forced to contend for his re-election against the active opposition of the protected interests in and out of his district; and as the character of the Democratic National Committee, by reason of the succession of Mr. Brice and Mr. Gorman to Mr. Barnum's leadership, is unchanged, he has not only not received the aid of his party leaders, although he has stood on his party's platforms, but he has met with strong opposition from Democratic leaders in his own State, who have doubtless foreseen the bitter struggle and the consequent peril to themselves which is now revealed by their party's outcry against the treachery of the "Conservatives." In spite of this opposition, Mr. Wilson has been elected six times by pluralities ranging from less than 100 to a little more than 2,000, and now he is before his constituents for the seventh time asking them to choose between his democracy and Mr. Gorman's.

Meanwhile the contest in the Democratic party has resulted in a great change. While protection is not driven out, it is greatly weakened. In 1884, 41 Democrats voted with Mr. Randall against the Morrison bill. In June, 1886, 36 Democrats in the House voted with Mr. Randall, and in December of the same year his following was reduced to 26. In 1888, only eight Democrats voted against the Mills bill, Mr. Randall himself not voting. The Democratic protectionist who dares to vote against his party's policy of tariff-reform has practically disappeared from the House of Representatives, and while a few (less than a half-dozen) remain in the Senate, who insist upon protection for their own special interests, even they have not the courage that animated Mr. Randall, whose manliness and sincerity were in glowing contrast to the tortuous and subterranean methods of his unworthy successors.

This change in the attitude of Democratic Congressmen, and recent popular uprisings in behalf of tariff-reform, have been brought about by the intelligent persistence of strong men, among whom, in some respects, Mr. Wilson is the strongest. In the Forty-eighth Congress, the men who made the most effective effort for the election of Mr. Carlisle believed that the Democratic party should have some other reason for its existence than opposition to the Republican party, and, having firm convictions on the subject of tariff-reform, they adhered to them. Of all these men, Mr. Wilson has remained a member of the House of Representatives, and has gone quietly to the front by force of character and ability, until he is the one to pluck the fruit of victory, —a victory that means more than its immediate consequences, for it has set the country moving in a direction from which it will never turn back toward McKinleyism.

The character of the chairman of the Ways and Means Committee is to be judged by the consistent, firm, and courageous part he has played in this ten years' struggle. Through it all, he has had faith in his cause, in the people of the district, and in himself. If any one in our public life is entitled to the much-abused name of statesman, it is Mr. Wilson. He is in public life because he belongs there. He went into it from the college. No one who knows Mr.

Wilson at all can doubt that the pursuits of the student are congenial to him. He knows books and loves them. Outwardly he seems the most placid of enthusiasts. His quiet manner suggests thoughtful repose. His conversation shows the full man that reading has made, and is lightened by the lambent humor that is the possession of those who have thoroughly enjoyed the fancies of literature. Those who do not believe in convictions, or who find in Mr. Wilson a difficult opponent, are in the habit of calling him " professor." It is, of course, not a serious crime to be a professor in this country, which boasts of its free schools as the basis of its political institutions. What these dealers in epithets mean is that Mr. Wilson is not a practical man, and that one who can make shovels and print cottons is a better lawmaker than one who knows the maxims of civil liberty, and who appreciates the full significance of the human movement which, after ages of fierce combat with the forces of despotism, at last brought forth this great self-governing Commonwealth. They are unconscious of the degradation to which their system has condemned the Republic, if a knowledge of price-lists and of cheap methods of production furnish a better preparation for the lawmaker than a knowledge of human endeavor in the art of government. There is nothing visionary in Mr. Wilson's mental processes. To whatever extreme the logic of his convictions might lead him, he is in no danger of going beyond the attainable. The bill that bore his name, and which was passed by the House of Representatives, did not represent his desires, but indicated the limitations imposed upon him by the slender Democratic majority in the Senate, and by the presence there of protectionists who made up that majority. There is nothing more intensely practical in statesmanship than the ability to fight strenuously for all that can be hoped for, and to accept the most that can be forced from a corrupt opposition. This is what Mr. Wilson has done; and if this is the work of a professor, it is among professors that the American people would better look for future statesmen.

It is an American idiosyncrasy that has grown stronger within the last thirty years, to demand, as an essential element of statesmanship, what is called executive ability,—the habit of mind which is developed by the management of a railroad. Whether Mr. Wilson could satisfy this demand may be doubtful. Men who are trained to reflect—to weigh one side against the other in order that they may not only reach a just conclusion, but also sustain it with argument—

are not likely to take on the practice of quick decision at fifty-one years of age. What we know of Mr. Wilson is that he is one of the best products of American political, social, and educational institutions; that he is capable of devoting himself to an idea to the point of sacrificing his chosen career if that be essential; that he is conscientious and laborious; that he possesses great firmness of character; that he does not look backward once his hand is on the plough; that he never yields so long as there is hope of conquering, although he never permits his passions to control his intelligence; that he is singularly honest and unselfish; that to him public station is an opportunity for public service, a Congressman's duty is to make laws for the whole country for the benefit of all the people, and he must not be turned from this duty by considerations of his own welfare or by the selfish desires of any of his constituents. Since he has become a leader the country has had an opportunity to learn that Mr. Wilson possesses these qualities, and most men who know him better and knew him sooner than the country were sadly disappointed that he was not made Speaker when Mr. Crisp was chosen. Perhaps it was for the best, however, that he remained to be the central figure on the floor of the House. His district has known Mr. Wilson so well that the whole force of protectionism throughout the whole country, which has more than once been concentrated on this single district, has been unable to overcome his slender majority. His constant re-elections show the regard in which character is held by the American people. There is no other man in public life in this country whom his home people would receive with such enthusiasm, the manifestation of affectionate honor, as greeted Mr. Wilson when he went back, a short time ago, to answer once more to the call of his district, and once more to renounce scholastic honors.

The chairman of the Ways and Means Committee is one of the most convincing orators of the public men of his time. He speaks with the eloquence of a full mind, and with a sensitive appreciation of the musical beauties of the English language. The effect which he produces on his audience in the House is deeper than that which any other political speaker of his day has wrought. Such scenes as those which followed his first and last speeches in the recent tariff debate have rarely been witnessed in that usually cold and indifferent assemblage. And it was doubtless due to his enthusiasm as well as his firmness that the House maintained its contest with the Senate as long as it did. But Mr. Wilson's oratorical power, considerable as it is, is not the quality which makes him one of the first of our public men. He displayed that when he was a young member. He then proved his mastery in debate, but a different and finer spirit animated his latest efforts when he felt that the cause to which he had devoted himself during his public career was entrusted to his keeping. In the earlier days he was not averse to answering jest with sharper wit, and to turning his opponent's ribaldry back upon its author; but in these latter days he has risen above the little personalities of debate, and has permitted nothing to divert him from the inspiration of his subject.

It is difficult to write or to speak of Mr. Wilson without betraying the strong friendship which he inspires. He is an amiable friend, a kindly antagonist, an avoider of scandal and gossip, a leader who does not assert himself or demand precedence, but who is where he is by force of his character and ability. He has not stormed the country, as he did not storm the body of whose majority at least he is the most distinguished member. He has simply done his duty with a rare and keen intelligence, and with a singular and unselfish devotion to what he has considered the right of the question which has seemed to him to be the most important in American politics. Whether his mental grasp is strong enough, and his view all-embracing enough, to enable him to fulfil the promise he has given, remains to be seen. But such men as he are needed wholesome influences in our public life.

HENRY LOOMIS NELSON.

My efforts to do something to lessen the appalling sum of human suffering and sorrow which the figures of infant mortality in New York but faintly indicate were begun in the summer of last year, when I opened a depot where pure milk, both in its natural and sterilized form, was sold. From this experiment I received such striking demonstration of the good that could be accomplished by raising the standard of the milk supply of the poor, that I resolved, if it were at all possible, to resume the work on a greatly enlarged scale this year. For the protection of the children of the poor, the milk must be sterilized before being sold.[1] I believed that if this could be done on a scale large enough to make an impression on the supply, the sum of infant mortality in New York might be sensibly reduced. I determined to make the attempt at least, and in opening six milk depots at the beginning of the past summer deliberately addressed myself to the task of reducing the death-rate of the city.

There is a great deal of waste in the world, but none quite so reckless as that of human life. Here in New York the lives of thousands of children are sacrificed every summer, simply and solely because they are fed with impure milk. Of people who die in the State of Maine every year, children under five years of age count for less than 20 per cent; of those who die in New York city, over 40 per cent are children under five years of age.

It is the mortality of June, July, and August that chiefly accounts for the large percentage of this annual harvest of death. Within a

---

[1] Here let me say that the penalty of disease and death, paid for the neglect of simple precautions in the use of milk, is by no means paid exclusively by the poor. Milk is not always good in proportion to the price paid for it, nor free from the germs of contagion because it has come from cattle of aristocratic lineage. The latter quality, as recent experience has shown, carries with it a special susceptibility to tuberculosis. In milk intended for infant nutriment perfect sterilization is an absolutely essential precaution; but, simple as the process is, it is not always certain, even in the homes of the rich, that it will be properly done. I hold that in the near future it will be regarded as a piece of criminal neglect to feed young children on milk which has not been sterilized.

radius of twelve miles from the New York City Hall, three children die during the heated term for every adult; and certainly two out of every three represent a sacrifice which it is a disgrace to our civilization to allow.   Within the area of what may be called the metropolitan district, the record of one week showed the total mortality to be 1,038, of which 713 deaths were under five years, 664 under two years, 529 under one year, and only 325 over five years of age. Here was 64 per cent of one week's death-roll composed of babies under two years, who drank but little water, and were almost wholly dependent on milk for their nutriment.   Could the " destruction that wasteth at noon-day" have been more palpably present than death in these children's milk-bottles?

The conditions of a wholesome milk supply are simple, but, like a good many other simple things, difficult of attainment.   These conditions are healthy cows, clean stables, clean and careful processes of milking, and the prompt transfer of the milk, in perfectly clean and close vessels, from the cow to the consumer.   In the milk supply of all great cities every one of these requisites is flagrantly violated. The inspection of cow-stables to detect the presence of disease is neither careful nor constant; milking is done in most cases under conditions indescribably filthy, and most of the milk consumed by the children of the poor is at least thirty-six to forty-eight hours old before it reaches them.   It is a simple matter to understand,—as Professor Sedgwick of Boston puts the case—

"—how this rich animal fluid—sterile at the start, but drawn by unclean hands into half-cleaned pails, and meanwhile sprinkled from above by the dust of the stable, by hairs, dandruff, dirt, and particles of excrement from the skin and udder of the cow vigorously shaken by the milker or brushed by his hat—becomes infested with organisms.   That these multiply swiftly and enormously in the warm and rich fluid, well aerated by the act of milking, is also a natural consequence of favorable conditions ; and, if we allow time also, the wonder is, not that it contains so many germs, but rather that it is still potable at all."

Mr. William M. Babbott, of New-York, who has issued an instructive little monograph on the connection between milk supply and disease, uses still stronger language in regard to the character of the milk sold in New York and Brooklyn.   He says:

"If milk gave the same outward appearance of decomposition or fermentation as is shown by vegetables. fish, or meat, more than three-quarters of all the milk consumed in the metropolitan district would be condemned as unfit for human food : if its pollution could be perceived, it would be loathed ; and if the disease germs could be as plainly seen as a pest-house, the death-dealing milk would be as soon dreaded and shunned."

It is unquestionably true that no plague by which the city was ever ravaged has yielded so plentiful a crop of deaths as that which is reaped from the seeds of contagion deposited in the infant system every summer by millions of noxious bacteria developed in milk.

The sterilizing laboratory which I established last year was this year very much enlarged, and every preparation was made to meet the demands likely to be made on it. The cows from which the milk was obtained were examined by the veterinary surgeon of the New York Board of Health, and the stables and dairies made a subject of careful inspection. The milk was iced in transportation and kept on ice till it was turned into the bottles for sterilizing. The apparatus used for the purpose was made under the direction of Dr. R. G. Freeman, of New York. The milk is exposed for twenty minutes to a temperature of 167° Fahrenheit. It has been demonstrated that tubercle bacilli die at 158° Fahrenheit, when submitted to that temperature for ten minutes. It is therefore reasonably certain that by this process all noxious germs in the milk are completely destroyed, while the nutritive qualities of this most perfect of nature's foods have not been in the slightest degree impaired. In the preparation of modified milk for infant feeding, two formulæ were adopted, one by Dr. R. G. Freeman, and the other by Dr. A. Jacobi. Both of these have been, and will during the winter continue to be, sterilized in six-ounce bottles, sold at a cent each. In addition to these modified milk foods, barley flour was sold. This was intended to meet a want, keenly felt by the poor, of wholesome nutrition at a price within their means, for children beyond the infantile stage.

During the hottest part of the summer the laboratory was kept running to its full capacity, night and day, to prepare sufficient sterilized milk to meet the demand. This was so active and so constant as to exhaust the stock in the depots daily, but it was a rigidly observed rule that, without respect to demand, no bottle of sterilized milk should be sold twenty-four hours after it had been sterilized. The Health Board's free doctors, the dispensaries, the " World's" free doctors, and nearly all the hospitals and charitable organizations, took an active interest in educating the people as to the value of sterilized milk. Order-books containing a hundred of the following coupons were placed without cost, and without restriction as to quantity, at the disposal of any physician giving his services freely to the poor, or to any charitable organization applying for them:

This coupon is good at any of the following depots:

Foot of East Third Street; 317 East Ninth Street; 147 Eldridge Street;
2½ Market Street; 201 West 63d Street; and 324 East 59th Street,
for

5 6-oz. bottles Milk and Barley Water, Formula No. 2; or
5 6-oz. bottles Milk and Lime Water, Formula 1; or
4 8-oz. bottles Sterilized Pure Milk; or
2 16-oz. bottles Sterilized Pure Milk; or
One-half pound Barley Flour and 2 8-oz. bottles Sterilized Pure Milk.

———o———

Deposit required on bottles from every one: 3 cents on each 6 or 8-oz.
bottle; 5 cents on each 16-oz. bottle.

NATHAN STRAUS.

———o———

This ticket is good for only one of the foods.

By permission of the Dock Department I erected on the pier at the foot of East Third Street, within a few feet of the milk laboratory, a large pavilion provided with comfortable seats, which were given to the unrestricted use of women and children. I also placed benches under the pavilion erected on this same pier by the Dock Department. My purpose in this was to furnish a free fresh-air resort for mothers who could not get through with their home duties early enough to catch a boat which sailed on schedule time. The tent was open all day up to midnight, so that at any hour a mother could bring her child and enjoy the fresh sea air without having tired herself out in a rush to catch an excursion, and probably unfitted herself for the proper care of the child. The central depot being situated on this pier, all the resources were at the command of those who used the rest and shelter provided. A physician assigned by the Board of Health was constantly in attendance. On hot days a thousand women and children could be found at almost any hour enjoying the shelter, and so impressed have I been with the benefit thus afforded that I have determined to use all my influence to have such outing-places, protected from the sun, erected on the piers that belong to the city. This can be done without interfering with traffic facilities, by putting benches on the roof of the pier, and covering them with an awning.

Free lectures under other auspices were given twice a week by experienced physicians, on the proper care and feeding of infants, and every opportunity was taken to bring home to mothers the knowledge that the best possible food for their children could be obtained at a nominal price. The sales of sterilized milk for babies at the six depots aggregated, up to the end of September, 280,000 bottles, or over 2,500 bottles a day. No record was kept of the number of sick children for whom sweetened and diluted sterilized milk in bottles was prescribed, but it was estimated that a daily average of 700 babies were fed on this modified milk. It is safe to say that some thousands of children, who were sick, owe their recovery during the summer to its use. On this point the returns of the Bureau of Statistics present eloquent testimony, as the following comparison between the number of deaths of children in New York under five years of age, this year and last, will show:

	1894	1893
January, February, and March	4,508	4,108
April, May, and June	4,521	4,386
July	2,560	2,796
August	1,559	1,686
September (to the 13th)	317	386

The summer of 1894 was a much more trying one for children than that of 1893. The average temperature of the latter part of June, of the whole of July, and of part of August was unusually high, and all conditions tending to the increase of the intestinal disorders which are chiefly accountable for infant mortality were correspondingly aggravated. As a matter of fact, the sanitary condition of the city had undergone no radical change, and the system of tenement-house inspection was not less thorough last year than this. Sick-children's funds, and other forms of charitable effort for the benefit of the poor, were not less liberally supported in the summer of 1893 than in that of 1894. All the external conditions, in short, led to the expectation of a higher death-rate in the summer of 1894 than in the one preceding; and, even had other things been equal, the increase of population would, without an increase of the rate, have been accompanied by a larger number of infant deaths. But it will be seen that since the opening of the pure milk depots the number of deaths among children has sensibly decreased. During the first quarter of the year there was an increase, as compared with 1893, of nearly 10 per cent—considerably in excess of a normal percentage—in the deaths of children under five years of age. For the second quarter, forty days of which were covered by the distribution of pure milk, the increase over 1893 was only a little more than 3 per cent. For the month of July there was a decrease, as compared with July, 1893, of nearly 8½ per cent in the number of infant deaths: for August the decrease was 7½ per cent, and for September

18 per cent. Allowing 3 per cent as the normal average of increase under the most favorable conditions, it will be seen that there has been a reduction of over 10 per cent in the summer mortality of infauts in this city.

Further analysis of the figures show results even more striking. The month of June started in with an exceptionally high mortality of children under one year. In 1893 this month showed 878 of these infant deaths: in 1894 the number rose to 1,076,—an increase of 22½ · per cent. Of children over one year and under two years of age, the deaths for June, 1893, numbered 247, and for June, 1894, 267,— an increase of over 8 per cent. Necessarily, it took some time to make the existence of the pure-milk agencies known to those for whose benefit they were intended, and to educate mothers into the necessity of having recourse to them. For July, when the system was fairly in operation, and its advantages generally known, the deaths of infants under one year numbered 1,918, as compared with 2,063 for the corresponding month of 1893,—a decrease of over 7 per cent. In the same month the deaths over one year and under two years of age were 381, as compared with 440 for July, 1893,— a decrease of over 11 per cent. For August the figures are equally suggestive, there being a decrease in the one-year class from 1,152 to 1,086, and in the two-year class from 402 to 265. This last decrease represents a ratio as high as 34 per cent, and as every mother knows the dangers attending the second year of infant life, the figures have a very direct bearing on what I must call the preventive average of infant mortality. I think I may safely claim that much of the diminished aggregate of children's deaths which happily distinguishes the summer of 1893 from that of 1894 has been due to the establishment of the pure-milk depots, and the very large decrease in August of deaths among children between one and two years of age would be quite unintelligible without this explanation. I make these assertions, not for the purpose of claiming personal credit for a work which has yielded me more pleasure than I can well describe, but with the hope that others may be tempted to enter the same field. It is much too large a field for any one man or organization to fill, but I have written to very little purpose if I have not shown it to be one in which there may be gathered a most abundant return for well-doing.

By way of divesting the public mind of the idea that sterilized milk was a medicated compound, and in order to supply poor people with a wholesome and strengthening summer beverage, I obtained permission to open booths for its sale in the public parks. There were nine of these, and soon I found that the demand for sterilized milk at a cent a glass was so great as to transcend the resources of my laboratory. This I had occasion to reinforce by the provision of another apparatus elsewhere for the preparation of one of the infant foods; but even then I was compelled to have recourse to the Appleberg Company for a supply of sterilized milk for sale at the park booths. Desirous as this company was to second my enterprise, the demand exceeded all possible supply by fully one-half, and what was lacking in the sterilized product had to be furnished in the form of raw milk from the dairies. At all of the regular depots I also sold raw milk in sealed cans. My purpose was to give a practical demonstration of the fact that pure milk can be obtained and sold at low prices. The demonstration has, I trust, been a convincing one, and its effect has undoubtedly been to elevate the standard of the milk sold by small grocers throughout New York city. With the advent of cool weather the depots were closed, but the sterilizing laboratory will be maintained during the year, so that any one desiring to obtain the sterilized milk, either in its simple or modified form, during the winter, can do so.

At the Park depots there were sold (up to September 30) 572,150 glasses at one cent each, and in the height of the season the number of people employed was 58. The sales of milk in all of the places (depots and booths) aggregated 400,000 quarts.

I have been frequently asked as to the possibility of placing such an enterprise as the one I have outlined on a commercial basis, that is, of conducting it at least without loss. I must say that my experience sheds but little light on such a question. I set out with the definite purpose of reducing the infantile death-rate of the city, and that could be done only by dismissing all considerations of trouble or expense. Every new depot that was added necessarily increased the cost of the business, for the expense of distributing the sterilized milk for babies to the branch depots was about as much as the price charged for it. The work, in short, as conducted, was one in which the only possible gain was that of human lives; but that is surely a gain to which all commercial and economical considerations must be held to be subordinate.

My work could undoubtedly be duplicated at a very much lower cost than it entailed. I had but little experience to guide me in arranging the details of the business, and the high price of milk which was a consequence of the summer drought, no less than the unexpected magnitude of the demands made by my customers, contributed to the increase of expense which in the future might be avoided.   Pure milk in its natural form could probably be sold without loss from one great depot situated close to the point of delivery by rail or steamer, at prices slightly higher than those which I established.   Milk in the sterilized form, put up in bottles for use in the nursery, would cost, on a commercial basis, quite double the prices paid for it at my depots.

I beg leave to repeat here what I have elsewhere said, that I consider the furnishing of pure milk the most important benevolent undertaking with which I have been connected, and I may be pardoned for referring with some personal satisfaction to the fact that my New York experiment has been in all of its details repeated with most satisfactory results in Yonkers and Philadelphia.

NATHAN STRAUS.

THE WAGE–EARNERS' LOSS DURING THE DEPRESSION.

IT is assumed in certain quarters that the wage-earner during the industrial depression has suffered beyond all recent precedent and more than any other class of people. Some think that his condition has been going from bad to worse so long, that the present social system is in serious peril, while a few do not hesitate to say that an industrial revolution is close upon us. The advocates of various social reforms or of social revolution, under whatever title they may be known, whether socialists, rationalists, populists, defenders of the single tax, or anarchists, point to the hardships of the wage-earner as evidence of their contention. And above all this din we hear the clamor of politicians of all parties over the terrible condition of labor. Governor McKinley recently said at Bangor, Me.: "Industry has been practically stopped. Labor has found little employment, and when it has been employed it has been at greatly reduced wages.' And this distinguished leader was saying only what has been uttered in equally strong terms by newspapers of high rank and from pulpits and platforms all over the country.

Now I think many citizens who have themselves shared in the losses of the industrial depression, either from the shrinkage of values, the diminution of profits, reduced salaries, lower rates of interest or idle money, smaller dividends and outright failures, are nevertheless more concerned about the sufferings of the wage-earners of the country than about their own losses. For the margin between income and cost of living among the laboring classes is often so small at the best that any reduction of income tells with unusual force. I venture, therefore, to give some results of an inquiry that I have made for my own enlightenment, and I do it more willingly because in all that I have read about the effect of the depression on the wage-earners, I do not recall any presentation of what appear to me to be some of the more important points of view.

The condition of the wage-earner in the manufactures of Massachusetts in 1893 is chosen for study because it is in this State and for this particular year that we have the fullest and most trustworthy information, and because it is commonly held that industries of this class have suffered beyond many if not most others. Though the conservatism of the manufacturer in Massachusetts may put him in better condition than the manufacturer in some other States, yet we may regard Massachusetts in this respect as fairly representative. It is certain that essentially the same principles of study will apply to most manufacturing sections of the country, and some of them to the entire United States, and it is my especial object to point to these principles.

Beginning with 1886, Massachusetts has published annually a remarkably valuable series of reports on her manufactures. The report for 1893, lately issued, is, so far as I know, the first report of the kind in the country that touches a year of panic and industrial depression. Returns were made from 4,570 establishments. They cover the production of goods in the 75 leading industries of the State to the value of $606,882,976, or more than 96 per cent of the value of all the goods made in the State as reported in its thorough census of 1885. No less than 4,397 of these establishments made returns in 1892 also, thus affording a basis for a fair comparison of the industrial situation in these two years.

We naturally turn first to the subject of employment. The largest number of persons at work in any one month of 1893 was in April, and was 319,818. There was a slight falling off in May, a considerable decrease in June, a much greater one in July, while in August and especially in September the loss reached great proportions. There were only 248,404 at work in September, or only 78 per cent of the number employed in April. In October there was a partial return to work, when 270,972 were employed, with a steady though small increase the rest of the year, leaving about 15 per cent of the high numbers at work in April idle during the last three months of 1893.

The unemployed were most numerous in the carpet industry, being 63 per cent in September, 28 per cent in October, and more than 17 per cent the rest of the year. In the leather industry they were 34 per cent in August, 35 per cent in September, and 22 per cent in December. In the manufacture of boots and shoes, one-fifth were out of work from August through the rest of the year. In the making of machinery 16 per cent of the number at work in April were idle in August, and 26 per cent in December.

Next comes the effect on wages. The total amount paid in wages in all these 4,397 establishments that reported in both years was $127,286,397 in 1893 against a total of $137,972,501 in the former year. This gives a loss of $10,686,104, or 8 per cent in the wages of a single year, although one-third of it had been as prosperous as preceding years. The Report says: "The average annual earnings per individual, without regard to sex or age, employed in the 75 industries, were $450.59 in 1892, declining to $434.17 in 1893, a decrease of 3.64 per cent." Caution is needed because of certain elements that vary from year to year, the chief of which are the relative number of males and females, of adults and children, and of day and piece hands. But the allowances do not prevent fair and instructive comparisons, if we assume that the 7.75 per cent of loss in total wages probably more nearly represents the actual loss in annual earnings, and remember the general upward tendency of wages. Nor should the reader forget that comparisons of daily or weekly wages are now abandoned by the best statisticians for the better basis of annual earnings, and earnings of the family are preferred to earnings of the individual as a basis for comparison. Unfortunately the latter method is not yet adopted in the annual reports.

But we may get a fairly good idea of the losses if we take annual earnings in a few typical industries: The wage-earner suffered most in making worsted goods. Here his average annual earnings fell from $369.26 to $244.08, or 34 per cent in a single year. The next heaviest loss was 5.45 per cent in making carpetings. In woollen goods the operative earned 4.8 per cent less than in 1892, or $371 against $389.54. The employee in the cotton mill got off with a loss of only 0.69 per cent in annual earnings, receiving $343.68 against $345.99 in 1892. In no other considerable industry did the average wage-earner meet so little loss in wages in 1893 as in the making of cotton goods.

The loss of time in the operation of the various industries is a matter of interest, too, because it shows the opportunity offered the wage-earner. In all industries this loss averaged 20.5 days out of the 306 possible in Massachusetts outside Sundays and legal holidays. Or, to put it in another way, the mills ran 276.4 days against 297.8 in 1892. Here, as might be expected, the greatest loss of time was in the carpet industry, whose mills were closed 56 more days in 1893 than in 1892. In woollens, the increase in idle time was 37 days; "in cotton, woollen, and other textiles," 49; and even the cotton mills lost 23 days more than in 1892. There were still longer periods of idleness in a few industries of lesser importance. As a whole, the establishments were run to only 59 per cent of their productive capacity in 1893, against 69 per cent in 1892.

Here, then, we find in a year whose first three months were as prosperous as usual, that a large number were out of employment— at one time 22 per cent of those at work in the best month; that there was a loss of nearly $11,000,000 in wages, or 7.75 per cent, and of 20.5 days in opportunity for work, while the actual idle time was still greater. These conditions enlarged the opportunities or necessities of the beggar and the tramp, and increased the temptations of the idle and the sufferings of the very poor. The account is a sad one, especially if we " leave these figures to tell their own story," as many are inclined to do.

But it is just this to which I object. Nothing can be more harmful or more unscientific than to be content with what popular leaders frequently call "a simple statement" of this kind. For the real meaning of these figures is not understood or even suspected until we go farther with them. Let us first turn them about so that we can see their counterparts, for, as has been said, "the knowledge of opposites is one."

If there were nearly or quite $11,000,000 less to be divided among the wage-earners in the 75 leading manufacturing industries of Massachusetts in 1893 than in 1892, or a loss of 7.75 per cent, then the complementary statement brings out the sum which they did get. It shows that there remained for the average man, woman, and child more than 92 per cent as much as there was paid in wages in 1892. The average annual earnings were more than 96 per cent as much, but we will not, for reasons already given, press this last figure. There may have been more uneven distribution, with severe reductions and downright want, as we know there was. But the great wage fund was kept up to 92 per cent of its amount in 1892.

Then, in the matter of employment, the picture is not altogether a dark one. For if in September, the month of greatest idleness, there were out of work 22 per cent of those at work in April, the best month of that year, this leaves 78 per cent still employed at a time when—besides the depression in business—vacation, repairs, and other similar special causes combined to keep many mills idle. And I think many will be surprised when they learn that the average number of persons at work in all these industries taken together, in the last three months of 1893, directly after the month of

extreme idleness, was seven-eighths the number having employment
in the last and most prosperous quarter of 1892. Yet such is the
fact, as any one may see for himself if he will work out the percentages. In other words, the great body of wage-earners in Massachusetts were kept at work when the depression was most severe, earning
in the course of the year nine-tenths of what they got the year before.[1]

Such a part of the real story should not go untold. Thanksgiv-
ing for remaining blessings is always a wholesome exercise amid loss
and trial. Yet many have never considered these complementary
facts at all. Even popular guides ignore them. We can afford to
smile at the extravagant utterances of such men as Coxey and Debs,
who hold the unemployed so close to their eyes that they cannot see
anybody else at all. But what shall we say of grave statesmen who
talk in language like the following? I quote from a recent speech of
Senator Hoar, as reported in the Boston " Transcript." He was addressing his own townsmen and speaking of the industries of their
own city of Worcester and of Massachusetts:

"The workmen have left the mill for the highway. The farmer and the
merchant are alike out of work. The statesmanship that lighted the furnace has
been succeeded by the statesmanship that builds soup-houses. The sturdy
demand of organized labor, proud, defiant, hopeful, demanding better wages,
more leisure, and better opportunity, has given place to the whine of the mendi-
cant and the sneaking footstep of the thief. The furnace fire has gone out, and
the incendiary fire is lighted. The hum of the factory is succeeded by the hum-
bug of the Democratic platform."

So far we have compared 1893 with the remarkably prosperous
year of 1892. We should next find the place of 1893 in the larger
periods of industrial movement. This will give us more light, but
I will not go into details. It is enough to say that the average earnings of the Massachusetts wage-earning population in 1893 were
larger than those of any other year since these reports were first made
in 1886, excepting only the two years of 1891 and 1892. Comparing returns from identical establishments, there was an advance in
annual earnings from $392.36 in 1886 to $452.21 in 1892. The
greatest increase was in 1891, after the tariff of October, 1890, and
perhaps in part due to its stimulus. A study of the fluctuations of
the wage scale of the " Report of the Senate Finance Committee"
shows a similar result. In other words the average wage-earner in
Massachusetts was better off in 1893 than in most former years, in

[1] In the good year of 1891, no less than 31,262 persons *in all occupations*, not
manufactures alone, were, on the average, idle 4.38 months.

spite of the depression of industry. Unfortunately no figures are yet available for 1894, nor of prices in 1892 and 1893. But the upward tendency at the close of 1893 toward greater employment is thought by most whom I have consulted to have been maintained since, though some think business dropped off in the summer before the revival in September, 1894. Wages probably have fallen more than in 1893.

The Report of the Senate Finance Committee has, however, pretty clearly shown that the general movement of prices is clearly downward, while the general direction of wages is strongly upward. The laborer thus always gets partial return for his loss in wages by the quicker fall of prices as soon as a panic or depression comes on. That the rise of wages does not necessarily carry up labor cost has long been asserted as a theory of political economy. It is now practically a settled fact. In Massachusetts the wage cost declined from 22.62 per cent of the selling price in 1886 to 21.66 per cent in 1893, or about 4.5 per cent as between the two years. As the base of comparison, the selling price, tends downward, this decline in labor cost is all the more significant.

We have thus looked at the condition of the wage-earner in 1893 on the positive side, and in comparison with the prosperous year immediately preceding and the period of eight or ten years to which 1893 belongs, and referred to the trend of prices which comes in to mitigate the severity of hard times. Let us now briefly consider the present period itself as it is related to the wider range of a half century or more. For this purpose the first Report of Mr. Wright as United States Commissioner of Labor is useful. It was made in 1886, just as business began to recover from the depression of 1883. Among the conclusions reached by the Commissioner of Labor at the end of his Report, two or three throw much light upon our present subject.

The first of these can be stated in the words of the Report itself: " It has been clearly shown that the depressions of the past in the manufacturing nations of the world have been nearly or quite contemporaneous in their concurrence." A table illustrates this conclusion. It arranges the crises and depressions in the United States and Europe by countries and years, showing that from 1837 downward this proposition has been increasingly true. Sometimes a variation of a year or two appears in the response of one or two countries to the general financial condition. The trouble sometimes begins in one country and thence reaches the rest in a year or two. But nothing but a war or other very exceptional condition seems to arrest the movement in its advance to all the great industrial nations.   Then, as most know, these depressions since 1837 occur with the greatest regularity every ten years, with a financial panic once in twenty years The years of distress are 1837, 1847, 1857, 1867 (showing only a slight disturbance), 1873, 1883, and now in 1893.   The great wars here and the condition of Europe carried us by until 1873.

Then, as to the causes of the troubles.   Speaking of 1857, the Report says: " Speculation, extension of credit, and all the usual accompaniments of financial disturbances ushered in the period."   And of that of 1873 we read:

"There had been a period of excessive speculation, especially in railroads and real estate; large failures following that of Jay Cooke, inflation of the currency, high protective tariff, large immigration, and the unnatural stimulus given to industry by the War, brought the monetary affairs of the country to a crisis, resulting in general distrust, fall of prices, and all the train of evils which follow such crises."

Of the depression of 1883 the Report said:

"The extent of the depression has not been so great as the popular mind conceived it.   An industrial depression is a mental and moral malady, which seizes the public mind after the first influences of the depression are materially or physically felt. . . . The severity of the present depression, while real and tangible, should be considered as in part moral in its influences."

Both a financial crisis and an industrial depression were, therefore, due to arrive in 1893, affecting the great manufacturing countries of the world, and brought about by the usual general causes reinforced by the special conditions that vary somewhat in different panics and depressions.   The wage-earner of to-day consequently must look at his condition as it appears in this larger perspective.   It may temper his judgment as to the extraordinary condition in which he now thinks that he is, though it may lead to serious reflections upon the currents beneath the waves that disturb us all.

Some notion of the comparative severity of the various periods of financial disaster may be gained if we compare the movement of the liabilities in the failures of critical years in the United States.   In round numbers they were $292,000,000 in 1857, dropping to $97,000,000 the next year.   They were $228,000,000 in 1873, averaging about $200,000,000 for six years during the adjustment to the specie basis.   Then they were again below $100,000,000, but in 1883 were $226,000,000, dropping to $124,000,000 the next year. But in 1893 they rose to $331,000,000.   The volume of business, however, has perhaps more than doubled since 1873, and of course is vastly greater than in 1857.   Certainly we know that in Massachusetts capital employed in manufacturing increased 48 per cent, and the value of products 29 per cent, in the ten years preceding 1885; and the rate of increase afterward was still greater.   In the first half of 1894 the liabilities in the failures of the United States were $101,578,152, as against $168,644,434 in the same half of 1893. We may then say that the distress of 1893 is hardly beyond all precedent, if indeed it has been as severe as in one or two earlier periods.

The movement of wages in these times of depression has become pretty well known.   It shows a marked rise of wages in the three years preceding the crisis of 1857, and that a slight fall came after it.   The scale, calculated on a gold basis, stood at 91.8 in 1853, and at 99.9 in 1857 before the panic affected it.   Before the great crisis of 1873, the scale indicated 133.7 in 1870, and 152.2 in 1872.   The rate usually holds up awhile after the panic begins, but falls later. Wages had fallen to 139.9 in 1879, rising to 152.7 in 1883, and dropping to 150.7 in 1885.   The last sharp rise began in 1889, and the index stood at 160.7 in 1891—the last year included in the Report. We may expect that it rose somewhat higher in 1892, and nearly held its own in 1893.   The movement of annual earnings in Massachusetts certainly supports this opinion.   Whether wages can be maintained without much loss, after a panic, as was the case in 1857, appears doubtful at least.   The aggressiveness and organization of labor are offset by the fact of the high point on the scale now reached.

I have not entered upon the important part of the field directly affecting the capitalist, though touching it in the matter of failures. The workingman should not forget that capital has shrunk in value; that dividends have been passed or diminished, or paid out of past accumulations; that profits have been less or disappeared, and the returns of interest upon invested securities have been small.   The capitalist may be better able to endure his severe losses than the workingman his idleness and lower wages, but he nevertheless in most cases suffers with him.   And let us remember that in the main we have dealt with the employee in manufactures, in which the working-people are held to suffer more than in most industries except in mining and transportation.   Generally working-people give so much attention to organized labor that they forget that this includes only a section of their own class, and that in turn is a small part of the grand army of toilers in the whole country.

This line of study leads us to see that the present real distress of the wage-earner, great as it may be, is neither out of all proportion to that of other periods, nor so extensive as to make us despair either of his own future or of that of the country. The vast majority of laboring people in the varied industries of Massachusetts, as well as in her manufactures, are neither going to the almshouse nor losing the greater part of their usual income as yet. The cheapest labor suffers most where the margin between income and necessary cost of living is smallest, and ignorance is content to live slovenly and from hand to mouth. Yet even in the lowest-paid industry of the State—in the cotton mills, where a lower class of operatives are found, and the great majority are women and children, and more than two from a family are usually at work—the average annual earnings in 1893 were $343.60 for each individual. With the low average of two wage-earners to each family, the income will, to say the least, compare favorably with that of farm-hands and many other classes.

The industrial situation, then, is not such as would lead us to despair. It is apparently as essentially sound and on the whole as healthy as it has been. Capital and Labor are riding together upon the waves which carry them up and down in an apparently rhythmic succession. The plunge follows the ascent, but the descent is not to continue forever. As things are, it must be accepted at its true value. Whether these successions are to continue or to be reduced to lesser proportions is a great problem. What is their cause is not clear. It may be in the adjustment of the economic material and mechanism. It may be in the hidden psychic factors of our civilization, pointing to a profound meaning in the characterization of Mr. Wright that an industrial depression is chiefly a mental and moral malady. But whatever the cause may be, it seems to me wise that the wage-earner—and everybody else, too—should learn to see his own distress in some sort of proper relation to the large movements with which it is inseparably connected.

This suggests a final consideration, which I think is worth serious attention. It is that, for the first time in a generation, a great industrial depression has come upon us at the precise time when it could be used as a makeshift in partisan politics by those who hitherto were interested in reassuring the people regarding their industrial troubles. Every motive of party interest affecting the politicians of the Republican party in 1873 and in 1883 made them anxious to allay excitement and restore confidence in the general soundness of industrial conditions.   But the rise of the tariff question, and the transfer of political power in 1892, wrought a great change.   For the first time since the War, the steady, honest, religious people, who are probably in the North more largely in the Republican party than in any other, have for the first time been stirred by their party leaders to magnify the evils of the industrial troubles of a disastrous year.   It has been easy to make a host of these and other people sincerely believe that these are the worst times they ever knew, and that political changes have been the chief cause of all their distress.   Those powerful influences which formerly were always found on the side of courageous hopefulness have for two years been thrown into the other scale. Probably no President since Lincoln met so difficult and complicated a problem as that which really confronted Mr. Cleveland at the beginning of his second administration in 1893.   The party which, in its constituency, principles, and practice, was best fitted for constructive work, has been transformed by defeat into a party of hostile criticism and obstruction, while its place is taken by one that had long been unused to power and was more experienced in the arts of opposition than in conservative progress.   Add to this state of things the disturbing elements of the socialistic movement in its various forms, and the chances of sane thought among the people on political and economic subjects have been seriously lessened.   The essential soundness of our political and industrial system has received stronger illustration than one might at first think, though the blighting effects of the partisanship of politics are keenly felt.   Indeed, if we learn to look more below the surface of things and farther out into their broad relations, the experience may not, after all, be too dearly bought.

SAMUEL W. DIKE.

FACTS TOUCHING A REVIVAL OF BUSINESS.

IT cannot be questioned that the severity of the panic of 1893 in the United States was increased by the doubts felt regarding the outcome of the silver and currency problems then actively under discussion, problems not yet fully solved. But aside from these reasons for financial anxiety peculiar to the United States, the widespread commercial depression reaching to every country of the civilized world indicated that general forces were at work whose effects would no doubt in any case have been traceable in America. To analyze a panic and show its causes is one of the most difficult of things, yet it is permissible to make one or two general statements under whose terms many minor causes may be covered. Perhaps "overvaluation" is the best single expression to explain so complicated a matter as the reasons for the panic of last year. In all quarters of the commercial world enterprises had become overvalued as regards the possible profits. This overvaluation may have come about through various causes. No doubt in the United States the tariff has been a minor factor. While industries in a new country must, from the nature of the case, be more speculative—using that word in its good sense— than in older and more settled lands, a highly protective tariff gives to business an additional uncertainty. If the census figures for manufacturing be accepted as approximately correct, the comparison of 1890 with 1880 shows interesting changes. While during this decade the population of the country increased, roughly, 25 per cent, the capital employed in manufacturing increased 121 per cent, and the value of the whole manufactured output 69 per cent. Having regard to the fall in the prices during this period, it is probable that the manufactured articles embraced in the census tables increased in quantity more than three times faster than the population. For this unduly stimulated activity the tariff is in small part, at least, responsible.

But the great factor in this increase of production in the United States as well as in other nations has undoubtedly been the more extended use of credit. The machinery for the collection and lending of money to business men has been brought to much greater perfection of late years, and there has been increasing willingness to lend

credits either in the form of money or of goods up to a larger proportion of the assumed value of the business than was formerly the
case. Those who had and even those who had not knowledge of
some particular industry, or those who saw chances for making money
in some scheme, found no difficulty in borrowing the greater part and
sometimes the whole of the capital necessary to enter upon the pursuit. Some of the census returns upon the true value of the real and
personal property in the United States will serve for a striking illustration of this extended use of credits. The North Atlantic States,
which are stated to contain one-third of the whole national wealth,
increased the value of their real and personal property from 1880
to 1890 almost exactly in proportion to their increase in population
—about 16 per cent. Montana, on the other hand, by the investment
of outside capital—that is, by means of credit—increased its wealth
1,000 per cent, an advance three times greater than its growth in
population. Colorado, a State often in the popular mind, in like
manner increased the value of the property within its boundaries
about 380 per cent, an increase more than twice greater than the
population. In these two typical Western States there is to-day going
on a further shifting of values on account of the changes in mining
and agricultural industries which do not yet seem to be complete.
Thus, by means of the abundance of credit, business in all branches
throughout the world became overdone. For a time production has
outstripped consumption. A fall in prices and in profits made necessary a revaluation of the properties and franchises involved, with the
consequent loss in many cases to both lender and borrower. The
effect of these general forces was heightened by the discoveries of new
methods of manufacturing in many lines of business, which so reduced
the cost of production as to render invested capital almost worthless.

Credit panics, we are told, come in cycles: it is certainly true
that the industrial advances of the modern world are due to the employment of credit,—a most efficient force, but one which we have
not yet learned how to control within safe limits. Following the discovery that the general business of the world had been overdone, and
that the range of values was too high, came liquidation; that is,
every one tried under pressure to pay off his debts. One way of accomplishing this was by the forced sale of such articles as were
available for that purpose. One reason for the low price of staple
commodities, noticeable of late years, lies in such forced sales. These
efforts resulted in the disasters of 1893.

The period after a panic is essentially one of readjustment of business to the changed conditions.   Whether this readjustment will continue for a long or a short time, or whether it will bear severely or mildly upon the community, are matters about which no one can prophesy.   The results depend upon the circumstances of each case, together with the combined effect upon business in general.   Of one thing we are sure: there is no doubt of the ultimate outcome.   The agricultural, mineral, and other resources of the United States are so great, and the natural intelligence and activity of our people so pronounced, that when once the level under the new conditions is found we shall have a period of prosperity in the United States such as perhaps was never before seen.   But while this is likely to prove true as a general prophecy, it is, after all, the individual men, the special company or the particular enterprise, with which business men and investors are most concerned, and in such cases it cannot yet be said that the capitalists have settled down to a belief in the permanency of present values in all instances.   It is this feeling of doubt regarding the future of particular enterprises during this period of readjustment which keeps money lying idle in the banks and makes the rate of interest on safe security so low in all the money centres of the world.

The low prices of many of our staple agricultural products make a serious factor in our problem.   It may be that wheat (for illustration) will continue low in price under ordinary crops for some time to come.   It is probably true that the United States will be found in the long run producing wheat as cheaply as any country; but agriculture, proverbially the slowest of all the great industries to yield to changes in the industrial situation, is particularly so in countries like India, Russia, and the Argentine Republic.   No one can tell how long it may be before the wheat supplies in those countries will fall off because of the loss of profit under continued low prices. Meanwhile new factors, such as the building of the Trans-Siberian Railway, are constantly coming up, whose effect upon the wheat supply of the world it is impossible to foresee.   As to the American farmer under these circumstances, it is to be said that the prices of the things he buys have fallen in something like the same proportion as the things he sells.   It is difficult to say whether, on the whole, he is worse off than he was five years ago; and, if so, whether his real loss of income is at all serious.   The Western farmer had one dubious advantage over his brother the storekeeper, in that his land was always available for greater borrowing.   The agriculturist who has gone into farming of late years, mainly on credit, or whose land is not in the fertile sections, may find it hard to make both ends meet. If so, in time he must give place to others who have better resources or have used better judgment.   But such a process requires time and presupposes some loss.

The Southern planter is, generally speaking, in better condition to meet a period of depression than before, in spite of the fact that cotton is low in price.   The wasteful methods under which cotton-planting was conducted entirely on credit at a cost of 15 or 25 per cent interest annually, are slowly giving way to new measures of financing and of cultivating the crop, which admit of a small profit though at low prices, a thing never before thought possible.   The Southern farmer, the present year, has grown corn enough for his own use, and in similar ways is more independent than formerly.   The railways may not earn so much, but the Southern people themselves will be found in better financial circumstances.   The pressure of a possible production beyond the consumptive demand is felt perhaps more severely in manufacturing than in any other line of industry.   Readjustment here will very likely be more prolonged, and may carry greater changes.   The discovery of cheap iron ore in the Mesabi regions of northern Michigan, for example, has brought the ironworks along the Atlantic coast face to face with the problem of existence. However the question may be solved, neither the Western nor the Southern nor the Eastern ironmaster is likely to yield easily.   Upon this question of the best location for the assembling of all materials which enter into the manufacture of iron depend other questions of importance, such as the continued supplying of coal, dry-goods, and other merchandise.

One result of the depression will be an increase in the tendency toward large corporations.   To manufacturers and business men confronted with a loss of trade both in volume and profit, a natural remedy is a combination which shall extract from the small volume of trade a profit large enough to compensate all the members.   So far as such a combination attempts to give badly located or poorly equipped factories a gain to which they are not economically entitled, the result in most cases must be merely a postponement of the inevitable.   But there are legitimate reasons for the formation of large companies; experience is showing that only in this way can the best results be obtained.   Although at first the consuming public be not allowed to share in the advantages of the combination through a re-

duction in the price of the product, yet such is likely to be the ultimate result, either through the workings of natural forces or by legislation.   But the point now to be considered is that until the dis-
tressed producers accept their losses and reorganize their business, or
take advantage of the temporary remedy of combination and thus put
themselves upon a financial basis which shall seem sound for a time,
the capitalist will be timid about loaning them large sums of money.
Of course the majority of our manufacturers, who have been prosperous and will be prosperous again, need have no fear so soon as
their strong position is recognized.

The reluctance of the capitalist to invest his money in commercial
enterprises until the readjustment shall seem to be over, is the important feature of the present year.   Indeed, in spite of comparatively large profits shown by many small enterprises in the years
previous to 1893, there has been of late a steady decrease in the returns received by investors in our large industries.   The railroads,
for example, have been carrying a growing volume of traffic with a
declining rate of earnings until transportation has become, commercially speaking, unprofitable.   This has come about, not so much by
the increase in the wages paid employees—though that must be considered—as by the continuous decline in the rates of freight, a decline
carried by competition and by legislation beyond all reason.   Nor is
stock- and bond-watering a satisfactory explanation of the small
average return now received on railway capital.   Roads built a dozen
or more years ago were commercially entitled to such an increase in
value as was obtained by neighboring industries in their territory.
Whether these companies pay high returns on small capital, or lower
returns on an increased capitalization, is immaterial: at any rate, of
late years railway earnings per mile of road have shown a continual
decrease.   It seems almost hopeless to expect a return of full prosperity until the question of the commercial right of the railway owner
to a profit is in the way of being settled.   It may be that an increase
in railway net income will come simultaneously with an increase in
the profitableness of the majority of our industries.

. The comparative steadiness of prices in the bond and share markets up to this time, and the reports of the improved volume of
business during the fall, tend to confirm the opinion already expressed
that the general basis of business values in the United States has not
been disastrously affected by the panic of last year, and that when
the readjustment is complete we shall again have a period of pros-

perity.   There is no doubt, too, that a large proportion of the firms and corporations in the United States will come out of the business depression without loss of credit.   This belief is the foundation for the present high range of quotations for the bonds of such companies as are considered to be beyond doubt.   But these high prices for " gilt-edged" securities are of themselves sufficient to deter investors from buying such bonds heavily, even supposing that they could be readily obtained—which is far from being the case.   There is no doubt also that many of the bonds and stocks now selling at low prices will advance in price when the majority of people believe that the commercial situation is settling down into normal conditions again. But until normal times approach, low-priced shares and mortgages may not appreciate greatly.   The difficulty here is the same as that already indicated, that there is uncertainty in the minds of the majority of investors as to the immediate future of the particular firms and companies whose commercial paper or bonds or shares such persons or institutions may be inclined to buy.   There may be doubt whether particular firms have not been overtrading; whether certain railways have not been capitalized too highly for the rate of profit which they are now obtaining on their traffic; and, in the case of large corporations of every kind, whether they are not arranging their accounts so as to show a paper profit from the year's operation while really borrowing money to meet deficiencies.   From the point of view of the money-lender, it does not alter the case to say that in many instances this latter policy is being pursued with the best of motives, and with confidence on the part of the managers or directors that if the period of depression can be tided over by the use of long-established credit, a few prosperous years will put the company back into its old position of soundness.   The purchaser of evidences of indebtedness, while believing, as he does and must, in the future of the general business of the United States, ought at the same time to be careful at this particular juncture to see that his money is loaned to companies which have, besides a fair prospect for the future, a really sound basis for credit during the period of dull trade.   The investor or the speculator who buys bonds or shares without this investigation may lose the whole or a part of his money; on the other hand, he who makes such careful investigation and buys with sound judgment at the time when the danger of failure is seen to be past, will unquestionably reap benefits from the general prosperity which, at some future time, all good judges are agreed, will bless our country.

The Forum

DECEMBER, 1894.

THE "BALTIMORE PLAN" OF CURRENCY REFORM.

THERE is a consensus of opinion that our currency-system,—or better, want of system,—is wrong. All political parties, all commercial interests, all labor interests, the debtor and the creditor agree that our currency system is ill-conceived, unresponsive to the various interests of our great nation, and prejudicial to renewed and stable prosperity. Here, however, harmony of opinion ceases.

Let us analyze our currency and the proposed remedies, which are various. There were in circulation on November 1, nine different kinds of money, nearly equally divided into gold, silver, and paper, classified as follows:

Gold Coin	$500,181,380
Standard Silver Dollars	56,443,670
Subsidiary Silver	60,242,999
Gold Certificates	64,252,069
Silver Certificates	331,143,301
Treasury Notes, Act July 14, 1890	122,715,396
United States Notes	280,474,705
Currency Certificates	54,045,000
National-Bank Notes	202,594,902
Total	$1,672,093,422

The gold currency needs no comment, for it is the currency of the nations, passing by weight and fineness.

Oldest of our paper money is the greenback—fiat money, pure and simple—issued by the Government and made a "legal tender at face value for all debts public and private except duties on imports and interest on the public debt," and used to defray the expenses of the war. In June, 1864, the volume of greenbacks reached $447,·

300,203. Everybody recognized them as a forced loan, justified only by the exigencies of the war; and on December 18, 1865, Congress, by resolution, approved the policy and plan then pursued by Secretary McCulloch for retiring them. The amount was reduced to $346,681,016, in 1878, when Congress forbade further contraction.

Next in point of age comes the national-bank note. President Lincoln, in his message to Congress in 1862, strongly seconded the recommendation of Secretary Chase to create a national banking system. Accordingly an act was passed in 1863 and revised in 1864. As a measure of currency reform it did not commend itself to Congress, as is shown by the debates and the votes. The national-banks were created, with authority to issue circulation based upon Government bonds, for the sole purpose of furnishing a market for such bonds, and thus enabling the Government to meet the financial exigencies incident to the war. This law was supplemented by a tax of 10 per cent imposed upon State-bank circulation in March, 1864. The national-banks rapidly increased, became large purchasers and permanent holders of Government bonds, and absorbed them from the market, thus appreciating their price and strengthening the credit of the Government. The plenitude and comparative cheapness of bonds and their high rate of interest rendered circulation profitable. This law accomplished the purpose for which it was created, but its framers did not contemplate providing a currency adapted to the wants of a great nation, nor did they succeed in so doing. These notes are receivable for all dues to the United States "except duties on imports," and for all payments by the United States "except interest on the public debt, and in redemption of the national currency," and are legal payment to national-banks.

The first coinage act of this country, in 1792, provided for the coinage of gold and silver at the ratio of 15 to 1, which ratio undervalued silver. In 1834 the amount of fine gold in the dollar was reduced so as to make the ratio 15.988 to 1. By this change the commercial value of the silver dollar exceeded the gold dollar, and logically the silver dollar was not coined and did not circulate. No one cared to avail himself of the free-coinage privilege so long as it took more than a dollar's worth of silver to make a dollar, and Congress in 1873 abolished the silver dollar, which had at no time, since 1834, entered into circulation. The development of trans-continental railways brought the vast mineral fields of the Rockies into market, and the production of silver enormously increased. Very soon after 1873 the commercial value of the two dollars changed places, silver rapidly declining.   Then came the cry, for the restoration of free coinage, from the mining interests, supported by that portion of our people that always favors more money.   They demanded the restoration of the free-coinage of silver in order that they might take to the mint less than a dollar's worth of silver and receive a legal tender dollar coin therefor.   This demand and the attendant political agitation resulted in a compromise measure in 1878, popularly known as the Bland Act, which was enacted into law over the President's veto.   Under its provisions the Government became a purchaser of silver bullion, and was obliged to coin from two million to four million dollars worth every month.   The coinage aggregated $378,166,795, and was coaxed into circulation by means of silver certificates, now in use, which are "receivable for customs, taxes, and all public dues." The coinage of this vast volume of depreciated silver alarmed the business interests, which sought relief through repeal.   The result was another compromise with free-coinage, July 14, 1890, whereby the Government purchased monthly a still larger volume of silver (4,500,000 ounces), stored it instead of coining it, and issued Treasury notes therefor, which were made a full legal tender.

These notes represented a gold dollar's worth of silver at the time of issue, and to that extent were better than the dollar coined under the act of 1878 which was at no time commercially worth its face value.   The rapidly growing premium upon bonds lessened the profit upon circulation, and induced a gradual contraction of bank-notes. This contraction disturbed those who believed that currency should keep pace with increasing population and commerce.   It alarmed those who always clamor for more money, believing that its plenitude has a stimulating effect upon the prosperity of a people.   It was this sentiment that forbade the further redemption of greenbacks, and was instrumental in forcing the passage of the Bland law in 1878, and compelled the acceptance of the compromise act in 1890, instead of absolute repeal.   The repeal came in 1893, wrung from an unwilling Congress by the business suffering of the country.

Our fractional silver coin was made subsidiary by Act of 1853 and is now legal tender to an amount not exceeding ten dollars.   The following statistics from the Mint Bureau, October 1, 1894, present the statement and the argument as to our silver legislation:

Total coinage of silver dollars under Act of February 28, 1878...... $378,166,793
Total cost of silver bullion used in such coinage...................   308,279,262

Seigniorage, or apparent profit.................................... $69,887,531
Bullion value of silver used in such coinage at present prices....... 186,207,289
Difference between actual cost and bullion value at present......... 122,071,972
Bullion purchased under Act of July 14, 1890, cost................. 155,931,002
Market value of such bullion at present market price............ .. 107,832,937
Depreciation in value of same 48,098,965

From these statistics it appears that, in addition to the more serious damage to general business and to our credit as a nation, our
silver legislation represents a loss to the people of this country, from
depreciation in value, of $170,170,937. That sum represents the
price of our homage to silver. It is in sharp contrast to the $73,-
000,000 paid into the Treasury by national banks as a tax on
circulation and more than $70,000,000 as a tax on deposits.

Note the inflexibility of this currency. Fixed amounts were
arbitrarily added each month, and. however great the stringency,
they could not be increased, nor, however great the plethora of
money, could they be withheld. And, since the Government can
put out money in exchange only for value or in payment for debt,
no Government currency can be flexible, elastic and responsive to the
varying wants of trade.

Having briefly sketched our currency as it is, let us examine the
prominent remedies proposed.

The most formidable and dangerous of the proposed remedies is the
free-coinage of silver dollars of present weight and fineness. The ratio
has not been changed since 1834, and, since silver dollars refused to
circulate as money from that date until their coinage was discontinued
in 1873, because they were commercially worth more than gold dollars,
it may be asked, Why do gold dollars circulate as money now, when
they are commercially worth more than double the value of silver
dollars?

The parity of the gold and·silver dollar is maintained because
it is the declared policy of the Government, formulated in statute law,
to maintain it. The Government is in the banking business. It
keeps a gold reserve to maintain its credit, and United States notes
and Treasury notes are convertible into gold upon presentation. So
long as the Government was purchasing 54,000,000 ounces of silver
yearly (Act of 1890) and issuing notes therefor redeemable in gold,
the country and the world distrusted its ability to maintain a gold
basis. This distrust precipitated the panic of 1893. Now silver
purchases have ceased, but the Government has of greenbacks, Treas-

ury notes, and national-bank notes (which are convertible into lawful money) in round numbers $700,000,000 of paper money (not to mention the $331,143,301 of silver certificates), all dependent upon about $60,000,000 gold reserve and on the general confidence that the United States will redeem its obligations in as good currency as is known in the world.   The credit of the Government maintains the parity.   This same greenback that now holds the keys to the gold vaults of the Treasury was worth only thirty-five cents in gold in July, 1864.   The credit of the Government has improved.   The meagre gold reserve, coupled with the Populistic tendencies of a large portion of our people, raises a distrust, however, which is the chief barrier to renewed prosperity.

The Government is no longer asked to buy the silver product, but to make a market for it by adopting free-coinage.   The bullion value of our standard dollar is to-day 49.44 cents.   The counterfeiter no longer needs to counterfeit.   He can produce a genuine silver dollar, both as to quality as well as to form and to design, and make more than 50 per cent profit by so doing.   Our gold dollar contains 23.22 grains of pure gold.   Our silver dollar contains practically sixteen times as much pure silver, viz., 371.25 grains.   The free-coinage of the present standard dollar containing $371\frac{1}{4}$ grains of pure silver means a dollar commercially worth less than fifty cents, but by the fiat of the Government made to pass for one hundred cents. It means that the seigniorage—that is, the difference between the cost of the silver bullion in open market and the face value of the money into which it is coined—shall hereafter inure to the benefit of individuals and not of the Government.   It means that an individual may take $100 worth of silver bullion to the mint, and, coinage free, obtain silver dollars with which to pay $200 worth of debt; and it would thus mean the repudiation of 50 per cent of existing indebtedness.   The sagacious instinct of trade would correct this wrong as to future contracts by doubling the price of commodities.   It means an inflation of prices without an increase of values.   It means a silver basis—silver monometallism.   It means that the $500,000,000 of gold now in circulation would go to a premium, would cease to circulate as money, and would simply become a commodity whether coined or uncoined.   It means a contraction of our currency equal to the amount of gold which ceased to circulate as money.   It means a general unsettling of values, the demoralization of business, a great injustice to present creditors.   Just what the effect would be upon business interests for each business to have one-half of its bills-payable and one-half of its bills-receivable virtually repudiated is a matter for speculation, and I trust the good sense and honesty of the country will leave it in the realms of speculation.

Another remedy for currency ills constantly before Congress is the restoration of State-bank circulation. Currency possesses value according to the area in which it will be accepted in payment of debts. Limit the area and you impair its value. Relegate this power to the forty-four sovereignties that compose this Union and you complicate this already complex question, contravene the spirit and tendency of the age, which seeks closer alliances and broader business relations, compel commerce to halt in its career to respect an artificial obstacle—State lines—and impose upon business a wholly unnecessary embarrassment. You create a new industry—money-changing—and, as in *ante-bellum* times, our State border would be dotted with brokers' offices, prepared, for a commission, to exchange bills issued in one State for those of another. Public interest and, I think, public sentiment will not justify the creation of a currency that is not national in its money functions.

Another proposition for giving the country a safe and adequate currency has recently been formulated by the bankers of Baltimore, acting as an Association. The principles underlying the proposition are neither new nor untried, but derive added importance from the endorsement of so important and conservative a city as Baltimore. The present national-bank law requires the deposit of United States bonds with the United States Treasurer as security for circulation, and allows circulation equal to 90 per cent of the par of such bonds. It provides one central place of redemption,—the United States Treasury,—thus making the notes of all banks alike good throughout the Nation, and it requires the deposit and maintenance with the Treasurer of a 5 per cent redemption fund. It redeems upon presentation the notes of failed banks, and has a prior lien upon their assets including stockholders' liability, to reimburse itself for such payments.

The Baltimore plan proposes to amend the National-Bank Act so as no longer to require Government bonds as security for circulation, but provide a safety-fund instead; to allow banks to issue circulation to 50 per cent of their paid-up, unimpaired capital, and, in an emergency, 75 per cent. All notes of failed banks are to be redeemed by the Government, as under the present law. A guarantee-, or safety-fund, equal to 5 per cent of the outstanding circulation is to be accumulated and maintained by gradual taxation upon such circulation. From this fund the Government is to redeem notes of failed banks. The Government also retains a prior lien upon the assets of failed banks, including stockholders' liability, as now provided by law, in order to replenish this safety-fund and protect itself against possible loss. Practically, the only change is to substitute a guarantee-fund for Government bonds as security, the other changes being incidental. The details are open to discussion and improvement, but I believe the principles to be right. The Baltimore plan has nothing to do with the money of ultimate redemption, whether gold, or silver, or greenbacks. It simply provides a bank-note currency redeemable in lawful money. Bank-notes are not legal tender, and should not be. A legal-tender quality would tend to keep them in circulation, prevent their return for redemption, impair their elasticity. A bank-note is a representative of value, by mutual consent performing the office of money, called into existence by some industrial need local to the bank of issue, and should appear and disappear at the beck and nod of such industry.

The principal defect in our present bank-note currency is the want of elasticity. The inability of banks, under existing law, to supply a currency commensurate with the wants of business, has given an opportunity for false theories of finance to come to the front and to command approval. It is not hazarding much to say that, had the National-Bank Act been amended in 1865, as now proposed by the Baltimore plan, and a currency responsive to commercial needs thus made possible, the country would have been spared the greenback heresy and the more substantial and serious injury to credit and business attendant upon silver legislation.

Suppose a bank wants to take out circulation. It is obliged to buy Government bonds as a basis. Four-per-cents are the best investment, and the bank buys $100,000, costing, at present prices, $115,500. The bank is allowed to take out circulation equal to 90 per cent of par—$90,000,—and it must deposit with the United States Treasurer a 5 per cent redemption-fund—$4,500. Thus, by investing and depositing $120,000, the bank is enabled to issue $90,000 circulation. By the operation the bank locks up $30,000 and diminishes its power to aid the public and its customers by such a sum. Could the defect of the National-Bank Act as the basis for a currency system be more glaringly illustrated? The same criticism applies to all currency based upon pledged stock or bonds as security.

The value of the securities must exceed the amount of currency issued, else the security fails.   The bank must invest more money in specified securities than the amount of currency it is allowed to issue. Such currency cannot be elastic and responsive to the varying wants of trade.   Currency should be issued against all the assets of the bank, not against any specified portion.   This is done by giving the note-holder a prior lien upon the assets.   Such currency is issued against the credit of the bank, may be increased when commerce calls and will flow back into the vaults of the bank of issue when its service is no longer required.   It is elastic.   Security and elasticity are the essential qualities of a perfect currency.   The currency proposed by the Baltimore plan is secure beyond question, for the Government is required to redeem at once notes of failed banks.   The Government would incur no risk of loss on account of such redemption, for the banks would provide and maintain a 5 per cent guarantee-fund from which to make such redemptions.   This currency would be perfectly secure without any obligation on the part of the Government other than the application of the guarantee-fund.

Let us examine our own experience since the creation of the national banking system as bearing upon the safety-fund principle. I am indebted to the Comptroller of the Currency for the following:

Average annual circulation of national-banks, 1864 to 1894	$282,801,252
Outstanding circulation of failed national-banks	17,819,541
Cost to general Government on account of national-banks as shown by the books of the comptroller's office	$7,610,169
Additional estimated cost	7,732,914
	$15,343,083
Tax of one-fourth of 1 per cent for thirty-one years	$21,917,093
Tax of one-fifth of 1 per cent for thirty-one years	17,533,674

In regard to this the Comptroller says in reply to my letter:

"These figures verify your conclusion to the effect that a tax on outstanding circulation of one-fifth of 1 per cent would have repaid the cost of the national-banks to the general Government, and also that a tax of one-fourth of 1 per cent would have redeemed the notes of all failed national-banks—in fact, a tax of two-fifths of 1 per cent would have been ample to meet both the cost of that system and the redemption of the notes of failed national-banks."

If an annual tax of two-fifths of 1 per cent would suffice to defray all expense and redeem every note of every failed bank for the past thirty-one years, a 5 per cent guarantee-fund maintained by the banks is certainly ample to protect the Government against loss in guaranteeing the redemption of notes.   But as further evidence let me quote the following, also from Comptroller Eckels:

"In further answer to your letter of September 13, you are respectfully advised that the loss to the general Government on account of circulation of failed national-banks, up to January 1, 1894, had there been no bond deposit, would have been $1,139,253.   Of this amount $958,247 represents the loss by banks whose trusts are still open and may pay further dividends, thus reducing the amount last named."

Under present laws the Government is bound to redeem all notes of failed banks and is given a prior lien upon the assets of the failed banks to reimburse such payment.   With this law in force and without bonds to secure circulation, the Government would during these thirty-one years have lost not exceeding $1,139,253.   An annual tax of three-hundredths of 1 per cent upon circulation would have covered this loss.   Surely a 5 per cent guarantee-fund maintained by the banks will make circulation perfectly secure.

The experience of thirty-one years of our Nation's history, years replete with many periods of depression, yet, withal, characterized by marvellous growth in population and unprecedented commercial and financial development, certainly constitutes a safe criterion upon which to base legislation for the future.

The State Bank of Ohio, chartered in 1845, having as many as thirty-six branches, illustrated the safety-fund principle.   Each branch was liable for the circulation of all, and was required to deposit with the Central Board of Control a 10 per cent guarantee-fund in money or bonds of the State of Ohio or of the United States.   This bank was very successful and its note-holders suffered no loss.

The safety-fund principle was proved sound also in the State of New York.   A free banking act was passed in 1829.   A safety-fund of 3 per cent was provided for the protection of note-holders.   By a mistake in legislation this fund was made to apply to all liabilities of failed banks, and hence, when the crash came, was utterly inadequate.   For twelve years there was no failure.   Millard Fillmore, Comptroller of the State, shows in his report that, had this safety-fund been limited to the protection of note-holders, it would have been ample, with several hundred thousand dollars to spare.

Just such a law as the one proposed by the Baltimore bankers is now in successful operation in the Dominion of Canada, except that the Canadian law allows circulation to the par of unimpaired capital, and the Government assumes no responsibility for the redemption of failed banks' notes beyond the application of the 5 per cent fund.   The law has proved eminently successful and satisfactory in Canada.   In the light of these facts no one can dispute the safety of the plan.

The deposits in national-banks are to their capital and surplus as $2,255,000,000 to $1,002,000,000. The deposits are more than double the capital and surplus combined, which means that more than two-thirds of the banking business is done upon deposits, and less than one-third upon the money of the stockholder. The national-banks, with over 300,000 stockholders, far from being monopolies, are great co-operative institutions, both as to ownership of stock and deposits. The borrowing season of one industry is offset by the surplus season of another. The extra demand from one section, while marketing its particular staple, is supplied from the surplus money of another section whose crop has been moved or whose special money wants have been supplied. This keeps money moving to and from our distributing money-centres. With our present inflexible currency-system, there is no alternative. Under the proposed law the banks of locality could increase their note-issue whenever the demand for money is active, and when the demand ceases such currency would naturally flow back to the banks' vaults, awaiting a renewed demand. This would in a measure save the expense of transporting money to and from money-centres and would tend to prevent the congestion of money in our large cities, with abnormally low rates and a tendency to speculation; and, on the other hand, it would tend to reduce the high rates for money in rural localities. An elastic currency is indispensable in time of panic. The only elasticity of our present currency-system consists in the auxiliary credits.

Ninety-two per cent of all the business transacted through banks in the United States is consummated by means of checks, drafts and other forms of credit. Hence, when credit is withheld, a money-stringency is easily created. Reliable data show that certified checks, cashiers' checks, certificates of deposit from banks, due-bills from individuals and corporations, all in round amounts, intended to pass from hand to hand as money and added to clearing-house certificates used in settling bank balances, were utilized to the extent of more than $100,000,000 during the recent currency-famine. This illustrates the defect in our currency-law, for which the Baltimore bankers have suggested the remedy. Under their proposed law, the banks would have met the situation with an increased issue of notes.

The free-silver interests criticise this plan severely, as they will criticise any plan that does not utilize silver. They have shrewdly utilized the evenly balanced condition of political parties and the popular clamor for more money to shape our monetary legislation since 1878; and, when a commercial crisis resulted from our suicidal silver policy, they maintained a deadlock in the United States Senate until commercial disaster and universal distress forced a vote and the repeal of the Act of 1890.

Another objection is that note-holders will have a prior lien upon the assets of a failed bank.   So they have now by the National-Bank Act.   Nearly all our State laws contain the same provision.   The prior claim of note-holders has long been recognized in Great Britain. It is a well-settled principle of currency legislation, and was well settled long prior to the passage of the National-Bank Act.   It gives note-holders an advantage over depositors, says the critic.   He is entitled to it.   Currency is the ingredient that assimilates all business transactions, reduces all barter to a common unit, and permits set-off and payment of balances.   The claim of a depositor is wholly a private contract, and rests upon an entirely different basis.   No man deposits money in a bank because the Government has given it a charter, but because of the standing of the bank.

As to the objection that banks would be organized in remote places solely for the purpose of issuing circulation,—remember that all circulation is issued by the Comptroller, who would enforce wholesome restrictions.   All provisions of the National-Bank Act as to payment of capital in cash, verified reports, and expert examinations, would still apply.   The Comptroller has power to withhold a charter if the character of the incorporators, the locality, or any good reason convinces him that good banking is not the purpose of the organization.

It is a recognized duty of the Government to supply its citizens with money which possesses debt-paying power, which when tendered by a debtor to a creditor must be accepted as extinguishing the debt. The Constitution reserves to Congress the sole power to coin money and to regulate the value thereof, and with the coining of gold and silver, I think, the Government's money-function should end.   Our own experience and the experience of other nations prove the wisdom of leaving the issue of auxiliary currency, paper money which does not possess legal-tender quality, under proper regulations, to the banks.   Our Government's credit would not then be measured by its gold reserve.   The national-bank note exemplifies the true principle of paper money, and, relieved from the unreasonable restrictions and given the elasticity embodied in the safety-fund principle, I believe it will prove a boon to our commercial interests, and relieve us from vexatious and injurious currency-agitation.   A. B. HEPBURN.

THE DEATH OF THE CZAR AND THE PEACE OF EUROPE.

THE norm of peace in Europe has been stated at a maximum of twenty years. This is not borne out by the facts. Taking the last three hundred years and counting only such tremendous conflicts as the Thirty Years' War, the Franco-Spanish War, the Wars in the Netherlands, the War of the Spanish Succession, those of the Austrian Succession, the Seven Years' War, the wars of the French Revolution and the Napoleonic Wars, the Crimean War, the Franco-Sardinian-Austrian War, the Prusso-Austrian-Italian War, the Franco-German War, the Turko-Russian War, there appear to have been more than one hundred years when the business of the world was killing. Should we count such minor conflicts as the wars of Grecian Independence and Italian Unification, the wars of the partition of Poland, the many wars of Russia and Austria with the Turks, those of the Scandinavian nations, and the numerous civil wars and revolutions everywhere, there would be a record of more than two hundred years of actual fighting in three centuries. The periods between great wars vary from one year to forty. Apart from the Malthusian theory, the most solid comfort to be derived from the rehearsal of all this slaughter lies in the fact that wars tend to grow farther apart, as they grow more potentially terrible. We may not be on the eve of a general disarmament, nor indeed, despite the example of the English-speaking nations, quite near an era of international arbitration; but it may be confidently claimed that the periods of war will be vastly fewer, and the intervals between wars markedly longer than heretofore. This means less waste of human life and less infliction of human suffering; for what exterminates armies is long and arduous campaigning, not general engagements, whatever their list of casualties.

In a certain sense, armies are provocative of peace, not war. It is the statesman or the journalist-politician who brings on war; it is the soldier who is compelled to conquer peace. The latter is the passive element, the former the active, however inverted these rôles may appear. If any one dreads war, it is the soldier of modern times;

not because he lacks stomach, for every young knight longs to win his spurs, but because he knows, if he has ever seen it, what war means.   The mercenary swashbuckler who lived on war is, happily, a creature of the past, unless his mantle has fallen on the over-excitable members of the press.   The citizen to-day protects his own fireside; and no one prays for peace more ardently than he upon whom the terrors of its rupture are first and most heavily to fall.

At no period of history has the world been so well equipped for war as to-day; at no period has every one more honestly desired peace.   It is always among the possibilities that a spark may set the structure aflame; but, though it would burn with a fiercer heat and a shorter, it is not so quickly kindled as of yore.   There is a disposition on every side to be less thin-skinned, which clearly makes for peace; and if the Socialist movement will occupy the attention of European statesmen at home so that they may have less leisure to brood over foreign encroachments or diplomatic provocations, then Socialism is *pro tanto* a blessing.

There is, in passing, a disposition to rob Socialism of the credit of such good as it is actually doing, by dwelling too much on the harm which its so-called offshoot, Anarchism, occasionally does; but the fact remains that Socialism, despite its rather disputatious congresses, is only the natural protest of the many to the arrogant rule of the few, and that it is, on the whole, gradually accomplishing the good which our Republic set out to do—to help the peoples govern them-selves.   In the good old *ante-bellum* days, when eighty per cent of all the property in the United States was owned by poor men, say those worth from five hundred to five thousand dollars each, Social-ism, let alone Anarchism, could find small footing with us.   Now that the Republic has become a plutocracy, and that eighty per cent of its property is owned by a small group, whose numbers are about as one to two thousand of the population, there is a better breeding-ground for both lawful and lawless creeds.   What the event will be at home, where our decentralization can barely put down riots, it is hard to say.

But this is wandering.   In view of the death of the Czar, what are the prospects of the interruption of a peace which has enabled all the Governments to prepare so stupendously for war?   Every nation has its internal troubles, financial and social; but, after all, the ques-tion put is the only international one, and on its answer depends the happiness of nearly every household in Europe.

Alexander III. of Russia will go down to future generations as a broad-minded man whose every instinct was firmly set for peace. In the thirteen years that he reigned, he earned the growing respect of the whole civilized world, and it is sad, indeed, that his life should have been cut short of even fifty years. For us Americans it is hard to appreciate the inner economics of Russia; but few of us know what the ignorant, heterogeneous population of the vast Empire is; and fewer can judge the difficulties incident to raising such a mass to a level with other nations. Whatever may be said of the home institutions, perhaps the Russian Empire may be gauged by the fact that more knees were bent in earnest prayer for the Great White Father than there could possibly be for any other man upon whom Death might set his mark. Despite Nihilism, Alexander the man and monarch was beloved; and, so far as his influence on foreign affairs was concerned, there is but one voice. He will be remembered as a ruler of exceptional common-sense, of quiet firmness, and of strong statesman-like views. An autocrat ruling over more than one hundred millions of souls, what he has said and done has had unusual weight.

In personal character and bearing he was strongly a Slav, and very devoted to Russia. Slavic methods of thought are not ours, and with equal intelligence and honesty it is not easy for a Slav and a Western European Aryan to understand each other in other than mere society problems. Keenly jealous of his prestige, it was largely the exclusion of Russia from what became the Triple Alliance that made him show the *rapprochement* for France which has been so eagerly coveted and so much exaggerated in Paris; but, for all this, there is no Germanophobia to be detected in his attitude. In his simple home-life, in his earnest habits of work, in his education, he was more like a German than a Gaul. He desired so to place himself as to have his voice in European leadership, which the Triple Alliance threatened to monopolize.

In frame the Czar was, in his youth, big, sound and athletic. He was fond of exhibiting his strength. He could, it is said, tear a full pack of cards in two, bend a ruble-piece, break a horse-shoe, or force in any locked door. Simple of habit, he had done no more of court ceremony than he must; and he keenly enjoyed plain fare and real toil. Like Gladstone, he used an axe; he would mow the grass on his lawn; his ministers have often found him hanging pictures or doing joiner-work. He was sincerity itself. Attentive to business, he rarely used a secretary, but jotted down his observations on state papers in his own hand. Though he received little and went out still less, he kept abreast with all that was going on in his own court and the world at large; and he dearly loved to hear the gossip of the day.

He was not a *gourmet*, but rather a hearty eater, preferring the plain Russian dishes, such as cabbage-soup. He was unapt to pay heed to his medical advisers. In his family-circle amiable and affectionate, kindly to inferiors and domestics, he was sober and somewhat stiff outside. While full of warm feeling, he found it difficult to utter words of praise; but he was able to give vent to his displeasure in very forcible Russian. For years he lived a life of worry:—the nation's financial straits, fear of attempts on his life, a natural habit of brooding over wrongs, care for the Czarina, who has been something of a nervous invalid. No one but his physician knew of the fatal disease under which he labored, and there was no little complaint in the court and army-circles that the Czar had given up the saddle, so that he no longer took part in military reviews, and that he gave each year less and less heed to palace-ceremonial.

The new Czar, Nicholas II., was born in 1868. By those who have known him informally, in his travels and elsewhere, he is said, while lacking the Romanoff physique, to be as strong as he is earnest and truthful, given to a fondness for scientific study, and interested in all that pertains to the good of Russia. More modern than his father, he is none the less pacific in habit of thought so far as the outside world is concerned; but, above all, he has the amelioration of Russia at heart, especially in what relates to the welfare of the middle classes and peasantry.

It is a tremendous responsibility which rests on the shoulders of the twenty-six-year-old successor to the throne of all the Russias; and, however sturdy may be his mental and moral equipment, he has not had the training which only years bring—years of trial, of danger, of yearning to do, and of failure in seeking to do, the right thing. We have had in the neighboring Empire a sample of what exuberant youth can be guilty of in unnecessary excess of inexperienced zeal; and we know that there is oftener wisdom in leaving undone than there is in doing. The one is the silver of speech, the other the gold of silence. Whether Nicholas II. will err in sins of commission or omission, and how he will, fill the throne of Alexander III., cannot yet be said.

The multiplicity of serious questions for him to face is appalling; and each of them is laden with the potentiality of peace or war.

Just what his personal sympathies are the public does not know. How he will adjust himself to the Triple Alliance and to its complement, the *entente cordiale* of Russia and France, with neutral England and her huge new appropriation for the navy as an enigmatical background, is yet to appear. How he looks upon the traditional Russian aspirations to the Balkan peninsula; how deeply he is imbued with Panslavism; how he views the Russian possibilities in the Corean war; how far he may desire to push forward Russian influence in the States abutting on India—all these are questions no one can answer for a while. Nicholas himself can scarcely be clear in the matter. It would seem that the internal economics of his vast Empire are complicated enough to keep his mind for some years from international entanglements. It is said that his father devoted much time to training the young Czar into his own method of thinking. He was scrupulous in selecting his governor, an old-fashioned, rigid, pious man. He watched over his associates. He strove to make him worthy of the crown. When a Nihilist bomb placed Alexander III. on the throne, the same dark anticipations were indulged in which confront us now. It was thought that the new Czar might be urged on by the young nobles' war-party to do some part which would interfere with general peace; but the strong, even current of his bearing was through his whole career one of the guarantees of quiet. May it be so with Nicholas!

There has been some recent prophesying of war, or, rather, strong hinting of its possibility. Some of this talk is idle, some of it vicious. To gag a few of the journalists would indeed be a public blessing. Such phrases as the " contagious influence of war," " the lust for slaying," " the intoxication which the sight of successful campaigns has on nations," and " the human tiger has tasted blood once more and the appetite grows with eating"—are surely noxious, even if flippant. If war is contagious, and European nations must rush to arms on account of the Corean struggle, why did our Civil War, which every week ate up more men than the entire campaign will cost Japan and China, not breed a conflict in Europe? Though wars are largely sentimental, nations do not plunge into them without a cause, real or imagined. Luckily the level-headed journalists do not indulge in such flourishes. I do not look for war out of any conditions now existing. There is no reason why the old Bulgarian sore should be prodded into activity so as to poison the political blood of Europe. Madagascar ought not to do so. The most proxi-

'mate set of factors which might so eventuate lie hidden in the Corean struggle and concern Russia and England.

Our British cousins very naturally look askance at everything Russia may do; that she is their prime opponent makes her course appear crooked, if not ignoble, in every instance; and the fact that Lord Rosebery paid a handsome personal tribute to the Czar in his Sheffield speech does not conflict with this popular mistrust of the Muscovite. But Russia has as much right to extend the borders of her garments as Great Britain has; and John Bull is not habitually slow to run up his flag on any available spot he may safely grab. Russia does no more.

Despite society imitation of her ways, there seems, at the moment, to be a curious antagonism to England manifested by all the powers, save Italy. . It is hard to trace this feeling to its source; but such *gauche* incidents as Lord Rosebery's recent reference to Agincourt do not tend to decrease it in France, any more than the irritating delays in the Madagascar business, or the continued occupation of Egypt. While there does not exist fuel enough to fan into a war-blaze even with France, Great Britain stands alone. Germany, in the event of war, would scarce lift a finger to aid her, and has lately been coquetting with Gallic susceptibilities; in fact, many people in France have begun to look on the loss of Alsace and Lorraine as ancient history. Thus Great Britain cannot boast an ally, and has the three strongest powers in a certain sense against her, a fact of which the recent refusal to listen to her suggestion for intervention between China and Japan was but a sign; and it is not improbable that, should Russia wish to seize a big strip of Manchuria, so as to straighten her Siberian railroad, she would be aided not only by Manchurian hostility to China, but also by the silence of Germany and Austria, who are not unwilling to see her Christianizing influence grow in those benighted lands, and by the consent of France, which might want Russia to wink at an increase of her own holding in Tonquin.

All this, added to the fact that Great Britain, while she can outweigh Russia by her Pacific squadron, cannot compete with her on land, seems to place the settlement of the Corean question rather in St. Petersburg than in London. That Japan shall not occupy Corea in permanency herself will surely be the insistence of both Russia and England; but if Russia saw fit to claim the right to guide the destinies of that peninsula, it might be hard for Japan alone to prevent it; and Japan and England will scarcely join hands. Russian
26

diplomacy is keen; and it is altogether probable that in dealing with the question so vital to her, Russia would know how to satisfy Japan by consenting to her taking her reward out of another part of China. Should this be so, England is scarcely in a position to do more than protest; and in case she demanded her slice, some territorial compensation near Hong-Kong and Shanghai would silence her objections.

The position of Great Britain was pointed out in THE FORUM for October by Dr. Geffcken. We Anglo-Saxons are wont to overrate ourselves. Inasmuch as our self-esteem has for centuries been coupled with the true colonizing fervor and with the habit of putting in big licks, the quality has been helpful, not only to us but to the world at large; but when we use this quality as an international yard-stick, we are not always happy in our figuring. We are impatient at being judged by a "foreigner." M. Paul Bourget, despite his generous keenness, makes many of us writhe. So with the English in matters international. They jeer at the estimates by foreigners of their position in the world's economy; and yet, to arrive at the truth of the military situation—and all politics is to a degree measured by the length and quality of the sword-blade—you may not overlook the conservative utterances of the leading continental authorities. We are all too provincial "to see oursel's as others see us."

Here I wish to maintain that the best American is he who has been fortunate enough to see the world and to be able to gauge both his country's faults and virtues by the measure of many other nations. Such a man returns home with a higher appreciation of and love for America, just because he sees her shortcomings. I do not believe in the expatriated American; but I do believe in him who intelligently views the world, and judges his country by the greater standard. An American yard is not six feet long, as we are fain to urge; but it is a good thirty-six inches—which is more than every other nation can boast.

No one disputes the greatness of England. It is only necessary to travel with her citizens to the climes where they civilize and broaden the world all round its vast circumference, to feel that were you not an American you would wish to be a Briton. She is indeed a mighty element in the welfare of the earth. But other nations have learned her ways while she has not learned theirs. Anglomania is not all imitation; it teaches many a lesson; and it is a serious question whether England can continue to be as relatively great as she has been. Continental nations have grown to be colonizers, and are gradually acquiring the knack of it.   A yet more trenchant idea is Dr. Geffcken's "key of the situation: namely, that the British Empire as it stands is *safe* only so long as it has supremacy at sea." This word cuts the knot of the problem.   It is not only the pre-eminence of England, but perhaps her safety, which might be at stake should she drift into a war.   The battleground of England is the Mediterranean.   She must hold this or forfeit her high-road to India, her control of the Suez Canal, her immense and easy superiority in commerce.   Russia has managed to slip some vessels through the Bosphorus; should this continue, she might yet gain a slight say-so in the Mediterranean; and with France as ally, and Italy neutral, England might be put to it to do herself justice.   Still Russia knows that she can best hamper England in the Orient; and she will not be lightly persuaded to try conclusions elsewhere.

John Bull is wise.   He stands alone, but he gets rated at a premium, and he knows how far he may go; and in the Oriental question he will not insist too much.   Were it possible for Great Britain and Japan to join hands, the union would outweigh Russia in the pending questions.   But as she did in 1861, England, prompted by commerce, has now chosen the losing side, and such a union is scarcely on the cards; it is vastly more probable that Russia will be able to play into the hands of Japan, enough to avert her suspicions and satisfy her demands, without losing her own hold on what she aims to get: a better climatic harbor than Vladivostok.   Russia can bide her time; and when her trans-Siberian railroad shall have got finished, she will be the power of the Pacific Orient.   It is, moreover, true that Russia makes friends of the peoples she subdues; a thing in which Great Britain often fails.   Though it is probable that the result of the Corean war will extensively modify commercial relations with the East, and will rub off some of the cuticle if not lop off some of the limbs of monstrous China, there is no reason why there need be any immediate change in the world's political centre of gravity. Japan has rightfully become a member of the sisterhood of nations; but she will play for a generation a modest part, except in the far Orient.

We Americans can but hope that Great Britain will retain her present position; it is a healthful one for the world's peace; but other nations are making gigantic strides in British specialties.   So long as her navy can hold head to any two others—a matter of present doubt—and is not too much scattered, she will maintain herself;

but she must beware of any complications which shall call for what other nations would deem a respectable land force. She has none. And what is more, when a few hours' fighting can entirely disable a fleet, as we have just seen done in the Yellow Sea, who shall predict the outcome of any naval encounter? It is no longer the old day of gunpowder and gin, of boarding-cutlass and human brawn: accident is king; and one lucky shot may disable a battleship full of mettle enough to win a kingdom.

Between France and England there always has been and always will be a series of little miffs; or, to use the French phrase, a succession of *moues;* and it needs more than this to breed serious trouble. Neither has anything to gain by war; the Gaul seeks it no more than the Briton; and, though the press on both sides of the Channel is full of little irritating thrusts, each will go a long way to avoid it. Could France be certain of active Russian support, a small incentive might suffice to make her cast her glove at Great Britain; but the Double Alliance is not of the strongest; and nothing but a clash on other ground between lion and bear would induce Russia to join in a French attack on her island neighbor. Bar France and Russia, Great Britain has no immediate prospects of drifting into war.

The mercurial German Emperor is again dealing in surprises. Since Bismarck's retirement, nothing so pictorial has happened as the dismissal of Caprivi and Eulenberg. If William II. could have his way, he would be a Barbarossa, with all the accompanying mediæval-isms. But this is his habit, and some months since he surprised us by again "sidling up" to France. Alsace-Lorraine is claimed to have become Germanized—indeed, part of the population is so; and though, at the outset of this Emperor's career, folks feared an outbreak of the bellicose Hohenzollern blood, or an error leading to equally grave results, he has now sobered down into a peaceful monarch. Socialism to-day in Germany is a factor in the peace problem. There exists no danger from her. The Emperor will be kept busy with his new team of ministers—behind whom he may himself hold the reins—for more months than he calculates. Poor old Bismarck now has a companion on the shelf. One can imagine his grim smile. Will he see a third one added to the row?

France will not attack Germany. Hatred used to be a good reason for wars; and a *casus belli* can be found hanging on even the smallest political disagreement. For twenty years "*Revanche*" has been thought to be such a reason; but the oncoming generations cry

"*Revanche!*" less lustily than their sires. Hatred of the bilious Briton, or revenge for a beating a quarter-century old, will not suffice to breed the feeling which generates war, even in Gallic breasts. Germany and Russia have no cause of quarrel, proximate or indeed within several removes; and it may be said that Austria-Hungary and Italy are not in a position to take the initiative in any question. They are mere lieutenants of the ponderous German captain. Italy would scarcely jeopardize her standing in the Triple Alliance by adding her fleet to England's.

There is no safety in predicting any turn in a game in which a youthful monarch holds a strong hand; but, though many rumors have been running around about the new Czar, Nicholas II., there seems no probability of his undertaking any inflammable rôle. Russia has so much more to gain by peace than war. Barely a third of her army has the new small-bore rifle, and it will be two years before the other regiments are so equipped. Her revenues are none too great. Russia needs her money for the trans-Siberian railway; and she ought not to blow it out of the mouths of big guns. No doubt there is tension in many of the international relations; but that is always present; and diplomats are growing more reasonable. It is probable that what has been said of the character of Nicholas is in the main true; and this should lead him to follow in the footsteps of his illustrious father and make Russia still the dictator of peace.

No man will be rash enough to say that war may not come. Every one of the continents has spots where an accidental outbreak, the blunder of an over-zealous servant, may work such a hardship, actual or ideal, to some great power as shall call for an excited demand for reparation. It is then that cool heads, if not thick skins, are in demand; and it is then that the effervescence of journalists in search of circulation or notoriety does most harm. The human animal, according to his kind, is the silliest of all animals, if we measure him rightly: I know of no other that is capable of such irrational freaks; and it is on these that peace or war hangs by a hair. But, to resume, I do not believe, despite all the talk, that there is in the present status of the world a set of conditions which will lead to early war. The sentiment of the leading rulers, statesmen and journalists does not trend that way.

THEODORE AYRAULT DODGE.

STATUS AND FUTURE OF THE WOMAN SUFFRAGE MOVEMENT.

THE argument for Woman Suffrage stands very much where it stood before the proposed Woman-Suffrage Amendment was rejected by the recent New York Constitutional Convention; and yet not altogether. The action of the convention indeed has thrown no new light upon it, but the lively discussion aroused outside the convention has wonderfully shaken up ideas, and has, so to speak, redistricted them according to many new party lines.

In this discussion, moreover, many latent ideas, of great yet unsuspected influence upon public consciousness, have been dragged into the open, and compelled to submit to tests of validity. Chief among such latent ideas is, naturally, the conviction of the universal, necessary, and irreversible inferiority of women. This idea was formerly patent enough,—indeed, has only just begun to disappear from the surface of society, and from the front rank of all social arrangements and of much philosophic theory. Nowadays, however, amid the general softening of manners and the spread of kindlier feeling, many men seemed to have almost forgotten that they were superior, until startled by the demand to accord to women the one seal of equality in a democratic community, namely, equal suffrage.

Nevertheless,—and this is most interesting to notice,—this conviction of the inferiority of women, though it be really the gist of all the opposition made by men to their enfranchisement, has been expressed only occasionally in the recent debates. A politeness which, in the premises, is fully as great an innovation as is the suffrage claim itself, has dominated the discussion and shifted the argument. Not contempt for women, but solicitude for the welfare of the State, is most frequently alleged as the reason for refusing suffrage.

Now in discussions in other countries on other propositions to extend the franchise, this question has been asked,—but then it has always meant: "Is it an advantage to the State that large masses of its population remain within its borders as aliens, unable to contribute the least share toward moulding social policy, prevented from having the faintest articulate opinion about the selection of public officials, one of whose most important functions is to reflect, measure, and express public opinion?" But when this inquiry is made about women, it is intended to mean, at its best, "What proof have you that women will 'reform' any of the undesirable situations, which have been so plentifully created by the political genius of men?"

When Senator Carey, of Wyoming, was invited by the Suffrage Committee of the recent New York Constitutional Convention to describe the working of equal suffrage in his State, almost the only question asked him by the committee was, "Have the women done anything to put down the gambling houses?" The Senator observed that gambling, being the characteristic vice of a mining community, could be outgrown only as the community became more civilized, and, in the diffusion of civilizing agencies, the four thousand woman voters of the State bore their full share. Moreover, they did not gamble themselves, and as they did vote, in this way at least they undoubtedly diminished the percentage of gambling voters. Still the question was repeated, until at last Mr. Carey, growing impatient, exclaimed, "I will tell you one effect of woman suffrage: Wyoming is the only State in the Union where the women school-teachers receive as high salaries as they would if they were men."

Women, too apt to be impressed by the dicta of their superiors, become themselves shy of urging their own advantage as a reason for their own enfranchisement. They prefer to promise that all sorts of moral improvements shall immediately follow upon this: that drunkenness shall cease, that gambling shall be abolished, that licentiousness shall be purified out of existence. I wish not to be behind any one in desiring the moral improvement of society, and I am also convinced that in many, though indirect, ways this will be furthered by the enfranchisement of women. Yet when, through modesty or an excess of caution, I hesitate to pronounce as certain anything which has not yet been proved, and refuse to rest the claim for woman suffrage upon the capacity of women for missionary work, I am accused[1] of giving away the whole case, and relying upon "arguments which would not convince a corporal's guard"! But when before, in the history of the world, was a right to citizenship made to depend on readiness to reform the vices of other people?

President Eliot observed in THE FORUM for October:

---

[1] New York "Tribune" review of "Common Sense Applied to Woman Suffrage."

"Universal suffrage prolongs in the United States the effect of universal education; for it stimulates all citizens throughout their lives to reflect on problems outside the narrow circle of their private interests and occupations, to read about public questions, to discuss public characters, and to hold themselves ready in some degree to give a rational account of their political faith. The duties of republican citizenship, rightly discharged, constitute in themselves a prolonged education, which effectively supplements the work of schools and colleges."

Of this "prolonged education" women are as universally deprived, as, in this country, men are universally admitted to it. What the result is of training women to believe that their business is to be personal,—always personal, nothing but personal,—and that the care of personal interests is their specialty, any one may easily observe who takes the trouble to observe women or to talk with them. Not "politics" alone is excluded from their mental horizon, but all public interests; and, if the public interests of the day, still more those of former days, which constitute history. Forbidden, at least officially and theoretically, to join in the social movements constantly organizing to produce real effects, women feel under no obligation to attain the exact knowledge which is required in order to produce effects. They lose, or never gain, a sense of reality beyond that of the members of their family or of their own interests, or feelings, or sensations. They remain indifferent to all knowledge beyond that of the concrete maxims necessary to carry on their daily private concerns, and are absolutely oblivious to general principles.

It is needless to add that there are many women, who, having been swept into currents of influence other than those of the general social situation, do not do any of these things, but quite the reverse. The women whose social instincts have thus developed spontaneously, and in the absence of the habitual and appropriate stimuli to development, are usually quite alive to the value of political rights, and are largely represented among the 400,000 women who recently demanded these in New York. Those who are not so alive, who continue to maintain the curious fiction that, though engaging in most useful public work, they are still remaining within the traditional private sphere of women, or that the branch of public affairs called political is something radically different from every other form, and especially from those enterprises in which the women engage,—such women decline at present to demand political rights for themselves, and sometimes, even, condemn with considerable asperity the other women who try to do so.

Once, women were not taught how to read, because pronounced forever incompetent for the priesthood. Now, though much more indirectly and less crudely, incompetency on the part of women for the franchise, for any share in the supreme social function, becomes a symbol for general unfitness, and for at least relative unfitness, in *all* social functions. This unfitness does not in reality exist. Moreover, every day it is less and less supposed to exist. The symbol, therefore, becomes a fraud,—a fraud organized in the very centre of our political system, and established as a fundamental part of the social machinery for the maintenance of justice. It is in vain to declare that it is of no consequence who administers justice, or who chooses the officials for administration. On the very threshold stands the question, Who has the right to conduct the administration? Violation of this initial right vitiates every step that follows. And are not these steps sufficiently vitiated, confused, demoralized? Can any citizen of New York to-day pretend that rights are so well maintained, that justice is so amply secured, through the administration of public affairs exclusively by men, that the fitness and sufficiency of men for popular government is conclusively demonstrated, and—by implication—that women are proved superfluous, and therefore unfit?

The revelations of universal corruption and of no less universal cowardice which are to-day appalling New York prove that the sense of justice which is the foundation of civic as of private virtue has become, for the time being, generally weakened, perverted, or altogether destroyed. It has been forgotten that it was as shameful to pay, as to receive, a bribe; as criminal to submit to blackmail, as to levy it; not more scandalous to carry on a conspiracy for crime than to maintain a conspiracy of silence by which crime should be condoued. The millions of money wasted, the widows terrorized, the orphans robbed, are yet an insignificant calamity beside the social moral rottenness which has rendered possible this prolonged, insidious, insolent criminality. A great shame has fallen upon New York. The splendid city stands like Phryne before the Areopagus, and the Public Prosecutor has snatched away her mantle to reveal,—not beauty, but hideousness!

In all the long roll-call of her misdeeds; in the dull selfishness which has counselled indifference to the commonwealth that private fortune might be aggrandized; in the stupidity which found a nobler field for ambition on the race-track or in the yacht-club, than in the public affairs of a magnificent realm; in the dense partisanship which has threatened to atrophy great parties into factions; in the vulgar greed which sees in the wealth of a metropolis only a field for plunder; in the reckless dishonesty which has tainted all administration; in the corrupt partnership with the criminal; in the brutal oppression of the innocent; in the brutal neglect of the helpless; in the perversion of all the machinery of justice toward the perpetration of injustice;—what part has been borne by women?

None! They, and they alone, are innocent of all these crimes and guiltless of all this disgrace. All that can be charged against women is that, excluded from responsibility, they have failed to feel responsible; that, forbidden to take any part in public affairs, they have usually obeyed the prohibition; that, trained to look upon New York as an assemblage of shopping-places, they have had no lofty ideal for their native city; that, encouraged or compelled to be apathetic themselves, they have infected with their own apathy husbands, and brothers, and sons; that, helpless to combine, they have often underbid their fellow-workmen; that, shut out from the sphere of public rights, they have often had feeble convictions of right or justice; and that when pressed too hard from above, or tempted too strongly from below, they have often abandoned their rocky foothold of ill-paid work, to slip into the sea of corruption seething around it, and added their own bodies to the putrescence!

In a democratic society, the government is the condensed expression of the collective activities of society. Of these activities it discharges the supreme function, the maintenance of justice. In doing so, it reflects and measures with considerable precision the moral sense of the community which chooses the government, elects its officials, prescribes their administration, and ratifies their laws.

But, in existing democratic societies, the activities of women are not included among those which government is expected to express. It follows, therefore, either that women are not members of society, or that the fundamental system of the State does not do, nor intend to do, what it professes to do. Yet by unanimous consent women *are* recognized as members of society, practically equal to men, notwithstanding tradition and theory. Thus both terms of the contradiction are simultaneously accepted. Again: according to the democratic idea, all the recognized elements of the social organism are enabled, at least to a minimum degree, to secure representation of their thoughts, wills, and respective situations in social institutions, and in social movements. If, in the democratic State, units whose force, intelligence, and virtue fall below the minimum continue to secure representation for their thoughts and wills, while units who possess this minimum, and much beyond, are excluded,—the fundamental principle of the State is contradicted. The State is thereby weakened.

The contradiction has been pointed out often enough during the last fifty years. Less often have been noted the ways, increasingly conspicuous, in which the weakness becomes manifest. Accustomed, in spite of profession to the contrary, to see government by all really carried on as government by some, men learn to acquiesce in the assumption of government by few. They may learn even to consider this a convenience; and it is true that sometimes the streets are then better swept. But governments do not exist chiefly in order to sweep streets, but to maintain justice among men. Though an oligarchy should sweep the streets to perfection, it could never condone its original crime of usurpation; and the poisonous influence of conscious crime would finally ruin even its power of street-sweeping. Exclusion of women from representation, after the democratic principle has been proclaimed, constitutes a contradiction of principle as positive as would the similar exclusion of any class of men.

Two questions arise: Why do not all women equally feel the pressure of this injustice? and, Why do some among them even protest against the "burden" of the suffrage? And what do those other women, who continue to press the claim for political equality, propose at this moment to do about it?

As to feminine opposition to political responsibility,—the claim to equality of position and opportunity made by the suffragists is based on a potential equality between the sexes, which is formally disallowed in existing social institutions, and often converted into an actual inequality under their powerfully distorting influence. Women whose capacities are cramped or atrophied by such influence suffer one kind of wrong. Women whose capacities have more or less escaped this influence, and attained a level of practical equality with those of men, suffer another kind of wrong, when they are forcibly maintained in a position of formal inferiority. And with both classes of women society suffers, by the loss of abilities, atrophied or repressed, and by the maintenance of assertions which even cursory observation shows to be untrue.

After the objection to citizenship as a "burden,"—perhaps as dangerous a sign as any of a widespread mental effeminacy and demoralization,—comes the second objection, that women should not vote, or do not want to vote, lest they might be outvoted by the "ignorant" and "illiterate." It is hard to see how any one can feel the force of this objection, and yet remain indifferent to the actual circumstances, in which women are being outvoted by ignorance and illiteracy all the time,—and that without the possibility of redress. There are, however, absolutely no facts upon which to base this oft-repeated objection. So far, wherever women have had the opportunity for full suffrage, they have exercised their right energetically, and evidently under the stimulus of the consciousness that unless they did so they might be outvoted, and men elected of whom they did not approve, or measures carried out to which they were opposed. Where women have been negligent of partial suffrage,—as sometimes, though far from always, in regard to schools,—it is because they have seen no issue at stake which necessitated their taking sides. They have not yet developed to the full stature of citizenship that implies the assumption of all responsibilities which fall of right to the citizen. Imperfect development of citizens constitutes one of the most formidable dangers of a democratic State.

The prevalence of misconceptions, the careless avowals of weakness and ignorance, the thoughtless inconsistency of current statement, all combine to show that the first need in regard to the enfranchisement of women, as of men, is education. Political education cannot really be secured without possession of political rights. Nevertheless, in default of these, the hope, the steady intention of obtaining them will often serve.

The work of the women who intend to continue the systematic agitation for the suffrage in the State of New York will be now mainly directed to efforts for the systematic political education of women. Suffrage leagues, as hitherto organized, have been apt to address themselves too little to education, too much to " campaign speeches." It is indeed difficult to persuade average citizens, either male or female, to study anything for which they have no immediate use. When the utility becomes obvious, the energy and interest are promptly forthcoming. The women of Colorado organized, all over the State, clubs for the study both of politics and of political science. The effective assistance, which, at the last election, the women of Colorado lent to the work of defeating the blatherskite candidate for Governor, shows an excellent practical result of such studies.

In New York City, curious object-lessons upon " women in politics" have been offered by the organization of groups of women,—many of whom had pronounced themselves " anti-suffragists,—to aid in the work of a reform election, under the leadership of men who had previously opposed, with considerable emphasis, the immixture of women in politics. Women who had been told that they should not vote were now urged to instruct men how to vote, or at all events to stand by them and see that they did their duty in voting. No more theoretically incongruous but practically admirable situation could have been devised than this, which followed so promptly upon the defeat of the claim by women to be allowed to exercise the rights of citizenship. It was a complete give-away,—and the most elaborate explanations can make nothing else out of it.

Out of this movement seems destined to rise some permanent organization of women in the city of New York, devoted to the interests of municipal affairs, and to the problem of showing how much public, *i.e.*, political work, women can accomplish *without* the franchise. The movement itself is in direct filiation with the movement started last spring, to secure a suffrage amendment from the Constitutional Convention. It is at this very moment assuming a permanent form, and planning a work intermediate between that of the old suffrage leagues and of the numerous organized groups of women, who, in one way or the other, as innocently as M. Jourdain, already speak the prose [of politics] without knowing it. It is extremely desirable to form a closely-knit yet widely ramifying organization of clubs for such meetings, properly systematized and sobered down to real work, throughout the State. A most famous historical model is offered for such clubs, in the Committees of Correspondence organized by Samuel Adams in Massachusetts in 1772, after the suppression of the provincial assembly had left the colony speechless. It was through the concerted action of five of these committees that the Boston Tea Party was successfully carried out.

Committees organized by the League for political education would have a fourfold work: 1, to create a focus of suffrage sentiment, by means of clubs meeting once or twice a month, for the study and discussion of current politics, of political institutions, of history, and, for the better educated, even of political economy; 2, to watch over the selection of candidates to the State Legislature from each Assembly and Senatorial district, to ascertain their views in regard to equal suffrage, and to endeavor as far as possible to create a public sentiment in favor of such candidates as will be found to favor their cause; 3, to enter into relation with all existing organizations of women—of which so many have sprung up just without the gates of the franchise,—to study their work and summarize its results, and at every available opportunity to urge the suffrage idea as the necessary and logical correlative of such work; 4, to continue the special work of collecting signatures to the suffrage petitions, which have already enrolled a number equal to more than a third of the voting population of the State, but which are destined to grow still further by incessantly new accretion. These committees, in all the Assembly districts of city or county, would report to the central organization of New York City, with which a vigorous correspondence would be maintained. The organization, co-operating with the elder suffrage leagues, will prepare to focus its action upon the State Legislature, which will be henceforth addressed annually on the enfranchisement of women, exactly as has been done for many years in Massachusetts, where, as every one knows, who chooses to remember, the suffrage was lost to women last year by only ten votes.

To the steadily expanding powers of women, citizenship can be denied only on the ground that its duties constitute a special sphere, walled off from the life, the thoughts, the daily concerns of the people of the State, that is, of citizens; or else that women, though involved in every transaction which takes place, in every interest which is to be defended, in every principle which is at stake, in every movement which goes on, are nevertheless absolutely uninterested, unconcerned, incompetent, the very highest among them below the level of the lowest who now enjoy citizenship. Either supposition is absurd, and cannot therefore indefinitely maintain itself against the reason of reasonable men. Some moment will arrive, some little interregnum of comparative party peace, when the Republicans will no longer be fearing to lose their grip on the State, nor the Democrats be fighting for existence; and when live interests will have shouldered their way to the front at the expense of those which shall have grown obsolete. Without other theoretical reason than exists now, but only in virtue of the expansion of new vitalities, resistance, :nined to a shell, will suddenly collapse; and the "gigantic revolution" will be effected as noiselessly as the fall of winter snow-flakes.

MARY PUTNAM JACOBI.

THE CHIEF INFLUENCES ON MY CAREER.[1]

THE most powerful influences over my life have been: 1. Literature; 2. Nature in Landscape; 3. The Graphic Arts; 4. Society. It
may seem strange that I should put human intercourse last, but the
reason is that I have lived very much in the country, both in England
and France, and especially in Scotland, where books and landscapes
were more easily accessible than cultivated people. Society, for me,
has been chiefly in London, and, in a minor degree, in Paris. My
debt to books is infinite and my love of reading seems to increase with
age. As for natural landscape, it has always been to me an unfailing
pleasure, an inexhaustible study, and a source of refreshment and
consolation. The Graphic Arts interested me first because they could
represent landscape more or less faithfully; not till later did I understand them as an expression of human sentiment and creative genius.

I was brought up in a part of Lancashire where the contrast between beauty and ugliness was, in those days, extremely strong. The
valleys, for the most part, were occupied by manufacturing towns in
which there was no visible trace of beauty or of art, but the neighborhood of Burnley, where I lived, was rich in natural beauty, still
unspoiled. There were the little rocky dells where the streams slept
in clear pools or plunged in miniature cascades, there were ancient
crags and cliffs, undulating green pastures, a noble old park with
stately avenues, and when I wanted a wider expanse I had only to go
out upon the moorland for a view of the Yorkshire hills with a
glimpse of the Irish Sea. I lived at that time in an old " house of
seven gables" that belonged to one of my uncles. The fields that
surrounded it were all meadow or pasture and they were bounded
by a rocky stream. A little further up the same stream was an
ancient hamlet with a gray old house where Spenser, the poet, was
believed to have lived during his sojourn in the north of England.
It is not absolutely certain that he lived there, but the amount of
evidence (I have not space for it here) is sufficient to establish a

[1] This paper has a melancholy interest because it is among the last products
of Mr. Hamerton's pen, if not the last. He died in London on November 5.—
Editor FORUM.

probability and so to give a poetic interest to the place. As to more modern celebrities, Turner had worked a few miles away and "Jane Eyre" was written by a young lady who was almost a neighbor of ours and who knew one of our friends. The Lake District was so near that I once rode to visit it on horseback, and the scenery of Craven, within a day's drive, had many literary and artistic, as well as historical, associations.

But however beautiful a country may be it teaches nothing by itself, not even botany or landscape-painting. Access to a city of some importance is absolutely necessary to the development either of a writer or an artist. I had this in Manchester. It was possible to go there by an early train, spend several hours, and return home in the evening. This kept me "in touch" with modern painting which was at least sufficiently represented there by the local and the dealers' exhibitions. Our northern manufacturing district with its numerous towns so close to each other and so intimately connected by railways is, in fact, like one enormous city, comparable to London, and as the race that created it is very industrious, enterprising, and intelligent, that region is far more favorable to mental development than the purely agricultural districts. As for London, I first became acquainted with it in the year 1851, but not intimately, as my relations had only distant acquaintances in the London society of those days, elderly people who seemed like icebergs to my boyish imagination. I took a dislike to the long and dismal streets with their rows of oblong openings in the dirty brick for windows. London has been greatly improved since those days and has now become, at least in some parts, a comparatively picturesque and interesting city.

As for the personal influences that acted upon me in childhood and youth, I never knew my mother who died very early and I lost my father in my tenth year. He taught me two things: to ride, and to read English aloud in a distinct manner. My appointed teachers, according to English custom, were a succession of clergymen. I read English easily at the age of four and began Latin at five-and-a-half but Greek was deferred till I was eleven. After my father's death, his eldest sister was my guardian and she very kindly grounded me in French. I remember afterwards that when I was at school at Doncaster I wanted to give up French, but she insisted on my going on with it, thereby, without knowing it, setting in motion a train of causes that ended with my residence in France. She exercised a very strong influence on my life in various ways, especially through the warmth of the affection I had for her and which is still to me like a religion. In those days the convenient words " Philistine" and " Philistinism" had not been invented, or at least not introduced into the English language, but I never knew any one who disliked what we now call Philistinism more. Some years later she said to me, " I know you will be an author and that is a good reason for diligence in your studies, as an ignorant author is a poor creature." She was always anxious that I should take good honors at Oxford, but when the time came for going there I found myself unable to sign the thirty-nine articles of the Church of England. The University " tests," so rigorously maintained in those days, were a sort of network ingeniously contrived for the admission of liars and hypocrites and the exclusion of all who were at the same time honest and more or less estranged from the Church of England. And so I missed the advantages that Oxford might have given and (a consideration of far more importance in my eyes) lost the chance of fulfilling what at that time was my guardian's most cherished hope and ambition with regard to me. My classical education had been carried on at two schools, Burnley and Doncaster, and under two private tutors, Dr. Butler and Mr. Hinde. Dr. Butler was a gentleman and a scholar, but he had a great affection for me and was too indulgent. Mr. Hinde, who had married one of my aunts, had been a tutor at Oxford (I mean what is called " a coach"). He was a man of remarkable classical attainments, and he exhibited an undisguised contempt for every one (including myself) who could not read Greek quite so easily as he did. However, he was an efficient teacher if not an agreeable one, and he would have made a Hellenist of me if I had stayed with him long enough. Unfortunately his influence over me was exactly the contrary of that which my guardian anticipated, for he let me perceive that a classical scholar could be a narrow and unjust critic of the English literature that I loved, so that I failed to see the advantages of classical scholarship in the general enlightenment of the mind. In another way, too, his influence was against my guardian's hopes for me, as his extreme intolerance of Dissenters and especially his firm belief in the future damnation of all Unitarians, made me, by a natural reaction, tolerant of heresy in all its forms, provided only that it was conscientious and sincere and free from a narrow spirit of sectarianism.

This repellent effect of what otherwise might have been encouraging examples produced in me a dislike to the exclusive pursuit of

27

wealth, as I had a friend (a distant relation), who was making a large fortune in business and so devoted to this object that he could hardly find a minute for anything else. His own wants were remarkably moderate, and his expenditure less than the interest of a sum equivalent to his income for one year. His habits appeared to me absolutely irrational, as he was accumulating money that he did not want and for which he had no use, while at the same time he was allowing the best years of life to slip by without seizing upon its innumerable opportunities. He had no time for anything, no time for travel, for reading, or for society. He gave as a reason for not getting married that he had " never found time to do the courting." This led me to a philosophy about money which differed essentially from his, and for some years I did not attach sufficient importance to it. One may value wealth for its good uses and dislike poverty, not because it has no luxuries, but because it is without leisure, privacy, or peace.

When I was about eighteen years old I determined to be a landscape-painter. I had always been in the habit of drawing and had learned almost from childhood what drawing-masters used to teach in those days. It did not amount to very much, but it helped to foster the intensely strong instinct of affection that I had for the scenery of the north of England and still more for the sublimer scenery of Scotland. This brought me under new influences, as it led me to make the acquaintance of some artists in London and elsewhere, while, for the time, I completely abandoned my classical studies just when they might have been most profitable and most effectual. However, the pursuit of painting gave me access to other ideas which were a great refreshment to my mind and increased my interest in nature. Besides this, it enlarged my acquaintance with mankind. Young gentlemen in England were then exclusively under the direction of clergymen. I had been so myself from the age of five to that of eighteen. In the provincial upper class at that time, artists were personally quite unknown, and were supposed to be idle and disreputable.

Two of the artists I first became acquainted with were Mr. Pettitt, a landscape-painter, and Mr. Leslie, the Royal Academician. Pettitt was a man of immense energy and industry, who kept a very large family by incessant labor: altogether an entirely respectable and manly character with a powerful, though uneducated, mind. His reputation as an artist was never brilliant, and it has not lasted, but he could earn a fair income by his strenuous toil and he spent nothing on himself. I first met with him in the Lake District, at Keswick, and he taught me more in about a week than I had learned from all previous teachers. After that, I worked in his studio in London. His way was to begin a picture, advance it a little, and then make me copy it twice on canvases of its own size. By this practice I very soon became intimately acquainted with his processes and could mimic his workmanship like a forger, so that he did not readily distinguish my copies from his originals. One day I put the copy on his easel, and he went on innocently working in the belief that it was his own picture until I told him. Still, his influence over me was not entirely beneficial. He had a passionate love of nature, but I had that myself already and did not require to have it intensified. What I needed was some idea of the distinction between art, as art, and the confused and intricate nature which supplies the raw material of art. This, Pettitt could not communicate to me, because his own conception of the duty of an artist was simply to copy nature just as it was and as accurately as the most unflinching out-door study might enable him to do it.

Mr. Leslie might have taught me far more about art, but as he was a figure-painter and I wanted to learn landscape, not having at that time any notion of extending my studies into art-criticism, I did not profit by Mr. Leslie's knowledge and experience nearly so much as I might have done. However, I owe him a debt of lasting gratitude for having taught me to appreciate, at least in some degree, the etchings of Rembrandt; and though I could not fully appreciate Constable in those days, still Mr. Leslie made me very intimately acquainted with his work, and so laid the foundation of an understanding of it that came to me afterward. Besides this, Mr. Leslie was a man of culture, at least in English, which he spoke and wrote not only correctly but with a certain taste and elegance that he had derived from the masters of the eighteenth century. His influence over me was in all ways a civilizing influence.

Luckily for me, I had another friend who kept me more in touch with my earlier education. This was Robert William Mackay, author of "The Progress of the Intellect as Exemplified in the Religious Development of the Greeks and Hebrews." As Mr. Mackay had a substantial private fortune, he could devote himself entirely to his studies with complete indifference to the sale of his books, which were published at his own expense and at a loss to himself, while even if their sale had been much larger the infinite labor he bestowed upon them must have made such writing as his an entirely

unprofitable occupation.   But, though Mr. Mackay did not work for
money, his authorship was far, indeed, from being the amusement of
a literary amateur.   His object was to create in the public mind a
better understanding of the history of religions by following them in
their growth, and he hoped that this better understanding might lead
to a wider toleration than that which existed in the still bigoted England of his time.   Unfortunately for the success of his attempt his
style of writing, though most sound and scholarly, was too learned
and not sufficiently entertaining for the general public, and so his
influence was confined to a small circle of readers, which, however,
included some of the best intellects in England, the historian Buckle
being amongst them.   No doubt Mr. Mackay may be credited with
some share in the great improvement we have since witnessed in the
liberality of English opinion, but whatever good he has done has
been effected indirectly, as the general public is naturally ignorant of
his writings, and even of his name.   My only regret is that Mr.
Mackay's influence over me was not still stronger.   He was one of
the most cultivated men in England, and it would have been easy for
me, under his direction, to go on with my intellectual culture without
suspending it, as I did at that time, in order to devote myself exclusively to painting.   However, it was something for me to be in constant intercourse with a superior intellect like his.

At Mr. Mackay's house I often met Mr. Watkiss Lloyd, a man of
very high culture indeed and a thorough gentleman, who had the good
sense to secure a competency in commerce before devoting himself
wholly to intellectual pursuits.   Mr. Lloyd was a noble specimen of
our English race, both physically and mentally.   He lived to be
eighty, and at seventy-six looked certainly twenty years younger.
His favorite study was Greek literature, and he wrote a history of
Greece which was never published, besides other works, of which only
a few have seen the light.   He had the gifts of a scholar, and if he
had only possessed the art of writing, which has often belonged to
his inferiors, he would have become celebrated, but his style was
difficult to read, being wanting in simplicity and lucidity.   He talked
well, and was a charming companion, with his kindness and humor
and amply abundant information.   Mackay had very poor conversational powers, though what he said was always worth waiting for.

I went to Paris in 1855 to study painting and improve my French.
There I met, among other people, my future father-in-law, who,
though not practically an artist, even as an amateur, had a far better

knowledge of the artistic element in painting than I had myself in those days, and he might have effected in me the necessary evolution if I had been rather better prepared for it.   I observed French art with some curiosity, but it had no influence upon me, and whatever advantage I got from Paris was on the literary side.   During this first visit to Paris, I became acquainted with Mr. Wyld, the painter, who had a very favorable influence upon me much later, but not at that time.   He was essentially an artist and I a naturalist, so that his work inevitably seemed to me too artificial.   But the advantage that I got on the literary side was very great, as I had suspended my studies in Latin and Greek and needed the discipline of another classical foreign tongue with a difficult grammar.[1]   By good luck I felt attracted to French, which afterwards brought me back to literary studies in other languages.

It is a wonder to me now that I could leave my books in Lancashire and go to paint from nature in the Highlands of Scotland with only half-a-dozen volumes in my hut.   I was trying very hard to become a photographic landscape-painter: that is, a landscape-painter who makes perfectly accurate portraits of the scenes which he professes to represent.   It was an interesting pursuit for two reasons: first, because there had been so little truthful landscape-painting in previous art, so that the aim had the attraction of novelty; and again, because I loved my favorite scenes so intensely that no degree of fidelity could be too perfect for my affection.   I was confirmed in these tendencies by Mr. Ruskin, who at that time believed that there was room for a new school of truthful landscape-painting, and his own drawings from nature belonged to it.   Some critics have represented me as his pupil or follower, but on a comparison of dates I find that I had done some careful topographic work before the publication of the fourth volume of " Modern Painters," in which he explained and advocated it.   It is scarcely necessary to add that topographic landscape-painting can have nothing of the charm or seductiveness of the pleasure-giving fine arts, which are emotional, and that, human nature being what it is, a topographic picture can no more affect people's feelings than a map.   From the purely artistic point of view I had, therefore, gone astray; I had not been led astray by Mr. Ruskin, but I had been confirmed by him in my error.   We may both of us be excused on the ground that all accurate draughtsmanship, if it is applied to land-

[1] If any critic says that French is easy I ask him if he can write it quite correctly.

scape, must lead to topography as inevitably as accuracy in writing leads to prose. An artistic landscape is a sort of visible music, admitting refinement but not accuracy of form, and requiring for its full effect upon the mind the harmonies of color and light and shade which present difficulties analogous to those of musical composition.

Marriage has always a great influence upon culture. It very frequently puts a stop to it altogether. As my wife was a Parisian with a strong taste for the classical literature of her own country, I became her pupil in French and she became mine in English. We made it a rule in our private conversation never to allow a fault in either language to pass uncorrected, and we read aloud to each other a great deal. At one time my wife read to me three or four hours a day. As we chose our books very carefully, this practice was almost an education in itself. We afterwards passed on to Italian together, with the help of a master. I then found, as Franklin had done before me, that the study of French and Italian had increased, in a conveniently unconscious way, my knowledge of Latin, and Latin led me back to Greek. This is mentioned without the slightest pretension to scholarship. In the use of languages I have one faculty which seems to be rather uncommon, that of keeping them entirely separated. When speaking or writing French, I am, for the time being, like one totally ignorant of English, as English words do not occur to me, and I never translate anything, not even weights and measures, or money, or the thermometer, from one language to the other, but think in each, independently. My marriage has certainly been most favorable to the continuance of my education in literature and even in the fine arts, as my wife has always been on the side of genuine art against the servile, literal, and unintelligent copyism of natural objects.

I have long had a taste for philology, and during the last five years this has been favored by my friend and son-in-law, Professor Raillard, who is a philologist of much learning and ability, with a happy instinct for original investigation and discovery. We have done a good deal of work together, and hope to do more.

It has been a great advantage to me to work in concert with Mr. Richmond Seeley, the publisher, in the management of the "Portfolio." His knowledge of business, of the fine arts, and of human nature has always been instantly at my service, and I have often been credited with merits that were the result of his suggestions.

During my residence near Autun my most intimate friend was Mr.

Stanislas Schmitt, at that time principal of the college there.   He talked with me on all sorts of subjects in French of the most classical purity, as he hated the carelessness and vulgarity of the present day which are ruining the beautiful French language.

I have lived so much away from England that my personal inter-course with English writers of eminence has been very occasional, though in some cases it was supplemented by correspondence.   Per-haps it would be claiming too much to say that Robert Browning, Mat-thew Arnold, George Eliot and R. L. Stevenson were friends of mine, but they behaved to me as if they had been both friends and neighbors.

When a man lives much in the country he is likely, if he reads, to be chiefly influenced by books.   In this way I have been strongly influenced by John Mill, whom I once met, but did not know per-sonally.   Mill had a power over all my thinking. ·

I became acquainted with Comte's " Positive Philosophy" in 1853. He has influenced me chiefly by his luminous statement of two laws.   The first is his well-known law that each of our leading con-ceptions, each branch of our knowledge, passes through three different theoretical conditions, the theological, the metaphysical, and the posi-tive.   The second concerns fine art, and divides it into three es-sential elements: 1. Observation with Imitation.   2. Idealization. 3. Expression.   These two laws still seem to me unassailable, and I value Comte's statement of them as a precious help in scientific thinking and in art-criticism.   The second may even be a guide in the practice of the fine arts.   But I never accepted Comte's religion, as, without being a misanthropist, I do not admire the human race sufficiently to worship it.

Mr. Ruskin intensified the love of nature, and at one time stimu-lated me in the study of the fine arts.   In art, however, we have long differed in opinion in a way that can be easily explained.   Mr. Ruskin has remained, at least in theory, faithful to the doctrine of Leonardo da Vinci that the best picture is the picture which most closely resembles the reflection of nature in a mirror.   My doctrine is that the art of the painter expresses his peculiar feeling and his special qualities as an observer, not by a generally indiscriminate fidelity, but by selection and emphasis, very frequently even by simple omission; and I say that a picture like a reflection in a mirror, without either selection or composition, would not have the qualities of fine art, but would be something like photography with the addition of color. Again, with regard to etching, it is an art which Mr. Ruskin has unsparingly condemned, whereas I have encouraged the study and practice of it in a volume which has been frequently reprinted, and also by the publication of etchings in the "Portfolio." Assuredly, as to this art, Sir Seymour Haden exercised a far stronger influence over me than Mr. Ruskin. As to the most important matters of all, Mr. Ruskin's intellect is, or used to be, intensely theological, but the longer I live the more evident it seems to me that we are all under the immediate dominion of natural forces that act unconsciously as the wind does when it either helps a vessel on its voyage and pleases the sailors or wrecks it on a rocky shore and drowns them, the natural power being equally indifferent in both cases, though in one it does good to men and in the other evil. I speak here of the action of natural law which we have innumerable opportunities for observing, and not of its origin, which we were born too late to see.

On the subject of natural law, especially in its relation to ethics, I owe more to Professor Huxley than to any one else. He has been the first to state with perfect clearness the true relation of man to nature, and though his statement of the case is neither devotional nor enthusiastic it disengages us from what is untenable in natural religion and sets human ethics on a higher plane. I value especially his Romanes Lecture of 1893, in which he plainly says that "cosmic nature is no school of virtue but the headquarters of the enemy of ethical nature," and that "so far forth as we possess a power of bettering things it is our paramount duty to use it."

Professor Huxley brings me to Mr. Frederic Harrison, whom he treated very unfairly. I occasionally met Mr. Harrison in former years, and we have renewed our acquaintance since. I wish I had known him from boyhood; the example of his energetic industry and ever active intelligence, with his cool superiority to misrepresentation, would have been valuable to me in many ways. He is a rare example of a man of the highest culture who is not in the least encumbered by his culture; another example is Mr. Gladstone. I have known scholars (Mackay was an instance) whose learning burdened them like a panoply of lead. Another great and rare quality in Mr. Harrison is the power of taking an equally keen interest in the past and the present. It is unfortunate for him that his advocacy of Positivism has put a weapon into the hands of his enemies who can so easily, though disingenuously, accuse him (a perfectly sane man) of sharing all the mental aberrations of Auguste Comte.

P. G. HAMERTON.

MAY A MAN CONDUCT HIS BUSINESS AS HE PLEASE?

A GREAT many valuable lessons will be learned from the Chicago strike of last summer; many suggestions for relief will grow out of it; and many questions, both ethical and economic, will be empha- sized by the experiences and the conditions attending it. While studying its phases, its origin, its course, and its close, two very far- reaching ethical-economic questions have been constantly in my mind. They can be answered to a certain extent—in fact, they have par- tially been answered. They are not wholly new questions, but in the near future, they will be urged by both labor and capital with in- tense interest in the answer to be given by society, for they strike at the fundamental principles of business-law and at the moral effects of conducting business rigidly in accordance with such law. They are:

1. Shall a man conduct his own business in his own way?

2. Shall the savings of labor be considered a reserve, from which labor must draw, in order to enable it to subsist during periods of depression or of adversity, while the reserve of capital is kept prac- tically intact under like circumstances, or, if drawn upon at all, in less measure than labor draws on its savings?

The first question was asked many centuries ago when a great employer of labor was trying to satisfy the workers in his vineyard that the man who worked one hour during the day should be paid as much as the man who worked all day. The question then was put in the following form: " Is it not lawful for me to do what I will with mine own?" A small strike was imminent on account of the payment of a full day's wage to those who had come into the vineyard at the eleventh hour. There seems then to have been no logical an- swer to the inquiry. The reasoning of the employer in asking this question was purely ethical, and the question itself apparently satis- fied the turbulent workmen.

The great employer of to-day, when asked to make some conces- sions to labor or to arbitrate differences which have arisen between him and his employees, declares that in order to win success he must have complete control of his own affairs; and he asks, " Shall I not

conduct my own business in my own way?" Under some circumstances the employee asks, "Have you the right to conduct your own
business in your own way?" Society has long since answered these
questions in some important particulars. It says to the property-
owner, the manufacturer: "You must not so conduct your business
as to injure the property of your neighbor, nor must you conduct
your business in such way as to injure the health of your neighbor.
No property-owner can do anything that will interfere with the rights
and privileges of his neighbor, whether these rights and privileges
come under the head of right to freedom from injury to property, or
the privilege of living without damage to health." These principles
are so old, and so well defined by precedent and by statute, that the
answer is complete and emphatic in so far as the two features named
are concerned; and no question is made as to the soundness, either in
ethics or in economics, of the position which society has taken in the
premises. A man cannot divert a stream, if by such diversion he
overflows the lands of his neighbor, without being compelled to answer in damages for his act; nor can he erect a manufactory whose
processes injure the health of the community. Law furnishes ample
remedy in either of these cases. In fact, the property-owner has no
clear, absolute title in himself to the property which he has bought
and paid for in full. Society can take it, under certain restrictions
and rules, by giving the owner, not the compensation which he asks,
but the compensation which society, through its organized forces,
considers sufficient. All the labor which the property-owner has expended and which is unseen goes for naught. The improvements
which he has erected, but which are not represented by tangible
entities, also go for naught. He must contribute something, when
his land is taken under the right of eminent domain, to the welfare
of society and accept the award of damages by the properly constituted authority. He, therefore, cannot administer his own affairs in
his own way in so far as the foregoing rules apply.

But the question which is much more far-reaching, and which will
inevitably be answered by society, relates to conditions of men rather
than to their material surroundings; and this question is: "Shall a
man or a corporation who does not, or is not able to, conduct his or
its affairs so as to avoid public disturbance, obstruction of trade, loss
of wages, or the lowering of the standard of living, be free from the
interference of society?" Will not communities say to the employer:
"If you cannot so conduct your business, or manufactory, or railroad

that public business be not disturbed or the standard of life interfered with, we shall take some part in the management, or insist upon some adjustment by which society shall be free from disturbance"? The broad answer will come in due time,—in fact, it has come,—not by revolutionary methods, but by the processes of reason, the application of justice, and the rule of right.

All attempts at conciliation and arbitration, whether they work under the form of law through boards established by the State or by the mutual consent of the parties involved in an industrial dispute, emphatically declare that society has the right to interfere.   When two parties to an industrial controversy by mutual consent agree to leave the matters in dispute to arbitrators, even those selected by themselves, they virtually agree that others may decide methods of business; and when the State has erected a Board of Arbitration instructed by law first to undertake conciliatory measures and, failing therein, to proffer its services as a Board of Arbitration, it has emphatically announced that it will interfere when the employer does not or is not able to conduct his affairs in such way as to avoid disturbance.   This action is based on the ethical position that the Government is bound to protect society and to secure to it peace and tranquillity.   The stoppage of traffic, the hindrance of business, the general disruption of peaceful relations, the violence and crime, which come logically in the train of an industrial dispute, are menaces to the welfare of society; and the State is in duty bound to do all in its power to prevent their recurrence.   And, since the power which the State has comes from the people, it is bound to exercise that power for the good of all, even if the individual suffers as a consequence.

The constitutionality of such acts cannot now be discussed, or, if discussed, denied.   The statute-books of the States and of the Nation and the decisions of the courts everywhere have established too many precedents to enable us to avoid the logical conclusion.   The enactments of the Interstate-Commerce Law, by which the Federal Government under certain circumstances undertakes to regulate freight-rates, is a clearly defined instance of the necessity of Government interference to prevent the disturbance of trade.   If it can interfere to prevent the disturbance of trade, can it not interfere to prevent the disturbance of society?   Cannot the State say to both labor and capital, "You must so conduct your affairs as to leave people at peace"?

It must be admitted at once that, in so far as the individual is concerned, the extension of this answer to the scope which it will take in the future is uneconomic. It is not good political economy, perhaps, but is it not good ethics? The employer or the employee may firmly believe that there is nothing in his conduct which warrants the interference of the public; but, if the public is subjected to great loss, to great inconvenience, to paralysis of trade, should not the individual who precipitates the difficulty be held responsible and accountable to the power which enables him to conduct his business or to perform his labor at all? And especially, when organized capital asks of the State peculiar privileges, under special acts or charters, and at the same time asks that individuals contributing capital be relieved from responsibility of the person, does not the question which has been suggested come with still greater force? And is not the answer that the State shall interfere made with greater emphasis?

The second question,—" Shall the undivided surplus profits of labor be drawn upon to sustain it in times of adversity, while the undivided surplus profits of capital remain practically intact?"—is not only an economic one but an ethical one, and is closely related to the first question. The laws of business and the true principles of political economy insist that profits once made shall remain intact. Of course large business houses, manufactories, and corporations engaged in production, if they are wise, look out for their reserves as well as for their dividends, and these reserves are used to offset deterioration of plant and to provide for the purchase of new machinery as invention demands it or as competition makes it necessary. An experienced and successful manager of one of the largest works in the country once told me that he had more difficulty in convincing his directors of the danger of declaring a dividend which should absorb all the profits, than he had in convincing his men that the conditions of production warranted a decrease in wages. I imagine this is quite generally true, because the stockholder, who is represented more intimately by the director, feels that all the profits of the concern should be divided; but the manager, who is responsible for the successful prosecution of the business, knows well that he must not only pay dividends, but must prevent too great a deterioration of his works.

Labor is paid its part of the profits through wages; and, if the individual laborers are prudent, self-denying, and imbued with frugal habits, they save money, which goes into the savings-banks. Probably in those States where savings-banks have been established, about 50 per cent of the deposits belong to the working-people. This has been demonstrated by investigation. These deposits represent the undivided profits of labor, its surplus in carrying on the productive industry. They constitute labor's reserve, carefully husbanded and wisely increased, for the purpose of meeting contingencies as they may arise,—not the renewal of plant, but to offset the deterioration which comes of exacting labor and of increasing responsibilities, and to make provision against sickness and old age. These reserves are as essential to the integrity of the business of a community as are the reserves of capital to prevent deterioration and waste of plant and for the introduction of new processes as they become necessary. Here, then, we have two reserves,—1. The undivided profits of business held by capital for legitimate purposes, and absolutely essential to the integrity of production; 2. The undivided profits of labor, which are as essential to the success of business as the profits of capital.

The trouble comes when, through depression, through competition, or other circumstances, wages are reduced; and, in so much as they are reduced, the possibility of keeping labor's reserve intact is lessened. If the necessity extend or continue, the possibility of keeping its reserve intact is not only lessened, but completely destroyed; and, in order to keep in condition to earn even enough wages to come up to the life-line, the reserves are drawn upon and in many cases entirely exhausted, in order that the processes of production may go on. Capital in the mean time rarely draws upon its reserve to sustain its productive processes, while it may and often does reduce the usual dividends; and sometimes its dividends may be wiped out completely, just as the surplus earnings of labor may be wiped out completely. But recently we have seen that labor has not only been obliged, under the depressed condition of business, to accept most serious reductions in wages, but to draw heavily on its reserve; while capital not only preserved its reserve intact, but did not suffer materially in its dividends, although it did meet current losses in its production. I am not speaking, of course, of losses on account of strikes.

This state of affairs is leading to the second question stated above, whether labor's reserves shall be exhausted in order to enable it to work, while the reserves of capital are kept practically intact. I do not know the answer to this question. The ethical view of it is clear; and even the economic view, which would insist that there shall be no answer, is quite as clear when economics only are considered; but the question indicates one of the chief causes of unrest that prevail in the ranks of labor. There is, at least, a suggestion of injustice, of unequal losses, and of over-drafts upon the side of labor. The injustice comes because labor is just as essential to production as capital, and neither can succeed without the full supplemental work of the other. It is idle for capital to say to labor, "If you do not wish to work for the terms I offer, you can go elsewhere." It is not only idle, but unjust and brutal. It is idle for labor to say to capital, "If you do not do so-and-so, we will not work." This, too, is not only idle, but it is brutal. The only result is the destruction of each by the other and the death of industry. In the question there is a deep, underlying ethical and economic significance; and the welfare of society, sustained peaceful relations of capital and labor, the prosperous conduct of productive industry,—are all involved in the adjustment, on an ethical and economic basis, of one of the most trying and at the same time urgent problems of the day. Industry cannot succeed, labor cannot prosper, progress cannot be continued, unless all the vital forces of production can be preserved in their integrity. The impairment of capital is the loss of labor: the impairment of labor is the loss of capital. These relations are reciprocal, but they are not identical. Will the wisdom of the day, will the re-writing of political economy, will the inculcation of higher and deeper ethical lessons, settle it? I believe so, most emphatically; but how and under what conditions this disturbing question will be answered is more than human wisdom just now can suggest. It may be that corporations and concerns engaged in productive industry will say to labor, "We will, with your assistance, establish a wage reserve-fund, by setting aside an equitable share of profits and an equitable share of wages, to be used in times of depression or of disaster for the purpose of keeping in healthful working condition the labor of the establishment, for preventing its dissipation, for avoiding the unequal draft upon labor's reserve, and even for conducting the works temporarily at a loss."

Some attempt has been made to answer this question through the methods known as industrial partnership, profit-sharing, co-operation, and other kindred means. While they are all good under some conditions, they have never been advocated as complete solutions of the difficulty; but the advocates of these palliative methods have clearly understood the ethics of the inquiry.

Labor would not contend so savagely against a reduction of wages under bad economic conditions if it felt morally certain that with restored conditions its share of the profits, which it receives in the form of wages, would be restored: for in the majority of cases it knows perfectly well that wages cannot be restored except by the most serious effort and contention. It, therefore, makes a strenuous fight against reductions, not so much on account of the reductions themselves, as on account of the certain knowledge that in order to restore what is reduced it must make another and a bitterer contest. Those concerns that increase wages voluntarily, when the conditions of production warrant, have little or no trouble.

These two questions which I have outlined, and which must receive the candid consideration of all men who care more for the welfare of society than for any individual member of it, indicate some of the underlying motives or reasons for labor controversies. Should they be settled on broad and logical grounds, the man who then so misconducts his business as to permit a strike to occur in his works will meet not only disgrace, like the fraudulent bankrupt, but the severe condemnation of the society from which he derives all his prosperity; and, with labor, he will be taught the lesson that that society which gives prosperity to them both will undertake to protect itself against individual encroachments upon its peace; for it is society that gives value to the production of labor. Without society there is no value: without industry there is no society. Labor makes things: society, competitive desire, gives them value. " Historical facts and evolutionary principles coincide with the proposition that the laborer is the member of society in and through whom that society survives; . . . and the wages of workers are to society what food is to the body—they enrich, strengthen, and make healthy the life-blood of the social organism." [1] The heart might as well claim that its functions alone are essential to the continuance of life, as against the claim of the stomach, as for either labor or capital to claim that its offices alone are essential to industrial prosperity and social progress. So society will answer these two far-reaching questions, in the interest of all and not of the individual. The answer will not come through revolutionary changes, but by a recognition of the ever-increasing intelligence of the men involved in industry.

At present the industrial world is disturbed by a succession of labor controversies, but these controversies must not be assigned to a supposed increasing antagonism, to retrogression, or to any anarchistic desire to destroy the grand results of past developments. On the other hand, it should be recognized that the man who works for wages has been taught to realize the conditions of a higher civilization, to

---

[1] James A. Skilton, Esq., in discussing "The Race Problem in the South."

appreciate, to understand, and to desire still greater mental, moral, and social progress; he has been taught, and by modern ingenuity enabled, to enjoy art, music, and literature; he understands that he is one of the sovereigns of the land, that he is a political and moral factor; and he now begins to comprehend that the labor question means simply the struggle for a higher standard of living. But, with all this, he finds that he still keeps the position of a wage-receiver in enterprises in which his skill as well as his hand is a necessity. The honest and the intelligent workman, so far as he is engaged in the controversies of the day, is practically the conservator of all the required forces of industry; but this man seeks in this conservation to become more closely allied to the factor of capital, which without him he knows to be dead material. He now comprehends, more clearly than he has comprehended at any other period, that he has outgrown the purely physiological relations which labor bears to production,—that is, the position of the animal; and he knows that he supplies the developed mental qualities of the man. Seeing this, he sees that he vitalizes the material side of production, which is capital. He, therefore, asks that he may become more closely associated with capital in productive enterprises, and desires also to secure a more liberal, and what most men would consider a more nearly just, share of the benefits arising from modern inventions than now falls to him.

The great problem of this age is how a new system shall be established, with perfect justice to capital and to labor, recognizing the moral forces at work contemporaneously with the industrial forces. I feel so sure that this problem will be solved on the broadest business basis, through the practical application of moral principles with economic laws, that I have little anxiety for the industrial future of the country. I know that no one element can come in as a panacea for ills, but I am morally certain that a combination of elements can be so applied, and will be so applied, as to relieve industry of the present apparent warfare and to answer practically the queries that have been propounded in this article. We are often confused in attempts to consider such questions, because progress has been so rapid that we fail to see the intelligence underlying industrial controversies. Ignorance, selfishness, perhaps dishonesty are all interwoven with intelligence, often so closely that it seems as if the unhappy conditions made intelligence subordinate; but the development will go on, and we shall see the results of society's answer in a better and greater and more equal diffusion of wealth.   CARROLL D. WRIGHT.

STOCK-SHARING AS A PREVENTIVE OF LABOR TROUBLES.

IT is not difficult to find men of intelligence above the average who maintain that there is no "labor question"; that, with the exception of a few refractory agitators, the laboring classes are perfectly satisfied; or that, if they are not satisfied, they ought to be. That the average wage-earner lives in greater comfort, is better housed, better clothed, and better fed than the richest nobleman of six hundred years ago, is undeniably true. It is true also that while in this century capital has had to content itself with a steadily shrinking interest-rate, the return for labor, viewed both in the light of increased wages and of shortened hours, has steadily risen. Let it be noted, too, that wages have risen despite the fact that the prices of commodities have greatly fallen. Yet a deep-seated, turbulent feeling of dissatisfaction prevails among the laboring classes; and there must be some defect of mental vision in the man who does not clearly see that dissatisfaction does exist and that it is rapidly growing.

Whence comes it? How explain this strange coupling of increasing physical comfort with increasing discontent? Many replies suggest themselves. The widespread ability to read, resulting in the wonderful multiplication of newspapers and books, and the rise of labor organizations in which large numbers of men can be readily appealed to, have given the agitator and the theorist a new opportunity.

We all recognize that fortunes have been piled up in this century as never before; that luxury and vain extravagance parade themselves with flaunting insolence; that an irritating class of the idle rich is being created; that the obligations of wealth are largely disregarded; and that the miserable standard which has been set up between man and man is that very wealth which is so unequally distributed. Taking these facts as a background, one set of theorists say to the labor classes: "All men are born equal. The French philosophers of the last century said so. Our Declaration of Independence says so. That all men are born equal as to rights and obligations no one disputes. Our universal suffrage proves that. You may never have saved a penny, and you may be generally ignorant, yet your vote counts just

28

as much as Mr. Vanderbilt's or as President Eliot's. But you are born equal also in all other respects; and, if you find any inequality, it is because somebody has stolen your equal share. This stealing will continue so long as individuals control capital and production. Make the state the only capitalist and the only producer, and then we may divide up the proceeds equally and we shall all be equally rich." —" Or equally poor," answers the critic.

Other theorists preach: " Money is wealth. The government-stamp makes money. Its stamp on fifty cents worth of silver makes it worth one hundred cents. Its stamp on a bit of paper makes it worth a dollar. We cannot have too much money. Those bad men in Wall Street and those greedy bankers throughout the country wish to contract the money-supply. That will make interest high. That will force wages down. Let us have all the money we want. That will bring good times. That will make wages go up."—" And make bread and meat and every other commodity go proportionately much higher," says the critic.

Another school plausibly urges: " Land is the basis of all food-supply and of all wealth. The benefits of all inventions and of all material human progress have gone principally into the pockets of the owners of the soil. The landowner robs both the capitalist and the laborer. It is growth in population which makes the increase in the value of the land. The state, therefore, which represents the population, is entitled to the increase. Individual ownership of land must cease. The good faith of centuries must count for nothing. The first owner of possibly a thousand years ago had no good title. The state recognized that title under a mistake. Now, although innocent holders, justified by the state's recognition, have again and again exchanged the fruits of their industry for that land, yet, to produce general prosperity, the state must confiscate it. No, it will not confiscate the land," explains this theorist," but it will confiscate the land-value."—" A distinction without any practical difference," exclaims the critic.

The advocacy of all of these and related theories have had their undoubted effect in stimulating discontent among the classes who work for wages. But there is another cause which lies deeper and which, however unrecognized, is yet the main reason for the present restless dissatisfaction and angry clash between the employing and the employed classes.

The personal tie which bound man to man under feudalism was,

in a large degree, kept alive under the industrial system which followed and which prevailed far into this century. So long as business
and manufacture were conducted on a small scale, every employer stood
in a close, personal relation to the man who did his work. Such a
relationship, as compared with the independence of the present time,
may have begotten too much dependence on the one side and too much
protection on the other, but the tie was something more than could be
expressed by a mere wage-equivalent. The workman knew his employer well, saw him frequently, worked at his side, could understand
what had given him a higher position; yet he did not feel that a
great social chasm yawned between them. That tie was human,
based on actual acquaintance between man and man, born of the daily
living touch of men actually working together. It represented something higher and better than a mere money-wage. It represented
loyalty, the devotion of man to man, the willing obedience to greater
knowledge and higher ability, the sense of intelligent human co-
working which sanctified and consecrated the strain of daily toil.

The nineteenth century ushered in a new industrial system. The
great giants, Steam and Electricity, could not be profitably employed
in the small industrial establishments of the past. The stock-company which made it possible for very many men to combine their individual capital in a common enterprise, was developed with startling
rapidity. This union of large capital and of business energy, which
the corporation effected, has called into life all the great enterprises of
our century; but it has also given the death-blow to the old spirit of
loyalty which prevailed between employer and employed and which,
in fact, was the spiritual cement that held society together.

The corporation is owned by stockholders, frequently widely scattered, who are bound together only by the pages of the stock-ledger.
In many companies these owners are only fleeting and temporary
owners, holding the stock speculatively, buying to-day and selling
to-morrow. The stockholders are represented by a board of directors who have the management, consisting of the president, the
vice-president, the general manager, and so on. These again,
in large companies, have their sub-officers, who finally come in
contact with the men that do the actual physical work of the business. The purpose of the corporation is simply the earning of dividends. The directors, if they have one ear open to the claims of
the workmen employed by the company, listen with a hundred ears
to the demands of the stockholders whom they represent. They do

not study the human hopes and needs which agitate their employees. They coldly study the credits and debits of the balance sheet. If earnings are large, the salaries of the president and of the manager may be increased, but the ordinary employee obtains no increase. If earnings decline, no cut is made in the salary of the officers, but they are instructed to reduce expenses. This means a reduced force, or reduced wages, or both. The reduction follows the line of least resistance. It falls on the powerless employee. In other words, the employee of a corporation is under the domination of an employer with whom he never comes in contact, before whom he has no voice, and from whom he can expect no consideration. He is simply a tool worth so many dollars a week so long as he is needed. How can any feeling of loyalty develop under such conditions? In any individual business, no matter how large, the employee, if he feels himself wronged, can as a last resource go straight to the head of the firm. But suppose the corporation-employee, if peradventure he could get a hearing, appealed to the president because of a reduction in his wages. The president, possibly expressing regret for the necessity of the reduction, would explain that the board of directors had decided the matter. The aggrieved employee could not get access to the board; but, even if he could, the directors would say that they were necessarily guided by the interests of the stockholders whom they represented. Is it not easy to comprehend that lack of genuine interest and ultimate antagonism are bound to take root where the tie of employment is a cold balance-sheet on the one hand and an uncertain monthly wage on the other?

A remedy must be found. Society cannot be tied together by dollar-bills. Yet corporate life and the concentration of capital in large enterprises are bound to continue and to expand. A new condition must be introduced which, in some degree, can take the place of the man-to-man loyalty of the past. To me there seems but one solution: *Make the employee loyal to the corporation; make him a stockholder and give him representation on the board of directors.*

Suppose a large corporation were to announce to its employees that, after a certain date, payment for services would be made at the rate of four-fifths in cash and one-fifth in stock of the company. It is at once evident that, if this labor-payment stock were not different from the regular stock of the company, the average American workman would, in his improvidence, soon transform it into money. This labor stock, therefore, should be made non-transferable, and void of value in case of sale or hypothecation. The non-transferability of this stock, on the other hand, should be offset by a guarantee that the company will redeem it at par. Should a labor stockholder voluntarily retire from the employ of a company, the option of a full year should be given for the redemption of his stock—to prevent embarrassment to a company in case a large number of employees should leave it simultaneously. The labor stockholders should be allowed to vote for one or more directors to represent them on the board. This representation would obtain for them a hearing before the controlling body, would tend to prevent hastily-considered action as affecting their welfare, and would enable them to receive direct, authentic information concerning the condition of the company. It is not necessary to discuss the details. The point I maintain is that, if the employees of a corporation are made stockholders, sharing in the prosperity and in the adversity of the company, having a voice in its management, and being fully informed as to the condition of the business, a spirit of co-ownership, of close personal interest, of loyalty, would be created which would make strikes most improbable, if not impossible. Every employee would feel that he was, to a degree, working for himself, that improved work would mean increased dividends and an increased value for his stock. His occupation would be invested with a deeper interest, a higher dignity. It would soon be recognized that it has been a waste of economic force to reduce man to the level of a tool. There must always be some incentive to call forth his best work, and there is no incentive like making him a sharer in the profits of his work.

We often hear an employer say: "My men want to work only eight hours, whereas I work ten or twelve or fourteen hours a day." But why is the employer willing to work so energetically? Because his extra work, as he believes, will result in extra profits. This incentive does not apply to the man who is employed for a fixed wage. He does not feel the spur which might energize him. He becomes dispirited, indifferent, careless. He does not give his best work because there is no heart in his work. But give him an interest in the profit resulting from his work, let him realize that increased economy and greater energy will bring an increase in his labor-return, fill him with a sense of co-partnership in the business, and you will have a transformed wage-earner.

Suppose the railroad employees engaged in the late strike had been stockholders in the railroads. Their impulse would have been to protect, not to destroy, the property of their respective companies. Their own self-interest would have been far better protection than United States troops. One of the commercial agencies estimates that the losses occasioned by the late strike will aggregate eighty-one millions. One-tenth of that sum held as stock-interests by the railroad employees would have made that strike an impossibility.

"But," says somebody, "your cure is simply profit-sharing." Yes, that is precisely what it is, coupled with a stockholding feature and with some voice in the management. In a way, it is not a new thing even in railroad management. The Paris and Orleans Railway in France tried it for many years, and it was extraordinarily successful until undue extensions and government interference destroyed its usefulness. Says Mr. Charles Robert:

"Applied as, for instance, it was in 1858 (this was fourteen years after its first introduction), association in the profits exercised a considerable influence on the *personnel* of the Orleans Company. The deep and lively feeling of a real and important solidarity of interests gave them the appearance of a great family. The employees looked after each other. They had constantly in mind the thought of an eventual profit to be shared, of a possible loss to be avoided. Thus every one showed the greatest care in handling baggage,. and, if an employee treated it roughly, it was a common thing to have a comrade say to him: 'What are you about? You will shorten our dividend.'" See the excellent volume by Mr. Nicholas Paine Gilman, "Profit-Sharing," p. 218: Houghton, Mifflin & Co.

In the Paris and Orleans Railway the employees had a profit-sharing but no stockholding interest. In none of the larger profit-sharing enterprises, so far as I know, has the stockholding plan been introduced, except in the *Bon-Marché*, the great mercantile establishment of Paris, which seems to be the most successful profit-sharing business ever attempted.

The great danger of the future is the socialistic danger. Its present expression is the rising tide in behalf of the nationalization of the railways. Make the railway operatives stockholders, and that question will magically disappear.

In this, as in all human actions, the policy of justice and of humanity will eventually be found to correspond and harmonize with cold self-interest. The best that is in men cannot be bought by a fixed money-wage, and it pays to get the best. When railroads and other great corporations take their employees into quasi-partnership by making them stockholders, and encourage their dignity and manhood by giving them representation on their directors' board, great strikes will be a thing of the past.   Louis R. Ehrich.

THE READING HABITS OF ENGLISHMEN AND OF AMERICANS.

To arrive at any exact statement of the quantity and quality of the favorite reading-matter of a whole nation is manifestly impossible. The likes and dislikes, the hopes and ambitions, the secret strivings and the mental processes of men cannot be represented by numerals. An attempt to discover what the English read along such lines would have an air of accuracy and deceive the unwary by that very assumption. It is, however, by no means impossible to collate facts and figures, and to bring to bear subsidiary matters upon the subject, to such an extent that one may arrive at a fair general impression.

There are, to begin with, a percentage of people in every country who do not read at all, or very little; there are others whose incomes and employments indicate that they probably limit themselves to a certain kind of reading; while, more useful still in such a discussion, every nation has a certain personality of its own, from which one may judge that this or that special form of literature would be best suited to satisfy its literary curiosity.

When we come to divide up the population of England and Wales for the purpose of discovering even roughly the number of persons whose reading is of little consequence, we find that about thirteen millions fall into this class, including five million school-children under fourteen years of age; a million paupers; a-million-and-a-half domestic servants; nearly three million laborers in the agricultural, fishing, and mining industries; two millions engaged in textile manufactures or employed as tailors, milliners, seamstresses, and shoemakers; to say nothing of a hundred thousand lunatics (some of whom write!). Although, even here, it were unsafe to say that what these thirteen millions of people read has no influence upon themselves or upon others, it is at least fair to conclude that whatever that influence, subjective or objective, may be, it is of small consequence.

This condition of things is due: first, to the lack of free educational facilities for children over fourteen years of age—there are practically no facilities; second, to the lack of free libraries—of which, later; third, to a well-defined, and to an American strange, but widely held, opinion, that the secular education of the masses does more harm than good; fourth, to the discouraging lead of the classes in all matters of education over the even now heavily handicapped masses, which leads these latter to look upon their past and present condition as necessary and permanent.

The English compulsory free-school system is of very recent date as compared with the American public-school system, which is almost as old as the state itself. The total number of schools receiving annual grants is 19,398. The number of children on the register of the Education Department was, according to the last figures made public, 4,755,835, of whom 3,682,625 were, on an average, in daily attendance. Of these only about 43,000 were more than fourteen years of age. The reason for this remarkably small number of children above fourteen years of age is, that this is the limit of age when a child is required to attend school, and then, too, because, as has been said, there is no school machinery, and very little encouragement, in England, for the education of poor children who wish to go on beyond the usual curriculum of children of fourteen. The American system of free education, by means of which a lad may go on from primary school to grammar school, from grammar school to high school, and thence to college, without any expense for tuition and very little for text-books, does not exist in England.

The annual running expenses of the British Empire amount to about $450,000,000; out of this large sum the total amount spent upon all educational agencies of whatever description is only $29,-201,455. The distribution of this fund is such that only a small percentage of the population of Great Britain are even in the way of fitting themselves to read anything but the most lamentably light and elementary literature. As a consequence of this policy, the percentage of adults who are, for all purposes of this discussion, practically illiterate, is probably very high. There are, unfortunately, no figures in the census returns which enable one to say exactly what that percentage is. The Home Office, however, in 1893, reported that of four-and-a-half-million total votes polled, one hundred and thirty-five thousand were illiterate. If one voter in every thirty-four is illiterate, one may be sure that, including the remaining women and children and non-voters, the percentage is very much higher; and these figures would be further borne out, did one care to make a calculation, from the fact that nearly 10 per cent of the men and nearly

12 per cent of the women in England and Wales; nearly 5 per cent of the men and more than 8 per cent of the women in Scotland (the Scotch school system is vastly superior to that in England or Ireland); and more than 23 per cent of the men and more than 25 per cent of the women in Ireland,—could not sign the marriage register.

Another phase of the subject that deserves notice, and to which some attention must be paid, is this: A very large number of intelligent people in England are altogether opposed to free general education. They are the Conservative—not to say the Tory—Old Guard in politics and in religion, who hold that the children, as of old, in each parish, should be taught to read and write and to say their catechism in the schools under the supervision of the clergy, and then earn a living as did their forefathers. This system, which is still in vogue, explains why so many well-educated German youths are employed as clerks in London, to the dismay of their English rivals. One may lay aside for this once the bugaboo of the statistician, which is the ever-present fear of generalizing from details, and assert that it would be difficult to find an American who is utterly opposed to free education for the people—so long as it is not carried to a foolish length. In England, on the contrary, there is almost a party of reactionaries, who scout the very idea that the education of the lower classes has benefited either those who have received it or those who have bestowed it.

The following figures show better than any expression of opinion the difference between England and America in this matter. The census of 1891 counted 606,505 men, and 765,917 women, of sixty-five years of age and upwards, in England and Wales, or a total of 1,372,422, of whom 401,904, or nearly one-third, received parish relief. Yet, over against this fact of the masses going from bad to worse as they grow older, set this other statement, viz., that in 1874, in a House of Commons of 658 members, 235 of them were Oxford or Cambridge university men, and 100 of them graduates of Eton alone; and in the present House of Commons of 670 members, 371, or more than one-half, are graduates of the great universities; while in the United States Senate there are 14, and in the House of Representatives 22, graduates of out dozen more prominent colleges, 36 in all. It would be difficult to put it more clearly that in England the classes are educated and rule, while the masses have little voice in administrative matters, and fall towards the end of their lives into helpless and rheumatic dependence, while in America the general average of prosperity is higher, though men of first-rate ability are probably fewer.

The last general fact, and perhaps not the least important, bearing upon this discussion, is the influence of climate upon reading. · No doubt the mild and equable temperature of England, which enables one to be out-of-doors, and consequently to take part in some form of out-of-door sport or labor all the year round, lessens the amount of reading. Other things being equal the inhabitants of a mild climate will read less than people who are, perforce, kept indoors many weeks of the year. No country in the world has such a never-ending round of sport in which so large a proportion of the population takes an interest as has England,—bicycling, grown to enormous proportions, all the year round; hunting, from October till April; racing, from early Spring till late Autumn; golf, which has developed from a game into a widely prevalent disease, all the year round; cricket, and tennis, from May till late September; shooting, from August till October; foot-ball (played, alas! by professionals, but as many as twenty thousand people attending on one game), from September until May; and besides these, coursing, fishing, boating, and a long et cætera of other pastimes. Nor are these sports confined to the rich and idle, or even to the well-to-do alone. It must never be forgotten, even by the most fervent opponent of an aristocracy, that England is to-day the most democratic country in the world, where the rights of the individual are more respected, and where the individual has more of personal freedom, than anywhere else in Christendom; for to miss this characteristic is to lose the explanation of many apparent anomalies. His lordship, the squire, the parson, and the butcher, the baker, and the candlestick-maker go galloping across the fields together after the hounds. The meeting-place is advertised in the local papers, and it is not necessary to wear pink to join in the sport; and one may see such a mingling of classes on terms of purely equine equality as one seldom sees in America. The same is true of the cricket-field, where the country magnate, the parson, and the young squires of the neighborhood play under the captaincy of some local tradesman's son, proving again that the genuine aristocrat is the best democrat, and that the snob and the prig lack something of being gentlemen. Indeed, the only people one hears talking much of what it is, and what it is not, to be a gentleman in England—or in America either, for that matter—are they who half suspect their own claims to the title. It may give some idea of the place of sport in English life to the sedentary American to say that it is difficult to find an Englishman between eighteen and sixty-five, in fair health and not supported by the rates, who is not a performer at some kind of sport or interested in some phase of it. Of the 673 reviews and magazines of a non-religious character printed in England, one in six is largely devoted to some form of out-of-door sport or occupation. Between 1880 and 1885, according to a private index kept in the British Museum, there were 266 books published on the one subject of sport or athletics; between 1885 and 1890, 412; and, although the figures for the last five years are not at hand, the number of books on the same subjects promises to be even larger—almost 40 books on golf alone appearing during the last five years. Nor does this list include books on topics germane to the subject, such as books dealing with voyages, geography, history, biography, and trade, of which there were 738 published in London in 1893 and probably more than a thousand during this last year. In a word, John Bull loves the fresh air. He is a sportsman, an athlete, a soldier, a sailor, a traveller, a colonist, rather than a student, and all the figures bear one out in making the statement. During those horrible days in the Crimea, these sport-loving " young barbarians" were " all at play," when they were not fighting; racing their ponies, getting up cricket-matches, and off shooting such game as there was. One family—the Pelhams—have hunted the Brocklesby pack of hounds for more than one hundred and seventy five years.

While Italy has twenty-one universities, Germany twenty, and France fifteen, each with a smaller population than England, England has only seven. On the other hand, the value of the sea-borne commerce of Great Britain and her colonies is $5,087,910,625, or double that of all other European countries combined, that of the United States being $1,866,280,000. The English control possessions in different parts of the world, aggregating 9,145,328 square miles in area, and 346,025,000 in population. They own foreign stocks to the amount of $3,819,035,000, or 23 per cent of all the foreign stocks in existence, yielding annually in interest $145,000,000, or at the rate of about $5.20 *per capita* of the whole population. A nation of students does not exploit itself along such lines. These people are the Romans of modern times, dull, vigorous, law-loving, law-abiding, and colonizers of the very finest quality, but not students.

When it is said that the English are, as compared with the Germans or even with their cousins in America, a non-reading race, we have still to give the facts and figures concerning the reading-population. To begin with, the census of 1891 for England and Wales groups under the heading, Professional Class, 926,132 persons; and of these it may be supposed that all are readers. Most startling of all, despite the fact that there are nearly a million more women than men in England, 555 in each 1,000 of the population are put down as unoccupied. This large unoccupied class in England—larger than that of any other country in Christendom—is due to the overcrowding—445 persons to the square mile in 1881, and 497 in 1891—and to the competition which forces people to be conservative and to be satisfied with a small but secure income, and to the civil-service system, which pensions off the servants of the state, there being 162,040 persons in England living upon state pensions amounting to $37,-944,465 per annum. In this connection it is suggestive to find that there are more than 130,000 members of London clubs alone, and we are not far wrong in guessing that one man in every forty of voting age is a member of a club, not including workingmen's clubs, free reading-rooms and the like. These, and many more besides, are the devourers of the newspapers, sporting-papers, and the magazines. And this brings one to mention the position held by the newspapers of England in the national life of the country.

The newspaper is a member of the family in England, and regularly comes to breakfast with the other members. The London "Times" is a kind of oldest son amongst newspapers, and "Punch," the jolly bachelor uncle, who makes occasional visits. Englishmen take their newspapers into their confidence, and have a naïf way of writing to them on all sorts of subjects. If an Englishman rows down the Thames and stops for luncheon at an inn and is overcharged, he writes to his newspaper, just as a little boy runs in to complain to his mamma of the rough treatment of his playmates; and later on this first letter is followed by others, in which the comparative merits and cost of light luncheons on the continent, in Seringapatam, in Kamchatka, and everywhere else where Englishmen have eaten and drunk—and where have they not done these ?—is discussed *au fond*. If horses stumble and fall in Rotten Row, there are letters on the subject which go into the matter of road-building, modern horsemanship, and the like, with quotations from Virgil and anecdotes of accidents that happened half a century ago. Half a dozen Englishmen go to Homburg. Finding that the golf links there are not to their taste, they sign a round-robin on the subject and send it to the "Times." Of late there have been many letters concerning the lynching of Negroes in our Southern States, and here again John Bull, with his ponderous disregard of the fact that he knows nothing at first hand, delivers himself naïvely, as usual, of his superficial omniscience. Not only the more serious weekly but also the daily newspapers give one the impression that they feel themselves to some extent responsible for the contemporary auditing of the accounts of the Day of Judgment. On the other hand, the better-class English newspapers do not indulge in rash suppositions, hasty generalizations, uncertain guesses at probable future happenings, and the daily exploitation of the personal affairs of notorious nobodies. And one may be permitted to say diffidently that perhaps this is preferable. If Mr. Balfour, for example, were to go abroad for a holiday, it would be considered vulgar to chronicle his doings and dinings, and absolutely brutal and boorish to write particulars of the dress and behavior of his sister—or of his wife, if he had one. The sense of fair-play of a nation of sportsmen does not permit an editor to torment even his enemy from behind a woman's petticoats.

There is no way of knowing with any exactness the comparative amount of newspaper-reading in England and America; but it is undoubtedly true that the Englishman takes his newspaper much more seriously than the American—first, because his newspaper is more accurate and more carefully written; and then, because the Englishman takes everything more seriously—even Mark Twain; and most notable of all, because of the wider sweep of interest, and the broader horizon offered to the English newspaper-reader, due simply to the fact that all the news and every interest of the whole British Empire are centered in London; and because, too, all Imperial politics are settled finally, not in forty-four different States, but in London. The English newspapers are, therefore, to be taken seriously into account when one estimates what, and to what purpose, English people read. Englishmen are *par excellence* the most careful travellers of the world. Men who are to write and men who hope to rule look upon a trip around the world as a necessary part of their curriculum. This reacts upon their newspapers and magazines, which receive weighty communications from experts, wherever a British interest is threatened, and whenever the British lion's paw is suspected of being used to roast somebody else's chestnuts. Nothing does more to keep up the tone of the daily press than this intimate and serious interest that so many Englishmen take in their newspapers, while the wide and varied interests of Imperial control—there is seldom a month when the army or navy of Great Britain is not in active service in some part of her wide dominions—give to the newspapers an heroic cast and a dramatic concern which in themselves supply the place of other literature. Therefore it is that, in casting about to discover what the English people read, one gives great weight to the fact that they are a nation who take their newspapers seriously, and in reading them become possessed of a great variety of information, and in the main accustomed to a sound style of writing and thinking. There are something like 1,882 newspapers published in England and Wales.

Judging, then, from these diverse facts brought to bear upon what the English read, what are we led to expect? What would such a fellow as John Bull read? Newspapers, novels, particularly novels of sport, adventure and travel, and, next, travels, history, biography, exploration, and then—because the great bulk of the English are Puritan still—books of a religious character. An analytical table of books which were published in London in 1892 and 1893 shows the following:

	1892.		1893.	
	New Books.	New Editions.	New Books.	New Editions.
Theology	528	145	459	74
Novels and Fiction	579	115	518	104
Political Economy, Trade....	151	24	71	14
Voyages, Geography.........	250	86	247	72
History, Biography..........	293	75	269	65
Poetry, Drama	185	42	197	37
Belles Lettres, Essays........	107	32	96	11
Sport......................	72	....	75	....

Out of this list of 2,309 books published in London in 1893, 1,435 of them were devoted to fiction, travel, biography, history, and sport.

To an American, particularly if he live in be-libraried Massachusetts, it must seem strange that, in writing of what John Bull reads, no use is made of library statistics. But when it is said that the first rate-supported library in England was opened to the public only in 1852, and that there are now only 165 such libraries, it becomes apparent how small a factor is this. In Massachusetts alone 248 of the 351 cities and towns have free public libraries, and there are besides 23,000 school libraries in the United States, containing 45,-000,000 volumes. A careful calculation shows that in 106 out of the total of 165 lending libraries in England, there were, in 1893, 389,698 net borrowers; and of these, on the average, nearly 80 per cent called for fiction and juvenile literature, and therefore what some 78,000 readers of the free lending libraries read, even if one could know, would be of small service in telling what the English people read. Mudie's Select Library and Smith's Lending Library have some 60,000 subscribers and probably 250,000 readers, and here again one-third of the books they distribute are novels.

In short, the only method which results, or can result, in anything like a satisfactory answer to the question, what the English people read, is the broad method of dealing with the nation as a whole. Doubtless there is here or there a governess writing a "Jane Eyre"; or a schoolboy wasting his time in preparing to write a "Vanity Fair"; or a dull boy at his arithmetic, who will some day be called The Grand Old Man, and make poetry of future budgets; or a young fop in Piccadilly, who may seem to belong to the class of non-readers, and yet who is destined to receive £10,000 for another "Lothair" and to make his Queen an Empress—who knows? At any rate we are not so enamoured of our figures, but we raise our hat to these exceptions to our rules. These countless exceptions to any and to every rule, the undoubted prowess of English scholars, and the maintenance of an uncommonly high average tone in matter, manner, and method in the English newspapers and periodicals prove fairly enough that, though the English nation is not a nation of readers, there must be a percentage by no means small, who demand, and who succeed in getting, a high class of reading matter for their daily consumption. On the other hand, it is equally fair to say that the 28,-000,000 inhabitants of a small island, who offer no facilities for the higher education of the poorer classes, who have a million paupers, a-million-and-a-half domestic servants, three million out-of-door laborers, two million working in mills, factories, and shops, and who have conquered and rule a population *in partibus*, outnumbering them twelve to one, cannot be spoken of as a nation of readers.

To one who is looking for a pat and hard-and-fast answer to the question "What do the English read?" the answer may seem to be lacking. It is not. The great bulk of the English read nothing, literally nothing, and he who knows something of rural England will agree to this; the casual and occasional reader reads, as we have shown, fiction, biography, history, travels, and no small amount of theology in a diluted form; the great middle class read, and trust, their periodical literature and their newspapers; the students, the real readers, who feed their minds as other men their bodies, read with more thoroughness and patience than our students. The entrance examinations for any college at Oxford, Cambridge, Edinburgh, or Dublin is trifling as compared with the entrance examination for Harvard University, but on the other hand both the classical and mathematical men who take the highest rank here go through an amount of reading that our men hardly dream of. England has nothing like the number of averagely well-read men that one finds in America; but America has nothing like the number of thoroughly well-read, widely-travelled, highly trained men in politics, and in all the professions, that one finds here. In America there is a widespread education of the hare; in England there is, confined to narrow limits, the education of the tortoise, and there is a fable that the world is poised upon the back of a tortoise! At any rate England carries a very heavy proportionate rate of the world's responsibility, and England and America together would seem to have little to fear from the future, for, after all, what men read is not a crucial test of their capacity. Who has not known men with enough university sheepskin to make a wardrobe of, who were vacillating incompetents? Who forgets how small were the libraries and the opportunities of Washington, Lincoln, and Grant? The English people are slow; in the main, dull; and they care little for abstractions in print; but if Mr. Benjamin Kidd's view of social evolution be correct, and the consensus of the competent apparently favors it, then the prosperity of a nation is not dependent primarily upon its intellectual alertness; and John Bull has little to fear from his lack of book-learning and his love of the open air.

PRICE COLLIER.

IS THE WEST DISCONTENTED? A LOCAL STUDY OF FACTS.

I AM asked to prepare for THE FORUM an article on the contented classes in Nebraska. The task is undertaken with pleasure, yet with no little trepidation. It is no small matter to run counter to public opinion; and especially to public opinion east of the Alleghanies. So much occurs west of the Mississippi that is really extraordinary, all conditions of life and growth are so wholly unlike those of the extreme East, that those who have had no personal experience in Western life may easily be divided into two classes: those who believe everything that they hear, and those who believe nothing that they hear. Both these classes seem to believe that extreme unrest and unreasoning and widespread discontent are our prevailing political, financial, commercial, and social characteristics.

There is need, perhaps, at the outset, of some fair, working definition of the word "contented." This ought not to exclude reasonable ambition,—the willingness and desire to change for the better; intelligent dissatisfaction with many existing social, civil, and political conditions. It may even include temporary discouragement, and perhaps take in a little reasonable and very natural grumbling about "hard times," "class legislation," "tariff-tinkering," "gold-bugs," and "silver cranks,"—according to the geographical or political locality of the grumbler. But it will not include that spirit which declares anything preferable to the present status, and substitutes revolution for evolution. Nor will it cover that other spirit—or want of spirit—that leads some men to forget their manliness; to declare that they have no chance in the world; that there is but sixpence a day difference between the man who works and the man who does not, and that the man who does not work generally gets the sixpence; that the struggle for existence is entirely hopeless; that they are "enslaved" by somebody or to something; that the world owes them a living, and that they propose by idleness to collect the debt.

The purpose of this paper, therefore, is to determine what proportion of Nebraska's population comes under the definition of "contented" as thus set forth. My duties as Chancellor of the State University have called me into nearly every town of prominence and my

29

executive journal shows about 10,000 miles' travel per year within the State. The purpose of this journeying has been to inspect the high schools which are accredited to the University; to attend farmers' Institutes and the meetings of the various State industrial and educational organizations; to make addresses in local lecture-courses or on various occasions; and to consult with people of in-fluence concerning educational affairs. One evening I have " as-sisted" at a reception in which *personnel*, toilets, and manners would do credit to any city in the Union. On the next I have ad-dressed a farmers' Institute in a little country town, and after the exercises have ridden nine miles in a farm wagon, wrapped up in a bed-quilt, with the thermometer ten degrees below zero, to spend the night with a farmer friend. I have talked with people in their stores and workshops, by the roadside, at their homes, in con-ventions, at church, and in school. The subjects of conversation have been almost as numerous as the people thus encountered. Because the University and its executive are entirely "out of politics," men and women have talked with me more freely than is usual except with warm personal friends. Many things have been said in confidence which the speakers would not repeat in public or even to a very few persons. It is no small advantage to come in contact during every academic year with 1,300 or 1,400 of the chil-dren of these people. In their relations to each other, in the way in which they go about their work, in the subjects upon which they write, in the questions which they debate, in their thinking and in the utterance of their thoughts, they reflect the home life pretty clearly. It is from this close and almost confidential relationship that the inferences and conclusions of this paper are drawn.

It is safe to say that there is a district school, representing the free State system, within walking distance of every Nebraska home. The last report of the State Superintendent shows 377 graded schools, of which about 70 are accredited to the University for more or less of the work preparatory to that institution, and probably 100 teach Latin and some advanced mathematics. There are 10 private or denomina-tional colleges of more or less reputation and standing, 10 private academies, and 6 private normal schools. In addition to these facilities for higher education the State maintains the University, with three colleges now established and an enrolment of over 1,300 students, and the State Normal School, where opportunity is given to prepare for teaching. The last official report of the State Superintendent showed over 6,000 public school houses, with nearly 5,000 districts holding six months' school or more.

All this has come to the territory practically within thirty years, or somewhat less than a single generation. That the people have not been able to do this unaided is shown by the fact that 54 per cent of the taxed acres and about 25 per cent of the taxed lots are mortgaged. It is not believed, however, that the State has exceeded 30 per cent of the greatest possible real-estate mortgage debt. The greater portion of our population came into the territory with little or no means, and has taken part in its development with slight resources other than an infinite capacity for hard work and that integrity of character which assures credit. On the whole the people are what are known as the common people; though one must confess that the common people with us are the most uncommon common people the world has ever seen. It is not probable that they have entered very deliberately or very consciously upon the task of State building. Each man has worked upon the wall against his own door until the defences of the city are complete. There has been a large amount of independent thinking and independent action. As the people have been drawn together in the towns, unity of 'purpose and definiteness of plan have developed; but we are still scattered and lacking in the strength derived from closeness of contact, man with man.

As to their manner of life, there would seem to be no better method of inquiry and investigation than to take concrete cases of which the most, and most accurate, information can be secured. If these cases are normal and typical, then inference and conclusion will come naturally and safely. Let us take, then, the city of Lincoln as fairly typical of the average Western town of its size; remembering that it is the second city of Nebraska. It has a population of 55,000. The use of the electric railway enables the city to spread out in every direction, and it probably covers three or four times the territory which would be occupied by an Eastern city of the same size. This means that in the residence portion there are almost no blocks of connected houses or tenements. In the very poorest part of the city there may be two houses to the lot (50 feet frontage) which gives from 8 to 10 feet between the houses, but even then the front of the house is from 15 to 20 feet from the sidewalk. There are, I think, only five, so-called, blocks of connected tenements or flats (rented houses); but these happen to be in the best part of the city and bring perhaps the highest rentals known in Lincoln. Very generally, therefore, there is one residence to a fifty-foot lot, and often the premises are even larger. The houses set back from the street and the streets are 100 feet wide. It will be seen that all these conditions give breathing-room and are conducive to health and comfort. It is a city of churches and schools; it has an excellent water system, miles of well-paved streets, electric lights and gas, a successful sewer system, a fine government building, two of the best opera-houses in the West, and several parks and pleasure-resorts.

The most costly residence portion is on and around Capitol hill. It is hardly likely that there will be much discontent here. It will be better, therefore, to take an average street and examine somewhat into its condition and that of its people. Let us take, then, one with which the writer is very familiar, four blocks north of the main business thoroughfare, and running directly through the University grounds east and west.

At the head of this street, lives a family of which the parents are of German birth and the children all American-born. Those now at home are the father, mother, and six sons. The oldest son is the business-manager of one of the evening papers, in which the father is a bookkeeper. Another son is an accountant in the University, one practises law, one is studying medicine, one is a post-graduate student and instructor in the University, where also the youngest is a student. The post-graduate student and the youngest son are employed on the newspaper during the vacation, and in other spare time. All are intelligent, industrious, frugal, temperate, and reasonably successful. They are undoubtedly ambitious for better things, but certainly cannot be said to be "discontented." Their nearest neighbor on the west is a practising physician and surgeon, one of the most successful in the city. He is on the governor's staff as surgeon-general of the State militia, takes considerable part and interest in public affairs, and is a very good all-around citizen. It would be hard to find a more contented or happy family than he and his wife and children appear to be. On the next lot is a comparatively small residence, occupied by an old gentleman with his wife and one or two of their younger children. They live in a very quiet way, and have a few rooms that they rent to students or others, and, so far as one can learn by occasional conversation, they seem to think this world a pretty good place in which to live and are in no hurry to leave it even though they have seen so much of it. Just beyond, on the corner, is a neat one-story cottage, occupied by a very old lady, who is partially, if not entirely, supported by her son. She may be seen quite frequently out in the garden among her flowers, which are chiefly noted for their old-fashioned names and colors. She has been a teacher and certainly loves nature and little children, and I feel pretty sure that nature and little children love her. I have never heard a word of discontent from her lips, though she may think the world is all awry, but if so, she does not show it.

Next to her home is a three-story frame residence just being completed. I have often stopped and talked with the workmen while the building has been going on. Of the two carpenters who are now finishing this work, one rides home every evening with his wife, who comes for him with a very neat little pony and phaeton, and is often accompanied by a bright-faced boy, evidently their son. I know where they live and how they live, and I think they are very good examples of American manhood and womanhood in what we sometimes falsely call the middle class—really the best class that we have. I know they read together evenings, and that he is reasonably well-informed in public affairs, and I do not believe that he is quarrelling with himself or his neighbors. His companion, a Swede, says he is discontented; he thinks the lot of the laboring man harder here than in the old country; and if he could get away he would certainly go back. Asked as to the cause of this dissatisfaction, he replied that at first he received large wages and thought he could soon own a home; that he had finally purchased it, but was somewhat in debt; that he disliked the continual paying of interest; and that now he did not get work enough to pay off what he owed. In the old country, he said with much apparent pride, he could not run in debt, he would have no credit, and he would be expected to rent and to remain a tenant. The man who was in charge and did most of the mason-work is an Englishman who seems entirely satisfied to have exchanged countries, and who feels himself a much freer and more hopeful man here than he could possibly have been at the old home. The one painter in whom I have taken enough interest to lead into somewhat prolonged conversation is a University student who is earning money during the summer to proceed with his work next fall. He is discontented: but it is chiefly the discontent which comes to the average intelligent American citizen because men of so little real worth so often find their way into public place and power. In fact, I think he is one of those horrible examples of the effects of higher education, which so constantly tends to make "independents" and

" mugwumps.' In the little story-and-a-half cottage next to this new house live the young man and the young woman who are building this home as a venture. The husband is a shipping-clerk for one of the large wholesale grocers of the city. His wife was, before marriage, a professional nurse with a long head and a warm heart. After their marriage she opened a students' club, and by good management has aided her husband in accumulating money with which to undertake the building of this University club-house. If she is not broken in health by over-work they will soon own this property free from debt, and will find it a source of more than fair revenue. They are busy and successful people, and such are rarely discontented.

Beyond them, still toward the University, are four or five small single-story or story-and-a-half cottages, occupied chiefly by men who labor " by the day." The only exception, I think, is a member of the fire department, whose wages are perhaps $50 a month. I do not know all these people, but I have not passed their homes four times a day for three years without learning much about them. There are children who are neatly dressed and who seem in good health and spirits. There are signs of comfort in the way of lawns and lawn-sprinklers, hammocks, window-screens, and fresh dresses for afternoon and evening. There is a good deal of companionship and neighborliness which speak of comfort and home-keeping. I have not heard these people complain, nor do I believe that they do.

Across the street is a larger house with larger grounds, occupied by a gentleman who is known as a capitalist; though I suspect his capital is not very large. There is every appearance of comfort, and as I meet him from time to time he seems cheerful and hopeful. On the next lot is a home in which lives a family consisting of father, mother, and three daughters. The youngest girl is still in the public school; the oldest is a graduate of the State University and is earning her way through the Albany (N. Y.) School of Library Economy; the second daughter is still a student at the University, and often sets type in order to meet her expenses. The father has some position upon one of the weekly papers, while the mother adds to the family income by caring for the few upper rooms in their house, which are rented to students or others. This family is thoroughly discontented—with intemperance, and with bad government, city, State and national; but it is about as intelligent discontent as one could readily find. I know them well enough to be sure that with all their material limitations they find life well worth the living, and make it better worth the living every day. Adjoining them is the residence of the city ticket-agent of one of the railway lines. He is a " rustler," as they say in this Western country; works hard, early and late; thinks his road is the best in the world; never lets a point in the business game escape him; and is steadily rising in the favor of his employers and of the community. He keeps a quiet family horse, which he drives with an easy phaeton; and he makes much of his wife and children,—and they make much of him. There is no discontent there.

The two blocks nearer the University are occupied in much the same way. There is a row of cottages which is given over chiefly to Germans. I am sure they enjoy life, for I see them enjoy it every day. The evening paper is thrown upon the porches; again there are the small lawns, flowers, and hammocks; and there are at least two pianos and one reed organ. On one of the porches I have noticed quite late at night two young people. They are not distinctly visible, for they are generally in the shadow of the porch, and there seems some confusion of outlines; but from what I happen to hear at times I suspect there is not much discontent there. In another house lives an old lady, comfortably supported by a daughter who is a stenographer. In the adjoining home there are two daughters who are clerks in one of the retail dry-goods stores. Several of these people let rooms; two of the best houses are owned by the man who built them, who is a mechanic, yet has managed to accumulate enough to be a landlord; in one of the others is a member of our Faculty; in another a newspaper man; another is occupied by a man who is a track-master and mechanic for one of our railway lines, but who owns his own house and I think three others in the vicinity; and in another lives an expert boiler-maker, who receives high wages.

Now I think these people, in their material conditions and surroundings and in their life and temper, are fair samples of the people who make up a Nebraska city or town. There are a few—a very few—streets in Lincoln that will doubtless show less comfort and less courage, greater limitations, more hopelessness, and more real suffering than does the one just described. But it is only fair to say that they will reveal also less intelligence, less will-power, less industry, less character; though it is often hard to tell which is cause and which is effect,—these two are so intimately connected and act and react so continuously on each other. On the other hand there are many portions of the city in which all the conditions of easy, comfortable, and contented life seem more distinctly present than in that section which I have tried to sketch. The latter certainly lies very close to the average line.

These conditions are practically those of the minor cities, towns, and villages; each, as compared with the city, minimized, photographed down, or looked at through the wrong end of the telescope. There are hundreds of communities in the State in which there is not a single family that can be called poor, in the sense in which that word would be used regarding a certain class of the population in New York, Boston, and Philadelphia. It is quite true also that none is rich, but one needs not more than a half hour's rapid walk about town to assure him that all are comfortable and that most are contented. Life is plain and simple, and even devoid of interest to those of us whose palates have been cloyed by the more highly spiced existence of a metropolis. But it brings much pleasure and solid comfort to those whose lines are cast in these quiet places. I know a banker who is also a good all-around citizen in his little town; being a member of the school board, a superintendent of one of the Sunday schools, president of a bicycle club, an active member of a gun club, and leader in the village band. I believe he gets more real enjoyment out of life, and in his way and place ministers more largely to the comfort and well-being of his fellows, than many whose names stand high among State or national officials. I know another, a householder and home-maker, who is superintendent of the city schools, organizer and leader in a branch of one of the great fraternal associations, a class-leader in his church, a stockholder in two small manufacturing enterprises and in one bank, and a member of the city council; and I am sure that he is a successful and a " contented" man, in any reasonable or true sense of that word. Such instances can be recalled almost without number in all the minor towns.

When one considers the agricultural part of our population there seems at first sight room for wide divergence of opinion because of an apparent wide divergence of conditions. Although this half of our population is carrying the heaviest burden in the fact that it deals altogether with a raw material (which always puts a man at a disadvantage), and suffers by shrinkage of currency, change of values, bad financiering at Washington, and frequent instances of bad government at home, it is, on the whole, gaining ground and strength from year to year. The last three years have been especially hard upon these people, and undoubtedly the greatest—and most natural—discontent is to be found in their ranks. It is true that a large number of them have undertaken agriculture with but little experience and almost no definite preparation and training for the work, and also that many who have had much experience have not the keenest intelligence. It is true that under one form of inducement or another many have undertaken agriculture in districts better fit, if not fit only, for grazing, and that many add to their lack of prepara- tion, of training and of intelligence, positive idleness and shiftless- ness. But it is also unquestionably true that there are large numbers of experienced, intelligent, industrious, hard-working, God-fearing men and women who, living with an enforced frugality which comes dangerously near absolute want, have found it a difficult task to make ends meet during the last few years. Some of them doubtless have lost hope; but even under the most discouraging conditions the per- centage is very small which really falls under our definition of dis- content,—the kind our Eastern friends think so prevalent. It is not probable that the hard times have borne much more heavily upon the farmers during the last few years than upon business men of all classes; but the farmers as a whole have had less reserve power with which to meet the struggle. Even in Nebraska, however, there have been fewer men sold off from their farms than have been sold out of their stores; there has been less money lost, in proportion to the amount lent, by those who have given credit to farmers than by those who have extended credits in the business world; and it is not too much to say that there has been more honesty and manliness in connection with financial transactions among farmers than among those in the business world. The farmer who can fail, yet continue to live as extravagantly as before, keeping his horses, carriages, and servants, and his place in all social functions, is a rare sight.

In order to make assurance doubly sure, I sent out a circular letter of inquiry regarding " discontent," to a hundred gentlemen of my personal acquaintance, who are fair representatives of the differ- ent sections, of the different political parties, and of the different material interests of the State. They were not chosen because I knew what they would write, but because I knew they would write honestly and intelligently and fearlessly. In this circular I expressed the thought that the normal condition of American life is certainly that of reasonable prosperity and rational contentment. I admitted, as we all ought to admit, the dissatisfaction of which every one must know something; but that we certainly ought also to know some-

thing in a clear and definite way of the high purpose and strong
hopefulness which must be prevailing.   Each letter contained a list
of twenty-six questions, to which I asked thoughtful and careful
answers, without reference to the present crop-failure, which is a local
disaster and temporary in its effects.   The questions covered such
subjects as the population of the city or county from which the
report was asked; the nationality of the population; the local indebtedness;   for what this indebtedness was incurred;   the percentages of
the people owning their homes or farms, of those heavily in debt, of
those reasonably well-to-do, of those reasonably successful in their
undertakings, of those better off now than they were ten or fifteen years
ago; how many are able to give their children much better opportunities (social and educational) than they themselves enjoyed when
young; how many are given to talking in a discontented way, how
many of these deeply and sincerely feel as they talk, how many of
the people are really and seriously discontented, and what are the
reasons and remedies for this discontent.   There was, of course,
much room for the exercise of individual judgment and opinion, for
inference and conclusion on the part of the writers; but such reports
were exceedingly helpful in preparing this statement.

The reports, with very few exceptions, confirm almost absolutely
the conclusions that I have drawn.   They differ somewhat in detail,
and they certainly differ as between the urban and rural populations.
But in all main points they agree, and upon some there is absolute unanimity.   For instance, there seems to be no question
that the people of this State are almost to a family better off than
they were ten or fifteen years ago.   As far as being able to give
their children better educational advantages than the parents enjoyed, all correspondents answer that the educational systems of
the present are far in advance of those of the past, and that the
child of the humblest citizen has better opportunities to-day than
most of the children of even the well-to-do classes of fifty years
ago.   There is a little feeling along social lines that the distinction
of class is more observable than a few years ago; but this is so slight
in Nebraska as to be scarcely noticeable.   As to those who have been
at least reasonably successful in their undertakings,—taking the years
as they go—it would seem that the general opinion is about 80 per
cent.   When one recalls Abbot Lawrence's statement, drawn from
his long observation in the business world, that 90 per cent of those
who go into business fail once, 80 per cent twice, and 70 per cent

three times, the latter going out of business altogether or else remaining as employees, it will be seen that the people of Nebraska are fully up to the average. If we understand by "very busy people" those whose time is fully employed in the fairly profitable affairs of life, the percentage seems to reach 85. If we understand by those who "take life easily and with reasonable comfort," those who are able to live without daily labor or effort or definite occupation of some kind, the percentage is very small. If, on the other hand, we refer to those who, by daily labor or systematic effort of perhaps eight hours, provide themselves and their families with the reasonable comforts of life, the percentage would show possibly 70 or 75. If we mean by those who are "reasonably well-to-do," those who own a farm of 80 or 160 acres, paid for or not encumbered for more than 20 or 25 per cent of its real value; or those who have a fairly successful, well-established business or profession; the percentage seems to be about 60. Very generally the children or young people are not drawn from the schools before the age of fifteen; and the percentage of those attending high schools, academies, and institutions of higher learning is quite as great as will be found in any of the older States. Our people realize that the times demand young men and young women who have the mental development, strength, and alertness which result from sound education. The increasing recognition of this is attested by the fact that in the State University the attendance has risen in three years from less than 500 to nearly 1,400; and by the further fact that even the hard times and the drought do not make any noticeable decrease in those numbers. All the public indebtedness of the State and of the counties and different localities has been incurred for public improvements. In Nebraska, as everywhere, there are always more or less carelessness and incompetency in the expenditure of such funds; but the reports seem to indicate that full value has been generally received, and that there is very little if any complaint because of such indebtedness. I have yet to hear a single instance of repudiation from any quarter of Nebraska. Our people feel that money thus borrowed for the purpose of erecting school-houses, churches, court-houses and other public buildings, is money well invested, and they will repay it.

I took pains to ask my correspondents to answer with more than usual care the questions, to which reference has already been made, referring to the discontent of the people of their several communities. The replies do not vary greatly, but where they do they are extreme in their divergence. Possibly five correspondents put the number of the discontented at from 80 per cent upwards of the population, and ten others say from 20 to 30 per cent. All the rest agree, however, that only from 3 to 5 per cent of the entire population are really and seriously "discontented." There is a general admission that a large number are given to talking in a discontented way. Unquestionably there is greater freedom of speech and there is a more general habit of criticism in Nebraska than in Maine or Massachusetts. But this only illustrates the saying that "freedom flourishes in the colonies." The people of Nebraska expect more and demand more than do many others; they feel that there may be and ought to be more in life for them than there is; they are more eager for financial success and material comfort, and more impatient at anything which looks like an unequal distribution of the results of productive toil. It is, therefore, but natural that they should be misunderstood by those who are somewhat more apathetic, to whom a change of theological or political creed seems like revolution itself, who "view with alarm" every forward movement of humanity, and who are more ready to accept the settled order of things as the only possible condition of existence. Such people naturally look upon any criticism and any real freedom of speech and action with distrust and suspicion, when these are positively healthful signs.

This, then, seems to be the conclusion of the whole matter. There is some discontent within the limits of Nebraska. In a new State, and especially in a rich State like our own, where all natural resources seem to be within the easy grasp of each and all, there have been great opportunities for acquiring a competence and even wealth. In most of these Western States money-getting has been easy. In the pursuit of wealth, some, by reason of extraordinary diligence, extraordinary shrewdness, or good fortune, have been more successful than others. With the unsuccessful, even though they have done more than fairly well, the sense of not being as far along in the race as those with whom they made the start is irritating. The rapid rise in values has unquestionably unsettled many men and made them discontented with conditions which we all know to be more nearly normal. The tenth commandment is undoubtedly often and badly shattered in Nebraska; but I fancy we are neither the only sinners nor the chief of sinners in this respect. Our people do not always wait to be deprived of necessaries before they complain, but are apt to speak, and speak sharply, if what may be termed the lavishness of supply is lessened. Men here, as elsewhere, are in haste to get rich; not simply to secure a competence. With many others the present complaining is hereditary, and comes to them with their New England blood. Most well-organized, normal New Englanders are always "on the road to the poor-house." The only difference between New England and Nebraska seems to be that, whereas in the former people go cheerfully and willingly and seem rather to enjoy the prospect (they rarely get there, of course,—those who are always talking about it never do), their descendants in Nebraska, with the same prospect in view and entertaining it just as sincerely as do their ancestors (which is not sincerely at all), grow rebellious at the very thought. With all this, however, it is quite a difficult task to avoid making out a case for contentment in one's own locality when the existing facts and conditions are studied carefully and in detail. Suffering, deprivation, and discontent are much like the ague,—"over in the next township"; and it is not at all unusual to find an audience applauding a speaker who tells them they are pauperized, when very few men in the audience would part with their possessions short of a sum represented by a big unit and three ciphers.

The discontent which really does exist, however, to any great extent and with any great power, is not so much discontent with one's individual lot as with the existing order of things. In our haste to build an empire in a night, we have not always guarded carefully the interests of all the people. We have only ourselves to blame for this; and part of our present ill-humor comes from a secret consciousness of this fact. Much, if not all, legal inequality might have been prevented by wise forethought and unselfish action on our part. It would sometimes seem as though our children could not possibly govern themselves any worse than we have governed ourselves, and that if they do not vastly improve in all methods of public administration they will suffer more than we do.

Out of such bitter experiences, however, and out of this kind of rational discontent, are evolved all human improvement and all advancement of the race. This kind of discontent seems to have naturally and properly become a powerful factor in American public life. But as for ourselves and our neighbors as individuals, and in our own individual and private interests and affairs, it is safe to say that 95 per cent of the people of this State fall easily under any thoughtful definition of the expression "contented classes."

J. H. CANFIELD.

WILL POLYGAMISTS CONTROL THE NEW STATE OF UTAH?

SIX times the people of the Territory of Utah have formulated a constitution and submitted it to Congress with an application for Statehood. Every time their petition has been refused. The seventh proposed constitution, framed in accordance with the " enabling act" passed by the last Congress, will be prepared and presented to President Cleveland for his acceptance or rejection during the coming year. For more than twenty years the Territory has had population and wealth sufficient to entitle it to a place in the Union. The population to-day is greater than the combined populations of the three adjoining States of Nevada, Idaho, and Wyoming. But for the institution of polygamy Utah would long ago have become a State.

It is now four years since the practice of polygamy was renounced by the Mormon people, in conference assembled, and the political party which united them was formally dissolved. The Liberal, or anti-Mormon, party continued its existence till November, 1893, when it, too, disbanded. Mormons and Gentiles, heretofore grouped into parties by local questions only, now ranged themselves by national questions and became members of one or the other of the great parties of the land. With one accord all the people of Utah, irrespective of politics or religion, petitioned Congress for admission as a State.

· The action of the Mormons in renouncing a fundamental tenet of their religion and disbanding their political party, at the bidding of their leaders, is without a parallel in our history. The question naturally arises, Might not this people, at the dictate of their Church authorities, with the same unanimity and readiness resume the practice of polygamy and combine again for political control of the local government, when Utah has become a State? True, under the enabling act the new constitution must inhibit polygamy; but statutory penalties and local enforcement are required to make any law effective. Would it not be easy for a Mormon legislature practically to nullify this provision of the constitution? Is it not possible, indeed, that in their zeal for Statehood the Gentiles of Utah are blind to the dangers that their action invites?

These are questions that many people outside Utah are asking. Their apprehensions are intensified by echoes from the present political campaign in Utah, in which Republicans and Democrats are trying to outbid each other for the Mormon vote. Nor is this solicitude allayed by the announcement that the late Territorial conventions of both parties unanimously favored woman suffrage,—an institution which existed in Utah for seventeen years and proved to be one of the strongest bulwarks of polygamy. To arrive at a definite conclusion it. is necessary briefly to consider the recent history of the Territory.

Polygamy was never regarded by the Gentiles of Utah with the same degree of abhorrence that it excited elsewhere in the world. The local Gentile hostility to the institution, it is true, was fierce and unrelenting. Yet Mormons who had been convicted and sentenced to the penitentiary for the crime of polygamy were never regarded by Gentiles with the aversion felt for other criminals. They were looked upon rather as blind and devoted adherents to a mistaken principle. In prison they were treated with respectful consideration by the guards and officials, and as far as possible they were employed as "trusties." The Gentiles attached no particular stigma to Mormons who had served sentences for polygamy, and by their own sect, of course, they were honored as heroes and martyrs. Quite different, however, was the feeling outside the Territory. The bitterest indignation prevailed against the iniquitous doctrine, and those who practised it or even believed in it were regarded as monsters. Tourists who came to Utah looked upon the Mormons with curious awe, and not infrequently with genuine fear.

Deeper than the resentment felt by the Gentiles of Utah against polygamy was that aroused by the union of Church and State in the Territory. The Church authorities have always strenuously denied that they exercised political power. Whether they did or did not, the effect was the same. In politics the Church was a unit. In business the distinction was less closely drawn, but most Mormon trade went into Mormon channels. This union of religion, business, and civil government awakened here, as it must anywhere, the fiercest opposition. This union of Church and State, however, was not the kind of evil that could be used with best advantage by the Gentiles in appealing to the whole Union. But polygamy satisfied this need because it shocked the moral sense of civilization. Consequently polygamy was made the scapegoat upon which the anti-Mor-

mon population of Utah piled its combined grievances. Another class
in the Territory joined with yet keener zest in the popular hue and
cry against polygamy. Officials sent from the Eastern States to official positions in the Territory as a reward for party service found
indiscriminate denunciation of the Mormons an excellent method of
perpetuating political power. It is notorious that not a few who
came to Utah poor men enriched themselves at the expense of the
Mormon Church. The shrinkage of the Church property escheated
by the government would itself unfold a tale of official rapacity.
Even the bench has not been free from charges of blind partisanship
continued to the present hour, with here and there ugly hints of corruption. Most of the Federal officials in Utah have been men of unimpeachable integrity and of rare personal courage in dealing with
one of the most pernicious institutions of modern times; but unfortunately there were some who took advantage of a righteous cause to
advance their personal interests. Curiously enough some of these
political vultures during the late campaign appealed, upon the
ground of past sympathy and protection, to the very people whom
they despoiled.

Polygamy among the Mormons had all the tenacity of a sacred institution. It was taught as a divine command, "a necessity to man's
highest exaltation in the life to come." For more than a quarter of
a century, the Mormon Church fought, with every weapon that it
could command, the laws directed against its favorite institution.
One by one, new and more rigorous penalties were enacted by Congress against polygamy. Finding women the most ardent champions
of the vicious practice (owing to their stronger religious convictions)
Congress, in 1887, took away their right of suffrage. The right of
dower was restored, in order that the first wife might always be able
to protect herself through her property rights. Federal machinery
for the enforcement of penal acts was steadily increased and strengthened. Deputy marshals watched, pursued, and arrested men suspected
of polygamy with the same zeal that Southern officers pursued fugitive slaves before the war. Indeed, the similarity of the two callings
led to the application of the term "underground" to those offenders
hiding from the law. Friends kept the refugees informed of the
movements of the officers. The news of a deputy's approach outsped
the officer himself. One Mormon who was captured and sentenced
to a term in the penitentiary after successfully evading the law's penalties for years, told me that he had outwitted the deputies dozens of

times through the warning of religious brethren. Often he had lain on the summit of a neighboring mountain and laughed in his sleeve as he watched his pursuers searching house after house in the village below in hope of finding him. He was finally surprised and taken through the treachery of a sister of a "plural" wife. On one occasion I was hospitably entertained on the frontier by a ranchman who cooked me an appetizing dinner with his own hands. He gave me to understand that he was a bachelor. I afterward accidentally discovered that he was a Mormon dignitary and had five wives. His first wife he did not like, and he dared not live openly with any of the others; so he pretended to be a bachelor, and he made stealthy visits to his favorite spouses at such times as he could best avoid the observation of the United States officers. President Woodruff of the Mormon Church was for some time himself "on the underground." Being a man of active temperament, he chafed under confinement. At one "station" he made it a practice to go out by moonlight and with a hand-sickle spend most of the night cutting grain, commencing in the centre of the field and working outward. In this manner he cut and bound a large field of wheat, until there was left standing only a fringe of grain on the outside which he dared not mow for fear of discovery.

By reason of the secrecy attaching to the marriage rite in the Mormon Church it was seldom possible to prove "plural" marriage. Nearly all the indictments had to be on the count of "unlawful cohabitation." Those convicted for this offence were commonly regarded as polygamists, and so considered in estimating the extent of the practice.

While able to evade the laws to a certain extent, the Mormons could not stem the tide of indignation which rose steadily against them. In the spring of 1890 a bill taking away the elective franchise from all Mormons was favorably reported in both Houses of Congress; and in July a bill was reported to the Senate providing for the appointment of all county officers in Utah by the Governor instead of their election by the people. The passage of one of the bills, or of both, was imminent. Idaho had already been admitted into the Union with a constitutional proviso disfranchising believers in the Mormon creed. Meanwhile within the Mormon Church a sentiment had gradually been growing against polygamy. Contact with the great numbers of Gentiles pouring into the Territory, strong enough by this time to carry the elections in both Salt Lake City and Ogden, made

30

many of the younger Mormons ashamed of their peculiar institution. Many children of "plural" wives, moved by sympathy for their mothers, were at heart embittered against the practice. Mormon influence in politics and business was directed against the young men and in favor of the older, even as it favored the Mormons at the expense of the Gentiles. The result was internal dissension and incipient rebellion against Church authority. More than this, there were many members of the Church who had no serious religious conviction, but remained within its pale for social or commercial reasons.

The Church authorities, under these circumstances, had a very difficult task laid on them. They did not longer dare to countenance polygamy in the face of the culminating wrath of the Nation and the opposition from within the Church. Neither did they dare directly to repudiate their old teaching by declaring "plural" marriage wrong in principle. The only practical line of retreat was the one adopted, whereby the President of the Church publicly "advised Latter-Day Saints against contracting any marriage forbidden by the law of the land." Nominally and theoretically, "plural" or "celestial" marriage remains a part of the Mormon creed, though its practice was suspended for all time. Those who argue that, because the suspension did not come in the form of a revelation, it must therefore have been but an artful subterfuge having in view the future revival of polygamy, fail to do justice to the President of the Church or to understand the embarrassing position in which he was placed before his people.

That the Mormons were sincere, both in renouncing polygamy and disbanding their political party, no one conversant with the affairs of Utah during the past four years can for a moment doubt. Their acts have confirmed their professions. The Liberals, or non-Mormons, by disbanding their political party and declaring for Statehood a year ago, emphasized their belief in the sincerity of their former opponents. The institution of polygamy would have gone down eventually of its own weight under the rush of Gentile immigration. The action of the Church only hastened the inevitable. In the days of its strongest hold less than ten per cent of the adult males of the Territory lived in polygamy. No "plural" marriages in any form are now taking place in Utah. It is a sin within the Mormon Church as within any other to live with more than one woman. The young man who should attempt it would find himself and his mistress (for such any "plural" wife would be regarded) subject to the same social ostracism from the Mormons as from society at large.

There is, however, another phase of this interesting question. With the division of the Mormons on National party-lines, the renunciation of their obnoxious creed and the inauguration of "the era of good feeling" in Utah, there has been a complete cessation of prosecutions for polygamy; and numbers of old-time offenders have resumed relations with their "plural" wives, with practical immunity from punishment. But the prop of polygamy, its social respectability and exaltation as a religious virtue, has been taken away. These old polygamists visit their younger wives precisely as a married man in an Eastern community might consort with a mistress—quietly and stealthily, not openly or boastfully as formerly. Their conduct is under the ban of the Church, and, since it is no longer justified by a religious principle, is regarded simply as an affair of lust or of affection for former associations too strong to withstand. We find a close analogy to this condition of things in the prohibition States where, in spite of stringent laws, the old toper undergoes any humiliation to secure his favorite beverage. Human nature does not differ greatly in New York, Massachusetts, Kansas, or Utah. But, with the passing away of the present generation, the last vestige of polygamy will disappear. No edict of the Church could restore it. Aside from the reasons already given, an insurmountable barrier in the way of its resumption is arising in the social amalgamation of Gentiles and Mormons. Intermarriages between the two classes have rapidly increased under the new conditions. Within a decade, the distinguishing characteristics of Mormonism will be no stronger in Utah than the distinguishing characteristics of Catholicism, Presbyterianism, or Methodism.

A strong evidence of the sincerity of the Mormon people and their devotion to principle was revealed in the recent political campaign. Many of the professional politicians who formerly inveighed most bitterly against the Mormons then protested with equal vehemence their former love and devotion. Having for years assailed Church influence in the State, these men recently appealed to religious prejudice in the hope of personal preferment. The following quotation from a political catechism that was scattered broadcast throughout the Territory, will illustrate the methods whereby it was sought to win the Mormon vote:

Who inaugurated the scheme to confiscate the property of the Mormon Church and to disfranchise the women of Utah? The Republican Party.

Who attempted to disfranchise the Mormon people? The Republican Party.

Who for thirty years refused Statehood to Utah? The Republican Party.

Who refused to give a majority of Utah's people a full representation in its National convention? The Republican Party.

Who brought about the return of the Church property? The Democratic Party.

Who obtained Statehood for Utah? The Democratic Party.

Who enfranchised all the Mormon people? Cleveland.

But appeals to religious prejudice during the recent campaign awakened only Mormon resentment and indignation. If ecclesiastics attempted to mount the hustings, they were compelled to take the same sort of knocks that laymen receive. No sort of religious interference was tolerated. Having been liberated from the religious yoke in political matters, the masses seem to have plunged into the opposite extreme of an independent delirium. Political contention ran wildest in the rural localities where the population is almost exclusively Mormon. Personal hostility waxed so warm that the President of the Mormon Church recently felt called upon to warn his followers against personal abuse in politics. Indeed, the recent campaign afforded a strange and unique spectacle. We saw a large body of our own citizens—Americans by birth or by long residence—undergoing political education in their maturity instead of in their youth. At the time the People's, or Church, party disbanded, the inhabitants of China could scarcely have been more ignorant of the principles of the two great political parties of the United States than were the masses of the people of Utah. The eagerness and absorbing seriousness with which they went to work to study the principles of government is one of the most hopeful signs of new Utah. To whichever of the national parties the Mormon voter gave his allegiance, he gave it with all the earnestness and enthusiasm of the new convert.

The best evidence of the remarkable change which has recently taken place in Utah is afforded by the growth of the public-school system. Five years ago there were practically only sectarian schools in the Territory. On the one side were the so-called public schools, where tuition fees were required, controlled, dominated and almost exclusively patronized by the Mormon people. The school-houses were cheap, primitive buildings, devoid of any modern conveniences and of many of the actual requisites of health. On the other side were the denominational schools, established by non-Mormon churches, and maintained chiefly by funds from missionary societies in the Eastern States. There was no pretence of system in the educational work. At best it was a mere makeshift. In Salt Lake City within half a decade there has sprung from these heterogeneous elements a public-school system which is thought to be one of the best in the country. The school-houses are commodious buildings, constructed with an understanding of school architecture. Both tuition and text-books are free. Of a total school population of 11,941 children, 88 per cent are in daily attendance upon the public schools, as compared with 27 per cent in 1889. In the country districts the advance has not been so rapid, but sectarianism is being rapidly eliminated from educational work, and a better class of buildings and teachers is provided. In the schools, too, as elsewhere, the distinction between Mormon and Gentile has been almost entirely obliterated.

The business influence of the Mormon authorities upon their people had become lax long before their political influence was weakened. Years ago the faithful were warned not to patronize Gentile stores, and later they were warned not to sell land to the Gentiles. But these warnings are now matters of ancient history in Utah, and with one accord all citizens, irrespective of creed, are working together to build up the Territory. A "home industry" movement has assumed gigantic proportions and has already made itself felt in a flattering material advance. In examining the *personnel* of recent incorporations I have observed that among the organizers of almost every stock-company are members of both religious elements. In Salt Lake City the line of demarcation on Main Street between Gentile and Mormon stores has been obliterated. Mormons and Gentiles trade indiscriminately at each other's places of business. Mormon merchants seek no longer the shadow of the Temple. All over the city the historic landmarks are fast vanishing. The long adobe houses with their various apartments for the different wives, the high fences of boulders and mortar, the all-seeing eye above the entrances to stores, the old wall that surrounded the city,—all these have already yielded to modern taste and improvement. More significant, however, than these material changes is the revolution that has taken place in the social customs, the business habits, the political opinions and the religious practices of the people. Utah is rapidly losing those strange features of life which made her an object of such fascinating interest to students and tourists; but to compensate for this loss she has placed herself in complete harmony with American thought and American institutions. GLEN MILLER.

THE NEW STORY–TELLERS AND THE DOOM OF REALISM.

EIGHT years ago, in writing on "Realism in Literature," I called attention to the then recently printed essays of M. Emile de Vogüé. That excellent critic, who has since been admitted to the French Academy, had in the essays referred to pointed out indications that realistic fiction—at least in France—was fast nearing the high-water mark, and he confidently expected that the turn in the tide would be followed by fiction of a purer, different sort. Only eight years have elapsed, yet no one can doubt that, so far as Realism is concerned, M. de Vogüé was a far-seeing observer. M. Zola, the arch-priest of the obscene rites of French Realism, has ceased to have any formative influence on French novelists; he has ceased to be called "*maître*," or to be imitated by disciples; his own books are still widely read, for obvious reasons, among which his talent as an advertiser is not the least; but they beget no warfare among critics and their power as literary epoch-makers has vanished. Even the stories of Guy de Maupassant, the Realist who presented his delicately-wrought immoralities to you with silver tongs, instead of Zola's coal-shovel, we were told the other day by another watcher of French literature, have lost their vogue: and yet Maupassant is but two years dead.

I refer first to France because France is still the initiator of novelties, whether in politics, literature, or millinery; and when she does not originate she is usually the first to give world-currency to what others have initiated. But the symptoms observed in France have been widespread, and the change they betoken is working most healthily in England and America. We violate no confidences in declaring that Realism in fiction is passing away. Eight years ago the "Realists"—who ought rather to be called the "Epidermists"—had the cry; to-day you have only to look at the publishers' announcements, or at the volumes in everybody's hand, to see what fiction is popular. Caine, Doyle, Zangwill, Weyman, Crockett, Du Maurier,—not Realists but Romanticists, not analysts but story-tellers,—are writing the novels which the multitude are sitting up late to read. And Stevenson and Crawford, whose reputation dates from the very heyday of Realism, have certainly not lost popularity during the past decade, while—worse and worse!—two separate popular editions of Scott, and new translations of Dumas *père*, have just come out, in spite of the assertions of the Epidermists that not even schoolboys could now be coaxed to read Sir Walter. Above all, Rudyard Kipling, who was so recently characterized by Mr. Howells as merely a young man with his hat cocked over one eye, holds the entire English-speaking world in fee as no other story-teller since Dickens has held it.

Now this change deserves attention, even from those of us who read very little current fiction, but who realize how important a symptom is the popular demand for it. To follow the statistics of the circulation of novels may lead to conclusions not less significant than do the statistics of the annual consumption of malt and fermented liquors. If you found, for instance, that the nation had in the course of ten years given up whiskey and taken to beer, you might be able to demonstrate the close relation between strong drink and crime; and so we may be sure that the change in taste which has led the public back to romantic fiction has for its basis something deeper than caprice. It is too soon to say how deep the meaning really is, or what may come of it, but it is not too soon to look back over the losing fight of Realism and to specify some of its traits.

In the first place, the tide turned much earlier than most of us expected. Ten years ago few of us dared hope that the exposure of Zola's plausible fallacy would so soon be generally agreed to. He had been captivated by the eminent physiologist, Claude Bernard, who found medicine an art and left it a science, and, reasoning from analogy, he had concluded that fiction might be subjected to a similar evolution. Observation and experiment, these were the two methods by which the " experimental novelist," subsequently miscalled " Realist," should produce his work. We all know with what vigor and plausibility Zola set forth this doctrine, which had all the more attractiveness in that it seemed to tally with the scientific spirit of the age. Everything was tinctured with science; the very word " scientific" had become a shibboleth: we had " scientific" clothespins, " scientific" liverpads,—why not " scientific" novels?

And in due time " scientific" novels came,—" Nana," " L'Assommoir," and the rest; but I suspect that Zola's literary philosophy would have achieved notoriety much more slowly had he not chosen topics either brutally obscene or horrible, which at once excited the jaded Parisian palate. And as the author of these works proclaimed that he was personally as impartial towards virtue and vice as a chemist is towards acids and alkalies, and that he did not make it his business to correct nature, but simply to photograph her, his aim being scientific truth, many persons read his abominations who could not have been induced to do so but for the seductive catchword "scientific." Many others read, and still read, Zola, regardless of any literary theory, to gratify their pornographic appetite; for it required no keenness to perceive that decency, modesty, sanctity,—conceptions which, after many painful centuries, the more civilized minority of the human race has begun to venerate,—could not protect themselves against the brazen presumptions of Realism. Zola and his fellows, at home and abroad, tore the veil away with an affectation of scientific impartiality even more repulsive than the downright prurience of the avowed worshippers of lubricity. Strenuously have they protested that their goddess is the naked Truth, but we may well ask, as we look at the product of their school, whether it has not been the nakedness rather than the divinity of Truth which has attracted them.

When Realism had thus assumed the proportion of a literary movement, the historians of literature went back to discover M. Zola's precursors. They traced, with what accuracy I know not, the roots of Realism down through Flaubert and Balzac to Stendhal. The disciples of the new school had no scruple in asserting that it was not only the school of the present and future, but that it would utterly supersede previous literature; its novels were to all previous novels as modern invention to old-fashioned handiwork. It would soon make even school-girls ashamed to admit that they enjoyed romances. Poetry, of course, could no more exist in its presence than frost before a blow-pipe. "There shall never be any more plots," was one of the edicts of the new law-givers. Not since the memorable conflict of the Romanticists and the Classicists had so pretentious a movement been seen; a movement, moreover, which affected, or tended to affect, not merely the writing of novels and all imaginative literature, but also our established views of morals.

I fear that we must confess that this Realistic movement has been, on the whole, less memorable than we should have predicted of a revolution which boldly took upon itself the task of creating a new

heaven and a new earth. It has certainly been less spectacular, amusing, and attractive than the Romantic movement which culminated
sixty-five years ago. Victor Hugo led that, as Zola has led this.
Hugo was very human, and abounded in qualities which drew enthusiastic disciples round him. We cannot think of Zola as a man
whom anybody can love; we think of him as a coldly calculating
doctrinaire, a chemist who has invented a process for making top-
dressing cheap and has the shrewdness to sell it at an enormous profit.
In France, the quarrel has been rather *banal*, not enlivened by any
such scenes as those which signalized the triumph of Hugo's supporters
at the production of " Hernani."

In America, however, the warfare has not failed to amuse us,
thanks to the wit of Mr. Howells. Yet even his wit has lacked
the picturesqueness of Théophile Gautier's famous flaming waist-
coat, which glows upon us from the records of the warfare of Romanticism. At the outset, however, Mr. Howells gave promise of
being both picturesque and lively. We all remember how, after his
first naïf declaration that the art of fiction as practised by Mr. Henry
James and himself is a finer art than that of Dickens, Thackeray, and
George Eliot, a burst of genial laughter swept over the continent and
re-echoed even in England. Mr. Howells did not directly name
himself, of course, but the implication was not to be escaped. The
public laughed because it thought it had caught a man-of-the-world—
one, moreover, who had been publishing books for a quarter of a century—in a perfectly indiscreet bit of egotism. The fact is, however,
that Mr. Howells told the plain truth,—the art of fiction as practised
by him and Mr. James is a finer art than that of Dickens or Thackeray,
just as the art of the cameoist is " finer" than that of the sculptor.

Mr. Howells, being thoroughly in earnest, probably did not mind
the laughter. At any rate no convert from one religion to another
could be more zealous than he was during five or six years. He bore
witness to his faith by example not less than by precept; and as he
had the good fortune to be able to use as a mouthpiece a magazine
with a very large circulation, he spread the gospel of Realism in a
brief time before multitudes who are usually slow to feel the direction of literary currents. Whatever opinion readers might have had
of the novel by Mr. Howells in the earlier part of the magazine, they
were sure to be informed in a crisp, satirical essay farther on that
only fools and old fogies tolerated fiction produced by other than
Realistic methods.

A propagandist as witty; resourceful, and assured as he, has not
for so many years together and from so conspicuous a pulpit preached
any literary gospel, good or bad, in America; and there were many
of us who, while we read very little of his novels, never missed one
of his monthly essays.   They were significant, if ónly as symptoms;
and then, perhaps the doctrine they uttered might be true.   At any
rate, it was very wholesome, if somewhat bewildering, at the start,
to have our venerable idols challenged, and to receive from the lips
of an evangelist the message which was to revolutionize literature,
casting out its false gods, dethroning its arrogant sovereigns, levelling
its exclusive aristocracies, and establishing a Simon-pure democracy
which should be run forever on scientific principles.   It took forti-
tude, until custom made us callous, to watch Mr. Howells, like another Tarquin, go up and down the poppy-field of literature, lopping
off head after head which had brought delight to millions.   The
Greeks, of course, were smitten very early: they are always the first
to excite the righteous rage of all sorts of reformers, and have been
demolished so many times!   Artistic principles—symmetry, grace,
condensation, beauty—went next: Realism, we perceived, knew not
beauty, and despised literary neatness as your true son of the soil is
supposed to despise those who indulge in soap and water.   Poetry,
too, had its death-warrant signed.   Even Shakespeare was not spared.
At his martyrdom, we knew that genius too must go, and soon
the dictum came that " there is no such thing as genius," that what
the unscientific foreworld called by that name is only a strong con-
genital predisposition *plus* indefatigable perseverance.

Incidentally we learned the tenets of Realism, and month by
month we were introduced to Spanish and Russian masters of the
new creed.   A little later than some of us, but earlier than the
masses, Mr. Howells discovered Tolstoi, and then we knew why
the Greeks and art and Shakespeare had been previously swept away.
For the great Russian, though he be in many aspects a master, has
certainly no inkling of the Greek conception of art, no spark of
Shakespeare's dramatic intensity.   The Greek made his effects by
selection, Tolstoi makes his by cumulation; the Greek's motto was,
" Nothing superfluous "; Tolstoi's is, " Put in everything, and then
add a little more."   If you think of Russia as a vast flat prairie land,
in which even a tree or hillock is an important feature, you may be
reminded of Tolstoi; if you remember Greece, with its infinite variety
of chiselled mountains and valleys, its individual headlands, its islands

and lovely bays, with a luminous sky above and beautiful color on all below, you have, in contrast with him, the Greek. No Greek could so have sinned against his instinct for symmetry as to write " War and Peace," a story, or congeries of stories, stretching through twenty-five hundred pages—the equivalent in space of fifty " Antigones" and of seven or eight Iliads. The Iliad is getting well on in years, and yet, if there existed a company for insuring the lives of literary works, some of us think that the Iliad would prove a better risk than " War and Peace ": for one good reason, it is only one eighth as bulky as the Russian masterpiece; and bulk is an element which will count more and more in the longevity of books.

I pause at Tolstoi, because Mr. Howells assured us that his works not only form the culminating glory of Realism, but practically render obsolete all other works not produced by that system. So we accepted the reign of Czar Lyoff, although for a while, after the immolation of Shakespeare and the great companions of our youth, the world seemed empty, lonesome. It was as if the sun had been stolen, and the thief had hung up a locomotive headlight in its stead. But, on closer examination of Tolstoi, we were surprised to find that he wrote almost always with a strong moral purpose; and this, we had been so often assured, was one of the foul practices of the old school of novelists which Realism would abolish. For, to the genuine Realist, virtue and vice are what acids and alkalies are to the chemist: therefore, he cannot prefer, cannot have, an ethical purpose.

Reading Mr. Howells's preachments month by month, while we could but admire his versatility in iconoclasm, and his unquestioning zeal,—he swallowed Tolstoi's " Kreutzer Sonata" and Zola's " La Terre," and smacked his lips, bidding us all do likewise,—we saw that we had to do with a very clever disciple and not at all with a master. As certainly as Mr. Howells is a more graceful and clever writer than M. Zola, so certainly is M. Zola profounder and more philosophical than Mr. Howells. The Frenchman had, indeed, thought out and formulated his system, and his essays in " Le roman expérimental" remain the chief document of the theory of Realism. Them, the serious student of literary and spiritual movements may consult, but Mr. Howells's critical writings take on more and more the aspect of being merely the register of the vagaries of a mind alert rather than cultured, and of a generous spirit which cannot resist becoming the champion of crude causes. Not impossibly, therefore, these writings of his will be valued less and less as orthodox Realistic tracts, and more and more as data for studying the psychological development of an interesting personality.

Nevertheless, Mr. Howells had the satisfaction, for the time being, of making Realism the chief topic of discussion, and of encouraging the belief in innumerable crude minds that you have only to report word for word the morning gossip of idle women on a summer hotel piazza, or the rusticities in wit and grammar of the patrons of the corner grocery, in order to produce a work beside which Shakespeare's pages look faded. Perhaps no higher compliment can be paid to Mr. Howells than to state that those who undertake to write about Realism in America will inevitably find themselves dealing with it as though it were his private property, instead of with the doctrines and assertions of a system. And yet for a dozen years a horde of Realists, great and small, have been filling the magazines with their products and turning out an average of two novels a day.

And now Realism—a movement which, but for the deep matters it involves, we might call a fad—is on the wane. It has been the logical outcome of our age, whose characteristic is analysis. Our modern science, abandoning the search for the Absolute, has been scrutinizing every atom, to weigh and name it, and to discover its relations with its neighbors. "Relativity" has been the watchword. Science literally knows neither great nor small: it examines the microbe and Sirius with equal interest; it draws no distinction between beauty and ugliness—having no preference for the toadstool or the rose, the sculpin or the trout: it is impartial; it seeks only to know. By observation and experiment, by advancing from the known to the unknown, science has begun to make the first accurate inventory of the substances, laws, and properties of the world of matter. Its achievements have already been stupendous. Its methods have dominated all the other works in our time; it was inevitable that they should encroach on the sphere of art and of literature.

Arguing from analogy, the Realist persuaded himself that the only means for attaining perfect accuracy in fiction must be experiment and observation, which had brought such rich returns to Science. He disdained anything except an exact reproduction of real life— hence his name, Realist. To him, as to the man of science, there should be, he declared, neither beauty nor ugliness, great nor small, goodness nor evil; he was impartial; he eliminated the personal equation; he would make his mind as unprejudiced as a photographic plate. To Pyrrhonism so thoroughgoing, considerations of interest and charm appealed no more than did considerations of morals or of beauty. The Realist frankly announced that the precise record of the humblest mind was just as important as one of Shakespeare's mind would be. So we have been regaled by our English and American Realists with interminable inspection and introspection of commonplace intellects; and if we have yawned, we have been told that we were still poisoned with Romanticism, and still had a childish desire to read about persons with high titles, moving in the upper circles. Realism, we were assured, was the application of democratic principles to fiction. When, on the other hand, the foreign Realists dealt chiefly in moral filth, we were chidden for our squeamishness, and informed that, since depravity exists, the Realist is in duty bound to make impartial studies of it.

I need not point out that such doctrines reduce literature, art, and morals to anarchy. The "scientific method," applied in this way, is not the method for portraying human nature. Only the human can understand, and consequently interpret, the human: how, therefore, shall a man who boasts that he has *dehumanized* himself so that his mind is as impartial as a photographic plate, enabling him to look on his fellow-beings without preferring the good to the bad, the beautiful to the ugly,—how shall he be qualified to speak for the race which does discriminate, does prefer, does feel? The camera sees only the outside; the Realist sees no more, and so it would be more appropriate to call him "Epidermist," one who investigates only the surface, the cuticle of life,—usually with a preference for very dirty skin.

And, in truth, he deceives himself as to the extent of his scientific impartiality. He, too, has to select; he cannot set down every trivial thought, cannot measure every freckle. His work is fiction— a consideration which he had forgotten. But since he is forced to select, he cannot escape being judged by the same canons as all other artists. Do they not all aim at representing life? Is *Silas Lapham*, produced by Epidermist methods, more real than *Shylock* or *Hamlet?* Will he be thought so three hundred years hence, or will he seem odd and antiquated, a mere fashion, like the cut of old garments? Only the human can understand and interpret the human; and our Epidermists also will, in time, perceive that not by relying on the phonograph and kodak can they come to know the heart of man. They have mistaken the dead actual for reality, the show of the moment for the essence, the letter for the spirit.

By the imagination have all the highest creations of art and literature been produced, and the general truths of science and morals
been discovered: for the imagination is that supreme faculty in man
which beholds reality; it is the faculty, furthermore, which synthe-
tizes, which vivifies, which constructs.   The Epidermist, whose forte
is analysis, discarding the imagination, has hoped by accumulating
masses of details to produce as sure an effect of reality, as genius
produces by using a few essentials.   Yet, merely in the matter of
illusion, this is an inferior method: if Mr. Kipling, for instance, can
in a paragraph illude his readers to the extent he desires, whereas it
takes Mr. Howells or Mr. James ten pages to produce an illusion,
the chances are ten to one against Epidermism as a means of literary
expression.

That heaping up of minute details which is proper in scientific
investigation has influenced immensely all our intellectual processes
for the past fifty years.   There was a time when theology was the
absorbing interest, and even non-theological works of that time, the
fiction and poetry, are inevitably saturated with theology.   We can
detect it plainly and can pronounce it just so far a detriment to the
novel or poem in which we find it.   So science has permeated our
time, encroaching upon, and inevitably vitiating, departments over
which it has no jurisdiction.   The multitude has been willing to
accept the products of Epidermism, because its own imagination has
been dulled, and it has come to suppose that observation and experiment were the only methods by which truth can be discovered.
Hence the tanks of *real* water and the *real* burglars and the *real* fire-
engines in our recent plays, and hence the predominance of Realism
in fiction.

But the knell of the Epidermists has sounded.   The novels that
are everywhere in demand are the novels with a story.   Individually, they may be good or bad—it matters not: the significant fact is
that the public taste has turned, and that that instinct which is as old
as the children of Adam and Eve, the instinct for a story, has reas-
serted itself.

Realism, therefore, has been a phase, indicating the decadence
of fiction, and not, as the Epidermists themselves believed, its regeneration.   It represents the period during which fiction has been enslaved by scientific methods, a period when the imagination has lain
dormant, and other—lower—faculties have essayed to do her work.
The novels produced by Realism will not, I suppose, occupy the

attention of the world sixty years from now to the same extent that the products of Romanticism still occupy our attention.   Certainly, the polemics of Realism have produced nothing so striking as Hugo's and Manzoni's and Heine's essays on Romanticism; nothing that has the lasting quality of Wordsworth's prefaces, or of Coleridge's criticism on Wordsworth.   I hazard the prediction that our children, if they ever turn the pages of the masterpieces of Realism, will wonder how we could once have read them: and that, not because they will find in those pages much that is nasty (under the plea of " science"), and much that is morbid, and more that is petty, but because the prevailing note is dulness.   Against dulness, the gods themselves have no refuge save flight.

Eight years ago all this was less evident than it is now.   We could not say with assurance eight years ago that the movement had reached its logical culmination.   To-day we can say this.   Doubtless its votaries will not abandon it suddenly; but when they find the story-tellers getting all the readers, they will know their doom. Epidermism has already found its true habitat in the sensational daily press: there, the kodak and the phonograph and the eavesdropper have untrammelled play; and moreover, the persons portrayed are really alive—which gives them an advantage against which the make-believe real people of Mr. Howells cannot in the long run compete; for if *realness* be the final test, the really real heroes of the newspapers must excel the make-believe real characters of Epidermist fiction.   What chance has *Silas Lapham* with the barber or bootblacks described, with illustrations, any day in the New York " Scavenger"?   Another product of Epidermism, the dialect story, will soon, we may hope, be banished from the magazines to the transactions of the dialect societies, which have been providentially springing up.   Of the shameless products—the obscenities and filth— we can at least predict that the time for foisting them, and all other matters not pertinent to fiction, upon us, under the plea of scientific impartiality, has passed; though doubtless from time to time some angel of the pit, some new Zola, will come to stir the surface of the cesspools of society.

Realism, or Epidermism, passes; but at least the example of sincerity which many of 'its devotees have given will not be lost.   And now, as the atmosphere is clearing, the dear and venerable masters greet us in their majesty undiminished.   Shakespeare—whose laurel has been prematurely claimed so many times by ardent partisans for the brows of ephemeral idols—Shakespeare and Dante, and the spokes-men of antiquity, confer serenely together. Near them, in another group, are Scott and Hawthorne and Thackeray, unconscious that they were so recently ostracized from Olympus. Could their words reach us, assuredly they would confirm the message written through all their books: " The lamp of Art differs from the lamp of Science; confound not their uses. Think not by machine or tool, which is material, to discover the secret of the heart of man, who is spiritual. The Real includes the Ideal; but the Real without the Ideal is as the body without life, a thing for anatomists to dissect. Only the human can understand and interpret the human."

WILLIAM R. THAYER.

CHRISTIAN MISSIONS AS SEEN BY A BRAHMAN.

MUCH criticism, adverse as well as favorable, has been published about Mr. Gandhi's article in THE FORUM for April, on "Why Christian Missions Have Failed in India." Prominent among the critics is Mr. Fred. Perry Powers, whose reply appeared in THE FORUM for June. Mr. Gandhi says that Christian missions in India have failed. Mr. Powers speaks of "The Success of Christian Missions in India." I must take the side of Mr. Powers and say that the business of the missionaries has succeeded.

How can an enterprise fail which is maintained by religion and supported by millions of good people who pay their money to continue it? Every year $14,588,354 are added to the capital invested in missions, according to Mr. Powers's statement. Hence there is no fear of the failure of missions until this vast amount is withheld by the Americans. The missionary gets good pay and lives better than an average well-to-do American gentleman. The friends of the missionary say: "Oh! the poor missionary! He receives only $100 to $200 a month!" This is a very small sum in America compared with its value in India; for a man who earns $100 a month in India can live as well as a man who has $1,000 a month in America. He can have five or six servants, a good house, free of cost to him, and a horse and carriage—at a cost of less than $100 per month. The missionary lives exceedingly well. He has no cares except the making of his reports and statements of the converts that he makes. In the morning he takes his breakfast; he walks in the church grounds, and looks to his flower-garden; then he sits in an arm-chair on the veranda, reading the Bible, newspapers, or a book; he eats a hearty luncheon and takes a good nap, the servant pulling the fan; he gets up at 3 o'clock in the afternoon, takes his Bible and goes to the town, followed by a pariah convert. He stands at the corner of a street, fixes his eye-glasses, and makes a sign for his pariah disciple to begin the work. The pariah, clad in American garments, excepting his head-dress, stands and exhorts his countrymen to embrace Christianity. While the Christian pariah goes on with his harangue,

31

the missionary looks with a smile of pride, first on the pariah and then on the people. When the Christian pariah exhausts his fund of exhortation and ends his oration, the missionary adds a few words. The better class of people look at him with pitying eyes, smile, and walk off to their homes. By this time it is the hour for dinner, and the missionary goes home. The talk and the walk give him an appetite for the good dinner that awaits him. After dinner he enjoys music or a chat with his wife, and then he retires, to get up in the morning to repeat the arduous business of the day previous. So the missionaries have not failed, and will not fail so long as Christians have money to waste in this useless way.

Let us now see to what extent the Christian missionaries have succeeded in converting the heathen of India. The missionaries first went with great zeal and a noble aim, and with sanguine hopes of converting the masses by wholesale. In their imaginations they regarded the Hindus as benighted, without any religion worthy of the name; and it did not occur to them that the hold which the Hindu's religion has on him and his whole life is a great deal stronger and more firmly rooted, because it is a great deal older and more elaborate, than the hold that the Christian religion has on Christians. This is the fundamental mistake made by missionaries, and the fundamental delusion held by the masses of Christians who contribute to the support of missions. They see in their dreams millions of Hindus, especially the Brahmans, coming to the church and kneeling to be baptized—welcoming the new religion. But when the missionaries reach India, these dreams dissolve and they meet a wholly different state of things. The higher classes of the Hindus are the proudest religious devotees found among men. They hold with greater firmness to their ancient religion and its literature than to life itself. For all other religions, indeed, but especially for the Christian religion, which is associated in their minds with the practice of meat-eating and wine-drinking, they have (to be frank) a profound and immovable contempt. The higher classes, particularly the Brahmans, have a religion of their own antedating the time set in the old Christian chronology when Adam and Eve were created; and its grand philosophy is studied the world over. Moreover the Brahman feels his immeasurable intellectual superiority to the Christian—indeed to any other man. In India, the routine of every-day life—food, clothing, customs, and manners—is all part and parcel of the religion. Dressing and eating and bathing—every act of life is a religious act.

Moreover, in the present Hindu religion one can find all the essential elements of all other religions. It is a vast pile of religions built up with the strongest spiritual cement, which has stood for thousands of years, challenging the storms of Buddhism, Mohammedanism, and now Christianity. Now and then faulty bricks in the structure, such as pariahs and other low classes, are "converted"; but this conversion, instead of weakening the old religion, polishes it, and takes away the dirt from it. It has stood innumerable attacks, as scholars who have made a study of Hindu religion know. The Hindus regard it as impregnable and everlasting. To preach Christianity to the Hindu, who had a religion and was civilized before the dawn of history, seems to him, therefore, the most ridiculous thing on earth —indeed, audacious.

All Christian missionaries to India must have met with this kind of a disillusion—at one period or another—if they have good judgment and any great degree of common sense.

When, therefore, it was found to be practically impossible to make great numbers of converts among the higher classes,—the Brahmans,—they naturally turned their attention to the lower classes, the lowest of which is the pariahs. The pariahs, the very touch of whom is polluting to a Brahman, are not allowed to live in the same streets with the higher-caste Hindu. They live outside the town. The missionary gave them food and clothing, and thus won their gratitude. He reminded them how low they were in Hindu society, and told them that if they became Christians they would raise themselves from their low station. Naturally some of the pariahs, more to get a status in life than on account of religion, for which they care very little, became Christians.

Here, in justice to the missionary, I must say that he has done much to lift the pariah, socially and mentally, by opening schools and educating those who became converts. The structure of Hindu society and religion—built on caste—is such that there is no such help for the pariah as the Christian missionary has brought to him.

When they opened these schools, Brahman boys also attended, and do to the present day, and a few Brahman boys have been converted to Christianity, not by convincing them of the superiority of the Christian religion, but by initiating them into meat-eating and wine-drinking. In one case—of a boy of sixteen—the first step was to give him sweet wine, which was very palatable to him. The first

day's glass made him pleasant; the next day's made him more pleasant; and the third day's gave the boy a strong taste for it.   He was in
ecstasy.   But all this while his parents were kept in utter ignorance
of his experience, for the Brahman is absolutely forbidden to taste
wine; they thought that he was simply studying English, and after
completing his studies they hoped that he would be able to support
them in their old age.   After a time the boy became attached to the
missionary, who had a magical influence over his young heart, and he
was persuaded to become a Christian.   The boy did not yet know
much about his own religion, so that he could not compare it with
Christianity, of which he had heard a great deal.   Hence he was an
easy victim—to the great agony and grief of his parents.   The boy
ran away from home on a certain day, and went to a Christian church.
The parents got information of him and went with tears to the missionary and implored him to give the boy back to them.   The boy was
married; his young wife would become a widow if he became a Christian.   She could not live with him, and nobody, not even his father
or mother, could eat with him, because he had lost caste.   He could
not enter the house of a Hindu, because he was polluted.   All his
mother's future hopes for him were dashed to pieces on the Christian
rock.   The missionary did not yield to the tears of the parents.   He
took a piece of meat, and put it into the mouth of the boy in their
presence and in the presence of the people assembled, and gave him
a glass of wine to drink.   It would be hard to imagine the sorrow of
the parents, the father-in-law, the mother-in-law, and the young wife,
to all of whom he now became morally and practically dead, because
by his conversion he lost caste and brought disgrace to both the
families.   This case was the talk of everybody in the surrounding
town, and it is painful for me to think and write about it.   I knew
this family personally.   It was wrecked.   The old father, who was
a revenue officer and the magistrate of the county, died of a broken
heart within six months, and the mother followed him within a short
period.   The young man's wife dragged out her life some years in
sorrow, and when she found that there was no other alternative she
went to her husband, but did not accept his religion; and she died
an untimely death.   This is not a solitary instance.

In this way the missionaries have made a very few converts among
the higher classes.   For a time, in consequence, the better classes of
people suspected the missionary schools and withdrew their children
from them, so that the missionaries, by attacking the prejudice of the

Hindus and interfering in their family relations one with another, as in the above case, have at times been the means of arresting and preventing normal progress in practical things in India, which the introducing of Western education and material civilization, without the Christian religion, would further.

The missionaries, then, make converts of the lowest classes by giving them bread and promising them money or employment.   Many of the missionaries to India, perhaps, never find out the real feelings of the Hindus: they are too ignorant.   At any rate, out of ignorance and out of other defects a vast literature of misinformation has been spread in Christian countries about the Hindus and their religion. There are those who think that the missionaries take care to keep their own countrymen ignorant of the good side of the Hindus.   Such misinformation has been spread, for instance, about the car of Juggernaut; the throwing of babies into the Ganges to be eaten by crocodiles; and the suttee or the burning of widows!   The current stories about the Juggernaut and the throwing of little children into the Ganges have not a particle of truth; and with regard to the suttee, this was practised only among the warriors in certain parts of India, and not among the Brahmans and other classes.   As to the car of Juggernaut, a few words describing this religious ceremony will not be out of place.

One of the religious festivals among the Hindus consists of the exhibition, on an appointed day, of the symbol of the Deity, which is mounted on a car elaborately decorated and drawn through the streets near the temple, followed by a procession with music and chanting.   This religious festival in many respects is like certain festivals of the Christian church in many parts of Europe, where, preceded by the cross, the priests and people march to the cathedral to do special honor to certain so-called relics which, by the ignorant, are supposed to possess miraculous powers.   The car bears the image of the Deity and is called by different names in different provinces; and in Orissa, Bengal, the name given is Jagannatha, signifying "the God of the Universe."   Since coming to America I have heard many startling stories about people throwing themselves under this car and being crushed to death.   I have seen such festivals many times, but have never seen or heard of any such thing happening. When the car, which is very high, is drawn through the streets, a man may have been accidentally forced under it by the crowd; or, perhaps, in a religious frenzy, some fanatic may have thrown himself under it, but if such a thing ever happened it was but the result of most ignorant religious fanaticism.

Mr. Powers says that the missionaries have done much for Hindu literature. To translate the Bible into the vernacular, which they murder outright; to print Solomon's proverbs; to publish small pamphlets saying that the Hindus are immoral, that their religion lacks moral precepts, and that every religion is bad except Christianity; and to put forth all sorts of books ridiculing the Hindu and praising Christians,—if this be improving Hindu literature, they have done more than enough. Unfortunately the missionaries are spoiling the language instead of improving it; for their translations are written without regard to Hindu grammar and are difficult for the Hindu to understand. The "missionary" language is proverbial among educated Hindus.

A Sanskrit poet says that critics are like insects that enjoy only the rotten part and not the good. Mr. Powers has spoken of the immorality of the whole Eastern people for want of a good religion. He has confused India with China, Turkey, Japan, Africa, and other countries, although India differs from those nations as much as she does from America.

Let me draw a parallel, touching morality and religion, Christian and Hindu—in order to get a proper point of view and to point out the ease with which wrong conclusions in such matters are drawn. Take your own good Christian nation of the United States. What is the state of morality? Read your daily papers and note the number of murders, train robberies, bank robberies (by burglars at night, and by the managers by day), elopements, shootings, cuttings, divorce cases, suicides, not to mention lynchings, and the roasting of Negroes alive. Count the number of saloons. Every corner of a block is adorned by their illuminations. "Dens" of vice exist, not only in New York, but in all large cities of America, where the grossest immorality is practised. I have not seen them, but I have been well-informed by many frank Christian Americans about these places. Christians will say: "Oh, these are not Christians who do this, and you see our country is filled with foreigners and unbelievers; we are trying to put down vice, and we have missions for the purpose." I grant that there are foreigners here too, and unbelievers, but they are all Christians, and when the time comes for numbering the Christians, you add them; and when their morality is in question you discard them. So, to complete the parallel, if some bad men are found in India among the low classes, they are Hindus, and the whole Hindu society and religion are reviled by the Christians; but if even a greater number are found in the Christian countries, they are not Christians.

Moreover, as a Hindu reads Christian history, it is full of cruelties such as shock the Hindu mind and cause doubt of Christian morality. How has your own nation in the United States treated the Indians? You have almost extinguished them, as you have done the buffaloes. Who by force brought the African to your shores? What became of the aborigines of Australia? How was India conquered, and by whom? Who snatched the kingdom of Hawaii from the Queen of those Islands? Who were the Crusaders? Who burned people at the stake and invented torturing-machines? Who were those who wished to burn Galileo for expounding the theory of the earth's motion? Who acknowledged slavery and practised it for many centuries, until it was stopped with a great deal of bloodshed by the liberty-loving Americans, and then rather for economic than purely religious motives? Christian history is full of instances, and Christian nations are the most aggressive and most intolerant people. These facts have much to do with the Hindu prejudices against Christianity. They therefore think that Christianity has been the curse of the whole world, especially the Eastern nations. It is the Christians who go among them to kill, rob, and teach the people to drink. If this conclusion be unjust, it nevertheless shows the insuperable difficulty that the Christian missionaries meet.

As for personal morality—this has not been affected by religion pure and simple in any country. Human nature is everywhere the same. If the Christian says that the Hindu religion is bad because, for instance, of polygamy, then I say that the Christian religion is worse for the same or a similar or a worse reason.

Christian missionaries have carried to India fine reports of the Christians that they left at home; and they carry to Western nations the worst reports of the so-called heathen abroad. The Hindus, therefore, think that all Christians in the Western nations are good people, and the Americans think the Hindus are all bad. Alas! both are mistaken. I found this out after I came and saw the Christians at home.

We admire the Western civilization in its material points. Our people have begun to open their eyes to the wonderful progress the Western people have made in material civilization, in which they have left us far behind.   You enjoy life better than we do.   We eat to live, and you live to eat.   The railroads are bringing the different nationalities in India together, and under the British rule and the spread of English education the hard lines of caste are slowly passing away.   We owe much to the Western civilization, and I am thankful to the British Government, which has done a great deal of good to our country.   We now have good railroads, schools, printing-presses, newspapers, telegraph facilities, and other things, but not in proportion to the needs of our enormous population.   Our lower classes, however, have not yet facilities for higher education.   They are so poor that a man cannot spare even half a dollar a month for the school fees of his child.   We want English free schools where no money is charged and where students are encouraged by scholarships. Americans can have no idea how poor the people of India are.   They live in small huts and have no cot or bedding.   Some of the lower classes cannot get a second meal a day, the first meal being a piece of bread or a little boiled rice.

Now if every dollar that the kind-hearted Americans spend on the missionaries were used in bringing up these lower classes by educating them, it would be the greatest charity in the world.   Building more railroads, teaching mechanics, electricity, and all kinds of manufactures; making sanitary improvements in the villages and towns to prevent thousands of people from being swept away annually by cholera and other diseases which have made India their home, —for those the people of India would bless the Americans.   In every poor man's house the praise of your nation would be sung, and the name " America " would be dear to them, and they would bless you from their hearts.   If your object is truly to improve the condition of India's poor, then, instead of teaching them religion, send teachers and open schools; give them education and let them select any religion they like.

But it is a sheer waste of money to spend it on the missionaries. It does not help the people.   On the contrary it only strengthens their own religious faith and creates international prejudice.   The people bitterly complain against them for their interference, not only in religion, but in politics too.   What benefit is it to India or America if a few pariahs are Christianized at an enormous cost?   I again affirm that it is a waste of money.   Send your missionaries to those who have no religion—for instance, to the interior of Africa and the South Sea Islands, and to the cities of the United States.

Let the aim of the missionary be to civilize and *educate* the savages and barbarians. To India send machinery instead of missionaries. Millions of people are kept back for want of education owing to intense poverty. Send good schoolmasters, mechanics, and scientists, and teach your practical arts to our people. This will cost you less than the missionaries.

But let us be friends, and, as children of one God, forget all differences of opinion. You have your religion and you think it the best. If it is the best, keep it yourselves. But do not revile other religions. As for faults, other religions have faults, but so has your own. Let us pray Him whom you call God, and I call Brahma, to send us enlightenment and make us love each other without consideration of caste or creed. But I assure you that you cannot thrust a new religion on an already civilized nation, whose religion is the cradle of religions; where the people are born to their religion and it is fostered through generations. Your money simply hurts their feelings and sometimes gets the curses of parents of boys who are converted by pious fraud. Christianity is best suited to the Western nations. As a religion we do not show disrespect to it, because every religion tends toward the same end, namely salvation. Christ taught beautiful things; and if all his teachings were strictly followed, the whole world would be a Paradise.

PURUSHOTAM RAO TELANG.

CHRISTIAN MISSIONS AS SEEN BY A MISSIONARY.

THE article which appeared in THE FORUM for April, 1894, on "Why Christian Missions Have Failed in India" attracted special attention because Mr. Gandhi (like Mr. Telang) is an educated Indian gentleman, and is supposed to speak from personal knowledge of India, if not from personal observation of missionary work. I should be extremely sorry to question the right of either Mr. Gandhi or Mr. Telang to criticise the missionaries of India or their work, and yet it ought to be said that residence in a country does not by any means carry with it knowledge of a country, with all that is going on among its people. Take, for instance, an intelligent graduate of Yale or Princeton, and ask him to write an article for the "Calcutta Review" on the present state of the Protestant churches in the United States; ask him whether any Italians have become Protestants, in what cities the Protestant movement is making most headway among the Bohemians, where the Hungarians are beginning to stir, how much has been done among the Germans, how much among the Spaniards and Portuguese, how the "slum work" is succeeding, and what is the present religious condition of the freedmen in Louisiana;—ask him to state his views on these questions, and in ninety-nine cases out of a hundred the intelligent graduate will be found as ignorant of the facts as if he had spent all his days in India. It is, of course, possible that an Indian gentleman may be found better informed in reference to religious movements in his own country, but the chances are all the other way. An Indian gentleman who moves in good society will never be seen in intimate personal contact with the classes among whom the missionary carries on his most successful work. He very rarely speaks to an Indian Christian, unless it be one in high position, and he seldom has an opportunity of seeing, much less inspecting, any department of missionary work. How far these remarks apply to Mr. Gandhi is seen in his extraordinary statement that not a single (Indian) Aryan had ever become a Christian!

Mr. Telang writes in a style which was current among European writers forty or fifty years ago, but which happily has now almost gone out of date. Sydney Smith set the first example in his famous tirade against the " consecrated cobbler" of Serampore, and for many years inferior men who could not distinguish between coarseness and wit seemed to think that the correct thing to do when writing on missionary topics was to resort to ridicule as a convenient weapon, even if a very weak one. The caricature of the American missionary and his " pariah convert" going to preach in the street was not intended —we must suppose—to be taken seriously, but it will serve to introduce a description of out-door preaching as it really is. If the reader will go to Beadon Square, in Calcutta, any Sunday evening in the year, he will find two or three Scotch missionaries, a Bengali attorney of the high court—a converted Brahman, by the way—a Bengali physician, and a few others, preaching in English to a large audience the majority of whom are intelligent undergraduates of the Calcutta University. In another public square, about two miles distant, two other groups of preachers, English, American, Bengali and Hindustani, will be found, and the people who gather to hear them are addressed by turns in three different languages. In all the large cities it is easy to find hearers who understand English, but the missionaries who resort to street preaching are, almost to a man, fluent speakers in one or more vernaculars.

Mr. Telang's statement that " a man who earns one hundred dollars a month in India can live as well as one who has a thousand dollars a month in America" is very wide of the mark. Very many missionaries receive much less than a hundred dollars a month, but at the higher figure the missionary receives about one-third of the salary of the chaplain next door, and one-fifth to one-tenth of the income of the station doctor. He sometimes pays more to the headmaster of his school than he receives himself, and always takes rank in income much below the average of the Europeans among whom he lives. He may have five or six servants, but one Irish or Swedish girl in America will do as much as the whole of them, and—including board —will cost about the same. As to having " no cares," the missionary is nearly always a burdened man, having, in addition to his own anxieties, to care for the endless interests of a score, a hundred, or perhaps five hundred families.

While speaking of these personal matters it may be as well to refer to Mr. Telang's accusation that the missionaries win their few Brahman converts by " initiating them into meat-eating and wine drinking." I can easily understand that Mr. Telang made this charge with a measure of confidence in its truth, for in a case of conversion such as he narrates all manner of incredible falsehoods are put into circulation; but it is necessary only to remark that nearly all missionaries are total abstainers, and that the Brahmans have no greater aversion to wine drinking than have the missionaries. Some Germans and a few English missionaries may not have adopted the rule of abstinence, but among the Americans I do not know of a single exception. It does sometimes happen that a youth is permanently separated from home and friends by becoming a Christian, not because he leaves them, but because they thrust him out. In a few cases I have known missionaries to act unwisely in giving shelter to youths under twenty years of age. The boy can legally claim freedom of conscience at sixteen, but it has never seemed to me quite right to advise a youth not fully grown to accept baptism against the will of his parents. In such cases an appeal is nearly always made to the courts, and no matter what the age of the convert, plenty of witnesses can be found to swear that he is under sixteen, while all manner of wild stories are put in circulation against the missionaries. Such cases, however, are rare. During the thirty-five years I have been in India, among more than eighty thousand baptisms in our own missions, I cannot now recall a single case in which a youth's baptism led to an appeal in the courts.

The American reader can hardly appreciate Mr. Telang's use of the word "pariah" in speaking of the convert that a missionary took with him to preach in the bazaar. Mr. Telang applies the word "pariah" to the convert preacher no less than six times. It is a term which belongs to South India, but since it has become anglicized it has come into general use, and is often applied by Europeans not only to the out-castes of Southern India, but to the meanest variety of dogs, the scavenger curs of the village. Not many Indian gentlemen of culture and refinement would apply it to a Christian preacher, but it sometimes happens that hostile writers try to identify all Christians with the out-castes, and especially those who before conversion belonged to one of the higher castes, by applying this term to them. The epithet as used by Mr. Telang was probably aimed less at this particular convert than at the general body of Indian preachers.

The pariahs of Southern India form a part of an immense division of the general community numbering about fifty million souls, or more than one-sixth of the whole population. These fifty millions are divided into many castes and sub-castes, and in recent years the term "depressed classes" has been applied to the whole mass, from the lowest scavengers to the more respectable artisans. The whole fifty millions are below the line of social respectability; and, although legally entitled to admission to the public schools, their children are practically excluded from them. Public sentiment would not tolerate their presence. The condition of these people is very hopeless, unless they can in some way escape from the hard lot which has fallen to them. Up to the advent of the Christian missionary in India, no door of hope had ever been opened to them, and Mr. Telang admits that this good office has been done for the pariahs by the missionaries.

The impression prevails very widely that these depressed classes can never wield much influence, even after becoming Christians; but that is by no means certain. The Brahmans are but a handful of the general community. In Northwest India, the chief seat of ancient Hinduism, the Chamars, or leather-dressers, a very low caste, are about equal in number to the Brahmans. What would the United States be to-day if the whole artisan population had been kept in a state of absolute ignorance and social degradation, from the first settlement of the country to the present day? When General Grant was President, and Henry Wilson Vice-President, the former visited Boston and was accorded a public reception. In driving in an open carriage through the streets it so happened that the President, the Vice-President, and the Governor of the State occupied seats in the same carriage with the Mayor. As they passed by, an Indian missionary said to a friend, "There go three Chamars!" General Grant had been a tanner, Henry Wilson had been a shoemaker, and Governor Claflin a leather merchant. Had Hindu caste prevailed in America these three men would have been lost to the nation, and Abraham Lincoln would have been obliged to spend his entire lifetime as a common day-laborer. India possesses within herself many of the elements which belong to a great empire, but she can never rise to a worthy position among the empires of the world while one-sixth of her people are kept in a state of dense ignorance, with every avenue of improvement rigidly closed against them. If the presence of three-and-a-half million slaves proved an incubus too heavy to be borne by the people of the United States, the presence of fifty millions of these depressed classes will prove—is proving—a burden which India cannot permanently endure. Mr. Telang frankly confesses that the hope and the help of these lowly people is in Christianity. With admirable candor, he says, "The structure of Hindu society and religion is such that there is no such help for the pariah as the Christian missionary has brought to him." If it were granted that the low-caste people are mentally and physically inferior to their high-caste neighbors, the fact would remain that India as a whole will be depressed by the injustice to so large a section of the community.

But are these people so very inferior in character and natural ability to the higher castes? To this question it is impossible to give a direct answer, chiefly for the reason that they do not constitute a homogeneous community. They differ from one another not only in different parts of the country, but often when living as sub-castes side by side. It seems almost certain that they are descendants of ancient tribes who were either conquered by more civilized Aryan invaders, or brought into India as camp-followers by these invaders. Hence they have not had a common origin, and many of them may have been Aryans themselves at a very remote period. Others belong to various aboriginal races, and hence differ as widely among themselves as their remote ancestors probably did. One thing, however, is very certain; many of them are men of fine physique, with very fair mental powers, and are abundantly able to hold their own in the battle of life when Christianity gives them a fair chance. Mr. Telang says the missionaries win these people " by giving them bread, and promising them money or employment." This charge is often made by opponents of missionary work, and hence the reader will no doubt be surprised when I assure him that the missionary who works among them is troubled much more by high-caste applicants for money and employment than by those belonging to the depressed classes. During the past four years I have been among tens of thousands of these people who are becoming Christians, and the one thing which they never ask for is money. Wherever I go they beg me to provide schools for their children, but not once in six months does any one ask for food or clothing, or even mention the subject of securing a higher social position.

In fairness I ought to say that the above remarks do not apply to all the divisions of the low-caste community. Some of them are cringing and feeble creatures, with many marks of inferiority stamped upon them, but so far as my own observation has extended it is not from such communities that converts are usually drawn. On the other hand those who become Christians improve rapidly and ask no odds of the Brahmans or the Mohammedans. I have seen a son of an extremely low out-caste preparing high-caste youths for university examinations. I have seen hundreds of Christian youths, whose parents had belonged to these classes in school and college with Hindu and Mohammedan boys, apparently on terms of good fellowship, and successfully holding their own in the keen competition of the school-room. I have seen many of them placed in responsible positions in the mission field, and acquitting themselves very creditably indeed. I may be too sanguine, but it is my deliberate opinion that the successors of the present generation of Christians will startle the Brahmans of the next century, by appearing on the scene as their competitors for every position of honor or emolument which the latter now hold.

It ought not to be supposed, however, that all converts in India have come from the lower classes. The Christian community has won a recognized position in the country, and in proportion to its numbers —excluding the so-called Portuguese and French Christians, whose ancestors became nominal Christians three centuries ago—stands fully abreast of any other community in the country. In proof of this I need only quote the following extract from "The Hindu," a leading Hindu paper of South India:

"We recently approved the statement of a Bombay paper, that the social eminence which the Parsees so deservedly enjoy at the present moment was due to these two causes: that their women are well educated, and they are bound by no restrictions of caste. These two advantages make themselves felt among our native Christian brethren, and it is probable that they will soon be the Parsees of Southern India. They will furnish the most distinguished public servants, barristers, merchants, and citizens among the various classes of the native community."

This is not the testimony of a missionary, or of a Christian, but of an enlightened Hindu writer who is able to take a broad and liberal view of the situation.

In forming an estimate of the native Christian community in India, a distinction should always be drawn between the converts of the modern missionary movement, and the larger community of nominal Christians whose ancestors more than two centuries ago were, for the most part, induced to become Christians under more or less pressure by the French, the Dutch, and especially the Portuguese authorities. The hostile attitude toward missionaries assumed and long maintained by the English authorities in India was not creditable either to their courage or foresight, but beyond all doubt it was the best thing that could have happened to the English and American missionaries. It is bad enough to have Church and State allied in Christian lands, but it is a hundred times worse in a non-

Christian country.   The Christianity which the Portuguese introduced into India was hardly Christian even in name.   The name of Francis Xavier is still revered in India, but the Roman Catholic missionaries of the present day would not think of resorting to some of the methods employed by that illustrious saint and his followers.   What might have happened, had Clive and Hastings taken it upon themselves to make the people Christians, we can hardly imagine, but it is cer-tain that any success on the part of such men would have been worse than absolute failure.   Happily for Christianity they did not make the attempt, and it was left to a lowly shoemaker, William Carey, to become the pioneer of the missionary enterprise, and hence this move-ment has been in operation only for a single century.

At the death of the Founder of Christianity there were about 120,000,000 inhabitants of the Roman Empire.   In India there are to-day 284,000,000 souls.   While I admit that the Indian converts of the century now closing are regarded with a measure of contempt by many intelligent Indians and Europeans, at the same time I venture to assert that the native Christians of India are more respected, are better known, and are more kindly regarded by the mass of the people than were the early Christians at the end of the first century after Pentecost.   We are too apt to forget that the Christians of the first century were constantly taunted with their low social position. It was charged against them, and probably with truth, that the majority of the whole community were slaves.   They had some great leaders, but not many.   Their existence was hardly known in the " society" circles of that day, and the " leaders of thought" could not have told the name of the Founder of their religion.   Gallio, who was one of the most accomplished scholars of his era, could not distinguish be-tween Paul and Sosthenes when they appeared before him in open court.   In India we have nothing corresponding to this.   The Chris-tian is an honored man in any public assembly.   The Christian com-munity is recognized in the National Congress, and Christian orators are among the foremost speakers at its annual gatherings.

Both Mr. Gandhi and Mr. Telang seem to be unaware of the change which has taken place among the mass of the people of India in their feelings toward Christian missionaries, especially in recent years.   At the close of the Mutiny a general distrust of missionaries was manifested in some parts of the Empire, but this gradually passed away, and a very different feeling now prevails, especially among the common people.   The missionary is regarded as the friend of the poor, the representative of public morality, and the promoter of re-form.   The common people are able to distinguish between spurious Christianity and that which is genuine.   In every European regiment a few dozen God-fearing soldiers were found, and in the regimental bazaars these men are usually well known to be different from their comrades.   Among the more intelligent classes the distinction be-tween nominal and real Christianity is understood to a surprising ex-tent.   Nor is there that strong aversion toward the missionaries on account of their " meat-eating" and disregard of animal life of which Mr. Gandhi especially speaks.   The sacredness of all life was a tenet of Buddhism, but that religion has long since ceased to exist in India, while in Burmah, where the people are still Buddhists, the use of fish as an article of food is universal.   The Burman explains his apparent inconsistency by saying that he never kills a fish, or causes one to be killed, but merely lays it on the bottom of his boat where it dies of its own accord!   When, some years ago, I chanced to live in a district infested by bears and leopards, my Brahman and Rajpoot neighbors never failed to send for me when a bear appeared in their grain fields, or a leopard among their cattle, and so far from being shocked when I came to their aid with two double-barrelled guns, their only complaint was that I was a very bad marksman.

The reader in America will probably be surprised to hear that Calcutta had a " Parkhurst movement" in progress before the present agitation in New York was commenced.   A little more than a year ago a great mass-meeting was held in the town-hall, in aid of this movement, which was attended by about 3,000 persons, representing all classes of the community, both Indian and European.   An American missionary was made chairman, on the nomination of an orthodox Hindu, a Justice of the High Court of Calcutta.   Among the speakers were the Parsee sheriff of the city, the European prin-cipal of the Jesuit college, one of the ablest and most respected physicians in the city, an Anglican clergyman, a Bengali Christian lawyer, a Mohammedan gentleman, and several other speakers.   The editor of the " Indian Mirror," who is a Brahman, and a gentleman who has never hesitated to criticise missionaries, including the chairman of the meeting, asked to be allowed to move the usual vote of thanks to the chairman.   In doing so this gentleman took occasion to ex-press the gratitude of his countrymen to the Christian missionaries of Bengal, saying, in substance, that the latter had again and again come to the help of the Indian people when their best interests were

32

in jeopardy; and, in the midst of enthusiastic cheers, he assured the whole missionary body that the multitudes for whom he spoke would not fail to appreciate those who had so uniformly shown their good will toward the Indian people. This is only one example of good feeling, it may be granted; but in the course of the last twenty years I have witnessed frequent demonstrations, in Calcutta and elsewhere, which were hardly less significant.

So far as I have noticed, all the Indian gentlemen who have recently written or spoken unfavorably of Christian missionaries, preserve a discreet silence in reference to missionary work among the women of India. Mr. Vivekananda has ventured to say of woman in India, that " from the Hindu standpoint she receives all her rights," but he did not explain that the orthodox standpoint was one from which women of the highest caste are viewed as on the same plane, intellectually, as the pariah. To the Christian missionary alone, the women of India are indebted for the door to education and intellectual progress which now stands wide open before them. No more difficult task has ever been undertaken in any missionary field than that of demonstrating to the people of India that their women could learn, that it would be safe to permit them to learn, and that it was of the first importance that schools should be provided for them. It would require a volume to tell the whole story, but suffice it to say that the field has been fairly won, that Hindu and Mohammedan ladies are now competing in many places with missionary teachers in the zenanas, that schools for girls are multiplying, that many influential gentlemen are deeply interested in the cause of women's education, and that there are now two institutions of college grade for women, while a third, under Hindu auspices, is about to be started. One of these colleges is non-sectarian, but most of the pupils belong to Brahman or other advanced Hindu families. The principal of this college is an accomplished Bengali Christian lady, whose education was chiefly received in a missionary institution. The third institution mentioned above is said to be intended as in some measure a rival to the flourishing Christian college for girls which has been for some time in operation in the same city. This, however, is by no means a discouraging omen to the missionaries. The more rival schools, the better evidence they have that their educational work has not been in vain.

I will mention only one other instance of an invaluable work accomplished by missionaries for the women of India, for which as yet but scanty credit has been given. I can remember very well when the first woman physician who had ever been sent into a non-Christian country arrived in India to take up the work of a medical missionary. Many readers will remember how much courage and perseverance were required by those women who ventured to act as pioneers of the medical sisterhood in America. The opposition which they incurred amounted to little short of downright persecution. If this was the case in the United States, it need hardly be said that the first female physician who ventured to offer her services to the women of India required a measure of courage, patience, and tact—to say nothing of professional skill—of the highest possible quality. Dr. Clara Swain was the pioneer upon whom this honor fell.

She arrived in India as late as 1870, and still remains engaged in her noble work. About the same time Dr. J. L. Humphrey made the first attempt to give Indian women a training in medicine. In this work he was ably seconded by Dr. Swain, and in due time it was fully demonstrated that the women of India could not only be persuaded to receive treatment from physicians of their own sex, but that they themselves could be trained for the medical profession, and thus a lucrative employment be found for them, and at the same time a service of unspeakable value rendered to the secluded women of India, who previously had been shut off from all medical aid.

Other women physicians soon followed Miss Swain, and in the course of a very few years all doubts with regard to the value of such services as these ladies were able to render had completely vanished. It thus happened that the way was prepared for what is now known as the "Dufferin movement." A returned woman missionary was honored with an audience by Queen Victoria, and ventured to speak to Her Majesty of the need of medical help for the women of India; and, when Lord Dufferin was appointed Viceroy, the Queen warmly commended the subject to Lady Dufferin, who chanced to be admirably fitted in every way for taking the lead in such a work. As soon as she arrived in India she took up the matter in earnest, made inquiries upon every hand, formed far-reaching plans, solicited aid from all possible donors, and in due time succeeded in establishing one of the most important humanitarian agencies ever introduced into India. The whole world has heard the story; and the fame of Lady Dufferin will forever be inseparable from her great project of giving medical aid to the women of India. It ought not to be forgotten, however, that but for the missionary women "the Dufferin movement" would most certainly never have been inaugurated. The possibility of such a movement was first clearly demonstrated, and nearly all the real difficulties involved were removed, before Lady Dufferin arrived in India.

Mr. Telang speaks in very severe terms of the "enormous cost" of missionary work as at present conducted, and calls the expenditure "a waste of money." On the other hand, I venture to affirm that, when the extent of the work and its results are fairly considered, it is the most inexpensive work to be found in the whole wide field of benevolent enterprise throughout the world. As I am at a distance from India, and have no statistics of other societies at hand, I must beg to be allowed to refer to the missions of the Methodist Episcopal Church in India and Malaysia, which chance to be under my super-intendence. The total number of missionaries employed in this field is 78, with 75 wives of missionaries, and 38 unmarried ladies. I omit these from the calculation altogether, as Mr. Telang pleads for education and other kinds of non-religious work. I omit the large staff of Indian preachers, churches and chapels, and even the medical and industrial features of the work. I omit also the four publishing houses, and all that is done in the way of preparing and distributing literature among the people, and after making all these omissions we have the following result:

We have 1,204 day-schools, 302 of which are for girls. It will certainly be granted that $100 a year is a very moderate sum to allow for each of these schools. We have 13 orphanages, and surely no one will object to an estimate of $20,000 a year for this item. We have also 18 cheap boarding-schools for the children of the poor, for which I put down the very moderate sum of $18,000, or $1,000 each. There remain 11 high schools, for which an estimate of $25,000 ought certainly to be accepted as very reasonable. We have thus:

Day-schools	1,204	$120,400
Orphanages	13	20,000
Boarding-schools	18	18,000
High-schools	11	25,000
Total		$183,400

The total amount sent out during 1894 by the two missionary societies which support this vast work was $229,917. According to Mr. Telang's estimate the married missionaries alone would have received $93,600, and when we add to this not only 38 unmarried ladies, but also more than 1,200 Indian preachers, four publishing houses, two colleges, one theological seminary, an extensive medical work, and various industrial enterprises, the reader cannot fail to see that an immense amount of valuable work is going forward at a cost which is so slight, when compared with American rates, that it seems ₐlmost nominal.

As one who has long been resident in India, I can understand, and to some extent sympathize, with Mr. Telang's feelings, when he sees the ancestral faith of his country challenged by the followers of what seems to him not only an alien religion, but a religion which the foreign rulers of his country, in the very nature of the case, seem to be constantly thrusting before him. The people of India have never been conquered by the English, and do not, in the proper sense of the word, occupy the position of a conquered people. A few Englishmen have built up a great empire in India, but in doing so they have as often been helped as opposed by Indian princes and Indian armies. The Government of India is English, and yet in a sense Asiatic. Mr. Telang may yet live to help to make laws for the empire. All this is true, and yet the aspiring Indian cannot but remember that the foreigner is in the land, that the highest places are his, and that the India of the golden age of Hinduism is steadily passing away. No people in the world are so proud of their ancestry as the higher classes of India, and it is not strange that many of them cling with desperate tenacity to their ancient traditions, and oppose Christianity as the embodiment of all the alien influences which seem more and more to endanger the very existence of all that has, from time immemorial, been most distinctive in the ideas and institutions of the country. The Indian's pride of ancestry is natural and, within limits, commendable, but it is at present a source of great weakness. It hinders his progress and makes him blind to the inevitable. It chills all feeling of real patriotism by trying to substitute an impossible past for a hopeful present and a splendid future. Happily, many leading men in India see this clearly, and not a few who decline to accept Christianity personally are practically adopting its spirit and commending its precepts. It is the only religious system ever propagated among men which is equally well adapted to every clime and every people, and in due time the people of India will discover that it is no more alien to them than the air which they breathe, or the rain which fills their magnificent rivers. It is the common heritage of all humanity.

J. M. THOBURN.

CHARITY THAT HELPS AND OTHER CHARITY.

OUR word "charity" has strayed far away from the χάρις of the Greek, which signified the treating of a person kindly, as if he were of the same kind or kin as one's self. It is chiefly with the desire to make clear this meaning of the word charity, and to urge a new standard of kindness, that I have gathered together a few of the stories of our neighbors of the College Settlement in New York City, as they have come to us through this last terrible year of distress.

The College Settlement is simply several young women who are trying to be friends to those who are near them, and we learn to know much of the lives of many of our neighbors. Many know something of the sorrows and sufferings of the poor, but it is a privilege given to only a few to know well their everyday home-life.

Through all the past year of distress, though the rich have given thousands of dollars, it is the poor who have given the most freely. "There is no way of calculating the kind deeds of neighbor to neighbor till the judgment day." The only natural form of relief is the help given by friend to friend. When a feeble old man without relatives and absolutely penniless was asked by a friend of mine if he ever suffered from hunger, "Never," he answered. My friend asked him, "What do you do?" and he replied promptly, "I go and get something." There was always ready for him in some neighbor's house a pail of soup or a bowl of coffee.

Scattered about among the tenements there are many who, in ordinary times, make a bare living by scrubbing floors and by doing washing for those who are better off than themselves. In a time of great poverty there is no money to pay for such work, and these people become helpless. One such old woman came to the housekeeper of a Chrystie-Street tenement and told of her great need. The housekeeper had neither work nor money to offer, but she sent out her daughter, who usually did the house-cleaning, to look for work. The girl obtained a temporary position in a large dry-goods store, and the

house-cleaning was given to the old woman, the mother simply saying, " Elsie could get a job when the old lady couldn't. "

In many a house a lodger who could no longer pay for a bed has
received shelter month after month.   One Russian Hebrew who had
been in the United States only nine months had three such lodgers,
and none of them could pay anything.   A young man out of work
received a bed from a friend for six months, and, now that he has
work again, he can pay his debts, and he can be counted as one more
saved from going down in this struggle for existence.

The cause of a friendless young fellow always appeals strongly to
the people of the tenements.   An effort had been made to find work
for a boy who needed it very much, but one day he came in to say
that if a position was found for him, he would like to have it given
to his friend; and another boy in the group explained, " You know
he's almost the same as an orphan.   His mother died when he was a
baby, and he has had a few step-mothers, and now his father is dead. "

A cobbler, who finds life a struggle much of the time, shared his
meals for several months with a young man who had just returned
from prison.   He said that he thought there was some good in the
fellow after all, and he would not be the better for starving.

It is hard, even for us who live among the poor, to realize fully
what it means to be out of work—the fruitless search for employment
day after day, the coming home at night unsuccessful, to see the
hard-earned savings growing less and less, the gradual going-down
step by step, seeing the children every day getting thinner and thinner, and to be powerless to help!   Parents whose children are all too
young to be wage-earners are most to be pitied.   One little girl expressed the feelings of many a careful mother as she said in trembling
tones, unconscious of the pathos of it all, " My mother says she cannot look at us, when she has not to give us to eat. "

It is a painful fact that charity has been made so repulsive that
even many of those who are in great distress are unwilling to accept
help.   One woman who was accidentally discovered without fire on
a bitterly cold day refused to receive coal from a relief society, even
though she had begun to pawn her bedding.   The neighbors have
often been kept carefully in ignorance of the new poverty which is so
hard to bear, and even the children have learned to be cautious as to
what they say.   Here in the Settlement the members of two children's clubs were asked to give up their Christmas presents in order
that the money might be used to buy shoes for other children, and

they gladly agreed to do so. One little girl was asked if she knew any one to whom she would like her present to go, and she answered in a whisper, "I know a little girl, but I must first ask her mother if I can give her name." A small boy came in one day with shining eyes and said, "I want to tell you something, but nobody else must hear." It was only a pathetic story of a neighbor's struggle with want. There is a pitiful sameness in these stories. After a few weeks or a few months of enforced idleness, all the money that has been saved is exhausted and all the furniture and clothing of any value is sold or pawned. Many of the "new poor" have pawn-tickets amounting to more than a hundred dollars.

Relatives and friends lend money freely. A sister who had no money lent her watch to be pawned. One man who had found work for a few weeks paid a third of his wages to the family upstairs, as he had borrowed from them a short time before, and he was now better off than they.

Even in ordinary times the rent is a large item in the living expenses; and, when there is no work, the thought of the rent becomes a horrible nightmare. The landlords have been unusually lenient. Perhaps in some cases leniency is only a choice of evils; for, even if the present tenant were evicted, the next one might be equally unable to pay his debts. We have, however, heard many a struggling tenant say, "Our landlord is a good man. He is never hard on us." Many of the evils of the tenements are due to the fact that the owner and the agent know but little of the circumstances of their tenants. They often leave the collecting of the rents to the housekeeper, usually some man or woman who receives the rent of three or four rooms in payment for the work of caring for the house. The best way to reform tenements is to place their management in the care of the best housekeepers. In the distress of last winter many a housekeeper took a little food every day to some tenant whose poverty was known to her alone. One housekeeper induced the landlord to give the rent for two months to a family in great need, and she told me in broken English, "Our landlord would have put out lots of people if it wasn't through me. I told the landlord it's because these people not got work." Every once in a while, families are forcibly evicted, and you will see a pitiable collection of household goods on the sidewalk. Often the mother sits there, and at her side is a plate into which the passers-by drop their pennies. One such plate held eighteen dollars before dark. It happens not infrequently that a friend in a little better circumstances will offer the rent of a room till something else can be found.   Many know that when the worst comes a relative or friend, or even perhaps a chance acquaintance, will take the children, but with a natural pride they put off as long as possible the evil day when they must confess themselves beaten in the struggle for existence.   I asked one man, who had formerly been an English butler, where his wife was, and he answered, "She has gone to Newark to some friends, but she did not go till she was clemmed with hunger."

A German family consisting of a man, his wife, and two children, lived comfortably in three rooms in a Stanton-Street tenement, until the man had no work and the woman became ill.   When the money was gone they went to live with a sister, all in one room; and the sister, by scrubbing and washing, kept the whole family together.

There lives in Orchard Street a family of pale, underfed children who have never had enough to eat.   As the father is an inefficient workingman, the only reliable sources of income are the wages of a half-grown boy and the little that the mother earns by washing; but the mother took in the entire family of a sister-in-law who had been evicted, and, when the sister-in-law's baby died, they managed somehow to pay the funeral expenses and thus to keep free from that last horror, the potter's field.   .

It has seemed to us sometimes that the whole world was unemployed, but occasionally our attention has been attracted to a man struggling to do double duty, because he was so fortunate as to have work.   Up at the top of a rickety tenement in Scammel Street, there lives a workingman who has had steady employment.   His cousin, however, was in trouble, and so the family made room for her and for her child.   She fell ill; and a nurse visiting the sick woman noticed that every day she found a strange woman and her children there.   Upon inquiring, she learned that they live in the tenement in the rear, and while the father went out every day seeking work, they were invited in, that the meals might be shared.   Thus one man who had work took care of two families besides his own through the greater part of the winter.

The owners of the small stores have done a great deal to prevent suffering.   Many of them have sold on credit, hoping for better times.   The bakers always give freely.   As one baker's wife said, "If there is no old bread, one must give new."   Giving is so natural that it is promptly forgotten.   I asked one German grocer if he gave away food, and he answered slowly, "Very seldom." When I asked him what he did when people came in and said that they had nothing in the house to eat, he answered, "Oh, I give them a few beans or a little coffee or a little rice, but not many come in. I don't think we had more than three a day all winter, though we did count twenty-six last Thursday, counting beggars and all." In our immediate neighborhood the small dealers showed themselves ready to respond to every demand upon their charity. At the beginning of the hard times a relief committee consisting of twelve men was organized by the United Hebrew Trades in Delancey Street. They collected nearly a thousand dollars, and contributions of supplies were made by many of the small dealers in the neighborhood. Forty thousand pounds of bread and six thousand pounds of meat, besides flour and potatoes, were distributed. Physicians gave their services, and druggists gave medicines. Tobacco to the amount of four hundred pounds was given, and two thousand tickets for shaving were sent in by the barbers. The indifference of the owners of some of the large retail dry-goods stores in Grand Street, two blocks away, was in painful contrast to the kindness of those who keep the small stores.

Many of the trades-unions were able to help their own members most effectively. The Tin- and Sheet-Iron Workers' Association numbers four-hundred-and-fifty members, and besides donating two hundred dollars when it was most needed, they lent one thousand five hundred dollars to be repaid to the Union, payments to begin three months after work was found. It is said that Typographical Union Number 6 distributed wisely ten thousand dollars. Many other unions did similarly efficient work.

Such are the scattered records of a few kind deeds. They are the merest fragments in the unwritten history of "the simple, quiet, kindly help of the poor to the poor." If the rich lived on the East side next door to poverty, they would catch the neighborly spirit. One of our neighbors who is considered rich by those about us saw the family of a musician evicted from the tall tenement next door, and he took them all in till the father could find work.

There is many a rich man seated to-day with easy conscience at a table shining with cut-glass and silver, who would be ready to stretch out a helping hand to those who need it, if they were not "all so far away." He is living in another world. What he does is to make his annual contributions to our charitable societies, and that is all. Some day we shall begin to calculate the evil resulting from such contributions. Again and again is it true of the charity of to-day that "it curseth him who gives and him who takes." On the one hand the poor man, sinking down into the mire of pauperism, realizes dimly the bitterness of his degradation, and takes the alms offered him with curses in his heart; while on the other hand the rich merchant or manufacturer, who is daily disregarding the health of little children and delicate girls, quiets his conscience with a large check in the name of charity. And society applauds the generosity of such a man, and his eyes are blinded. "It is so tempting to the rich to think that by giving a check for the support of a social scheme, poverty may be abolished, and they be left free to enjoy their wealth. They always hope that something, *not themselves*, may meet all needs." It is very easy to make friends with those who have had few opportunities, for they are by nature frank and outspoken; and through every such friendship there comes a chance of escape out of the narrow conventional life of the rich into the broader, simpler life of the great human family.

Many years ago a young man said that he truly wished to enter into life, and the great Teacher told him to go and learn of those who had few possessions, but he turned away sorrowfully. It was true then, as it is true to-day, that the rich man, shut up in his own little circle and so cut off from the larger human life, is himself the greatest sufferer.

One is often asked the question, "What can the rich man do for the relief of suffering?" I believe that there is but one answer: Let him give not alms but himself, and the wisdom comes with the giving. I knew a young apprentice in a great machine-shop who was stricken down with consumption. His parents were old and feeble, and it was only through the gifts of his employer that his last days were made comfortable, but more to them all than the gifts was the fact that the employer came himself to the little home in the East-side tenement, and spoke friendly words. From every such natural friendship there grow more and more chances for helpfulness, and for that truest charity of all charities—the treating of others as if they were of our own kind.

JANE ELIZABETH ROBBINS.

BRIEF ESTIMATES OF NOTABLE NEW BOOKS.

f Frances
Cobbe, by
hlf. 2 vols.
iton, Mifflin &
4.00.

RECENT books are richer in Biographies, Reminiscences, and Letters than in any other department. Easily first in this group is the autobiography of Miss Cobbe, which is a very cheerful record of a life that has been "an interesting one to live," an interesting one, too, to know in so frank and familiar a way; for it has been a very active, sane, and cheerful life, covering a most important period. The book gives much information about most of the notable men and women (especially English) of the last fifty years, and letters from many of them. It has, besides the charm of cheerful reminiscence and entertaining gossip, a more serious value, for her life very forcibly illustrates the great widening of the range of women's activity and influence these fifty years.

Booth. Rec-
ons by his
:er, Edwina
h Grossman.
y Co. $3.00.

Attractive, too, is the handsome volume of Letters of Edwin Booth, together with his daughter's Recollections. These letters, to his daughter and a group of his most intimate friends, show the playful, familiar qualities of the man rather than his serious reflections on his art or on any subject. Many of them are commonplace; and, although they are all interesting, they owe their interest rather to the personality of Mr. Booth than to the matter of the letters themselves. But they contain passages of permanent value.

e of Charles
Brace, chiefly
his own let-
dited by his
er. With por-
Scribner.

The record of the life and work of the late Charles Loring Brace, so told by selections from his letters as to have much of the charm of an autobiography, is as inspiring a book— inspiring to the most unselfish activity—as could be made of the life of any private American citizen of the last fifty years. Mr. Brace's chief work, of course, was the establishment and maintenance of the Children's Aid Society, but the same spirit that moved him to this work shone through all his life and activity.

e Manners of
mericans, by
'ollope. 2 vols.
Mead & Co.

It was a happy idea to republish Mrs. Trollope's classic volumes of 1832, which irritated our ancestors, and which have been a precious boon to our historians. This is a book that has a legitimate claim to a second lease of life. To this day no book more interesting has been written about American manners.

Since the death of Thoreau, nine volumes have been pub- Familiar Let Henry Davi reau, edit Frank B. Houghton, 1 Co. $1.50. lished of his manuscripts and fugitive pieces, and this volume of letters makes the tenth. A collection of his letters appeared thirty years ago, selected to show the philosopher rather than the man. This present collection includes letters illustrating particularly his " domestic and gossipy mood." The editor has not rejected the common and trivial, desiring to present " this piquant original just as he was." The book is in every way well edited.

In " The Early Public Life of William Ewart Gladstone," The Early Life of W Ewart Gl by A. F. I Dodd, Mead $1.50. Mr. Alfred F. Robbins has dealt only with Mr. Gladstone's career down to 1840, " with an amount of detail which has not before been attempted." The book gives evidence of thorough work, with frequent references to original sources. Mr. Robbins has permitted many of Gladstone's early contemporaries—and such a plan is cruel to many of them—to give their estimates of him in their own words.

General Hyde's well-written volume of very interesting Following th Cross, by W. Hyde, brigadier-g of volunteer traits. Ho Mifflin & Co personal reminiscences of the civil war is well worth reading, in spite of the many similar volumes that have caused a temporary satiety with this kind of literature.

An important biography,—important as a biography as The Life of Defoe, by Wright, prir Cowper Sch ney. Anson Randolph & lustrated. $8 well as for its bearings upon both literature and history, is Mr. Thomas Wright's " Life of Defoe." By reason of its scholarly work, its fulness, and its style, it may at once be accepted as the standard life of Defoe.

·Very welcome to the most cultivated readers will be the Eighteenth Vignettes, series, by Dobson. Dod & Co. $2.00. second series of " Eighteenth Century Vignettes," by Austin Dobson, which contains studies of last century subjects and men by the greatest living master of that period. There are no literary essays nowadays done with a surer hand or a more delicate touch. Very excellent, too, are Miss Guiney's A Little Engli lery, by L Imogen Gt Harper. $1. essays, her subjects falling within the same period—gathered into a dainty volume. At once solid and graceful, too, is Mr. Horace E. Scudder's " Childhood in Literature and Art,"

od in Litera-
and Art, by
.e E. Scudder.
hton,   Mifflin
$1.75.

Greek, Roman, Hebrew, Early Christian, Mediæval, English, French, German and American, and a separate essay on Hans Christian Andersen—nine essays of wide range, some of which readers of " The Atlantic Monthly" will pleasantly re- call.   And of our American literary essayists none now at work

dy Fire, by
lton   Wright
, second series.
  Mead & Co.

is more useful than Mr. Mabie, further evidences of whose graceful faculty of compressing sound literary judgments into brief space is given in this latest collection of papers on a very wide range of topics.   Mrs. Oliphant's running review

:torian Age of
h Literature,
rs. Oliphant.
Lovell, Cory-
o. $3.50.

of writers of the Victorian era, great and small, is both bio- graphical and critical; more interesting than profound; a most excellent sketch and a book of great practical utility, especially to young readers, or as a first sketch for older readers.   A very practical book has grown out of Mr.

lege Woman,
harle s F.
g. The Baker
lor Co. $1.00.

Thwing's own work as President of the College for Women of Western Reserve University—full of the common sense and helpfulness that are the outcome of very earnest personal experience.

s in Plaster,
the collection
rence Hutton.
r. $6.00.

Accompanying the ghostly but interesting pictures of the death-masks of many historic persons is Mr. Hutton's gossipy text about the persons and the masks and the features and characteristics suggested.   The volume is one of the most attractive books of the season.

ded Gates, and
   poems, by
as Bailey Al-
  Houghton,
& Co. $1.25.

The pretty volume of Mr. Thomas Bailey Aldrich's re- cent poems bears the title of his ringing warning that appeared a little while ago in " The Atlantic Monthly"—" Unguarded

ooks of Song,
chard Watson
:. The first
iete collection
r. Gild e r's
. Illustrated.
ry Co. $2.50.

Gates." It contains also " Elmwood" in memory of Lowell, and other recent poems.   Into one volume Mr. Gilder has gathered his preceding five books of poetry, with some new poems, making a single complete edition of the author's poems to date.

Against Com-
ealth,   b y
r y Demarest
' d.   Harper.

Mr. Henry Demarest Lloyd, whose writings in analysis of monopolies, and in hostility to them, especially in criticism of the Standard Oil Company, have engaged him for some years, now issues in much larger bulk than hitherto his study of the rise of this company and an explanation of his indus- trial philosophy, which is, that " monopolies have become a despotism over the public." The book is a stout volume, full of testimony given before investigating committees, all so used as to make a narrative and written in a very emphatic style.

"A primer of science of city-government" is Mr. Conkling's own description of his very practical and useful book, which sets forth the central facts of municipal organization and administration. It is a most opportune manual, the best as well as the latest.

City Govern the United by Alfred R ling. Appl $1.00.

The lectures delivered at Yale by Professor Allen, of the Episcopal Theological School at Cambridge, on Religious Progress, make a notable summary of the advance of Christian thought and of its present status and its outlook, and are one of the most notable contributions, in fact, to religious literature of the year.

Religious P by Professor Allen. Ho Mifflin & Co.

Important also are the Rev. Arthur T. Pierson's lectures delivered in Scotland last year, narrating and reviewing in a practical and inspiring way the work done in every land by Christian missionaries. It is a stirring story, told with spirit and sympathy. Accompanying his book is a religious map of the world.

The New Act Apostles; or t vels of Mod sions, by Ar Pierson. Th & Taylor Co.

Dr. Carus's book is an explanation of Buddhism—it might be said *is* Buddhism, since much of the book is a translation of the Buddhist sacred writings, but so selected as to give a consecutive and proper understanding of them.

The Gospel of according t Records, tol Paul Caru Open Court ing Co. $1.

There have been issued in two volumes the discussions of the International Christian Conferences held in Chicago, 1893, under the auspices of the Evangelical Alliance. Vol. 1 contains the Addresses of Greeting and Responses, the Addresses setting forth the Condition of Protestant Christendom, Christian Union and Co-operation, and the Church and Local Problems, and Vol. 2 contains the Evangelistic, Reformatory, Social, Educational, and Miscellaneous Addresses.

Christianity cally Applie theDiscussio Internationa tian Con held in Chica under the of the Eva Alliance f United Sta vols. The Taylor Co.

Mrs. Miller, who in a certain sense has the bird-world as her personal property for loving interpretation, has written plainly but sympathetically a practical book about the care of pets—birds and other; and nobody could do the task better.

Our Home Pet to Keep The and Happy, Thorne Mill lustrated. $1.25.

A volume of short stories and sketches of Scotch life, in dialect, published first a little while ago in England under

the Bonny
Bush, by Ian
ren. Dodd,
& Co. $1.25.
the *nom de plume* of Ian Maclaren, shows so true a touch of humor and of pathos that these sketches have already taken their place along with the best of the considerable volume of recent Scotch literature. These scenes of simple life are pictures no reader will easily forget. Some of them strike very deep down into the fundamental emotions.

Among the beautiful volumes of the month are Theodore Child's "Wimples and Crisping-Pins," studies in coiffure and ornaments (Harper, $2); an elegant two-volume profusely illustrated edition of "Hypatia," from drawings by William Martin Johnson—very handsomely manufactured in every respect (Harper, $7); a two-volume edition of "Memoirs of the Duchesse de Gontaut," translated by Mrs. J. W. Davis (Dodd, Mead & Co., $5); a very elegant edition of Tennyson's "Becket," illustrated by F. C. Gordon (Dodd, Mead & Co., $2); a very handsome edition of "Holland," by Edmondo de Amicis, translated from the Italian by Miss Helen Zimmern (and this translator is worthy of the picturesque and most interesting author), very beautifully illustrated (Porter & Coates, $5); a convenient and pretty edition of "A Tale of Two Cities,' illustrated by Edmund H. Garrett (2 vols., Dodd, Mead & Co., $3.50).

From A. C. McClurg & Co. come two interesting translations— "Tales from the Ægean," being short stories of Greek life by the foremost modern Greek writer, Demetrios Bikélas, translated by L. E. Opdycke ($1); and "Jewish Tales," by Leopold von Sacher-Masoch, translated from the French by Harriet Lieber Cohen ($1)— both very excellent and interesting. Another convenient translation of note, "At the Ghost Hour," consists of four dainty little volumes, each containing a tale from the German of Paul Heyse, translated by Frances A. Van Santford, with many decorations by Alice C. Morse (4 vols. in case, Dodd, Mead & Co., $2).

There comes from William Beverly Harison (New York) the useful educational series of historical summaries: "The Evolution of Empire Series," in which Mary Parmele condenses history with unsurpassed skill, making a first sketch of each nation's history within the space of about a hundred pages of large type; "The Theory and Practice of Handwriting," revised edition, being an explanation of the practice of vertical writing and of its far-reaching importance by its originator, Mr. John Jackson; and Klemm's excellent relief-maps, in paper.

The Forum

JANUARY, 1895.

ARE OUR MORAL STANDARDS SHIFTING?

SocIAL philosophers and social reformers do not always realize that what people think they ought to do is, in the long run, more important than what they really do. The religious persecutors, with all their monstrous attempts to punish inward opinions by outward pains, at least foresaw the effect of letting new standards of right and wrong come into the world. What is done in America to-day is, therefore, not the measure of the people's uprightness: the mass of crime and folly which the morning paper brings to our unwilling notice may mean only that the reporter dwells on what seems most shocking. On the other hand all the current reprobation by laws, editorials, and sermons may not prove that public gambling is contrary to the accepted principles of morality, in the face of the open existence of bucket-shops and gambling houses. There is one, and only one, practical national moral standard: the conviction of the average person as to what is right and wrong. That conviction may be God-given at our birth; it may be implanted by our mothers, by our churches, or by our schools; it may be beaten in by a policeman's "billy"; but the actual American morality of the Nation is simply the "average man's" stock of convictions.

In many directions the average man has raised his own standard during the last hundred years, and is still raising it. To have abolished political privileges; to have accepted religious toleration; to have made drunkenness disgraceful; to have learned to treat the pauper, the lunatic, and the prisoner with humanity; to have destroyed slavery,—these are his splendid achievements. The country has accepted such new principles as right, and stands by them.

33

Churches begin to realize that they must appeal to this average intelligence and sense of right, and therefore ministers dwell lightly on the acceptance of doctrine and on religious observances, and strongly on good works; they look less to proof-texts for the edification of their hearers, and more to the truth.   While in the ordinary private affairs of life moral standards are on the whole advancing, the old standards no longer apply to the political and social matters which now absorb so much attention; for the foundation of the Nation's judgments is undergoing a change.   Yet politics and government and labor questions and public order are as dependent as religion upon the average idea of what is praiseworthy and what is iniquitous; they are all moral questions.

One of the evidences of a moral shifting is that so many people suppose that private and public affairs have two standards: that it is wrong to use an employer's time for private gain, but right for a public officer to draw his salary and then leave the regular duties to a deputy; that it is wrong to secure a privilege for one's self by bribing a city council, but right to subscribe money to a campaign fund to buy votes for a party's advantage; or that a distinction may be made between the private and public character of public men. Americans seem rather more prone than formerly to consort with Thomas, Richard and Henry, if thereby they get aid or amusement. The leading idea of a book which is said recently to have sold a hundred thousand copies in the United States seems to be that, if you can contribute to the entertainment of people, they are to receive you and make you a friend, no matter what your character.   The scoundrel Svengali is courted by three respectable Englishmen, and allowed to acquire a fatal influence over their *protégée*, because he can play a folding flageolet.   Think of the Svengalis in American politics, perfectly well known to be consorts and partners of thieves and unjust persons, and yet accepted in political and even personal fellowship by honest men!

In matters of government all good Americans know themselves to be like the Neolithic Man:

> " We are going to live in cities and build churches and make laws;
> We are going to eat three times a day without the natural cause;
> We are going to turn life upside down about a thing called gold;
> We're going to want the earth and take as much as we can hold."

Wherever a thousand of us are set down together—in a California mining-camp, or a Dakota prairie, or a Sandwich Island,—we know how to form an orderly community with open discussion, parliamentary practice according to Jefferson's Manual, and legislation by a majority vote,—of white people. Free government depends upon the acceptance of this wholesome dictum of majority rule; to refuse to abide by it is an evidence of moral obliquity. There are many evidences of the decline of the old-fashioned, good-tempered agreement to come to a decision and take the consequences if one is out-voted. For instance, filibustering, the commonest engine of the minority, is essentially immoral, because it denies the right to reach a conclusion. It is also a very common practice for minorities of a city council or legislature, or of the House of Representatives, to hold off and refuse to permit the organization of their body; the practice seems to strike the public mind as an amusing trick, instead of a betrayal of popular government, and practical anarchy. "If the minority will not yield, the majority must, or there is an end of government."

Another very interesting and significant change of public standard is seen in the growing impatience with legal and constitutional methods of bringing about a change of laws. There is hardly a State constitution which may not be amended within two years, or a city charter which may not be altered within a year, or a law which can-not immediately be repealed if the community demand it. The experience of New York City in saving Central Park from the speed-way shows how the worst legislatures cower before a plain indication of the people's will. Yet Americans grow more and more impatient. We know so well the power of organization in politics, and the difficulty of getting legislation when opposed by powerful interests, that we all wink at breaches of the law; that is, the unpopular statute is practically abrogated by ignoring it. From this condition of befogged morals springs such an episode as the recent impudent request of nearly fifty of the leading business men of Denver that the enforcement of the laws against gambling be suspended. If Colorado likes gambling, let it repeal its laws, and invite Eastern people to come and live in such a paradise; but to retain the law and then to suspend it is a case of what the philosophers call " both being and not being."

" The horseleech hath two daughters, crying, Give, give." Americans appear to grow more disposed to illustrate the proverb by living on the Government. Of course the whole theory of rotation in appointive and non-political offices is that the party in power has a right to pay for the private services of its followers out the public treasury. A recent Governor of the State of New York put this practice in its baldest form when he approved a corrupt public contract so as to pay off his election expenses. The ordinary state of mind as to pensions is similarly low. A few months ago a distinguished soldier, diplomat, and statesman defended the action of a man who was drawing a pension for total disability while an active member of the United States Senate. " The law," said he, " makes no distinction; it does not recognize the possibility of mental labor by a man physically disabled." " But," it was objected, " might not the Senator look at the matter simply as an honest man?" " You might as well say that I have no right to the pension that I draw," replied the General. The discussion ceased at that point; but the wonder remained that men of wealth and station and public spirit should take, and encourage others to take, payment for their own gallantry. There is no effective public sentiment even against notorious pension frauds. In what community would a person be esteemed who gave information against a widow who had married again and still drew her pension? Yet any of us would notify the police if he saw the same woman stealing ribbon at a counter.

This lack of moral alertness is seen likewise in the tariff question. The stanchest upholder of a tariff intended to encourage national industries, or to retain the home-market, or to raise wages, may blush at the influences by which the last two bills have been shaped. Under the McKinley tariff the free list increased nearly two hundred million dollars and tariff taxes fell off by twenty-seven million dollars. Yet it is deservedly unpopular because of the general belief that many duties were introduced at the demand of persons who had rendered service to the leaders of the party in power. That unpopularity did not prevent Senators of the other party from doing the same thing, apparently in the belief that their constituents would not be seriously disturbed. In this, as in other moral questions, the responsibility lies not in the greed of the few, but in the acquiescence of the many. To depend upon the Government to keep up the profits of one's business by successive enactments is sufficiently demoralizing; to permit extortion by our representatives is morally the same as to extort.

The relations of employer and employee in this country had for many years a unique and happy experience. In colonial times there were no workmen, in the modern sense, but handicraftsmen; their social status is indicated by the traditional term " help," for distinctions between master and man were of little account when all worked side by side. The Colonies never knew the European systems of trades-guilds, and there was a constant incentive and opportunity to rise from employee to employer. The right of the workman, as of every other man, to go where he liked within the Union is inserted in the Federal Constitution, along with that right of free trade between States which loosed the bonds of the producer. There was every incentive to a man to labor, to improve, to move about, to save money, to "work out his own salvation with fear and trembling." So well established was this industrial freedom that the country easily adjusted itself to the change of commercial conditions brought about by the development of manufactures and transportation on a large scale. Until about six years ago the whole system seemed founded on the following simple and well-understood principles, acknowledged by masters, men, and the public as natural and right, as a sort of un-written code of labor law: The relation of employer and employee is one of mutual advantage; the business supports them both, and the usual feeling is one of good will. Workmen may freely organize unions for any lawful purpose that seems good to them; and they have a right to remain outside such unions if they please. In case of differences a strike is a reasonable method of enforcing the work-man's opinion, provided there be no violence. A man is free to fol-low any trade for which he thinks himself fitted, and to leave service and to seek other service at his discretion. On the other side, the master has a moral right to increase or diminish his force or to close his works according to his judgment of the business: but not to dis-charge a faithful man from mere personal dislike. A man out of work is temporarily unfortunate, but will soon find something to do; a man who will not work for a fair wage when work is provided is a tramp and needs nobody's sympathy. On the question of wages, there must be an agreement: masters ought to pay what the business can afford; men must try to keep him up to paying a just rate. The whole relation is not one of contract or duress; it is a mutual agree-ment terminable at immediate notice by either party.

In the above statement there is no attempt to state or to discuss the economic principles of capital and labor; but simply to set forth what the public seemed to think about it, say as late as 1888. Al-ready at that time the ground was prepared for a great change. In-dustry was rolling into larger masses. Consolidations, leases, com-binations and trusts made masters fewer, and brought the men into personal relations with hired managers, instead of proprietors. Trades-unions began in like manner to aggregate into powerful national organizations. Then came the great Southwestern railroad strike, the first of the general strikes. Ever since, it has been evident that a new spirit is abroad. What is the present state of the average mind as to the right and wrong in the relations of capital and labor?

The writer was for the year from August, 1893, to September, 1894, at a distance from the country, and caught only faint rumors of what was going on at home, except for the explosion in Chicago, of which the echoes penetrated everywhere. On his return he was amazed to find how different was the tone of public sentiment. So far as can be gathered from the unconscious indications of the newspapers, and from the utterances of many intelligent men who are neither employers nor employed, the following is a fair statement of the present average opinion: Industry is warfare, in which labor and capital are each trying to tear away spoils from the other. The right to strike includes the right, by all means short of violence, to prevent non-strikers from taking the places of strikers; the unemployed member of a labor union deserves public aid; the non-member of a union who accepts a place vacated by a striker is a "scab," and does not deserve protection, though public order is a good thing too. Employers are necessarily hostile to their laborers, and withhold all that they possibly can of wages or of consideration. In case violence occurs in a strike the responsibility lies with the employer for not yielding to the strikers; but a particular striker who kills or burns does very wrong. It is the duty of the State to see that workmen have "a living wage," to interpose in labor troubles, and to compel the employers to accept arbitration; but it is hardly just to compel workmen to accept the arbitration, if it go against them. Maintenance of the peace by force of arms is a brutal and dubious expedient. In any case of trouble between a corporation and its workmen the presumption is that the corporation is wrong.

Is it too much to say that this statement of principles is more moderate than the actual convictions of at least one-third of the people in the Northern States of all classes and pursuits? The farmers of the Northwest hold railroads responsible for most of their ills; the large class which lives by supplying working-people with the necessaries of life naturally sympathizes with them; and thousands of conservative people of the middle class, who have little to lose or gain from strikes, appear convinced that "labor needs protection." The notion that labor and capital are by nature antagonistic to each other is perhaps helped out by another principle which has been busily enforced by certain politicians. For two centuries and a half the importer and exporter had been looked upon as a public benefactor; and the "benevolent merchant" is the hero of Sunday-school books. Now we are passionately assured that the importer is engaged in an unpatriotic and immoral business: that there is a rightful national profit and advantage in selling goods, but none in buying them. In the same way people see the profits of the employer, and do not realize that he can make nothing except by permitting others to make something. Into the profound discontent with corporations and their management the limits of this paper do not permit inquiry: there must be reason for it, or it would not be so widespread; but it neither justifies nor explains the plain tendency to look upon "capital" as the enemy of "labor."

To the dissatisfaction with corporations is probably due the remarkable change of public sentiment toward strikes. The old-fashioned strike was a cessation of work, more or less complete, by the employees of one concern or at most of the allied workers in one town. Such movements have been a very powerful and legitimate means of keeping up wages and preventing oppressions, and even when nominally unsuccessful they have often been effectual in compelling employers to recognize the money-value of a good understanding with their men. Hence the public has endured the inconvenience, provided the methods were peaceful. Now the very word has taken another meaning. Says Professor Ely in a discussion of strikes in the October FORUM: "They are a species of warfare and must be viewed somewhat in the same light in which we look at war in general." This was not true ten years ago; it is true of many of the recent strikes; and they have been occasions for the use of force on both sides. To the public mind a "strike" has come to mean a disorderly and passionate contest between two powerful parties; and the average man has a new set of opinions upon such struggles.

In the first place the public has come to accept the long-disputed contention of the workmen, that the "master workmen," "walking delegates," or other representatives of the unions ought to be received by employers as the responsible persons with whom they are to deal in case of disagreements. Since the unions almost always include men from several or many establishments, this system means, of course, that negotiations are to be carried on with persons whom the employer has, perhaps, never before seen.   It is useless to struggle and object: the *agora* of public opinion, which is the highest tribunal in the United States, has decided that the old personal relation of the " boss" with his " hands" must give way to a system of diplomacy between ambassadors of the employers and delegates of the employed.   Yet here arises a question of serious import and growing difficulty.   What is to be the status of those who refuse to join the unions?   The old notion was distinctly that they were to be unmolested, and it is not plain yet that the average man expects them to join or else be excluded from employment.   Probably people do not realize the importance of a change by which public sentiment no longer protects the man who prefers to work in his own way by personal agreement with his own employer.   The obligation to join a trades-union, whether enforced by boycott, by brickbats, or by exclusion from the privileges of arbitration and protection which are given to unions, is an obligation which is directly contrary to the most ancient principles of American government.   It is a revival of mediæval guilds, and restrictions on labor; it is the formation of an *imperium in imperio*.   It is a deadening process, tending to ignore the natural differences of capacity and strength between men.   It is a part of that pressure toward uniformity which is the most dangerous symptom of American democracy.   There is but one society to which men must belong, whether or no; and that is the State.

The same influence is at work at the other end of the industrial system, only there the small manufacturers and tradesmen protest against it, while the workmen seem to welcome it.   Why should not the same rule be applied to both parties?   Combination and organization are practically established by both corporations and workmen; may they not be legalized, while securing to all those who prefer to stand out the fullest protection against any discriminations?   Many small concerns may still flourish if allowed equal transportation facilities: many thousands of workmen may be prosperous in their own way, if protected from boycotts.

Everybody knows the reply of the English barrister to the judge who interrupted him with: " But that's not the law, you know."— " It was the law, your Lordship, till your Lordship spoke."   A few days ago it would have been safe to say that whatever might be the desire of the Nation as to arbitration in labor disputes, no system could be accepted the results of which were not equally binding on both sides. The Report of the Commissioners on the Chicago strike necessitates new public sentiment and a new moral law. " It is the duty of the Government to have them [the railroads] accept the decision of its tribunal, even though complete reciprocal obligations cannot be imposed upon labor." The doctrine itself is not new; it has repeatedly been put forth by ardent advocates of State interference: but its acceptance by disinterested and able men is a thunderbolt. A court with powers to require railroads to pay specified wages and to retain specified employees is in itself a reversal of old-fashioned ideas as to the contract nature of service. A recommendation that the workmen be neither bound to accept the wages thus fixed nor to remain in service, even for a day, nor to observe in any way the convenience of the travelling public in the time or manner of their strike, may possibly be American morals, but it certainly is not the morals of even two years ago.

Perhaps the most significant change of the public conscience is with regard to violent acts of all sorts, and especially violence accompanying strikes. Murderers were once treated as beasts; then as dangerous men; and now more or less as heroes. It is hardly fair to make the average man responsible for the shameful celebrity given to criminals; but there certainly is a bluntness of the public conscience as to the moral duty of keeping order. " No army of mercenaries deserves popular support," says a highly educated literary man, in discussing the use of troops in Chicago; and he adds, " If these trusts and corporations that make a business of lobbying know that an army stands at their beck and call, an army that asks no questions, that simply shoots straight when the word is given, the task of doing equal and exact justice will be impossible." This is sufficient evidence of a dangerous tendency to look upon corporations and millionaires as the only people who have anything to be defended by military force. Jefferson said as long ago as 1787: " I hold that a little rebellion now and then is a good thing, as necessary in the political world as storms in the physical. . . . Let the people take arms, pardon, and pacify them. . . . The tree of liberty must be refreshed from time to time with the blood of patriots and tyrants." In 1808 he wrote about the opposition to the Embargo in New England: " I think it so important an example to crush these audacious proceedings and to make the opposers feel the consequences of individuals daring to oppose a law by force." Even he was compelled to appeal to the *ultima ratio regum* when he had the responsibility of preserving the Union; for he saw at last that armed disobedience is disorganization.

In a case like the Chicago strike the question is not whether force shall be used,—that was settled by those who attacked the railroad shops and trains,—but whether unlawful and uncontrolled force shall yield to force directed by law. The chief evil of mobs is not that they destroy property and life, but that they encourage lawlessness: a mob is simply a momentary military organization, acting without a constitution; it is a despotism of the worst, because of the most irresponsible, kind. Despotisms sometimes have good objects in view; but they are force, and have to be met and repelled by force whenever they attack established governments. To admit that there may be orderly mobs or justifiable mobs is to admit that the time has come for a political revolution. "Many impartial observers," says the Report on the Chicago Strike, "are reaching the view that much of the real responsibility of these disorders rests with the people themselves and with the Government for not adequately controlling monopolies and corporations, and for failing to reasonably protect the rights of labor and redress its wrongs." This statement is in effect the assertion that labor, after an honest effort, has been unable to secure adequate laws, and therefore that a breach of the law is morally justifiable. If it be correct, the machinery of popular government has broken down, and the experience of mankind shows that in such a case the workingman loses most. The reign of law, the *régime* of ballots instead of bullets, is the triumph of the organized many over the powerful few: to teach the nation that there is any better way of reaching its ends than by discussion and legislation is to give up, and to go back to the "law of might" of the Middle Ages. Has the moral standard of the American people so far drifted from its moorings?

ALBERT BUSHNELL HART.

THE HUMILIATING REPORT OF THE STRIKE COM-
MISSION.

IT is probably safe to say that in no civilized country in this century, not actually in the throes of war or open insurrection, has
society been so disorganized as it was in the United States during
the first half of 1894; never was human life held so cheap; never
did the constituted authorities appear so incompetent to enforce respect for the law. The social fabric seemed to be measurably near to
dissolution, and the country was not far from the verge of anarchy.

During the coal strikes whole counties lay terrorized at the mercy
of armed mobs who committed incendiarism and murder where they
pleased and with impunity. The vagabond forces of Coxeyism swept
across the country levying compulsory alms on peaceful communities,
stealing trains, taking forceful possession of the operation of railway
lines, openly defying the laws and the military power of the United
States. In Colorado, the officers of the State, where they did not
sympathize with, were totally powerless to reduce to submission, the
miners who were intrenched in frank and undisguised insurrection
and daily perpetrating crimes of violence against life and property—
crimes of which the story has not yet been told and probably never
will be told in all its brutality and horror. In the strike on the Great
Northern Railway, by which 4,000 miles of line were temporarily
paralyzed and vast stretches of country were left without communication with the outside world, deeds of lawlessness were done of which
the perpetrators could not be convicted because the sympathy of communities was with them and against the enforcement of the law.

The spirit of social and industrial unrest seemed to culminate in
the great railway strikes of June and July, which, originating in
Chicago, spread southward as far as the Gulf of Mexico, eastward
almost half-way to the Atlantic seaboard, and westward to the Pacific
coast. The original pretext for the strikes was, according to the
leaders, a controversy, involving chiefly a question of wages, between
Pullman's Palace Car Company and certain of the employees in its
shops. This pretext, however, was thrown aside in the very earliest

stages of the trouble, which rapidly developed, first into a general warfare (or boycott) of railway employees of almost all classes against such railway companies as operated Pullman cars; secondly, and almost immediately, into a still wider conflict between the various classes of railway employees and practically all the railway companies of the West; and, finally, into a condition of widespread disorder in which, for the space of more than two weeks, the operation of some 70,000 miles of railway lines, on which were employed about 300,000 men, was either wholly or partially suspended; property of the value of millions of dollars was wantonly destroyed; many lives were sacrificed; armed mobs held possession of railway tracks and yards; trains bearing passengers, including women and children, were deliberately wrecked,—not for purposes of robbery but simply as a measure of retaliation against the railway companies and against society; the laws of the United States and the injunctions of Federal courts were set at defiance; the forces of individual States were powerless to preserve order, and in no less than eight States the military power of the General Government had to be used to move interstate commerce and the United States mails.

In its last stage the uprising was not confined to the employees of railways. For some days it was uncertain whether the cause of revolt would not be taken up by all classes of organized labor throughout the country. Leaders of organizations, not at all connected with railways, did not hesitate to threaten that if the Government interfered to enforce the laws, such interference would be the signal for a general rebellion. When the crucial moment came, wiser counsel happily prevailed. Some isolated classes of workmen, entirely disconnected from the railway service, did throw themselves hot-headedly into the fray, believing that others would follow; but the general industrial revolution by force of arms was temporarily averted.

During the period of suspense the situation was more critical and more menacing than anything which has been seen in the United States since the close of the Civil War. It is not surprising that the events of those days should have awakened in many quarters grave misgivings as to the stability of our form of government, and serious doubts as to the adequacy to our present political conditions of that instrument on which our Government is founded, and which sets forth in its preamble that one of the objects for which it is framed is to "insure domestic tranquillity."

There have been strikes before, involving vast interests and bitterly contested, but none fraught with such sinister significance as those of last July. What caused the most profound alarm in all thinking minds was not any individual incident of the uprising, so much as the fact that the spirit of discontent and of despair should have so far saturated large masses of the people of our country as to make such things possible,—not anything which was done, so much as the method of its doing and the narrow escape from what was undone.

Whence comes this discontent? What are its causes and how has it attained such growth? How are we to check it? These questions every man was asking, and on the finding of a satisfactory answer to them seemed to depend (and still depends, for the temporary quiet is no assurance of permanent security), not the prosperity only, but the very existence of our institutions.

When, therefore, on July 26, the President, exercising the authority conferred upon him by the act of 1888, announced the appointment of a Board of three Commissioners to make investigation into the causes and conditions of the recent disturbances, his action was generally applauded. It is rarely that a temporary commission has such important duties laid upon it as were laid upon Carroll D. Wright, John D. Kernan, and Nicholas E. Worthington. And in proportion as their responsibility was great, so was their opportunity. The country had suddenly found itself face to face with the most serious danger that had threatened it for a quarter of a century. The events of the preceding months had developed not merely a local bitterness or a temporary irritation on the part of a certain number of employees against their individual employers, but a deep-rooted and widespread hostility on the part of great masses of our population against the whole scheme of constituted society. To the Commissioners was entrusted the task of unravelling the threads of this tangled skein of hostility and bitterness, and of laying them in orderly wise before the President and the people, showing which strand should be picked up here and which one severed there, until all might be knit together again into a harmonious fabric of peace and amity. To them was given the opportunity to render a service, not to the country only, but to humanity,—a service in the rendering of which they would have written their own names large on the history of the social evolution of the world. ' It was a splendid chance; and they were left untrammelled in their choice of means to improve it.

To those who watched the course of the Commission's investigation, it became evident from the outset that the three members of the Board had no recognition of what it was that was given into their hands. But, even after it was seen that the best could not be hoped for, their report was still awaited with anxiety. Though they failed to grasp the magnitude of the charge that was laid upon them, they might yet, it was hoped, do good service; for an accurate and faithful setting forth of the facts within the narrower field to which they confined themselves would still be of no small economic value.

In such a setting forth of facts, two qualities above all others would be essential: absolute truthfulness or accuracy of statement, and entire freedom from prejudice or partiality. That these should be the two qualities which are most conspicuously lacking from the report which we have received is not only a public calamity but partakes of the nature of a national humiliation.

Through the daily and weekly press of the country, attention has already been called to a number of minor errors of fact in the report, —errors many of them of individual insignificance and assuming importance only collectively as evidence of the astonishing carelessness of detail with which the document was compiled. Other misstatements there are, however, which are of a graver nature. It is not possible within the limits of a single article to canvass in detail all the errors which the Commission has made. It must suffice rather to take one or two of the more radical misstatements.

The Commission says (on page 36): "Throughout the strike, the strife was simply over handling Pullman cars, the men being ready to do their duty otherwise." From a document which was placed in evidence before the Commission, let us pick out in outline the course of events during the eight or ten crucial days as they bore upon the operation of the Wabash Railroad. Abstracting from the document in question we find:

June 29—At 7 P.M. the switchmen at Chicago stopped work without notice.

June 30—In the forenoon the switchmen at St. Louis did likewise.

July 1—The engineers and firemen between Chicago and St. Louis went out. The freight conductors and freight brakemen at Decatur did likewise.

July 2—No freight was moved on either the St. Louis or Detroit division. Engines at various points were stoned. No trains in or out of Decatur.

July 3—All switching engineers at East St. Louis went out.

July 4—Trouble experienced at Springfield, Ill., and Ashley, Ind. The company had plenty of men willing to work, but had no protection. The company tried to take some new men to Ashley, but the strikers ran them out of town.

July 5—Some gangs of section men struck. Strikers set fire to a caboose at Litchfield at 2 A.M., and shortly after that a car-repairer's oil-house was burned, and shortly after that the freight-house was set on fire.

July 6—Trains coming into Chicago were attacked by a mob at Thirty-fifth Street, and nearly all windows in cab, coaches and parlor car were broken. No one hurt so far as known.

July 7—A mob went to the company's tracks at Halsted Street, Chicago, and proceeded to run cars from side tracks to main track and turn them over. They turned over ten or twelve and also piled on the track timber, ties, and any other material they could get hold of as obstructions, and tore out a few rails. At other points trains were generally moving under protection of the militia.

And so on. These records apply only to the lines of the Wabash Railroad between St. Louis and Chicago and Detroit. They were in evidence before the Commission. It was also in evidence before the Commission that *no Pullman cars are handled on these lines.*

A similar record of desertion and obstruction and violence was placed in evidence in relation to the Michigan Central Railroad, on which no Pullman cars are hauled; also in relation to the Lake Shore and Michigan Southern Railroad, on which no Pullman cars are hauled; also in relation to the Chicago, Milwaukee and St. Paul Railway, which (while it does happen to have in operation four Pullman cars recently inherited among the assets of the absorbed Milwaukee and Northern road) is on notoriously unfriendly terms with the Pullman company.

It might have suggested itself to the intelligence of the members of the Commission that, if the desire of the American Railway Union had been only to coerce the Pullman company, the first action that it would have taken would have been to discriminate sharply between the patrons of that company and those who were opposed to it—while thwarting and obstructing to the best of its ability all such companies as handled Pullman cars, to have done all in its power to assist and facilitate the operations of these companies which were already the Pullman company's enemies, or competitors. But that was not the object of the leaders of the strike. The hauling of Pullman cars and the interests of the Pullman employees were matters of indifference to the leaders of the American Railway Union.

Perhaps the most picturesque incident of the strike occurred when the contractors who had in charge the removal of dead carcasses from the stock-yards at Chicago appealed to the mayor of the city for assistance in hauling a train, loaded with rotting bodies, away from the yards to the station where they were to be disposed of. The mayor, it will be remembered, instead of furnishing police force sufficient to move that train in spite of the strikers, made request of the President of the American Railway Union for an order to the strikers to permit its removal. The President of the American Railway Union issued the order " in the interest of public health, " and the train was moved.

Does the Commission suppose that these carcasses were hauled in Pullman cars? If " the strife was simply over the handling of Pullman cars" why was there ever any trouble at the stock-yards? The handling of Pullman cars had no more to do with the attack of the American Railway Union upon the railways than had the muddying of the stream in Æsop's fable to do with the lamb being eaten by the wolf. And the wolf, also, it will be remembered, said that that was what " the strife" was all about.

Again, on page 28, the Commissioners say, " Until the railroads set the example, a general union of railroad employees was never attempted. " It is difficult to believe that the United States Commissioner of Labor can be entirely ignorant of the history of railway labor organizations during the last twenty years. Yet the United States Commissioner of Labor was chairman of the Commission which made this report, and anything more flatly perversive of the facts of that history than the above statement can hardly be conceived. The " general union of railroad employees" has been attempted again and again. Attempts to achieve it—whether by consolidation or federation of existing orders or by the creation of a new order to absorb all others—have never ceased. Since the organization of the order of the Knights of Labor there has never been a railway strike of any magnitude in which a union more or less general (and always extending far beyond the limits of one class of labor or the employees of a single road) has not been in some measure achieved.

The statement quoted is part of the attack made by the Commissioners upon the General Managers' Association of Chicago. It is curiously characteristic of the purblind view which the Commissioners take of all the circumstances of the strike, that they insist on treating it as if it had been a controversy between the American Railway Union on the one hand and the General Managers' Association on the other. They ignore the fact that about twenty thousand miles of railway line (employing, at a guess, one hundred thousand men) were involved, which were owned by companies not members of the General Managers' Association, which could not under the rules of the organization be members owing to their geographical position. Except the Atchison, Topeka and Santa Fé Railway, no transcontinental line is represented in the Association. To limit the inquiry into the conditions of the quarrel on the part of the railroads to an examination of the share borne by the General Managers' Association is absurd. Apart from the falsity of the statement that the organization of that association " set the example" for, or antedated, the attempt to make a general union of railway employees, the sage misgivings to which the Commissioners give vent as to the legality of the association are as irrelevant to an elucidation of the essential principles underlying the strike as they are ridiculous in law.

After the American Railway Union had declared its gratuitous warfare upon the railway interests, the representatives of the lines centring in Chicago which were members of the General Managers' Association met in response to a call for an " emergency meeting." At that meeting it was decided to make use of the machinery of the Association to withstand the attack made upon the railways, and the various lines; members of the Association then pledged themselves " to resist the boycott in the interest of our existing contracts and for the benefit of the travelling public, and to act unitedly to that end." Thenceforward the American Railway Union had, so far as the lines centring in Chicago were concerned, to reckon with the Association. The Association did not either then or thereafter represent such lines as the Southern, Union and Northern Pacific, which had to make the best fight that they could single-handed.   To pretend that the strike was a measure of retaliation against the Association is not only pre-posterons, but is immediately seen to be false on the face of the facts —facts which were in evidence before the Commission.   It might be added that had the lines in Chicago failed to " act unitedly" as they did, the destruction of life and property and the danger to society would have been incalculably worse than they were.   Next to the President of the United States and the military which did duty in Chicago, it is to the General Managers' Association that the gratitude of the American people is chiefly due.

The mandate to the Commission extended to the examining into the " causes" and " conditions" of the disturbances, and to the suggestion of the best means for their adjustment.   No statement could well be more misrepresentative of the causes of the strike than the phrase of the Commission which would represent the employees as uniting in protest against the union of the railways; no statement could well be framed to more completely distort the conditions of the strike than that wherein the Commission declares that the strife was simply over handling Pullman cars, the men being ready to do their duty otherwise.

34

During those terrible days of June and July, 1894, there was one supreme issue, and one only, at stake. Above and beyond all particular controversies as to wages and as to the relations of individual employees to individual employers—above and beyond all party sympathies or economic prejudices, the one great question was of the ability of this Government to suppress insurrection. On the one side was the party of lawlessness, of murder, of incendiarism, and of defiance of authority. On the other side was the party of loyalty to the United States. For all the treason, the violence, and rebellion, the Commissioners have no word of condemnation—the strife was simply over the handling of Pullman cars! There is not one word of praise for those who in the time of peril upheld the dignity of the nation and the sanctity of the law; but there is abundant vituperation of the " rank injustice" of corporations and the " unlawful and dangerous combinations" of the " monopolies" against the " rights of labor." The Commission sneers at all that is good in the institutions of Pullman—at the library, at the system of medical attendance, at the " sanitary and æsthetic features" of the town. It scourges the General Managers' Association and questions the competence of the Federal Courts to take the action which they took for the restraint of lawlessness. But for the leaders who prompted to insurrection and sheltered violence there is no word of reprobation, but only apology and extenuation, as of a parent pleading for the venial peccadilloes of a petted child. There is no chapter in the report of the Commission which is not an incentive to discontent and an excuse of violence. It says:

"Such dignified, manly, and conservative conduct in the midst of excitement and threatened starvation is worthy of the highest type of American citizenship, and with like prudence in all other directions will result in due time in the lawful and orderly redress of labor wrongs. To deny this is to forswear patriotism and to declare this Government and its people a failure."

What was this " dignified, manly, and conservative conduct?" It was the conduct of the strikers at Pullman—their conduct in failing for several weeks so far to overstep the restraints of law as to demand the intervention of the military. That they took part in rioting and violence later, is forgotten. That because " until July 3" they refrained from such extremity of lawlessness as to compel their suppression by military force—for this their conduct is " worthy of the highest type of American citizenship." Verily, if American citizenship knows no loftier ideal than this, the time for despairing of the Republic has almost come.

For the ill-digested mass of matter which the Commission has lumped together at the end of its report as its "recommendations" for the "best means of adjustment" of such controversies in future, the best that can be said of it is that all that the Commission says has been said many times and better in countless magazine articles and in the daily press.   That any recommendations should be based on so gross a misunderstanding of the conditions in regard to which they recommend, is almost an impertinence.   For the main suggestion which they make (one already familiar enough to the public mind) for the establishment of a permanent Strike Commission, it is a measure against which there has heretofore been no such serious argument to be advanced as is now furnished by the example which this temporary Commission has set.

If the achievements of men are to be measured by their opportunities, then is the performance of the Commissioners a thing almost beyond pity.   They had it in their power to give us a document which should be of service to the world and to mankind, which might have marked an epoch in the world-wide struggle for the alleviation of social discontents.   In place of it they have given us a document which is untrustworthy in its statements of fact, ignorant and uncomprehending in its scope, and in its spirit cowardly with the cowardice of the politician who sets the applause of the worst element in the population above the aims of patriotism.   That such a production should be in danger of taking its place among our public documents is a humiliation to the people of the United States.

HARRY PERRY ROBINSON.

GRAVE DANGER IN OUR PRESIDENTIAL ELECTION-SYSTEM.

For more than a hundred years our Federal Constitution has been in full operation; and yet ninety years have elapsed since the proposal and adoption of any amendment to that instrument except those three which abolished human slavery and closed the Civil War. Not a single State of the Union shows such stagnation in constitutional reform. On the contrary, our increasing States, each in its own jurisdiction, have modelled and remodelled their fundamental institutions, to check legislative and other abuses and yield more closely to popular control; yet the antiquated machinery of the Federal Government still creaks on in its operations unchanged, exposing us repeatedly to the dangers of national anarchy and confusion.

I speak of constitutional machinery alone; for as concerns the general scheme of our government and the general distribution of State and Federal powers, I offer no criticism. Our fathers framed wisely in those latter respects, and custom and precedent have aided the development of good results. A national policy may well be an elastic policy, leaving much for contingencies to shape. It is not to the fundamental system, then, of our American Union, but to the mode of bringing rulers and representatives into power, that I would ask the reader's attention. The recent proposition to choose Senators by the people of a State is well worth considering; so, too, are some of those checks upon legislative action now so common in our modern State constitutions, such as might, for instance, prevent a mere casual majority in the two branches of Congress from annexing foreign territory or admitting new States capriciously without reference to popular approval or sanction. I confine myself here to desirable reforms in the method of Presidential elections, and in the relation of both Presidential and Congressional terms to the popular elections of a biennial November.

In the first place, our anomalous method of choosing the Chief Executive by electoral colleges has become, in the course of a century, not only a senseless but dilatory and dangerous duplication. We know how utterly the expedient of 1787, for obstructing popular suffrage on a national scale, has failed of its original purpose; and how truly, in consequence, the quadrennial assemblage of our present age, when millions of voters undertake on an autumn day to choose by their own ballots a President and Vice-President of the United States, has become in spirit a complete perversion of what the Constitution itself intended. Yet the letter of that instrument remains; and the people of each State still choose, after all, simply Presidential electors, just as the several legislatures chose them formerly, and as South Carolina's chose them continually down to the Civil War. So far as Federal fundamental law is concerned, a State legislature may still at any time take the direct choice of Presidential electors to itself, depriving the State voters of such suffrage; and more than this, Presidential electors, whether popularly chosen or not, have only a moral obligation to cast their votes afterward, in the college, for the candidates previously designated. The whole sanction, in short, upon which popular expression rests in the selection, every four years, of President and Vice-President of the United States—the whole assurance of legal title to a valid succession—is each individual elector's own pledge of honor to vote in the college as he was chosen to vote in November.

The original provisions of our Constitution, indeed, were soon found so faulty with respect to Presidential elections in other particulars, that after the famous tie vote in 1800, between Jefferson and Burr, when President and Vice-President were not named apart, those provisions had to be amended. But two prime evils of the original plan still confront us, showing how utterly unsuited are those provisions to the present republican age: (1) Colleges of electors still elect the Executive; and consequently the choice of a Chief Magistrate is not legally made in early November, but about a month later; and in addition to the injurious delay, the voter who casts his ballot for electors at the polls is exposed not only to peculiar misconceptions concerning his own functions, but to the far more insidious danger that corrupt and crafty politicians may yet, at some later crisis, when voting runs close, baffle the wishes of the people. (2) Nor does a plurality of votes, even in the electoral colleges, finally elect the President; for the Constitution still adheres to the eighteenth-century rule requiring a complete majority, in default of which the eventual choice devolves upon the Legislature, or rather upon one branch of it. To this latter solecism, common enough in State politics a hundred years ago, but long since repudiated upon bitter State experience, public attention has not been drawn as it should be. All American experience is to the practical conclusion that, desirable though a majority choice must always be, it is much better to let the candidate who has a popular plurality on the first trial at the polls come in over all competitors, than to vote over again, or to refer the ultimate selection of a Chief Magistrate elsewhere.

Nor is it to an incoming Congress, but to a retiring one, and often in effect to a defeated and dishonored one,—and in fact, to a House of Representatives, voting by States, which was constituted two years earlier,—that our Federal plan confides this momentous choice of a President whenever no candidate has received an electoral majority. What State would trust any assembly for so solemn an arbitrament short of that Legislature which was chosen at the time when the Executive was voted for? Our national perils in this respect have been less only because the national choice was more seldom; but with each new election the results at stake become more tremendous and the temptation to trifle with public opinion more pronounced. Whenever, as happened in 1892 and may happen again, some third party is strong enough to carry a State or two, or political issues have temporarily faded out, and the choice lies chiefly as among individuals, "bargain and corruption" may once more be the cry over an election by the House, as it was in 1825, and with far more substantial reason. Two years ago, during the last Presidential canvass, and while the chances appeared close in October, two distinct conspiracies, for forestalling final results and controlling the succession in case the choice should devolve upon a House already Democratic, were divulged by the press to augment the popular uneasiness. One was for the friends of the third candidate to keep the eventual election for the colleges to decide in December, by causing their own Presidential electors to invite bids for Populist principles from the two highest candidates, and then turn the scales as between them. The other plan was from another quarter, to resist all choice by the House as then constituted, upon the claim that its representation had not been based upon the new census of 1890, and ought, therefore, to be changed. From such dangers, which might otherwise have become positive ones, a sweeping majority of electoral votes for Mr. Cleveland delivered us.

Still another constitutional change is highly desirable in the same connection, and, I might add, for all our biennial elections to Congress, in order to give symmetry to our national system of government and to adapt it to this modern age. We should abridge the present long interval which elapses between the popular vote and the entrance of a new Administration and a new Congress upon their several responsibilities. Considering that a new Presidency lasts but four years and the term of a new Congress but half that time, our present waste of national energy is very great, and needlessly so. We have profited much in the advance of popular suffrage by leaving tests and qualifications in all national voting to State discretion. We have gained in national concentration by compelling a uniform day to be observed throughout the Union for choosing the Presidential electors. But another change still more desirable (could only a constitutional amendment be had) would be to bring a newly elected Administration more speedily into power, and a newly chosen House of Representatives and Congress besides.

Ever since 1804, "the fourth of March," originally an accidental date, has been graven into the very tablet of our Federal Constitution. That day of the month and year, with its variable weather, is hardly suitable in the Potomac latitude for out-of-door pageants and parades, as we well know. In fact, inauguration-weather at Washington on the two latest occasions was as unfit as possible for the military procession and the ceremonials at the east front of the capitol. But what then? Some have seriously proposed, in propitiation of the weather, that the Constitution be so amended as to inaugurate each new Executive toward the close of spring. But this would be reform in the wrong direcion. Mere ceremonials, anywhere or at any time, are liable to capricious weather, and may readily conform to circumstances. The paramount interest, however, of the people of this Union is to have their declared will carried expeditiously into effect; and from that preferable point of view, whatever Constitutional amendment substitutes some other date for the fourth of March will require America's inauguration day to be moved backward and not forward.

Constitutional reforms are, indeed, difficult to carry; but this is, more than anything else, because the people are not aroused to considering them. Where the change proposed is not likely to excite party opposition, nor to inflame State or sectional jealousy, it is worthy, at least, of consideration and effort. State constitutions have borne much salutary improvement; and we ought not to persuade ourselves that constructive inspiration in whatever pertains to the welfare and stability of the whole Union perished with the Revolutionary fathers. Let us set ourselves, then, to repairing the weak joints of this constitutional armor, where almost all else is strong. The present basis for an electoral proportion by States has its merits and need not be exchanged for a numerical poll of the whole Union; but, in either case, we should sweep out, once and for all, this dangerous and superfluous electoral college, and set each State to devoting the month which follows the November vote to its own official registry of State results. We should abolish the present intervention of a House of Representatives, or reduce it to the remote contingency of a tie between the candidates, trusting, as in State elections, to the rule that a popular plurality shall elect, once and for all. The House of Representatives, and the Congress, to revise results and formally announce the choice, should be the incoming and newly chosen, and not the outgoing, one; and all concerting opportunity for mischief between a Congress and an Administration already delegated to retirement—all such opportunity as embarrassed and paralyzed the country so greatly in 1860 if not in 1876—should be reduced to a minimum. With a month gained by the abolition of electoral colleges, it would not be difficult for a newly chosen Congress to enter upon its functions at New Year's; and for the new Executive in alternate Congresses to be installed then or soon after, following the common example of the States. An adjournment of Congress, long enough to give a new President time to make up his Administration and formulate a policy, might perhaps be provided; but the United States is scarcely a representative government at all, if public agents elected to meet existing conditions must invariably begin their work under later ones, at the same time that they are liable to stand long in the way after they have been superseded.

JAMES SCHOULER.

IS THE EXISTING INCOME TAX UNCONSTITUTIONAL?

IN the discussions that have followed the re-enactment by Congress of an income tax, the proposition has been frequently advanced, and supported by lengthened argument and citations, that the tax in question is unconstitutional, and therefore illegal,—because it is a direct tax, and not in conformity, as respects assessment and levy, with the clause in the Constitution of the United States (Article 1, Section 2) which requires that "Representatives and direct taxes shall be apportioned among the several States which may be included within this Union, according to their respective numbers"; and in the ninth section of this same article, the above provision is in effect reaffirmed in the following terms: "No capitation, or other direct, tax shall be laid, unless in proportion to the census, or enumeration, hereinbefore directed to be taken."

If now the existing income tax is a direct tax, and has not been laid and apportioned as the Constitution clearly requires, then clearly it is unconstitutional and illegal, and all provisions for its imposition and collection are void. But is the income tax a direct tax? The United States Supreme Court had this question fairly and squarely before it for consideration in 1880,[1] and held that under the definition of a direct tax as expressed in the Constitution, an income tax was *not direct* but *indirect*, and, accordingly, that its imposition and collection were not unconstitutional. The exact language of the court was as follows: "Our conclusions are that *direct taxes*, within the meaning of the Constitution, are only capitation" (poll) "taxes, as expressed in that instrument, and taxes on real estate; and that the tax of which the plaintiff in error complains" (*i.e.*, an income tax) "is within the category of an excise or duty." This decision, it may here be remarked, was in opposition to the opinion of every economic or financial writer or authority from Adam Smith down; and inferentially also to the opinion of Alexander Hamilton,[2] who

---

[1] Springer *v.* United States, 12 Otto, 102 U. S. Reports, S. C., p. 586.

[2] See Hamilton's brief in the carriage case of Hylton *v.* United States, 1794; Hamilton's Works, Vol. VII., p. 848.

helped to frame the Constitution. In all the debates in the British Parliament also, it is doubtful if any British statesman can be named who has ever spoken of an income tax as other than a direct tax. But be this as it may, the opinion of the Court, as above cited, is the law of the land, or determination of what the law means; and, until it is reversed, there can be no more interest or profit in discussing the constitutionality of the income tax from the predicate that it is a direct tax, than attaches to the time-honored school-house debate as to whether rum or war have been productive of the greater evil.

But there is another point or basis, on which the constitutionality of the existing income tax may possibly be impugned with success, which does not seem to have hitherto attracted public attention, and which is worthy of consideration.

To appreciate and understand the involved issue, it is essential to obtain in the first instance a clear view of the incidence of an income tax. Upon what does such a tax fall? One American writer of repute on economic subjects assumes "*faculty*," or the native or acquired power of production, to be an equitable basis for taxation; and his answer might be that it falls on "faculty." But "faculty" is not an entity, and a tax to be productive must be assessed on something that is material or an entity. A little reflection must satisfy us that an income tax is always a tax on property, for in default of any property there will be no income or basis for taxation; wages, salaries, interest, rents, gains, or profits in business, as elements of income, being simply terms characterizing the different manifestations or forms of property.[1]

It may also be regarded as an economic axiom that when a government taxes the income of property, it in reality taxes the property itself. In England and on the Continent of Europe land is taxed on its yearly revenue, or income value, and these taxes are always considered as land taxes. Alexander Hamilton in discussing the taxation of incomes derived from property goes even further, and in asking the question, "What is property but a fiction without the beneficial use of it?" leads to the inference that property, and the income derived from it, are substantially one and the same thing.[2]

---

[1] "Income for services is money (property) in the form of wages, commissions, brokerage, etc."—Hillard, Law of Taxation.

[2] The following court decisions are also pertinent to this question : "All must

With this brief exposition of the true and sole objective of an income tax, attention is next asked to the eighth section of the first article of the Federal Constitution, which reads as follows:

"The congress shall have power to lay and collect taxes, duties, imposts, and excises, to pay the debts and provide for the common defense and general welfare of the United States; *but all duties, imposts and excises shall be uniform throughout the United States.*"[1]

We have, therefore, a clear and imperative constitutional mandate as to the manner in which the Federal Government must assess an income tax in common with all other duties and excises; and the question of next importance that presents itself is, Do the provisions for assessing the present income tax conform to such mandate? And the answer turns on the definition, or interpretation, of the term "uniform" in its application to taxation.

The framing of such a definition has not been free from difficulty, and has often come up before the court for determination. The late Mr. Justice Miller, in his Lectures on the Constitution, discusses it at some length, and states his conclusions as follows:

"A tax is uniform within the meaning of the Constitutional requirement, if it is made to bear the same percentage over all the United States,"—and again, "When they" (the statutes) "use the words 'taxes must be uniform,' they mean uniform with regard to the subject of the tax; . . . that is, different articles may be taxed at different amounts, provided that the rate is uniform on the same class everywhere, with all people and at all times."

To complete this argument, it only remains to consider what is meant by property of the same class. The answer to this is, obviously, property which immediately or directly competes in open

perceive that a tax on the sale of an article imported only for sale is a tax on the article itself."—Chief Justice Marshall, 12 Wheaton, 439.

In the case of Weston v. City of Charleston, the U. S. Supreme Court decided that when a State was prohibited from laying a tax on United States stock it could not evade the prohibition by laying the tax on the income of the same and of other stocks.

"A devise of the income of land is in effect the same as a devise of the land itself."—9 Mass., 372; 1 Ashmead, 136. "A devise of the rents and profits of land or the income of land is equivalent to a devise of the land itself."—Washburn on Real Property, 2,752.

In the case of Dobbins agt. the Commissioners of Erie county, the court decided that the emoluments of an office could not be taxed if the office was exempt.—16 Peters, 435.

[1] If the omission of the word "taxes" in the last part of this section may seem to limit the application of the injunction of uniformity, the decision of the United States Supreme Court in the Springer case above noticed, that an income tax "is within the category of an excise or duty," certainly divests such omission of any application to this form of taxation.

market. The force of competition is not dependent upon the quantity owned or produced by few or many persons, but upon the aggregate quantity of similar property offered in market, whether produced or owned by few or many persons. On the ground of eminent judicial· authority and common sense, territorial uniformity by taxation must therefore imply and involve absolute uniformity and equality of taxation on like values and quantities.

If an income tax is laid at the same rate or percentage upon all incomes, there would be no question as to its uniformity and compliance with the constitutional provisions. On the other hand, if such a tax is laid as the present income-tax law proposes, with discriminating incidence or with different rates or percentages on different incomes, there would seem to be no ground for assuming that it was invested with uniformity, or was in compliance with the constitutional mandate. Let us suppose, for illustration, three farms designated as A, B, and C, owned by three persons, producing the same products, or the same class of products—wheat, corn, potatoes, and the like—and returning a profit or income to their respective owners from the sale of these products under the same competitive conditions. Let us suppose further that the profit or income from the farms A and B is in each case $4,000; while the profit or income from farm C, owing to a greater area of land cultivated, or greater energy and skill on the part of the owner, is $8,000. Under the present discriminating income tax the profits or income of the two farms, A and B, and of two persons, under an exemption of $4,000, would be free from all income taxation; while the profit of the competitive farm C, producing the same income as the other two farms, would be subject to a tax burden, on half its income or profit, of two per cent, if, as assumed, the farm happens to be in the hands of a single owner. The aggregate of the value or income of the property is the same in both cases, but the incidence of taxation is made dependent upon the circumstance of making the assessment upon two persons rather than one. This is not equality of burden on competing property, or on immediate competitors, but may be fairly characterized as robbery.

Under the operation of natural laws, larger quantities will be owned and produced in one State than in another. Colorado and Texas have large herds of cattle, Illinois has large cornfields and large distilleries, Louisiana large sugar plantations, and New England large factories, owned by single persons. Two States may, and in some instances do, have nearly equal *per capita* wealth in the aggregate; but in the one the wealth may be made up of capital invested in numerous small industries adapted to soil and climate, while in the other, owing to different natural conditions, there may be great concentration of capital in a few hands and in few industries.

Thus, in the case of the income tax enacted during the war period, seven States in the year 1869—Massachusetts, New York, New Jersey, Pennsylvania, Ohio, Illinois, and California—possessed forty per cent of the assessed property of the United States, and had just about forty per cent of the population. But at the same time these same seven States paid fully three-fourths of the entire income tax levied by the Federal Government upon the people of the whole country; or, to put it differently, the States which had sixty per cent of the wealth and population of the country paid only about one-fourth of the income tax.

There is another clause of the Federal Constitution which is pertinent to this subject, namely, Article V., which provides that private property shall not be taken for public use without just compensation. It must be conceded that this is a limitation on the power of Congress. There must be a line between the taking of private property for public use and taxation; but how can that line be drawn except by the rule that taxation means uniformity of burden on competing avocations and competing property? A decision of the Supreme Court of New Jersey some years since seems to have a direct bearing upon the unconstitutionality of discriminating burdens, on the same class of persons or property. Thus the New Jersey Court said:

"A tax upon the person or property of A, B, and C individually, whether designated by name or any other way, which is in excess of an equal apportionment among the persons or property of the class of persons or kind of property subject to the taxation, is, to the extent of such excess, the taking of private property for a public use without compensation. The process is one of confiscation and not of taxation" (36 N. J., p. 66, 1872).

A word in conclusion on the subject of exemptions, which all modern systems of income taxation have recognized to the extent of discriminating in favor of persons in receipt of comparatively small incomes, and which, being effective in producing discrimination and inequality in taxation, may be regarded as constitutionally illegal: An exemption is freedom from a burden or service to which others are liable; but an exemption for a public purpose or a valid consideration is not an exemption except in name, for the valid and full consideration, or the public purpose promoted, is received in lieu of the tax. Nor is an exemption from taxation a discriminating burden on those who pay an income tax, provided the person or institution benefited by the exemption is a pauper, or a public charitable institution; for then there is consideration for the exemption, and it is justified as a matter of economy, and to prevent an expensive circuity of action in levying the tax with the sole purpose of giving it back to the intended beneficiary of the Government. The avoidance of this unnecessary circuity of action is not, moreover, an injury but a gain to those who pay the tax. It cannot, however, be seriously claimed that a man having $100,000 of productive capital, and receiving from it $4,000 of annual income, is entitled to receive support from the Government as a public pauper.

The United States Supreme Court, in the case of Loan Association *v.* Topeka, held that our Government, State or National, cannot impose taxes for the purpose of fostering any *private* business or enterprise. Taxes can be imposed only for public purposes; and, when they are imposed for any other purpose, the Government acts the part of a highwayman and takes forcibly the property of A and gives it to B. In short, there is the same reason why all exemptions of like property from taxation should be based solely on the ground of a public purpose, as that all taxes collected should be for a public purpose.

Finally, the principle involved in this question of discriminating income taxation is one that affects the foundation and continued existence of every free government, namely, the equality of all men before the law. Any exemption whatever, under an income tax, be it small or great, except to the absolutely indigent, is purely arbitrary; and the principle once allowed may be carried to any extent. Any exemption of any portion of the same class of property or incomes is an act of charity which every patriotic American citizen ought to reject upon principle and with scorn, except under circumstances of great want and destitution. Equality and manhood, therefore, demand and require uniformity of burden in whatever is the subject of taxation.

DAVID A. WELLS.

DICKENS'S PLACE IN LITERATURE.[1]

It is a fearsome thing to venture to say anything now about Charles Dickens, whom we have all loved, enjoyed, and laughed over: whose tales are household words in every home where the English tongue is heard, whose characters are our own school-friends, the sentiment of our youthful memories, our boon-companions and our early attachments. To view him in any critical light is a task as risky as it would be to discuss the permanent value of some fashionable amusement, a favorite actor, a popular beverage, or a famous horse. Millions and millions of old and young love Charles Dickens, know his personages by heart, play at games with his incidents and names, and from the bottom of their souls believe that there never was such fun, and that there never will be conceived again such inimitable beings, as they find in his ever-fresh and ever-varied pages. This is by itself a very high title to honour: perhaps it is the chief jewel in the crown that rests on the head of Charles Dickens. I am myself one of these devotees, of these lovers, of these slaves of his: or at least I can remember that I have been. To have stirred this pure and natural humanity, this force of sympathy, in such countless millions is a great triumph. Men and women to-day do not want any criticism of Charles Dickens, any talk about him at all. They enjoy him as he is: they examine one another in his books: they gossip on by the hour about his innumerable characters, his never-to-be-forgotten waggeries and fancies.

Yet here in my path stands an inexorable editor bidding me include Charles Dickens in this small series of mine on the "Victorian Writers." And how could we avoid some notice of one whose first immortal tale coincides with the accession of our Queen, and who for thirty-three successive years continued to pour out a long stream of books that still delight the English-speaking world? When we begin to talk about the permanent place in English literature of eminent writers, one of the first definite problems is presented by Charles Dickens. And it is one of the most obscure of such problems; be-

[1] Copyright also in England.

cause, more than almost any writer of our age, Charles Dickens has
his own accustomed nook at every fireside: he is a familiar friend, a
welcome guest; we remember the glance of his eye; we have held
his hand, as it were, in our own.   The children brighten up as his
step is heard; the chairs are drawn round the hearth, and a fresh
glow is given to the room.   We do not criticise one whom we love,
nor do we suffer others to do so.   And there is perhaps a wider sympathy with Charles Dickens as a person than with any other writer of
our time.   For this reason there has been hardly any serious criticism
or estimate of Dickens as a great artist, apart from some peevish and
sectional disparagement of his genius, which has been too much tinged
with academic pedantry and the bias of aristocratic temper or political antagonism.

I am free to confess that I am in no mood to pretend making
up my mind for any impartial estimate of Charles Dickens as an
abiding power in English literature.   The "personal equation"
is in my own case somewhat too strong to leave me with a perfectly "dry light" in the matter.   I will make a clean breast of it
at once by saying, that I can remember reading some of the most
famous of these books in their green covers, month by month, as they
came out in parts, when I was myself "in my 'teens."   That period
included the first ten of the main works from "Pickwick" down to
"David Copperfield."   With "Bleak House," which I read as a student of philosophy at Oxford beginning to be familiar with Aristo-
telian canons, I felt my enjoyment mellowed by a somewhat more
measured judgment.   From that time onward Charles Dickens threw
himself into a great variety of undertakings and many diverse kinds
of publication.   His "Hard Times," "Little Dorrit," "Our Mutual
Friend," "Great Expectations," "Tale of Two Cities," were never to
me anything like the wonder and delight that I found in "Oliver
Twist," "Nickleby," and "Copperfield."   And as to the short tales
and the later pieces down to "Edwin Drood," I never find myself turning back to them; the very memory of the story is fading away; and
I fail to recall the characters and names.   A mature judgment will
decide that the series after "David Copperfield," written when the
author was thirty-eight, was not equal to the series of the thirteen
years preceding.   Charles Dickens will always be remembered by
"Pickwick," "Oliver Twist," "Nickleby," and "Copperfield."   And
though these tales will long continue to delight both old and young,
learned and unlearned alike, they are most to be envied who read him

when young, and they are most to be pitied who read him with a
critical spirit. May that be far from us, as we take up our
" Pickwick" and talk over the autobiographic pathos of " David
Copperfield."

This vivid sympathy with the man is made stronger in my own
case in that, from my own boyhood till his death, I was continually
seeing him, was frequently his near neighbour both in London and
the seaside, knew some of his friends, and heard much about him and
about his work. Though I never spoke to him, there were times
when I saw him almost daily; I often heard him speak and read in
public; and his favourite haunts in London and the country have
been familiar to me from my boyhood. And thus, as I read again
my " Pickwick," and " Nickleby," and " Copperfield," there come
back to me many personal and local memories of my own. The personality of Charles Dickens was, even to his distant readers, vivid
and intense; and hence it is much more so to those who have known
his person. I am thus an ardent Pickwickian myself; and anything
I say about our immortal Founder must be understood in a Pickwickian sense.

Charles Dickens was before all things a great humourist—doubtless the greatest of this century; for, though we may find in Scott a
more truly Shakespearean humour of the highest order, the humour
of Dickens is so varied, so paramount, so inexhaustible, that he stands
forth in our memory as the humourist of the age. Swift, Fielding,
Hogarth, Sterne, and Goldsmith, in the last century, reached at times
a more enduring level of humour without caricature; but the gift has
been more rarely imparted to their successors in the age of steam.
Now, we shall never get an adequate definition of that imponderable
term—humour—a term that was invented to be the eternal theme of
budding essayists. We need not be quite as liberal in our interpretation of humour as was Thackeray in opening his " English
Humourists"; for he declared that its business was to awaken and
direct our love, our pity, our kindness, our scorn for imposture, our
tenderness for the weak, to comment on the actions and passions of
life, to be the week-day preacher—and much more to that effect.
But it may serve our immediate purpose to say with Samuel Johnson
that humour is " grotesque imagery": and " grotesque" is " distorted
of figure: unnatural." That is to say, humour is an effort of the
imagination presenting human nature with some element of distortion
or disproportion which instantly kindles mirth. It must be imagina-
35

tive; it must touch the bed-rock of human nature; it must arouse merriment and not anger or scorn. In this fine and most rare gift Charles Dickens abounded to overflowing; and this humour poured in perfect cataracts of " grotesque imagery" over every phase of life of the poor and the lower middle classes of his time, in London and a few of its suburbs and neighbouring parts.

This in itself is a great title to honour; it is his main work, his noblest title. His sphere was wide, but not at all general: it was strictly limited to the range of his own indefatigable observations. He hardly ever drew a character or painted a scene, even of the most subordinate kind, which he had not studied from the life with minute care, and whenever he did for a moment wander out of his limits, he made an egregious failure. But this task of his, to cast the sunshine of pathos and of genial mirth over the humblest, dullest, and most uninviting of our fellow-creatures, was a great social mission to which his whole genius was devoted. No waif and stray was so repulsive, no drudge was so mean, no criminal was so atrocious, but what Charles Dickens could feel for him some ray of sympathy, or extract some pathetic mirth out of his abject state. And Dickens does not look on the mean and the vile as do Balzac and Zola, that is, from without, like the detective or the surgeon. He sees things more or less from their point of view: he feels with the "Marchioness": he himself as a child was once a Smike: he cannot help liking the fun of the Artful Dodger: he has been a good friend to Barkis: he likes Traddles: he loves Joe: poor Nancy ends her vile life in heroism: and his dog worships Bill Sikes.

Here lies the secret of his power over such countless millions of readers. He not only paints a vast range of ordinary humanity and suffering or wearied humanity, but he speaks for it and lives in it himself, and throws a halo of imagination over it, and brings home to the great mass of average readers a new sense of sympathy and gaiety. This humane kinship with the vulgar and the common, this magic which strikes poetry out of the dust of the streets, and discovers traces of beauty and joy in the most monotonous of lives, is, in the true and best sense of the term, Christ-like, with a message and gospel of hope. Thackeray must have had Charles Dickens in his mind when he wrote: " The humourous writer professes to awaken and direct your love, your pity, your kindness—your scorn for untruth, pretension, imposture—your tenderness for the weak, the poor, the oppressed, the unhappy." Charles Dickens, of all writers of our age, assuredly did this in every work of his pen, for thirty-three years of incessant production. It is his great title to honour; and a novelist can desire no higher title than this.

There is another quality in which Charles Dickens is supreme—in purity. Here is a writer who is realistic, if ever any writer was, in the sense of having closely observed the lowest strata of city life, who has drawn the most miserable outcasts, the most abandoned men and women in the dregs of society, who has invented many dreadful scenes of passion, lust, seduction, and debauchery; and yet in forty works and more you will not find a page which a mother need withhold from her grown daughter. As Thackeray wrote of his friend,— " I am grateful for the innocent laughter and the sweet and unsullied page which the author of 'David Copperfield' gives to my children." We need not formulate any dogma or rule on such a topic, nor is it essential that all books should be written *virginibus puerisque;* but it is certain that every word of Charles Dickens was so written, even when he set himself (as he sometimes did) to describe animal natures and the vilest of their sex. Dickens is a realist in that he probes the gloomiest recesses and faces the most disheartening problems of life: he is an idealist, in that he never presents us the common or the vile with mere commonplace or repulsiveness, and without some ray of humane and genial charm to which ordinary eyes are blind. Dickens, then, was above all things a humourist, an inexhaustible humourist, to whom the humblest forms of daily life wore a certain sunny air of genial mirth; but the question remains if he was a humourist of the highest order: was he a poet, a creator of abiding imaginative types? Old Johnson's definition of humour as " grotesque imagery," and " grotesque" as meaning some distortion in figure, may not be adequate as a description of humour, but it well describes the essential feature of Charles Dickens. His infallible instrument is caricature—which strictly means an " overload," as Johnson says, " an exaggerated resemblance." Caricature is a likeness having some comical exaggeration or distortion. Now, caricature is a legitimate and potent instrument of humour, which great masters have used with consummate effect. Leonardo da Vinci, Michael Angelo, Rembrandt, Hogarth use it; but only at times, and in a subsidiary way. Rabelais, Swift, Fielding, use this weapon not unfrequently; Shakespeare very sparingly; Goldsmith, and Scott, I think, almost never. Caricature, the essence of which is exaggeration of some selected feature, distortion of figure, disproportion of some part, is a potent resource, but one to which the greater masters resort rarely and with much moderation.

Now with Charles Dickens, caricature—that comical exaggeration of a particular feature, distortion of some part beyond nature—is not only the essence of his humour, but it is the universal and ever-present source of his mirth. It would not be true to say that exaggeration is the sole form of humour that he uses, but there is hardly a character of his to which it is not applied, nor a scene of which it is not the pervading " motive." Some feature, some oddity, some temperament is seized, dwelt upon, played with, and turned inside out, with incessant repetition and unwearied energy. Every character, except the walking gentleman and the walking lady, the insipid lover, or the colourless friend, have some feature thrust out of proportion, magnified beyond nature. Sam Weller never speaks without his anecdote, Uriah is always " 'umble," Barkis is always " willin'," Mark Tapley is always "jolly," Dombey is always solemn, and Toots is invariably idiotic. It is no doubt natural that Barnaby's Raven should always want tea, whatever happens, for the poor bird has but a limited vocabulary. But one does not see why articulate and sane persons like Captain Cuttle, Pecksniff, and Micawber should repeat the same phrases under every condition and to all persons. This, no doubt, is the essence of farce: it may be irresistibly droll as farce, but it does not rise beyond farce. And at last even the most enthusiastic Pickwickian wearies of such monotony of iteration.

Now, the keynote of caricature being the distortion of nature, it inevitably follows that humourous exaggeration is unnatural, however droll; and, where it is the main source of the drollery, the picture as a whole ceases to be within the bounds of nature. But the great masters of the human heart invariably remain true to nature: not merely true to a selected feature, but to the natural form as a whole. Falstaff, in his wildest humour, speaks and acts as such a man really might speak and act. He has no catch-phrase on which he harps, as if he were a talking-machine wound up to emit a dozen sounds. Parson Adams speaks and acts as such a being might do in nature. The comic characters of Goldsmith, Scott, or Thackeray do not outrun and defy nature, nor does their drollery depend on any special and abnormal feature, much less on any stock phrase which they use as a label. The illustrations of Cruikshank and Phiz are delightfully droll and often caricatures of a high order. But being caricatures, they overload and exaggerate nature, and indeed are always, in one sense, impossible in nature. The grins, the grimaces, the contortions, the dwarfs, the idiots, the monstrosities of these wonderful sketches could not be found in human beings constructed on any known anatomy. And Dickens's own characters have the same element of unnatural distortion. It is possible that these familiar caricatures have even done harm to his reputation. His creations are of a higher order of art and are more distinctly spontaneous and original. But the grotesque sketches with which he almost uniformly presented his books accentuate the element of caricature on which he relied; and often add an unnatural extravagance beyond that extravagance which was the essence of his own method.

The consequence is, that everything in Dickens is " in the excess," as Aristotle would say, and not " in the mean." Whether it is Tony Weller, or " the Shepherd," or the Fat Boy, Hugh or the Raven, Toots or Traddles, Micawber or Skimpole, Gamp or Mantalini —all are overloaded in the sense that they exceed nature, and are more or less extravagant. They are wonderful and delightful caricatures, but they are impossible in fact. The similes are hyperbolic; the names are grotesque; the incidents partake of harlequinade, and the speeches of roaring farce. It is often wildly droll, but it is rather the drollery of the stage than of the book. The characters are never possible in fact, they are not, and are not meant to be, nature; they are always and everywhere comic distortions of nature. Goldsmith's Dr. Primrose tells us that he chose his wife for the same qualities for which she chose her wedding gown. That is humour, but it is also pure, literal, exact truth to nature. David Copperfield's little wife is called a lap-dog, acts like a lap-dog, and dies like a lap-dog; the lap-dog simile is so much overdone that we are glad to get rid of her, and instead of weeping with Copperfield, we feel disposed to call him a ninny.

Nothing is more wonderful in Dickens than his exuberance of animal spirits, that inexhaustible fountain of life and gaiety, in which he equals Scott and far surpasses any other modern. The intensity of the man, his electric activity, his spasmodic nervous power, quite dazzle and stun us. But this restless gaiety too often grows fatiguing, as the rollicking fun begins to pall upon us, as the jokes ring hollow, and the wit gets stale by incessant reiteration. We know how much in real life we get to hate the joker who does not know when to stop, who repeats his jests, and forces the laugh when it does not flow freely. Something of the kind the most devoted of Dickens's readers feel when they take in too much at one time. None but the very greatest can maintain for long one incessant out-pour of drollery, much less of extravagance. Aristophanes could do it; Shakespeare could do it; so could Cervantes; and so, too, Rabelais. But then, the wildest extravagance of these men is so rich, so varied, so charged with insight and thought, and, in the case of Rabelais, so resplendent with learning and suggestion, that we never feel satiety and the cruel sense that the painted mask on the stage is grinning at us, whilst the actor behind it is weary and sad. When one who is not amongst the very greatest pours forth the same in-extinguishable laughter in the same key, repeating the same tricks, and multiplying kindred oddities, people of cultivation enjoy it heartily once, twice, it may be a dozen times, but at last they make way for the young bloods who can go thirty-seven times to see "Charley's Aunt."

A good deal has been said about Dickens's want of reading; and his enthusiastic biographer very fairly answers that Charles Dickens's book was the great book of life, of which he was an indefatigable student. When other men were at school and at college, he was gathering up a vast experience of the hard world, and when his brother writers were poring over big volumes in their libraries, he was pacing up and down London and its suburbs with inexhaustible energy, drinking in oddities, idiosyncrasies, and wayside incidents at every pore. It is quite true: London is a microcosm, an endless and bottomless Babylon; which, perhaps, no man has ever known so well as did Charles Dickens. This was his library: here he gathered that vast encyclopædia of human nature, which some are inclined to call "cockney," but if it be, "Cockayne" must be a very large coun-try indeed. Still, the fact remains, that of book-learning of any kind Dickens remained, to the end of his days, perhaps more utterly innocent than any other famous English writer since Shakespeare. His biographer labours to prove that he had read Fielding and Smol-lett, "Don Quixote" and "Gil Blas," "The Spectator," and "Robin-son Crusoe." Perhaps he had, like most men who have learned to read. But, no doubt, this utter severance from books, which we feel in his tales, will ultimately tell against their immortality.

This rigid abstinence from books, which Dickens practised on sys-tem, had another reaction that we notice in his style. Not only do we feel in reading his novels that we have no reason to assume that

he had ever read anything except a few popular romances, but we
note that he can hardly be said to have a formed literary style of his
own. Dickens had mannerisms, but hardly a style. In some ways,
this is a good thing: much less can he be said to have a bad style. It
is simply no style. He knows nothing of the crisp, modulated, balanced, and reserved mastery of phrase and sentence which marks
Thackeray. Nor is it the easy simplicity of " Robinson Crusoe" and
the " Vicar of Wakefield." The tale spins and the incidents rattle
along with the volubility of a good story-teller who warms up as he
goes, but who never stops to think of his sentences and phrases. He
often gets verbose, rings the changes on a point which he sees to
have caught his hearers; he plays with a fancy out of measure, and
turns his jest inside out and over and over, like a fine comic actor
when the house is in a roar. His language is free, perfectly clear,
often redundant, sometimes grandiloquent, and usually addressed
more to the pit than to the boxes. And he is a little prone to slide,
even in his own proper person, into those formal courtesies and obsolete compliments which forty years ago survived amongst the superior
orders of bagmen and managing clerks.   .

There is an old topic of discussion whether Dickens could invent
an organic and powerful plot, and carry out an elaborate scheme with
perfect skill. It is certain that he has never done so, and it can
hardly be said that he has ever essayed it. The serial form in parts,
wherein almost all his stories were cast, requiring each number of
three chapters to be " assorted," like sugar-plums, with grave and
gay, so as to tell just enough but not too much, made a highly
wrought scheme almost impossible. It is plain that Charles Dickens
had nothing of that epical gift which gave us " Tom Jones" and
" Ivanhoe." Perhaps the persistent use of the serial form shows that
he felt no interest in that supreme art of an immense drama duly un-
folded to a prepared end. In " Pickwick" there neither was, nor
could there be, any organic plot. In " Oliver Twist," in " Barnaby
Rudge," in " Dombey," in " Bleak House," in the " Tale of Two
Cities," there are indications of his possessing this power, and in
certain parts of these tales we seem to be in the presence of a great
master of epical narration. But the power is not sustained; and it
must be confessed that in none of these tales is there a complete and
equal scheme. In most of the other books, especially in those after
" Bleak House," the plot is so artless, so *décousu*, so confused, that even
practised readers of Dickens fail to keep it clear in their mind. The

serial form, where a leading character wanders about to various places and meets a succession of quaint parties, seems to be that which suited his genius and which he himself most entirely enjoyed.

In contrast with the Pickwickian method of comic rambles in search of human "curios," Dickens introduced some darker effects and persons of a more or less sensational kind. Some of these are as powerful as anything in modern fiction; and Fagin and Bill Sykes, Smike and poor Jo, the Gordon riots and the storms at sea, may stand beside Victor Hugo for lurid power and intense realism. But it was only at times and during the first half of his career that Dickens could keep clear of melodrama and somewhat stagey blue fire. And at times his blue fire was of a very cheap kind. Rosa Dartle and Carker, Steerforth and Blandois, Quilp and Uriah Heep, have a melancholy glitter of the footlights over them. We cannot see what the villains want, except to look villainous, and we fail to make out where is the danger to the innocent victims. We find the villain of the piece frantically struggling to get some paper, or to get hold of some boy or girl. But as the scene is in London in the nineteenth century, and not in Naples in the fifteenth century, we cannot see who is in real danger, or why, or of what. And with all this, Dickens was not incapable of bathos, or tragedy suddenly exploding in farce. The end of Krook by spontaneous combustion is such a case; but a far worse case is the death of Dora, Copperfield's baby wife, along with that of the lap-dog, Jip. This is one of those unforgotten, unpardonable, egregious blunders in art, in feeling, even in decency, which must finally exclude Charles Dickens from the rank of the true immortals.

But his books will long be read for his wonderful successes, and his weaker pieces will be entirely laid aside as are the failures of so many great men, the rubbish of Fielding, of Goldsmith, of Defoe; which do nothing now to dim the glory of "Tom Jones," "The Vicar of Wakefield," and "Robinson Crusoe." The glory of Charles Dickens will always be in his "Pickwick," his first, his best, his inimitable triumph. It is true that it is a novel without a plot, without beginning, middle, or end, with much more of caricature than of character, with some extravagant tomfoolery, and plenty of vulgarity. But its originality, its irrepressible drolleries, its substantial human nature, and its intense vitality, place it quite in a class by itself. We can no more group it, or test it by any canon of criticism, than we could "Pantagruel" or "Faust." There are some works of genius which seem to transcend all criticism, of which the very extravagances and incoherences increase the charm. And Pickwick ought to live with Gil Blas and Tristram Shandy. In a deeper vein, the tragic scenes in "Oliver Twist" and in "Barnaby Rudge" must long hold their ground, for they can be read and re-read in youth, in manhood, in old age. The story of Dotheboys Hall, the Yarmouth memories of Copperfield, little Nell, Mrs. Gamp, Micawber, Toots, Captain Cuttle, Pecksniff, and many more will long continue to delight the youth of the English-speaking races. But few writers are remembered so keenly by certain characters, certain scenes, incidental whimsies, and so little for entire novels treated strictly as works of art. There is no reason whatever for pretending that all these scores of tales are at all to be compared with the best of them, or that the invention of some inimitable scenes and characters is enough to make a supreme and faultless artist. The young and the uncritical make too much of Charles Dickens, when they fail to distinguish between his best and his worst. Their fastidious seniors make too little of him, when they note his many shortcomings and fail to see that in certain elements of humour he has no equal and no rival. If we mean Charles Dickens to live we must fix our eye on these supreme gifts alone.

FREDERIC HARRISON.

THE ANATOMY OF A TENEMENT STREET.

I. The Street.

BULFINCH STREET is about one-eighth of a mile long, and fifteen feet wide from curbing to curbing. Brick and wooden houses are in about equal proportion. Many of the wooden houses are thirty years old—a few small ones are still older. The brick houses, which are four-storied, belong to a later period. The street is in a transition from wood to brick. Not more than a block to the right is a street whose houses are all of wood—this is Bulfinch Street as it was. Not more than a block to the left is a street whose houses are all of brick—this is Bulfinch Street as it is to be. The half of the street known as Upper Bulfinch stubbornly resists the march of progress; several of its wooden houses even have little grassless yards at one side. The brick houses of Lower Bulfinch, however, stand wall to wall in evidence of the increase in land values: eighteen-fold within the century is the record of a spot not far away. The residents of the houses with side-yards dry their clothes therein; the others must use the roofs. Three small one-and-a-half story houses are each occupied by a single large family, the rest by three to ten families each.

Tenements have from one to six rooms, most of them three. Rents of three-room tenements vary from $1.75 to $2.50 a week. One of the best of these is the second floor of No. 9 Upper Bulfinch, rent $2.50. The kitchen is a 12x15 room, lighted by a single window which overlooks a 5x8 back-yard, odorous of the garbage-barrel. It has a rough, unpainted floor; high, dark-colored mopboards; painted walls, a small sink with a water-faucet, a fair-sized dish-closet and a diminutive chimney-cupboard. Out of one end of the kitchen opens an 8x10 room with a tiny closet, and two tiny windows overlooking the back-yard. Like the kitchen this has dark woodwork, painted walls, and an unpainted floor. The third room is about the same size as the kitchen. Its two windows command the street, and it alone, of the three, gets sunlight enough to have a real cheerfulness. This cheerfulness is increased by bright wall-paper and white woodwork. The floor once had paint, but it shows few traces of it now.

Two small holes in the wall serve for clothes-closets.   All the rooms are low and have whitewashed ceilings.   Between the front room and the kitchen is the stair-landing, lighted by a ground-glass window in the day-time, not lighted at all at night.

In this tenement live the MacGregors—father, mother, and six boys and girls.   The front room is sitting-room and parlor.   As the show-room of the house it has pictures and a carpet.   It has to be used as a bedroom, however, by Mr. and Mrs. MacGregor and the two youngest.   The vulgar disguise of the folding-bed has not yet invaded Bulfinch Street; consequently the functions of the room as a chamber rather overshadow its other functions.   The rest of the MacGregors are packed away at night in the small back-room.   The stair-landing, so far as the landlord allows, is used for storing slop-pails, swill-buckets, and other articles not likely to be stolen.   The MacGregors have the good sense to take no lodgers.   The same cannot be said of all their equally cramped neighbors.   Number 9, and all the other houses of the street, are connected with the city water and sewerage systems; but none of them has gas, hot-water heaters, bath-rooms, or—trifling but portentous detail—fly-screens.   One badly kept water-closet, located in the cellar, has to answer for all the families of a house.   Padlocked wood-boxes and coal-bins, as many as the number of families, are also in the cellar.   Many of the cheaper tenements are squalid and out of repair, and have such defective drainage that the city Board of Health would find plenty of cause for action, should it take the trouble to investigate.

Bulfinch Street is between, and at right angles to, two of the great highways of the city, which are given over to business, factories and tenements.   The original dull-gray paint of the wooden houses has grown duller and grayer with age, where it has not entirely disappeared by peeling; the bricks have lost their pristine freshness; the blinds have faded from green to a color sombre and unnamable.   Nevertheless, if the street has not brightness, it has scraps of picturesqueness—a dormer window to which a discouraged plant or two is clinging; a shingled, unpainted, weatherbeaten house-side bearing a dove-cot and green trailing vines; and terraces of roofs crouching about the base of a lofty church with true old-world humility.

The rough cobblestones with which Bulfinch Street is paved are rendered well-nigh harmless to the feet by the accumulations of dirt in their interstices, as well as by the miscellaneous rubbish of every conceivable description with which they are more or less thickly strewn

—rubbish which might prove the key to the cipher of scores of human lives, if the man appeared with wit enough to use it. True, a member of the Street-Cleaning Department occasionally stalks through in the wake of the garbage cart, selecting from the litter with the glance of a connoisseur such occasional pieces as seem consistent with his dignity, but such a visit makes no perceptible impression.

II. The People.

In Bulfinch Street live about 450 persons—a hundred families. Of this hundred, three-fourths are Irish, and of these three-fourths less than half are Irish-American. Seven families are from Canada, five from Scotland, and five are native American. Of the remaining eight families, two are German, two Italian, one English, one Hebrew, one French, and one Negro. In religion, eighty-one families are Roman Catholic, ten Protestant, and one Jewish; the rest claim no church whatever. Of the heads of families, more than half are common laborers. Six are carpenters, four teamsters, three storekeepers, two hostlers, two masons, two engineers. Here are also a lineman, a carriage-washer, a fireman, a lather, a roofer, a cobbler, a piano-maker, an organ-varnisher, a machinist, a sailor, a fisherman, a bridge-builder, a bartender, a cook, and an employee of the city Street Department. Highly skilled labor, it will be observed, is very scantily represented, so that the men must be very few who make a wage of $2 a day the year round.

A majority of the mothers work out as washwomen or scrubwomen. Some are dishwashers and seamstresses. One keeps store, one is a nurse, another a dressmaker, and two, at least, sell liquor. Others take in work to do at home. Very few confine themselves to their own housework. The bulk of the young men are not content to follow in their fathers' footsteps, but try to enter what they consider more genteel callings. They become, among other things, cheap clerks, bartenders, ushers or ticket-sellers at theatres, assistants in pool-rooms and managers of little cigar-stores. Now and then a Jack-at-all-trades appears. Jim O'Brien, an erratic genius of thirty, living at No. 15, has been successively grocer's boy, telegraph messenger, blacksmith, wheelwright, coachman, teamster, bartender, and saloon scullion. The girls and young women, eager as the men for genteel work, scorn all sorts of domestic labor. They are, however, eager enough to marry. Consequently, they marry young, and after a few years of child-bearing are only too glad to wash windows and scrub floors as their mothers did. The boys nearly all sell papers, and on Sunday mornings a few black boots also. They are errand boys on Saturday, drive parcel-delivery wagons and wear the uniform of the Western Union; but these employments are looked upon as temporary expedients. The thing really desired is a place, no matter how humble, in some monster mercantile establishment. As a rule nothing but the law keeps them in school, so keen are they to earn money and become merchant princes.

The body, physiologists tell us, is renewed every seven years, so in just about that time is the population of Bulfinch Street renewed. Within limits, the people are nomadic. The Whitings have changed their residence sixteen times in eight years, and there are many more families like them. Moving from house to house in the street is perpetual. And, once a family is out of the street, it describes a sort of circle in its migrations, eventually getting back, as a rule, to the identical point it started from. In the summer, Bulfinch Street men occasionally work in the country on the farms of relatives or friends; but there is practically no emigration to the country and very little new blood comes in from the country. In the matter of worldly possessions, also, there is a very unstable equilibrium in Bulfinch Street. Fluctuation is constant between comfort and poverty. Two-thirds of the families are on the lists of one or more charitable agencies. Of these, one-third are hopelessly dependent, another third periodically so. Very few of the independent third have bank accounts of any size.

It is a favorite pastime of a certain class of charitably disposed persons to assign all the poverty in the world to a single cause, usually a sin (or what these persons consider such), frequently, too, a sin they themselves have no mind to. But in reality things are not so very simple as they would have them seem. An individual misfortune may proceed from a group of causes, and in a body of four or five hundred people so many groups of causes are at work that it is impossible to make any one cause fit even a majority of cases. The most that can safely be done is to enumerate such of the causes as have appeared with a fair degree of clearness. Low wages, of course, is often a prime cause (oftener than capitalistic philanthropists are ready to admit); though not so often, perhaps, as irregularity of employment. For the man with steady low wages at least knows what *not* to depend on, and, given a fair amount of intelligent will power, will "cut his garment according to his cloth," while the man fitfully employed is always on the brink of a precipice. Again, both low wages and unsteady work are sometimes due to inefficiency or unreliability of the worker, so these also must be reckoned as causes.

Death makes widows and orphans in Bulfinch Street as elsewhere. Of both, the street has more than its quota, and these almost without exception are on the charity books. Economically considered, accident and illness are—for a time—the same as death; they are causes of poverty that must be convincing. When Mr. Johnson, a carpenter living at No. 35, was paralyzed by a fall from a staging a dozen years ago there was no longer a bread-winner for Mrs. Johnson and her five children. From that single point of view Mr. Johnson might as well have been killed by the fall. That the Johnson family were paupers for ten years after was no fault of his. Three summers ago Mr. Reagan was taken to the hospital very ill of kidney trouble. Mrs. Reagan was at that time in the last stages of consumption. Josie, aged fifteen, the eldest child, had bronchitis. The family not only got badly behind with their rent, but they were obliged to sell their bedding and clothes for food. It was hardly to be wondered at.

Improvidence works sad havoc with the family exchequer, and the havoc, cruelly enough, is as great when caused by inculpable ignorance as by wanton extravagance. Wasteful cooking, buying on instalments, mortgaging furniture at exorbitant rates, and other equally disastrous practices are far too common. When John Gorman, of No. 40, died, his wife received a $400 death benefit. She indulged in the luxury of a $110 funeral, and within a year was in need.

Overproduction of children is another source of trouble. Whether the children live or whether they die, they are about equally expensive. The more desperate the family circumstances the faster the children come. And yet nature seems to smile on this form of improvidence in the long run. Children are transformed to bread-winners by time. Thus, the family dragged down at first by its surplus of children is often exalted by this very thing at the end. Comfortable old age comes quite as often to the heads of the large families as to the childless couples, since the latter have no bread-winners to call on when they themselves cease to win bread.

The multiplication of charities (which paralyze effort), old age (seldom adequately prepared for), chronic intemperance of one or both parents, laziness, desertion by the husband—all these causes of poverty are amply illustrated in Bulfinch Street. Even United States pensions have worked damage there. In the light of these few facts the folly and factitiousness of the hard and fast lines drawn between worthy and unworthy by charity experts is plain enough.

III. THE LIFE.

During its thirty years or more of comparative seclusion, Bulfinch Street has developed a life of its own that is far from being the dull, inhuman thing that popular opinion assigns to a tenement-house district; and this life resembles no one thing so much as the life of the typical New England village. Of course such a parallel must not be too much emphasized. It is valuable solely as a help to a comprehension of a manner of existence remote from the groove in which our conceptions of life naturally run. This little community of 450 people has: (1) A small bake-shop opening out of Mrs. Flanagan's kitchen and presided over by Mrs. Flanagan herself, who, like Miss Hepzibah Pyncheon, is apprized of customers by the tinkle of a little bell. (2) A cobbler's shop installed, as cobblers' shops are apt to be, in a tiny, dimly-lighted shed. The cobbler is an old, gray, spectacled, long-bearded man who is very much of a philosopher and an epigrammatist withal—the most flaring sign of his shop, " No trust, no bust," being an admirable example of his epigrammatic powers. The shop is a rendezvous for other (though inferior) philosophers and wits, and this is as it should be. (3) Three stores, two groceries in basements and one on a corner, with bread, kindling-wood, milk, and salt pickles for staple articles of traffic, but without the intellectual glory—peculiar to the country corner grocery—which is divided between the cobbler's shop and the three kitchen bar-rooms of the street.

Like the calm of a village is Bulfinch Street's atmosphere of deliberateness. Nervous prostration is unknown even by name. Joanna Murphy, a parchment-faced, swaying-gaited, thirty-years' resident, who buried her husband from this street and from it sent her children out to make their way in the world, frequently consumes half-an-hour in going from her house to the little bake-shop. On her way she chucks the little children under the chin, delighting their baby souls with grotesque, Celtic baby talk. Everybody speaks to her and she speaks to everybody. Nor is this sociable dawdling confined to Joanna. Rarely do men or women go by an occupied door-step or window without " stopping to pass the time of day." There is the same borrowing of butter, sugar, etc., from door to door as in the village; the same calling in of neighbors' children to run errands, the same use of " Miss" for " Mrs.," the same habit of loud talking, the same cautious spending of pennies by the children, the same eagerness to exhibit one's own bruises or deformities, the same eagerness to show the sick and the dead to strange visitors, the same superstitions, the same, or rather a fuller, worship of the tea-pot, the same feeling of isolation from the rest of the world, the same pride in the petty things that differentiate one family from another, the same bragging over bygone prosperity. The women of Bulfinch Street talk across the street as village women across back-yards, hold informal receptions on the door-steps, go about bareheaded or with little shawls over their heads—never with hats on, except when they are going as far away as the avenues—array themselves in the figured shawls that all country women wore a score of years ago and some wear still. They are quick to note a stranger and almost equally quick to ask him his business. They scrutinize him from the second, third, and fourth story windows, and when he is out of sight, talk him over.

But the most significant expression of the spirit of village-life in Bulfinch Street, and a truly beautiful one, is the readiness of neighbors to help each other out of trouble. Prudential motives force this exercise of brotherly love to be kept so far out of sight in streets of this kind that, as a rule, its amount is absurdly underestimated. The well-dressed visitors of charitable societies, however remote from charity their fabricated excuses for calling may seem to be, are yet known for what they are—a charity picket-line.

Eighty-year-old Bridget Mulcahy, toothless, but still bright-eyed, may be seen almost any fair day smoking her pipe on the stoop of No. 20. Her husband, Jim, a day-laborer, died eighteen years ago. For seven years before his death he was blind, and his misfortune, joined to his good-nature, made him a favorite. Soon after Jim's death Bridget dislocated a shoulder, thereby permanently losing the use of her right arm. She became destitute. The neighbors lent her many things (cooking dishes and a comforter among them) and after a little, Michael Roe, who was himself behind with his rent, gave her a home in his family. Then her friends, " the boys from Ireland," " put up" a raffle for her which netted $40. She rented a cellar room for fifty cents a week and took in two girl lodgers at ten cents a night. From that time to this she has lived in a cellar or a garret and shared her room with girl lodgers; but she has depended largely for her support upon the raffles which the " boys" have continued to " put up" for her once or twice a year. Three years ago, Michael Roe, by that time a widower, was stricken down with a fatal sickness. Then the "boys from Ireland" got their heads together again and "put up" a benefit ball for Bridget's former benefactor. Tickets were fifty cents each and the ball netted $75. There was something left toward funeral expenses when the old man died. Then another ball was given for the benefit of his orphan children.

Raffles and balls are not the only Bulfinch Street methods of fulfilling the law of Christ. The Talbots had been in the street only a week, when their little boy died. Nevertheless, the neighbors went in with their sympathy as soon as a white rosette was tied to the doorbell. Frank Whitney, hopelessly in consumption, but possessed of a superstitious dread of going to a "home," has been taken in by Thomas Wood, who promises to keep him as long as he lives. The little help about the house that Frank can give Tom's wife is Frank's only possible return for the kindness. Neighbors send in little treats to the sick, share with each other the good things they have humbugged out of the charities, "mind" each other's children, lend their cooking-stoves, take in, for a time, evicted families, or women and children when the father is on a dangerous spree, and shelter unfortunate women during confinement.

There are a freedom and a flexibility about Bulfinch Street life that are quite unknown in the old-fashioned village. Familiar as village life is, it would scarcely tolerate a woman's combing her hair on the sidewalk, or such a race between married women, holding their dresses to their knees for greater freedom of movement, as Bulfinch Street witnessed and applauded a few weeks ago. It is significant of much, too, though a trifle in itself, that no Bulfinch Street woman would think of washing on Monday, if it chanced to be a holiday. In fact, self-sufficient as its local life appears to be, Bulfinch Street does not by any means escape the influence of the metropolis that surrounds it. The life of the great city acts constantly and strenuously upon it. Before all else stands the influence of the church. And, because Bulfinch Street Protestants are only one in ten, and many of these hopelessly irregular in church attendance, it is fair to speak of the Catholic church alone—St. Stephen's—which splendidly dominates this and scores of other streets. Upon its stalwartness the people lean, and without its ceremonial sanction few important events occur in family life. By its pomp and circumstance this little band of vulgar people is brought into a conscious relation with nearly two thousand years of glory that is past, and with the present glory of Catholic Christendom—a relation that extends to a

36

sense of ownership. Mysterious as the true nature of this relation and the true value of this ownership may be to them, it is none the less inspiring. These people "believe in soul." They are "very sure of God," Christ, the Virgin, the saints, the Pope. A great deal to be sure of at this end of the century!—enough, certainly, to impress their imaginations with the perpetual presence in the world of a Power, not themselves, "that makes for righteousness," enough, too, to lift them now and then out of themselves into union with that Power. Furthermore, the church, and the church only, to any considerable degree, diffuses the warm glow of ritualism over a life that otherwise would have little beauty and poetry in it.

How far the offices of the church affect the imagination is illustrated by the good Catholic mother with five children who only "counted them four" until the youngest had been christened. Bulfinch Street tradition demands at the ceremony of confirmation a new dark suit and a soldier cap for boys, and a white dress and white slippers for girls. When, after many days of anxious preparation on the part of parents and relatives, the trim procession moves along the sidewalk of the avenue or up the church aisle, each boy with a white satin ribbon on his left arm and each girl with a white gauze veil, "they show like troops of the shining ones." That day brings presents of nickels and dimes and confectionery from godfathers, godmothers and benevolent grannies. Rarely, it is easy to believe, does a boy grow into so hardened a villain as not to recall at times with a glow of true feeling the day of his confirmation; never does a mother forget the confirmation of her boy.

Extreme unction distinctly sobers, for a moment at least, the whole street. Then the priest becomes the visible messenger of Destiny. The grim, popular phrase, "anointed for death," goes up and down. The sign of the cross is made, a prayer is murmured. Relatives who are not near enough to be torn with grief take a harmless vanity in the prominence into which their family name is brought and in the assurance that all things are being done decently and in order. Weddings and funerals, though very important occasions in the life of the street, are so familiar as joyous and melancholy ceremonials that they need not be enlarged on here. The observance of Fridays and Holy Days and Lent, as well as Sundays, is another factor in making religion palpable; and the Sunday-school and the sodalities play a prominent part in the lives of the children. The very money this church relation costs enhances its value as a religious force.

The permanent value of the sort of education given by the public schools is seriously questioned in many quarters, and justly.   But that the schools with all their defects materially modify the ideals of the children for the better is clear from the way in which, during the school season, they talk about their school work, and bring their out-of-school disputes to the touchstone of the teacher's dictum.   The city evening schools unfortunately get very little patronage from Bulfinch Street.   Nearly all its youthful ambitions are of the very near sighted order.   But the theatre is much patronized by all.   In its influence upon the young it comes after the church and the school alone.   The two theatres close by are the only ones much attended —another evidence of the strength of neighborhood habit.   Both are low-priced and present an almost uninterrupted repertory of highly moral melodramas whose sombreness is lightened by " variety" between the acts.   As these people detect neither the improbability of the plots, the fustian of the sentiments, nor the crudity of the art, the influence of the plays they hear may be adjudged, in the main, uplifting.   Other outside factors of more or less importance are labor organizations, benefit and insurance orders, newspapers, prize-fights, races, ball-games, and ward politics.

Bulfinch Street family life differs in important respects from the family life of the typical village, in nothing more, perhaps, than in the parents' treatment of their children.   Although the children have quite as much direct attention from the mother as in the wealthy city families which employ nurses, and, as in the village, they see quite as much of their fathers as do the children of men whose business cares exclude everything else, still the children are not properly attended to.   Vicious cruelty is rare.   Mothers lavish affection enough upon their babies, but they are ignorant and thoughtless and, above all, over-indulgent.   If the family is eating corned-beef and cabbage and the baby cries for it, the baby gets it.   So with green fruit, liquors, and other equally unsuitable things.   Anything rather than have the baby cry!   Drugging is occasionally practised, usually for this same reason.   Tiny creatures, one and two years old, who ought to be in bed at six o'clock, are allowed to creep or toddle around till ten; and children of four or five years are sent on errands as late as eleven o'clock.   Parents who have themselves never been able to save money are not likely to insist on their children's doing so.   True, several of the small boys have saved money for the Fourth of July and the circus.   Little Mamie Flanagan (daughter of the proprietor of the bake-shop) has been saving for several weeks to get her pet dog licensed.   Teddy Jameson is hoarding for an utterly impossible bicycle.   But these are exceptions for which the parents are scantily responsible.   Inconsistencies are common, of course.   The very parents who take real interest and pride in their children's prog- ress at school keep them out whenever it happens to suit their own convenience; other parents make their children lose whole terms by being too careless or bigoted to have them vaccinated.

Besides the progress of the younger generation, shown by its es- chewing manual labor, are occasional signs of change in the taste or in the code of etiquette of the elder.   A house that makes any pre-: tensions at all to gentility is pretty apt to have some gaudy plush furniture and a few cheap lithographs or chromos.   It is sure to have a plush album.   Mrs. Kimball, of No. 1, buys bottled beer and has it delivered at the door; she has grown too high-toned " to work the growler."   Mrs. Butland regularly washes off her sidewalk.   Mrs. Boland and Mrs. MacGregor have peep-curtains; Mrs. O'Brien and Mrs. Conlon lace curtains, and Mrs. Jackson a $2.00 copy of Scott's " Lady of the Lake," not to mention a flamboyant subscription-book, " Ireland in Poetry and Song," and Moore's " History of Ireland." Mrs. O'Toole's Katie has a blackboard in her bedroom and Mrs. Budlong's Josie is taking lessons on the violin.   Mrs. Grogan has stopped going without stockings.   And while Mrs. Brannigan still smokes a pipe and Mrs. Quinn still uses her apron as a handkerchief, they are both a little ashamed; they do these things on the sly.

In amusements the children of Bulfinch Street are easily first as elsewhere.   Among them are gaunt, pale, dirty, ragged, undersized, vermin-infested specimens.   There is an occasional cripple, mute or half-wit.   The majority have to sell papers, run errands, mind the baby, forage for wood, and do other equally tiresome things.   They are perpetually liable to summons and scoldings from doors and win- dows, and occasionally liable to " clubbings."   Their most radiant sports are shadowed by fear of the " cop," for whom they are obliged to set a watch at each end of the street.   In the school season their fear of the truant-officer is still greater, inasmuch as the blessed old privilege of " playing hookey " at the risk of one or, at most, two thrashings (at school and at home) is no more.   Truancy is now bar- barously classed as a crime and may result in six months' imprison- ment or, if obstinately adhered to, in imprisonment till the age of twenty-one.   In spite of all these drawbacks the children of Bulfinch

Street, taken as a whole, appear as buoyant and happy as other children and, in this matter at least, children are no dissemblers.   They
squat as readily in the middle of a street as they do on a chair or a
door-step, play without stint in the dirt and yet, with a laudable catholicity of taste, take quite as keen a pleasure in fine raiment, when
they happen to have it put on them, as if they were accustomed to
it.   The older boys hie away to a distance to play ball, fish, swim,
steal rides and despoil aristocratic gutters and ash-barrels of fruit and
finery.   The younger boys occasionally visit a small park, about a
quarter of a mile away, to give a dog a swim in the basin of a fountain
or to take turns in riding a rickety wooden bicycle.   The girls, too,
stray away at times, impelled by milder motives.

But, in general, the sports of both boys and girls are confined to
the street or its immediate vicinity.   Leap-frog, hide-and-seek, mar-
bles, peg-top, jack-stones, stick-knife, cat's-cradle, duck-on-a-rock,
shinny, snap-the-whip, and blind-man's-buff are as familiar to them
as to other children.   They have the same pets (not perhaps in as
great numbers)—dogs, cats, doves, rabbits.   Some of their pastimes
are as distinctly perquisites of city life, as bird-nesting, for example,
is of life in the country.   Such are: seeing games of the national
baseball league and the sports of the big athletic clubs, stealing
rides on electric cars, practising high-kicking on the fenced-in roofs,
dancing the skirt dance; above all, going to the theatre.

They revel in plays of the imagination; they play house, horse,
school and cars; they play white man and Indian with a few clubs,
some dirty colored flannel and, for a scalp, a shred of a fur carriage-
robe; they play circus with their dogs and cats; funeral with a dead
rat; Salvation Army with a tin pan and a shattered, quavering old
zither; Christmas tree with a dilapidated clothes-horse; and Robinson Crusoe with a tattered parasol.   They get up shows and charge
pins for entrance.   Furthermore, they have a healthy fondness for
a reasonable amount of fisticuffs.   The gang known as " the Bulfinchers" thus settle a baseball dispute with the gang known as " the
Greenies"; or they prevent " the Greenies" from giving a " show" in
which the " Bulfinchers" are reported to be satirized.   If one were to
be only a child and die in early life, it were as well, perhaps, to be
born in Bulfinch Street 'as anywhere.   Such minute details of the
Bulfinch Street child-life ought to be taken for granted rather than
recorded.   But the artificial lime-light of sensationalism has been so
often thrown upon the children of the poor, they have been so long

regarded as weaklings or monstrosities, instead of natural children, that nothing can be taken for granted.

The German and Italian poor have a commendable habit of taking many of their pleasures out by families. Not so the people of Bulfinch Street. Large numbers of family men forsake their families for the saloons and kitchen bar-rooms; a few for the theatres. The rest smoke their pipes stolidly in the windows, on the doorsteps or in the kitchen, too tired to move about, too ignorant or hampered by insufficient light to read. The men who go to the saloon are not necessarily the worse; they may be simply the more enterprising. They go, no doubt, because they are thirsty, but also because of a strong social instinct. And in at least one of the saloons frequented by them, there is considerable mental stimulus in the talk at the tables.

There are women in Bulfinch Street who work out regularly during the day and wash, iron, and sew far into the night for their own families. These are exceptions. As a class they have more leisure than the women of better-to-do streets. They ignore utterly the trifling household cares that worry the life out of the conscientious middle-class housekeeper, and they have no burdensome society obligations. They are always gossiping on the stairs. They stop for a chat at the grocery or the beer-shop. They often take possession of their doorsteps in the forenoon, and hold them until bedtime, leaving them only for meals or other more animated door-steps, sometimes pretending to sew, sometimes without even that pretence. A few women take their pleasures in the kitchen bar-rooms with the men, and some of these have brutal faces. But the faces of the majority of the Bulfinch Street men and women are neither wicked nor wretched. They express stolid, animal content.

The young men and women, more sophisticated than their elders, dress in their best and betake themselves to the avenues: the young women to attend the dancing assemblies or theatres, or to flirt up and down the avenue sidewalks; the young men to be where the young women are and to visit the saloons and pool-rooms besides. If they remain in the street after work-hours they keep on their old clothes as their parents do. The policeman on his beat is as much a godsend to the young woman as he is to the traditional park-nurse. And there is curb-stone lovemaking with the local beaux.

After the supper-hour, though with less noise, perhaps, than in the forenoon, the activity of the street reaches its height. In spite of absences on the avenues, men, women and children are all very much

in evidence. The children, especially, instead of showing weariness as by good rights they should, have, at this time, some of their
wildest frolics. When it is dark, gas-lamps are lighted, one at each
end of the street, and one in the middle, making just light enough
to throw most of the street into shadow. The lower light is used as
a loafing-place nightly by a gang of young toughs, among whom are
several " students. " In the phraseology of the neighborhood a " student" is a " bum" with a home, as distinguished from a common lodg-
ing-house " bum" or a tramp. The middle light projects from the
most respectable and exclusive house of the street. The upper one
has been preëmpted for the evening by a group of fourteen- to fif-
teen-year-old boys who are giving selections from the most impassioned scenes of the plays of the week. As an exhibition of memory, rather than of mimetic power, the performance is truly marvellous.

Music sounds on every side. Jack Caddigan plays a harmonica,
Tom Bullard an accordeon, and Tom Wood's cornet is always to be
depended on for excruciating versions of all the " home classics."
Jack O'Toole's father, a veteran of the late war, has kept a genuine
army trumpet all these years, upon which Jack, who aspires to be a
veteran himself some day, performs a few calls with considerable
skill. Pat Geoghegan, at No. 12, is rendering some real Irish songs
in a sort of tuneless recitative teeming with weird Celtic melancholy.
Eighteen-year-old Katie Rafferty follows him with half-a-dozen popular concert-hall melodies, delivered with the strident voice and ultra-
serious air peculiar to concert-hall soloists; these are all vigorously
applauded from the street. Six months ago Katie sang at an " am-
teur night" at the nearest of the two theatres. Since then she has
affected a professional swagger.

Early quitting of work on Saturday afternoon gives the men time
to rest and to change their clothes before evening. Saturday night is
a lively occasion in the bar-rooms, the favorite night for avenue assemblies and for newsboys at the theatres. More people forsake the
street in consequence, and from seven until eleven it is quieter there
than on other nights, in spite of much passing in and out with pails
of beer and Sunday provisions. After eleven o'clock, the aspect
of things changes. Intoxicated merry-makers straggle in. Jim
O'Grady has an attack of vomiting on the sidewalk. Young Jerry
Flannagan rattles the shutters and pounds the door of the bake-shop
in vain. His mother will not let him in. She is giving him a much-

needed lesson.   Mrs. Mahoney and Jim White fall to fighting in the alleyway beyond the cobbler's shop and are separated by having the contents of a slop-pail poured over them from above.   Old Dolan, crazy drunk, emits such an unearthly series of yells that the people of Green and Cumston Streets, who ordinarily pay no attention to drunken yelling, come in to investigate.   At No. 27 and No. 40 carousing will go on until morning, and it will be a wonder if indoors does not become so cramped before then that an adjournment will be made to the roof.

The efforts of the people of Bulfinch Street to distinguish Sunday are very noticeable.   No family permanently ignores it.   And if any do so, temporarily, it is an infallible sign that they are "down on their luck," or that one or both parents are on a protracted spree. Owing to the presence of the men, a fuller sociability and much indulgence in music, Sunday is more like an ordinary evening than an ordinary day; but in certain respects it differs from either.   The newsboys have to rise even earlier than usual in order to get their papers folded and be at the church gates with them by 6.30,—the closing-time of early mass.   All make great efforts at fixing up. The men shave, put on white shirts, polish their square-toed shoes, and conscientiously make themselves physically uncomfortable. Then, very ill at ease because of their unwonted smartness, but with a proud sense of being gentlemen—that is, wearing good clothes and having nothing to do—they sit about in their shirt-sleeves, read the papers and smoke, not the every-day pipe, but perhaps a cheap cigar.

Sunday is almost the only day on which it is possible to tell exactly how the children look, for then their faces are scrubbed and polished.   A new toy is brought out for them or a new cart turned over to their use, and they are expected, except for the restraint that a consciousness of fine clothes naturally imposes, to frolic as vigorously as on week-days.   The women array themselves in dresses of astounding fits and colors.   Widows' weeds are, as a rule, dirty, crumpled, and rusty from overmuch wear or neglect.   Occasional instances appear, however, of excellent taste in dress, particularly among the young women.   The young men, however, deck themselves out loudly and clumsily.   Brand-new clothes, whoever wears them, never fail to attract the attention of the neighbors.   When Jack O'Toole appeared in his first long-trousered suit, a new derby hat, a standing collar and an ambitious tie that nothing could keep from climbing the collar, every one took note and guyed him merci-

lessly. Old Mag Maguire, " happy Mag, ' the street calls her, drunk
as she was, saw the humor of the situation and plastered him with
burdocks in her mirth. All day long, poor Jack's face betrayed his
misery, and his attempts to appear manly grievously miscarried.

Grown-up married children come home to the Sunday dinner.
Here and there a devoted mother reads aloud stories of the saints to
her children. Excursions are made by a few to the parks and the
beaches. Many are attracted to the theatres by the " sacred concerts, "
or stereopticon lectures in the evening. Most important and distinctive of all are the church services—early mass from 6 to 6.30, low
mass from 9 to 9.30, high mass from 10.30 to 12; and to one or another of these services nearly every Catholic finds his way.

Such is the summer life of Bulfinch Street. The winter life is
not essentially different. The principal scene of action is then transferred from outdoors to indoors. There is a little less sociability and
poverty gripes harder—that is all.

IV. MORALS.

Of the moral side of Bulfinch Street something must be said.
The saddest feature of the life is, oddly enough, the very thing that
makes it superficially bright,—the perfect content with a low standard
of living which springs from an extreme poverty of ideals. This is
evidenced by nothing so much as the ignoble things that kindle pride.
The men, in particular, take their drudgery unquestioningly, though
they feel no pleasure in it. There is more hope of progress in the
rash, anarchistic discontent prevalent in certain other poor districts.
For this discontent, however misdirected, and however dangerous (for
a time) to social order, has at least some upward-moving vitality in
it, inspired as it is by the sense of justice which is here almost entirely
lacking. One of the saddest manifestations of this sad satisfaction
is a benumbing of the energies of the young, when they leave school,
or when, outside incentives to work being taken from them by the
necessity of bread-winning, they are left practically at the mercy of
their immediate environment. Growth is at once arrested and rarely
recommences. Content becomes positively as well as negatively harmful, when it results, as it does here, in a moral denseness which amounts
to an absolute inability to make distinctions,—to appreciate that anything whatever may not be done that does not bring reprisal from the
priest or the policeman. And the church, in spite of its uplifting
power along many lines, seems to be partially responsible for this.

Once this moral denseness is appreciated most of the moral defects of the people are easily understood.   The most salient of these and, by all odds, the most disastrous is untruthfulness.   Among themselves in their simple, neighborhood life, the people of Bulfinch Street are so natural and so loyal that frankness and honesty prevail to a large degree, partly, perhaps, because there is so little to be gained by crookedness that it has not seemed worth while.   But their relation to so much of the outside world as they are in any way physically dependent on—principally employers, landlords and the visitors and agents of charitable societies—is one tangled web of deceit. Anything and everything asked is freely promised: in part, it may be, out of a false notion that a refusal of any kind is not good breeding.   But promises once made are done with; thereafter they are naïvely ignored.   Successful perjury is venial.   Mrs. Jenkins, for instance, almost begged to be allowed to swear in court that her Frank was a hopelessly stubborn child.   She was really proud of his being quite the reverse.   But she desired to have him committed for stubbornness instead of truancy, her reason being a more or less well-grounded preference for the institution to which stubborn children are sent to the one devoted to truants.   That in perjuring herself thus she would not be doing a mother's full duty she never had a glimmering.   Men and women, unasked, assert that they would not touch a drop of liquor for the world, though they drink as a matter of course and are, at bottom, nòt ashamed of it.   They have learned by hard experience that there is an absurd lack of distinction on the part of their would-be benefactors between drinking and habitual drunkenness.   It is only natural that they should utilize their dearly earned knowledge to the best advantage.   The parents, of course, are imitated by the children.   More than that, many of the children are forced to be steady deceivers for the benefit of the parental purse.

One is obliged to wonder how much of this chronic untruthfulness is due to real moral depravity and how much to well-meant intermeddling in their affairs by the well-to-do; since this intermeddling has not only made it pay well to deceive, but, as in trampdom, has made success in deceit a thing to be mightily proud of.   Temptations to easy living are hard to resist and are none too much resisted in any grade of life.   These people must not be judged too harshly for yielding to their peculiar temptation.   This easy lapsing into deceit may be in some degree a matter of race, but that it is not entirely so is plain enough from the fact that it is as pronounced in the other families of Bulfinch Street as in the Irish families. It is certain that the charities are responsible for a part of it. It is equally certain that there is little hope of developing integrity in Bulfinch Street, until private charitable impulse, instead of indulging in the exquisite luxury of giving, shall practise the difficult self-denial of leaving the people there, in matters of finance, to their own natural, noble village communism. It may as well be confessed, also, that many of the charity visitors have resorted to diabolical sharp practice in ferreting out damaging facts under the guise of friendship. These have found apt pupils, so apt that they are now being fleeced by their own tricks. Servility, another striking defect, is really only another phase of this deceit used for commercial ends. Flattery and cajolery have been put at a high premium, as well as direct deceit, by being too often mistaken for gratitude and bountifully rewarded as such.

Energy and persistence—strenuousness of every sort—is lacking. But this may be so far due to purely physical causes that it is hardly safe to treat it from the moral point of view. Overwork and poor food alone are enough to undermine any sort of original sinew.

Intemperance is found in both sexes, and as much in the one sex as in the other. Speaking broadly, everybody drinks more or less. A majority, it may be, drink to excess now and then. On Christmas or on the Fourth of July it is *comme il faut* to be drunk. But this is not habitual drunkenness nor anything like it. Habitual drunkards are, unquestionably, in a small minority. A few of the boys, however, are already inebriates. Only the other day two, fourteen years of age, were sentenced to a considerable term for drunkenness. The causes of intemperance are many, but the chief are bad food, over-work, unemployment, poverty, ugliness on the part of the husbands, shrewishness and slatternliness of the wives, and " pure cussedness."

Sexual immorality exists here as everywhere, but it is not common enough to be appalling. There are no houses of prostitution. There are loose women who, as the neighbors express it, " have men hanging round them," and there are some couples living in *union libre*. The home-life of the latter, however, cannot truthfully be said to be any less well-ordered than that of their more conventional neighbors. Mrs. Brannigan's Jenny, aged thirty-three, is officially known by the name of Mrs. Duncan, from Jim Duncan, with whom she has been living for several years; but her three children all bear the name of Brannigan. Rosa Brackett, now twenty-one, at fourteen a homeless orphan in a dance-hall, was taken in by John Belasco and given a home. She has lived with him ever since. They have two children. In conversation, the people have a refreshing habit of calling a spade a spade. Pregnancy is nothing to be ashamed of, and does not force retirement from society. Conventional sensibilities would be shocked by the vulgarisms of Bulfinch Street, but deliberate obscenity is not more common than among the better to-do.

It has been the purpose of this study to show what is, not what ought to be, in Bulfinch Street. A detailed programme of reform would be grotesquely out of place here. But the conclusion forces itself that the social elevation of Bulfinch Street, if it is to be achieved at all, will be achieved most quickly and most easily by an open-minded, inquiring, humble coöperation with its healthy native forces —more especially sociability and neighborly helpfulness. If these forces may somehow be directed so as to come into vital contact with new ideas, the standard of living will be raised all along the line and life will be splendidly enriched. The natural and the best way of bringing about this vital contact, since the local feeling as well as the lethargy of Bulfinch Street forbid reaching far out after the ideas, is to bring the ideas to it. This involves the opening of Bulfinch Street branches for the dissemination of the ideas of the larger life—local centres of learning, manual and technical training, the fine arts, morals, religion (using the term broadly). In this enterprise, neighborhood traits must be appreciated, neighborhood tradition reverenced, and neighborhood pride and support appealed to. This, if anything, will prevent growth from being arrested; may even cause it to recommence where it has been arrested. If these conditions are fulfilled and the affair be absolutely divorced from charity, it is a matter of little difference how or by whom these local centres are established.

· If, however, this raising of the standard of living of Bulfinch Street necessarily involves the loss of its splendid human qualities, it is hardly worth while. The stupid, comfortable, self-satisfied, unsocial respectability of the city middle classes is not a result to make large sacrifices for. There are those who love Bulfinch Street as it is, and these pray that, whatever else may happen to it, it may not come to that. The world has enough of that sort of thing already.

ALVAN F. SANBORN.

THE CRUX OF THE MONEY CONTROVERSY: HAS GOLD RISEN?

THAT gold has acquired in recent years a greatly increased purchasing-power or command over commodities, no one is insane enough
to deny; but that it has been the result of any change in economic or
industrial conditions operating directly upon the metal-mass itself, no
one will admit who has investigated the subject with the single purpose of ascertaining the facts underlying the phenomenon. Its explanation, therefore, should be sought for, by inductive methods,
among the complex industrial conditions which have produced a fall
in prices, and not by an arbitrary or gratuitous assumption, based on
mere illation, that such a fall is the result of an appreciation of gold.
When this shall have been done it will undoubtedly appear that the
alleged appreciation is simply *an effect* resulting from, and not *a cause*
producing, the phenomena observed.

At the very threshold we are confronted with a fact that admon-
ishes us of the dangers of hasty conclusions. It is not to be denied
that gold is, of all known substances, the least subject to changes
either physical or economic. It possesses all the elements of stability
of value in a more eminent degree than any other product of nature,
or than any product of man's ingenuity. It is, therefore, pre-
eminently suited to the purposes of a " standard" measure of value,
whose paramount and most essential characteristics are immutability
and exemption from physical and economic changes.

At the next step of our inquiry we encounter another important
fact scarcely less discouraging to the theory that gold has risen. And
this is, that within the period in which it is alleged this change has
occurred.—say since 1865, the year following that in which prices
attained their highest point both in this country and Europe—we find
that while there was, for a time, a decline in the product of gold of
about 10 per cent as compared with the phenomenal output for the
first fifteen years following its discovery in California and Australia,
there was an increase of 100 per cent in the product of silver during
the same period, and a combined increase of both metals of 16 per
cent. And yet, within the period of fifteen years following that of
the maximum product of gold—and during this increase of the joint

output—prices both in this country and Europe fell to the lowest point of the century up to that date, 1878. We find further that, following this temporary decline in the product of gold, a very notable increase in that metal occurred, nearly equalling for the past eight years the average of the maximum product for the fifteen years from 1851 to 1865, and for the past three years exceeding it by over $12,000,000 per annum; while, for the past eight years silver has increased, as compared with the same period, over 300 per cent; and the joint increase has been 70 per cent in excess of the product of the period of maximum output, and for the past three years, 100 per cent.

Adopting Dr. Soetbeer's tables up to and including 1879, and the tables of the Director of the Mint since that date, we find that for the twenty-eight years from 1866 to 1893—the period of the so-called "contraction of the currency," and of falling values—the world's product of gold exceeded $3,276,000,000, or $116,000,000 *in excess of the product for 358 years* from the discovery of America to the year 1851; while the product of silver aggregated $3,063,000,000, making a joint output of $6,339,000,000, or an excess of over $3,781,000,-000, or 150 per cent, as compared with the joint product from 1851 to 1865, the period of maximum output in the history of the metals to that date, and of the inflated prices alleged to have resulted therefrom. This excess greatly exceeds the increase of either commerce or population for the same period, and if there is any foundation for the theory that prices are dependent upon the volume of money in circulation as compared with the volume of the commodities upon the market, then prices should have advanced to a figure never before witnessed in modern times; instead of which there has been a depression wholly unexampled.

It may not be uninteresting to give here a *résumé* of the product of the metals for the century, as it may afford some idea of the alleged "contraction" that has occurred and upon which the theories of existing industrial depression have been founded. We state the annual average product of each metal, the combined average output, and the total product for the period designated:

Period.	Annual average output—gold.	Annual average output—silver.	Total annual average.	Total product—gold and silver.
1801-50, 50 years...	$15,750,164	$27,205,424	$42,955,588	$2,147,779,407
1851-65, 15 " ...	130,428,400	40,086,400	170,514,800	2,557,723,000
1866-80, 15 " ...	118,217,310	79,887,606	198,104,916	2,971,580,736
1866-93, 28 " ...	117,002,855	109,391,682	226,394,537	6,339,047,036
1886-93, 8 " ...	124,039,162	163,944,250	287,983,412	2,303,866,300
1891-93, 3 " ...	142,667,766	197,190,666	339,858,432	1,019,575,300

The mint reports of leading commercial nations show that the coinage of the metals considerably exceeds their total output, to say nothing of the amount consumed in the arts. But this is so largely due to recoinage, that it is impossible to ascertain the net annual additions to the stock of metallic money. As, however, the consumption in the arts does not greatly differ from year to year, it is believed that a statement of the output will indicate, with sufficient accuracy, the relative supply of metallic money.

But whatever serves the purpose of effecting exchanges and distributing the products of industry, practically performs the functions of money and, to that extent, relieves the pressure of "demand" upon the money-mass. And we find that, within this period of falling prices, the increase of uncovered paper money, which, though a mere arbitrary "sign of value," subserves the purpose of effecting local exchanges, has been even more remarkable than the increase of metallic money, and is altogether unprecedented in monetary history. To this, we may add also the abnormal increase of "banking power" among leading commercial nations within the same period, which, though not necessarily involving an increase of the money-mass, creates a powerful agency for effecting exchanges and facilitating the operations of borrowing by the aggregation of small savings and the utilization of credits based upon material wealth, and, to that extent, increases the effectiveness of the currency.

Hume, in explaining the circumstances which tend to reduce the rates of interest, has well elucidated this idea. He says:

"In order to have in any State a great number of lenders, it is not sufficient nor requisite that there be a great abundance of the precious metals. It is only requisite that the property or command of that quantity which is in the State should be collected in particular hands, so as to form considerable sums, or compose a great moneyed interest. This begets a number of lenders and sinks the rate of usury."

And Mulhall tells us that "since 1840 the banking of the world has increased about eleven-fold, that is, three times as fast as commerce, or thirty times faster than population."

If, to these instrumentalities, we add the vast sums represented by the bills of exchange arising from the phenomenal expansion of commerce and travel within the same period, or growing out of the enormous carrying trade of the world incident thereto—the underwritten risks—international dealings in funded securities, foreign loans and speculative stocks, all which, to a greater or less extent, perform the functions of money in the transfer of credits and the liquidation of balances, we shall have a volume of the various "signs of value" wholly unexampled in the history of the world. The logical tendency of this should have been to produce a rise in prices or, *e converso*, a fall in the value of money. On the contrary, we are confronted with a great fall in prices, as alleged, from an appreciation of gold.

As these things all tend directly to relieve the pressure upon the money-mass, we are unable to discover anything in the economic conditions of the past twenty-five years tending at all to an appreciation of gold. As heretofore observed, the exchangeable value of that metal, like that of other commodities, arises from its utilities; chief among which are its uses as a "standard measure" of value in liquidating the balances of international commerce, or of rating the exchanges which arise from it. It has already been shown that six times the amount of gold is employed in foreign commerce that is so used for local circulation and the arts combined. And to the extent to which it has been superseded for such purposes by these various instrumentalities, has its "utility" been impaired; and the logical effect would be its *depreciation*, or fall in value.

But there is yet another, and even more important, consideration to be taken into account, tending to the same result. We allude now to the immensely increased *effectiveness* of gold as a medium of exchange, both in foreign and domestic commerce, arising from the increased rapidity in the transfer of credits resulting from the increased facilities of rapid transit by ocean cables, telegraph, railway and steamship service. They have not only minimized the time required for the transfer of credits, but have greatly multiplied the operations of exchange by cross bills and arbitrages which the perfected mechanism of commercial methods, incident to these improved facilities, have made practical. Fortunately, this is not a matter of theory or speculation, but is susceptible of absolute proof.

Immediately following the cessation, in 1866, of the abnormal exports of silver to the Orient, which had been draining Europe since 1853, a series of events followed in rapid succession that not only revolutionized Oriental exchanges that had so long controlled the market price of silver, but also produced important modifications in the commercial methods of the Western world. In that year the Atlantic cable was laid, connecting Europe with this continent. Three years later, in 1869, the Suez canal was opened and cable communication was established throughout the Orient. During the same year, the golden spike was driven in our first transcontinental railway, and the steamship line from San Francisco to China was established. In the meantime continents were being ribbed with railways, the atmosphere was being webbed with telegraph wires connecting every important commercial centre, and in this girding together of hemispheres and continents with cables, the whole commercial world may be said to have become one vast clearing-house whose daily transactions were flashed to every financial centre—relieving financial tension and adjusting balances by the instantaneous transfer of credits that, within a few years, had required weeks, and in many instances months, to effect. The industrial development and commercial expansion that followed this revolution in commercial methods imparted unwonted energy to every department of human industry, the substantial and visible evidences of which are to be found in the unparalleled increase of the material wealth of the world within the last thirty years.

Following, now, this line of inquiry, let us see what was the effect of these important changes upon the movements of the precious metals in the adjustment of the balances of international commerce, for which we are now told the supply of gold has become inadequate. For this purpose we will compare the "movement" of the merchandise commerce, *i.e.*, the gross imports and exports, of Great Britain, France, the United States, and British India—aggregating over 40 per cent of the commerce of the world—for the quinquennial periods of 1860 to 1864 and 1886 to 1890, the one just preceding, and the other closing with, the period of falling prices and industrial depression. We will state also, for the corresponding periods, the movement of treasure and its percentage of the merchandise moved, as well as the world's product of gold and silver. It is deserving of notice that during the first period the movement of silver was 40 per cent of the whole, while in the latter it was 45 per cent; showing, that notwithstanding its alleged demonetization as a currency, it still continued to perform its functions as a commodity in commerce, which has always been its chief use. And it would doubtless have been still greater but for the large amount of overvalued coin held by this country and France, which is excluded from international commerce in consequence of the heavy "seigniorage" with which it is charged:

Period.	Movement of merchandise.	Movement of specie.	Per cent. of specie moved to merchandise moved.	Product of gold and silver.
1860–64	$18,568,736,213	$3,143,656,271	17	$792,350,000
1886–90	36,204,527,385	2,717,334,783	7¼	1,284,291,000
Difference	$17,635,791,172	$426,321,488	9¼	491,941,000

37

The increase of merchandise moved was 95 per cent; the decrease of specie moved was 13 per cent; the decrease of the percentage of specie to merchandise was $9\frac{1}{2}$ per cent; and the increase of the production of gold and silver was 62 per cent.

To show, now, what has been the economizing effect of the improved mechanism of international exchanges and the increased efficiency of the metals in effecting them, we have but to make a very simple calculation. If the merchandise moved during the latter period—1886–1890—had required the same amount of specie for the settlement of its balances as in the first period—1860–1864—(17 per cent) then the commerce of these four countries alone would have required about $6,155,000,000 for that purpose—an amount equal to *the entire product of the world for the thirty-one years from 1860 to 1890.* But they actually employed only $2,717,000,000, or $3,438,000,000 less. This is equivalent to an increased efficiency of 126 per cent in the amount of specie employed.

But let us reverse the calculation. At 17 per cent, the $2,717,-000,000 of specie actually employed in the latter period, would have moved something *less* than $16,000,000,000 of merchandise; whereas, it actually did move over $36,200,000,000, or $20,200,000,000 *more.* As compared with the first period, this amount of merchandise was, therefore, apparently moved *without the employment of a dollar of specie.* Or, in other words, to that extent, the metals only served the purpose of " standards" of value for rating the exchanges which were " settled" by cross bills and arbitrages, and not by the payment of specie, or the direct employment of gold. It will be observed that this excess of merchandise moved is, also, equivalent to an increase of 126 per cent, and, of itself, is nearly $2,000,000,000 *greater than the entire commerce* of the countries designated, during the first period. We thus have, then, for the period covered by these movements, an actual increase of 62 per cent in the joint product of the metals, and 126 per cent in increased effectiveness, or 188 per cent in both volume and effectiveness; as against 95 per cent increase of commerce, and less than 40 per cent increase of population.

But the countries designated are much above the average of the commercial world in the movement of the metals relatively to commerce, as their exchanges were largely for account of other nations. While for these other nations we cannot now ascertain these movements for the first period, there is no difficulty in doing so for the second. We have, therefore, selected eleven of the more important of these countries, which, during the latter period, moved about the same amount of merchandise as the four countries first designated. We find that it aggregated something over $36,100,000,000 in merchandise, but less than $940,000,000 in specie, or $2\frac{6}{10}$ per cent, instead of $7\frac{1}{2}$ as in the case of the first group, during the latter period. For the remaining countries the movement was doubtless still less. We may, therefore, safely assume that for the fifteen countries designated, representing fully 90 per cent of the commerce of the world, the average movement of specie during the latter period did not exceed 5 per cent of the merchandise. Of this, about 60 per cent was gold and 40 per cent silver, which would give us about 3 per cent for the former, as compared with the movement of merchandise commerce.

But if we take into account the vast volume of international exchanges heretofore indicated, as arising from operations other than those pertaining to the movement of merchandise, it will be readily perceived that gold does not directly effect 2 per cent of the international exchanges of the world, and, to the extent of 98 per cent, serves only the purposes of a "standard of value" by which they are rated. Its functions, therefore, in such cases are only those of "numeration and arithmetic," which was the Scythian philosopher's idea of money among the Greeks, as quoted by Hume. Its employment, therefore, for such a purpose, produces no more effect upon the exchangeable value of the metal as a commodity, and exerts no more influence upon prices, than the fluctuations in value of dry-goods would have upon the length of a yard-stick, or the speed of a train of cars would have upon the length of a mile. It simply performs the functions of a numeral in estimating value, and not as a material recompense or exchangeable equivalent, as when employed as a "measure" of value. For as such, it can be as readily made to express a thousand millions as a single unit, and, as heretofore explained, would as effectively perform that function if it were only a theoretical unit by weight, as in the form of coined money which in such cases is only regarded as a commodity.

When, therefore, writers upon the science of money undertake to establish mathematical relations between the volume of circulation and general price-levels within given periods of time, they strangely overlook or disregard the obvious considerations which arise from the fact that the exchanges effected by metallic money, considered simply as a "standard" of value, vastly exceed those effected by it as a "measure" of value in which it becomes the exchangeable equivalent of the things it measures. They apparently fall into the error of reasoning upon the hypothesis that all the exchanges effected are cash transactions, and thus ignore that vast volume of operations that are effected by mere credits, and are ultimately liquidated by the " unearned increments" of trade when realized at a future day. This fundamental law, as they are pleased to call it, also eliminates from the calculation all those factors which arise from the numberless vicissitudes and contingencies which beset industry and its products, but in no wise affect the stability of money. It is, therefore, nothing but a postulated fallacy, for which no verification can be found in commercial history. The examples relied upon prove, upon investigation, to be mere coincidences and can be clearly traced to other causes. It is equally at variance with the fact that while metallic money possesses an unlimited self-repeating power in effecting exchanges, both as a " standard" and a " measure" of value, commodities soon reach the ultimate consumer, and disappear from the market. Its effectiveness, therefore, depends much more largely upon the density of population, the subdivisions of labor and the diversity of its products, the activity of trade and the facilities of rapid transit, than upon its volume. When these obvious and important considerations are taken into account, it will not be difficult to detect the fallacy that underlies the specious formulation of this moss-covered paralogism of " economic science," incrusted though it be with " high authority." So palpable is this fallacy that it would be altogether undeserving of notice, did it not constitute the basis upon which bimetallists have founded all their wild theories as to the origin of existing industrial depression, and the remedies they propose for it.

But there is much additional evidence to be found, indicating the great abundance of money and other signs of value that performed, in part, its functions during this period of falling values, that is wholly incompatible with the idea of an appreciation or rise in value of gold. Prominent as such may be instanced the universal decline in the rates of interest in all the financial centres of the world, as indicated by the rise in value of funded securities. In this connection we may quote the sagacious observations of Hume in his chapter on " Interest":

"If we consider the whole connection of causes and effects, interest is the barometer of the State, and its lowness is a sign almost infallible of the flourishing condition of a people. . . . Those who have asserted that the plenty of money was the cause of low interest, seem to have taken a collateral effect for a cause; since the same industry which sinks the interest commonly acquires great abundance of the precious metals. . . . But though both of these effects, plenty of money and low interest, naturally arise from commerce and industry, they are altogether independent of each other."

In whatever aspect, then, we view the subject—whether from the physical properties of the metal and its comparative immunity from change either economic or physical, whether upon the line of the industrial phenomena resulting from its produce and distribution, or as a controlling instrumentality of international commerce—we fail, alike, to discover anything in the economic conditions prevailing during this period of falling values tending in the slightest degree to an enhancement of the value of gold. We are thus, again, brought squarely to the question, Has gold appreciated or risen in value? or, Is the apparent phenomenon of its increased purchasing power the mere assumption of an effect for a cause, or the substitution of a mere theory for a material fact? It is assumed that prices depend upon the volume of money in circulation as compared with the exchanges to be effected by it. Prices, we are told, have fallen—*ergo*, the volume of money has been "contracted." Silver is money, silver has been demonetized—*ergo*, demonetization is the cause of "contraction" and of the fall in prices. Such seems to be the logic, the Alpha and the Omega, the Genesis and Apocalypse of the inspired economic wisdom and revelation of economic truth upon which it is proposed to found the most far-reaching and radical changes in our monetary policy.

There is an important technical difference between a "standard' and a "measure" of value which, though independent in the nature of their functions, become often united in the operations of exchange. As heretofore explained, gold, considered as a "standard," is not necessarily a coin, and is to be regarded only as an immutable unit of magnitude that does not express any "relation" of value to other commodities, but with reference to which all other things either rise or fall in value in accordance with the economic conditions affecting the question of "supply and demand." There is a wise maxim of the Roman law that has come down to us from the "Institutes," that fully recognizes this essential principle, and which declares that "things are estimated by their value in money; but money is not estimated by its value in things" (*Res per pecuniam æstimantur, et non pecunia per res*). The obvious justness of this maxim will be at once accepted by all who recognize the technical nature of a standard of value as it relates to the terminology of monetary science, as well as to those exact methods of reasoning which are essential to intelligent action in our daily transactions.

All idea of fixity or immutability in a standard of value must be abandoned if we are to go back to the primitive methods of barter, and gold coins, as standards of value, are to be regarded *only* as exchangeable commodities whose "value" is to be determined by the "relations of value" that subsist between them and other commodities with which they may be compared or for which they may become exchangeable.   In that event, instead of having one fixed and unalterable standard, we should have a hundred or more different standards, all varying from day to day, and all depending upon different economic conditions, which, for the time being, would be wholly unknown but which would give us a hundred or more different values of money at one and the same time, and yet no one would be able to determine what its true value was until he had gone through an elaborate and impossible process of ascertaining the so-called "general average" of the aggregate "relations of value" subsisting between money and the various commodities which had participated in the transactions of trade at any given time.   The moment we lose sight of the essential principle of absolute *fixity* in a standard of value, with reference to which all other things only rise or fall, and assume that such a standard is the thing which rises or falls in value in accordance with the constant variations of commodities, which are subject to an infinite number of contingencies,—we enter a realm of limitless speculation wholly incompatible with any logical analysis of economic phenomena.   And it must be seen that the whole of this theory of the appreciation of gold is thus made to rest entirely upon a process of reasoning which wholly disregards the innumerable contingencies to which the products of industry are subject, and which, to a greater or less extent, affect prices favorably or otherwise.

Whether gold has risen in value or not, possesses but little significance as an abstract question, and is important only in so far as it relates to the assumption that it has resulted from "contraction" of the currency produced by demonetization of silver, and becomes the basis of a dangerous change of policy founded upon that conclusion. All true theories of economic science are formulated upon a concretion of observed facts as developed by industrial and commercial phenomena, while this assumption eliminates from the diagnosis of existing maladies all those economic, physical, and social factors which so largely control the phenomena observed.

In attempting, therefore, to discover the true cause of the general fall in prices, or of the industrial and commercial depression resulting therefrom, it is important to consider those portentous changes that have occurred in the economic conditions of the past quarter of a century affecting, for better or for worse, all the activities of human industry.   Among these we may enumerate, as specially applying to this country, the enormous increase of productive energy, by reason of the abnormal increase of population which, by immigration alone, exceeds that of thirteen such States as the State of Maine—an empire within itself.   Within the same period there have been issued over 430,000 patents for new inventions and labor-saving devices, immensely stimulating, while reducing the cost of, production.   To these agencies may be added an abnormal increase in the facilities of rapid-transit, exceeding 440 per cent, since 1860, greatly cheapening the cost of transportation, while stimulating competition among home producers by making all the industrial and commercial centres accessible to all sections of the country, and, to that extent, reducing prices.   Within the forty years from 1850 to 1890, while population in this country increased but 170 per cent, foreign imports increased 346 per cent, domestic manufactures 820 per cent, wheat 366 per cent, all cereal crops 305 per cent, raw cotton 267 per cent, horses 278 per cent, horned cattle (not including milch cows) 221 per cent; thus showing a mean average increase of more than 200 per cent in excess of the increase of population.

If, then, the law of " supply and demand" possesses any potency or influence in determining general price-levels, here would seem to be a partial solution, at least, of the phenomenon of falling prices, wholly independent of any question pertaining to the supply of money or its relations to the volume of commodities dealt in.

But, apart from these obvious considerations, every so-called table of prices, compiled for the purpose of indicating the general rise or fall of the same within given periods of time, is radically defective and misleading in so far as it substitutes for a true average a mere numerical mean of a given number of incommensurate units of quantity, and respective prices, varying from a few cents to hundreds of dollars per unit, the true average of which is not infrequently the very reverse of the result shown.   For it is scarcely necessary to state that any general average of prices that does not determine the relative proportion of each commodity to the aggregated volume of all the commodities embraced, and which it is impossible to ascertain from ordinary market quotations, must be fatally defective, and can, at best, indicate only the general *course* of prices downward or upward as the case may be. And this is proved by the fact that all such tabulations present precisely the same phenomena.

They all show that while some commodities have risen, others have fallen. And they show, as often as otherwise, that those that have risen were produced, wholly or in part, as raw products, from those that had fallen, and *vice versa*—thus clearly proving that the fluctuations are not the result of any *uniform* law—such as contraction of the currency, as alleged,—but arise from complex industrial, social, and physical conditions operating with greater or less energy upon the several industries represented.

To determine, therefore, whether the increased purchasing-power of gold has resulted from a change in economic conditions affecting the metal itself, or its relations to industry and commerce, or, upon the contrary, is due to the numberless and complex conditions which affect only the products of industry, it is not sufficient to compare it merely with the price levels of *perishable* commodities which are affected by such a vast number of contingencies and conditions that are purely fortuitous in nature; but it should be compared with the more permanent forms of property that constitute material wealth, and which, by nature, are comparatively exempt from the casualties to which perishable commodities are subject, and which, therefore, possess to a greater or less extent those elements of stability which have always characterized gold itself.

It was suggested by some of the earlier writers upon political economy that human labor would furnish the best basis for a standard of value. And while it was shown that such a " standard" would be subject to many insuperable objections, it is undoubtedly true that both " capitalized" and " wage" labor, that enter so largely into the value of all the products of human industry, furnish a much more stable standard of comparison than many of the perishable commodities that are employed for that purpose.

If, then, we compare the value of gold, as measured by its purchasing power, with the prices of leading funded securities founded upon material wealth and national credit—with farming-lands, towns and city property—or with the wages of labor as paid in leading industries, and which, in this country alone, largely exceed *annually* all the metallic money of the world, we shall find that so far from gold having " appreciated" or risen in value during the period of

" falling prices" designated, it has *perceptibly depreciated and shows a marked loss of purchasing-power.* This will be clearly indicated by the following statement of the value of farming-land and live stock and the wages of factory-hands as shown by the census returns for the past forty years:[1]

	FARM LANDS.		LIVE STOCK.	
	Gross value.	Value per acre.	Gross value.	Value per head.
1850.....	$3,272,000,000	$11.14	$544,000,000	$7.28
1860.....	6,645,000,000	16.27	1,089,000,000	12.24
1880.....	10,197,000,000	19.02	1,577,000,000	13.03
1890.....	13,279,000,000	21.31	2,419,000,000	14.63

There is no way of determining the increased value of town and city property, but it is within the knowledge of every intelligent person that it has been relatively much greater than that of farming-lands.

ANNUAL WAGES PAID IN THE FACTORIES OF THE UNITED STATES.

	No. of employees.	Total wages paid.	Average per capita.
1850...............	957,059	$236,755,464	$247
1860...............	1,311,246	378,878,966	288
1880...............	2,732,595	947,953,795	346
1890...............	4,711,832	2,282,823,265	484

While we cannot ascertain definitely the increase of wages in other industries, it is known to be very considerable. We find, for example, that in 1880, 286,593 teachers in public schools received an average salary of $195 per annum, while in 1890, 363,922 teachers received an average of $251—equivalent to an increase of nearly 30 per cent. Railroad traffic also furnishes further proofs of the general rise in wages. The census year of 1889, as compared with that of 1879, shows that the " operating expenses" of the rail system of the United States rose from something less than 58 per cent of gross earnings, to over 66 per cent; and they increased nearly 24 per cent in excess of the increase of earnings. And while this increase in percentage is, to some extent, due to the reduction in rates of transportation, operating expenses consist so largely of labor that it is evident that a marked increase of wages in this important branch of traffic must have taken place.

[1] We omit the census of 1870 for the reason that, apart from its being one of the most defective ever taken—bearing internal evidence of glaring inaccuracies—all values are given *in currency,* which was then at a considerable discount. And as the premium on gold fluctuated daily, while prices were not changed more than two or three times a year, any attempt to reduce census values to a gold basis would be grossly misleading. The increased valuations of 1880, therefore, represent the increase of two decades.

If, in addition to these evidences of the loss of purchasing power of gold, we consider the increased value of funded securities, as measured by the rates of interest on market prices, representing, as they do, such vast investments of capital,—it is difficult to see how the conclusion is to be evaded, that the value of gold, *as compared with all the more stable and permanent forms of material wealth, has perceptibly depreciated.* And, as we indicated at the outset, the explanation of the phenomenon of a fall in prices must be sought among those complex economic conditions which arise from the physical or social forces to which industry and commerce are subject, *wholly independent of their relations to existing monetary conditions.*

Conceding this, it necessarily follows that the whole fabric of economic fallacies that has been reared upon the basis of this synthetic theory of industrial depression vanishes into thin air, and the imposing array of unassimilated facts and unconnected theories by which the attempt has been made to sustain it becomes a mass of mere postulated vagaries, born of empiricism and nurtured by popular delusion.

LOUIS A. GARNETT.

SAN FRANCISCO, CALIFORNIA.

THE PAY AND RANK OF JOURNALISTS.

JOURNALISM in the United States had its beginning in 1690, when an adventurous citizen of Boston printed the country's first newspaper, and was promptly forbidden by the colonial authorities to issue a second number. As late as 1775, the number of papers in the country was only thirty-nine,—all weekly but one, which was semiweekly. The Revolution was fought and independence gained without a single daily newspaper. There were journalists at that time merely in a groping and premonitory sense.

It is easy to understand that papers were not multiplied in those days because they were profitable. As a rule, they hardly paid expenses, and had in their outlook no logic of continuance. The field was restricted, the conditions precarious, and competition close and disheartening. When an editor was made a postmaster, as sometimes graciously happened, it was chiefly gratifying to him on account of the opportunity that it furnished to improve his newspaper and to take patronage away from a rival one. Most of the papers were chronically in debt. The proprietors, who were also the editors, resorted to all kinds of devices for driving the wolf from the door. Franklin proposed to marry a young lady, whose parents had permitted his attentions, if they would furnish him five hundred dollars to pay off a mortgage on his office; but they refused, saying that the business was a poor one, that the types would soon wear out and new ones would be wanted, and that his failure was only a question of time. However, the newspapers kept on increasing in spite of all drawbacks and vicissitudes until in 1830 they numbered a thousand.

When De Tocqueville visited the country in 1831, he noted the fact that almost every hamlet had its newspaper, which he accounted for mainly by the influence of the liberty of the press, and the absence of licenses, securities, and stamp duties. "The facility with which newspapers can be established," he said, "produces a multitude of them"; but he went on to point out that the competition prevented any considerable profit, and thus deterred "persons of much capacity" from engaging in such undertakings. Even if they had been a source

of wealth, he suggested, writers of ability could not have been found
to conduct them all. "The journalists of the United States," he declared, "are generally in very humble position, with a scanty education and a vulgar turn of mind." He had no indulgence for their
"open and coarse appeals to the passions of their readers," their
neglect òf principles in order to assail the characters of individuals,
which he pronounced to be "a deplorable abuse of the powers of
thought." It seems strange that with his fine sagacity he did not
discover the extenuating circumstances in the case. The American
press had then barely passed the elementary period. It was still
comparatively tentative, and more or less at the mercy of its own un-
disciplined energies. There was as yet really no profession of journalism; there were no journalists in the true meaning of the term.
The papers were principally devoted to political controversy, and
most of them were directed by men who regarded them exclusively
as means to ends in that relation.

In the memorable political campaign of 1840 there were 1,400
papers to stimulate public interest and advocate the claims of the
contending parties. The staff of the larger daily had been increased
from an editor who wrote the leaders, corrected the communications
and read the proofs, with an assistant who did the local work, to two
editors and two reporters, whose compensation was about the same in
an average sense as that received by the stage-drivers of the period.
Most of the smaller dailies and a majority of the weeklies lived in a
hand-to-mouth fashion, and salaries were contingent upon receipts
adapted to a low tone of expectation. Horace Greeley concluded, as
the result of experience in this campaign, "that the right sort of a
cheap Whig journal would be able to live," and so he started one,
printing 5,000 copies of it and "nearly succeeding in giving away all
of them that would not sell." The idea proved to be contagious.
There was a gradual cheapening of rates; and a corresponding increase
of patrons ensued.

Then came the telegraph and the railroad to accelerate newspaper
progress, and put the business upon a substantial basis. The principal dailies had four editors and five reporters each. There was one
salary of $2,500 per year to attest the commercial reputability of
journalism and to fire the ambition of the profession—for it had now
become a profession to the extent that it represented chances of steady
employment, and required certain technical qualifications for the performance of its duties. But the papers with receipts larger than

their expenditures were yet exceptional. Where there was one in that happy state, there were twenty that hovered on the verge of bankruptcy and could be kept going only by peculiar fertility in financial expedients. Generally speaking, there was a suggestion of indigence associated with the press. The editor was looked upon in a degree as a pensioner, and a man to be pitied, and it too often happened that he was obliged to justify the estimate by humiliating appeals for assistance that a better appreciation of his services would have obviated. It is a wonder that so many of those thus situated bravely and patiently endured the stress when they could have escaped from it by consenting to be something else than journalists.

During the decade from 1850 to 1860, the number of American publications was doubled, reaching an aggregate of 4,051, including 387 dailies and 3,173 weeklies. The organization of the New York Associated Press invested news-gathering with increased importance, and signalized the feature of journalism that was eventually to make all others subordinate. More men were required year after year as writers for the papers, and they were mostly recruited from the ranks of the printers. The rates of pay advanced, in the cities, to a level with those prevailing for the better grades of mechanics; but in the towns and villages, the remuneration still remained ironically small, journalists being hired by the month, like farm-hands, and their wages, with board and washing, running from $12 to $20, part or all of which was paid in orders on the stores. Newspaper profits in those days were derived principally from subscriptions and job-printing, with the publication of the delinquent tax-list as an annual bonanza. When merchants advertised, they did it in a spirit of benevolence, as a service of charity, with the same feeling that they made donations to the cross-bearers of clerical poverty. The editor was paid grudgingly, and considered worthy of support in the proportion of his ability to be combative and vituperative, according to the prolixity of his utterances, and the measure of his facility in "goads, thorns, nettles, tails of wasps." He was expected to be continually quarrelling with other editors, and never to permit himself to be outdone in personal derision and calumniation; and as often as he fell short in this respect the dread penalty "stop my paper" began to shrivel his income.

The Civil War was the surpassing impetus of our journalism, the influence that revealed its latent possibilities and put it in the way of realizing its true potentialities. There was a great popular thirst for information about a contest that vitally concerned every family in the land. For each soldier that enlisted, the papers gained a new sub- scriber, and the aggregate increase of patronage gave them means to materially enlarge their operations, to augment their public useful- ness, and to pay better prices for the work done upon them. The collection, adjustment, and dissemination of news that had never been excelled in interest and importance, and the discussion of events and issues that absorbed the attention of all classes, afforded them the opportunity to make themselves not only desirable but indispensable —not only popular but profitable. They discharged their debts, and attained the felicity of a regular balance to their credit in the bank. The people bought papers as they bought bread and other necessaries of life; the value of advertising as a business investment was discov- ered; and journalists were accorded a place with teachers, lawyers, and physicians in the assessment of the standing of the different pursuits. After the war closed, the advantages thus secured were retained and extended. In 1870, the publications of all kinds numbered 5,871, of which 574 were dailies and 4,295 were weeklies. The next ten years swelled the total product to 11,314, and of these 971 were dailies and 8,633 were weeklies, showing an increase of 584 of the former and 5,460 of the latter in twenty years, or more than the whole number of both that had existed ten years before.

There are now in the United States, according to the latest statis- tics, in round numbers, 20,000 publications, issued at varying inter- vals from daily to quarterly, of which 1,855 are dailies and 14,077 are weeklies. These publications are reported in the census of 1890 as representing an aggregate capital of $126,269,885, employing an average of 106,095 persons, paying wages to the amount of $68,- 601,532 per year, using materials that cost $38,955,322, and turning out a product valued at $179,859,750. This exhibit is to be re- garded, it is proper to say, with considerable allowance for lack of full returns when the census was taken, as well as for increased busi- ness since that time; but it is approximately trustworthy and fur- nishes a fair general view of the financial resources and transactions' of the American press. It is impossible to separate the wages account in such a way as to show what sums are respectively expended in the business, editorial, and mechanical departments; it can only be said that they grow larger in the order named, and are regulated by differ- ent theories and conditions in different localities. For similar reasons an exact statement of the pay of journalists, the established profits of the profession as such, cannot be made.   The matter has not yet been reduced to a basis of uniformity.   Hardly any two papers have their staffs arranged alike, and no two papers, even in the same place, pay the same prices for given kinds of service.

To begin with Boston, where our journalism had its origin over two hundred years ago, the salaries of editors-in-chief and managing editors, the two positions being combined in some cases, range from $2,500 to $6,000.   Several of the men thus employed are part-owners of the papers, as is true with respect to a large proportion of the dailies throughout the country.   Editorial writers are paid from $35 to $50 per week, with an average of about $40.   City editors get from $25 to $50 per week, with an average of $40.   Literary and other critics are paid from $25 to $35 per week.   Copy-readers average $5 per day.   Some reporters do not receive over $10 per week, while others command as much as $35: the average is from $18 to $20.   Space-writers, who do special work and are paid by the column, sometimes make $100 a week, but more frequently not half of that sum, and their average may be put at from $35 to $40, according to their fortune in finding acceptable material.   The salary-lists in Philadelphia are about the same as those in Boston, with a few exceptional cases where personal considerations make a difference in favor of certain editors or writers.   A corresponding average, less ten to fifteen per cent, prevails in Baltimore and Washington; and in the smaller cities of New England, New York, Pennsylvania and New Jersey, journalists as a class, excluding amateurs and makeshifts, earn from $600 to $2,000 per year.

In New York City, the salaries are higher than anywhere else, partly because of the superior standard of proficiency, and partly because the cost of living is greater there than in any other large city. One editor-in-chief has the same salary as the President of the United States, $50,000 per year, and others receive from $10,000 to $12,000, or more than members of the Cabinet.   Managing editors are paid from $100 to $150 per week, or a better compensation than that of Senators and Representatives in Congress.   Editorial writers get from $50 to $75 per week as a rule, and in cases of rare ability as much as the average salary of a managing editor.   City editors receive from $50 to $75 per week, and in a few instances $100.   The pay of news editors is about equal to that of city editors.   Literary, theatrical, and musical critics average $50 per week.   Copy-readers are paid from $40 to $45 per week.   Reporters earn all the way from $15 to $60 per week, with an average of $40, and space-writers of particular talent have been known to make as much as $125 per week; though the limitation of topics and the pressure of competition usually keep their incomes down around those of the best-paid reporters.   There are some writers for syndicates of newspapers, men with names that have a certain value, who earn from $5,000 to $6,000 per year; and there are others of first-class technical capacity in various lines whose salaries occasionally reach $5,000.   The pay of all classes of journalists averages 10 per cent lower in Brooklyn than in New York City.

The salaries of managing editors in Chicago range from $2,500 to $7,000 per year, the average being about $4,000.   Editorial writers are paid from $40 to $75 per week.   Night editors get from $35 to $60 and in one case $75; copy-readers from $30 to $40.   City editors are paid $40 to $60, with assistants at $30 to $40.   Financial and commercial editors receive from $35 to $50; and dramatic and literary editors, who usually give a portion of their time to other work, about the same.   The pay of reporters is from $15 to $35 per week, with an average of $25.   One managing editor in St. Louis gets a salary of $150 per week, the largest in the country outside of New York City, and the others get from $40 to $60; editorial writers receive from $30 to $50, with one or two instances of higher figures; city editors, $35 to $40; news editors and copy-readers, $25 to $35; reporters, $12 to $35, with an average of $20.   The general range in Cincinnati is 20 per cent lower than in St. Louis.   In the smaller cities, where the divisions of service are not so definitely marked, the salaries run, with occasional exceptions, from $10 to $40 per week in the West, $10 to $30 in the South, and $15 to $50 on the Pacific Coast.   Most of the managing editors of the dailies in these cities depend upon the profits of the business for their income.

Taking as a basis of computation the scattered data thus presented as to the pay of journalists employed on daily papers, and taking proper account of special deviations, the averages for cities of over 400,000 inhabitants, in which the journalism of the country is best organized and most significantly representative, the averages may be stated as follows: managing editors, $5,000 per year, equal to the average salary of bishops of the various churches, and only $500 less than that of brigadier-generals of the army; editorial writers, $3,500, equal to the salary of an assistant Secretary of State at Washington, and more than the average salary of college presidents; city editors, $2,500, only a little less than the salary of a secretary of legation at one of the leading courts; news editors, copy-readers, and space-writers, $1,800, matching the pay of a captain in the army or a junior lieutenant in the navy; and reporters, $1,200, as much as the average income of the majority of those engaged in any commercial pursuit. For cities of over 200,000 and less than 400,000 inhabitants, these averages need to be lowered from 10 to 15 per cent, and for cities of less than 200,000 about 25 per cent. The average pay of journalists of all kinds on all of the dailies is to be put at $1,500. That is to say, a competent man can always earn that much, with chances of more in proportion to the degree of his ability and his ambition. The big prizes are comparatively few, as in all professions, but there are subordinate ones that are well worth striving for, and that are to be had as fast as they are earned by meritorious service.

The remuneration in daily journalism would probably be higher, at least in some departments, but for the fact that it is to a considerable extent the refuge of the mediocrity that is continually failing to make a living in the other professions. There is a certain amount of hack-work to be done on every newspaper, which calls only for the kind of talent that knows how to put simple words together as a child constructs them with alphabetical blocks, and this is eagerly seized at pot-boiling prices by clientless lawyers, patientless doctors, and parishless clergymen. These impecunious intruders seldom or never get beyond the desk of the reporter. They are in the profession, or the vestibule of it, not because they like it, or are adapted to it, but merely because it means daily bread to them. Another depressing influence in this respect is the fact that many of those who think nature intended them for journalists are mistaken, and yet they do not find it out, but continue to work for small wages wherever their limitations will permit, thereby helping to make cheapness a fixed factor in the problem of general averages. Then there are young men who would become good journalists if they had patience and perseverance, but who accept other forms of employment with the hope of improving their condition, and thus add to the considerations which unfavorably affect the adjustment of salaries, and the orderly development of values in that relation.

That branch of journalism which pertains to paid correspondents deserves separate notice. The voluntary correspondents came in at an early date, and have been sufficiently numerous ever since. A famous editor complained over a hundred and fifty years ago that the liberty of the press was construed by his subscribers as implying " that

38

a newspaper was like a stage-coach, in which any one who would pay had a right to a place," and this view still prevails to some extent. Every community has its spontaneous benefactors who enjoy serving it by writing communications to the papers on all kinds of subjects, not omitting the personal delinquencies of their neighbors. But such matter is now mostly consigned to the ravenous waste-basket at the editor's elbow. The correspondence that is available is that which regularly employed men supply, principally by telegraph, from different points. Those stationed at leading news-centres receive salaries of from $40 to $75 per week; the others are paid according to what they furnish, at the rate of from $5 to $6 per column. One of the St. Louis papers has the largest staff of correspondents in the country —1,500—and their earnings aggregate $60,000 per year. A great many journalists find in this sort of work the opportunity to increase their income, since preference is usually given, for obvious reasons, to men holding positions on other papers.

It is by these correspondents that the news-gathering is mainly done, which is to say that upon their alertness, discretion, and fidelity largely depends the success of the press in its most important function. The old theory that it was the chief province of the newspaper to publish political essays, and help politicians to get offices, has been exploded, and in the place of it we have the demonstrated fact that it is the essential business of a newspaper to tell daily and as accurately as possible the many-featured story of current events, with such comments as shall serve to instruct and entertain. It must pursue a ceaseless and vigilant quest for late things, novel things, interesting things; it must ransack the universe for the unexpected that is always happening somewhere. The spirit of public curiosity and anticipation is imperative and insatiable and will have what it craves. Much that is trivial creeps into the news columns, unquestionably, and that may be lamentable, but it is not the fault of the newspapers. They tell what there is to be told, not what there should be to tell. The poet Whittier, who was also an editor, was fond of relating that an old Quaker once said to him, " Greenleaf, we must accept things; we must even accept ourselves. " That is the philosophy of the newspapers, modified by reasonable discrimination; and in carrying it out, the correspondents perform the principal service.

The 14,077 weekly papers in the United States include about 4,000 that are devoted to special interests—agricultural, financial, commercial, mechanical, scientific, literary, and religious—some of which pay salaries of from $20 to $50 per week, and, in a few cases, where superior technical ability is required, $60 to $75. The others, not counting weekly editions of the dailies, are known as "country papers," and are mostly published in towns of less than 3,000 inhabitants. In cases where they employ writers, which are exceptional, they pay from $10 to $15 per week. Generally, they are owned by two partners, one of whom does all the writing and the other manages the business. The majority of these papers are good properties, with receipts averaging from $4,000 to $6,000, and profits of from $2,000 to $3,000, per year. They are obliged to render much gratuitous service, but they are duly respected and commended for it. The country editor, like his city brother, is no longer snubbed and left to the casual Samaritans. He is courted now, and feared, and he gets his pay as other folks do, and can support a family and live in his own house; and, when he dies, they bury him with flowers and music and grateful talk about what he has done for the town.

It is in this branch of the profession that the best practical experience is gained. The country printing-office is really our only school of journalism, and its graduates are found everywhere, and hold responsible positions on all the metropolitan papers. There is no other place where preparatory general training for the duties of the profession can be obtained, where a young man can learn to be an all-round journalist. In the large city offices, the division of labor, and particularly the assignment system as to reporters, tends to place men in grooves and keep them there, making them proficient in only one of various essentials, chilling their enthusiasm, and delaying and preventing their promotion. Such hindrances are unavoidable, perhaps, in the organization of newspaper forces for the accomplishment of the best results, but they are to be regretted, nevertheless, because they specialize talent that should be generalized, and detract from the advantage of thoroughness which in all professions, as well as trades, has so much to do with the matter of employment and earnings. In the country offices, on the other hand, a man plays all the parts in turn, and is drilled for every kind of work. He is not thereby made a finished journalist, competent to fill any position, but he gets a grasp of the profession as a whole, and can more readily adapt himself to its diverse requirements than one who lacks this discipline.

A comparison of the pay of journalists with the pay of the members of other professions in different parts of the country and collectively shows that journalism pays better than is commonly supposed. There are not so many journalists as there are lawyers and physicians with incomes of $10,000 and more per year; but there is a larger proportion of journalists than of either lawyers or physicians, with incomes ranging from $2,000 to $3,000 per year. Only a small percentage of journalists work for salaries as low as $500 per year; but there are thousands of ministers who have to be content with that meagre stipend. The average pay of teachers is only $800 per year, or little more than half as much as that of journalists employed on daily newspapers. It follows that the young man who enters journalism with an aptitude for its duties, and a disposition to compass success by deserving it, is more likely to make money and save something for a rainy day than one who selects law, medicine, theology, or teaching. He cannot hope to accumulate wealth, but he can count upon earning at all times a comfortable living, with a margin to spare for luxuries. His tasks are sure to be arduous, confining, and harassing, but fascinating in their way at the same time; and there is to be added as a point of no little importance the satisfaction of belonging to a profession that bears close and potent relations to all the interests of life, to the happiness of mankind, and the destinies of nations.

HENRY KING.

THE LABOR CHURCH: RELIGION OF THE LABOR MOVEMENT.

I AM asked to give a concise account of the origin, history, and future prospects of the Labor Church.

It was the confluence of two lines of thought that led to its birth —the first religious, the second social. Compelled to abandon the evangelical Christianity in which I was brought up, the one purpose of my life became the development of a conception of religion which should be at once rational and spiritual, and which should make God a living reality in both personal and national affairs. After three years spent in Australia, America, and England, in which I struggled to solidify my ideas, and to prepare myself for a Unitarian pulpit, I had to abandon the attempt and return to business life. After three years of business life, I was driven by internal necessity to the comparative seclusion of the edge of a small country town in England. After three years in the country, God had become a reality to me—in nature, in my home, and in my own life. After another three years I found myself the minister of the Upper Brook Street Free Church in Manchester, having previously worked some eighteen months as assistant-minister to Philip Wicksteed, in London.

Although occupying a Unitarian pulpit, and immensely indebted to Unitarian friends and institutions for many privileges, I felt compelled always to avow that I could not take the Unitarian name. Unitarianism is the last word of reason, operating upon a traditional belief. It belongs to that which is passing away before the aggressive energy of the New Life. So much it is necessary to say to make my own position clear; but it is equally necessary to add that all along the line Unitarians have assisted me with a generosity which could probably be found in no other church.

On the first Sunday in June, 1890, my ministry in Manchester commenced. Before the first year was completed, the conception of the Labor Church was formed. In order to explain its formation I must take up the second line of thought.

In the three years of my life as an architect I became profoundly

dissatisfied with competition.   I felt myself and my profession degraded by the conditions under which I had to work.   Ardently
desiring to serve my fellow-men, no amount of sophistry could convince me that my work was any true and helpful service.   Others
could do it as well as I could, and needed it as much to keep them
and their families from want.   If I succeeded in securing a client,
my brother was unhappy and impoverished; if he succeeded, I was
unhappy and impoverished.   The thought that I might be compelled
to spend my life in such ridiculous and inhuman rivalry became intolerable.   The burden of it, combined with the impossibility of
facing the religious problem under such conditions, drove me into the
country.   I could not take up the social problem seriously until the
religious problem had been dealt with.   If life in itself was not good,
no social reform could mend it.   Three years of country life gave
me the beginnings of that reasoned conviction which I needed.   In
London I faced the social problem.   The result was a slow but sure
drift toward Socialism as the next step needed to approximate man's
outward condition to his inward development.   Hence I came to
Manchester a Socialist.

Like some new St. Christopher, I sought to serve God in the person of the strongest; and that strongest I found in the Labor Movement.   Here we have manifested the real vital energy of our time.
Before the fierce activity of this growing force, all the old powers are
bending the knee.   It is a new life which demands a new interpretation; and with it to urge them forward, Religion and Science and
Politics are reaching newer and truer conclusions.   It is the commanding genius of our age, which on all sides compels new canons
of criticism and a fresh set of rules for the Art of Life.

Here, then, it seemed to me, God was occupying his most advanced position for the further unfolding of human destiny; and on
this conception it was that the Labor Church was founded.   Henceforth a church, to have any reality to me, must not merely be one in
which the aspirations of Labor were sympathized with; it must be a
church established in the very heart of the Labor Movement.

The first Labor-Church service was held in the Chorlton Town-
Hall, Manchester, on Sunday afternoon, October 4, 1891.   I spoke
on " The Programme of the Labor Church."   The hall, which seats
600, was nearly full.   The service consisted of a hymn, a reading, a
prayer and an address, in the same order as at any popular service,
but with a difference.   The hymns were distinctly social as well as

religious, some even bordering on the revolutionary.   The reading
was James Russell Lowell's poem, "On the Capture of Certain
Fugitive Slaves near Washington."   The prayer was entirely free
from the usual phraseology.   Indeed, it was applauded!   On the
second Sunday, Robert Blatchford, editor of the "Clarion," gave
the address.   The throngs who came to hear this unique master of
the hearts of the people were so great as to make it impossible to go
successfully through our programme.   On the following Sunday we
adjourned to the People's Concert Hall, with seats for 1,600 people,
and I spoke to a great crowd on "God in the Labor Movement."   On
the next Sunday, Ben Tillett was the speaker, and so we went forward.   Early in November a demand arose for organization.   The
following principles were then drawn up to embody the ideas on which
the movement was founded; and at a special meeting called to consider the basis of our work and membership, they were explained, discussed, and unanimously accepted:

1. That the Labor Movement is a religious movement.
2. That the religion of the Labor Movement is not a class religion, but unites
    members of all classes in working for the abolition of commercial slavery.
3. That the religion of the Labor Movement is not sectarian or dogmatic, but
    free religion, leaving each man free to develop his own relations with the
    Power that brought him into being.
4. That the emancipation of Labor can only be realized so far as men learn both
    the economic and moral laws of God, and heartily endeavor to obey them.
5. That the development of personal character and the improvement of social
    conditions are both essential to man's emancipation from moral and
    social bondage.

In January, 1892, the "Labor Prophet" was started as the organ
of the movement, being published monthly and sold at a penny per
copy.   A Labor-Church hymn-book followed, and more recently a
tune-book has been issued.   Labor-Church tracts have also been
published, and many thousands of handbills explaining our aims and
principles.   In July, 1892, a Labor Church was opened at Bradford,
and others soon followed.   In every case the demand for a church
has been entirely local and spontaneous.   In July, 1893, the
first Conference of Labor-Church delegates was held in Manchester, a
Labor-Church Union was formed, a constitution adopted, and a council appointed to carry forward the work of the movement.   Fred
Brocklehurst, who had formerly assisted me in the work, was appointed general secretary to the Union.   Mr. Brocklehurst had
studied at Cambridge with a view to entering the Church of England,

but immediately upon taking his academic degree he threw himself wholly into the Labor-Church movement.

At the time of this Conference fourteen Labor Churches had been formed, of which ten were represented. Four were too poor to send delegates. The formation of a Union so early in our career was made necessary by the break-down of my health, and the development of questions which could be dealt with satisfactorily only by the churches collectively. After renewed efforts to return to public life, I have been compelled finally to abandon the attempt, and to confine myself almost entirely to writing, and to the development of such work as can be carried on through the medium of the "Labor Prophet." In this work I have the able assistance of Mr. H. C. Rowe, who is corresponding secretary to the Labor-Church Union.

There are now nominally twenty-four Labor Churches in existence, reaching from Dundee in the North to Plymouth in the South, and we hear of several towns in which Labor-Church services are about to be inaugurated. Only in a dozen towns are there fully organized churches with an enrolled membership. In other cases the church is little more than a Sunday meeting of the Labor Party, usually with the prayer omitted. In most towns the Labor Movement is too poor, both in men and money, to maintain two separate organizations. Indeed, in every direction, the financial difficulty is always with us. At the same time, although my own work depends upon outside sympathizers for support, the churches themselves are self-supporting, and the life of most of them is very vigorous. In Manchester, Bradford, Halifax, Leeds, and some other towns, the Labor Church has a vitality to which all things are possible.

In connection with several of the churches adult classes are held, libraries have been formed, and very poor children are fed and entertained in the winter and taken into the country in the summer. The publication of the hymn-book and the tune-book has enabled them to develop very hearty and characteristic singing. Solos, glees and anthems often form part of the service. Social gatherings are frequently held on Saturday evenings in winter. At the present moment we are going forward with the formation of Sunday schools.

The influence of the Labor Church upon individual life and upon the Labor Movement has undoubtedly been very great and very beneficial—far more so than a stranger casually attending a Labor-Church service would conceive to be possible. Shut out as I now am from personal contact with the whole movement, I am apt to become unduly critical of its weaknesses; but I am repeatedly assured by friends, who know what they are talking about, that the church is doing a great work, and that my own estimate of its efficiency is unduly modest.

From the point of view of my own high ideal, the Labor Church is an organized opportunity for the promotion of a real living religion, which we have not yet the speakers to take advantage of. For the most part our speakers are politicians first and foremost. What we are now waiting for is the development of a few prophets, in whose hearts God lives and moves, and on whose lips the Living Fire has been placed. To create a conscious demand for this type of man, and to help toward his development, is now the fixed aim of all my work.

In the Labor Church the basis is being laid for a great religious revival. The very fact of its existence is a perpetual call to a higher life. Meanwhile it has provided a platform and an organization for the development of the Labor Movement at its best, and this opportunity is by no means being wasted. Beyond this I have good reason to know that my own line of work is touching many a heart, and that life and God are being made real to those who had lost their way. It is in these individual souls that the future of the movement lives.

Moreover, the Labor Church has taken root in America, and under circumstances that justify the greatest hopes. Early in the present year, Mr. Herbert N. Casson commenced Labor Church services in Lynn, Mass. He has since been joined by his brother, Mr. Charles W. Casson, who is organizing a church at Providence, R. I. These two young men, the latter of whom visited me recently, are of the true apostolic type. Both have come from the Methodist ministry, and have thrown off their orthodoxy without losing their religious enthusiasm and faith. This latest development justifies the conviction which I had at the first, that if the Labor Church had anything real in it, it would become in time an international church.

The Labor Church, as I conceive it, is an institution which I shall not live to see in its full development, but of its future I have no fear. Though necessarily identifying itself with a passing stage of God's work in the world and of man's activity, beneath its temporary force lies a conception which will apply in varying shape to all times alike, and with an ever-deepening significance as the ages pass. When the Labor Church is no longer needed, because the Labor Movement has fulfilled its mission, the conception underlying it will take on higher forms in the better age which it has helped to bring.

JOHN TREVOR.

TO ANCIENT GREEK THROUGH MODERN? NO!

It is difficult not to sympathize with the feeling of an educated Greek who sees the language of his forefathers laboriously and in-effectually taught by aliens whose pronunciation falls upon his ears as a strange and barbarous dissonance. One readily comprehends, too, the naïf enthusiasm of the elderly traveller whose own Greek is oxidized an inch thick, and who is awe-struck to find children and cabmen familiarly speaking what he innocently fancies is the mys-terious idiom which he failed to master by years of painful drill.

These respectable feelings of the English traveller in Greece and of the Greek traveller in England or America have frequently found expression during the last few years in appeals to the educational public to adopt the modern pronunciation and the teaching of Greek as a living language by natives of Greece. The national susceptibil-ities involved and the genuine enthusiasm for the best things of the mind that pervade these pleas make it an ungrateful task to com-bat them, especially when they are so temperate in spirit and digni-fied in form as the paper on teaching Greek as a living language in the October number of THE FORUM. But the uncontradicted propa-gation of erroneous opinion in matters of education is never safe in a country governed in the last resort by public opinion. If the teachers of Greek remain silent, there is danger that the zeal of some sudden convert among our trustees or college presidents may insist on intro-ducing disorganizing experiments into the already sufficiently confused Greek departments of our schools and colleges. It is fitting, then, that some one who is familiar with both sides of the question should make a plain statement of the facts as to the relation between ancient and modern Greek and the educational value of the latter.

And first let me dispose of an *argumentum ad hominem* with which the discussion of the question is frequently embarrassed. It is claimed that the opposition to the reform is due to the habits and interests of the teachers of Greek who are unacquainted with the modern pronun-ciation and are committed to a mistaken tradition.

But the fact is that a respectable and increasing number of American professors of Greek have studied at Athens and reject the so-called reform, if they do reject it, *en connaissance de cause*. At one time I spoke modern Greek, and am still able to follow a lecture in that language, and my unwillingness to see the modern pronunciation introduced into our class-rooms is due simply to the conviction that it is unscientific and displeasing to the ear, and that the association of the study of classical Greek with the modern form of the language offers no compensating gain for these disadvantages.

The matter of pronunciation is really of comparatively slight moment, though it is always put in the forefront of this debate and cannot therefore be passed over in silence. The philological question need not be examined here. It is admitted that we do not know exactly how Sophocles or Demosthenes pronounced. And there is some room for difference of opinion as to the precise dates at which the vowel-sounds characteristic of the modern pronunciation came in. But there is substantial agreement among philologists that the pronunciation described in the introduction to Professor Goodwin's Greek grammar is far nearer the utterance of the ancients than that heard at Athens to-day. The assertion that this pronunciation is more agreeable to the ear will probably be thought a mere subjective prejudice of habit. I have heard lectures on the Greek tragedians at the University of Athens, and have associated freely with students of philology there. In no single instance did I find a modern Greek student who had any appreciation of the verbal melody of Greek poetry, or who was able to read Pindar and Æschylus metrically. And it can hardly be denied that the monotony of the modern Greek vowel-system would sadly impair, if it did not utterly destroy, the music of the vowelled undersong of fluent Greek. Pronunciation, however, as I have said, is a minor matter. If modern Greek is of really great intrinsic educational value, or a considerable aid in the acquisition of the older language, we should probably consent to suppress our prejudices and to reconcile our ears to the sacrifice of something of the rich vowel harmonies of Homer, Pindar, and Æschylus. The value of modern Greek, then, is the real issue.

The continuity and persistent vitality of the Greek language through a period of twenty-eight recorded centuries is an imposing historical phenomenon, and has called forth eloquent utterances from Gibbon, Mrs. Browning, Professors Jebb, Blackie, and Freeman, and from many others who have been or might be quoted in this controversy. To the mature student of universal history it is an inspiring and significant fact. What a fascination one felt in reading one's first Greek newspaper at Athens and noting that perhaps five-sixths of the words as they stood on the printed page in accent and spelling were possible ancient Greek! But the guardians of higher education are obliged to make distinctions and reservations that would be discourteous in the passing tourist and are perhaps pedantic in the magazine writer. And the essence of the distinctions relevant here is that we do not require our youth to study Greek because it is " a living language spoken all through the Levant, possessing a contemporaneous and daily increasing literature and an ably conducted newspaper press." There is no lack of languages possessing an ably conducted newspaper press and spoken over wide empires, which it is convenient for tourists and commercial gentlemen to know, but which we cannot study in the few brief years allotted to disinterested culture. If we select Greek rather than Russian or Japanese, it is because it is the noblest language that ever lived on the lips of men and the vehicle of the most original, stimulating, and artistically perfect literature of which history holds record.

Now the language and literature of modern Greece, however estimable the place they hold among the minor languages of southeastern Europe, have nothing of this distinctive nobility and beauty, and their study tends only to confuse the student's perception of these supreme qualities in the ancient tongue. The resemblance of modern to ancient Greek has been much exaggerated. It lies wholly on the surface. And the statement that the difference is far less than that between Chaucerian and modern English, while partially true to the letter, is wholly misleading in spirit. Indeed, there are two modern Greek languages: the rude dialect of the people, which is too remote from ancient Greek to be of any service, and the conventional language of the newspaper and public school, which is an artificial restoration, very convenient for practical purposes, but anathema to the philologist and an abomination to the man of delicate literary sense. Plato could not read a paragraph of a modern Athenian newspaper. If the professor of ancient Greek is able to read the modern Greek newspaper at sight, it is because he translates English, German, and French idioms into Greek vocables of the insipid dialect of the post-classical age as he reads. For the delicate and precise mechanism of the ancient syntax is substituted a clumsy, imperfectly developed, analytic structure; the pure native classical idiom is replaced by a grotesque mixture of all the idioms and worn-out newspaper metaphors of Europe; and the meanings of all higher spiritual words are confused by associations with the translator's equivalents in French or German: κόσμος, for example,—shades of Pythagoras! —meaning *peuple*, or company, by contamination with the French *monde*.   To fix the associations of this hybrid jargon in the mind of the young student is to bar access forever to the perfect purity and propriety of the older tongue.

And for what educational end is this injury to be inflicted?   To facilitate the acquisition of a few vocables which with proper training the student can learn easily enough in the class-room.   For this and this only it is that lends plausibility to the contention that Greek should be taught as a living language by natives of Greece.   The claims put forward for modern Greek in its own name are urged only *pro forma*, or are due to an amiable but undiscriminating patriotism. The number of those who really need to speak modern Greek or find occasion to read a modern Greek book is insignificant.   All educated Greeks speak French or English.   But it is felt that practically effec- tive command of Greek is not obtained by the systems of teaching now in vogue, and it is vaguely hoped that, approached by the familiar methods employed in the study of modern languages, the college Fetich would lose some of its terrors.

Professor Blackie is quoted as saying that by these methods more of the language can be learned in five months than is now acquired by the assiduous labor of many years.   Of course, this could be even approximately true only if knowledge of the language was measured solely by fluent command of the few hundred words employed in the simplest conversation.   Absurdly exaggerated as the statement is, however, it contains a challenge that must be answered.   And the answer involves the explanation of some misconceptions that attach to the study of Latin as well as Greek.   Something of the charges must be frankly admitted.   There is much inefficient teaching of this as of other subjects, and much wasteful pre-occupation with abstract grammatical futilities usurping the place of direct study of the con- crete facts of the language.   But in abatement of this we must remem- ber that our students of Latin and Greek are not mature men.   They are boys, learning to use their minds, and their positive achievement is at first necessarily slight in any study that demands more than simple memory.   The more rapid progress that sometimes seems to be effected by the employment of so-called natural methods must be attributed to the longer hours demanded by these methods, or to the limitation of the study to the simpler aspects of the subject, or in some cases to the contagious enthusiasm of the teachers.

There is much exaggeration as well as misconception in the charge that the faithful labor of years fails to give the American student the power of reading ordinary Greek and Latin. The young Greeks themselves, it appears, require six or seven years of training in order to read intelligently authors like Sophocles and Thucydides, and my recollection is that the men at the University of Athens did not interpret Æschylus any better than some college juniors whom I have known. Where the results of eight or nine years of study prove nugatory, it will be generally found on inquiry that the study had not been continuous, or that the student's interest in the substance and thought of the authors read has not been properly aroused. The importance of this last point can hardly be over-estimated. Any bright boy can learn to read ordinary narrative Greek and Latin—fables, Cæsar, or Xenophon—as readily as he learns to read German. If he fails, it is because amid the tempting solicitations of the various studies on the modern side he is not properly stimulated to make the effort. But a large part of classical Greek and Latin literature is not ordinary narrative. It is the loftiest epic, lyric, or drama, the most impassioned and thoughtful oratory, the subtlest philosophy. It is literature of a type that students who prattle very prettily boarding-school French or German, and read light comedies or novelettes, would not think of attempting in French or German, or even in English, for that matter. And the problem of the Greek teacher is first to teach the boy rapidly to read easy prose like Xenophon,—which is, after all, no great trick, if the student can be induced to try; and secondly, to lead him gradually to the intelligent enjoyment of the higher forms of literature with their involved and subtle modes of expression. It is here that the real difficulty and the real educational rewards are found. And to this end natural methods, conversational exercises and modern Greek contribute nothing. They at the best would somewhat shorten the process of gaining familiarity with the commoner words and idioms that occur in the simplest narrative prose.

The advocates of modern Greek, like the advocates of natural methods, begin by loudly proclaiming incontrovertible facts which unfortunately have no relevancy to their particular demands. They rightly insist that in the study of language the ear must be trained as well as the eye, but they are oblivious to the fact that the student's ear may be accustomed to the sound of Greek as well by reading the

Anabasis aloud and hearing his teacher quote Homer, as by chatter-ing guide-book phrases about the weather in modern Greek. They urge that the language should be made of living interest to the student, but they fail to see that the real life of Greek is in the mas-terpieces of the literature, and that it is through the intelligent inter-pretation of these that the student's dormant enthusiasm must be awakened.   Vigorous teaching of conversational trivialities in modern Greek is perhaps better than inert and mummified teaching of Sopho-cles.   But the power to read and appreciate Sophocles is what we want, and there is really no serious reason why we should not have it.

The obstacles to the ready reading of Greek, assuming the indis-pensable drill in the elements, are mainly two: lack of vocabulary, and insensibility to the complicated evolution of the thought and the subtle forms of expression that characterize much of the world's higher artistic literature in all languages.   The first difficulty can be overcome by any intelligent student who reads faithfully under good guidance for two or three years.   The few hundred words that on the most favorable assumption would be used in conversational exer-cises are insignificant in comparison with the far larger number that must in the nature of things be learned in a purely literary way.   A conscious effort to master the vocabulary by frequent reviews, judi-cious etymologizing, reading aloud, apt citation of parallel passages, and other devices that will suggest themselves to the practised teacher is all that is needed.   The other difficulty can be met, in the case of young and immature students, only by gradually initiating them into the appreciation of the elaboration of the expression and the imagina-tive coloring of the thought that mark high poetic and reflective liter-ature.   And this education, one of the best fruits of classical culture, is just what is evaded or postponed by natural methods or by the substitution of the analytic and trivial modern Greek for its nobler ancestor.   The student fails—when he fails—from want of apprecia-tion of delicate literary art, or inability to apprehend the peculiar and subtle logic of the higher rhetoric of poetic expression.   I have not infrequently known a young student who missed the meaning of a passage of Æschylus or Pindar which he has construed with literal ac-curacy, to receive immediate illumination from a pertinent parallel from Milton or Shelley. But instead of patiently initiating the stu-dent into this difficult and noble *lingua franca* of genius by faithful and sympathetic teaching, we are asked to substitute for it a courier's parrot-like familiarity with a commonplace modern newspaper dialect.

There is indeed a sense in which Greek should be taught as a living language—a sense indicated in the words of Lowell, which are
irrelevant to Mr. Gennadius's contention, though relevant to mine:

> "If the classic languages are dead, they yet speak to us with a clearer voice
> than any living tongue.   If their language is dead, yet the literature it enshrines
> is crammed with life as perhaps no other writing, except Shakespeare's, ever
> was or will be."

It is of this life that the Greek teacher should make himself the interpreter, rather than waste his limited opportunity on the futile endeavor
to galvanize a few commonplace phrases of the language into a jerky
conversational resurrection.   And this the English teacher of Greek
can best do by interpreting his authors in their relation to our own
national tradition of culture and our own rich poetic inheritance.
Greek literature touches our modern life in two chief ways: first,
through its universal liberating human quality, whereby it has always
appealed to ages of awakened spiritual life like the Renaissance and
our own; and secondly, through the historic influence that it has exercised on the finest English poetry and the profoundest English
ethical and philosophic thought.   In these facts the teacher who has
himself entered into the glorious literary heritage that is the birth-
right of every Englishman will find the suggestions of a natural
method of making Greek a living tongue in the only sense possible
or desirable for American students.

PAUL SHOREY.

MOTHERHOOD AND CITIZENSHIP: WOMAN'S WISEST POLICY.

"MEN are not wise enough, nor generous enough, nor pure enough to legislate fairly for women. The laws of the most civilized nation depress and degrade women."

In the heat of the debate on the subject of woman suffrage, these words of George William Curtis were flung broadcast in the campaign documents. Now that the debate has been silenced, for the time, they are used less aggressively, perhaps, but fully as persistently, by those who feel that they are suffering from the injustice of denial of a legitimate claim; even if not used, they are harbored in the thought of the disappointed woman suffragist as a conclusion proved by the issue of the New York Constitutional Convention.

Alas! that women do not realize that by this arraignment of men they condemn themselves. Is their vision too limited to discern that the more proofs they bring forward of the folly, selfishness, and impurity of men, the more conclusively they are proving, at the same time, that women are not wise enough, as yet, to legislate for themselves?

Every man who legislates has been conceived of woman, has been influenced by her life, her thoughts, her spirit, during his pre-natal existence; has had her impress on his dawning soul; has been led and guided through the first unfolding of his life by her hand; has had his susceptible young heart first in her keeping, his awakening thought first beneath her sway. And if, at last, he grows up to make laws which depress and degrade her, there must be some lack of grace or wisdom, some error of nature or of life in woman, which had better be met and overcome as the first step toward her emancipation; that when it comes it may stand upon a firm foundation, upon the impregnable rock of her own fitness and character.

Evolution is better than revolution; and if the women who lavished their enthusiasm and their activity to secure the right of suffrage be wise, they will now turn their splendid energies into the channel of their opportunity. They will so educate the sons of the present

39

generation that the suffrage, if desirable, will be granted to their daughters as a logical and natural sequence, without the counterbalancing evils, and without the opposing obstacles, that would retard and imperil the use and potentiality of their new privilege, antagonized by the men whom they have fought, and unaided by the men whom they have not convinced.

Warfare and aggression are unlovely methods, and by them women sacrifice much that they can ill afford to lose; whereas, if they are wise, they will wait the opening of the door. A greater gain, long coming, is worth a partial good at hand. There is a surer way, a better road than by suffrage toward the obtaining of her rights, and to her more complete emancipation. It may take more courage, it may require more patience, but by these qualities she justifies her claim.

The discussion that echoed through the land a few months ago failed to touch the vital point. Between the suggested alternatives, —viz., an unsexed woman on the one hand, and a slave of man, or frivolous coquette, on the other,—it lost the reality of woman's mission and high destiny, which she herself has helped to minimize. Much of the complaint that is poured forth as argument for woman's enfranchisement is a tacit admission on her part of inappreciation of her own present opportunities.

Protests from woman that she has little scope because she is not man; that, debarred from coöperation with him, she is confined to patchwork and cooking; that her sphere is limited,.narrow, and circumscribed because it has not his larger interests, is as if the mighty element of water should struggle with fate because it was not air. Let it remember that it is a part of the force and power of the universe, different from air, but no less potent. To woman is given the mission of maternity, the basic fact of mortal life: not the mere bearing of children in an accidental, incidental way, but the mission of the perpetuation of the race; the direction and shaping of the race; and, until she understands and studies to fulfil her trust to the utmost, she has failed in her obligation and privilege.

As long as men are unjust to women, carelessly selfish, and cruel, as they too often are, woman is sending forth proofs to the world of her own incapacity and failure. And she has no right to ask,— nay, by her revealed lack of a sense of justice, she forfeits her right to ask,—to be made ruler over more things, until she has been faithful to those already committed to her charge.

Many women have asked with scorn, "Is the whole duty of woman that of child-bearing?" Some women have even been heard to ask, "How much better am I, then, than an animal?" Little better if she can ask this question. The physical burden laid upon woman in the economy of nature must be a factor in the argument that woman's mission is distinct and separate from that of man; for it hampers women with limitations, which increase with the delicacy and fineness of their organisms, setting them in a measure apart; but it is only a detail of the larger function of maternity. The full, wide, spiritual mission of motherhood is the dignity and the opportunity of the sex.

Could any power be greater than that which God and nature have given woman of ploughing the ground, and sowing the seed in her son's heart? Could any representation be more to her advantage than the impress of her own personality which she may leave upon him, if she has turned all the forces of her mind into an intelligent effort to make that impress deep and lasting?

If the argument be advanced that a large proportion of the race is unmarried, and childless, and that, therefore, for them there is no such opportunity, the answer is self-evident,—every man who lives has been born of a woman; and if each mother did her share toward making her son reverent and just enough to legislate more fairly for the sex, and toward giving him a consciousness of her ability and capacity, so that in the end he would gladly grant whatever she might logically claim, the result would be the same for the childless woman. She, therefore, may energize her more fortunate sister for her task, and that will be *her* opportunity.

How do women fulfil the mission of their lives, which—be it welcome or unwelcome,—has been divinely ordered? By a false and foolish sophistry, and a shallow prudery, it is something too often approached in ignorance, concealed and veiled as they draw near to it: —this mighty mystery which is the portal for the race. The whole education of women is often a tissue of half-truths, "ever the blackest of lies." Girls trained by mothers for wifehood are kept in ignorance of the real design of their lives. The preparation for marriage is an equipment, greater or less, for all things worldly and unworldly; but instruction or mention that marriage "was ordained for the procreation of children" has seldom been given. If the young woman has not been too busy with the bridal garments, and the preparation for the feast, she may have read the old and solemn form of the Holy Ordinance, and wondered vaguely what these words meant; or she may have an embarrassing secret knowledge— gathered from unwise sources—of the wonderful economy of nature; and is half ashamed of knowing what she should have investigated with more zeal, and with as pure intent as she had studied the flowers, or followed the courses of the stars.

That this miscalled innocence pleases the new husband, and is to him an evidence of purity, is but a proof, moreover, that his mother has failed to teach him true standards of estimate. Purity is not negative, but positive—as all moral force must be. Ignorant, she bears her child; uninformed, and often unthinkingly, she rears him, as an "aside" to some active motive in her life of fame, fashion, or religion. Even if her every motive be absorbed in him, and she be a devoted mother, the pattern of domesticity, in her very excess of virtue she often loses the higher conception of a broader righteousness in her work; she may coddle and fondle and pray over her child faithfully and devoutly, may neglect no care of his physical well-being, and yet be all-unmindful of the far-reaching issues she has in her keeping; and, in the moulding of the plastic stuff she has in her hand, be indifferent to the bents and imprints that are to militate against her in the future. Nay, she even encourages and deepens them. Be she a servant of the world, her ambitions for his worldly advancement and for his social prestige will make her tolerate and encourage in its incipiency that which she will deplore in its growth. This is a failure of her moral obligation. But she has failed, as fully, in her intellectual obligation, if she has not made herself the utmost that she may become in all ways; and if she has not instructed him—first thoroughly understanding herself—concerning the full sanctity, dignity, power, and place of woman. "My boy must sow his wild oats, all boys do," sounds shocking to the thoughtful matron, when it comes, as it so often does, from the lips of women who draw young men in their train to facilitate the process; but the "My son knows best, I am only an ignorant woman," is an equal failure in another direction.

It is not enough for woman to be good. The sole obligation of woman in her equipment for her mission is not goodness. She has a mind as well as a soul; and a woman has no more right to let her intellect revel inconsequently, or lapse into lazy lethargy, than she has to let her morals. That, as a rule, she has failed somewhere in the circle of her duties, her own estimate of, and claim against, men plainly show.

And while so many *are* failing in their obligations, either morally or intellectually, it would seem that there could be but little gain, and much risk, for woman if she succeeds in obtaining the suffrage. The women who are expected to be stimulated by a granted franchise to a more active knowledge of the political life about them, and to a wider interest in deeper subjects than their feminity has hitherto permitted, would sadly disappoint those who are earnest in their prophecy that they would be so stimulated. The woman who has not, without the franchise, kept herself informed that she may instruct her son, that she may meet her husband's mind, that she may throw her influence with her friends into the scale for righteousness, would not be apt to be awakened from her indifference by an added duty. To vote may, or may not, be a right or duty of woman, but it cannot be a remedy for all the evils she urges as her reasons for demanding it. Woman may be equal, may be superior to man, but she must prove her superiority in the duties she is obligated to perform, before she is ready to assume new ones.

Until woman gains truer wisdom than she now shows in her shaping of man, and develops greater strength than she now has in her holding of man, she is weakening the power of her accomplishment, and the probability of her success, in desiring functions and activities that have, heretofore, been confined exclusively to men. This is by no means a lack of appreciation of woman as she is; rather the highest appreciation; the life of the average woman, bearing and rearing children, organizing and conducting households and charitable institutions, flashing and scintillating in the social sphere, sharing and solving petty problems and graver questions that are poured into her ear, all at the same time,—proves that she has both strength and wisdom in a degree not often realized.

But the measure of possession is the measure of obligation; and, having these powers, she should be even more potential and influential than she is, in many ways. Especially the women of the United States, whose social growth has been as free as the spirit of the land; who have drawn, through heredity and intercourse, the varying forces of the differing types,—the vivacity of the French, the domesticity of the German, the romance of the sensuous South, and the balance and practical ability of the English.

How measureless the good to all mankind if the aroused interest and efforts of women could now be turned toward obtaining eman-cipation in a broader, truer way; toward a more intellectual appre-hension of their own possibilities and present far-reaching opportu-nities; toward a more intelligent bearing and rearing of sons; toward the training of girls to be more thoughtful and intelligent mothers. Let discussions and exhaustive study on marriage and maternity be begun; let organized investigation be started for finding, and the electrified energies of women be turned toward considering, how they may better shape the work of their own hands. Let them keep before themselves, if they will, the determination to obtain the most complete enfranchisement in the future; but let them re-member that to have had a path opened up the mountain-side before starting to climb is a surer and, in the end, quicker way of reaching the summit.

And above all let the ideal of true womanhood be held high before the world's daughters. Woman must compass in herself a trinity: physical well-being, because she is the mother of the race; mental well-being, because she has its youth to teach; spiritual well-being, because to her keeping have been given souls to save.

The complete woman understands to inspire, reaches to love, stoops to heal. Radiant, she goes forth and bathes the world "in smiles of glee;" tenderly she holds close the little child, sheltering its head upon her breast and singing lullabies, crooning soft songs, as though there were no other life but this. When new need arises, some vexed, grave question, some serious problem to be solved —on a sudden this brilliant creature, this careful mother, is the clear-brained, earnest thinker, who brings her faculties of delicate discernment and swift-winged intuition to share and lift the load of him she loves. She weighs, considers, comprehends the intricacies, the financial difficulties that fence him in, the subtleties of the political ambitions that lead him on. Nor is she, for this power of mental grasp, the less a clinging, passionately complete woman when the hour comes for soul to speak. Ah, no! She loves the better that she *is* the more; for highest force comes but from highest powers.

Beneath all the phases of the life she lives,—when she adorns the feasts, when she lights the home, when she shares the conflict of the market-place and the public arena by her sympathy—she glows with the light that has its issues within, that glorifies the common-place and illumines the every-dayness of life.

The woman who is really earnest, unselfish and single-minded will be willing to wait,—confident in the justice and truth of her own convictions,—and to utilize the present quickening of minds for a process of regeneration as the prelude to a real emancipation. And the woman who is self-seeking and dissatisfied, who says,—and too many have been heard to say it—"My lot is bondage to man; for woman is but little worth," may have eyes, but she sees not the possibilities of her own high destiny.

KATRINA TRASK.

A NEW AID TO POPULAR EDUCATION: FREE TRAVEL-LING LIBRARIES.

THE New York State travelling library system is a direct development of the work of the public library. The local library lends one book, the travelling library lends a hundred; the local library lends to a person, the other to a community; one lends for two weeks, the other for six months. In this way the State library becomes the parent of libraries.

This system was made possible by legislation of the State of New York in 1892. The University law of that year authorized the Regents to lend for a limited time selections of books, from the duplicate department of the State library or from books specially given or bought for this purpose, to public libraries under State supervision, or to communities meeting required conditions. Out of $25,000 appropriated for free libraries, a portion was at once set apart by the Regents to buy and prepare books to be lent under their rules.

The rules then adopted provide that a selection of one hundred books may be lent for six months to the trustees of any public library in the State under Regents' visitation, on payment of a fee of five dollars to cover the expense of cases, catalogues, record-blanks, and transportation both ways. Where no such library exists, the books will be lent on petition of any twenty-five resident taxpayers. In their petition an owner of real estate must be named as trustee, who must be personally responsible for the books. Libraries may be lent to the officers of a university-extension centre, reading course, or study club, if registered by the Regents. A later rule offers selections of fifty volumes for a fee of three dollars.

It was decided to begin with ten libraries of a hundred volumes each. The libraries were chosen with reference to their educational value, without disregarding a reasonable demand for recreation. In these days, fortunately, science is becoming more and more capable of popular illustration, new books of history and travel have the fascination of romance, while fiction is burdened with the most serious problems of humanity; so that in making up a library the task of preserving an even balance between information and amusement is by no means so difficult as it would have been twenty-five years ago. Books of reference and periodicals were ruled out, but a few bright sensible books for children were accepted. The tastes of professional men were not ignored; a few significant books on social science or economics were carefully sought. But all these were a small minority. After these, in order of importance, came books about the useful arts, about natural science, books of travel, biography, letters, history, and fiction, which were added in quantity and quality to suit the needs of "the general reader." It was obvious, too, that the requirements of different communities must greatly vary. There are some communities where even the old familiar books would be unknown; in others nothing but the latest would serve. To meet different needs, three libraries of the ten were made to include a liberal allowance of the older favorites, such as Scott, Thackeray, Dickens, Holmes, Prescott, and Parkman, which were excluded from the other seven; and one library was made up wholly of the books of the year 1892.

At length, after much revision and consultation at the State library, one thousand volumes were chosen and distributed into ten groups as nearly equal as possible in the range of subjects, in literary merit, and in attractiveness. The percentage of each kind of literature was: Fiction, 22 per cent; History, 18; Biography, 13; Travel, 11; Science and Useful Arts, 9; Sociology, 5; Religion and Ethics, 4; Fine Arts, 3; other literature, 15.

Since the first ten lists were made up, later books have been constantly bought to supply additional libraries. The later libraries have been of fifty volumes instead of one hundred, to permit the more frequent appearance of a new library and a wider range of choice to the borrower, or the borrowing of a small library at less cost. The choice of books rests with the Book Board, made up of five members of the staff of the New York State Library.

In addition to the general libraries, special-subject lists have been prepared; a set of fifty and a set of twenty-five volumes in each subject. Economics, Agriculture, French History, and United States History have been already taken up in these selections, besides lists in Literature, to cover Regents' reading-courses. The general lists now number eighteen; the special lists, nine. The university-extension libraries also should be noticed. Any registered extension-centre may obtain one hundred dollars' worth of books for reference, selected by their lecturer, on the same terms as a travelling library. The same privilege is extended also to registered study-clubs and reading-circles. As fast as these books are returned, they are arranged as a distinct library to meet future requisitions.

The first purchase of books consisted of two sets of each of the ten general libraries. As the demand increased, other sets of the same were needed, and several have been duplicated ten times. Cloth-bound editions have been used. The price of single volumes has varied from forty cents to five dollars, list price. The average cost is a little less than one dollar a volume.

Books are made ready for circulation as in a well-equipped public library. The catalogue-note on each book is intended to give in the briefest form a clear idea of its scope and character. Every copy of the printed catalogues contains the rules for local circulation, and these are supplied in quantity with each library sent out. A simple system of charging borrowed books is indicated in the rules, and book-cards and readers' cards, specially designed for the purpose, are supplied. All cards are returned to Albany with the books, enabling the central office to keep full statistics of the use of each volume. An oak bookcase, with neatly panelled doors and a lock and key, is furnished with every fifty books. There is sent also a plain oak cabinet with a single drawer with compartments to hold cards, and the like. This outfit, with cards and packing-cases, costs about fourteen dollars for every hundred volumes.

The first travelling library went out February 8, 1893. In eight months, up to October 1, 1893, 24 libraries had been sent out. In the second year, up to October 1, 1894, 101 had been sent; a total of 125. They went to 86 places. Of these 125, 43 were sent on petition; 40 to public libraries; 22 to academy libraries open to the public; 18 to university-extension centres; 2 to individual borrowers. In all, 11,900 volumes were sent out, of which 9,600 were included in general libraries, 950 in subject libraries, and 1,350 in university-extension libraries. Forty-four of these libraries, aggregating 4,400 volumes, are still out, leaving 7,500 volumes which have been returned without any loss or serious injury. One missing book, costing seventy cents, was paid for by a trustee.

Complete statistics of the circulation of 5,300 volumes are at hand. Their total circulation was 15,358, an average of 290 readers to each 100 volumes, in a period of six months. The smallest circulation was 66, the largest 609. One 50-volume library circulated 338. The number of borrowers was 4,392, showing an average of three-and-a-half books to a reader. The details of circulation of the different libraries show great variation.

The library which had a circulation of 609 in one place had 186 in another; that which had 598 in one place had 122 elsewhere. The library that had but 66 in one place had 476 in another, showing that the circulation was determined by local conditions. Let us note a few examples. The library that reached the highest mark of 609 in six months was in the small village of Havana, in Schuyler county, where a library association had been organized by women a few years ago and had four or five hundred well-read books. But their books were growing old, subscribers were few, and they were at the point of discouragement when they petitioned for a travelling library, and made their own library free. The next highest circulation—of 598—was reached in Ogdensburgh, where a newly chartered public library of 3,000 volumes is under the care of the principal of the public schools, who, with his teachers, has guided an enthusiastic group of readers. Three successive libraries have gone to an academy in Canandaigua, and, under like active influences, have reached circulations of 339, 504, and 476. At Peru, a small station on the Au Sable Railroad where books were very scarce, a circulation of 490 was recorded, one reader taking 38. The lowest circulation of 66 was in a place where the demand was cut off by a prosperous library of 5,000 volumes. Nineteen places have already had two successive libraries, five places have had three, Fort Plain has had four, and Plattsburgh five. From this beginning Plattsburgh has now a promising public library just chartered, whose trustees are preparing for use their first purchase of $400 worth of books. Six public libraries chartered within the year began by petitioning for travelling libraries.

Many interesting items might be gleaned from the record of individual books. For example, Mrs. Burnett's "Surly Tim" had fourteen readers in one place, and eleven, nine, three, and two in others, and none at all in another. "That Lass o' Lowrie's" was taken out by seventeen in one town, and fifteen, four, two, six, and twelve in others. "Henry Esmond" was read ten times, and "The Virginians" nine times, in one place, and neither was called for in another. The circulation of fiction was 52 per cent of all; but the books of fiction in the library were only 22 per cent.

In the department of Travel the popular books are: "The West from a Car Window," 18 readers; "Boy Travellers in Africa," 16;

"Tramp across the Continent," 15; "On Canada's Frontier," 14; "Tenting on the Plains," 12; "Knockabout Club on the Spanish Main," 12.   In Popular Science, only one goes above 11, and that is "Feathers, Furs and Fins," at 16 calls; "Electricity in Daily Life" has 10; "Horse Stories," 11.

Books on Social Science were usually read by two or three persons in a place.   The highest records in this class are: "How the Other Half Lives," 8 readers; "Children of the Poor," 6; "Who Pays Your Taxes?" 6; "Girls and Women," 6.   In Biography, the favorites are: Butterworth's "Lincoln," 13 readers; Coffin's "Lincoln," 11; Holmes's "Ralph Waldo Emerson," 11; Hale's "New England Boyhood," 11; Schurz's "Lincoln," 10.   Plainly, Lincoln is the hero. In other literature, "Over the Tea-Cups" had 15 readers; "A Connecticut Yankee in King Arthur's Court," 13; "My Summer in a Garden," 10.   In History the war stories are in the ascendant. Page's "Among the Camps" had 17 readers; "Boys of '61," 13; "Blue-Jackets of '76," 11; "Battlefields and Victory," 10; "Battlefields of '61," 8.

A list of the neglected books is not without interest; but a large number of trials would be needed for a fair comparison.   When Library No. 10 had gone out and returned ten times, there was but one of its books unused in any place.   That was Adams's "Three Episodes of Massachusetts History."   This would not have occurred in ten Massachusetts towns.   In the same library Merry's "Select Fragments of Roman Poetry," a book in Latin, had a reading in three different places.   Keene's "Literature of France" was read in only one place, but by two readers.   The number of neglected books is always reduced by further returns.

There is little to choose between the libraries in regard to popularity.   The most popular has been the library which consists wholly of books published in 1892.   But if the library that stands at the foot of the list in popularity had gone to the same places as the other libraries, I have no doubt it would have stood as high.

If, now, we turn to see how many books were taken by a single reader in six months, we find in one place,—Peru,—38 books charged to one name.   At Harkness, the next station to Peru, a girl of thirteen took 32 books, and a neighbor's boy of fifteen took 25.   Other places show readers who handled 31, 27, and 24 books each.   We cannot be sure that they read them, but it indicates at least the insatiable book-hunger that prevails in some localities.

As a general indication of the appreciation with which the travel-ling libraries have been regarded by those who have used them, a few expressions are quoted from letters received:

"There was a great deal of interest in our last library, and I believe, when we get another, nearly all the books will be out at once."

"This is a country school district.   Some of our people have never read books of any kind, and few have had the opportunity to read books like these."

"Interest is increasing. . . . Circulation has a steady growth."

"The circulation has greatly increased."

"We shall certainly get another next winter and every winter."

"The number of readers of our local library has increased tenfold."

"Increased interest in every direction. . . . It has led to the establishment of a reading-room."

We may say that 25,000 books have been read as a result of these travelling libraries. They have been good books and have left their mark on a multitude of minds. These libraries have everywhere promoted an interest in good reading, and have already led to the establishment of some important local libraries. They have been cordially received and are more in demand now than ever before. As a public investment they have fully vindicated the wisdom of their projectors and have proved worthy of the continued interest of the State. The system admits, too, of indefinite enlarge-ment. Special-subject libraries may be multiplied as fast as they are wanted; and the addition of general libraries can keep pace with the publication of good books. The State of New York can well afford this offer of books to her citizens, which is at once generous and, in the highest sense, profitable; and the plan is confidently commended to the consideration of other States.

WILLIAM R. EASTMAN.

PROPER TRAINING AND THE FUTURE OF THE IN-DIANS.

LATE in the forties a party of Winnebago Indians camped on Honeyoy creek in Walworth County, Wisconsin. They were on their way to Chicago to meet the authorities of the Federal Government. As they arrived at the ground the few weary horses were burdened with packs; old men and women were foot-sore and disconsolate; mothers with children on their backs sank down to rest as they reached the brink of the creek; and tired children toddled into camp and sank to sleep. A few of the more vigorous men and women prepared a scanty evening meal. Some days later the same Indians returned, but their condition was very greatly improved. The women were dressed in calicoes, the men in blankets, even the children had shoes, and a spirit of happiness prevailed. From a hill which was covered with a burr-oak grove a great spring gurgled and its rill ran through a meadow into the creek. In a glade near the spring the Indians established their canvas town of tents arranged in a circle. In the centre they placed the camp-fire. It was historic ground to them: the spring was a fountain at which their forefathers had quaffed, the groves about were the hunting-grounds of their ancestors, and in the creek their fathers had caught fish. On this sacred spot the tribe lingered for more than a week, hunting and fishing by day, dancing and feasting by night.

This temporary Indian village was on my father's farm, not a mile away from our new house. My mother and elder sisters visited the camp, taking me with them, and I gradually learned that the new wealth with which they seemed so glad was a part of the price of the ancient tribal homestead, and that the right to our new home was acquired through the Government from these self-same Indians. The little creek, now obstructed by a mill dam, was once beset with fish snares, and the strip of ground on which we had planted our apple orchard had been their rabbit preserve. I can yet remember how deeply these facts were impressed on my mind, as my mother gathered them from two or three Indians who could speak English.

This was my introduction to the Indians of the United States. Since that time I have lived among them and travelled much in their country, so that nearly one-half of my time has been passed with these people. I have seen most of the tribes of the United States. I have wandered with them in the woods, ridden with them across the plains, climbed with them over mountains, visited their homes, slept in their camps, and studied their languages, habits, customs, and mythology. For twenty-five years I have had associated with me on exploring expeditions and in the work of the Bureau of Ethnology a number of men who, like myself, have been making a life-study of the North American Indians. These investigations have extended from the Eskimo of the Arctic circle to the Maya of the tropics. As the result of these researches we have published about fifty volumes of reports of all kinds. Of course, therefore, my interest in the " Indian problem" is profound.

The most pertinent and interesting aspect of the subject now is that with reference to the efforts that have been made to educate the Indians. These experiments have now been going on a sufficiently long time to enable us to reach something like a clear conclusion as to whether any considerable proportion of the North American Indians may ever be expected to merge themselves into our American life as civilized men, or whether these agencies for educating and civilizing them will at most do only a good service to a few individuals—an inconsiderable number of the whole—and the great mass of Indians will be left gradually to disappear as civilization presses in around them in an ever-narrowing circle; and I am asked to give my judgment on this matter.

At first I began to collate the statistics of Indian education, and I prepared a number of tables to show the progress made in schools—under such headings as " The growth of Indian schools from decade to decade," " Money expended in the establishment of schools," " Money expended in the maintenance of schools," " Attendance from year to year." I then began a statistical article and attempted to draw some lessons from it. Then I found myself in a confused state of mind. The statistics seemed hardly to be related to the transformation which I had observed in the Indian tribes during the last forty-five years. There are some things that cannot be numbered. I have seen scores of thousands of Indians pass from the state of savagery to a half-civilized condition, and a smaller number into practical civilization. Under my own eye thousands of them, naked the greater part of the time, but gaudily dressed in fantastic pelts, furs, and feathers on gala days, have thrown aside these gauds and adopted the costume of civilized man. Men by the thousands who were snaring rabbits in their youth and my youth are now guiding the plough; girls who were picking berries then are now churning butter. Boys and girls who were speaking in languages native to only a few hundred persons, are now speaking our common tongue. Medicine-men who were practising sorcery when I was a boy are dead, and in their stead physicians employed by the General Government are administering quinine. Scores of thousands of people subject to the superstitions of sorcery and to the attendant methods of torture by which evil spirits are supposed to be driven out, are now submitting to rational treatment for disease. Few of the old men and women speak our language; usually the children speak it, and in another generation one homogeneous tongue will replace the multiplied jargons of savagery. These facts and many more I could not tell in tables of statistics, so I put my notes in the waste-basket and commenced again. The statistics remain in the reports of the Indian Bureau. I will tell my story without them.

More money has been paid to extinguish Indian titles than to extinguish the titles of foreign nations, and the cost of Indian wars has been greater than the cost of foreign wars. In treating with foreign governments we have employed our ablest statesmen; so in treating with Indian tribes we have always employed men of high character. In looking over the list of the men who have made treaties with the Indian tribes we find such men as Jackson, Harrison, Cass and many others who have served in the councils of the Nation. We have always been liberal in our bargains, giving to the tribes moneys in excess of the values of their lands at the time when they were purchased, and at the same time confirming to them the title of portions of their lands as reservations. As the country was redeemed to civilization these reservations have developed in value by unearned increment, so that many tribes have become comparatively wealthy and nearly all are well-to-do.

This policy of extinguishing Indian titles by purchase has necessarily involved great expense, and as we are rapidly cutting down the reservations the expense is growing from year to year. Sometimes we have purchased directly from the Indians and paid in instalments, and sometimes we have sold Indian lands and held the funds in trust to pay the principal and interest in instalments. The Indian appropriation for the current fiscal year, for example, aggregates the sum of $10,750,486.03, made up of the following items:

Expense of supporting Indian agencies and furnishing gratuitous supplies,	$1,776,010.84
Fulfilling treaty stipulations	2,936,846.53
Payment of principal and interest of trust funds	1,509,236.66
Purchase of lands	2,467,697.00
Support of schools	2,060,695.00
	$10,750,486.03

From the above it will be seen that the expense of supporting the Indian agencies, together with all gratuities, is less than $2,000,000, while we pay this year nearly $3,000,000 to fulfil treaty stipulations, and $1,500,000 due Indians as trust funds, and for newly purchased lands $2,500,000.   Thus, nearly $7,000,000 are paid under treaty obligations, all solemnly promised to the tribes by diplomatic officers of high standing, approved by the President of the United States, and, finally, confirmed by the Senate, as if the treaties had been made with foreign nations.

But more than this: in making these treaties or bargains with the tribes, the negotiating officers have usually represented to the Indians that agencies would be established and that they would be taught the industries of civilization, and that their children would be taught in schools established by the General Government.   Sometimes these items are stipulated in a general way in the treaty; but in the history of the treaties it has usually been recorded by the officers making the treaties that such requests were made by the Indian tribes, and that such promises were made as an argument to induce them to part with their lands, so that all the expense now incurred by the General Government is practically a debt due to the Indian tribes in fulfilment of promises made by the Government and its authorized agencies. Whether the policy be wise or unwise it cannot be abandoned; it is fixed upon the country.   No Congress can fail to make the appropriation without disgrace; no party can with impunity fail to fulfil the obligation incurred.

What effect is this having on the Indian himself?   Will he become a beggar and a vagabond?   Does he feel himself a pauper degraded by receiving alms from the white man?   On these questions hangs the wisdom or folly of the policy adopted by the Government of the United States in its management of the Indians.   All other nations have adopted a different policy in dealing with aboriginal savage peoples.   We have treated with them as sovereign nations, and

40

have purchased their lands at comparatively high prices; other nations have treated savages exclusively as wards and paupers, with no rights which the white man was bound to respect.   The effect of these two policies on the development of Indian character is great.   The Indians to the North and South of us have been comparatively peaceful and have accepted the position assigned them as a degraded and depend-ent race.   The Indians of the United States have carried themselves with pride and defiance, demanding their rights and fighting for them when they must.   On the frontiers our Indians have sometimes been abused, out in general they have held their own, and altogether they have received from the Government a justice which, though some-times tardy, has usually been ample, and more than ample, for this reason: whatever might be the conflict which arose between the white settlers and the red tribe, in every dispute the Indians had for their support the sentiment of the people of the whole United States, which was sure sooner or later to be expressed by the officers of the General Government.   It was impossible to grant the Indians all they asked. They desired to be left alone in the quiet possession of their lands. The march of civilization could not thus be checked.   Realizing this the people of the United States have encouraged the invading settlers to make new homes and assured them of protection; and in carrying out this policy treaty after treaty has been made with the Indians. Petty wars have arisen from time to time, and as soon as an Indian tribe discovered the hopelessness of such a contest treaty negotiations were begun, they demanding payment for lands, we yielding a price which at the time was ample and often more than ample.   So we have paid to Indians, never numbering more than four hundred thousand souls, more than three hundred millions of dollars, and have yet secured to them lands which by increase of value through unearned increment are now worth more than were the lands origi-nally claimed by them.   Treated in this manner the Indians have not become mendicants and criminals.   They have retained their self-respect; they are proud of their ancestry and glory in the virtues of their race.

Many schools of this country had their beginning in attempts to educate the Indians; even Harvard University was first an Indian school.   After the organization of the Federal Government many at-tempts were made to educate the Indians, some by the Government but many more by individual enterprise.   Perhaps some good was done in this way, but in the aggregate the early attempts were disappointing, as the schools established were not endowed with long life. Why they disappeared so soon after their founding is now made plain, but at the time it was not understood, and failure carried consternation into the minds of many good people. From the first it was not properly known that the Indians were not a homogeneous people. The white man did not know that he was dealing with hundreds of distinct governments, hundreds of distinct religions, and hundreds of distinct languages. That which was accomplished for one little tribe had no further influence by extending beyond its boundary. The distinctions between tribe and tribe were as radical as those existing between any one of the tribes and the invading Europeans. The Scriptures, translated into an Indian tongue after years of missionary toil, could be read by only a few persons. The labor of translating the Bible and the accessory religious books into five hundred or a thousand different languages, and of training missionaries to preach and teach in all these languages, was an undertaking too great even for religious enthusiasm. For such reasons the early methods devised for civilizing the Indian tribes largely failed. Schools failed and books failed. Progress was made to the extent that the Indians came in contact with civilized man and learned his ways and industries, but it was acculturation, not education, by which the advance was secured. The triumphs of civilization, the power of prosperity, the wonders of industrial art, all made a deep impression on the Indian, and from them he learned much, but from the school and books he learned little.

A time came when this was changed. When all the valleys of the United States were settled and all the Indians were assigned to small reservations, when the buffalo were killed, the hunting-fields ploughed, the fishing-grounds navigated, and the Indian absolutely stranded on the shore of civilization where he must live under new conditions or die, the problem was presented to his mind in a new light. Fortunately at this juncture the right men came to the front. Pratt of Carlisle, and Armstrong of Hampton, were men who grasped the new conditions and devised a system of education that has since been accepted and is being rapidly developed, the results of which are potent in directing Indian life into civilized channels. The old education was literary and religious; the new education is industrial.

To learn a trade fifty years ago it was necessary for a boy to serve as an apprentice for seven years, to become a journeyman, and at last a master workman. There were many trades, and no common method by which they could be taught by one person to a number of people working together. That day has departed. Machinery does the special work of all trades. This change from hand-work to machine-work constitutes the greatest epoch of human history since the art of making fire was discovered. All skilled work is done by machinery; years of training are no longer required to learn a trade, and if the boss employs men under the plea of apprenticeship they are set to do work which the masters do, and they can do it just as well.

The differentiation of trades has been replaced by the invention of machinery, so that the skilled workman is now the skilled machine. There must yet be a few special workmen, but the great body of mechanics are machine-tenders. In this manner a new and universal trade has been developed. By this transformation labor has become mobile so that it can easily pass from one theatre of operation to another. What is now needed is a general deftness by which a man may turn from one operation to another as the call arises, and this general deftness is the universal trade. This was the Carlisle and Hampton idea, and it is the principle which is at the basis of industrial education first systematically developed in the highest grade through the agency of our polytechnic schools, but now it has found its way into the public schools and is gradually permeating the whole system.

From Carlisle and Hampton the new education has spread through the West so that a number of special institutions have already been established in proximity to the Indian reservations, while others have been founded upon the reservations themselves.

Their influence is already widely manifest, for the young Indians are everywhere drifting into a new industrial life. They are becoming farmers, and learning to use the plough, the cultivator, and the harvester. They are becoming lumbermen, and fell trees, navigate rafts and saw timber; they build houses and manufacture furniture, and in a multitude of ways are learning the universal trade. The young Indians from Hampton and Carlisle, and to a slight extent some of those trained in the later schools, are taking their positions as special laborers in the higher grades. The full fruition of this policy does not yet appear; in fact, the policy is not yet universal. Some schools have not been transformed, others are in progress of transformation: only a few are fully fledged industrial schools. Teachers competent to inaugurate the system have not always been found, but the work has fairly begun and the beneficial effects are already seen.

About 20,000 Indian pupils are now under instruction, some in good schools, some in fair schools, and some in nearly worthless schools, but all are improving. The system of education adopted extends beyond the school-house. Farmers and other instructors are now employed to teach the Indians the practical arts of life. To a large extent the moneys due to Indians under treaty stipulations are not directly paid in currency, but are expended for them by the Government agent in the improvement of their homes and the purchase of necessary current supplies. If an irrigating canal is to be constructed the Indians are employed to dig it for themselves and paid fair wages for their work, and then they own the canal. Instead of building houses for them the Government pays them by the day's work to build their own houses, and treaty obligations are thus fulfilled. So on all the reservations the Indians are set to work, and by every possible means made to toil for themselves rather than made the beneficiaries of sums of money. Young Sioux that fought Custer now drive teams at the Government agency; Navajo that fought Kit Carson are now digging ditches; and Apaches that fought Crook are now husking corn.

The pioneers of industrial training for the Indians had the wisdom to discover the changed conditions and they said, " We will train boys and girls for the new industrial life." For this purpose many were brought from their reservations to Carlisle and Hampton. The experiment soon proved successful, and now such schools are established on or near the more important reservations. Still the work of enlarging the labor schools is in progress. Now, the Indians are taught to work, and to speak and write the English language and certain rudiments, all of which are well calculated to prepare them for industrial life. Not all the schools are thus transformed, but the metamorphosis is well under way. There are some schools on the old plan, and the national authorities assist many that have been established as denominational enterprises for religious instruction, but the contagion of good example is working, and it will not require many years more to complete the revolution, when the purposes of Indian education will be industry and an understanding of English speech, not sacraments and creeds, and when it will be taught that an honest day's labor is a moral duty. In the meantime the Methodists, the Baptists and the Catholics will develop their schools and teach the Christian religion as it is interpreted by the various sects, and plant a new religion which is a characteristic of the highest civilization.

J. W. POWELL.

THE INCREASING COST OF COLLEGIATE EDUCATION.

THE increase in the number of students in American colleges in the last two generations should be still further augmented. The period of education, too, should be lengthened for most boys and girls, men and women. Of the students at any one time enrolled in the public schools of the United States only twelve per cent graduate, and the private academies and seminaries exhibit as low a percentage of graduates as seven. Many college classes show a decrease of one-fifth, and I have known classes to have only one-half as many men upon the Commencement platform as stood together in the Freshman year. We ought to do all that can be done to have the pupils of the grammar-school enter the high-school, cause students of the high-school to complete the course, and urge graduates of the high-school to take degrees at the college.

It is never to be denied that many men and women do not want a college education. It is also to be granted that if a person does not want a college course the college does not want him. He would probably be hurt by the college, and he certainly would hurt the college. And yet most persons would be glad of an education if it could be had. The most evident reason which prevents worthy men who desire a college training from getting it is the cost. Mr. Benjamin Kidd, in his " Social Evolution," says:

"Even from that large and growing class of positions for which high acquirement or superior education is the only qualification, and of which we, consequently (with strange inaccuracy), speak as if they were open to all comers, it may be perceived that the larger proportions of the people are excluded—almost as rigorously and as absolutely as in any past condition of society—by the simple fact that the ability to acquire such education or qualification is at present the exclusive privilege of wealth."

In one view of the question the cost of a college education is high. The average cost to the student per year at the better college is larger than the total income of the average American family. The cost, too, has greatly increased. I have lying before me tables which indicate the cost of education in certain respects at three such old and representative colleges as Harvard, Yale, and Dartmouth since their foundation.   I shall begin with the former.

From 1825–30 the average annual expenses of a student at Harvard were $176, of which half went for tuition and half for board and room; from 1831–40 the average was $188.10; from 1840–48, $194; 1849–60, $227 ($138 went for board and room); in the 'sixties it jumped from $263 to $437, two-thirds of which went for board and room; in 1881–82 the average expense to an economical student ranged from $484 to $807, the latter sum including a few more material comforts, and in 1893–94 these last figures had been slightly reduced.

At Yale the increase of expenses was nearly in the same ratio, the average for the opening year (1821) being $175, and the average for 1893 being $687.50.

Eleven catalogues of Dartmouth College which I examined mention no expenses prior to 1822, in which year the cost of tuition was $26, other expenses amounting to about $75.   This scale of expense changed little until 1862, when tuition cost $51, and other expenses amounted to about $101.   In 1892 the figures were higher, tuition being $90 and other expenses about $191.

At the risk of inflicting too many figures upon the reader I venture to give certain further facts in reference to the increase of bills at a few other colleges.   In 1830 the total expenses per student at Waterville, Hamilton, Amherst, Brown, and the University of Pennsylvania ranged from $84 at the first named to $180 at the last; in 1893 from $275, or more, at Waterville to $335, or more, at the University of Pennsylvania.   President Lord, of Dartmouth, wrote in 1830:

"Our students have just now commenced reform with an excellent spirit in regard to their diet.   Several boarding-houses have been opened upon the principle of strict temperance, and perhaps fifty or sixty young men have good living for $1 to $1.12½ per week.   It may be understood that boarding may now be had in our most respectable families for $1, the student consenting to a moderate, but in all respects sufficient bill of fare, and which will insure the 'mens sana in corpore sano.'"

These facts necessitate the conclusion that every element of the cost of an education has in the last sixty years increased three or four fold. The following notes taken from the college-books of Harvard show the contrast between the simplicity of its early days and the more costly necessities of the present:

May 22, 1727.—Tuition charge advanced from ten to fifteen shillings per quarter.

Sept. 8, 1778.—Tuition raised to 40ˢ a quarter.

Dec. 15, 1778.—Assessment as follows: To Hancock Professor 16ˢ: to Tuition £5 5ˢ 0ᵈ: to the Monitors 2ᵈ: to gallery money 6ˢ. Also, on the Junior and Senior Sophisters, for Library £1 5ˢ 0ᵈ; for Hollis Prof. Math. £2. Reckoning is always by the quarter.

(Money is greatly depreciated at this time.) Assessments were levied for various purposes, permanent and occasional; votes on this subject are numerous. This custom makes it impossible to fix the charges satisfactorily for any extended period.

Oct. 14, 1805.—Tuition for Seniors and Juniors $5.50 a quarter; for Sophomores and Freshmen $4.50.

Aug. 7, 1806.—Tuition doubled—twice as much as preceding quarter.

Dec. 16, 1806.—10ᶜ assessment on each student attending the French instruction.

Sept. 13, 1811.—Tuition increased one quarter part.

1667.—"The cook, receiving provisions from yᵉ Steward at current prices, shall deliver the same out, to yᵉ scholars, advancing an halfe penny upon a penny." "The Butler, receiving his beer from yᵉ Steward, single beer at 2ˢ, & double beer at 4ˢ yᵉ barrell, shall advance 4ᵈ upon yᵉ shilling."

1702.—Steward allowed to ch'ge two pence 3 farthings for each "part."

1724, Apr. 14.—Steward may charge 6 pence per *part* the current quarter.

1732, Nov. 7.—Food increased: Steward may charge 10 pence half penny for a part at noon: other meals remain the same.

1737, Apr. 6.—Provisions dear: so charged 16ᵈ a part at noon, 10ᵈ at night: bread to be 5ᵈ a loaf.

1741, Apr. 15.—Dearness of provisions. Steward to ch'ge 2ˢ a part at dinner, 15ᵈ at night.

1748, Oct. 19.—Particular management of Commons, and the price, left to be ordered by the members of the corporation resident in Cambridge.

1750, Aug. 15.—Prices of Commons fixed: Bread—two pence per loaf. Dinner —five pence, one farthing ("of which ⅓ part is allowed for sauce"). Beer—one penny a quart. Supper—three pence, one farthing.

Commons to be as follows: "Two sizzes of bread in the morning, one pound of Meat at Dinner wᵗʰ sufficient sauce & half a pint of Beer: & at Night, That a Part Pye, be of the same Quantity as usual, & also half a pint of Beer, and that the Supper Messes be but of four Parts, tho' the dinner Messes . . . be of six."

It cannot be said that this increase of cost can in any way be avoided. It is simply a part of the increase which belongs to the cost of living in a simple and rural community to living in a community whose relations are more or less elaborate. The college is a part of the community; it is moved by all that moves the community. The ordinary family of the community is spending several times as much money as the family of the community of two generations ago. The college-man does as the family does of which he is a member. It is also to be said that the cost of the administration of a college has vastly increased. Though complaints as to the present small salaries of college professors abound, yet these salaries have increased quite as rapidly as most incomes. At the period of the American Revolution the average salary of a professor at Harvard was £200. Early in the century the salary was $1,500 and remained at that figure till 1838–39. At this time it was increased to $1,800. In 1854 it was raised to $2,000. In the next twelve years it was by successive increments so increased that in 1866 it was $3,200. In 1869 it became $4,000. The maximum salary now paid in the college is $4,500, and in the Law School $5,000.

The most expensive part, in certain respects, of a college to-day is the laboratory and the library. The laboratory is wholly a new creation, and the library in its present extensive relations is also new. The library of Harvard College cost for the year for which the last report is made $50,000. What a laboratory costs it is hard to separate from other elements of expense. But each college is spending in scientific instruction and in scientific apparatus many times what it expended some years ago. All this increase of cost must directly or indirectly increase the cost of an education to each student.

Yet the cost to a student for an education does not consist only of the amount of his formal fees and of the cost of board and room. The expenses which are called incidental are now in a few colleges larger than all others. Not a few college men of an economical turn find that when they have added together the three things,—the cost of tuition, room and board—that the expenditure of the whole year will be represented by this sum multiplied by two. Now there can be no doubt that the cost of an education is keeping many men from receiving it, and the question therefore recurs, Can anything be done to open the way to boys who want to go to college but who cannot pass through the narrow financial doorway?

In answer it is to be said, first, the cost of an education to the student should not be lessened by lessening the cost of administration or of instruction or by diminishing the efficiency of laboratories and libraries. Such a diminution would represent the diminution of the worth of a college course. It would also represent a change which the colleges themselves would not endure. Secondly, a decrease should not be secured through a decrease in the fee for tuition. The fee for tuition now represents only a part of the cost of the tuition itself. President Coulter has recently gathered together certain very suggestive facts upon this point, which are well worth careful study. From his table, which shows, among other interesting things, the cost, above fees, to the leading American universities of educating their students, I have selected a dozen of the largest institutions, and I find that the average cost per student over and above fees to these twelve colleges is $245. The figures I used in this computation range from $128 at Vassar to $400 at the Leland Stanford, Jr., University.

But on the positive side it may be said, first, that the cost of an education may be secured through the increase of endowment. This increase of endowment and the consequent increase in income would allow a decrease in the amount which the college receives from the student. Second, the same result might be secured by a tax laid upon the people for the benefit of the college. The State university is the result of a public tax. Should the State lay a tax upon itself for the benefit of more than one college?

In answer to the second of these two questions it is to be said that one university supported by the State is sufficient. Ohio has three universities which are supported in part out of the public chest. Those who are best acquainted with the education of this great State believe that it would be for the advantage of the State and of education if the money now given to three colleges could be given to one. Not a few colleges in each State are denominational, and the chief reason for their existence is the denominational reason. No tax should be assessed for the promotion of such interests.

In respect to the method of decreasing the cost of education through the increase of endowment it is to be said that such increase has seldom resulted in such decrease. For, as a rule, every college has need of all the funds it can possess for filling up urgent needs. But there is a method, the opposite of this, which might result in allowing a poor boy to come to college. It consists in the increase of tuition fees. As has been said, the present fee for tuition represents only a share of the cost of tuition. Why should not the fee be increased to represent the entire cost? Why should there not be a payment in money of the cost value of instruction? Any reason which can be given for paying less than a college education costs is a reason which I apprehend would overthrow most economic theories. The American people have come to expect that the American college shall give an education at less than its cost. This expectation should cease. It has arisen from the free public school system. Every American child goes to the public school without a direct expenditure on the part of the parent. The parent does not feel the indirect taxes which he pays for his child's education. It is hard, therefore, for him to pay the fee at the college to which his son or daughter goes upon graduation from the high-school.

It is also to be said that the price of instruction at the college is higher than the price of many secondary or even primary private schools. One hundred and fifty dollars is an extreme price for tuition at the college, but twice one hundred and fifty dollars is an extreme price for tuition at certain private schools. But there are two special reasons for the increase of fees. The one of less force is that not a few rich men are not willing to give their money to afford the sons of other rich men an education at less than its cost. A friend of mine with whom I was recently conversing said to me, " I can give you, if you wish, a large amount of money, but that amount of money would go for the benefit of the son of Mr. A. or Mr. B., who is perfectly able to pay all his son's fees at their full amount." The force of the reasoning cannot be easily set aside, as the truth of the fact cannot be denied. But the special reason for this increase lies in the fact that money would thus be had for the benefit of men who could not pay for a college education. If the American college could increase its tuition fee to $500, there are not a few men in the college who would be willing and able to pay this fee, and who ought to pay this fee, for the fee represents simply what the education costs. With the present endowments and with the increase of endowments sure to be made, these payments would allow each college to offer an education to men who are not able to pay for it, at a very small cost. Thus, every poor boy in America who wants an education could receive it.

CHARLES F. THWING.

THE FINANCIAL YEAR AND THE OUTLOOK.

THE opening of a new year finds the American people still struggling toward better times, but with a clearer prospect ahead than a
year ago. That prophecies made soon after the panic, regarding the
speedy return of prosperity, were falsified by the events of the year
1894, we know. It was easy to prophesy by drawing discriminating comparisons with the conditions which followed the panic of
1873. That memorable period of liquidation caught the country
unawares. It came upon us after a time of high prices: it found the
affairs of the great business and banking houses so intertwined that
the fall of one was followed as a necessary sequence by the suspension of another, like the tumbling of a row of blocks.

Such conditions were wanting in the panic of 1893. For three
years business may be said to have been, in general, preparing for
the storm. Prices of commodities declined; liquidation had already
begun in the more speculative lines, and the affairs of the majority of
merchants and mercantile houses were in better shape than at the beginning of the distress of twenty-five years before. The expression
common last summer that it was a "rich man's panic" meant, if it
meant anything, that it was the more fanciful and uncertain valuations which were at first and most disastrously affected. The news
which reached us in November, 1890, that the old London house of
Baring had been obliged to beg for money to meet its obligations because its funds were locked up in unsalable and speculative securities, was a notice served upon the financial world that a re-valuation
of all enterprises and all business must be had. We should have had
our panic following soon after that confession, had it not been for
the bountiful crops in the following year, crops which were phenomenal both in yield and in prices because of crop failures in other parts
of the world. Nature's bounty in 1891 was great enough to carry
us through the succeeding year, so that it was not until May, 1893,
that liquidation in the United States fairly began. No doubt the
delay softened the blow to many, besides helping to change the character of our panic.

It is the peculiarity of a new country to be speculative. Development means risk: great profit or great losses followed the establishment of new enterprises, especially in our younger States west of the Mississippi and Missouri rivers. Not only was this development, as we now know, pushed in advance of the real consumptive requirements, but, as we now see, the very activity of this development created an extra and large demand which ceased at the moment this activity itself stopped.

From 1880 to 1890 there were built in the United States approximately 75,000 miles of new railway. If we consider for a moment what this means, how many tons of steel and iron for rails and track construction, how much material and land for equipment and terminals, how much demand for food supply to laborers engaged in production, and, not least, how much revenue to the older railroads which carried the breadstuffs one way and the required iron and wood the other; and if we think that the same thing was going on as to mining and a thousand other pursuits, we are prepared to see how far our activity reacted upon itself, until at last the question of the ultimate market for all this output was forced upon us. It was the stoppage of this development which restricted trade so severely in the year just closed—the withdrawal from the iron furnace of the railway orders and from the manufacturer of the demand for supplies and machinery. Credit and our national optimism had hurried us on faster than the disposal of the national products had warranted, while the old and large profit made by the farmers in our great staple crops accelerated the pace.

The year 1894 would have seen more disasters had not the panic found us in better condition than in 1873. Our salvation from a worse fate lay in that fact of unconscious preparation. Business after the Baring liquidation could be, and was, gradually reduced to the curtailed demand; there were no entangling financial alliances to hinder such curtailment. Each firm or corporation met its own conditions, and with the exception of such business men as had spread out their sales or manufactures beyond their resources, the failures were not comparatively large. Wages were reduced either by direct cuts or by discharges, while in the latter case no doubt the incompetent suffered most. 'It is the belief of most of us that prosperity will come again to the United States; how long it will be delayed no one can tell. By this phrase we mean that the mineral, agricultural, and general resources of the country are such that development will begin again, slowly and cautiously at first, but gathering greater momentum as more markets open to the new or increasing products. Our advance has been so rapid that a steady business seems to us like a decline.

The year has taught us some healthful lessons. Continued success had made us as a nation believe that we could do anything without harm—that we were an exception to all economic law. No Asiatic or South American country could tamper with its currency without experiencing the ill effects, but the United States could get close to our silver precipice without danger of falling over; Spain, Italy, and Portugal could get into trouble with their national credit, but in the United States no apprehension need be felt because the foreign money-lender had fears regarding the intention of the Federal Government to pay in gold and on demand. Such small matters were beneath us: but we have had a rude awakening. Our people are beginning to see that good faith and prosperity, like liberty and union, are one and inseparable. Nor did we believe that any injustice to ourselves lay in juggling with the currency.

The greenback heresy of thirty years ago was the father of many of the wild proposals made in recent years. "Why should not the Government set its printing-presses going when it had debts to pay?" It needed a panic to force upon us the lesson that a government can no more manufacture money from nothing, than can an individual business man pay his obligations by assets of his own conjuring. Then, too, we shall probably never again see in the United States a high protective tariff. It *is* possible for a nation to interfere to a certain extent with the flow of trade without material harm: it *is* possible for so great a country as our own to increase in wealth for a time even though commerce should be artificially restricted. But manifestly such a policy has its limits. We have been trying to pull ourselves along by the straps of our own business boots, and the outcome in mechanics or economics is innocent as to the athletic side but barren of lasting results.

It is useless as it is unnecessary and indeed impossible to forecast the future. Trade regulates itself. What we need at the present is not speculation on the future of commerce, so much as determination to look our problems squarely in the face as they arise, and to maintain our credit at all hazards. The condition of the United States treasury two months ago was enough to make the patriotic American blush. We need reform of course—and the prospect now seems

brighter—but we need also a set of Congressmen who would appreciate the argument that the credit of the United States, strong as it is,
requires proper legislation before it becomes practically available.
We should never forget that sentiment and fact are so intertwined in
the fabric of public and mercantile credit as to make the drawing of
a dividing line impossible.   If we would have full confidence, both
elements must be considered.

But no doubt these general problems will be put in a fair way to
be eventually solved.   Faith in the American people forbids any
other conclusion.   We may hold this opinion the more unhesitatingly
because the history of the past year has taught us truths about public
and private finance which were formerly passed over or ignored altogether.   We may expect that trading and manufacturing, now having found or finding the new level, will go on with increasing
volume.   Inventions will play their important part.   New uses for
old things will be found.   Cheap iron ore will permanently cheapen
iron and its manufactured products.   Structural steel, for illustration,
already having shown a wonderful advance for the last decade, is no
doubt destined to further triumphs, especially under late improvements of styles and processes of manufacture.   There is no reason
why large buildings alone should have the new steel frames, or why
steel should not supersede wood in much of our future construction.

Even in trade the path to prosperity lies through improvement.
The much-aspersed "department stores," for example, will at least
teach retail grocers that they must put more brains into their business.
There is no necessary connection between a corner grocery and bad
taste or uncleanliness, though in too many instances an observer
would be led to believe so.

As to our great agricultural interests we may think of their future
with encouragement.   We may believe that in some way the American farmers will "meet the market," and at a profit too; though the
days are over when an immigrant could buy a farm on credit and
pay for it in two or three years from his crops.   Farming will be
more like other businesses, requiring capital and training; but considered in this light it will be made profitable.   If the present occupants cannot answer these conditions, they must give place to others
who can.   All improvements in farming of late years have been in
the direction of better utilization of the horse, not in the line of a
change of motive power except in threshing.   The man who shall
invent a new motor for the farmer—either through the application of

electricity or in some other way—a motor which shall drive his plough and his mowing machine, run his farming operations generally, and get his produce to the nearest railroad market, will do much to solve our national trade problem.   As to our railways, it is to be said that disasters have taught economies not before thought possible; though earnings are yet too low for safety.

An improvement here through permissive pooling would at once be felt among the three million of persons directly dependent upon transportation for food and clothing, and also among the manufacturers who look to the railways as the principal customers for their now seriously restricted product.

While, therefore, the depression of 1894, following the panic of 1893, has proved a bitter experience for the commercial interests of the United States, nothing but our own folly need lead us to distrust the future.   The problems before us are not to be lightly regarded. They demand careful economic thought and good financial judgment. Nor need we expect at once a revival of the volume of trade and prosperity of former years.   Above all we must as a people forever abandon the delusion that nature's generosity to us and our own supposed superiority have placed us above the financial and commercial laws which govern the rest of the civilized world.

The Forum

FEBRUARY, 1895.

SHOULD THE GOVERNMENT RETIRE FROM BANKING?

"The government note, a bad, unsound, untrustworthy currency, persecutes society at every turn and brings loss on all but gamblers. . . . Not an hour should be lost by any legislature who has any knowledge of the nature and working of money to arrest the plague and sweep away inconvertible money."
—*Bonamy Price.*

THE popular opinion, now widely expressed in intelligent quarters, that the United States Government should go out of the banking business, is based upon the fact that one of the important functions of banking has been assumed and practically monopolized by an institution totally unfit for its performance.

The term bank, as used here, should be distinguished from the term banker. Prejudiced writers constantly confound the two. A bank is an extremely essential part of the business structure. The capital stock of a bank, furnished generally by hundreds of people the majority of whom are in moderate circumstances, is a small proportion of the whole. The most important element is the deposits, which are contributed by a large part of the community. In respect to deposits, then, the people are the bank. The banker, as generally understood, is the paid officer who looks after the interests of the entire institution. Banking profits are not proportionately large, and go to the stockholders, who are again the people. Private bankers with capital of their own are comparatively few in number and cut but a small figure in the United States as compared with incorporated stock banks. These private bankers issue no notes, and are not benefited or affected directly by laws relating to banks. Laws which injure the banks do harm to the whole community; whereas laws which contribute to the proper working and prosperity of the banks help radically the whole people, especially those who depend upon daily labor for their wages.

The business of banking may be divided into three principal operations: (1) The receiving of money on deposit; (2) the loaning of the same on security of collateral or names; (3) the issuing of notes for circulation. In speaking of the United States Government being in the banking business, reference is made only to the latter feature, the note-issuing part of the business. The currency troubles in the United States are mainly due to the assumption by the Government of this prerogative, which as properly belongs, under certain restrictions, to individual associations as does the right to manufacture the necessities of life. That is to say, the experience of generations of trading people has demonstrated that the Government, from its very nature, is as unfit to issue the circulating medium required by commerce as would be the faculty of a young ladies' seminary to conduct a great war.

We hear frequently the natural inquiry, Why should the banks issue currency? Why cannot a great government, with unlimited resources as a background for taxation, best maintain this instrument which affects the daily life of all the people? The answer is that currency is one of the tools of trade; and, whether good or bad, it is controlled or acted upon by the laws of trade, which are as immutable and as powerful as are any of the great laws of nature. Proud kings and powerful states have endeavored to pervert these laws by creating something out of nothing, and to wrest to themselves the benefits which are the reward of industry alone and which belong to the whole people; but, in every instance, these great laws have in the end, long confined by false conditions, broken away with the force of bursting cyclones, leaving behind them death, destruction, and ruin.

Money is one of the tools of trade, but in all banking transactions, for instance in the United States, metallic and paper money are used only to the extent of about 6 per cent of the whole. How is the place of money taken as to the other 94 per cent? It is made up of checks on banks, bank drafts, and other like instruments of exchange. The business of the United States, then, is done to this great percentage by bank machinery, which has grown to its present perfection as a result of the operations and development of commerce through the ages. The bank is as much the machine of trade as money is its tool. If this machinery did not exist, it would make necessary the

use of actual money in every transaction.   This great business is
done with immense economy by banks, safely, smoothly, and in fabulous amounts.   Actual coin is used to an extent of about $1\frac{1}{2}$ per
cent, paper money to about $4\frac{1}{2}$ per cent, but the other 94 per cent
is just as much in effect money as if it were actually coin.   Let
us call it check-money, if you please.   The check-money, then, is
used for the larger transactions, and paper money and coin for the
smaller.

New, what is the difference between check-money and bank-
notes?   The first is an order of the depositor on the bank to pay a
larger sum, the second is an order of the bank on itself to pay
a smaller sum; in effect, there is no difference.   One is payable to
order, the other to bearer; one is as safe as the other, as convenient
and as justifiable.   Commerce is to-day using check-money to an
extent of 94 per cent out of 100 per cent of its transactions.   Is
there any objection to giving it the privilege of using $4\frac{1}{2}$ per cent
more and furnishing, through perfect machinery adapted for the purpose by the experience of all time, all the paper money needed?

The bank-note, if sent in every day for redemption (as a check
is) and as it should be sent in under any proper system of bank
currency, becomes identical, in almost every respect, with the check.
The validity of check-money is based on representatives of wealth
deposited in the bank: so is that of the bank-note issued by the bank.
Check-money will be issued to the extent that trade requires it in
a community: so will the bank-note.   Check-money will stay out
only so long as it is needed and will come back again for redemption
from other banks who want the money: so will the bank-note, under
the daily redemption arrangement which is essential.   Check-money
circulates in the neighborhood where it is needed: so will the bank-
note, if redeemed daily.

The increase in the number of bank-notes is regulated thus by
the requirements of trade and the desire of the banks to get them
out, because of the profit there is in the operation.   Their decrease
is effected by the pressure brought to bear by other banks, who,
striving to force their own notes out, send the notes of other banks
in, and the total amount kept out can thus never be more than trade
actually requires.   The regulation of volume is automatic.   We see
thus the uses, the convenience, the essential propriety of notes
issued by banks.

Does the Government, usurping this function of the bank in going into the banking business to the extent of note-issuing, fulfil, with its paper issues, the mission of the bank-note? Emphatically no. The Government is made 'up of representatives of the people, not chosen for any peculiar business qualification, but on account of a variety of attainments, in most cases political. Now the currency has essentially to do with business—with commerce—and the regulation of it must be thoroughly in accord with the needs and requirements of trade. True, we have many students of finance and practical financiers in our own Congress. I venture to say that the Committee of the House on Banking and Currency is one of the best-informed bodies of men on financial subjects to be found in any government. They are thoroughly cognizant as to what *should* be done, but partisan pressure, expediency, the wishes of constituents, weigh heavily. Most of all comes to them the question, What will pass? Can this or that, no matter how good, be put through? The fact stands that one bad man, or a few ignorant or vicious legislators, are enabled to block the whole body of Congress; and at just the point when prompt and sound action is imperative they stand in the way, with the whole country in peril. We had such a state of things in the criminal tardiness of the silver-purchase repeal. Given a body like this, subject, too, to change from period to period, so that a wave of Populism and Anarchy may at any time cast up temporarily an unreasonable and dangerous representation, we turn over to them the privilege of issue—the very life-blood of trade and commerce. In addition to the dangerous element, we have the Representative who is impelled by the demands of honest but ignorant constituents. Except he be a born statesman, he necessarily sinks to the level of the voters who elected him.

There comes now a grand emergency like war, and the pressure for money is very great. There are conferences and conferences, sound council and weak council, but the easy way prevails, and the Government is authorized to create a paper currency, and the poison of fiat money enters the blood, never wholly to be eradicated. We then have the greenback. The business of making a note-issue was thus started in this country. It has never permanently stopped since. The danger, of course, lies always in over-issue; but, with admirable firmness and decision, the limit of $400,000,000 was regarded throughout the War. But at these figures, gradually reached in an ascending scale, the greenback was productive of wild inflation, speculation in trade, extravagance in living, recklessness of expenditure, and final collapse with widespread ruin, bearing hardest upon the hand of labor. Then came slow and painful recovery. It has been computed that the War cost us eight hundred millions more than it would have cost if there had been no greenback. This is what we have already in the past to thank the greenback for.

Now let us note what follows this first warning. A cancellation of the greenback is begun. But the working poison—the deadening comfort of inoculation—stops it. Specie payments are resumed. But the eruption appears in another form: in fiat silver, the Bland dollar. No harm seems to follow, and back again we swing in the delirium of 1890 to paper. Once more the legal tender—the Treasury note. Now the fever is high again and we plunge with a crash into '93, and for a second time the issues are stopped—the second warning. But we have, nevertheless, not stopped soon enough. We have the over-issue. The necessity is upon us to maintain these over-issues. From the conditions thus produced every person in the United States is suffering more or less to-day.

The bank, issuing notes, depends upon its business depositor to take what he needs of them to pay out in the conduct of his business. This puts them into circulation. No more are taken out than business needs. Another business depositor, getting more of them than he needs, brings them back to the bank, where they are retired. Business thus regulates their volume. The Government bank has no depositors and can get its notes into circulation in no such way. It has no automatic method of getting information as to how much money is needed by trade, and could not act upon it if it had. The Secretary of the Treasury, ostensible Manager of the Bank, has his hands tied. The Government currency once out stays out; and, as if natural conditions were not strong enough to keep it out, the legal tenders, when they come in for gold, must by law be paid out again.

The tendency of an irredeemable Government currency is to drift to the money centres, and there, when its volume is too great for the uses of legitimate trade, to incite to inflation and speculation. Once at the great centres it stays there, and this is the cause of the dearth of money in the West and South. It is the real reason for that honest cry (of which dishonest leaders take advantage and fan into a dangerous flame)—the cry for more money—which ever and anon sweeps into a whirlwind, now for silver, now for State money, now for fiat money, for people's money, money on farm mortgages, money *per capita*, by the barrel, tons of it, millions and millions! I do not wonder that our Representatives from those regions which have been denuded of the natural right of a community, the right to bank-notes, feel that they must heed this cry.

There is a good honest remedy for all this. It is through the permission of note-issue to banks, without specially pledged security, under proper general supervision. We have this supervision in almost complete perfection in the national system. But the banks are now held down to an issue of 90 per cent against par of bonds. There is no profit in this and so no relief, because banks will absolutely refuse to put out a single note voluntarily unless there is a profit in it. The issue must eventually be not against bond security, but against the general assets of the bank with provision for daily redemption, so that the notes will stay to do their work in their own neighborhood, thus clothing them with all the advantages claimed for State-bank issues, but with none of the dangers.

The real want thus met, the dangerous, ignorant, but honest cry for money will cease. Above all and before all, Government money, the legal tenders, must be wiped out. They are danger-breeders, inoculated with fiat poison, clumsy, unscientific and out of place. The Government must go out of banking, a business which it is manifestly unfitted for, and a business which has proved disastrous to governments in every historical instance. It must adopt once more the high and only prerogative of a state with regard to the issue of money, namely, the stamping upon precious metals the state's certificate of their weight and fineness.

WILLIAM C. CORNWELL.

WHY GOLD IS EXPORTED.

THE large and continued exports of gold from the United States to Europe during the last few years and recently, at seasons of the year in which imports of the metal should rather have been expected, have called forth much comment and anxious inquiries as to the reason of the movement. Under ordinary circumstances and for a long series of years it was considered natural to *export* gold in the spring, when our crops of cereals and cotton, etc., had been marketed, and to *import* gold in the last quarter of the year, when the exports of these commodities again came into active operation after the new crops had been garnered. During the last few years, however, these normal conditions have undergone a gradual change. First, the autumnal imports of gold began to decrease, then to cease entirely, and finally were superseded by an actual outward flow of gold in the midst of the full export season of our products.

Whence this great and important change? Did we import so much more merchandise, coincident with the decrease in value of our articles of export? Did a vast amount of our railroad and other securities come back to our country to be paid for here?

To a certain extent these were the factors that caused gold to leave us, and the first impetus to cause our securities to come home was undoubtedly given by the Baring collapse in 1890. But these factors no longer exert their influence, in so far as the merchandise balance has turned largely in our favor, and the flood of American securities back to this country has virtually ceased. It is argued that Europe has no longer large quantities of our securities to return; but while it is true that Europe's holdings are very considerably reduced, there is still owned abroad a vast amount of our securities, especially those of the well-managed and dividend-paying railroads such as the Pennsylvania, Illinois Central, New York Central and other Vanderbilt properties. It has been claimed that France, Germany and Russia were vying with each other to accumulate gold in preparation for an eventual war, and that Austria was drawing gold from us in order to carry through its currency reform and the adoption of a gold standard.   All these statements have truth in them, in-asmuch as these countries, for one reason or another, wanted or re-quired gold.   But why should they not only look to the United States for it but actually succeed in drawing it hence, instead of from Great Britain, or from each other?   Desire to attract gold is not sufficient: there must be some right to call for it.   Temporarily gold may flow from the country in which a lower rate of interest prevails to the country in which a higher one can be obtained, and as Great Britain has had the lowest rates for money, it is thence that the bulk of the requirements of other European nations should have been taken.   Such *temporary* movements were seen during our panic of 1893, when the unusually high interest rates attracted a large amount of gold from Europe, only, however, to be lost again as soon as interest rates dropped to the low figures which generally follow in the wake of such financial disturbances.   In order not only to attract gold temporarily, but to retain it permanently, there must be an actual, matured debt, which cannot be settled in any other way than by payment in gold, the only universal measure of value.

If it be true that, as stated above, Europe no longer sends us large quantities of securities, and since the merchandise balance is very con-siderably in our favor, whence then comes this unsettled debt which keeps clamoring for payment in gold, and which, it seems, we can liquidate with nothing else?   The explanation is simple enough, but as the items that go to make up this debt are not subject to statistical verification, and are nowhere officially reported, they are but rarely quoted and not sufficiently taken into account when the subject is debated in our press and in the halls of Congress.

The United States owe to Europe (apart from the ordinary mer-chandise balances as evidenced by the Custom House returns) annu-ally:—

1. For money spent by American travellers abroad, about.........	$100,000,000
2. For freights carried in foreign ships, about....................	100,000,000
3. For dividends and interest upon American securities still held abroad, minimum...	75,000,000
4. For profits of foreign corporations doing business here, and of non-residents, derived from real estate investments, partner-ship profits, etc., about....................................	75,000,000
Total..	$350,000,000

These figures have been carefully gone over and represent a very conservative estimate, so that the actual total is more likely to be larger than smaller, making no allowance whatever for undervaluations of merchandise imported into the United States.

In order to pay this vast annual indebtedness to Europe the balance of trade in merchandise would have to reach at least this sum, but it has never done so. The merchandise balance (including exports of silver) in our favor in 1894 was $264,000,000, and large as this was, it still left a very large amount to be paid for. This balance could be paid only in securities or in gold. So long as European creditors were willing to take our securities or reinvest their balances in American enterprises, there was no inordinate call for gold, but as they no longer seem to wish to take our securities to any extent nor to make permanent investments here, there is nothing left but to ask for and insist upon payment in gold.

And this leads up to the other question: Why do they not wish to take our securities or make investments in our enterprises? Simply because the developments in our railroad management have filled would-be investors with disgust and anger, and above all because they are dismayed at the condition of our Treasury and our currency, and fear that if they leave or invest money here, they may not be able to get back as good money as they gave. They have no doubt of the good intentions of the Government to uphold the parity of gold, silver, and paper, but they cannot help doubting its ability, under the present conditions, so to do. Thus, fear is one of the main causes, and this fear will not be dissipated until we are on a sound basis, and no basis is sound that does not provide for a redemption of all currency in the money of the world—*gold*.

Without desiring to touch upon the respective merits of gold and silver, as money metals, it must be conceded that so long as we wish to deal with, and attract the capital of, the great nations that have been creating and accumulating wealth for centuries before the United States existed, we must be ready and able to pay in the same measure of value adopted by them, rightly or wrongly, and that is *gold*. It is not sufficient to have a form of money that may be acceptable to *our* people: it must be *universally* acceptable. The same feeling that prevails in Europe is making itself felt at home, and as a consequence capital here is also reluctant to enter upon new enterprises, and business is stagnant, and money, withheld from fructifying use, commands but nominal rates of interest.

That the people of the United States require European capital for the full development of the great resources of our country there can be no doubt, and we cannot hope to attract it before we succeed in getting our currency upon so sound a basis that the world will recognize our ability to redeem every pledge at its fullest international value.

According to the report of the Secretary of the Treasury there have been redeemed in gold, since the resumption of specie payments in 1879, about $260,000,000 of greenbacks, but as they had to be reissued instead of being cancelled when so redeemed, the amount outstanding has not been reduced, and they can continue to draw gold from the Treasury up to the point of absolute exhaustion. The fear that this stage of exhaustion may be reached, and *all* the gold in the country be gradually drawn from us, is at the root of our present troubles.

That this fear is not imaginary, but actually exists, is evidenced by the fact that various foreign insurance companies, domiciled here, have orders from the home offices to remit immediately all premiums collected; that mortgages on the best property, owned by foreigners, are not renewed at maturity, but the proceeds ordered home; that bankers, when offering good bonds, receive the reply that clients are no longer investing in American securities; that real estate purchases in New York arranged for by foreign corporations have been abandoned.

If the millions of greenbacks redeemed in gold within the last fifteen years had been cancelled, instead of being reissued, a gradual contraction of our circulating medium would, it is true, have taken place. But as we were continually adding to the circulation, first by the annual coinage of $24,000,000 to $30,000,000 in silver dollars, and then by the annual issue of about $54,000,000 of coin certificates, this would have been rather an advantage than otherwise. We are suffering rather from too much, than from too little, money. The desire in certain sections of the country for a debased currency, or what is called "cheap money," is the consequence of the desire to pay existing debts as easily as possible. But have these debtors given the question a thought of how and under what onerous conditions new debts will have to be incurred when such money has become the basis of transactions?

Much stress is laid also upon the necessity of giving to our currency more elasticity than it now possesses. While this certainly is extremely desirable, the paramount duty, at present at least, is to take the Government out of the banking business, and to provide for *safety*, leaving the question of arranging for a more elastic circulating medium to be worked out with care and circumspection by able financiers when the country is not under the pressure of requiring speedy legislation to maintain the high standard of its credit, and thus avert any possibility of disaster. In order to ameliorate the situation, and to gain the confidence of our best customers so that they will readily trade with us, giving us their wares for our products, and place their surplus in American investments of every kind and shape, two things must be done. Corporate management must become more honest, reliable, and circumspect, and, above all, our currency must be put upon an absolutely sound basis. The time for experimental financial legislation is past. In any plan for reform it should be provided that greenbacks and coin certificates (Treasury notes), when redeemed, shall be cancelled, and not reissued, and they should be funded into a low-interest-bearing, long-time, *gold* bond that will find a ready market both at home and abroad, especially if it be issued in small denominations.

The resumption of specie payments in 1879 was followed by great imports of gold and an era of general prosperity. May we not expect, therefore, without being too sanguine, that when the United States Government can prove to the world at large that it intends to be, as it has hitherto been, honest toward its creditors and amply *able* to satisfy every claim upon it, the outgoing tide of gold will cease, to be followed by an incoming tide, carrying with it renewed enterprise, full employment for labor, and prosperity for all?

ALFRED S. HEIDELBACH.

THE PROGRAMME OF GERMAN SOCIALISM.

FOR many years, and at present perhaps more than ever, so much silly or malicious nonsense has been written and is being written about our Social Democratic movement, that I consider it my duty to accept the invitation of the editor of THE FORUM, and to state briefly what we are and what we want. Social Democracy has become such an important factor in our whole political life that the course and essence of German and European politics cannot be understood without a knowledge of the Social Democratic movement. Caprivi, the late Chancellor, said once in the Reichstag, that all legislative measures of the Government were framed from the point of view of the effects they were likely to have on Social Democracy; and thus it was confessed, by the head of the Imperial Government, that Social Democracy is the axis around which the political world of Germany is revolving.

I am asked to write on our "working" programme. If this should imply that we have two programmes—a working or practical programme and a theoretical programme—then I should have to disappoint the readers of THE FORUM; for we have but one programme, the one containing our principles and their application. We do not admit any distinction in principle between theory and practice— if the theory is right, practice cannot be opposed to it, practice being nothing else but applied theory.

After the last congress of our party—at Frankfort-on-the-Main —our adversaries reproached us with having two programmes, one pronouncing the last consequences and aims, and the other discreetly hiding them and exhibiting a brilliant set of fascinating delusions: the former for ourselves, for the initiated, the latter for the common herd. What fools we are taken for! In our principles lies our strength, and twenty-four years ago, in a treatise on the "Land Question," I plainly and unreservedly said, and proved, that hiding our ultimate aims would be suicidal stupidity, and that the truth and logic contained in our programme constitute the irresistible strength of our party.

Of course, when we have a village-meeting we do not give a lecture on Marx's " Capital," but we speak about the villagers' economic and social situation, about the debts of the small peasants, the wages of the agricultural laborers, the misery in which they both have to live, and the reason why. We show the working and action of capitalism, how capital destroys property,—the property of all those who have to live on their handiwork; how property is in a state of constant warfare, how small properties are devoured by big properties, —the small farms by the big farms; how of the five and one-half millions of *soi-disant* landed proprietors in Germany according to the later published statistics, half a million at the utmost have still real property of their own, and how the others are proprietors only in name, who will soon disappear, swept away by the crushing power of capitalism. And if we succeed in getting the ears of our hearers, we win them.

It is stuff and nonsense to talk of the " anti-collectivist peasant": the big land-owners are anti-collectivists, like the big manufacturers and merchants; but the small peasants are quite as open to our doctrine as the small tradesmen of the towns,—and the agricultural laborers quite as much so as the industrial laborers. What renders the propaganda more difficult in the agricultural, than in the industrial, districts, is principally a question of space and time. The agricultural population is more dispersed, so that we cannot reach the masses so easily as in the town; people must be taken *en detail*, which of course takes longer and requires more patience and pains than spreading the propaganda in the towns where the masses are concentrated.

No, we have no double programme, as we have no double truth and no double moral. What we *will* we say, and our deeds correspond to our words. Our adversaries cannot say this of themselves; their actions belie their professions. Theory and practice—one for us—are for them separated by a wide gulf, in which honesty is drowned and out of which rises the basest hypocrisy. They talk sanctimoniously of religion, order and morality, and in the same breath they call for measures of oppression, by which the greatest party, comprising one-quarter of the whole German nation, is outlawed, civil war virtually proclaimed, and the laboring classes helplessly delivered over to the clutches of capital. Instead of practising charity, they ask for charity—that is to say, for alms out of the pockets of the laboring people, alms for the rich taken from the poor! Here you have the political secret of our *Junkers*, who, united to the industrial magnates have, under the glorious government of Bismarck, in the shape of duties on corn and industrial produce, of "benefices" on spirits, sugar, etc., robbed the German people not of millions, but of milliards; who conspired against Caprivi, because as an honest man he tried to diminish their "profits"; and who, after the overthrow of Caprivi, are now moving heaven and hell to bring back the golden times of Bismarck.

Our programme has always been a "working" programme. We never lived and dreamed in cloud-land. We always traded and worked on the solid earth. We applied our principles to all forms of life; and by this we won the masses.

Do you think that the nearly two millions of men who voted for the Socialist programme on the 15th of June, 1893, and to whom must be added nearly a million of voteless young men between 20 and 25 years—do you think they are a mob of "discontented" people who do not know what they want and, like silly children, only know what they do not want? Think what these numbers mean! They represent one-fourth of the entire body of active, that is of voting, electors, and consequently one-fourth of the entire population of Germany,—an Empire of twelve-and-a-half millions in the Empire of fifty millions. And not the worst fourth! The best, the cleverest workingmen of Germany are Socialists. The towns and provinces in which we have most adherents are the intellectual centres of Germany, and yield the smallest number of criminals; while on the contrary all those parts in which the *Junkers* and other saviors of religion, order and morals predominate—the East Elbian provinces, including the "German *Vendée*," Pomerania—have, according to the official statistics, the highest criminality and the lowest intellectual scale. And he must be very superficial who thinks this to be a mere accident.

Our programme, therefore, consists of a declaration of principles and of the practical and concrete demands founded on these principles. We do not want to abolish private property; it is only private property in the instruments of production that we want to abolish, because it gives the possessor power over his fellow-men and renders them economically and politically dependent on him. Labor is to be organized nationally and internationally, to the benefit and in the interest of all, with equal rights and duties for all. Instead of private production and speculation we want to have all the economic functions of society performed by, through, and for the commonwealth. The commonwealth is to be substituted for the private speculator, who has only his own private interests at heart. Thus, our Democratic Socialism is not to be confounded with the "state-socialism," of which we hear so much in recent years. No word has ever been more misused than the word "socialism." The Bismarckian police laws for insuring the workmen against sickness, accidents and invalidity have nothing whatever to do with Socialism; they are in reality nothing but a reform (and not a good one) of our poor laws. And as to the state-socialism, favored by Bismarck and by many reactionaries in the highest position, it ought in truth to be called state capitalism—the state, governed by our *Junkers*, is to abolish all private property in the instruments of production (railways and mines included), and is to be put in the place of all private proprietors—the state is to become the sole proprietor, the sole capitalist, the sole master who makes the people work and slave for the governing classes. The essential criterion of Socialism is the abolition of wages-work, for which is to be substituted the system of associated work, of fraternal coöperation.

Socialism has been accused of aiming at the oppression of personal liberty. Now I beg you to look at our programme, and you will see that every point of it is a striking refutation of this childish reproach. What do we ask for? Absolute liberty of the press; absolute liberty of meeting; absolute liberty of religion; universal suffrage for all representative bodies and public offices in the state and the commune; national education; all schools open to all; the same opportunities of learning and education for all; abolition of the standing armies and creation of national militia, so that every citizen is soldier and every soldier citizen; an international court of arbitration between the different states; equal rights for men and women—measures for the protection of the working classes (limitation of the hours of work, sanitary regulations, etc.) Can personal liberty, can the right of the individual be better guaranteed than by this programme? And can any honest democrat find fault with this programme? Far from intending to suppress personal liberty we have the full right to say that we are the sole party in Germany that fights for the principles of democracy.

And something else is demonstrated by this programme: that we want the legal, constitutional transformation of society. We are revolutionists—no doubt—because our programme means a total and fundamental change of our social and economic system; but we are also evolutionists and reformers, which is no contradiction. The measures and institutions we demand are to a great extent realized already, or on the point of being realized, in advanced countries, and all are in harmony with the principles of democracy, and, being thoroughly "practical," they constitute the best proof that we are not as we are depicted—brainless fellows, who disregard the hard facts of reality and who are going to break our heads on the granite bulwarks of state and society.

The founders of your great commonwealth were quite as much—and very similarly as we are at present—misrepresented and calumniated by the tyrants of their time, and persecuted too. From the beginning of our movement we had to encounter the hostility of the Government and the ruling classes. Without intermission we have been persecuted. Hundreds and hundreds of times we have been condemned for crimes which in free countries are unknown or are even regarded as duties of free men; for example, for pronouncing our opinion, for demanding our rights, for making use of our rights.

Under the rules of the infamous *Socialistengesitz* years of prison —the millennium of Bismarck!—were imposed on us, and thousands of us were driven from our homes and families, outlawed and ruined. And what for? For taking part in the elections. For distributing voting tickets. For meeting without the permission of the police, who did not permit any meeting. These are all, artificial crimes—crimes created expressly to destroy our party.

But all persecutions were in vain. Our party continued to grow. When Lassalle died thirty years ago his followers in the whole of Germany did not count 7,000. Now we have nearly 2,000,000 socialist electors—that is, men above 25 years of age. The growing and grown-up population below this age, not having the right to vote, is not included in that number, and the young generation, our future citizens, in all towns and in a large part of the country are socialists to the marrow.

The following figures will show the growth of Social Democracy. At the general elections since the foundation of the German Empire we had votes:

Year.	Number of Socialist votes.	Mandates gained.
1871	124,655	2
1874	351,952	9
1877	493,288	12
1878	437,158	9

Year.	Number of Socialist votes.	Mandates gained.
1881	311,961	12
1884	549,990	24
1887	763,128	11
1890	1,427,298	35[1]
1893	1,786,738	44[2]

These figures speak for themselves. With the exception of the elections of 1878 and 1881, when the Bismarckian reign of terror was at its climax, and when our members were not yet accustomed to the new tactics made necessary by the lawless brutality of our oppressors, we see a constant rise; and the next election—of 1884— shows again a great increase, and the last election under the Socialist law—that of 1890—brought us at the head of all other parties, and broke the power of Bismarck, the *major domus* of the Hohenzollerns, whom the new Emperor would never have been able to shake off without this tremendous judgment of the German people. In the number of mandates the progress is not so steady, because, owing to our imperial law of election, there is much room for accidents in the distribution of the mandates.

The following figures will give you a comprehensive picture of our two last elections:

On the 20th of February, 1890, there were cast the following votes:

The Social Democrats	1,427,298
The Centrum (Catholics)	1,309,565
The National Liberals	1,169,112
The Progressists	1,147,863
The Conservatives	919,646
Free Conservatives	457,936
The Poles, Danes, etc., together about	750,000

On June 15, 1893, there were cast the following votes:

The Social Democrats	1,786,738
The Centrum (Catholics)	1,468,457
The Conservatives	1,038,555
The Free-Conservatives	438,435
The National Liberals	996,980
The two broken branches of Progressists together	924,920
The Anti-Semites	263,861
The Poles, Danes, etc., together about	750,000

If the election of 1890 overthrew Bismarck and his majority, the election of 1893 dealt a stunning blow to militarism. The Reichstag of 1890 had been dissolved for refusing to sanction the

[1] By a supplementary election we gained one mandate more: 36.

[2] By supplementary elections we gained two mandates more, so that we now have 46.

42

new military bill.   The questions before the German electors were,
Is our immense standing army again to be increased and the people
crushed by fresh taxation?   Or shall we break altogether the yokes
of standing armies, and prepare for a general disarming by an international congress?   And the answer was that out of a total of 7,674,-
000 voters, in round numbers, 4,350,000 voted against militarism
and 3,330,000 for it,—a majority of more than 1,000,000 against
militarism in the home of militarism.   That is indeed a great fact—a
great victory won by civilization, and won under the guidance of
Social Democracy, which is the representative of all popular demands,
the champion of Liberty, Peace and Humanity.

    This constant growth of our party, this growth under persecu-
tions of every kind, in times of peace and in times of war, under
common law and under exceptional law, is without parallel in history.   You have had many "booms" in your gigantic commonwealth,
but booms do not last long: they are like a hurricane swiftly increasing in strength and swiftly dying out.   Our Social Democratic movement is now—as far as we can fix for it a beginning, a birthday,
so to say,—more than thirty years old, and it is continually growing.
The Chartist movement in England, which in some respects had
most resemblance to it, did not last half that time, and had already,
after the lapse of ten years, passed its zenith.   Such wonderful growth
is the proof of wonderful vitality; it would have been impossible,
if Social Democracy were not the natural result of circumstances, the
natural fruit of our social and economic development.

    Nobody can swim against the tide of time, nobody can make it turn.
And the tide of time is the working of the elementary laws governing the social and economic world.   The tide is with us, to be sure.
We owe much to the faults and the shortsightedness of our enemies;
and Bismarck, by his remarkable talent for disorganizing everything
and making everybody uneasy and discontented, has certainly done
much to promote our cause (as part of that power, which always
strives for the bad, and always does the good, like Mephistopheles).
But we should never have had any lasting success if the "logic of
facts" had been against us.   Persons have nothing to do with it.
Hero-worship is the pastime of political children.   If we rob history
of all its "heroes," we only clear it of so many myths.   Before the
sharp eye of critical science the heroes disappear, and we find that
our civilization is the collective work of mankind,—work done by
myriads of generations,—and that mankind would be just as far ad-

vanced as it is had all the great conquerors, kings and other heroes, of whom history tells us, not lived at all. If a political, social and economic system is doomed, that is to say, if it has become opposed to the vital conditions and interests of society, no man and no power can prop it up. The old Roman Empire died under the best Emperor not quite as fast as under the worst. No heroes could have averted the final catastrophe. We agitators of to-day do not pretend and cannot pretend to be greater agitators than Ferdinand Lassalle. We know that we are not his equals. And yet our successes are far greater than his. Why? Because in Lassalle's time capitalism, quite new then in Germany, was in its infancy, and had not yet shown its capacity for destroying property. The immense majority of workingmen and all small trades-people (the agricultural population was then still slumbering) believed stanchly in the gospel preached by Schulze-Delitzsch: that the interests of capital and labor were in full harmony, and that by dint of diligence and economy anybody could become a well-to-do and independent proprietor. Now, thirty years later, capitalism has made such a revolution, and its effects are so evident, that there is no workman and nearly no tradesman in Germany who still believes in that beautiful but untrue children's tale; and honest Schulze-Delitzsch, once "the king in the social empire," is to-day forgotten.

Facts are not only stubborn things, but also great agitators and stern, convincing teachers. And if the facts speak such a powerful language as to show that in Germany, millions of ruined "existences" —the destruction of our small trades-people and peasants, not your middle classes—demonstrate so forcibly the nature and working of capitalism, then you cannot wonder at the wonderful successes of Socialism in Germany.

Being the youngest power on the immense battlefield of the *Weltmarkt* (world's market), Germany has in the last thirty years made giant strides in industrial development; she has got ahead of all other countries, with the exception alone of England and the United States; and having entered the fight as the weakest power, she has had to suffer most, and the number of victims is with us the greatest. And all the victims come to us, the "party of the discontented," as Social Democracy is dehominated by thoughtless scoffers.

Yes, we are "the party of the discontented." All the discontented come to us for help—all who have been wrecked in this our "best of all possible worlds," all whose hopes have been blighted, and who have discovered that their misery is caused by our irrational, in-human and unjust social and political institutions.   Jeer at the "dis-contented"!   Have all beneficial reforms of which history tells us, has all human progress, been brought about by contented people?   No; the discontented were at all times the pioneers of progress.   Discontent has always been the whip that drives mankind forward.

And those that come to us, come with open eyes and by their own free will.   It is an act of *courage* to enter our ranks, for it is an act of opposition, of rebellion even, against the powers that be.   So we have only tried people, people of character and resolution.   The millions of Socialist electors have been represented by hostile papers as confused, weak-brained fellows, who do not know what Socialism is.   That is a scandalous injustice.   The fact is, our electors are on the average more conscious of what they aim at, and more consistent in their doings, than the electors of any other party.   Every one of our electors and adherents in general has an idea of the fundamental principles of Socialism, while the members of the other parties, none of them excepted, in their immense majority do not belong to their party from conviction, but are at the command of some authority—the priest, clergyman, *landrath*, *burgermeister*, landlord, mill-owner, or whatever name the authority may have.   Our electors never swerve; they stick to the red flag, and neither threats nor promises will bring them into any other camp.   The Conservative, the National Lib-eral, etc., electors are most of them ready to change their party if their authority changes.   We had a most ludicrous example when last year at the bidding of anti-Semitic officials many thousand con-servative electors voted for anti-Semites and against the Conserva-tives, who had found out that the anti-Semitic movement, Bismarck's pet, had become rather troublesome.   Well, the "boom" of anti-Semitism is a thing of the past—it has only prepared the way for Socialism in districts which we could not reach at once.   Anti-Semitism, the "Socialism of the stupid," has been sowing, and Socialism reaps.   If you want to see "voting cattle," in the *literal* sense of the word, visit Germany at our next election, and walk about in one of the rural districts on the day of polling.   You will see human beings put in cars like calves sent to the slaughterhouse, and driven to the place where the next voting-box is, where the hu-man beings are taken from the car and marshalled to the voting-box into which they have to deposit the tickets given them by their "chiefs."   These voting cattle may be Conservative, National Liberal,

Catholic, even Progressist—of this one thing only you may be sure: they are not Social-Democrats.

Social Democracy goes its own way, and it bows to no " *sic volo sic jubeo*" but that of duty. We have our firmly established tactics, which have led us from success to success, from victory to victory. We fight our battles on our own ground and with arms that render us invincible. We do not and shall not allow ourselves to be enticed into mad adventures, where defeat would be sure. If we accept a challenge, as we did that of the Berlin Brewery Ring, then we fight it out, and our adversaries will learn to their detriment that we have well calculated our strength and theirs. The late beer boycott was the greatest struggle of this kind of class-warfare ever waged in any country. It was a real "trial of strength," and we brought to its knees one of the most powerful organizations of employers.

Socialism is in every respect the opposite, the antipode, of Anarchism. Anarchism in its two practical significations means first idolization of *I* and the unbounded right of the Individual; and secondly, resulting thereof, the right of each Individual to enforce his will by any means—the religion of brutal force, the propaganda of the deed. In each of these forms we combat Anarchism on principle. I have no time now to enlarge on this theme. Suffice it to say that we Socialists know and teach that no Individual has either the right or the power to impose his will on Society. Neither a Bismarck nor a Ravachol, neither Czar nor Emperor, can alter the laws that govern human society. And we know and teach that we have to organize the working classes for class-war against the capitalist classes; and we know and teach that "individual fight" in the shape of killing and maiming individual adversaries is criminal folly and can never lead to any revolutionary result. We have from the beginning warned against the anarchistic tactics, which in fact are only in the interest of our enemies and directed by them. If we except the lunatics and the blustering spouters, nearly all "practical" Anarchists (of the "theoretical" ones, being most harmless and inoffensive people, I do not speak here) have been and are still police-agents. Mr. Puttkamer, Bismarck's police-minister, told us frankly in the Reichstag that he preferred the Anarchists to the Socialists; and indeed he had succeeded in raising a crop of anarchistic " *lock-spitzel*" or *agents provocateurs*. But we spoiled his game and Germany has neither Anarchists nor "*attentats.*" To recompense us, we are to have a new gagging bill, which, if it became law and had the effect intended by its authors, might produce Anarchism. But it will not. I do not know whether the Reichstag will accept the bill in some form—in the present, certainly not. What I know is that no gagging bill will have the intended effect; and the import-ance of the present bill is principally a symptomatic one, as showing the utter absence of statesmanlike thought in our so-called states-men. Our reactionists—they call themselves " Conservatives"—are indeed the twin brothers of the Anarchists. Instead of believing in the "blessed bomb" or the "saint dagger," they believe in the holy trinity of Infantry, Cavalry, Artillery, aided by a subsidiary army of policemen, public prosecutors and Star Chamber Judges. That is the whole difference, and it is a difference only in quantity, not in quality. The gagging bill, as proposed by the Government, is simply a law of proscription. Every man in Germany can be put in prison for years if his opinion is not to the taste of his judge—that is the long and the short of this monstrosity.

Add to this the attempt to drag me before a Court of Law be-cause I did in the Reichstag that which was my right and my duty —and you have the temper, the mind, and the sense of our Imperial Government. The prosecution against me is judicially an impossi-bility, and politically an outrageous blunder. And you know the words of Talleyrand: " Worse than a crime, a blunder." Many Gov-ernments have survived a series of crimes, none a series of blunders. And this prosecution is perhaps the biggest blunder that could be committed; for it puts the Government on the horns of the dilem-ma—ignominious retreat, or a disastrous conflict with no chance of victory.

Germany is not in a social crisis alone; we are also in the midst of a decisive political crisis. The German Constitution is the most ridiculous anomaly in the world. The pyramid of the Em-pire has universal suffrage for its base, and is crowned by the " Pickelhaube." Democracy at the bottom, Absolutism at the top—how can that agree? The two hostile principles cannot exist peace-ably together; they must fight, and they will fight it out to the end. The English fought it out two hundred and fifty years ago, the Frenchmen a hundred years ago, and we slow Germans are now at it. And we Socialists have to bear the brunt of the battle. Our middle class has not had the courage or the opportunity to conquer civil liberty. So we Social Democrats have the double mission which is already expressed by our name: to fight for democratic institutions as well as for social emancipation.

The struggle between Socialism and our Government reminds me of the fable of the Goblin and the Peasant. A Peasant had in his hut a Goblin, who did him no harm, and did him even much good; but he hated him and wanted to drive him out or destroy him. He chased him, he hit at him, but instead of breaking the Goblin's skull, he broke his own furniture. At last, in his blind fury, the Peasant set fire to his house, in the hope to burn and so surely to kill his enemy. The hut became a heap of ashes, and when he left it in his cart, chuckling at the thought of having at last got rid of his enemy, he discovered the Goblin sitting behind him and laughing in his sleeves, quite happy and quite comfortable.

Our rulers can break the furniture and burn the house—Socialism is beyond their reach, Socialism is a necessity. And necessity knows no law but *its own*.

W. LIEBKNECHT.

THE SOCIAL DISCONTENT—I. ITS CAUSES.

THE year 1894 contained an occurrence which, though it marked no change in the seat of empire or in any ruling dynasty or even in the dominance of party, was attended by no wars or portents in earth or sky, was heralded by no boom of cannon or blare of trumpets, yet might with no slight warrant be regarded as one of the most significant occurrences in human history. It was no mere expression of a theory, but was in the nature of a demonstration, peaceful, legal in form at least, and without any pressure from necessity, that the old order of the world, under which from time immemorial the strong have dictated to the weak, has, with at least one great people, passed away, and that an era has been entered upon wherein the weak dictate to the strong. The demonstration was in the passage by the American Congress of the law taxing all incomes of over four thousand dollars a year. An income-tax law is no new thing, but this one differs from preceding ones in that it was passed without pressure from armed revolution, or from war, military establishment, increasing national debt, or any emergency whatever. There were, it is true, some deficits in revenue to be met, but despite all the stupid and interested arguments, they could easily have been met by other and usual forms of taxation, or *a fortiori* by this one without exemption of comfortable incomes. There is no respectable doubt that the tax was imposed purely and simply by a desire among vast numbers of voters that their share of the taxes should be paid by the rich. This, though among the least noisy of the many illustrations of the growing social discontent, is probably the most portentous. The matter has reached a point where its discussion in almost any form may be of use, though the papers are so full of it that a writer undertaking it without a self-distrustful smile would show himself probably lacking in humor. But the papers necessarily treat it very fragmentarily, and I venture to believe that very few of the readers of anything but " Labor organs" begin to apprehend the nature of the ignorance, credulity, and prejudice at the bottom of the social discontent, or, on the other hand, the honesty and self-respect in the same position. I shall try to illustrate both by circumstances which, whenever I have had occasion to tell them to such people as the majority of those who read this Review, have aroused surprise.

First, however, I shall attempt to summarize the principal causes (which have all been mentioned right ånd left) of the recent rapid growth of the social discontent, and after giving the illustrations I have alluded to, of the chaos of popular ignorance, prejudice, honesty and self-respect, I shall attempt to indicate the economic doctrines which, in such a soil, furnish sustenance for the discontent.

Its recent rapid growth has had for its most general cause one which I think I saw pointed out in the "Evening Post" in a profound and admirable application of Sir Henry Maine's great generalization. The writer attributed the growth of the discontent in modern times not only to the growth of education and the tendency to think, but more generally to the change of the vast masses of mankind from the condition of status to that of contract. The slave, the thrall, the serf accepted their conditions in dogged silence; but as the laborer has increased in opportunity to contract for his services, his discontent has kept pace. And now, at last, he is agitating schemes to rise superior to the policy of contract, although that policy alone has made possible his progress, and the progress of civilization itself; he wishes to dispose of all property by fiat, not knowing that that policy kept his forebears enslaved, and if returned to (which fortunately it cannot be) would bring general slavery back again.

A reason why the discontent has grown fastest of all in Germany, France, Italy, and America, would be suggested by the fact that of late years those nations have increased the protectionist features of their tariffs. The laborer has been put under the most expensive and onerous of all forms of taxation, his industries have been subjected to abnormal stimulation and collapses, and naturally he is writhing, without, in this regard, knowing what is the matter with him. He is learning, though.

The discontent in America, however, where it is still less than at least on the continent of Europe, has had, among others, three special causes,—first, the spectacles constantly before the working classes, owing to our facilities for the sudden acquisition of wealth, of people of their own grade enjoying luxury and some sort of position; second, the growing snobbery of the press; and third, excessive immigration from countries where harder conditions than ours have given more occasion for discontent.

I have heard President Cleveland's maintenance of order in Chicago during the strike, called a war on labor in the interests of capital, and Altgeld lauded as the peer of Lincoln and Washington, and these sentiments were rapturously applauded. The speaker was a foreigner. All the rational, temperate, helpful discussion of this class of questions that I have heard from workingmen, has been from Americans; with but one exception, all the crazy, destructive talk has been by foreigners. American social discontent is, in its worst form, of foreign manufacture. Indeed, the American laboring-man is hardly any longer a leading characteristic of this country. When he was, he did his work, saved his money, enjoyed and advanced his life, and spent no thought upon any agency for doing so but his own energy and frugality. What passes for the American laboring-man now consists largely of importation from inferior conditions, with inferior education and balance, a childlike dependence on government, and a fixed intention, through it, to better his condition at the expense of somebody else. Yet I by no means intend to say that the native has had no share in the social discontent of this later day. Under it, he has set Yankee ingenuity at work the country over, but most effectively in the South and West, on schemes for getting suddenly rich,—he has been a Populist and an inflationist, I do not think very often a full-fledged socialist: he has too much of that same Yankee sense for so great a fallacy. But he has generally been law-abiding, good-natured, and, in intention at least, constructive: seldom destructive, never anarchistic. And when his minor follies have been demonstrated, he has been quick to see the signs and change his vote. It is not often, however, that he is now merely a laboring-man without capital, and I hardly know how far to attribute to him the opinions I am to speak of later.

The spectacle of h... erstwhile bench-mate in a brand-new high-back victoria, with a big diamond in his shirt front and another on his finger, does not tend to keep the workman at ease in his humble estate; and the spectacle of such people acting in the various political councils—from those of the cities up to Congress itself—tends to make the man still at the bench think his " opinions" on public and economic questions as good as anybody's.

As for his wife, one of her chief consolations in her intervals of rest, has become the so-called " society news" which has lately been occupying increasing space in all the papers, and even inspired the creation of some papers especially for its setting forth. The nauseating stuff has now reached the point where, though many people of position despise it, the mails of the city editor are weighed down by the applications of the *noveaux riches* to have their doings chronicled; their crushes and gorges are described as "elegant entertainments," and even the country papers call it a "*fête* of some of our young society people," when· the clerks of the village butcher and grocer take the seamstress and the milliner for a straw ride. This sort of thing is bearing more fruit in "labor troubles" and mad legislation than is taken into account by the editors who purvey it believing it at worst merely foolish. To the workman's wife, or daughter, it makes no difference that the vast majority of the people so chronicled are not really "society"; and so far as they are her own quondam associates (which is quite far), the irritating stimulus is all the more effective.

Now for a few illustrations of the state of popular intelligence and character in which the discontent has taken root. Once last winter I heard a socialist haranguing the Sunday-night audience in the hall of the University Settlement Society in Delancey Street, New York. The audience consisted almost entirely of working-people, well-fed, well-dressed, and, I doubt not, with money in their pockets. The speaker's theme was that Socialism was the only avenue of advance open to the working classes, because, according to Lasalle's "iron law of wages," under the system of private property and wage-payment, the utmost the wage-earner ever could hope for was the very least that would keep body and soul together and in wage-earning order. And there sat the well-dressed, well-fed, well-to-do audience of wage-earners, and calmly swallowed that statement, while in their own persons they flatly contradicted it. In the discussion which followed, not one of them questioned it. On this basis of stupid untruth, and with reiterations of the equally untruthful statement that the present economic system is inevitably making the rich richer and the poor poorer, the speaker, amid frequent applause, built up his argument for Socialism. After he got through, and the topic was open for general debate (the educational process in vogue there being to give both sides a hearing and trust the truth in the long run), one of the audience stated a few of the facts gathered by Atkinson, Wells, Giffen and other investigators, which entirely obliterate the speaker's argument. But his defence, amid general enthusiastic applause, was that the investigators had evidently doctored their figures in support of "capitalism."

Another time, when conciliation and arbitration were under discussion, the secretary of a tailors' trade-union said that he did not
believe in them, because, although the workmen were always right,
the arbitrator sometimes decided against them.   At first, of course,
I thought he was joking, but he was not.

So much for the ignorance, credulity, and prejudice of those
workmen: now for their self-respect.   Nothing said by the speaker
during that first evening met with heartier approval than that the
workman does not wish charity, and that charity is deteriorating to
self-respect and working-power.   And I do not think that the hearty
endorsement of these sentiments was promoted by anticipation of the
speaker's following remark, that what the workingman does want is
justice,—which, it was soon made plain, in the view of the speaker
and the majority of his audience, consists in an even division all
around.

One more illustration of the spirit of independence and fairness
which underlies all the prejudice and gullibility of those people:
somebody was talking to them one night about getting ahead in the
world, citing the facts and saws new to them, though familiar to
most who will read this, of " twenty-five years from shirt-sleeves to
shirt-sleeves"—that nine-tenths of the employers were once laborers,
etc., etc.   All in the audience whose employers began as wage-
earners were asked to hold up their hands; then all whose employers
got their businesses by inheritance or otherwise than through their
own work and savings; and lastly, all who did not know how their
employers reached their positions.   The first show of hands largely
outnumbered both the others, and the speaker thought he had made
a pretty fair case to stimulate and encourage his audience.   But
when he was laid on the table for dissection, the first operator, a
cheerful looking little workingman of about fifty, said he thought it
was bad to advise young workingmen to try to get rich.   In his
opinion, " The fellows that get rich are the mean low-down chaps who
never stand treat or go to a ball-match or take a glass of beer."   The
reception of these observations was rather a tribute to their humorous
element than an expression of popular opinion one way or the other.
But there was a thundering burst of approval when a gentleman well
known in reform works chimed in with the preceding speaker, saying: " I don't believe in encouraging the poor man with fruitless
hopes.   Not one in ten can ever get rich, any more than one in ten
million can ever be President.   Their best way is to stick to their

own class and do what they can in it, like Joseph Arch and John Burns." The advice was open to question, but the sentiment receiving it was not.

The laboring-man's general position on economics, every intelligent newspaper reader, if he has thought about it, knows for himself; but unfortunately, notwithstanding its wide treatment, there are hosts of educated and influential people who have not really thought about it. Certain facts regarding our social situation need iteration and reiteration until iteration becomes sufficiently damnable to disturb the large majority of intellectual people who are peacefully sitting, reading physical science and the classics, on a crust covering a mephitic chasm or, as many think, a volcano.

This article is confined mainly to the fallacies in the wage-earner's reasoning, but before going into them more specifically I wish to state most emphatically that I do not by any means think that all his causes of discontent are fallacious. My position is almost the opposite: I think most of the hardship of the workingman's position comes from causes as substantial as those that make the difference between a man five feet high and one six feet high; but I think many of his views are as mistaken as would be those of the little fellow if, instead of making the best of his stature, he were to deny the difference, and at the same time attribute it to the big fellow's tyranny. The big one does impose on the little one sometimes, but the law is protecting him better every day; and probably just as often, in these times, a lot of the little ones get together and impose on a big one, and when he invokes the law, shriek that the law was made for him alone.

I hope that stating some of the mistakes of the less fortunate man will not be taken to imply lack of sympathy with him: but to do the best for him, the first essentials are to confine belief to the reasonable, and effort to the possible.

The workingman generally believes five fallacies as firmly, and in some cases as religiously, as his forebears believed in Heaven; and as his belief in Heaven has grown very indefinite, he holds the beliefs that take its place, all the more strongly, passionately, bitterly. He believes, first, that the world is his, for he made it; second, that it has been taken from him by the superior strength and cunning of his employer; third, that it is constantly being taken in greater and greater degree—"the rich richer, the poor poorer"; fourth, that if he can put himself in his employer's place, he can get it back; fifth, that by his ballot (not to speak of intermediary and ancillary meas- ures, such as strikes and boycotts, and making the master's income pay the workingman's taxes), he can put himself in that place, and he is going to do it.

Let us look at these beliefs a little.

First: his reasoning is that all wealth is in material things—im- proved farms, crops, felled trees, quarried stone, roads, railways, buildings, manufactured goods and chattels. All these were obvi- ously made by "Labor." No one but the laborer ever put his hand to them. To whom, then, can they by right belong but to Labor? The representative of "Labor" is, as a rule, oblivious of such facts as that an ordinary laborer cannot dig a ditch straight without some superior intelligence over him—that if you show a laborer a dead tree and a live one, and tell him to cut down the dead one, he is as apt to cut down the live one (as actually happened in my experience), and think he ought to be "paid for his time," and to get the pay too. He is, of course, still more oblivious that the com- forts of the laborer's life are put within his reach only by the cheap production possible under large industry, that large industry must be managed, that the amount of production varies vastly more with the capacity of the manager than with that of the laborers—that of two enterprises with equivalent plant and equivalent labor, one will fail and the other prosper because one manager is good and the other bad—that, in short (not to attempt the proof in detail), after aver- age wages, rent and interest are paid, the rest of the product is as much the outcome of the manager's brains as (in one sense) the whole product is the outcome of the laborer's hands.   Laborers gener- ally have some sort of recognition that management, tools, material, and buildings are necessary, but they do not see why a manager or capi- talist should have any larger income than a laborer; while they claim that every man should have what he produces, they are blind to the somewhat recondite facts that whenever a factory "pays," as dis- tinguished from a factory that does not pay, what the first pays is simply what the manager produces, in the second the manager pro- duces nothing, and in both alike the laborers produce what pays their wages.   Though this is theoretically correct, theory of course does not work out more exactly in economics than it does in physics, or as exactly. But there is no more extravagance in the theory that under free competition wages measure the laborer's product, than in the theory that the speed of falling bodies increases as the square of the distance. Neither case ever actually happened, but the latter would happen in a perfect vacuum, if there were such a thing, and the former would happen in perfectly free competition, if there were such a thing. Competition is generally free enough for practical purposes, however, and is growing more so—an improvement more obstructed by the laborer than by the employer, and obstructed to his disadvantage. Still less than the facts already alluded to, do the laborers realize the more remote facts that the very existence of the factory, the kind of machinery it uses, the kind of goods it produces, its periods of great and small activity, the purchase of material and sale of product in the best markets, the giving and obtaining of credit, the anticipation of changes of fashion and of good times and bad—that all these things can be successfully determined only by one man in a thousand, that most men who attempt to determine them fail, and that upon the degree of success in determining them, more perhaps than upon the more immediate functions of superintendence which the workman constantly experiences, depends the success of the enterprise. Workmen generally have heard of coöperative production, but they have a very imperfect knowledge of the fact that it has generally failed because the coöperators did not possess enough of the manager's genius, or because, through the meddling of too many owners, they did not give that genius full play; and they are equally ignorant of the correlative truth that where coöperation has succeeded, it has generally been in the industries requiring least of the manager's genius. The enormous production from invention is, theoretically, a little better understood by workingmen than the production from management, but, under their prejudices, the right of invention to its own production is practically ignored. And why should it not be ignored by them, when it is so imperfectly apprehended among the presumably higher intelligences who direct legislation?

The laborer's (I always feel a protest when I use the word or one of its synonyms in a sense restricted to hand-labor—as if the brain did not well know a toil and a weariness that the hand is a stranger to) the laborer's incapacity, then, to recognize the share of production due to management and capital, leaves him no alternative but his second fallacy—that the share which capital and management get is filched from him; and that the instruments of production have been filched from previous laborers, and are now, instead of blessings ready for the man who comes naked into the world, engines to extort the lion's share of his production.   He fails to appreciate that the capitalist's tools and material, and the landlord's land and buildings are theirs, remotely if not proximately, by the same right that the laborer possesses his own wages or the product of his kitchengarden, if he be wise enough to live in the country and have one:—namely each man's right to what he himself produces—the very right that he, wrongly in most cases, blames his employer for violating—the very right that he ignorantly violates whenever he claims a share of what the employer has really produced.   To him who has no property, " property is robbery."   Nine persons in ten—(would it be too much to say ninety-nine in a hundred?)—have virtually no conception of " making money" but that of making it out of somebody else—no realization that " a good trade is good for both sides"; the rank and file of mankind believe that every fortune is an aggregate of petty advantages filched from other men.   Of the truth of Mallock's generalization which, whether correct or not, is in the right direction, that the wage-earners make five-thirteenths of the product and get seven, most men have not the remotest conception.   There is a vague general impression that a portion of the world is in possession of all the powers and all the facilities, and simply makes the rest of the world do the work, and, after giving that rest enough to keep it alive, pockets everything left over. Hence the bitterness of " the social discontent."   And alas! this bitterness often grows from ground more substantial than such narrow views: for the powers of intelligence and capital are often abused.   But the bitterness also grows—I sometimes think that most of it grows—from a tradition.   What vague reflections of ideas working-people have, and what ideas they reflect, date mainly from Karl Marx; their teachers as a rule know nothing later and want to know nothing later; and the horrors told by Marx of the infancy of " the great industry"—of women and children worked and starved as their employers would not work and starve cattle, of the economic fallacy (though Marx did not know it was one) that there is profit in the over-time of a dying child —all these horrors were enough to turn stronger brains than Marx's.   Among the ignorant, the tradition of those miseries survives as a present reality, just as many of the old Know-Nothings I remember, and many of the A. P. A., I presume, attribute to the Catholic Church of to-day all the infamies of the Inquisition and the mediæval priesthood.   And with the stupefying facts of Marx and his school, survive their equally stupefying theories.

The third fallacy : " the rich richer and the poor poorer," is entirely a survival from Marx and his school.   When the individual industry was changing into the great industry, it was true—as much because steam was throwing people out of employment, as because employers had not learned justice and the wisdom of justice, and laborers had not learned combination.   That it has not been true for more than thirty years, probably more than fifty, is, as already said, abundantly proved by Giffen, Wells, Atkinson, and others.

Fallacy number four springs naturally from fallacy number two. If the employer is not a producer, if he virtually does nothing, anybody can do that: so if the laborer can get himself into the employer's place, he can do what the employer does, and get what the employer gets.   This he can do whether he gets into the place individually or in his aggregate capacity as " the State."   That the employer holds the place by using powers that the laborer (with the rare exception who eventually becomes a manager) cannot use, because he does not possess, hardly enters any laborer's head.   He thinks it is all the magic of " capital."   Still less does he reach the broader conception that if the manager, instead of being called by natural selection, were to be called by ballot, in the present state of political capacity, the share of wealth which the managers produce would, in most cases, not be produced at all, and that which the laborers produce would be materially lessened.

The fifth fallacy is that, in our present grade of political capacity, the laborer can get himself, as " the State," in the manager's place at all.   He intends to get in as " the State," because he regards that way as quicker and easier than the arduous way of industry and frugality which, ignore it as he may, put his employer or his employer's ancestor there.   He cannot carry out this intention for at least four good reasons: First, the socialist's theories being out of balance, and therefore unworkable, will be proved so in piecemeal trial long before there is any danger of general adoption: consider the recent history of the United States—greenbackism and grangerism and silverism and McKinleyism and Altgeldism and Populism.   Details are superfluous.   What the last two " landslides," probably the greatest in our history, meant, was simply that people were working up to a proper understanding of these things.   For the same reason, socialists have never agreed

43

among themselves long enough to accomplish much, and never will. Glance through any good history of Socialism. Rae's is probably the best. It is simply a series of accounts of combinations and dissolutions. A parliament assembles perhaps two or three times, differences arise, the organization splits up, new ones are started by the fragments, they run two or three years, more disagreements, new splits, new combinations. The life of any political party that ever accomplished anything but a revolution is immense in comparison; and a successful "revolution" is not on the socialist cards, however much it may be in their mouths; for despite all their talk, those who can at any one time agree on anything are an insignificant minority.   Again, property-owners not only outweigh but outnumber the foes of property, and in an increasing rate. It may justly be said that many property-owners have voted for the special socialistic crazes just enumerated. True, but it is a long way from voting for such fragments of socialistic doctrine, whose recoil upon private property is too devious to be generally appreciated, to directly voting for handing all productive industries over to "the State." Yet I do not wish to be too optimistic. These outbreaks of fragmentary Socialism do a great deal of harm—the panic of '93 was no trifle, and it was due to two socialistic crazes: silverism and protectionism. The latter's damage was, of course, not directly attributable to the craze itself, but to the apprehension of the withdrawal of a vicious stimulant, a thing which is often physiologically impossible without death.   Finally: the importance of economics in education is at last recognized, and the increase of such education is fatal to such inconsistencies as Socialism.

Next in importance perhaps to the five concatenated fallacies before enumerated, is a group of three that are specially active in fomenting the social discontent—that high wages cover the whole question, that wages are a small part of cost, and that the rate of wages depends on the volition of the employer.

The first is so simple that its wide bearings may well excite surprise. The laborer seldom reflects that he is a consumer as inevitably as he is a producer—in fact, more inevitably, for he can, and often does, live without producing, but he cannot live without consuming. Oblivion of this fact is the root of the wasteful opposition to prison labor and imported labor, and is also one of the elements of the protectionist craze, so far as employers still succecd in keeping their men under that delusion.   In production, too, this oblivion does harm in several ways.   One of them is in the habit of scamping and slouching in order to "make work."   If workingmen always labored directly for each other, they would see how scamping work is for the mutual disadvantage; but in manu- facturing the master's goods, or in building his warehouse, their im- agination cannot ordinarily follow waste down step by step until it appears in the prices of their own supplies; in scamping the tene- ment, they cannot see the waste raising their own rents; or in build- ing the rich man's palace, they cannot see waste resulting in the destruction of capital which, if preserved, would increase the demand for the poor man's labor.

Could the laborer be brought to understand these things, he would be better prepared to understand that it is an injustice to him- self as a consumer, as well as to his competitor as a laborer, that his wages should be any higher than an equally productive competitor is ready to take; that not only is it for the greatest good of the greatest number that all men should be employed at whatever prices the market will sustain—that no man should be left to starve in order that another man's wages may be kept high, but that it is also for the greatest good of the greatest number that those wages shall be the lowest which the productive capacity of the laborers warrants. That wages will be at least as high as that capacity warrants, can in our day ordinarily (I say ordinarily, not universally) be left to the competition of employers, which, helped a little by the trade-unions, is generally "free."   But that wages shall be as low as production warrants cannot with equal safety be left to the competition of the employees: for the trade-union machinery generally tries to restrain that competition more than employers try to restrain competition for help.   Yet just as far as any influence succeeds in forcing wages above the normal, just so far the wage-earner must pay for the prod- ncts of all trades, including his own, not only the excessive wages, but in addition all middlemen's commissions on them.

This fallacy I have just been treating prepares the way for the hatred of the " competitive system" characteristic of the working people and of the sentimentalists who befog them.   It is natural of course that those who do not succeed under a system should be less alive to its good side than to its bad one, and so it is no wonder that wage-earn- ers should be oblivious of the two facts that employers seeking help bid wages up as much as laborers seeking work bid them down; and that competition lowers the prices of the things that wages are spent for, vastly more than it lowers wages. Notwithstanding these facts, it is, at first sight, very easy to say that an altruistic society would be very much happier than a competitive one. But the fact is that when we say that, we simply don't know what we are talking about: so far as we know, no one ever saw a purely altruistic society, and the difficulties and contradictions involved in imagining one reduce the whole conception almost to the level of a pseud-idea. Yet I firmly believe that we are moving in the direction of one. I believe too that probably the best thing in human nature is altruism. The sentence is glib enough: but after all, I cannot think of altruism, and I do not believe anybody can, as a thing of any value unless it is accompanied by the capacity to do something and give something. The very least it can give is sympathy, and that is of no value unless it comes from a character of some positiveness. The truth is that, in competition and altruism, nature has been evolving two sets of virtues as opposite as male and female, and has even made the respective predominance of them characteristically male and female. Yet just as a man is a poor creature without sympathies, so is a woman a poor creature without courage, enthusiasm—in short, what we call character. Now character—that which does and resists, as distinct from the intellectual apparatus it does it with, is a product of the competitive system; and just as, in Doctor Johnson's judgment, "God might have made a better berry than the strawberry, but never did," so we may assume, if we want to, that God might have made a better system for developing character than the competitive system, but in human experience he certainly never did. And yet side by side with the competition, *and really as a consequence of it,* has grown up the sympathetic side of the soul. If there had been nobody left behind in the race—nobody to help and pull along, and even bandage and nurse—there would have been no chance for the altruistic sentiments to grow. So inextricably are all departments of our nature and of our environment intertwined, that we cannot think of altruism itself, let alone energy, courage, initiative, endurance, as anything but products of the competitive system.

Yet the wage-earners propose to do away with competition, and think they *can* do away with it, by a stroke of legislation. They might as well attempt to do away with gravitation. The two began together when our cycle of evolution began and the particles of star-dust rushed to their centres. There was conscious competition as soon as there was conscious need of food. Through its corollary of natural selection, it has evolved man himself and all his virtues, and it will not cease until its own processes, helped by others that are growing, have brought the race to a stage where the majority is capable, instead of a stage like the present where the majority is incapable. Then perhaps the help that the capable majority lends the incapable minority will be as adequate, as is now inadequate the help that the present capable minority lends the incapable majority.

Those who hate the competitive system, rich and poor alike, probably will not receive these ideas of it without a long course of education: but they can at least be taught the simple economic workings of that system for the poor man's good, and so something be done to stop his crazy efforts to overthrow it, with all their destructive recoils.

The wage-earner's concentration of view upon only his own wages, keeps him blinded by another prevalent fallacy: that wages are a small part of cost. The workman seldom thinks of the wages that preceded his, on material, and must follow his all the way to the final market.

On the foregoing limited conception is based the third fallacy of which I spoke: that the payment of high wages, or at least a "living wage," is a matter solely of the employer's volition. The relations of laborer and employer are too generally regarded as concerning only those two parties; and two other parties are left out— the community in general and, at times, the unemployed workingman. Whether wages are forced down by justice to men seeking employment, or by consumers refraining from buying until prices fall, the employer is blamed as if he were responsible, and there is an era of discontent, and perhaps pillage, arson, and murder.   I heard this fallacy preached one night by a philanthropist universally known and respected for intelligence and practical self-devotion. It was apropos of a recent refusal of the hatters and tailors to advance wages. I asked what those employers were to do in times when people generally incline to wear their old hats and old clothes. The answer was: "If they pay high wages, their employees will wear more hats and clothes."

I asked: "Do you mean that the employer can pay for the material in the clothes worn by the laborer, and also for the laborer's rent, food, and other outlays, out of the profit he can make on the clothes he sells him?" I was answered by a virtual change of subject.

This brings me to one of the most painful and hopeless features of the whole situation. The reasoning just given is a fair specimen of the economic reasoning generally characteristic of educated and refined people whose sympathies with the poor are strong enough to lead them to go down and take off their coats and work among them. Not only are such people all subject to their native danger of being swayed by sympathy, but those the least subject to it see so much of suffering and injustice, that their sympathies are specially stimulated, and they come to believe suffering and injustice to be the invariable lot of the less fortunate classes. Their natural bias becomes identical with that of a leading physician whose specialty is the diseases of women, who told me that he believes marriages are generally unhappy. Of course those he saw the inside of, generally were. So to the philanthropist working among the poor, the cases of employers' injustice are constantly brought, and the first postulate of his economic reasoning is that the superior is always wrong and the inferior always right. Thus these very guides of the poor, themselves become among the chief fomenters of the social discontent, and the chief believers in delusive short cuts out of it.

I hope to say something next month of the practical ways out.

HENRY HOLT.

HAS THE PROFESSION OF THE LAW BEEN COMMER-CIALIZED?

I HAVE been requested to give my views to the readers of THE FORUM on the subject, Has the Profession of the Law been Commercialized? Like most sociological questions, it does not admit of an easy or absolute answer in categorical form.

The general question which sociologists are putting to themselves, Is civilized society growing better or growing worse? is answered one way or the other according to the tendency of the observer's mind or according to the class of facts to which he particularly directs his attention. The slums of London or Paris or New York present us with a sombre picture of human depravity. The leisure classes of society, whose main object in life is to amuse themselves, now and then give us glimpses of a refinement of vice reminding us of the days of the Roman Empire. On the other hand, no one would seriously contend that these glimpses of vice fairly represent the character of modern polite society, nor would any one seriously deny that the general tone of the leisure classes is better on the whole than it has been in previous epochs of the world's history, where equal wealth and equal leisure prevailed. So those who take a broad view of civilized society are encouraged to believe that the slums are no worse to-day than the slums of former times, while the great body of the modern community is healthier, wiser, and better than at any previous period. In like manner, when we look at any particular class or profession, we find evidence on the one hand of decadence and on the other of improvement. The profession of the law is no exception to this rule.

In the hurry and bustle of this end of the nineteenth century we must expect to find more or less change in the methods and character of the profession of the law, as well as in every other calling in life. We cannot expect that lawyers of the present day should follow the methods of the lawyers of the end of the eighteenth century, any more than we can expect the same of physicians or even of the clergy.

Tempora mutant et nos mutamur applies to members of the legal profession as to all other men. Daniel Webster, travelling in a stage coach, is subject to an entirely different set of conditions from the modern leader of the Bar, whirled as he is from city to city on the limited express. The high pressure of life in this day and generation must affect the work and the spirit of lawyers as well as of other busy men. Much work must be got through with in little time, and labor-saving appliances are becoming more and more necessary.

The active practitioner in one of our great cities must also avail himself of the services of juniors and assistants in order to accomplish his daily tasks. He must delegate much of his work, or most of it will go undone. Even in the matter of examining authorities and of preparing briefs, it would be a useless waste of time and energy for him to attempt to cover the whole ground without assistance. The multiplication of Law Reports is a marked feature of the day. Chancellor Kent doubtless had read every decision of any importance reported in the various State and Federal Reports of his time. He certainly had read and probably knew almost by heart every reported decision in his own State. Such a thing is now physically impossible. No lawyer in the State of New York can have read, or, if he has, can remember, all the reported decisions of the various Courts of this State. It is almost incredible that any one, unless of phenomenal application and memory, can have mastered the cases even of our Court of Appeals since 1846, as found in the 142 volumes of New York Reports, not to speak of the volumes of Johnson (Law and Chancery), Paige, Cowen, Barbour, Hun, and a dozen or more other series of reports. When we add to this the 154 volumes of the United States Supreme Court Reports, vast numbers of State Reports and Federal Reports, as well as the English Reports, the mind is bewildered by the very enumeration of their titles, not to speak of their contents. Text-books and digests of decisions are of absolute necessity at the present day, and skilled assistance in collecting and analyzing decisions and preparing briefs is almost equally a necessity to a lawyer in very active practice.

The vast and complicated affairs of great corporations and of great corporate trusts, such as those, for instance, which modern railroad companies or trust companies undertake, call for an amount of professional advice and labor which necessarily requires a great expenditure of time and effort on the part of the counsel engaged in looking after the interests at stake. Such time and effort demand a commensurate compensation.

There has been much criticism of the large fees paid, or supposed to have been paid, to many of our leading lawyers. Some of such criticism is just, and some is unjust. There are, it must regretfully be admitted, many cases in which counsel take advantage of the existence of trust funds in the hands of a Court for administration to obtain, through the good nature of the Judges, allowances largely in excess of the value of their time and labor. There are, also, many cases where counsel have charged excessive fees to estates. In most cases, however, where large fees are paid or large allowances made, it will be found that there are vast pecuniary interests at stake and great responsibility incurred. Besides, it is not generally understood, but, as already indicated above, it is nevertheless the fact, that such fee or allowance frequently represents, although nominally paid to one man as counsel, the work of many men acting together with the counsel to whom the fee is paid—junior partners and salaried clerks—all of whom have given time, labor, research, and thought to the questions involved.

Then, too, the expenses of a lawyer in active practice in one of our great cities are heavy. High rents must be paid, especially in New York City, for offices in convenient localities. Other necessary expenses are also to be incurred. The modern law-office, equipped with stenographers, typewriters, and telephones, must, of course, be a much more highly organized business enterprise than the old-fashioned law-office; just as the modern railroad train must be more highly organized than the old-fashioned stage coach. There are to-day, nevertheless, thousands of able lawyers who do a large professional business in a quiet, simple, old-fashioned way. These men do a referee business, or the business of a Master in Chancery, or exclusively a Court business. In our great cities, however, it is usual to have firms of lawyers, combining the functions of solicitors and counsel, where usually one or more members of the firm appear in Court, while others attend to the office work, the drawing and preparation of papers, the conferences with clients. These different functions in England are separated between distinct classes of the profession—the solicitor and the barrister. In this country these two classes are combined in the same individual, though one man will, by natural selection, take up the work of the advocate or barrister, while the other will more naturally take up the work of the solicitor or attorney. The distinction is not, of course, a hard-and-fast one, for many of our ablest lawyers do more or less of both kinds of work. But the combination of the two functions in our great law firms is sometimes overlooked in measuring the magnitude of the fees received by such firms.

It will readily be seen from all these facts that the income of leading lawyers is apt to be greatly exaggerated in the public mind. Gross income is one thing; net income, after rent, expenses, clerk hire, and division with partners have been deducted, is quite another thing.

A further significant feature of modern practice is the formation of title guarantee companies. These have greatly interfered with the work of the old-fashioned conveyancer and real-estate lawyer. Formerly, every title had to be examined by some individual lawyer, or firm of lawyers, the records searched, and a certificate of title given. Now, this work is very largely, and in some places exclusively, done by companies formed for that purpose, who employ lawyers on salaries, or on stipulated compensation, for the purpose of examining the records and certifying the title.

It has been suggested that in the legal profession, as well as in other lines of activity, "the individual is disappearing in favor of the large organization," and that additional difficulties are presented to men just entering the profession. To a certain extent this is true. On the other hand, the very growth of organization furnishes opportunities both for the older and the younger men. It not only remains the case now, as it was in Daniel Webster's day, that there is "plenty of room at the top," and that individual lawyers of learning, ability, and force are at a high premium; but there is a growing demand for young men of brains and character and industry as law assistants and title examiners in the corporations above referred to, and as clerks and junior partners in our great law-firms.

The very nature of the work required of the lawyer prevents the complete extinction of the individual. The fierce contests of litigation call forth the highest qualities of individuality. In no sphere of human activity is the rule of the "survival of the fittest" more perfectly exemplified. The man who succeeds in the long run is the man who deserves to succeed. He meets his brethren of the Bar, as the knights of old met their compeers, in the open tournament. Whether he wins or loses in a particular contest, the character of his mettle is seen and known and accurately measured. The lawyer who impresses himself upon the judges and his brother-lawyers as a man of force and learning is the man whose aid and counsel are sought in future contests. Sham and shallowness and pretence are sure to be discovered. No permanent success can be built up except on the foundation of solid worth.

The work of the advocate is not merely nor mainly the reading and citation of statutes and authorities: it is the analyzing and marshalling of testimony; the logical reasoning upon legal principles; the clear and forcible presentation to the court of the facts and the law of the particular case in hand. Mere rhetorical glitter, mere oratorical brilliancy, are daily growing less effective; close argument and accurate and lucid expression are becoming daily more influential in the determination of the complicated questions of modern litigation.

It follows, then, that intellectual individuality must be, and must continue to be, the paramount force in the higher ranks of the profession in the trial and argument of causes before courts and juries, —and especially in the cold, dry atmosphere of appellate tribunals. Not only so, but in office work, the man of constructive ingenuity, with the grasp of mind to master complicated details, with the soundness of judgment to measure the practical workings of a scheme, with the knowledge of legal principles necessary to avoid dangers and pitfalls, with the patience and industry to perfect and carry out his plans, is the man who is sought after in organizing great corporate or commercial enterprises; in reorganizing and reconstructing insolvent railroads and other corporations; in drawing important contracts involving large pecuniary interests.

The young man, too, as already indicated, finds in some respects a readier opportunity than of old. It is true that starting by himself, in a great city, without influential friends or connections, " hanging out his shingle," as the old phrase goes, he has a hard and long struggle for recognition . He is lost in the crowd. There is, however, a great demand for " bright young men," as I have already remarked, as clerks and junior partners in large law firms where the seniors are overworked and are more than ready to turn over a large part of their work to their assistants, and are, as a rule, ready to recognize and encourage any special ability that may be displayed in the management of such work.

I hesitate to write this, for I do not like to say anything to stimulate the *hegira* of young men to our great cities, and especially to the city of New York. My belief is that the average young man

will do better, in the long run, in a smaller community, where character and attainments are sure, sooner or later, to win recognition;
and where the rewards of a successful lawyer in social importance
and influence are relatively greater, and where a moderate professional income procures a larger degree of comfort and independence.
In our great cities, opportunity has much to do with success; but
opportunity is of no avail without an ability above the average, enabling the man to impress himself upon his seniors at the Bar as a
man of force.   The pecuniary rewards of success are, of course,
much greater in our large cities than in smaller communities; but the
average rewards are less and the possibilities of failure greater.   In
other words, the "struggle for existence" is more severe.

In view of the situation that I have endeavored to summarize,
the question still remains whether the practice of the law has
been in fact commercialized?   I suppose it must be admitted that
on the whole there has been a growing tendency among the profession to desire big fees, and to seek after a large income rather than
to pursue the law as a science.   In our great cities it has become
increasingly difficult to get the leaders of the Bar to forego lucrative
practice for the sake of positions on the Bench, where the salaries are
limited and are much less than the income of such men at the Bar.

On the other hand, I am sometimes amazed at what seems to me
to be the high standard of professional spirit still remaining.   Our
busiest lawyers are willing to sacrifice time and effort in public matters, without reward, or expectation of reward, of any kind.   It is
not infrequent for a lawyer in the highest ranks of the profession to
give advice or take charge of litigation where the entire amount involved would not pay him a reasonable fee for the time actually
spent in doing so because he becomes interested in the case or in
the questions involved, or because his sympathies are appealed to on
behalf of one who has suffered injury, or who has rights requiring
vindication.   To the credit of the Bar, too, it must be said that there
are still men found who are willing to take positions on the Bench,
even upon the pitifully meagre salaries given to the Judges of our
Federal Judiciary in the Circuit and District Courts.   The wonder is
that so many able and learned men have been found to adorn the
Bench, and when one considers that a United States Circuit Judge,
for instance, is frequently called upon to grant, and does grant, an
allowance to a single counsel in a railroad foreclosure suit largely in
excess of his own salary for an entire year, one realizes vividly

the pecuniary contrast between the Bench and the Bar.   It speaks volumes for the *morale* of the American Bar that it has given to the Bench so many of its ablest men, and that such a thing as a judicial scandal occurs but once or twice in a generation.   Judges on a salary of $6,000, or even $4,000, a year have under their control great railroad systems, in the hands of receivers appointed by them, where millions of dollars are involved and where the decision of the Judge on a single motion affects enormous pecuniary interests, and yet there has been scarcely an instance in the last twenty years where a Judge has been even suspected of profiting pecuniarily by his judicial conduct, or even of taking advantage of the situation to make money by speculating in stock the price of which would be affected by his decision.   It is too much to hope that such a state of affairs will always exist.   The fact, however, that it has existed thus far is something in which the American Bar may well take great pride.

My conclusion on the entire matter is that the practice of the law on the whole has not as yet been commercialized.   The tendencies are undoubtedly in that direction.   In this, as in every other sphere of society, a man will judge of the future according as he is by nature an optimist or a pessimist.

WILLIAM B. HORNBLOWER.

THE OUTLOOK FOR DECORATIVE ART IN AMERICA.

The recent competition for the decoration of a new court-room in New York City presented certain features that promise favorably for the future of a national art. This was the first effort of the kind ever made here, and it attracted much attention. After a public exhibition of the competing designs continuing for several weeks, many of them were shown for ten days in the gallery of the Century Club, in New York, and thence sent to the Pennsylvania Academy of the Fine Arts, in Philadelphia, where they were discussed with as critical an interest as they had been in New York and in a spirit intended to stimulate a similar movement there, where also a court-room is to be decorated. Why this departure in the direction of mural painting is such a marked one, why we have not made it before, and how largely it may influence our future art, are questions that may fairly claim consideration.

It is, perhaps, not quite fair to say that we have never, as yet, attempted anything that stands for mural decoration in this country; for there have been certain efforts with this purpose in view; but they represented rather a concession to the conventional demand for sumptuousness and display in public buildings of an official character, than any truly æsthetic instinct which seeks first of all architectural appropriateness and harmony as a *sine qua non*. The Capitol at Washington received many years ago this kind of enrichment. Huge pictures were done on the walls by foreigners imported for the purpose, although work by a few native painters also is to be found there. Strictly speaking, such paintings are not decorations at all, although these historical compositions remained for long years the most important examples of mural painting that we possessed. But this is not decoration, which is to say, that form of painting wherein the artist subdues the resources of his art to harmony with the surroundings: the works were merely painted pictures of given subjects executed on the wall. These compositions bear no proper relation to the architectural plan they were supposed to aid and ornament; they do not show any well-intended effort on the part of the painters to preserve the aspect of structural integrity of surface, a quality that should be present in all ornamentation of this nature.   In the paint-ing of a picture an artist obeys his own taste and instinct, while in a decoration he makes these subservient to the surrounding conditions imposed by architecture—two very different things.   If this distinction be borne in mind, it will greatly help our point of view.   Later work than that spoken of at Washington has been done by Mr. John Lafarge in Trinity Church, Boston, and in St. Thomas's, New York; and by Mr. William Morris Hunt, in the State House, Albany.   Until within the last ten years, however, mural painting has been but spar-ingly employed by us; and even during this time the opportunities for decorative work have been few.   Five or six years ago the Church of the Ascension in New York City acquired a noble altar-piece from the hands of Mr. Lafarge.   The World's Fair at Chicago also gave a chance to several of our painters for work on a large scale which, considering the conditions of haste and inconvenience to which they were subjected, proved, on the whole, that our artists possess the true decorative instinct—a bright promise which needs only fair oppor-tunity for fulfilment.   In addition to these examples, the following are among the hotels in New York City that have been ornamented murally by some of the best-known painters, who, for lack of demand for work on a larger scale, had before busied themselves mainly with the production of easel pictures: the Plaza, the Imperial, the Wal-dorf, the Savoy, and the Fifth Avenue.   Drawing room, recep-tion room, ball room, dining room and café have afforded spaces, and received at times appropriate and successful decoration.   In some of the finest residences, too, there may be seen interesting mural work by American painters; although when one notes how frequently abroad such commissions are given to artists of distinction, the fact strikes us forcibly that we are still far behind in the æsthetic impulse.

In Europe, the Baudrys, the Cabanels, the Laurenses, the Bonnats and the Constants are as naturally chosen to use their intellectual and artistic accomplishments in the service of embellishing the interiors of private mansions of men of taste and fortune, as they would be to paint portraits, or to execute commissions for smaller works.   This custom of calling upon the ablest painters for large decorations has prevailed, more or less, in all the best periods of art; and Leonardo could, with equal felicity, trace the subtle and evasive charm in the countenance of the Gioconda, or cover the refectory walls of Santa Maria delle Grazie with the dignified and impressive " Last Supper of Our Lord." Michelangelo, summoned to Rome by Pope Julius II., filled with sublime figures the pendentives and lunettes of the Sistine Chapel. Raphael would paint a Madonna at one moment, and at another, turn his facile hand to peopling with pagan beauties the ceiling of the Farnesina. Correggio, at Parma, could picture with sensuous and glowing life the stories of mythology, or reveal, in boldest foreshortening of figures, a rapturous vision of the Ascension on a dome of San Giovanni. The fact that the Venetians of their time did not like frescoes in no way prevented those great portrait painters, Titian and Tintoretto, from making noble compositions of heroic proportions—a certain form of decoration that was demanded and which they supplied; and Veronese revelled in the sumptuousness and splendor of contemporary life which he painted also on a gigantic scale. Nearly two hundred years later, Tiepolo, that most brilliant of decorators, painted ceilings in churches and in palaces with matchless art. The names of Venetian merchant princes whose houses were thus adorned come down to us to-day, not as mere money-makers, but because, as men of taste, they encouraged art and thus linked their names with the immortals. If material prosperity thus stimulated art in the past, why should it not do so now?

From the few instances given of decorative work already produced by us, it will be seen that we have reached a point in building when, in the houses, hospitals, churches, hotels, theatres, colleges, and courts of justice that are projected, the growing needs of the people require something more than the adaptability of plan to the purpose it serves. In a word, we have passed the period in architecture of accepting only what is necessary, and we now demand that our taste shall be consulted in the matter. We have been strictly utilitarian long enough, and there is a present disposition on the part of the public to go beyond the obviously practical in the art of building, and to recognize the practicality of appealing to the mind. This is a great step, and it is full of encouragement.

Although I do not say that our artists have, as yet, given us largely of the decorative quality—mainly, perhaps, for lack of opportunity—still I am convinced that they have never before been so well equipped to do so. The discrimination in presenting what is most salient and typical, while leaving realistic studies for the portfolio, is taking art out of the sphere of the pictorial and definite, and into the realm of the imaginative and suggestive. The sentiment of things, and not the things themselves, is what vivifies, stimulates and inspires.   Each man then becomes individual; he does not reproduce, he interprets; and in the proportion that his mental gifts are superior, in just that degree you will mark superiority in his art.

Now it is this power of abstraction, so valuable, and indeed so essential in all decorative composition, which makes the expression " *le grand art*" in France a synonym for decoration, and its pursuit and practice there of the highest importance.   Let us concede then, that until the present we have had no intimation of a "grand art," but have limited ourselves to easel work and an occasional historical subject or panoramic landscape.   Artists here for more reasons than one have been somewhat slow in approaching this broader field.   Perhaps the greatest immediate obstacle to the production of work on a large scale is the lack of space to exhibit canvases of great extent.   If an artist feels a subject in heroic proportions he has no incentive to attempt it, for he knows that the opportunity to exhibit a composition of unusual size is practically *nil*.   In France one is not handicapped by such considerations.   Sixty or one hundred feet of space will be given there to a work, should this be necessary, if it possess sufficient merit to be shown at all.   I have known brilliant young men, so poor that they were obliged to paint, to sleep, and to take most of their meals in the close quarters of their studios, who would stretch a canvas to the full limits at their disposal—perhaps twenty-five by fifteen feet—project upon it some biblical, mythological, or historical composition, and put a year of earnest work on its production, economizing closely to defray the expenses of materials and models, knowing that when finished it would not be excluded from the spacious walls of the *Palais de l'Industrie* on the score of dimensions merely.   It is only too obvious that lack of exhibition space is one cause, and an important one, why we have attempted so little of the kind of work that is an essential preparation for the even greater achievement of mural design.   If it were possible to secure some building, of the area of Madison Square Garden in New York, for instance, in which to hold an annual exhibition of the fine arts, the stimulus given to mural painting and works of importance tending in that direction would undoubtedly be great.   I feel confident that ambitious painters would take heart if assured of exhibition room, and that subjects which they feel " *en grand*" would be produced by them in consequence of this assurance.

It is the business of the decorator, the mural painter, to bear in mind, when working in restricted quarters as he frequently does, the

44

position in which his painting is to be ultimately seen.   If he fail to
do this he fails in all, so far as the decorative quality of his work is
concerned; and it is only in an exhibition hall of ample proportions
that the result may be judged with fairness.   There are many painters
who do not care to confine themselves wholly to easel pictures; and
it is doubtless true that with adequate provision for the exhibition of
heroic canvases or large mural motives and designs, these would be
forthcoming, to the inevitable enrichment of our art.   For it is on the
lines of decoration that a high standard of drawing is maintained, a
great breadth and simplicity of painting demanded, and that splendid
power of deduction and synthesis called for which divests the forms
of nature of all that is not inherently large and noble.   It is thus
that the highest qualities of art are conserved and protected from the
littlenesses which, in its more restricted practice, too often creep in to
degrade.   For this class of work calls upon the painter to reject or
to choose from that great arsenal of the natural world where all his
facts are stored, and, after passing them in review, to select those
that he may bend most perfectly to his will, which he in turn has
made subservient to the architectural scheme.   To apparently annihilate compulsory limitations of area; to relieve the monotony of the
regular and equal proportions that architecture, of necessity, imposes
—these are among the problems with which the mural painter has to
deal; and it is this exacting and intellectual demand that gives added
dignity to the achievement, rendering such exercise of hand and
brain worthy to be entitled " *le grand art.* "

Another reason, which lies deeper than the prohibitory lack of
exhibition space, has prevented our developing this noble art.   It is
one also that may not perhaps be so immediately remedied—viz.,
the want of general public instruction in the elements of drawing and
painting.   Primary schools in France give pupils an elementary
acquaintance with art which creates a demand later on for some kind
of graphic supplement to the legends and facts of history that they
have absorbed at school.   Then, too, local pride tends to foster the
art instinct there as perhaps in no other country.   A youth in any
distant *département* or unimportant French town who shows peculiar
aptitude for drawing and painting is often encouraged and aided by
a public purse to continue the cultivation of his gifts in the art
schools of Paris.   As records of his progress there and in recognition
of this assistance, he sends home from time to time examples of his
work, which become the property of his native place.   I was often

surprised, when first living in France, to come across paintings of superior quality in the museums of comparatively insignificant towns, and it was only after a prolonged sojourn there that I learned the source of these unusual acquisitions. They proved to be oftentimes the productions of a local genius who, on the road to fame, had acknowledged municipal benefactions by perhaps a " success" from the Salon, or the customary contribution expected of him by the authorities. Might we not here in our own country follow some such course with profit?

It is no great matter of surprise, then, that we, as a people, have but recently awakened to the larger purposes of art. And many of these larger purposes are served through the medium of decorative paint-ing. The sweep and requirements of decoration are boundless, its function wide and all-embracing; for its mission is to adorn the various activities of life with appropriate and harmonious illustration. Despite the drawbacks which have hitherto impeded our advancement in mural art, there is still for us, owing to the force of native talent, an encouraging outlook which heralds even brilliant results.

Perhaps in no other sphere of artistic effort is there so much de-manded of the painter as in this very one of mural embellishment; and I sincerely believe that it is a branch which, if better understood, would be more generally regarded with the high respect that is due to it. In the first place, the pursuit of this art implies a life of sub-jection on the part of the painter; he works each moment tram-melled by conditions that are not of his own making but of those who have gone before him, both architect and builder, leaving behind problems which he alone must confront. In addition to this, his ex-haustive studies from nature must necessarily have been of wider range than those of specialists in art—the painter of figures only, or the portrait, marine, animal, or landscape painter. All these elements are likely to be called for in the execution of some interior design; and these must be made so subservient to the requirements of mural fitness that they become practically of another world in matter of color and a certain conventional synopsis of form. Then, too, in point of subject alone, scenes of fable, history, legend, or classic idyl, biblical story or splendid epic, must find a sympathetic harbor in the mind of the painter who would acceptably fill the rôle of grand illuminator of the present and of the past.

The general prevalence of large fortunes has given us the right to expect that a portion of this treasure will be expended by its owners after the manner of enlightened possessors of wealth in Europe, viz., by calling on those whose taste and study have prepared them to beautify and embellish our dwellings; and not the home only, but all those places where humanity meet to carry on the functions of a civilized existence.   First of all, let me mention a few that are now being thus ornamented: Sir Frederick Leighton is engaged in decorating an important panel of the interior of the Royal Exchange, London; while Bowdoin College, Maine, and the Boston Public Library have recently employed a number of our own artists to adorn their walls; and in the case of the latter institution the services, as well, of that veteran French mural painter, M. Puvis de Chavannes, have been secured to make a series of designs for the enrichment of the staircase.   This is surely encouraging.   But our museums, opera houses, music halls, not to speak of libraries, hospitals, and railway stations, are, with few exceptions, practically barren of mural ornamentation by professional painters.

These large opportunities are still open, nay, they are multiplying; but bequests to hospitals and universities will in time make them realizations in these institutions, and I expect to see even railway stations become a factor in disseminating a taste for the fine arts. Few places could be made more inviting to high effort on the part of the decorator than these utilitarian structures.   Here the waiting passenger—the untried youth starting out to face the world, and the newly landed immigrant—might find something in these pictured panels to cheat the hour, stimulate ambition, or to encourage hope. Stations should be built to accommodate this work; and as a means of carrying art's message to the masses this method would be unsurpassed, thronged as these places are daily with hosts which scatter to the four quarters of the land.   Our banks also might be appropriately decorated; for subjects suggesting the various business activities that create them, and from which they draw the "sinews of war," may be illustrated on their walls with much effect and pertinence.   And where could themes from history, biography, the classics, be more fittingly delineated than on the walls of institutions of learning?   Great events of the past should there be pictured by a master, and thus salient points of history impressed on the student's memory, while at the same time he would make a step in æsthetic culture.   Portraits of great men, too, will not be out of place here— scientists, inventors, poets, writers of fiction, historians and statesmen looking down from their frames might become sources of inspiration and incentive to those who are preparing themselves for the various labors of the world.

The propriety of illuminating the walls of colleges and churches is so obvious that it will be enough to mention the fact here that these precincts in most civilized countries have been peculiarly favored in this matter, and I will cite only the Grand Opera House, Hotel de Ville, the Sorbonne and the Panthéon in Paris, as the more recent recipients of this distinction.   During the past twenty years the interiors of these three buildings have in some instances received the crowning work of a painter's lifetime, notably in the case of Baudry at the Grand Opera House; and it is a significant fact that, with slight exceptions, the honor of such commissions has been awarded to men of acknowledged achievement and highest reputation in their art.

But the culmination of the decorative spirit will perhaps be reached only when the architect, the painter, and the sculptor work together from the inception of the structure to its completion.   From the present condition of things this sounds like a dream—it may become a reality.   Should a building be projected here in which the arts of architecture, painting, and sculpture might go hand in hand from start to finish, it may not be too much to say that it is well within the possibilities of the American temperament to set a model for the world.   It is indisputable that such a course pursued by a people in any special department of intellectual effort tends to perpetuate a high standard of accomplishment in that particular field, and thus secure a present, and promise of future, excellence that holds them up to the admiration of mankind.   This excellence we may make our own by intelligently improving our splendid opportunities.   For, to briefly recapitulate, the multifarious occupations of a young and growing country will be used as suggestive themes reducible to lofty treatment by means of mural art.   In this art, as I have already shown, business enterprise may be turned to æsthetic account, and transportation, freight-traffic, and agricultural pursuits become fit subjects for noble illustration.   So, too, will scholarly research, religious life, the diversions of society, and all the amusements and recreations of mankind be brought to the service of an art that shall be as omnipresent as light itself, and in a certain sense as vivifying.

FRANK FOWLER.

A RELIGIOUS STUDY OF A BAPTIST TOWN.

SUMMER loiterers along the Sound shore of New England, especially such as have made excursions in the country lying about Watch Hill, have pleasant memories of drives under the elms of the fine old Rhode Island town of Westerly, famous for its granite and its thread. Visitors in recent years have watched the rising here of the walls of an imposing church. The autumn witnessed its completion and consecration. Should a passer-by to-day, attracted by the roll of music, step in, he would find at the organ, as likely as not, a maiden of dark face like those in the altar pieces before which generations of her mothers worshipped in Italy. It is not the church of her mothers, however, for the marble-cutters who have come to Westerly are of that class of Florentine craftsmen who leave their religion in its Roman home, and whose wives and daughters easily accept the forms of what they believe a purer worship.

The congregation of Christ Church is, indeed, as interesting in composition as is in religious history the town of whose changed and changing conditions the new church is a monument. For Christ Church, as a dominant religious fact, is new; the old fact was the dominance of another religious body, whose idea is the exact and logical opposite of that of which the Episcopal Church is the exponent. That body still exists, and is strong, but the community is gradually outgrowing it, and its rival and enemy is gaining from it; and a condition is passing away which merits being photographed before it vanishes. In this quiet village is none of the perplexing problems of the administration of religion with which crowded populations struggle; here is no wide arena in which religious divisions work dire political effects; but here exist, side by side, the extreme representatives of the two ideas which are in contest in the religious world; and here to-day is to be found perhaps the most interesting ecclesiastical picture which any American community affords.

The village has six Baptist, and two Roman Catholic, churches; an Episcopal, a Congregational, and a Methodist church; a congregation of Plymouth Brethren, another of Adventists, and a Theo-

sophic Society.   Of the Baptist churches, three are of a sect which it
will be the purpose of this paper to study, and one is " Christian,"—
the *i* is pronounced long in Westerly.   The other two have no reason
whatever for living apart; a quarrel over temporal matters a few
years ago furnished the opportunity for an exhibition of the Baptist
devotion to the principle of division.   The order of precedence observed in the list probably represents the order, as to numerical importance, of the denominations.   Should the three sects of Baptists be
regarded as separate denominations,—and they do not affiliate,—they
would lose the first place.

An appearance of unusual good-fellowship is maintained among
the Protestant denominations generally.   They have sometimes
joined forces for local mission work,—relieving their feelings subsequently by laying the failure at one another's doors.   They even
unite in " protracted efforts" of revival,—falling out only over the
distribution of the spoils.   The familiar differences of theology and
practice which elsewhere divide Christians become here, however,
minor and unimportant in the presence of a controversy which rends
the religious, social, and commercial life of Westerly to its foundation.   The one great fact concerning the town, the shadow upon its
existence, the block in the path of its progress, the strange, distress-
ing and bewildering occurrence which weekly chills its religious enthusiasm, is the observance of different holy-days by two parties, who,
denying each other by their most apparent feature, keep up the
ghastly farce of calling each other " brother."   Three of the Baptist
churches keep Saturday, and disregard Sunday.

The membership of these societies constitutes, if not now numerically half the community, practically more than half of it.   It includes the proprietors of large machine shops, and many shopkeepers
and employers of labor.   Until lately, it was impossible on Saturday
to make a purchase at a single retail shop in town; the supplies for
the day's table had to be bought on Friday.   On Saturday, Sunday-
keeping Christians are embarrassed in their work by the cessation of
labor on the part of half the population, as on Sunday, Sabbath-keep-
ers are by that of the other half.   No device could more completely
disorganize society or disturb business.   The consciences of Sabbath-
observers are offended on every Saturday by the behavior of their
neighbors, while on Sunday, Lord's-Day Christians are awakened
by the scream of factory whistles, go to church to the unedifying
music of lawn-mowers, pray and sing amid the shouts of boys at

play, and listen for the benediction over the rumble of carts. It is a singular sensation for New England Christians, sons of the Puritans, to reflect that while they are at worship, drills are resounding in the quarries, and that the machinery of the factories is in operation.

Only this mere sketch is necessary to enable the imagination to picture correctly the state of things which obtains in Westerly. One of the evil results of the strife between the two days is that many of the village people keep neither. A considerable number of Englishmen have settled here. They are chiefly operatives in the machine shops, and are compelled to work Sundays. They will not go to the Saturday services, and they soon learn to use their day of rest in turning an honest penny. After a few appearances at evening prayer Sunday night, they are apt to give up all church attendance, and all regard for sacred times; then, from year's end to year's end, their wives never see them in other than their working clothes.

The desecrators of the Lord's Day in Westerly are protected by special statutes. Their chief congregation has about four hundred members, and is presided over by a minister of great activity, learning, and ability. His people are intelligent and moral, and have high spiritual ideals. Many First-day people of this generation are children of Seventh-day observers of the last generation, and intermarriages are common. These facts soften the asperities of the situation, and obscure the critical character of the issue.

Who are these people? They are the modern representatives of a long line of dissenters from the teaching that there is in the world a Church of Christ. They claim succession from the Ebionites and the Nazarenes of the first century of this era, the Hypsistarii of the sixth, the Cathari, the Petrobrussians and the Passagii, all Protestants before the " Reformation," and the Anabaptists, the most consistently and logically Protestant of the sects that arose after Luther. Their descent from the last is indisputable. The Anabaptists were able to denounce the attitude of the mass of the Reformers as half-hearted and inconsistent, pointing out that they had failed to follow the Protestant principle to its ultimate result. Their especial execration was launched against the practice of infant baptism, which they characterized as a diabolical invention, utterly incompatible with pure Protestantism. For, if it be inquired how the Catholic Church of Christ chiefly proclaims the unity of the family of men, it must be replied: " By taking in its arms the yet unconscious babe, and solemnly and authoritatively pronouncing it a child of God; so uttering for each new-born man humanity's glad welcome into its redeemed and consecrated fellowship." But Protestantism, which is a system founded on the individualistic view of society, cannot admit that a child is entitled to be called a child of God, except in virtue of some voluntary personal act on its own part. Consistency demands that Protestants put away infant baptism, therefore; they can practise it only as magic. The contention against it has been led by the various branches of the Anabaptist sect;—nowadays we courteously omit the first syllable of their ancient designation. The Baptists are, therefore, the most consistent Protestants.

Among Baptists in England there developed, during the reign of Elizabeth, the further idea that Protestantism was still incomplete so long as the Church was acknowledged in the keeping of its chief festival, the Lord's Day. These thoroughgoing men pointed out that the observance of the first day of the week rested upon precisely the same authority as that for the holy-days which had been abolished among dissenters, and they demanded the restoration of the Jewish Sabbath. This position, like that of opposers of infant baptism, is absolutely valid from the Protestant standpoint, and it was defended with ability. I find that the Crown deemed it wise to command replies from learned Churchmen. Among Independents, Baxter and Bunyan wrote against it, but not with the skill of Nicholas Bownd, who, in a book issued in 1595, set forth for the first time the theory that the fourth commandment remained in force, but might be applied to Sunday instead of Saturday. A majority of the Puritans and Baptists were content to be inconsistent. Embracing the compromise proposed by Bownd, they were successful in impressing a Sabbatical character upon the feast, and the illogical institution known as the Puritan Sabbath came into being. It is not Protestant, and it is not Churchly, and observers of the seventh day point out that the test of time has stamped it an absurdity and a failure. All that religious enthusiasm and civil enactment could do for the Puritan Sabbath has failed; the world will have none of it.

Roger Williams organized Rhode Island as a Baptist commonwealth in 1639. In 1671 a separation occurred in the Baptist church at Newport, part of the members seceding to set up a Seventh-Day congregation. Somewhat later, similar societies arose in Pennsylvania and in New Jersey. Rhode Island has been the chief seat of a not unsuccessful propaganda. The Newport church is now extinct; the building is used as a place for relics. There are now seven

Seventh-Day churches in the State; one in Woodville, one in Rockville, two in Hopkinton, and three in Westerly, whither, from Newport, the body of original Sabbatarians emigrated.

What we see in Westerly, then, is the result of the Protestant principle followed to its conclusion. We see this in actual existence, side by side with bodies which have retained more of the Church idea. Since Christ Church is representative of a reformed Church which is not, accurately speaking, Protestant, it will be of interest to remark its relations with the Seventh-Day Baptists.

The Seventh-Day minister, at the invitation of the rector and the bishop of the diocese, has participated in the Church service. The rector has preached in the Baptist place of worship; but, when he did so, the minister absented himself, so disclaiming responsibility. He described only the general position of Baptists when, replying to the rector's inquiry as to the character in which he was recognized by the Baptist congregation, he told him that he preached on his own responsibility, without recognition of any sort. Logical Baptists cannot regard a visiting clergyman as a minister,—indeed, not as a Christian. The Westerly minister has informed me that a Mussulman or a Buddhist would speak to his congregation on the same footing as a Christian priest.

One is tempted to remark here upon the vast emptiness of the outcry against Episcopalians for their attitude in the matter of "ministerial reciprocity." No indignation is expressed at Baptist intolerance, and yet no Churchman would deny the Christian character of clergymen outside his communion, however he might be constrained to regard their ministerial authority. It happens that the very relations we are considering were the occasion of the enactment of the canon which denies ministers of other denominations the right to officiate in congregations of the Episcopal Church,—the canon which has lately been the object of so much discreetly inspired and carefully fanned wrath.

In 1870, the Reverend Mr. Hubbard, then rector of Christ Church, agreed with the Baptist minister of the town to exchange duties for once. Accordingly, Mr. Hubbard conducted service at the Baptist meeting-house, while the Baptist minister appeared in the chancel of Christ Church in surplice and stole, and performed the full service, including the functions of absolution and benediction. The Baptist minister had promised, as an acknowledgment of their courtesy and liberality, to throw open his communion-table to Episcopalians.

His congregation forbade the carrying out of the promise.   Mr. Hubbard was brought to trial before an ecclesiastical court, which found that his procedure, however injudicious, was in violation of no existing statute.   Thereupon, the General Convention of the Episcopal Church in the United States, meeting the following year, enacted what is now Canon 17, Title I., Digest of Canons:

"No Minister in charge of any Congregation of this Church, or, in case of vacancy or absence, no Churchwardens, Vestrymen, or Trustees of the Congregation, shall permit any person to officiate therein, without sufficient evidence of his being duly licensed or ordained to minister in this Church: *Provided*, That nothing herein shall be so construed as to forbid communicants of the Church to act as Lay-Readers."

This is the subject of much recent and present controversy.   A symposium of the opinions of a number of bishops upon it, gathered by an enterprising sectarian journal, the secret enemy of all attempts to heal the wounds of Christ's body, has been placed before the world as if it were the final word upon the whole subject of church reunion.   Whatever may be the individual opinions of bishops, the fact is, the word "officiate" in the canon, on which its force depends, has never been given an authoritative interpretation.   The most churchly view would not look upon preaching, for instance, as "officiating."   Certainly the canon should be interpreted in the light of its origin.   That it was the result of the Westerly affair, while not now generally remembered, is certain from the statements of those who were familiar with the circumstances of its enactment, among them one, at least, of the most eminent canonists of the church.   It is an interesting and striking fact that the canon which has been denounced as the chief barrier to Christian unity should have originated in an attempt to force relations between a representative of the Church, and of the extreme left of Protestantism.

From this village proceeded, two years ago, a remarkable series of messages, conveying proposals of peace to other Christian bodies. The Seventh-Day Baptist General Conference met in Westerly, in 1892, and issued addresses to the official bodies of the Episcopal, the Congregational, the Presbyterian, and the Baptist churches.   The addresses were composed with great skill and impressiveness.   There is reason to suspect their sincerity as proposals for union, but there can be no doubt that their clear logic was most embarrassing to recipients who were engaged in an attempt to connect the Lord's Day with the Hebrew Sabbath.

The address sent to the National Council of Congregational Churches was not acknowledged by the secretary, and it is not known that it was presented to the Council, though a private letter from Dr. Fisher, of Yale University, shows that it was received. The Baptist associations generally ignored it. One clerk wrote that he could not present an address from a church in error. The clerk of the General Assembly of the Southern branch of the Presbyterian Church wrote that he had received the address,—no more. The General Assembly of the Presbyterian Church of the North did not even acknowledge it.

The reception accorded the address in the General Convention of the Episcopal Church was, I am assured by the chairman of the committee charged with its promulgation, " courtesy itself." The Bishop of Rhode Island interested himself in the matter, the secretaries of both Houses wrote that it would be a pleasure to present it, and it was in due course read before the Bishops and the Deputies. The former referred it to their Committee on Memorials, the latter to their Committee on Christian Unity; and these committees now have it under consideration. The polite consideration paid to the memorial was marked, and it was the subject of much kindly comment in debate on related questions.

The behavior of the Episcopal Church, in such contrast with that of other denominations, is accounted for by the fact that it alone is not implicated in the absurdity of supporting a Christian feast by a Hebrew reason. To it Sunday is just such a day as are Easter, Christmas, Epiphany, and the Saints' Days, and depends for its character solely upon the decree of the Church. Except for the few particulars in which Protestantism has invaded it,—chiefly in the introduction of the Decalogue into the Office of Holy Communion, which requires the reading on Sundays of the command to keep Saturdays,— a performance which leaves an ill taste in the mouth of most priests,— it does not pretend that the Lord's Day is a Sabbath.

Of course, it is impossible for the Episcopal Church to do more than give the proposal of the Seventh-Day people a polite reply. Between these two bodies, the logical representatives of two ideas, the issue is perfectly clear. They understand each other perfectly, and have the mutual sympathy of opponents who recognize each other's sincerity in a quarrel which is irreconcilable. For the whole issue between the Church and Protestantism focuses itself in the contest between the Lord's Day and the Sabbath. One is witness to the authority of the body of redeemed humanity to make laws supersessive even of Mosaic commandments; the other is the individual-istic denial of such authority. The Lord's Day is Christian; the Sabbath is not. I now venture to inquire whether the sect of Seventh-Day Baptists, affiliating with Judaism, does not reveal itself as a lapse from the religion of Jesus? In this inquiry is involved the question whether Protestantism, considered logically, is not essentially un-Christian.

The Seventh-Day Baptist Handbook rebukes " an age which talks gushingly about salvation through faith." The Handbook traces with pride the genesis of the body it represents from the heretical sects before mentioned in this article. Of these, the Ebionites and the Nazarenes regarded the Jewish law as obligatory, branded St. Paul as an apostate, and denied the divinity of Christ. The Hyp-sistarii blended a Greek paganism with the worship of fire. The Cathari held the Persian doctrine of a good and an evil god, and taught that the evil one created the visible world; part of them worshipped the devil, and railed against Jesus as a false prophet. The Petrobrussians were insane iconoclasts, and the Passagii practised circumcision and denied Christ's divinity.

At the Seventh-Day General Conference of 1886 a minute was adopted, setting forth that while a few might dissent, it is neverthe-less the general belief of the denomination that Christ will come again, and that, while some might think otherwise, the prevailing belief is that there will be resurrection. It seems there is doubt about it. The Sadducees had a similar doubt.

The Christian Creed is unknown to the religious assemblies of these people. The Westerly minister cannot affirm his belief in its statements. He, however, began a course of lectures upon it a few weeks ago, but was interrupted at the first one by a deacon who rose and protested, declaring that he hoped to see the day when all creeds shall have perished. This deacon did not protest when recently a Hebrew, visiting the town, attended by invitation the Seventh-Day service, and being called upon to pray, did so, according to his faith, in Hebrew.

It is a fact complimentary to the Baptists that their denomination has produced far more than its share of Hebrew scholars. The Sab-bath-Baptist clergy-list shows the names of authorities on Hebrew out of all proportion to its size. The Westerly minister himself is a past-master of the language and literature. His monograph on the " Song of Songs" is to be ranked with the works of Ewald and

Oettli; it won Mr. Daland the friendship of Franz Delitzsch, and gave American scholarship a European reputation.   He is the editor of a periodical named " The Peculiar People, " devoted to Hebrew interests.   Its motto is: *Judæus sum: judaici nihil a me alienum puto.* It is impossible to withhold sympathy from the purpose of this paper, or to be uninspired by the enthusiasm with which the editor holds up the ideas of the adoption of the Hebrew tongue by all the scattered people, and the re-establishment in Palestine of a Hebrew commonwealth.   Its importance for us is that in its columns the belief of a man who stands at the head of his sect finds unimpeded expression. He here, over and over again, in every form, and with every emphasis, declares that Christianity is a Jewish creed, expresses the hope that no Jew will join a Christian church, and exhorts Christians to turn from their errors to the purer faith of Judaism.

If this is the logical outcome of Protestantism, what is Protestantism?   Let us confess: It is an admission that divisions among men are normal. . It is a negative which presumes the existence of something besides itself.   Protestantism cannot exist unless there is something against which to protest.   It recognizes that " something, " appeals to it, confesses it a prior fact, every time it names its own name.   Its wickedness is that it does not, and cannot, anticipate the extinction of that against which it protests, for in that extinction the possibility of Protestantism would become extinct.   It regards division as natural and necessary.   Disintegration is its principle, its product, and its doom.   Protest begets protest, and ever into further division divided bodies take their way.   The end of the process is not reached until absolute individualism is attained.

But individualism is just what Christianity contemplates as the evil from which men are to be saved.   Its ethics teach that personality is achieved only in association.   Its grandest proclamation is the paradox that a grain of wheat, except it fall into the ground and die, abideth alone; its supreme symbol is the Cross, the witness lifted above the centuries that the very death of one for the race is the victory for the one and the race alike.   So the mission of Christ was the founding of a Kingdom.   That was the word most often on His lips.   He did not set going a set of pious sayings.   He wrote not a line, save once in the sand.   He founded a Kingdom.   He told scores of parables explaining what the Kingdom was like.   He was accused of being a King.   He affirmed before his judges that such He was. The inscription over the cross proclaimed Him the head of a Kingdom. Every act of His was to lift men up from individualism, and make them members of a divine Society. Any principle which ends in individualism, therefore, if allowed to run its course, is bound to reveal itself as un-Christian.

Seventh-Day Baptists are better than their logic would make them; let us hope every Christian sect is. Baptists, most consistent of Protestants, are still saved by their glorious inconsistency to be worthy and noble members of the Church which their theology would deny.

But may not this pursuit of its logic do something toward reclaiming us from our infatuation with a pernicious principle? Is it not time we perceived the essential weakness of a negative designation? There is much in the form of statements, and there is much in names. How long do we propose to continue playing into the hands of the papal church by yielding to it the most noble of appellations, and contenting ourselves with the most ignoble? When every Christian body begins to boast of every catholic feature it can claim, and all together put away that common name which confesses Rome a greater fact, we shall be far along toward the day when at last our groping hands will meet.

WILLIAM BAYARD HALE.

STEPS TOWARD GOVERNMENT CONTROL OF RAIL-ROADS.

THE relation of the Chicago strike and its influences in the development and extension of certain fundamental principles constitute it an epochal event in the labor movement and in the industrial development of the country. Probably no new thought has grown out of it, nor are there any new principles being developed by it, but the strike has emphasized certain principles which have quietly grown into activity, and they are now forcing attention. Principles that have been crystallized into law are now being approved or attacked, as the interests and the ideas of writers dictate. What was considered by large bodies of business men as essential in the government, management, and operation of railroads is now considered by many as revolutionary, although these principles have already quietly taken their place in the body of laws governing the land. The purpose of this paper is to show how the Chicago strike has emphasized some of these principles, their logical extension to other features than those to which they have been already applied, and their influence upon the growth and development of the idea of governmental control, and of industrial arbitration.

The Chicago strike was not constructive of new principles or systems, or destructive of those already existing; but it did emphasize some principles which were not recognized as even existing. The vast proportions of the forces enlisted in a gigantic strike for supremacy are sufficient alone to constitute the Chicago affair an important event without reference to its influence upon legislation and the principles applicable to the management of railroads. As time goes on its influence is being felt in several directions, strengthening and illuminating the contentions of parties on either side of the contest, and drawing careful and critical attention to principles intimately connected with the supremacy of the Federal Government, and its relations to the government, management, and operation of railroads.

The strike has crystallized public sentiment upon a question which has often been argued but never settled,—that relating to the *quasi-*

public character of railroad employees. The country now thoroughly recognizes the absolute necessity of considering railroads as representing not only their own interests but the interests of the public, and that, as they obtain their charters by public consent and are thus and by the nature of their business *quasi*-public corporations, their employees are to a degree *quasi*-public servants and must have a status under the law independent of their status as employees of individual corporations. It has stimulated anew the inquiry which was first made some years ago, during the troubles on the New York Central Railroad and on the Southwestern system, as to how railroad employees can be brought within the influence of statutory provision to such an extent as to be held accountable to the public as well as to their employers. Stability of transportation, stability of business in securing constant delivery of supplies, security in preserving life through such supplies, all demand an answer to the question, and demand emphatically such legislation as will place the railroads and their employees on a basis where they shall recognize their allegiance to the public. I believe that the Chicago strike, in developing legislation which shall accomplish this great purpose, will be worth all it has cost, even admitting the accuracy of the estimates of public journals, chiefly " Bradstreet's," that it involved a loss of over eighty million dollars.

One of the chief reasons why the Chicago strike emphasizes vital principles lies in the fact that it constitutes a subordinate element in a revolution which is quietly taking place in this country, and which accords with that phase of a revolution depicted in an editorial[1] on the recent Report of the Strike Commission in " Harper's Weekly," where it was declared that " the most momentous stage in every revolution is that which takes place silently in the popular mind." The strike was a subordinate phase of this kind of revolution, because there preceded it a revolutionary measure far more significant than that growing out of the Chicago strike, and which is being supplemented by one still more significant.

It is not necessary for me to say that I approach this part of my subject from a standpoint entirely opposed to state-socialism as a system. I have no faith in it, no adherence to it, and no fondness for it, for I believe that as a system state-socialism means the destruction of industry and the retrogression of society. Nor need I assert that I approach it from a point of view antagonistic to what is

[1] "Revolutionary Statesmanship," "Harper's Weekly," November 24, 1894.

45

known as compulsory arbitration. I have no faith in compulsory arbitration as a system for the settlement of labor troubles. I approach it, further, from the point of view that neither the Federal nor State Governments can or ought to be allowed, as a rule, to regulate rates of wages or prices of commodities.

Notwithstanding these professions, I am not afraid of state or any other form of socialism, but I am ready to re-examine these propositions to which I am opposed and, if expedient, to apply some of the features involved in each of them. In what respect, therefore, does the Chicago strike become a subordinate element in a revolution which is now going on?

In 1887 the Congress, at the demand of the shippers of the country, and in their interest as it was supposed, made the declaration that all charges made for any service rendered or to be rendered in the transportation of passengers or property on interstate railroads, or in connection therewith, or for the receiving, delivering, storage, or handling of such property, should be reasonable and just, and every unjust and unreasonable charge for such service was prohibited and declared to be unlawful. This declaration was made in the "Act to Regulate Commerce," approved February 4, 1887. The Act not only made the declaration which I have recited, but gave power to the Interstate Commerce Commission, created by it, to carry out its principles. It established the machinery for the regulation of freight rates over all the interstate railroads of the United States, and, as a logical result, over all railroads. This declaration has become to all intents and purposes an authoritative interpretation of the Constitution of the United States, because it has been sustained by the courts. In a certain sense it explains the Constitution. The legislative declaration was made under the clauses of the Constitution providing for the general welfare and for the regulation of commerce between the States, and it enlarges the Constitution through interpretation because of the necessity for such enlargement.

The Congress of the United States, acceding to the demands of the shippers of the country, recognized that existing conditions were in conflict with a moral sentiment comprehending the justness and the equity involved in the transportation of commodities essential to the welfare of the people. But this declaration was emphatically socialistic, it was compulsory arbitration, it was emphatically a law regulating the prices of commodities through the price of services. I understand the position of the courts in sustaining this, and believe the position to be correct, and that is the old principle of regulating pikes, tolls, etc.   The declaration of the law was not the declaration of a new principle, but it was the crystallization of an old principle into Federal legislation, with the proper machinery for carrying it out, and the machinery as well as the declaration makes it state-socialistic in character, makes it compulsory arbitration, because it undertakes not only to regulate the affairs of corporations but to arbitrarily adjust the contracts made in connection therewith. What is the consequence of this, as shown in another step in that silent revolution which is taking place?

There is now pending in Congress a measure which has passed the House of Representatives by a very strong majority; it is very socialistic, as much so as any legislation that has been considered favorably by any government in the closing half of this century. As a state-socialistic measure it equals the compulsory insurance legislation of Germany; as legislation establishing the most rigid and stringent laws for the most compulsory of compulsory arbitration it has no equal.   I refer to the pooling bill (H. R. 7,273) now pending in the Senate.   I have not a word to say on the merits of this bill, of its necessity, of its effects, or against it.   I cite it only to show the second phase of the silent revolution to which I have referred. This pending legislation is demanded at the instance of the shippers and the railroads of the country, and its passage is being aided by a powerful lobby in their service.   The railroads base their advocacy of the bill on the claim that it will be to the interest of the shippers to have such a law.   The bill provides for a great trust, with the government of the United States as the trustee.   It provides that the roads of the country may enter into contracts, agreements, and arrangements, which are enforceable between the parties thereto as common carriers, for the regulation of freight pooling, and that under proper rules of procedure every such contract, agreement, or arrangement may be changed or abrogated by the Interstate Commerce Commission.

When the first bill to regulate commerce was passed the great and powerful wedge of state-socialism, or so far as control of railroads is concerned, was driven one-quarter of its length into the timber of conservative government—of that government which means democracy.   The pending bill, the moment it becomes a law, will drive the wedge three-quarters of its length into the timber.   There will then be needed but one more blow to drive the wedge home, and that blow will come at the instance of business and not of labor—entire governmental control of all the railroads of the country instead of partial control under the laws now existing or proposed. With twenty-five per cent of all the railroad interests of the country now under the control of the Government, through its courts, it is but a very short step to that final blow which will send the wedge its full length and bring entire governmental control. This blow will be struck in the most seductive way. It will come through a demand that the Government shall take charge of the roads, not purchase them—shall take charge of the roads and out of the proceeds of the transportation business guarantee to the existing stockholders of the roads a small but reasonable rate of dividend. Under such a seductive movement the stockholders themselves, conservative men, will vote for the striking of the blow. All this, as I have said, will be at the demand and in the interest of the railroads and of the shippers, and not of the labor involved in carrying on the work of transportation, as the demand of to-day for the enactment of the pooling bill is alleged to be largely in the interest of the shippers and of the public welfare. Will the railroads now consistently demand, and keep their lobby employed to secure, the extension of the same principles to labor, and thus give their employees the status of semi-public servants and thus help to prevent or reduce the number of strikes on all interstate roads, and logically on all roads?

The Act to Regulate Commerce, approved February 4, 1887, was followed by an act creating boards of arbitration, approved October 1, 1888. This act embodied to a certain extent the suggestions of the President in a special message to Congress, of date April 22, 1886, in which the creation of a board of arbitration for the purpose of settling disputes was recommended. The provisions of this act, however, were in the main simply administrative. The Act contained no declaration of principle like that embodied in the Act to Regulate ·Commerce. Under the arbitration act of 1888 no action was ever taken until the appointment of a Commission to investigate the Chicago strike; in fact, the Act had been on the statute-books a long time before it was known to many, and at the time of the Chicago difficulty was practically forgotten. It had never been considered a revolutionary measure in any sense, or one that could by any means overturn existing institutions or subvert the principles of our Government. In comparison with the Act to Regulate Commerce it was a tame affair, for the interstate commerce act was decidedly revolutionary, as already pointed out, while the arbitration act had no elements of the kind in it from the first to the last section. It will be seen by what has been said that the Federal Government has committed itself to the principle of regulating the business of transportation through the regulation of freight rates, the terms and conditions of contracts pertaining thereto, by establishing proper machinery to execute the declarations of law and principle, and, in fact, making the Government the trustee of a great transportation trust. It has also committed itself, in the Act of October 1, 1888, to the principle of adjusting labor controversies by arbitration. It has asserted its right to control to a certain extent the business of the railroads of the country because of the necessity of such control in securing stability and peace. The Act to Regulate Commerce has, in effect, made the railroads comprehended by it *quasi*-Federal corporations. The Act of October 1, 1888, creating boards of arbitration, recognized the necessity of adjusting difficulties, but it did not go far enough. It does not place the employees on interstate railroads in the position of *quasi*-public servants, because the law has made no declaration of principle, but simply provided a board to which parties can resort in case of controversy. Something more is needed,—something in the nature of the declaration contained in the Act to Regulate Commerce,—to place railroad employees in a position where they must to a certain extent recognize the public and the railroads as their joint employers.

I can now answer why it is that the Chicago strike is exerting an influence as a subordinate phase of a silent revolution—a revolution probably in the interest of the public welfare. It is because it emphasizes the claim that there must be some legislation which shall place railroad employees on a par with the railroad employers in conducting the business of transportation, so far as the terms and conditions of employment are concerned; it is because the events of that strike logically demand that another declaration of law and of the principles of the Federal Government shall be made; a declaration *that all wages paid, as well as charges for any service rendered in the transportation of property, passengers, etc., shall be reasonable and just.* A declaration of this character, backed by the machinery of the Government to carry it in effect, would give to railroad employees the status of *quasi*-public servants. The machinery accompanying such a declaration should be modelled on the interstate commerce act. It should be provided that some authority be established **for** the regulation of wage contracts on railroads. I would not have the machinery of the law for the regulation of such matters provide for a compulsory adjustment, as now provided for the adjustment of freight rates, but I would have such machinery that there would be little inducement under it on the part of railroads to pay unjust and unreasonable wages and on the part of employees to quit work when they were just and reasonable.

A bill (H. R. 8,259) is now pending in Congress which makes the declaration as to just and reasonable wages and provides for the submission, by agreement, of all differences relating to the terms and conditions of employment on railroads to a properly constituted tribunal, but I submit that this step in the silent revolution now going on is a subordinate one, and that should the principle involved be enacted into law, as I trust it will be, it could not be considered as another blow, but only a light tap, on the wedge of state-socialism; it could be considered as a phase only of the great blow now contemplated by the pooling bill. If this measure for the regulation of wages on interstate railroads, which places the employees in the position of *quasi*-public servants, amenable to the public as well as to their incorporated employers, is considered by any one as a piece of state-socialism, I can only refer to the other features of the revolution already in active operation. I think I recognize the distinction between governmental adjustment of freight rates and like adjustment of wage rates, and I fully agree that while the Government can fix the compensation of its employees, it cannot and ought not to attempt arbitrarily to fix that of the employees of railroads; but I further recognize that it is the right and duty of the Government to prevent the interruption of interstate commerce and the obstruction of the mails, and that in the exercise of this right it ought to have a voice in making the terms and adjusting the conditions of the employment of the employees engaged in such service. This it can do through some such machinery of law as that provided in the present Act to Regulate Commerce. The prosperity of our railroads is a necessity upon which business stability largely depends, and every reasonable means which can prevent disaster should be considered.

I read in an interesting editorial from "The Nation" (November 22, 1894), on the Chicago strike, that "Nothing is more needed at this crisis than the practice of treating the working-classes as business men fully capable of managing their own affairs, and not as children who are being put upon by their elders," etc. The enactment of a law such as that indicated would place the employees of railroads upon a business basis and would recognize their capacity to conduct properly their own business in connection with the business of their employers, and if it be said that it would recognize them as children who are being put upon by their elders, what shall be said of the interstate commerce act and of the pooling bill? Can it be that merchants and shippers are children who are being put upon by their elders and must be coddled?

In the broad and patriotic message of the President, already referred to, there occur the following passages:

" Under our form of government the value of labor as an element of national prosperity should be distinctly recognized, and the welfare of the laboring man should be regarded as especially entitled to legislative care. In a country which offers to all its citizens the highest attainments of social and political distinction, its workingmen cannot justly or safely be considered as irrevocably consigned to the limits of a class and entitled to no attention and allowed no protest against neglect. "

" The laboring man, bearing in his hand an indispensable contribution to our growth and progress, may well insist, with manly courage and as a right, upon the same recognition from those who make our laws as is accorded to any other citizen having a valuable interest in charge; and his reasonable demands should be met in such a spirit of appreciation and fairness as to induce a contented and patriotic coöperation in the achievement of a grand national destiny. "

" While the real interests of labor are not promoted by a resort to threats and violent manifestations, and while those who, under the pretext of an advocacy of the claims of labor, wantonly attack the rights of capital, and for selfish purposes or the love of disorder sow seeds of violence and discontent, should neither be encouraged nor conciliated, all legislation on the subject should be calmly and deliberately undertaken, with no purpose of satisfying unreasonable demands or gaining partisan advantage. "

" The present condition of the relations between labor and capital is far from satisfactory. The discontent of the employed is due in a large degree to the grasping and heedless exactions of employers and the alleged discrimination in favor of capital as an object of governmental attention. It must be conceded that the laboring men are not always careful to avoid causeless and unjustifiable disturbance. "

I commend these wise utterances to all legislators, to all employers, to all employees. They contain the principles which will lead to industrial peace and to the continuity of industrial prosperity. These principles have been emphasized, since they were announced by the President, by the British Royal Commission on Labor, under the conspicuous chairmanship of the Duke of Devonshire; and the Hon. C. C. Kingston, Q.C., Premier of South Australia, in an elaborate article on Industrial Agreements and Conciliation,[1] has

[1] See "Review of Reviews," December, 1894.

made an able argument in their support; in fact, if the Premier had had the pending arbitration bill before him and had held a brief in its favor, he could not have more thoroughly advocated it than he has in the article referred to. He points out that if one hundred individuals entering into one hundred separate agreements are entitled to secure their enforcement, there is no reason why one agreement, made on behalf of the same individuals acting collectively, should not be afforded recognition, and he thinks that in these days of highly organized trade associations the question of industrial agreements and conciliation is second to none as affecting the prevention or settlement of industrial disputes. Such disputes, in the absence of surrender by either party, can be ended only by agreement between both. But he wisely asks the question, What assurance is there to either master or man, in the absence of any binding treaty, that war will not be again declared at any moment? We must agree with Mr. Kingston that organizations, whether of masters or men, should be afforded the same facilities for combination and agreement as are given in the case of ordinary joint-stock companies, and to this end he would have unions, or associations of unions, made capable of registration and of *quasi*-incorporation.

The bill now pending to provide for arbitration, and for the further incorporation of labor organizations and for their recognition, is in direct line with this argument of Mr. Kingston, who believes that a union should act through a committee, and an association of several unions through its council, or whatever its executive board may be. He points out with great force that on the occasion of great strikes the public cries out for conciliation. He therefore urges that boards should be established in anticipation of the differences they are designed to prevent, for when war has been declared and the disputants, as it were, are at each other's throats, each hopeful of ultimate success, they are seldom in the mood to listen to peacemakers. As well might it be attempted to organize a fire brigade in the midst of a conflagration as to provide for an effectual system of arbitration in the middle of a strike. These are the views of an able statesman, and they are gratifying indorsements from the antipodes, from a country which is making great progress in all labor legislation, of the principles laid down in the President's message of 1886. Carried into effect, it must be conceded that they constitute a feature, although subordinate, of the silent revolution which is leading the country into governmental control. Opposed as I am to the taking over of the railroads by the Government, and believing fully in the interstate commerce act, I cannot avoid the logical results of the movements which are now going on.   My chief purpose now, however, is to call the atten-tion of the public to the demands of the railroads and the merchants and shippers themselves for the control of our railroads by the Fed-eral Government, and to the subordinate influence which the passage of an arbitration bill must have in securing such control, and, fur-ther, to insist that governmental control on one side shall not be conceded while leaving the doctrine of *laissez faire* to have its full operation upon the other element, labor.

The Chicago strike must be recognized as a factor in producing the changes in Federal law now going on, for it is dissipating a good deal of the haze which has hung before the eyes of both labor and capital; it is teaching the public the necessity of placing labor and capital on a strong business basis of reciprocal interests, but interests which recognize the public as their chief master.   The discussion of the personal equation in the great Chicago strike has nothing to do with the principles involved.   Action must be taken on the side of law and order, without reference to individuals, recognizing, how-ever, that law and order mean the welfare of the nation and are based on principle and not on specific, individual acts, and that govern-ments must adopt from various systems those features which are ap-plicable under the conditions and necessities of the time, whether they are taken from a system of Government already in existence or one that may be advocated purely on theory.   The experience of the American Government, which has adopted more socialistic ele-ments than any other, is a sufficient guaranty of the conservative em-bodiment in labor legislation of the best ascertainable methods on which the majority of men can unite, not as partisans in the interest of labor or capital as such, but as patriots endeavoring to secure free-dom from strikes, riots, intimidations, and violence of all kinds, which must be condemned by all right-minded men.   The dictates of lofty patriotism should be the power to demand measures for their prevention.   One of these measures comprehends industrial concilia-tion and arbitration.   The warmest friends of this measure, however, do not claim that it is a complete remedy for labor troubles.   They do claim that it is an effective balance-wheel and that it will secure better and firmer relations than now exist between the two great ele-ments of business, and on a business basis.

CARROLL D. WRIGHT.

COLORADO'S EXPERIMENT WITH POPULISM.

PRIOR to the year 1892, Colorado was considered, on national issues at least, a reliable Republican State—in presidential elections always Republican. In 1882, and again in 1886, a Democratic governor was elected, but the other State officers were Republicans. The election of 1892, however, revealed a remarkable change of sentiment among the people; and the following analysis of the total vote for governor for each of four successive elections will furnish food for reflection:

	REPUBLICAN.	DEMOCRAT.	PROHIBITIONIST.	POPULIST.
	Percentage of whole vote.	Percentage of whole vote.	Percentage of whole vote.	Percentage of whole vote.
1888.....................	53.87	42.67	2.28	1.18
1890.....................	50.11	42.38	1.28	6.23
1892.....................	41.39	9.54	1.88	47.19
1894 (unofficial).........	53.	4.12	1.50	41.38

It would appear from this table that the Democratic party has been almost obliterated in Colorado. It is a fact, however, that in the last election a great many Democrats voted the Republican ticket as the only practicable way of defeating Populism—this notwithstanding the fact that in 1892 more than three-fourths of the Democratic party went over to the Populists, and that more than one-sixth of the Republicans did the same, with the result that Davis H. Waite was elected governor with a complete corps of Populist State officials. The Populist party did not, however, have equal success in the legislative elections of that year. In the house of representatives the Republicans had a majority. In the senate they had a plurality which could be overcome only by a combination of Populists and Democrats. Colorado's experiment in Populism is, therefore, an experiment in administration, and not in law-making.

The Populist movement in Colorado is not identical, either in causes or development, with the corresponding movement in Kansas, Nebraska, and the South. The real influence which suddenly swelled the Populist vote from 6 per cent to 47 per cent of the total vote of the State, is found not in the Ocala platform of the Farmers' Alliance, nor in the vagaries of the Omaha platform, but in the attitude of the two great national parties on the question of bimetallism. The voters of Colorado of all parties are practically unanimous in the advocacy of bimetallism. Long prior to the National Conventions of 1892 there had developed an intense sentiment that the policy of gold monometallism was destructive not only to the interests of Colorado, but to manufacturing, producing, and commercial interests throughout the United States. In the hope of influencing national policy, "silver clubs" were organized throughout the State in the winter of 1891 and 1892, the members of which were pledged to vote for no presidential candidate who was not committed, and whose party was not committed, to the free coinage of silver. Delegates and organized committees labored with the Republicans at Minneapolis, and afterward with the Democrats at Chicago. Their efforts were fruitless. Then followed the Populist Convention at Omaha, with a declaration in favor of bimetallism, but with a demand for paper money, to be distributed in accordance with the sub-treasury scheme of the Farmers' Alliance, "or a better system" (*noscitur ex sociis*). Here, then, was a national party pledged to the free coinage of silver. Thousands of Colorado voters turned to it, not because they accepted its doctrines on other subjects,—for they ignored them,—but for the purpose of protesting against the attitude of the two dominant parties on the one subject of coinage. At the ensuing election the Weaver electors received a plurality of nearly 15,000 votes in Colorado, and the Populist candidate for governor was elected by a plurality of 5,436. Thus Colorado soon found herself subject to the full sway of a Populist *régime*.

From the foregoing statement it will be apparent that Populist ascendancy in Colorado was accidental. It did not represent the judgment of the great mass of citizens. The peculiar doctrines of the Populist party have no hold on those who, by their enterprise, their investments, and their labor, have done and are still doing so much to develop the wonderful and varied resources of the State. It was with a shock of surprise that vigorous and enterprising, albeit conservative, Colorado suddenly discovered that she had put her neck into the yoke of Populist control.

Since the character of a State administration must usually be, and in this case was, determined by the policy and conduct of the man who happened to be chief executive, it is fair to inquire whether any peculiar or radical features should be attributed to the party and its principles, or to the idiosyncrasies of the man. After a gubernatorial career of nearly two years, Governor Waite sought a renomination. The State Convention of his party gave it to him with great unanimity and boundless enthusiasm. At the ensuing election he received more than 40 per cent of the total vote of the State. These facts can be considered only as an approval and ratification by his party of his public acts.

The dominant idea which permeates the Omaha Populist platform and its immediate predecessors is a concentrated paternalism. The Government ownership of railroads, of telegraph lines, of telephones: the reclamation by the Government of lands held by corporations and by aliens; the abolition of banks; the direct issue of full legal-tender paper money, not supported by a coin reserve; the lending of this money to the people on the security of "imperishable farm products," stored in Government warehouses,—these are characteristic features of Populism. The party also appeals to and emphasizes class distinctions. It calls for a "union of the labor forces of the United States"; it declares that "'if any will not work neither shall he eat'"; it sees naught but wickedness in the two great parties, and alleges that "corruption dominates the ballot-box, the legislatures, the Congress, and touches even the ermine of the bench."

Colorado in its State administration under Governor Waite gave an illustration of the practical operation of these Populist principles. Paternalism manifested itself in the assumption that the Governor is "the Government." Class distinctions were emphasized and increased by the announcement that the rich have had their day and turn about is fair play. The courts, if they differed from the executive in the construction of constitution or statutes, were corrupt usurpers. Under such influences the spirit of anarchy was fostered and grew apace, and the State was brought to the very verge of civil war. Is this indictment sustained by the facts?

In the first year of Governor Waite's administration there is little that requires comment. His inaugural message, although colored by populistic sentiment, was a strong address, and as conservative as could be expected from a disciple of the Omaha creed. Its most radical feature, perhaps, was the recommendation that a railroad commission of three members be created, with power "to hear and determine complaints, *without recourse to the courts.*"

The Governor's intemperate utterances in the summer of 1893, which gave to him and to his State an extended and unpleasant notoriety, have been unduly exaggerated. Words which, when taken with the context, show only a rhetorical but injudicious emphasis, have been construed as manifesting a spirit of bloodthirsty violence. Their practical effect, however, was to create in the outside world a distrust of Colorado, and among the conservative people of the State they created a feeling of apprehension as to what a Populist administration might do in the emergencies of the times. This apprehension was justified by subsequent events.

Under the laws of the State of Colorado the Governor appoints the three members of the Fire and Police Board of the city of Denver, and these appointments are made " with power of suspension or removal at any time for cáuse, to be stated in writing, but not for political reasons." Under this provision of law, the Governor made, from time to time, various changes in the *personnel* of the Fire and Police Board. These changes resulted in considerable friction and some litigation. Finally the Governor attempted to remove two of his appointees, who denied his authority so to do. The merits of the controversy between the Populist Governor and his Populist appointees do not concern us. Suffice it to say, that these members of the Fire and Police Board claimed that the real reasons for their removal were political, and that the assigned cause was a mere pretence. They refused to surrender their offices until the right thereto should be judicially determined and, in the meanwhile, obtained an injunction restraining the new appointees from interfering with them in the discharge of their duties. It is doubtless true also that, in anticipation of armed attack, they prepared for armed resistance. It should be said, however, that these officials at all times averred that if it should be judicially determined that they were not entitled to their offices, they would immediately surrender them.

The slow-moving process of the courts, however, did not, in the opinion of the Governor, furnish an adequate remedy. Notwithstanding the fact that the Supreme Court had promptly upheld the executive power in a previous controversy over appointments to the same Board, the Governor determined to carry out his purposes by force. He construed his constitutional power " to execute the laws" as including the power to forcibly induct his appointees into office without the intervention of civil process. His views upon this subject can be best illustrated by extracts from his own official statement. He says:

"That by the constitution of the State of Colorado the undersigned is charged with the duty of executing the laws. . . . That, acting upon the belief that he was authorized to carry into effect any order of removal that he might make in conformity with law . . . the undersigned . . . as commander-in-chief of the militia of the State of Colorado, upon the 14th day of March, 1894, duly called upon a number of the military forces of the State of Colorado to assist in the enforcement of the laws of the State, and in the removal of said Orr and Martin from the positions so wrongfully held by them. . . . The said military force was directed to proceed to the said City Hall in the city of Denver, and demand of the said Orr and Martin that they vacate the offices and apartments so unlawfully withheld by them, and that they desist and refrain from further interference with, or control over, the officers and patrolmen of the Police Department of the city of Denver, or the officers of the Fire Department of the city of Denver."

After speaking of the preparations of·Orr and Martin for armed resistance to this military demand, the Governor further states that he deemed it his duty to call upon all of the National Guard of the State of Colorado to place themselves under arms in their respective armories, subject to call.

"How great a matter a little fire kindleth!" A controversy over two petty municipal offices sets a whole State in uproar. Although the law provides ample machinery for the swift determination of titles to office, this machinery is not employed. A military demand is made, and military force is at once used to enforce the demand. Gatling- and Napoleon-guns are trained on the City Hall, and the military forces of the city are drawn up in battle array before it. The militia of the entire State are ordered to their respective armories to await the orders of the commander-in-chief; and, in the midst of the tempest, the Governor calls also for United States troops. The correspondence in the War Department of the United States will show some of these events in a peculiar light. The Governor calls for United States troops to assist him in "preserving order and preventing bloodshed." Upon their arrival he demands that they be placed under his orders to assist him in "taking possession of the City Hall," that is, to induct his appointees into office. He learns to his dismay that United States troops can be subjected to the command of no other than a United States officer, and that they can be used only for prevention, and not for aggression. He then requests their removal. But, under the judicious control of the wise and experienced commander of the Department of the Colorado, they remain, and by their presence constitute a protection against further violence, a guaranty of safety for life and property.

Finally, under the urgent solicitation of citizens, and by the advice of General McCook, which we may well presume was supported by the moral effect of the presence of United States troops not subject to the orders of the Governor, the Governor was induced to submit the matter to the Supreme Court of the State, under a constitutional provision permitting the executive in certain contingencies to call upon that body for its opinion. It is a strange commentary upon this Populist administration that it should become necessary, in this year of grace 1894, for the Supreme Court to re-enunciate principles which lie at the very foundation of civil liberty. It is in the following manner that the Court commented on this strange proceeding:

"Will it be contended that it is the duty of the chief executive of the State to install into office, by force, if necessary, every county, precinct, or municipal officer whom he may deem entitled to such office, in advance of the determination of any controversy that may arise concerning such office? A proposition so fraught with danger to every principle of free government cannot for a moment be entertained ; and, if such power cannot be lawfully exercised by the Governor acting in his civil capacity, *a fortiori* is the use of military force to that end by him as commander-in-chief unauthorized. . . . We repeat that by no rule of construction can the power and duty imposed upon the Governor 'to execute the laws' be held to authorize the forcible induction of an appointee into office. . . .

"Monarchical and despotic governments can undoubtedly proceed more speedily than a representative government in the enactment, administration, and execution of the laws. Reasonable delay is the price we pay in order to secure the protection and vindication of personal and property rights under a government like ours ; and when it is once conceded that the hardship resulting from such delay justifies a resort to the summary exercise of arbitrary power, either by the civil or military authority, then will justice be dethroned, and despotism or anarchy usurp her seat."

It may well be supposed that such display of military force in such a cause, the contempt expressed by the chief executive for the established courts, and his assumption of arbitrary power caused great ferment in the public mind, and greatly increased the difficulties and hardships of industrial and commercial life, already prostrated by the general pressure of the times.

But, under populistic misgovernment, even more serious troubles were imminent. As early as February, 1894, differences arose between miners and mine-owners at the great gold camp of Cripple Creek, resulting in a strike of the most virulent kind. At an early stage this strike developed into armed opposition to any working of the mines except on terms dictated by the miners' union. Later, mine bosses and foremen were driven away. Miners who advised concessions were in several instances grossly maltreated, in ways too

horrible to relate, and were ejected from the camp. From the inception of this trouble, the active and expressed sympathies of the
Governor were on the side of the miners, and they were thereby em-
boldened to deeds of violence which certainly would not otherwise
have been committed. Early in the strike, the sheriff in attempting
to serve process was met with armed opposition, and after resorting
to the usual means of assistance he called upon the Governor for aid.
The militia were sent in response to this demand, but very soon afterward the Governor, publicly alleging that he had been deceived by
the sheriff and by false representations had been induced to order out
the military, withdrew them. From that time on the miners looked
upon him as their champion. The conservative people of the State
considered that the chief executive was aiding and abetting lawlessness.

There is no need to write a detailed account of the "Cripple
Creek War." It should be stated, however, that hundreds of honest
miners took no part in, and had no sympathy with, the disgraceful
procedings that took place. Many of these were compelled to leave
the camp until the "war" was over. Many others were, against their
will, impressed into service. The evidence seems indisputable that
many of the leaders of the movement were ex-convicts and known
outlaws whose right to be called "miners" was doubtful. The
authorities of El Paso County finally determined to enforce the law
at all hazards, and the sheriff appointed a large number of deputies
to assist him in so doing. The "miners" immediately extended their
organization, gathered arms and ammunition, invaded private houses
for the purpose of gathering munitions of war, and unceremoniously
appropriated them wherever they found them. They stopped travellers on the highway and searched them for arms. They built fortifications on "Bull Hill," and gathered a force variously estimated at
from 1,000 to 1,800 armed men. At the first approach of deputies
they blew up the shaft and shaft-houses of a large mine. A portion
of their number went out to meet the deputies and made a night
attack upon them, resulting in loss of life.

Now, what is the attitude of this Populist administration in the
meanwhile? The Governor is openly and even over his own signature in the public press charging the Sheriff with gathering an unlawful assemblage, because he had included in his list of deputies
men from other counties than El Paso. His Adjutant-General, who
happens to be a lawyer, is appearing for and defending, in the

courts of El Paso County, certain of the "miners" who had been already arrested. The Governor's private secretary, in a published interview, encourages the strikers in their resistance to law in words like these:

"The majority of the men on Bull Hill are animated by the conviction that they represent a vital principle. They haven't the slightest fear of death. There are scores of those men who believe that if they fall in the impending battle, their blood will be the seed which will redeem the cause of labor to the world."

It is during this period that the expression "D—n capital" is attributed to Governor Waite.

Finally a force of 1,000 armed deputies is gathered in camp a short distance from "Bull Hill," and a battle seems imminent. At this stage of the proceedings the Governor visits "Bull Hill," where he is cordially welcomed. Divers reports exist of his sayings and doings there, and, according to newspaper accounts, certain violent words which then dropped from his lips became a rallying-cry for the "Bull Hill" battalions. He finally came back bearing overtures of peace. He came as the ambassador of "The Free Coinage Miners' Union, No. 19, W. F. M. A.," duly appointed by writing bearing the seal of the order.

Under the active influence and pressure of certain citizens brought to bear on both parties, a compromise of the original differences was finally arrived at, and further bloodshed was avoided. After the agreement of compromise was reached, the Governor sent a strong body of militia to the scene of conflict, to stand between the belligerents, and with orders to strictly limit the number of arrests which the Sheriff should be permitted to make.

Throughout this proceeding the Populist Governor, in accordance with the spirit of the Omaha platform, seems to consider himself as representing not the whole people, but a special class; not employer and employee, but employee against employer; not labor and capital, but labor as against capital. He himself recognizes this fact and attempts to justify it. In a subsequent campaign speech, he remarked:

"I said when I was elected Governor, and many times since, that in the administration of my office I should look after the interest of, and legislate for, the laboring man and woman. Fault was found with me that this would be class legislation. Well, what if it is? Is it not the truth that for thirty years the two old parties have been legislating for the creditor class? It is true, and turn about is fair play."

Observe, in passing, that the Governor, having before assumed judicial

46

power, now assumes, perhaps unconsciously, that he can also exercise
the duties of legislation.   The trinity of governmental powers converge
in him.   This assumption that governmental policies, having swung to
one side, must now, like a pendulum, swing to the opposite extreme,
is the cardinal vice in the Populist doctrine.   Out of this assumption
springs the evil genius which has shaped the course of Colorado's
Populist administration.

In December, 1893, the Governor called a special session of the
General Assembly.   His principal purpose was to have a law enacted
which should make foreign silver coins a legal tender in Colorado.
With this was coupled a proposition that contracts payable in gold
should be prohibited.   It is unnecessary, perhaps, to say that these
suggestions dropped still-born, and were by the legislature quickly
consigned to oblivion.

The Populist policy of administration could be illustrated by
numerous other acts of minor importance, but the foregoing are
surely sufficient.   That Colorado suffered in her credit abroad and
in her enterprise and investments at home is but the necessary corollary—too intensely verified by actual experience.   While all the
world has suffered from causes which are world-wide, Colorado has
had the additional burden arising from the spirit of anarchy fostered by executive authority.

Colorado is, however, rich in resources.   This wealth of resources can be developed only by the harmonious coöperation of capital and labor.   The existence of such natural sources of prosperity
serves to strengthen among the people of Colorado a conservative and
law-abiding spirit, and in no State of the Union will there be found
a stronger spirit of business integrity and faithfulness in financial obligation than among those who bear the burden of taxation,—State,
county, and municipal.   There was, therefore, a universal feeling of
indignation prevalent in the State when it was found that, by the
accident of 1892, there had been invoked the spirit of misrule,
setting labor and capital at variance, breathing violence, and casting
an odor of discredit upon the State.   This feeling of indignation
was especially strong in the cities and in the agricultural counties,
where tremendous majorities were given against Governor Waite in
the recent election.   His defeat would have been far more over-
whelming, except for the support he received from mining counties,
a support which is sufficiently explained by facts already related.

In its State convention preceding the late election, the Republican party declared: "The paramount issue in the State of Colorado is the suppression of the spirit of anarchy, the restoration and maintenance of law and order." Upon this issue the battle was fought, and the victory won. The silver question was a minor issue, and rested on the proposition, asserted by the Republicans, that the people's party is "the most insidious foe to the restoration of the free coinage of silver, in that its platform demands an extensive issue of paper money not based upon, or redeemable in, either gold or silver."

The Eastern press makes an egregious error in assuming, as has frequently been done of late, that the Republican victory in Colorado denotes defeat of the silver cause. It does not imply the slightest diminution of bimetallic sentiment. Certainly, a party which wins its victory under the leadership of such men as Senator Teller and Senator Wolcott can hardly be said to have grown less zealous in the cause of bimetallism. The Republican party of Colorado believes in gold and silver coin as the legal-tender money of the country, and as the basis of currency issues. It looks with some amusement at the present proximity of extremes—the bankers at Baltimore and the Populists of the Farmers' Alliance—the one advocating a paper currency based on stockholders' liability and bank assets (for example, bank buildings, furniture and fixtures, and bills receivable); the other advocating a paper money issued on the security of "imperishable farm products," such as wheat, cotton, and tobacco. It wonderingly inquires whether we shall depend in future for our money supplies "upon the quartz mills or the pulp mills of the country." The combination of doctrines labelled "Populism" furnishes, however, no panacea for existing ills. Colorado is not likely to repeat her experiment in Populist government.

JOEL F. VAILE.

THE GREAT REALISTS AND THE EMPTY STORY-TELLERS.

WHO that has read Rousseau's "Confessions" will fail to remember the emphatic avowal that he was unfitted for life by the reading of novels? To be sure, the novels he read were of a highly romantic, or, as it is euphemistically called, "idealistic," kind, which represented a condition of things that never was on land or sea. And it was not an occasional excursion the boy, Jean-Jacques, undertook into this delightful region of high-colored improbabilities; but he took up his residence there and dwelt there, making only reluctant visits to the "sordid" reality which surrounded him. He devoured romances with a ravenous appetite for the intoxication which he craved, and craved more and more. He sought refuge in a fictitious world of resonant speech and mighty deeds from the *petites misères* of a small *bourgeois* existence in Geneva. Like the opium-habit the craving for fiction grew upon him, until the fundamental part of him had suffered irreparable harm.

It is barely possible, of course, that Rousseau, in looking back upon his past life and trying to account for its vagaries and misadventures, exaggerates the effect of his intemperance in the matter of fiction. He may have had a taint from his birth, making him nervously unstrung and liable to excesses. But, even making allowance for this, I find his avowal interesting and significant. He is not the only one who has experienced detrimental effects from dwelling too long in the pleasant land of romance. As soon as a man—and particularly a child—gets acclimated there, he is likely to become of very small account as far as reality is concerned. He becomes less and less able to apply sound standards of judgment to the things of this world; and as the success in life for which we are all striving depends primarily upon this ability to see things straight and to judge them clearly, no one can escape the conclusion that a large consumption of romantic fiction tends distinctly to disqualify a man for worldly success. A habit of mind is produced by the frequent repetition of the same or similar impressions; and if, while young, your thoughts move among absurd and lurid unrealities, and your eyes become accustomed to the Bengal illumination of romance, you will be likely to tumble about like a blundering bat in the daylight. Many a time, I will warrant, you have had this very experience of waking, as from a delightful dream, when your novel was finished. The world and all your daily concerns look pale, dreary and vaguely irritating, while your mind is yet vibrating with the courtly speeches of some fascinating d'Artagnan, to whom life was but a stage for gallant adventures, or with the clash of Ivanhoe's sword or the impossible heroism of an impossible Esmeralda. The youth who gets his mind adjusted to these styles of speech and action and the motives which they imply will be severely handicapped in dealing with affairs which require a nice discrimination of practical values. He will find it next to impossible to command that supreme concentration of effort without which no great achievement is accomplished. He will lapse into mediocrity, even though he may have been equipped for distinction.

"But," you will object, "this escape which romance affords us from life's dreary round of cares and duties is not only delightful but beneficial: it refreshes the mind, satisfies a latent craving for the heroic, which we all have, and sends sun-gleams from an ideal world down into our gray, monotonous existence; it is like canvas-back, terrapin, and champagne to a man who is wont to dine on porridge and red herring."

Well, there is a good deal to be said for this view. But, in my opinion, it is unsound. As the world is now constituted, the little margin of superiority by which a man secures survival and success is so narrow, that the very smallest advantage, gained or squandered, may be decisive as to his whole career. Therefore, all education should be primarily directed toward securing as intimate an acquaintance as possible with one's environment, so that one may be able to utilize it most effectively. I freely admit that this is not the aim of our present educational system, which flounders helplessly between the old humanistic curriculum and the new scientific studies. But a new light has dawned upon our darkness, and education is being reformed about as fast as academic conservatism will permit. This by way of a parenthesis, which, however, has a direct bearing upon my contention. The most modern novel—which should not be confounded with the romance—has set itself this very task of exploring reality, and gauging the relative strength of the forces that enter into our lives and determine our fates. It is, therefore, a powerful educational agency, and is being utilized as such in at least one of our great universities—by Professor Brander Matthews, of Columbia College, who gives an annual course of lectures on "The English Novel." It does not act as an opiate dulling our interest in everyday affairs, but it sharpens our observation and enables us to detect the significance of common facts and events. The reader is a wiser and, perhaps, a sadder man, when he rises from the perusal of such a book, as, for instance, "Middlemarch," which illuminates one of life's most vital problems and enables him to deal with it more intelligently when it presents itself for his solution. For it is only a poor, spluttering, tallow dip nature has provided you with for the exploration of that intricate labyrinth, matrimony; and no Ariadne's thread will ever lead you safely out, if once you have had the hardihood to enter. In "Middlemarch," the intimate history of two typical marriages is related. In the one case, the husband's career is wrecked by the hard, exacting selfishness of the wife who is a very harpy disguised as an angel. In the other case a noble and lovable woman is led by her very nobleness into a no less tragic mistake, and here it is the husband who is the Moloch in whose arms the wife finds a slow, but no less torturing martyrdom. How many thousands, if not millions, of lives there are which intersect this story at innumerable points! It is as if an electric torch had been thrust into the innermost recesses of our lives, throwing its fierce glare upon ourselves and all our surroundings. I can imagine no more profitable reading either to young or old than this great epic of matrimony.

I have chosen "Middlemarch" as an example of the modern realistic novel, because I know none, unless it be Thackeray's "Vanity Fair," which deals so searchingly with typical persons and conditions, and so scrupulously excludes everything that does not appertain to the experience of the average human being, in the sphere of society with which it deals. Many excellent persons will, no doubt, disagree with me, if I avow the opinion that "Vanity Fair" is also, in a sense, educational, though it requires a higher degree of maturity to detect and profit by its lesson. By lesson I do not mean a pointed moral at the end—a *hæc fabula docet*—but merely a deepening and widely ramifying acquaintance with reality. Instead of blinding one to the forces that govern the world, novels of this order reveal them. Instead of counteracting the logic of life, they enforce it.

I am distinctly conscious of being indebted to Thackeray for having led me out of the "moon-illumined magic night" of German
romanticism (in which I once revelled) and accustomed me, by degrees, to a wholesomer, though less poetic, light.   Vividly do I remember the distaste, the resentment, with which as a youth of twenty
I flung away "The Virginians" at the chapter where Harry's calf-
love for Maria is satirized.   Like a sting to the quick was to me the
remark about his pressing "the wilted vegetable" with rapture to his
lips, or was it his heart?   The delicious, good-natured ridicule with
which the infatuation of Pen for Miss Fotheringay is treated in
"Pendennis" hurt and disgusted me.   I felt as if the author were
personally abusing me.   For I was then at the age when Pen's madness seemed to verge more nearly on sublimity than on foolishness.
Accordingly I had a low opinion of Thackeray in those days.

But for all that, I could not help reading him; and, truth to
tell, I owe him a debt of gratitude which it would be difficult to
over-estimate.   He saved me from no end of dangerous follies by
kindling in me a spark of sobering self-criticism, which enabled me
to catch little side-glimpses of myself, when I was on the verge of
committing a *bêtise*.   He aroused in me a salutary scepticism as to
the worth of much which the world has stamped with its approval.
He blew away a good deal of that romantic haze which hid reality
from me and prevented me from appraising men and things at their
proper value.   Though no crude Sunday-school moral is appended
to "Pendennis," "The Newcomes" or "Vanity Fair," he must be
duller than an ox to the subtler sense who does not feel in the pervasive atmosphere of these books a wholesome moral tonic.   And who
can make the acquaintance of Colonel Newcome without having the
character of the man stamped on his very soul and feeling a glow of
enthusiasm for his nobleness, uprightness and lofty sense of honor?
It is because he is so touchingly human, so pathetically true, that he
makes so deep an impression.   And as for Clive and Rose and the
Campaigner, their fates have an educational worth beyond a hundred
sermons.   Though Thackeray does not often scold his bad and questionable characters (as does, for instance, Dickens), and though he permits an occasional smile to lurk between the lines at Becky Sharp's
reprehensible cleverness, there is nowhere any confusion of moral
values; and the voice that speaks has a half paternal cadence of genial
wisdom and resignation.

Among the other novelists to whom I am indebted for a clearance of vision, I cannot omit Tolstoi. He is a more strenuous and commanding personality than was Thackeray; and the moral he teaches is more direct, insistent, importunate. I am speaking now of his early works, which were written before he became a prophet. Not that—though disagreeing with him—I honor him less in this capacity than in that of a writer of fiction: but his work as a social reformer lies beyond the scope of the present article. It is as the author of "Anna Karénina" that he has his title to immortality. I have heard many good people call this wonderful novel immoral, because they have the notion that every book which touches upon the question of sex is *ipso facto* immoral. Nothing can, to my mind, be sillier than this. The novelist has to take life as he finds it, and he would produce a false, distorted picture if he were to omit a factor which plays so tremendous a part as sex. The morality depends upon the spirit in which the author deals with his subject. "La dame aux Camélias" is immoral, not because the heroine is of the *demi-monde*, but because Dumas *fils* violates the logic of life in representing her as a lovely and sentimental creature, and capable of as pure and exalting a passion as a woman who had never sinned. Likewise Mürger in "Scènes de la vie de Bohême" and Du Maurier in "Trilby," fascinating though they are, extol the grisette, implying that an occasional lapse from virtue is, on the whole, a venial affair and leaves the core of the character unimpaired. Musette in the former novel and Trilby in the latter are rose-colored lies and are the more dangerous because uncritical youth will take them to be types of their kind and will never suspect how untrue they are, how far removed from reality. No, then give me rather Zola's "Nana," which states the unvarnished fact with brutal directness; or even Daudet's "Sappho," which details the whole direful experience, from the first intoxication of the sense through the years of gradual disillusion to the utter blighting of the soul, exhaustion and ruin. No one will feel tempted to embark in so perilous an enterprise, after having received so lucid an exposition of the consequences; while I know more than one young man in whom the seeds of corruption were sown by Dumas and Mürger. These writers are immoral, not because they deal with sin, but because they deal with it untruthfully; while Zola and, in a less degree, Daudet, who give an exact and vivid reflection of an ugly reality, become unintentional, if not unconscious, moralists.

Among these faithful and unflinching chroniclers of life Tolstoi is the foremost. He is the greatest living moralist, because he pierces

deeper into the heart of things than any contemporary writer. Nowhere have I found in him an instance of prevarication. Without
a word of preaching, he enforces in " Anna Karénina" the inexorable
law that all anti-social relations are destructive of character, destructive of happiness, destructive of life itself. When the individual, in
pursuing its lawless pleasure, imagines that it is drinking in deep
draughts the very fulness of life, it is really engaged in reducing and
diminishing its fitness for life—in eliminating itself from the struggle for existence. It is engaged in demonstrating its unfitness for
survival. Thus Anna's sin destroys her by a relentless necessity,
first, because it brings her upon a war-footing with society, which is
founded upon the family and must, in self-protection, resent affini-
ties that controvert this fundamental institution; secondly, because
the insecurity of the relation itself and the consciousness of its ab-
normality induce perpetual excitements, which, by ruining the nerves,
upset the mental balance and make sane and tranquil conduct impossible. What profound psychology Tolstoi displays, and what fine
reticence, too, in the account of Anna's moral deterioration! How
insidiously and gradually she entangles herself in the net which drags
her to perdition!

There is something almost appalling in the rigorous veracity of
this great and patient Russian with the toil-worn hands and the tragic
face. There is a vast murmur of human activities in his novels, a
busy clamor of human voices, a throbbing turmoil of human heart-
beats,—so much so that one appears to have lived through his books
rather than to have read them. Never did I suspect the closeness of
man's kinship to man and the identity of human experience, in
spite of race, climate and country, until I read Tolstoi's remarkable
autobiography, entitled, " Childhood, Boyhood, and Youth"; and
after having finished " Ivan Ilyitch" I actually began to develop the
symptoms of the mysterious malady which killed the unheroic hero
of that extraordinary novel. To be sure, I had had a fall from my
horse the week before, and that may have given color to my illusions.

How unutterably flimsy and juvenile, romantic fiction, such as
Stevenson's tales of villanous wreckers and buccaneers, Haggard's
chronicles of battle, murder and sudden death, Conan Doyle's accounts of swaggering savagery and sickening atrocities, and S. R.
Crockett's sanguinary records of Scotch marauding expeditions, appear to me, compared with Tolstoi's wonderfully vivid and masterly
transcripts of the life we all live! Amid all the shouts of the fight-

ers and the clash of arms there is, to me, a deadly silence in the popular novel of adventure. The purely artificial excitement leaves me cold and a trifle fatigued. I see everywhere the hand that pulls the wires. It is a great dead world, whose puppets are galvanized into a semblance of life by the art of the author.

"But," the critics will tell you, "you must be a poor prosaic soul if you do not feel your pulses tingle with delight when you read of heroic adventures and daring deeds." Well, that depends primarily upon what they call heroic. When I read in Rider Haggard of two Englishmen who killed fifty or a hundred or five hundred Zulus, or in Conan Doyle's "The White Company" of four Britishers and a Frenchman keeping an army of six or seven thousand at bay, or in Walter Scott of Ivanhoe's tremendous feat of arms, I am not a particle stirred, first, because the deeds do not seem admirable, and secondly, because neither Ivanhoe nor the Zulu-killing young Britishers are to me alive; for which reason it is of small consequence what they do. When, on the other hand, I read in Tolstoi's "War and Peace" the account of the siege of Sevastopol, during which daring acts were frequent, I am deeply interested, because it all bears the stamp of authenticity, and it is interpenetrated with a warm, red-veined humanity. That is war as it is, written by one who draws upon his own experience, and knows whereof he speaks. But who will pretend that Walter Scott, splendid *raconteur* though he was, represented with even a remote degree of correctness the life of the Middle Ages? And still less can Rider Haggard, or any of his romantic *confrères*, lay claim to verisimilitude or fidelity to anything but their own desire to excite and amuse. The reading of their books tends to the awakening in the young of the feudal ideal which it has cost the world such a deluge of blood and tears, partly to get rid of. For that we have not wholly gotten rid of it the popularity of these very authors sufficiently proves.

I shall probably be charged with exaggeration if I say that the recent aristocratic development in the United States, with its truly mediæval inequality between the classes, is in no small measure due to this recrudescence of the feudal ideal among us, which is again, in a measure, due to the romantic fiction that our youth of both sexes consume. It is the feudal sentiment of good Sir Walter and his successors which makes our daughters despise the democracy which their fathers founded, and dream of baronial castles, parks and coronets and a marriage with a British peer as the goal of their ambitions. It is the same feudal sentiment which makes their mothers share and encourage their aspirations and equip them, in Paris, with all the ethereal ammunition required for the English campaign.   Half the novels they read glorify these things, and it would be a wonder if the perpetual glorification did not produce its effect.   For the idea that literature of amusement is a neutral agency which affects you neither for good nor for ill is a pernicious fallacy.   What you read, especially in youth, will enter into your mental substance, and will and must increase or impair your efficiency.   Much you will outgrow, no doubt; but there always remains a deposit in the mind which you will never outgrow.   It is, therefore, of the utmost importance that that which you read should tend to put you *en rapport* with the present industrial age, in which, whether you like it or not, you have to live, rather than with a remote feudalism, whose ideals were essentially barbaric, and certainly cruder and less humane than ours.   It is your comprehension of the problems in your own existence and in that of your unheroic neighbors—what the romancers contemptuously call the prose of life—which makes you a useful and influential citizen; while preoccupation with what is wrongfully conceived to be its poetry produces wrecks and failures.   It is because the romantic novel tends to unfit you for this prose of life that I condemn it; and it is because the realistic novel opens your eyes to its beauty, its power and its deeper significance that I commend it.

HJALMAR HJORTH BOYESEN.

STUDENT HONOR AND COLLEGE EXAMINATIONS.

ON a warm day in June some years ago, a number of students of a well-known college were seated around a large table in the examination-room. Each had a set of printed questions to which answers were to be written within a prescribed number of hours. Before handing in his paper the student was required to sign a printed statement in these words: "I pledge my word of honor that in preparing these answers I have not received aid from any person, book, manuscript, or any other source whatever." Two students, who may be designated A and B, were seated opposite each other. After several hours A had nearly completed his task, while B was still perplexed over a question. Suddenly a gust of wind swept through the open windows. Scores of sheets of paper were scattered in confusion through the room. A's paper fell upon the opposite edge of the table, and by an ill fate the answer to the question over which B had been so much puzzled was uppermost. The involuntary glance of a moment gave the clue he had in vain sought. He found himself unable to sign the examination-pledge, except by omitting entirely the question on which aid had been thus so unexpectedly rendered. This omission caused his paper to be graded below the passing mark, and failure in a single subject at a final examination determined his loss of the baccalaureate degree. The professor who graded these papers was a man whose justice was unquestioned and whose kindness was unbounded, but B's delicate sense of honor was such as to make him unwilling to offer any explanation of his failure. He bore his mortification in silence, and not until many weeks afterward was the truth made known.

This is perhaps an extreme case. I was a classmate of the unfortunate student, and gently criticised him for his failure to secure the lenient consideration that was justly due. Martyrdom for an abstract principle is honorable; but martyrdom without the use of all honorable means to prevent it is not necessary. The error was one of head and not of heart. But it was far less worthy of condemnation than the more common one which may now be detailed by way of contrast.   Two students, C and D, are seated next each other in the examination-room.   C is a good memorizer, but not infallible.   He writes out a faulty demonstration, employing an incorrect diagram, and one or more absurdities are introduced through the faithful reproduction of unrelated statements committed to memory from his text-book or lecture-notes, or brought into the examination on concealed bits of paper.   D, who admires his friend's apparent brightness, furtively copies the faulty diagram and demonstration, line for line, symbol for symbol, word for word.   Each writes his signature to the pledge that during this examination no aid has been given or received; or perhaps he has eased his conscience by affixing his signature before writing out any answer.   The pledge presupposes the existence of a "word of honor," but, in the absence of any adequate conception as to the meaning of such a phrase, quibbling is to be expected.   On the following day the examiner's attention is unavoidably attracted to the remarkable coincidence that two papers should include identically the same errors in both form and statement.   Each student is privately summoned, and an explanation is demanded.   Conviction at once follows, and the nature and extent of the punishment are determined by local precedent.

It is probably within the truth to say that shortly before the beginning of every summer vacation a majority of those who are engaged in the work of instruction, whether in colleges or preparatory schools, have their attention called, directly or indirectly, to cases of dishonesty in examination.   The evil is widespread, but in colleges at least it may now be confidently said to be diminishing.   Probably it will never wholly cease so long as periodic written examinations continue in vogue, nor, indeed, so long as students are subjected to any kind of examination whatever.   In civil life, courts of justice and prisons are as necessary to-day as they were in the days when Roman law was becoming formulated as a basis for future codes.   Human nature among students is substantially what it was and is among their parents. In the competition of business, of politics, of professional life, men are continually trying to gain prizes with the least possible expenditure of labor.   The virtue of truthfulness is praised in the abstract, but truth is so commonly sacrificed in the pursuit of profit that in certain kinds of business its violation is assumed as a matter of course, and strict integrity is looked upon as the characteristic of a simpleton.   Students are not superior to the world around them; they cannot be held to a standard superior to that of society at large.

It is quite generally agreed that no student should be held responsible for mental deficiency.   He had no agency in determining
his inheritance, whether in mind or body.   But the laws of nature
operate without pity, and he who is intellectually weak is naturally
deprived of the opportunity to enjoy what the world accords to
power.   So it is also in regard to morals.

There are many young persons who have no conception of the
obligation implied in a" word of honor."   Such a conception is not
innate, but rather a product of culture.   The moral sense needs direction and cultivation.   The current standard of honor is to a large
extent arbitrary, an outcome of popular sentiment, and hence liable
to change with the growth of civilization.   This is abundantly shown
in changes that have been developed within a single generation in our
own country.   The " code of honor" forty years ago made duelling
obligatory under certain conditions; and this is the case still in
Europe.   Such a code is now little else than a memory in America.
The rapidity with which change in popular sentiment has made laws
against it effective is a sufficient indication that change in the student
sense of honor may be developed; and the current standard twenty
years hence may become generally as high among American students
as it is already in a few institutions to which reference will presently
be made.   The change will not be an outcome of prohibitory college
legislation, but rather of growth in college freedom.   In the ordinary
business of life the man who is convicted of palpable mendacity or
any other form of flagrant dishonesty loses caste among those whose
good opinion is most worth retaining.   The sin brings its own natural punishment, even though called only " the sin of being found
out."   Among those who claim to be educated, who wish to maintain leadership in the industrial, political, or social world, dishonesty
is costly and dangerous.   Honesty based upon principle is above all
things to be desired.   But even apparent honesty, based upon an
intelligent conception of policy, constitutes a long step toward the
attainment of a healthy tone of honor.

With a view to investigating the tone among American colleges,
so far as this can be manifested in the standard of student honor in
examinations, a list of questions was prepared and sent to a member
of the faculty of each of forty-three institutions of higher education in
every section of the United States.[1]   Of those addressed only one

---

[1] The following is the list of institutions selected : Adelbert College, Agricultural College of Iowa, Alabama Polytechnic Institute, Amherst, Brooklyn

failed to respond.   The list includes a majority of the leading American institutions, though not all of those having a high standing.   It
is fairly representative of all parts of the country, and little would
have been gained by multiplying applications.   The results of the
information received are summed up as follows:

I. Out of forty-two correspondents only one writes that his examinations are exclusively oral, this course being adopted because
it makes cheating difficult.   In two other cases it is stated that they
are mostly oral.   In eight cases they are both oral and written, the
natural inference being that about equal value is attached to each
method.   In nine cases the examinations are mostly written, and
in twenty-two cases wholly written.   This shows that in the leading
American colleges the method of written examinations is the rule, of
oral examinations the exception.   Forty years ago oral examinations
were the rule, and written examinations the exception.   Each plan
has its own advantages.   If cheating is to be prevented by vigilance
alone, the oral examination is better.   But happily this necessity is
not always present.   In a large number of cases each teacher is at
liberty to examine in any way that may seem to him best, without
being bound down to any inelastic rule.   If a daily class-record is
kept, it is best to make such a combination of grades in advance, review, and examination work as to cause the student to find his own
interests promoted by constant attention to duty rather than by
" cramming" for an examination.   But the keeping of a daily class
record implies much recitation; and by many teachers, especially in
the higher departments, recitation-marks are deemed a clog rather
than an aid.   Without them a good teacher is still able to judge
regarding the attainment reached by his students.   It is not possible
to dispense with examinations; but for the method of conducting
them no rule can be laid down as deserving of universal application.

II. Twenty-nine correspondents write that the student is not required to make any statement that his work has been independently
done.   Thirteen write that a pledge is required to the effect that no

Polytechnic Institute, Brown, Case School of Applied Science, Colby, Colgate,
Columbia, Cornell, Dartmouth, Harvard, Johns Hopkins, Massachusetts In-
stitute of Technology, Northwestern, Ohio State University, Princeton, Rens-
selaer Polytechnic Institute, Richmond College, Rose Polytechnic Institute,
Rutgers, Smith, South Carolina College, South Carolina Military Academy,
Stevens Institute of Technology, Trinity, Tulane, Union College, U. S. Mili-
tary Academy; the Universities of California, City of New York, Georgia,
Michigan, Pennsylvania, Rochester, Tennessee, Texas, Virginia, Wisconsin;
Vassar, Williams, Yale.

aid has been given or received; and each of these thirteen expresses his conviction that the writing and signing of such a pledge has a decided influence in preventing dishonesty.

III. In twenty-one cases comes the statement that among the students a strong popular sentiment against "cribbing" exists. In twelve cases this feeling is said to be not strong. In nine cases the reply is given that a student disgraces himself if he cribs in an examination for honors, but that in the estimation of his fellow-students he is considered justifiable in cribbing if his class record has not been high and the effort in examination is merely to escape being conditioned. This distinction of course has no ethical basis. To win an honor by cheating is obviously an offence against honest competitors, altogether apart from the self-degradation involved in falsehood. The student who merely passes is not on this account a person of distinction, but if he does so by dishonest means he may quite naturally incur the contempt of the man who has failed honestly. At best he has recorded his disbelief in the importance of truthfulness as an element of manly character. It is encouraging to note that a majority of the replies indicate a strong sentiment among students against any form of cheating in examination. A considerable proportion of these writers intimate that this feeling is growing in strength; that cheating was formerly more common, but that a decided reaction against it has been lately developed. The monthly college journal is an index and at the same time an important agency in bringing about these changes. Its editors are usually selected from the better class of students, and their influence in such matters is nearly always for good.

IV. To the fourth question—whether there is among the faculty any sentiment that cribbing should be prevented rather by the vigilance of the examiner than by an appeal to the honor of the student—the answers were in some cases less direct than was desirable, because a single writer, while giving his own impressions, felt naturally some hesitation about speaking for others without special consultation. The general preference of the faculty was in seventeen cases said to be in favor of the honor system, and in eleven cases in favor of that of vigilance. In six cases the simultaneous application of both systems was advocated, and in eight cases the members of the faculty were said to differ among themselves in relation to this subject. A few quotations from the replies may be here given.

"I think the faculty are divided, though I feel sure that a majority believe that simple vigilance, unaided by the students' moral support, will not be effective. For myself I believe that temptation should be removed, so far as possible, by separating the seats and by a certain amount of watching."

"If you adopt the honor system, do not spoil it by doubting the word of a student. An honored professor once told me that he required a written pledge to the paper, 'but,' said he, 'we watch them too.' This is a mixture worse than either plan alone."

"Both methods are used. I am sorry to say that, human nature being weak, an appeal should be made, *and* the instructor should be *present* and *watchful.*"

"We employ proctors to assist the examiner. I object to putting students on their honor by means of a written pledge or affirmation."

"Cribbing is so uncommon here that I know of no sentiment one way or the other about watching against it. For myself I choose to trust the honor of our students, and I think that I can safely do so. Where watching is depended upon, a certain class of students would rather enjoy evading such vigilance, while they would not cheat if put upon their honor."

"It is considered so grave an offence to cheat that the accusation is not hastily made. It is a matter for serious consultation, just as serious in college life as it would be in the outside world to accuse a woman of want of chastity. So soon as a professor begins a system of espionage the student feels at liberty to outwit him if possible. Such espionage would be felt here to be equally degrading to both professor and student."

V. The fifth question—as to whether a student who signs a pledge which is handed in with his paper is permitted to leave the examination-room before completing his paper—was left unanswered by about a dozen of those who in response to the second question had written that no pledge was exacted of the student. In eleven cases it is stated that no permission is granted the student to leave the room during the course of an examination. In eighteen cases it is stated that such permission is accorded when any reasonable ground for it is presented. If the espionage system is in force, it is natural to suppose that a student would feel himself at liberty to seek aid if temporary leave of absence is granted. If the honor system is in force there is no reason why he should be trammelled. In an American university where I spent some time as a student, and where the honor system is in full force, it is not uncommon for students at mid-day to leave the examination-room in order to eat dinner. The work is resumed in the afternoon, and occasionally a student leaves a second time for supper, and finishes his work by gaslight. Despite the abundant opportunity for cheating, so high is the standard of honor, so vigilant are the students, and so relentless in crushing offenders, that less than half a dozen cases of dishonesty in examination have been detected within the last forty years. No proctors are needed in such an atmosphere. The written pledge is appended to every examination-paper, but only in obedience to a wise custom and not as a necessity.

47

VI. To the question as to the maximum and minimum penalties in cases of conviction of cribbing, the answers are naturally somewhat varied. Where the honor system exists, the penalty for its violation is rightly more severe than where the student is subjected to espionage. To abuse a trust is a graver offence than to outwit a police officer. The maximum punishment inflicted for cheating in examination is expulsion, summary and unconditional. This is assigned as the usual punishment in twelve of the institutions enumerated. In several others the offender is not publicly expelled, but permitted quietly to withdraw. In others the punishment is graded according to the circumstances of the case, the maximum being suspension for a year or more, and the minimum suspension for a single term. In all cases the offender's examination-paper is rejected, so that he is thrown back a year or required to stand a subsequent extra examination. In addition to this the student is suspended for six months, three months, or in one institution only two weeks. Sometimes the infliction of a penalty is left to the judgment of the professor in whose department the offence has been committed, especially if the offence is so very rare that no " usual penalty" is provided for it. This last remark applies to each of the two women's colleges, and to at least two Northern institutions for young men.

Of the six quotations given above, the second and last are from Southern colleges, the other four from Northern institutions.

In Southern colleges generally, the traditional standard of honor in the examination-room is very exacting. The following extract is from a letter written by a professor in a well-known Southern college. It is only one of a number of accounts from different sources, all of which indicate the same spirit.

"On one occasion a young man of talent, from one of the best families in the State, committed the very unusual crime of cheating in an examination. The faculty knew nothing of it. His class held a meeting and appointed a committee to wait on him at the hotel whither he had gone on hearing that he had been detected. This committee notified him that he would not be allowed to enter the College limits, but allowed him to send a dray for his trunk. He informed the committee that he had fallen into temptation and felt the disgrace keenly, but that they were right and he would leave. The students notified the faculty of the occurrence and of their action, and asked that for the sake of the offender's family he be not publicly expelled, but that he be dismissed. The faculty thanked the students, and indefinitely dismissed the young man. Repentant, but feeling that the stigma would cling to him, he soon left the State."

The conclusion must not be drawn from this incident that in Southern students there is any inherent moral superiority over their

friends in Northern colleges. College honor is largely the outcome
of tradition.   It would be aside from our purpose to inquire into
the causes which have produced the very noticeable difference be·
tween the standards applied in the examination·room in certain representative universities, North and South.   The present investigation
has revealed the fact that some Southern students, who had been
scrupulously careful to avoid even the appearance of evil at home,
where the honor system prevails, have speedily yielded to temptation after entering Northern institutions in which the system of espionage was applied.   The risk of severe punishment in the one case
is great; in the other it is small. What is by common consent
criminal and disgraceful in the one place is in the other regarded as
objectionable but often pardonable.   A young man quickly adapts
himself to his surroundings. It is to be hoped that Southern col·
leges will never give up a tradition so creditable as the honor sys·
tem.   It is a subject for congratulation that its growth at the North
has lately become so marked.

An additional word of comment may now be made about the
subjects embraced in paragraphs II. and IV., above.   Thirteen
writers state that the students in their colleges are each required to
sign a pledge that no aid has been given or received during the examination.   In every one of these institutions the honor system is in
force.   In eleven cases the majority of the faculty are said to be in
favor of depending upon vigilance rather than honor. Quite naturally they favor no pledge. The student who would deliberately cheat
would not be deterred by the formality of signing his name to a
falsehood.   But when a student of fairly good character is tempted,
the presence of a pledge is an aid to him in resisting temptation.   It
is well to furnish to all students the same style of examination-paper.
At the head of each sheet may be printed a few instructions suffi·
cient to remove the necessity for asking questions, and then the pledge,
with a blank to receive the signature, which should be appended on
each sheet just before the paper is handed in to the instructor.

VII. The answers to the seventh and eighth questions—as to the
best means of securing practical honesty in the rendition of examination-papers, and asking for suggestions—although varied, indicate re·
markable unanimity on certain points. To secure practical honesty in
examination-papers, the proper course to pursue depends very largely
upon the spirit of the community, the past history and traditions of
the college, the average age of the students, and the general culture of a

controlling majority of them.   The evil of dishonesty in examinations is almost invariably more prevalent among the younger than among the older students, and more formidable in institutions with inelastic curricula than in those where there is wide range and reasonable freedom in the election of studies.   If a student is compelled to take a subject which is distasteful to him, the temptation is very strong to employ all available aids to get through, whether these are lawful or not.   At Harvard University, for example, where the opportunities for election increase with the student's length of stay, it is well known that strict surveillance is necessary at the admission examination, but that this necessity rapidly diminishes with each successive year spent at the college.   The habit of cheating is acquired in the preparatory schools everywhere, though in some of the best of these it is largely under control.   Newly-arrived freshmen are not apt to view any subject from the standpoint of the senior or the post-graduate, who has a definite aim and a manly feeling of personal responsibility.

There is much unanimity of opinion that the only effective means of securing general honesty in examinations is the development of high moral tone in student society.   If this does not already exist, no rule for its attainment can be laid down beyond the exercise of tact and sympathetic personal influence on the part of the faculty and all others who should naturally take an interest in the students. If the disposition is manifested to treat every one of these as an honorable gentleman just so far as he warrants this assumption, then in most cases the disposition to cheat is taken away.   To repose a trust produces generally a desire to honor that trust.   The sooner such mutual confidence is developed as may warrant the complete withdrawal of espionage, the better it is for all.   At both Cornell and Princeton universities the experiment has been begun, within the last two years, of leaving to the students themselves the control of all cases of discipline necessitated by human weakness in examination.   The same plan has been carried out for many years in the South Carolina College, the Universities of Georgia and Virginia, and many other Southern colleges.   It has but lately been introduced in a modified form into the University of California.   At Williams College, last summer, the faculty responded favorably to a proposition of the sophomore class to permit the experiment to be tried at least with this class during the coming scholastic year.

The chief difficulty to be encountered in carrying out the plan of student self-government is twofold: students are naturally and rightly indisposed to act as informers against each other, and the majority of them have not the degree of maturity that is needful in a judicial investigation.   As to the first of these obstacles I may quote from a letter of a professor in one of the Southern colleges just named.

"I feel that it is not improper in this connection to call attention to the traditions of Southern schools and colleges.   It has always been the law that a pupil shall not inform on his fellows to the teacher.   In fact some of the best Southern school-teachers have made it an invariable rule to punish a pupil who reports his fellow.   This of course refers to ordinary offences.   But it is also held that if one is guilty of a disgraceful act, the student body deals with him, either by expelling him or handing him over to the governing body.   This is an entirely different thing from tale-bearing.   It is a by-law of this college that a student shall not be required to inform on his fellow.   But a student who is accused by the faculty of an offence may be called on to affirm or deny.   A refusal to answer a charge is considered by the faculty a confession of guilt.   A denial is generally accepted, but if such denial be a falsehood the student body would be expected to preserve its honor by getting rid of the offender.   If the student body is not actuated by these high principles, it is naturally impossible to carry out such a course.   There is, so far as I know in the South, an unbending rule regarding cheating in examination.   Where the students do not take the matter in hand, the faculty never fails to do so.   But the latter prefer to let the students deal with such cases if they will.   A student does not wish to bring himself under suspicion, and he avoids suspicious acts.   He knows that there are those among his companions whose censure is worse in student life than the censure of the faculty."

The details and limitations of student self-government must necessarily vary in different colleges.   In the University of Georgia and in Cornell University there is a university court composed of one member from the freshman, two from the sophomore, three from the junior, and four from the senior classes.   The president of the university or some one or more members of the faculty are also members of this court.   In the former any violation of faith is made the business of the class to which the offender belongs.   To the court is submitted in writing all testimony relating to the case, and a majority of two-thirds is necessary to convict.   Such a students' court or committee exists also at Princeton.   It gives to the delinquent the option of leaving college quietly or of being reported to the faculty for discipline.   A Princeton professor writes:

"The general impression is that the plan as sketched above is more effective than any practicable watching by the faculty.   I think the proper way is to appeal to the honor of the student, and, whenever the offence is detected, to cut off the offender as unfit to associate with gentlemen.   I should not 'watch' and 'suspect' students, but should act decisively when a case of cheating is found out."

Experience at Cornell University has been substantially in accord with that at Princeton.

"The friends of the new system place their faith chiefly in its ability to elevate the standard of student honor to such a point that no one will have the
hardihood to cheat in the presence of his fellows."

The success of these experiments in both North and South warrants
the confident hope that, within a few decades at most, the system of
espionage at college examinations will be completely abolished, and
students everywhere will be entrusted with the maintenance of such a
standard of honor as is worthy of young gentlemen. The great majority of them are opposed to cheating, whether in the examination-
room or elsewhere. In society at large, criminals are the exception
rather than the rule, and honorable men resent the imputation of association with criminals. The laws must still provide for the exceptional college criminal, and it is not to be expected that all offences
will be detected and punished under any system. But in proportion
as espionage is relaxed should the punishment for abuse of confidence
be increased. Merely to condition a student for dishonesty, or to
suspend him for a few weeks, is equivalent to assuring him that his
offence is unimportant. Expulsion from the society of gentlemen is
what has been found most wise in those colleges where the standard
of college honor has been sustained with the best success. If this
penalty be deemed too severe for those in which no traditional hostility
to cheating has yet been developed, suspension for a year or for a
term would seem to be as little as the nature of the offence warrants.

In all cases, whether the honor system or that of espionage is in
force, due regard should be had for the removal of all unnecessary
temptation in the examination-room. If possible, students should
be sufficiently separated to afford each one abundant elbow-room;
conversation should be discouraged; and no one should move from
one seat to another without good reason. These precautions imply no
distrust of the student; they serve merely to protect him from falling
accidentally into some situation that might prove embarrassing. It is
much easier to avoid a false position than to explain it.

No reform has ever yet been accomplished without giving rise to
new problems. That of self-government in colleges has already made
the moral tone of these far better than it was in the days of our fathers.
Hazing, cheating, drunkenness, and gambling have not yet been abolished, and perhaps will not disappear entirely during the twentieth
century; but with the progress of the last thirty years we have no reason to be discouraged. It is quite reasonable to expect at least equally
rapid progress during the remaining few years of the present century.

W. LE CONTE STEVENS.

TRUE AMERICAN IDEALS.

In his noteworthy book on "National Life and Character," Mr. Pearson says: "The countrymen of Chatham and Wellington, of Washington and Lincoln, in short the citizens of every historic state, are richer by great deeds that have formed the national character, by winged words that have passed into current speech, by the examples of lives and labors consecrated to the service of the commonwealth." In other words, every great nation owes to the men whose lives have formed part of its greatness not merely the material effect of what they did, not merely the laws they placed upon the statute books or the victories they won over armed foes, but also the immense but undefinable moral influence produced by their deeds and words themselves upon the national character. It would be difficult to exaggerate the material effects of the careers of Washington and of Lincoln upon the United States. Without Washington we should probably never have won our independence of the British crown, and we should almost certainly have failed to become a great nation, remaining instead a cluster of jangling little communities, drifting toward the type of government prevalent in Spanish America. Without Lincoln we might perhaps have failed to keep the political unity we had won; and even if, as is possible, we had kept it, both the struggle by which it was kept and the results of this struggle would have been so different that the effect upon our national history could not have failed to be profound. Yet the nation's debt to these men is not confined to what it owes them for its material well-being, incalculable though this debt is. Beyond the fact that we are an independent and united people, with half a continent as our heritage, lies the fact that every American is richer by the heritage of the noble deeds and noble words of Washington and of Lincoln. Each of us who reads the Gettysburg speech or the second inaugural address of the greatest American of the nineteenth century, or who studies the long campaigns and lofty statesmanship of that other American who was even greater, cannot but feel within him that lift toward things higher and nobler which can never be bestowed by the enjoyment of mere material prosperity.

It is not only the country which these men helped to make and helped to save that is ours by inheritance; we inherit also all that is best and highest in their characters and in their lives. We inherit from Lincoln and from the might of Lincoln's generation not merely the freedom of those who once were slaves; for we inherit also the fact of the freeing of them, we inherit the glory and the honor and the wonder of the deed that was done, no less than the actual results of the deed when done. The bells that rang at the passage of the emancipation proclamation still ring in Whittier's ode; and as men think over the real nature of the triumph then scored for human-kind their hearts shall ever throb as they cannot over the great-est industrial success or over any victory won at a less cost than ours.

The captains and the armies who, after long years of dreary cam-paigning and bloody, stubborn fighting, brought to a close the Civil War have likewise left us even more than a reunited realm. The material effect of what they did is shown in the fact that the same flag flies from the Great Lakes to the Rio Grande, and all the people of the United States are richer because they are one people and not many, because they belong to one great nation, and not to a con-temptible knot of struggling nationalities. But besides this, besides the material results of the Civil War, we are all, North and South, incalculably richer for its memories. We are the richer for each grim campaign, for each hard-fought battle. We are the richer for valor displayed alike by those who fought so valiantly for the right and by those who, no less valiantly, fought for what they deemed the right. We have in us nobler capacities for what is great and good because of the infinite woe and suffering, and because of the splendid ultimate triumph.

In the same way that we are the better for the deeds of our mighty men who have served the nation well, so we are the worse for the deeds and the words of those who have striven to bring evil on the land. Most fortunately we have been free from the peril of the most dangerous of all examples. We have not had to fight the influence exerted over the minds of eager and ambitious men by the career of the military adventurer who heads some successful revolu-tionary or separatist movement. No man works such incalculable woe to a free country as he who teaches young men that one of the paths to glory, renown, and temporal success lies along the line of armed resistance to the Government, of its attempted overthrow.

Yet if we are free from the peril of this example, there are other perils from which we are not free. All through our career we have had to war against a tendency to regard, in the individual and the nation alike, as most important, things that are of comparatively little importance. We rightfully value success, but sometimes we overvalue it, for we tend to forget that success may be obtained by means which should make it abhorred and despised by every honorable man. One section of the community deifies as " smartness" the kind of trickery which enables a man without conscience to succeed in the financial or political world. Another section of the community deifies violent homicidal lawlessness. If ever our people as a whole adopt these views, then we shall have proved that we are unworthy of the heritage our forefathers left us; and our country will go down in ruin.

The people that do harm in the end are not the wrong-doers whom all execrate; they are the men who do not do quite as much wrong, but who are applauded instead of being execrated. The career of Benedict Arnold has done us no harm as a nation because of the universal horror it inspired. The men who have done us harm are those who have advocated disunion, but have done it so that they have been enabled to keep their political position; who have advocated repudiation of debts, or other financial dishonesty, but have kept their position in the community; who preach the doctrines of anarchy, but refrain from action that will bring them within the pale of the law; for these men lead thousands astray by the fact that they go unpunished or even rewarded for their misdeeds.

It is unhappily true that we inherit the evil as well as the good done by those who have gone before us, and in the one case as in the other the influence extends far beyond the mere material effects. The foes of order harm quite as much by example as by what they actually accomplish. So it is with the equally dangerous criminals of the wealthy classes. The conscienceless stock speculator who acquires wealth by swindling his fellows, by debauching judges and corrupting legislatures, and who ends his days with the reputation of being among the richest men in America, exerts over the minds of the rising generation an influence worse than that of the average murderer or bandit, because his career is even more dazzling in its success, and even more dangerous in its effects upon the community.

Any one who reads the essays of Charles Francis Adams and Henry Adams, entitled " A Chapter of Erie," and "The Gold Conspiracy in New York," will read about the doings of men whose influence for evil upon the community is more potent than that of any band of anarchists or train robbers.

There are other members of our mercantile community who, being perfectly honest themselves, nevertheless do almost as much damage as the dishonest. The professional labor agitator, with all his reckless incendiarism of speech, can do no more harm than the narrow, hard, selfish merchant or manufacturer who deliberately sets himself to work to keep the laborers he employs in a condition of dependence which will render them helpless to combine against him; and every such merchant or manufacturer who rises to sufficient eminence leaves the record of his name and deeds as a legacy of evil to all who come after him.

But of course the worst foes of America are the foes to that orderly liberty without which our Republic must speedily perish. The reckless labor agitator who arouses the mob to riot and bloodshed is in the last analysis the most dangerous of the workingman's enemies. This man is a real peril; and so is his sympathizer, the legislator, who to catch votes denounces the judiciary and the military because they put down mobs. We Americans have, on the whole, a right to be optimists; but it is mere folly to blind ourselves to the fact that there are some black clouds on the horizon of our future.

During the summer of last year, every American capable of thinking must at times have pondered very gravely over certain features of the national character which were brought into unpleasant prominence by the course of events. The demagogue, in all his forms, is as characteristic an evil of a free society as the courtier is of a despotism; and the attitude of many of our public men at the time of the great strike last July was such as to call down on their heads the hearty condemnation of every American who wishes well to his country. It would be difficult to overestimate the damage done by the example and action of a man like Governor Altgeld of Illinois. Whether he is honest or not in his beliefs is not of the slightest consequence. He is as emphatically the foe of decent government as Tweed himself, and is capable of doing far more damage than Tweed. The Governor, who began his career by pardoning anarchists, and whose most noteworthy feat since has been his bitter and undignified, but fortunately futile, campaign against the election of the admirable judge who sentenced the anarchists, is the foe of every true American and is the foe particularly of every honest workingman. With such a man it was to be expected that he should in time of civic commotion act as the foe of the law-abiding and the friend of the lawless classes, and endeavor, in company with the lowest and most abandoned of the class of office-seeking politicians, to prevent proper measures being taken to prevent riot and to punish the rioters. Had it not been for the admirable action of the Federal Government, Chicago would have seen a repetition of what occurred during the Paris Commune, while Illinois would have been torn by a fierce social war; and for all the horrible waste of life that this would have entailed Governor Altgeld would have been primarily responsible. It was a most fortunate thing that the action at Washington was so quick and so emphatic. Senator Davis of Minnesota set the key of patriotism at the time when men were still puzzled and hesitated. The President and Attorney-General Olney acted with equal wisdom and courage, and the danger was averted. The completeness of the victory of the Federal authorities, representing the cause of law and order, has been perhaps one reason why it was so soon forgotten; and now most of our well-to-do shortsighted people actually forget that when we were in July on the brink of an almost terrific explosion the governor of Illinois did his best to work to this country a measure of harm as great as any ever planned by Benedict Arnold, and that we were saved by the resolute action of the Federal judiciary and of the regular army. Moreover, Governor Altgeld, though pre-eminent, did not stand alone on his unenviable prominence. Governor Waite of Colorado stood with him. Most of the Populist governors of the Western States, and the Republican governor of California and the Democratic governor of North Dakota, shared the shame with him; and it makes no difference whether in catering to riotous mobs they paid heed to their own timidity and weakness, or to that spirit of blatant demagogism which, more than any other, jeopardizes the existence of free institutions. On the other hand, the action of Governor McKinley of Ohio and Governor Matthews of Indiana entitled them to the gratitude of all good citizens.

Every true American, every man who thinks, and who if the occasion comes is ready to act, may do well to ponder upon the evil wrought by the lawlessness of the disorderly classes when once they are able to elect their own chiefs to power. If the Government generally got into the hands of men such as Altgeld and the other governors like him referred to, the Republic would go to pieces in a year; and it would be right that it should go to pieces, for the election of such men shows that the people electing them are unfit to be entrusted with self-government.

There are, however, plenty of wrong-doers besides those who commit the overt act. Too much cannot be said against the men of wealth who sacrifice everything to getting wealth. There is not in the world a more ignoble character than the mere money-getting American, insensible to every duty, regardless of every principle, bent only on amassing a fortune, and putting his fortune only to the basest uses—whether these uses be to speculate in stocks and wreck railroads himself, or to allow his son to lead a life of foolish and expensive idleness and gross debauchery, or to purchase some scoundrel of high social position, foreign or native, for his daughter. Such a man is only the more dangerous if he occasionally does some deed like founding a college or endowing a church, which makes those good people who are also foolish forget his real iniquity. These men are equally careless of the workingmen, whom they oppress, and of the state, whose existence they imperil. There are not very many of them, but there is a very great number of men who approach more or less closely to the type, and, just in so far as they do so approach, they are curses to the country. The man who is content to let politics go from bad to worse, jesting at the corruption of politicians, the man who is content to see the maladministration of justice without an immediate and resolute effort to reform it, is shirking his duty and is preparing the way for infinite woe in the future. Hard, brutal indifference to the right, and an equally brutal shortsightedness as to the inevitable results of corruption and injustice, are baleful beyond measure; and yet they are characteristic of a great many Americans who consider themselves perfectly respectable, and who are considered thriving, prosperous men by their easy-going fellow-citizens.

Another class, merging into this, and only less dangerous, is that of the men whose ideals are purely material. These are the men who are willing to go for good government when they think it will pay, but who measure everything by the shop-till, the people who are unable to appreciate any quality that is not a mercantile commodity, who do not understand that a poet may do far more for a country than the owner of a nail factory, who do not realize that no amount of commercial prosperity can supply the lack of the heroic virtues, or can in itself solve the terrible social problems which all the civilized world is now facing. The mere materialist is, above all things, shortsighted. In a recent article in THE FORUM, Mr. Edward Atkinson casually mentioned that the regular army could now render the country no "effective or useful service." Two months before this sapient remark was printed the regular army had saved Chicago from the fate of Paris in 1870 and had prevented a terrible social war in the West. At the end of this article Mr. Atkinson indulged in a curious rhapsody against the navy, denouncing its existence and being especially wrought up, not because war-vessels take life, but because they "destroy commerce." To men of a certain kind, trade and property are far more sacred than life or honor, of far more consequence than the great thoughts and lofty emotions, which alone make a nation mighty. They believe, with a faith almost touching in its utter feebleness, that "the Angel of Peace, draped in a garment of untaxed calico," has given her final message to men when she has implored them to devote all their energies to producing oleomargarine at a quarter of a cent less a firkin, or to importing woollens for a fraction less than they can be made at home. These solemn prattlers strive after an ideal in which they shall happily unite the imagination of a green-grocer with the heart of a Bengalee baboo. They are utterly incapable of feeling one thrill of generous emotion, or the slightest throb of that pulse which gives to the world statesmen, patriots, warriors and poets, and which makes a nation other than a cumberer of the world's surface. In the concluding page of his article Mr. Atkinson, complacently advancing his panacea, his quack cure-all, says that "all evil powers of the world will go down before" a policy of "reciprocity of trade without obstruction"! Fatuity can go no further.

No Populist who wishes a currency based on corn and cotton stands in more urgent need of applied common sense than does the man who believes that the adoption of any policy, no matter what, in reference to our foreign commerce, will cut that tangled knot of social well-being and misery at which the fingers of the London free-trader clutch as helplessly as those of the Berlin protectionist. Such a man represents individually an almost imponderable element in the work and thought of the community; but in the aggregate he stands for a real danger, because he stands for a feeling evident of late years among many respectable people. The people who pride themselves upon having a purely commercial ideal are apparently unaware that such an ideal is as essentially mean and sordid as any in the world, and that no bandit community of the Middle Ages can have led a more unlovely life than would be the life of men to whom trade and manufactures were everything, and to whom such words as national honor and glory, as courage and daring, and loyalty and unselfishness, had become meaningless. The merely material, the merely commercial ideal, the ideal of the men " whose fatherland is the till, " is in its very essence debasing and lowering. It is as true now as ever it was that no man and no nation shall live by bread alone. Thrift and industry are indispensable virtues; but they are not all-sufficient. We must base our appeals for civic and national betterment on nobler grounds than those of mere business expediency.

We have examples enough and to spare that tend to evil; nevertheless, for our good fortune, the men who have most impressed themselves upon the thought of the nation have left behind them careers the influence of which must tell for good. The unscrupulous speculator who rises to enormous wealth by swindling his neighbor; the capitalist who oppresses the workingman; the agitator who wrongs the workingman yet more deeply by trying to teach him to rely not upon himself, but partly upon the charity of individuals or of the state and partly upon mob violence; the man in public life who is a demagogue or corrupt, and the newspaper writer who fails to attack him because of his corruption, or who slanderously assails him when he is honest; the political leader who, cursed by some obliquity of moral or of mental vision, seeks to produce sectional or social strife—all these, though important in their day, have hitherto failed to leave any lasting impress upon the life of the nation. The men who have profoundly influenced the growth of our national character have been in most cases precisely those men whose influence was for the best and was strongly felt as antagonistic to the worst tendency of the age. The great writers, who have written in prose or verse, have done much for us. The great orators whose burning words on behalf of liberty, of union, of honest government, have rung through our legislative halls, have done even more. Most of all has been done by the men who have spoken to us through deeds and not words, or whose words have gathered their especial charm and significance because they came from men who did speak in deeds. A nation's greatness lies in its possibility of achievement in the present, and nothing helps it more than the consciousness of achievement in the past.   THEODORE ROOSEVELT.

THE BARNACLES OF FIRE INSURANCE.

To all owners of destructible property, insurance has become a necessity. The premium is a tax we cheerfully impose upon ourselves if it be reasonable and paid to insurers who are always ready and willing to replace what may be destroyed. According to official reports, sixty of the wealthiest corporations doing a fire-insurance business in New York State received $822,000,000 for premiums in the last ten years. After paying $500,000,000 for losses, $280,-000,000 for expenses, and making the legal provision for returning premiums paid in advance, they wound up the business of the decade with an aggregate net loss of $10,000,000. No widespread conflagration had occurred, for brave firemen, assisted by excellent appliances, were able to prevent a disastrous spread of the flames in many thousand cases of serious danger; nor had the average rates for premiums diminished; yet our insurance business continued to degenerate, as the following figures of the National Board of Underwriters show:

In 1891, the ratio of loss by 258 companies was 61.23 per cent of premium receipts.
" 1892, " " " " 251 " " 62.08 " " " " "
" 1893, " " " " 244 " " 66.93 " " " " "

In German cities it costs from 4 to $7\frac{1}{2}$ cents per $100, annually, to insure stone or brick dwellings, against a proposed rate of 10 cents here; mercantile risks there cost $6\frac{2}{3}$ to $22\frac{1}{2}$ cents per $100; here an average of 60 cents. Although their premiums are considerably lower, German insurers earn, while ours lose, money. In Austria the business must be profitable, or the government would not contemplate engaging in it for revenue. A comparison of some foreign conditions and business methods with those prevailing here may suggest measures of reform which we could advantageously adopt.

In Germany the person who wants to be reimbursed for the full value of his property when destroyed by fire must insure such value and pay the premiums on it; it is understood that he is coinsurer to the extent that he does not pay. When he insures a stock of merchandise for $50,000, which is wholly destroyed and is found, upon investigation, to have been worth $100,000, he can claim only $25,-000.   Our companies have recently encouraged this system in a modified form, by requiring merchants to insure 80 per cent of values, in which case no more can be recovered.   But the foreign coinsurance system is preferable, because it is obligatory to its full extent; it either increases the premiums or diminishes the losses to a greater degree and induces the insurer to be more cautious.   Losses are adjusted in Europe with more care; when several companies become involved in a fire they select a representative to act for them all: the executive officer of the corporation which has the largest amount at stake or is the most reputable is chosen.   To this arbiter the claimant must bring conclusive evidence of the previous existence and actual value of his stock,—his books and papers, sworn depositions of experts, or whatever testimony may be required.   After careful examination of all surrounding circumstances, the officer makes an award which forms the basis of settlement.   The decision is not influenced by outside considerations: a grand duke and personal friend of the Emperor recently recovered five thousand marks for a painting (supposed to be by Rubens) which was insured for fifty thousand, because the expert found that it was only a copy.

Our custom formerly was, when losses were compromised by the payment of a lump sum, that the agent sold the salvage through some auctioneer, with whom he was apt to arrange for a division of the profits; now, the underwriters have formed, for their mutual protection, a company to dispose, at best possible prices, of their damaged goods.   When a number of small companies are interested in a large fire, it is customary for the assured to engage an expert, to whom he pays a commission on whatever he may recover.   Under his direction he prepares a proof of loss, which must be affirmed by oath, and which is usually for more than he is entitled—or expects—to receive.   For example, during a recent fire, smoke penetrated a stock of linens insured for $325,000: the assured claims $32,500, although his own adjuster found the damage so slight that he advised the acceptance of $3,250 as a compromise.   Every company hires its own adjuster, who receives a fee of from $10 to $25 per diem and travelling-expenses as long as he is so engaged; instead of expediting the settlement he often pretends to wrangle over the value of trifles until he is bribed to surrender the interest of his employers to the assured. Where large companies only are interested they may agree to leave the settlement to a committee of salaried experts, but among these are often men who will be influenced in their decision by unworthy motives. Even officers of insurance companies crave popularity so that they forget, in their anxiety to please clients, what is due to their stockholders. The value of property destroyed by fire in the United States in 1893 exceeded $150,000,000,—considerably more than half of the present value of our entire crop of wheat. From the assured down, every person in any way connected with a fire seems only to study how much he can make for himself out of the underwriters. If losses were adjudicated under the direction of a single honest and efficient man, the result would be a more impartial—certainly more economical—settlement.

When we compare the haste in which buildings are erected here with the care bestowed on them abroad, we find another explanation of the frequency of fires. In German cities, when the plan of a new house has been approved by the authorities, officers are detailed by the building-police to watch over its erection. These may come at any hour, without notice, to see that the work is done according to well-established sanitary and fire-protection laws; they can order changes or the removal of the entire building if they deem it essential, and on its completion must make a final report, to be approved by the magistrates, before the owner is permitted to occupy the premises.

Our cities no longer allow the erection of frame structures [1] within certain fire limits; we have as good building-laws as exist anywhere, but they are not always properly executed. In New York about 3,000 buildings are constantly in course of erection at one time, while about 7,000 are being altered; and forty inspectors are employed by the building-department to see that all this work is properly done. It is absolutely impossible for the inspectors to perform their duty properly, because each one is obliged to watch over 75 new and 175 old buildings. I learn that contractors have been known to place the burnt-clay linings for flues, required by law, on the sidewalk, not for actual use, but merely to deceive inspectors should they happen to pass; when the work was finished, the material was carefully returned to the builder's warehouse. The imperfect insulation of electric wires has for a long time been a source of serious danger; fires constantly occur from this cause, though methods have been im-

[1] There were in 1891, buildings: of brick or stone: of frame.

In London	557,134	None.
" New York	82,323	32,692
" Chicago	69,849	51,808

48

proved. New York has for several years had a law on its statute-books prescribing how this work must be done; but, no appropriation having been made by its city authorities for the proper inspection of such work, the law cannot be enforced.

In Europe fires are of rare occurrence except in cities which, like Berlin, have recently grown with American rapidity. In 1890 the loss caused by fire in Berlin amounted to only 22 cents per head of population, against a loss of $2.81 per head in New York, $2.44 in Chicago, and $1.89 in Brooklyn, during the year of which we have the last reports. In France the person in whose house a fire originates through negligence is responsible for the loss caused thereby to his neighbors. It may be difficult to establish this rule here, but we can be more careful than we are. Statistics show that 30 per cent of all our losses is caused by exposure to other burning property.

Successful underwriters will examine adjoining buildings with the same care that they bestow on the property they insure; but they ought to be more circumspect in the examination of risks before writing them, and remember that an ounce of prevention is better than a pound of cure. Proper inspection may often cost more than the amount of the premium; still it is foolhardy to hazard the loss of a thousand dollars in order to gain two or three, and written applications should be insisted upon in such cases, especially from strangers. Premiums charged by "industrial companies" for insuring lives are also small; yet the applicant for insurance must make a detailed statement and submit to a medical examination besides. Applicants for fire insurance should answer questions pertinent to the risk, and contracts obtained by means of false representations should be void. This precaution would have a tendency to diminish the number of incendiary fires, which increase with the recurrence of every period of business depression,—it is estimated by the New York "Financial Chronicle" that almost 9 per cent of the losses sustained last year was due to incendiarism. A man who has pressing obligations to meet, and a property insured for its full value, is often tempted to set it on fire, collect the insurance-money, and get rid of his debts. When the crime is committed by a man who has borne a good repu-tation it is seldom detected and never punished. Although, accord-ing to fire-marshals' reports, five thousand incendiary fires took place in 1893, only four persons were convicted in New York, and only one in Chicago; and they belonged to the ranks of hardened criminals who make incendiarism their occupation. Such villains will hire rooms, move goods into them, and ostensibly sell them long enough to give the place a certain air of respectability; then, during some dark night, they will take away whatever is of value, set fire to the rest, and claim more than the whole was ever worth. The " East Side" of New York has an unenviable notoriety for this class of crime. Some equally disreputable insurance-broker is frequently a confederate; after procuring a policy he retains it in his possession until the fire; then, becoming adjuster, he makes the best compromise he can with the insurer, and divides the plunder with the assured. The goods saved from fires, which are damaged so that they can be used only for deception and ought to have been destroyed, are eagerly purchased by certain dealers, who are always prepared to supply to incendiaries such crooked wares on short notice.

Underwriters now habitually inquire into the antecedents of persons who apply for insurance and are unknown to them. This information is usually derived from mercantile agencies, and Mr. C. C. Hine keeps, for their convenience, a black-list of men who were burned out more than once and whose characters are suspicious. A movement is on foot also to establish a bureau of information for the exclusive use of fire companies. The National Board of Underwriters has provided a fund of $100,000, from which, every year, rewards are appropriated for the detection of incendiaries. From this fund only $2,225 were paid last year for the conviction of thirteen persons,— a result which must disappoint the members not less than the public.

In the greater part of Europe the cause of every fire is investigated by a special police; in Massachusetts a law has been enacted which creates a State fire marshal, who is charged with the same duty. He must begin the investigation of every fire within two days of its occurrence when in Boston; when in other places, within a week, personally or by deputy; he has the power of a trial justice to summon and compel the attendance of witnesses; he can enter into buildings at reasonable hours for the purpose of examination, and order the removal of dangerous material. Similar laws should be passed by every State in the Union or by the National Government, and insurance companies should be prohibited from settling a loss unless the fire has been promptly reported to the authorities; and they should refuse to settle, wherever there is a reasonable doubt as to the cause, until they have received a report of the official investigation. In Germany, companies are not permitted to pay losses which have not been examined by the fire police.

Agents are sometimes so anxious to secure commissions that they will accept doubtful risks even from strangers. In Boston, a notorious woman already guilty of incendiarism had been suspected of planning a similar crime; while she was under the surveillance of a female detective, to whom she had confided her scheme, the Boston agent of the same company she expected to defraud and who employed this detective, accepted her application for an additional policy of $500 on the very property she wanted to burn in a few days!

One Saturday afternoon a well-appearing man walked into the office of the newly appointed agent of a Boston company in a New England town, and insured his mill for $20,000; with the contract there arrived in Boston, on Monday morning, the news that the mill had burned down on Sunday. This loss would have been saved if the agent had not been too anxious to secure a commission. Had he first referred the application to the company, it would have been refused, as his character was known. He has made a fortune by fires in woollen mills, lives in good style, and is respected by some of his neighbors on account of his liberality to churches.

In Europe the contract for insurance, which we call a policy, cannot be rescinded; an agreement once made must run its stated period and can be cancelled by neither party. This custom makes the insurer more cautious before he writes the policy; he does not part with it until he receives the premium, which may then be considered as earned, except in case of fire. Here the assured may surrender his policy at any time and call for the return of part of the premium; the insurer may cancel the contract when he refunds the premium. So long as the character of our risks is subject to unexpected change, it is questionable if our underwriters would be safe in adopting this European custom, but we can learn something·from their system of agencies.

All companies in Germany employ a number of " general agents," one in every important commercial centre, who alone is empowered to issue policies. These agents are either salaried clerks, who have long been in service and are thus rewarded, or they are chosen among the reputable merchants or bankers of the locality. They consider the appointment a distinction; they are paid by a commission of 15 per cent on premium receipts; they return 10 per cent to sub-agents for procuring the business; what is not absorbed from the rest by clerk-hire represents their perquisite. Sub-agents are chosen among small tradesmen and subaltern civil officers; they must have a good reputation and occupy a social position, and one agent can represent only a single company. In this way an efficient and honest management of agencies is secured.

Our large companies employ at least one agent in every important town, involving a staff of thousands of persons, each of whom receives a commission of 15 per cent on his receipts, irrespective of losses, and has authority to issue policies. As the profits of these men depend exclusively on their receipts, they have every incentive to increase them. When losses occur they may regret them, but this cannot interfere with their income; they will be slow voluntarily to cancel a risk, after they have accepted it, even when it becomes doubtful, because doing so would diminish their earnings. It is true that the companies employ also special salaried agents who travel about to inspect and control the risks taken by local agents, but it is difficult to form a correct opinion of the hazards surrounding each venture in the short time the special agent can devote to each place. Almost every resident agent represents from five to twenty different companies, and divides his favors among them according to his personal interest; often he loses money for every one. If a merchant were to pay a clerk, working not for himself alone but for competitors as well, a commission larger than his profits, such action would generally be considered a sign of impending failure. Insurers will follow this policy without regard to the ultimate consequence: I know that companies continue it in States where they have not earned a dollar in twenty years. When some method is devised which identifies the interests of the agent with those of his employers, the agent will be more careful in the inspection of risks and reject those which are doubtful.

Forty years ago there existed, in all parts of the country, numerous small companies, with capitals ranging from $100,000 to $500,000, divided in small shares among the greatest possible number of holders. Thus the owner of every share of stock exerted himself to bring the business of his friends and customers to his own company and to diminish its loss in case of accident. By such watchfulness, losses were kept down, while receipts were large enough to warrant a distribution of fair dividends besides the accumulation of a good surplus. It then happened that a director in one of these good old-fashioned associations conceived the idea of allowing some poor relative, unable to earn a livelihood for himself, to attend to his insurance business for him; another director desired, in this way, to

assist a customer who had failed. At the solicitation of such influential men, officers were persuaded to pay these genteel beggars
a small commission on their regular rates, and the system of brokerage was inaugurated. Not more than 5 per cent of the insurance
business was done through brokers forty years ago; less than 5
per cent is done now without them. Of the old companies but few
remain, and a great part of the business is concentrated in the hands of
comparatively few large corporations in New York, in Hartford, and in
Philadelphia. At home it is done through brokers; outside through
agents; and the commission paid these middlemen amounts to 18 per
cent of the receipts, one-half of the entire expense. There is no reason
why the brokerage at least could not be saved; almost everybody
knows enough to insure his own property; the published reports
of the standing of responsible companies are accessible; and rates are
established for a majority of risks. But the influence of brokers has
become so great that the officers in some companies actually discourage direct application, and if a customer happens to find his way to
the office of such a company he is introduced to some favorite broker,
with whom the officer divides the commission. Only where insurance
is difficult to procure are brokers useful to the insurer: this is true
where a large risk of a specially hazardous nature must be placed, or
where a great deal of valuable merchandise is concentrated in a small
district like the dry-goods centre of New York. In such cases the
greater benefit accrues to the assured, and the commission should be
paid by him. This is virtually done now, but in a roundabout way,
so that it enhances the price of desirable insurance to those who do
not need the assistance of a broker. Risks could be accepted more
cheaply by as much as the brokerage amounts to, if all underwriters
were to agree to pay none. The person who should continue to employ a broker should also pay him; he would then know what his
service cost him; probably he would also discontinue paying his premiums through him. Not everybody is aware of the risk involved
in this practice, —it consists in being obliged to pay the premium
twice if the broker should fail to turn it over to the company. It
may be more difficult to inaugurate a change so radical than to grade
the commission to be paid as follows:—

Twenty per cent for premiums on dwellings: the amounts are
small and difficult to collect. The reason why a larger commission is
now paid is chiefly due to the fact that tariff rates on dwellings have
not yet been established; meanwhile officers take them at ridiculous

prices and pay as much as 40 per cent commission to secure them. Although a dwelling-house burns every hour, this class of risks is considered the safest.

Ten per cent for premiums on ordinary mercantile risks; it takes less time to procure them, and the amounts are larger.

Five per cent for the high premiums of special hazards which applicants are usually more anxious to place than insurers are to write.

The premiums paid annually in New York City for insurance amount in the aggregate to $7,000,000, and the brokerage to about $1,000,000. This is more than the companies earn themselves, and more than is paid for similar service to any other class of middlemen who employ no capital and assume no responsibility.[1] Among several thousand so-called brokers in New York City, only about twenty-five have sufficient knowledge of the business; they probably receive 75 per cent of the brokerage distributed, and they usually divide it with favored customers, so that their net profits will scarcely exceed the percentages which I propose. But to encourage them further, and to enlist the coöperation of their ambitious but so far less fortunate competitors, I would pay them at the end of each year a contingent commission of 10 per cent of the amount which every company has earned on the business which the broker brought in that period, on condition that it exceeded five hundred dollars,—I would so limit it to avoid the opening of accounts which are not worth the trouble.

The greatest benefit the insurers would derive from this system of graded and contingent commission would be obtained by applying it to their agents, because it would naturally ally their interest with that of their employers; more of them would concentrate their efforts on behalf of a single company, and the ridiculous custom of calling a man an agent who tries to serve a dozen masters at the same time would soon terminate. The president of the Continental Fire Insurance Company made a praiseworthy effort at reform in this direction for five years. But he had to abandon it, because those of his agents who represented other companies at the same time were required by those companies to return to the old form of compensation.

[1] It is hardly fair to consider here the commissions paid to canvassers for life insurance. That they are larger is due to the circumstance that few persons will insure their lives unless solicited. The commission paid marine-insurance brokers is 5 per cent.

While this experience shows that my plan is correct in principle, it also shows that it cannot be applied under existing circumstances because of the opposition of officers of our largest companies, who are so jealous of each other that they cannot be induced to adopt the most sensible reform measure unless arguments can be used more forcible than any that have yet been tried.

When I have referred to insurers, I mean the executive officers of insurance companies, who direct the affairs of their respective organizations as if they owned the business, although they usually have but a small pecuniary interest in the corporation.[1] If shareholders will not soon adopt measures for proper management, they will see their capital and surplus vanish like that of eight hundred and seventy-eight fire insurance companies whose assets have gone up in smoke since 1860. Recent improvements, like automatic sprinklers, have resulted in saving property; and other conditions have been so favorable that when the losses of 1894 are added the figures will be less formidable than in the previous year; but a business conducted on wrong principles cannot thrive.

Underwriters refer with pride to a rise of mercantile rates which they have recently managed to enforce after a struggle of years. That measure has increased the tax on commerce without any corresponding improvement in the profits of insurance. Instead of planning to increase receipts, they ought to see how they can reduce losses and current expenses.

While every insurer has an interest in these reforms, and can help to bring them about (1) by dispensing with his broker wherever that is feasible, in order to reduce premiums; (2) by guarding his property and that of his neighbors against fire; (3) by agitating in favor of laws which will make property more secure, and by assisting in their proper execution,—it must be remembered that more serious considerations also urge reform, since the business, as it is now carried on, (1) encourages idleness, by paying more for service than it is worth; (2) offers a greater indemnity for goods which have been burned than their previous value, and thus encourages their destruction; and (3) it is hedged in on many sides by corruption and fraud to an extent which must engender immorality.

LOUIS WINDMÜLLER.

---

[1] Executive officers of French and German corporations must deposit in the company's safe certificates of stock commensurate with their responsibility before they can enter upon their duties.

INDEX.

Lightning Source UK Ltd.
Milton Keynes UK
UKHW020850110119
335238UK00009B/932/P